ALFRED HITCHCOCK

Centenary Essays

Edited by Richard Allen and S. Ishii-Gonzalès

bfi Publishing

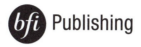

Acknowledgments
It is our pleasure to acknowledge the following individuals who have contributed to the publication of this volume: Renata Jackson provided an indispensible index, Alexandra Seibel helped us with bibliographic research, and the sterling efforts of our editors at the BFI, Andrew Lockett and Tom Cabot, ensured that the book would actually be published in Hitchcock's centenary year. Finally, we wish to thank David J. Owens and Bridget Sisk for their moral support of our endeavour.

First published in 1999 by the
British Film Institute
21 Stephen Street, London W1P 2LN

Reprinted 2000

The British Film Institute is the UK national agency with responsibility for encouraging the arts of film and television and conserving them in the national interest.

Cover design: Squid Inc.

Set in Minion by Fakenham Photosetting Limited, Fakenham, Norfolk
Printed in Great Britain by St Edmundsbury Press, Bury St Edmunds

British Library Cataloguing-in-Publication Data
A catalogue record for this book is available from the British Library
ISBN 0–85170–735–1 hbk
ISBN 0–85170–736–X pbk

Contents

Introduction

As the title indicates, this volume commemorates the centennial of Alfred Joseph Hitchcock, who was born 13 August 1899 in London, England, in a lower middle-class district of London's East End called Leytonstone. This centenary provides us with the ideal occasion to consider the nature of Hitchcock's achievement as a film-maker, the relationship between the artist and the authorial persona he partially (and ingeniously) manufactured, and the relationship of the director's work to the larger political and economic forces that shaped it. It also happens to coincide with the end of the twentieth century, a century whose paradigmatic art form, we would immodestly claim, is the cinema, just as some have suggested that the novel was paradigmatic of the nineteenth – each congeals in their aesthetic form the socio-cultural aspirations of the epoch. And, to continue in our immodesty, we would like to suggest that Hitchcock is the cinema's exemplary artist.

We are not asserting that Hitchcock is a greater film director than, say, Eisenstein, Lang, Welles, or Renoir. However, although we agree with Gilberto Perez that the amount of critical and theoretical attention which has been lavished on Hitchcock is 'in excess of any other director's fair share', it seems less important to us to draw from this the conclusion, as does Perez, that Hitchcock is not deserving of his reputation as it is to speculate on the nature of this 'excess' and the possible meanings to be extracted from it.[1] We might add that Perez overlooks, as well, the fact that Hitchcock remains, even after his death nearly twenty years ago (in 1980), one of the most popular, not to mention easily identifiable, directors in the entire history of the medium – indeed, the term 'Hitchcockian' has become a single-word synonym in contemporary advertising campaigns for a masterful control of the mechanisms of suspense as well as a guarantor of audience satisfaction. All of which is to say, contra Perez, that Hitchcock's reputation is not merely attributable to his academic fetishisation, and, hence, can not be explained and contained through such an articulation. What we wish to propose here instead is that the endless fascination with Hitchcock (both inside and outside the academy) is related to the ways in which the director and his œuvre have come to embody or represent the possibilities of the medium itself. As Lindsay Anderson remarked in 1949, 'Hitchcock's long career is *intimately* bound up with the history of the cinema'.[2]

Before we examine this hypothesis in more detail through a discussion of the essays contained in this volume, we would like to briefly recapitulate for the reader the trajectory of Hitchcock's career and the conditions governing the emergence and development of Hitchcock scholarship. Hitchcock's birth coincided, as we know, with the arrival of the new mass medium of motion pictures. The first commercial film screening took place in December 1895 when the Lumière brothers' *Workers Leaving the Factory* was projected at the Grand Café in Paris (the first public screening of a motion picture in Britain would come a couple of months later in February 1896 at the Great

Hall of the Polytechnic Institution in London). Although there is no clear date given for when Hitchcock saw his first film, it is evident that he had seen more than a few by the time he was a boy of ten or eleven. He was not alone. By 1913, as Donald Spoto reports, there were, in London alone, approximately four hundred venues (including skating rinks) in which to watch movies and the weekly attendance rate was roughly eighty thousand.[3] As a teenager, Hitchcock was already studiously reading not only the emergent movie magazines targeted at its legion of fans but the American film industry journals. After a stint at the Henley Telegraph and Cable Company and night courses for non-matriculated students at the University of London (where he took classes in art-history, drawing, political science, among others), he was hired by the Famous Players-Lasky at Islington in 1920 as a title-card designer. Hitchcock's apprenticeship in the art of film-making was nothing if not practical. Hitchcock spent the next six years taking on a variegated series of tasks, including production manager, art director, scenarist, editor, assistant director, before completing the direction of his first feature, *The Pleasure Garden* in 1925. (An earlier attempt at film directing, in 1923, was aborted due to the quickly deteriorating status of the studio which then employed Hitchcock.)

The British film industry at the time of Hitchcock's engagement was reliant on stage and literary adaptations directed with little cinematic flair or innovation. Conservative, even moribund, it was one which construed the role of the film director as being akin to the theater director: dramatising for an audience the creative ideas of another. From the outset of Hitchcock's career he was insistent that the creative importance of the film director should be acknowledged, and he self-consciously and self-interestedly promoted this view. In a 1927 open letter to the *London Evening News* he wrote:

> The American film directors under their commerically minded employers have learnt a good deal about studio lighting, action photographs, and telling a story plainly and smoothly in motion pictures. They have learnt, as it were, to put the nouns, verbs, and adjectives of the film language together. But even if we conceive the film as going no further as an art, it is obvious that what we must strive for at once is the way to use these film nouns and verbs as cunningly as do the great novelist and the great dramatist, to achieve certain moods and effects on an audience … Film directors live with their pictures while they are being made. They are their babies just as much as an author's novel is the offspring of his imagination … when moving pictures are really artistic they will be created entirely by one man.[4]

Hitchcock's early film-making career in Britain was extremely prolific: in the space of thirteen years he made twenty-four films. In early films such as *The Lodger* (1926), which the director considered 'the first true "Hitchcock film" ',[5] and the first British sound film *Blackmail* (1929), Hitchcock revolutionised English cinema by uniting popular storytelling traditions, with their roots in the Victorian sensation novel and detective fiction, with the visual style of European art cinema – German expressionism and Soviet Montage.

Lindsay Anderson, while ostensibly celebrating the superiority of the British films to the Hollywood productions, wrote that Hitchcock's strength was as a storyteller and that his films are not interesting 'for their ideas nor their characters'.[9]
But it is clear, at least with hindsight, that what is most interesting about these works are

Hitchcock's attempts to translate the stories that he is telling into the idiom of film – into the realm of 'pure cinema'. Pure cinema is, like 'the MacGuffin', one of Hitchcock's cherished terms to discuss the distinctive quality at work in his films. For Hitchcock, 'pure cinema' is a narrative told in purely visual terms: it is a distillation of the perceptual power particular to the experience of watching a movie, and this 'pure cinema' is achieved through montage, the creation of *ideas* through the assemblage of images: 'the purest form of cinema … is called montage: that is, pieces of film put together to make up an idea. When the film was originally invented, when cutting was invented, it was the juxtaposition of pieces of film that went through a machine that displayed ideas on the screen'.[7] The works of the British period are littered with such ideas (indeed, Anderson's essay is replete with examples), and it is the director's persistent refinement of this endeavor which explains in large part the success and enduring appeal of these early films.

Hitchcock's success in Britain brought him, in 1939, to Hollywood under the aegis of the producer David O. Selznick with whom he remained under contract until 1947. During this period he directed ten features and two shorts which serve as his contribution to the Allied war effort. Hitchcock, supremely aware of the connection between technological and stylistic innovation, found in Hollywood the means to augment his stylistic repertoire, especially through the use of complicated camera movement as a strategy of both character identification and authorial comment. After a brief period of independence in the late 1940s, during which time he made his 'experimental film' *Rope* (1948), Hitchcock returned to the safety afforded by a studio contract (the safety, that is, of not losing one's own money) to make such films as *Strangers on a Train* (1951), *Rear Window* (1954) and the remake of *The Man Who Knew Too Much* (1956). Hitchcock also became involved at this time in television production with the CBS series *Alfred Hitchcock Presents*, which began its ten-year run on network television in 1955. This series dramatically increased Hitchcock's name recognition and popularity with the general public, even as his film work strained toward ever-darker themes and more daring stylistic innovations. It is during this period that he directs *The Wrong Man* (1957), *Vertigo* (1958), *North by Northwest* (1959), *Psycho* (1960) and *The Birds* (1963).

The late phase of Hitchcock's career is both coincident with and productive of a shift in the general perception of popular film from mass entertainment (or, as Clement Greenberg would put it, 'kitsch') to serious art form. This is brought about in large part through the dissemination of auteur theory, first articulated by critics writing for *Cahiers du Cinema* in the 1950s who, rather scandalously, proposed the director in popular cinema as a source of expression and meaning as complex and moving as any in contemporary art (one article by Jean Domarchi favorably compared Hitchcock's *Under Capricorn* (1949) to James Joyce's *Finnegan's Wake*). One of its high points was the publication in 1957 of Eric Rohmer and Claude Chabrol's book-length study of Hitchcock's first forty-four films (wittily referred to by Albert J. LaValley as the 'original sin' of Hitchcock criticism).[8] In this monograph, the authors argue that far from being simply a showman-entertainer (the orthodox reading of Hitchcock in the Anglo-American context), Hitchcock was a profound Catholic dramaturge of guilt and redemption and that the moral complexity of his films came through the imbrication of content and form. As they write at the conclusion of their study, 'Hitchcock is one of the greatest *inventors of form* in the entire history of cinema. Perhaps only Murnau and Eisenstein can sustain comparison with him when it comes to form. ... In Hitchcock's work form does not embellish content, it creates it. All of Hitchcock can be summed up in this formula.'[9]

As extravagant as the auteur critics could sometimes be, there is no doubt that their contribution to film history and Hitchcock scholarship is fundamental. As Robin Wood pointed out in his book *Hitchcock's Films* (1965), the first serious study of the director in English, critics of the period had no problem discussing such figures as Michelangelo Antonioni or Ingmar Bergman as auteurs but omitted the work of commercial directors from consideration. The auteur critics, on the other hand, challenged the very division between the work of a 'serious' artist and the work of a popular figure such as Hitchcock (among other Hollywood contract film-makers). Their insistence that the terms of the debate had to be interrogated and reformulated permanently altered the way that films, in the Anglo-American context, were studied and discussed. There is no doubt as well that the emergence and wide-spread acceptance of auteur theory fueled the institutionalisation in the mid-1960s of cinema studies as an academic discipline – in the context of literature departments, where the auteurist program had a receptive audience, and in the context of film schools, where the idea of the director as auteur spawned a new generation of film directors. In both environments, Hitchcock became a pivotal influence. It is as if, as Robert Kapsis has argued, belatedly, and through developments in critical taste that he was not in a position to control, Hitchcock finally gained the recognition of the role of the director that he had always believed he deserved – even if it was in a language that Hitchcock himself could not always appreciate.[10]

The importance of auteur theory to the establishment of film studies is indisputable, yet as any historically-minded student of cinema very well knows, it did not take very long for auteur theory itself to become *passé* (at least in academic circles). However, unlike many of the other Hollywood directors championed by the auteur critics (e.g. Nicholas Ray, Anthony Mann, Budd Boetticher, Howard Hawks) the interest in Hitchcock not only survived the heyday of the *politique des auteurs* but flourished through the various paradigm shifts which have constituted the short history of this field – from textual analysis to apparatus theory to feminist–psychoanalysis to poststructualism to the recent ascent of cultural studies. Through all these disciplinary changes, Hitchcock and his silhouette have remained. It is as though each methodological field must, at some point in its elaboration, turn its attention to the director's œuvre, must test its precepts against or alongside the film-maker's own. Hitchcock continues to solicit prodigious critical attention – as both this volume and its supplementary bibliography attest.

*

For the purposes of clarification, we have organised this collection into four broadly conceived areas of critical inquiry. Part I explores the figuration of Hitchcock's authorship both without and within his texts. The continuing importance of auteurism may seem odd or anachronistic to those readers familiar with the influential theoretical developments that have sought to displace the author as the sole or even significant source of meaning in a film. However, successive polemics against authorship have served less to render the author obsolete than to make author-based criticism more sophisticated, more aware of the complex and multiple ways in which authorial intention bestows meaning upon and is inscribed within a film.

In Chapter One, Thomas Elsaesser suggests that auteurist critics generated three different Hitchcocks: Hitchcock the moralist, an idea first articulated in Chabrol and Rohmer's pioneering study and refined with a more humanist/therapeutic slant by Robin Wood; Hitchcock the modernist-formalist, a perspective suggested by Peter Wollen who emphasised Hitchcock's preoccupation with narrative structure and plot mechanisms and linked them to the theme of the unconscious; and Hitchcock the aesthete, proposed by Raymond Durgnat in his book *The Strange Case of Alfred Hitchcock* (1974). Elaborating upon Durgnat's insights, Elsaesser connects Hitchcock's preoccupation with form for form's sake to the authorial persona Hitchcock projected outside his works, as a means of squaring the pre-auteurist and self-cultivated idea of Hitchcock the superficial showman with the post-auteurist images of the modernist-formalist and moralist. Elsaesser's Hitchcock is a conservative, roguish, aesthete-dandy, whose clothes make the man in a manner that demonstrates authorial identity as an effect of calculated appearance in much the same way that his preoccupation with formal structure, with rhymes and repetition (as in *Strangers on a Train*), produces character identity and relationships as an effect of surface and chance. Both persona and films display a cultivated sense of unseriousness that, for Elsaesser, has the paradoxical force of a moral stance.

Paula Marantz Cohen, in the next essay, refines her argument about Hitchcock and character first proposed in *Alfred Hitchcock, The Legacy of Victorianism* (1995) by comparing Hitchcock to Henry James and the respective relationships each artist had to the medium in which they worked. Cohen argues that each stretched the boundaries of their chosen field with respect to the portrayal of character, but in opposite directions, as befits the differing conventions of each art form which they struggled to transform. Cohen develops the contrast through a detailed discussion of Hitchcock's *Rear Window* and James' *Portrait of a Lady*, both works that focus on the way in which character can effect and be effected by its environment. In *Rear Window* the consciousness of the central character, L.B. Jefferies, is transformed by his sympathetic involvement in the lives of the people across the courtyard. Hitchcock realises this novelistic conception of character development against the grain of a medium that insists on surface rather than depth, action rather than reflection, by mobilizing to the fullest the visual resources of the medium to articulate character consciousness. By contrast, in *Portrait of a Lady*, James amplifies a novelistic conception of character to a point that reveals the limits of human (self-) understanding. With a rich inner life and all the freedom to choose, Isabelle Archer, James's heroine, nonetheless completely misreads the qualities of the man who becomes her husband. What both works have in common is the equilibrium they sustain between the inner and outer that Cohen considers essential to a coherent story and a sense of character.

William Rothman returns, in his contribution, to the argument of his 1982 book *Hitchcock – The Murderous Gaze* by way of a comparison between Hitchcock's *Psycho* and its recent so-called 'shot-by-shot' remake (1998) by Gus Van Sant, and in the process articulates the theoretical underpinnings of his book in the writings of Stanley Cavell. Rothman compares Hitchcock and Van Sant in order to illustrate the distinction between the systematic use of film form to carry authorial intention and meaning that is characteristic of Hitchcock (for example, his use of the '////' motif), and the degeneration of form into a series of meaningless marks or empty quotations in Van Sant. Rothman notes that his preoccupation with the works that bear visible signs of authorship that mediate our response to the fictional world contrasts with the claims made by Cavell for cinema. By presenting to us a fully realised world from which we are nonetheless excluded, cinema, for Cavell, invites us to meditate on the condition of our skeptical isolation in order to overcome it. Cinema tranforms our relationship to the human beings it depicts independently of human intention. Rothman's Hitchcock, however, is a director who self-consciously inscribes his own signature on every frame in such a way that subordinates our access to the world of the film to his artistic vision. The critic who seeks to understand Hitchcock's work is thus required to acknowledge his authorship and in that way bring their own critical voice into being.

In Chapter Four, Susan Smith takes up Rothman's concern with the formal inscription of authorial point of view in Hitchcock's work through a close analysis of his 1936 English film *Sabotage*. Smith demonstrates how the external acts of sabotage carried out by male protagonists of the film, Verloc and the Professor, serve to express their unacknowledged wishes to be rid of social and domestic responsibilities and are ultimately acts of self-sabotage. She argues, furthermore, that the complex meaning attached to sabotage is given added significance through the various ways in which the saboteurs in the text act as authorial surrogates for Hitchcock. Smith identifies three levels of authorial surrogacy. First, Verloc and the Professor reproduce Hitchcock's portly profile embodying Hitchcock, the man. Second, a series of analogies made in the film between sabotage and film-making suggest that the film-maker, Hitchcock, is like a saboteur. Third, just as the Professor disavows his sabotage activities, Hitchcock, in his interviews with Truffaut, seeks to disown his own role as saboteur-film-maker by disclaiming a defining sequence in his œuvre – the killing of Stevie, the boy protagonist. Hence, even the persona Hitchcock projected in his interviews and elsewhere has its correlate in the film. Smith concludes her analysis by contrasting the responses of the spectators in the text to the act of sabotage to the responses of the more sophisticated, critically detached, viewer solicited by Hitchcock's film.

Thomas Leitch, proposing to complete the diagram first elaborated by Andrew Sarris (who introduced the auteur theory to American readers in articles written in the early 1960s for *Film Comment*), discusses Hitchcock's authorial persona as the outer circle of auteur theory in contrast to the 'inner circle' which, for Sarris, is where we encounter the true auteur. The director's long-running TV series *Alfred Hitchcock Presents* has been largely ignored by Hitchcock scholars, but Leitch argues that the relationship between the director's wry, scripted commentaries and innovative performances at the beginning of the show and the stories that follow offer a key to understanding the way in which, in the case of Hitchcock, the outer circle penetrates the inner and helps bring it into being. Leitch argues that unlike his movies, where the congruence between morality and the law is thrown into question only to be restored, in many of the TV shows, including some Hitchcock directed, criminal behaviour is not punished. Instead, it is left to Hitchcock, the wry, genial host of the show, both to frame and complete the story in a way that the aloof, witty and ironic impresario becomes, in the imagination of the audience, the producer or director of the work. More generally, Leitch demonstrates the way in which Hitchcock's role as presenter becomes the defining feature of the television shows through the exaggerated discontinuity between the nature of the presentation and the content of the shows, the subordination of all other figures in the host segment to two-dimensional props, and the self-conscious performativity through which Hitchcock always emerges as a persona beneath, rather than the actor of, a role.

The essays in Part II are concerned with issues pertinent to the field of aesthetics: what is the relation between the artist and his/her art (in what way can we conceive of art as a form of self-expression); how do we account for the contents of aesthetic experience and the nature of its effects on the art work's beholder; what is art's specific value as perceptual experience.

In Chapter Six, Peter Wollen offers us three hypotheses for interpreting *Rope*. The first hypothesis considers the anguish of childhood in general and an English private school education in particular on the later artistic productions of both Hitchcock and Patrick Hamilton. The second comprehends *Rope*'s *tour de force* as an exemplification of Hitchcock's desire to experiment with the perceptual and cognitive limits of the cinematic medium. The use of the camera-instrument as an integral component in the text's composition is read as an extension by other means of the rhythmic qualities of cinema explored in the early abstract films of Survage, Eggeling and Lye, and in Eisenstein's application of overtonal montage in *The General Line* (1929). *Rope*, in this formulation, becomes part of a genealogy which culminates in Michael Snow's *Wavelength* (1967). The third hypothesis suggests that *Rope* be understood as the ultimate expression of Hitchcock's fascination with both moving trains and the effects of claustrophobia – except that here it is the film's spectator who is placed in the position of the train passenger who comes to experience, through the film's duration, the devastating effects of travel anxiety. Wollen does not reconcile these readings; rather, it is left to the reader to synthesise them or not, to choose one reading over another or not. Wollen (implicitly) suggests that the power of Hitchcock's work lies in this very oscillation of possibilities.

Joe McElhaney makes a similar claim for *Marnie* (1964), a film which is typically situated in Hitchcock scholarship as either the director's last great work or the film which marks his decline. The author proposes that what makes *Marnie* a fascinating work is related to its director's attempt to satisfy a dual impulse to be both classical and modernist. McElhaney's essay precisely delineates how *Marnie* makes manifest this juncture between classical and modern cinema: the classical is figured through both the director's adherence to the logic of melodrama and the structure of classical narrative film (which have worked so well for him in the past); the modern in a modernist cinema of surface and tactility found in the works of such directors as Antonioni and Bresson. The modernist cinema, according to McElhaney, is to be understood not as other to Hitchcock's own film practice but as its natural consequence. Here the author elaborates Gilles Deleuze's contention that it is Hitchcock's development of the 'mental-image' (which takes us beyond affect and perception to the register of intellection and interpretation) that precipitates the 'time-image' found in modern cinema. Hitchcock thus recognises something of himself in the cinema of the modernists and he wishes to explore this relation. It is the singular way in which this exploration is inscribed in the film which makes *Marnie* a significant Hitchcock text.

Deborah Knight and George McKnight begin Chapter Eight with a general consideration of the nature of suspense, its particular formal qualities, and the imaginative projections at work in its narrative unfolding. The authors illustrate, through a detailed reading of four Hitchcock films, how Hitchcockian suspense diverges from the prototype theories of suspense proffered by Dolf Zillman and Noël Carroll. Both Zillman and Carroll argue that suspense requires a moral empathy between the audience and a particular character, and that the experience of suspense is generated out of the spectator's fear of an immoral outcome when this character is placed in a perilous situation. Although Carroll's argument allows for a more nuanced understanding of morality than Zillman's (since Carroll argues that morality is contextually determined by the individual narrative), neither version can sufficiently account for the complex, shifting levels of morality and immorality found in Hitchcock's works, particularly *Vertigo* and *Psycho*. In these two late works, the 'focused uncertainty' which characterises the suspense plot is conjoined to an uncertainty about a character's motivation or intentions. What these films elucidate are the ways that Hitchcock perfects and then moves beyond prototypical suspense to achieve something completely unforeseen: suspense in the service of shock and tragedy. It is exactly in this 'move beyond' that Hitchcock achieves his distinction as master.

The next two essays, by Brigitte Peucker and Slavoj Žižek, read Hitchcock's aesthetics in relationship to psychoanalysis and hence are concerned with how the art work serves as a container of hidden or repressed truths that the critic-as-analyst unravels. According to Peucker, the repressed truth of Hitchcock's œuvre is the male's simultaneous attraction to, and fear of, what is construed as the female's lack – a lack which signifies both castration and death, or, death as castration. Her essay thus considers how the director's work both acknowledges and disavows its own fascination with these themes. It is acknowledged to the extent that Hitchcock recognises a fundamental accord between the art of cutting, montage, and murder (its apogee being the shower sequence in *Psycho*). It is disavowed to the extent that this castration is usually figured in, or as, the female body (either through a diegetic death or through her presentation in fragments), and in the way that Hitchcock's films place the stasis of painting and sculpture in opposition to the ceaseless forward movement of the cinematic image. In other words, this preoccupation with femininity (castration) and immobility (death) can only be articulated through a displacement which consigns its attractions elsewhere, as the life-negating attributes of the other. The paradox of art's apotropaic function, though, is that it can only ward off or defeat these forces by bringing them to realisation, into the space of representation. The artist can only come to resist the seductions of the abyss through its evocation in his art. And this evocation, once put into circulation, always threatens to provoke what the text nevertheless must ceaselessly deny.

Whereas Peucker reads Hitchcock's work as fundamentally in alignment with the symbolic order (the socio-cultural realm of language and meaning), Slavoj Žižek finds in the director's work a radical challenge to the conventions or demands of this order. Žižek, who interprets Hitchcock's films in the light of his distinctive reading of Lacanian psychoanalysis, articulates the way in which the symbolic is subtended by a realm of non-meaning (which Lacan called 'the real') that at once enables the symbolic order to exist and yet permanently threatens its dissolution. Hitchcock's films, according to Žižek, are exemplary for the way they elucidate the strain put upon the symbolic by the real – a strain which manages to denature the transparency of vision and the cohesive fabric of social reality. This is done through the intrusion of a blot-stain which reveals what is uncanny (*unheimlich*) within the picture. This disruption does not occur through a fantasy of overturning the symbolic order – exemplified in such avant-garde strategies as Brecht's alienation-effect – but by following the logic of this order all the way through. As Žižek says elsewhere, Hitchcock's subversion 'consists in dispelling the lure of [a] false "openness" – in rendering visible the closure as such'.[11] There is then in Hitchcock not a false 'openness' but a true (ideo)logical (en)closure which is made to tremble under the weight of its own resolution. Hitchcock's aesthetic strategy is to reveal, stylistically and thematically, how the real is always already there, always already a part of the picture – and he does so with the appearance on the narrative horizon of a blot-stain.

The last essay in this section, George Toles' '"If Thine Eye Offend Thee...": *Psycho* and the Art of Infection', asks us to reflect on a connexion between Hitchcock's *Psycho* and two classic literary texts, Edgar Allen Poe's 'Berenice' (1835) and Georges Bataille's *Histoire de l'œil* (first version published in 1928). Each work explores the metaphor of the eye as it traverses and transforms the space of its narrative enunciation. Our obsessive fixation with the eye, Toles explains, is related to its metaphoric status as the meeting point of the exterior and interior, the objective and subjective; it is where we come to penetrate – to devour – the external world but it is also where we are most vulnerable to the world's violent intrusion (think of the tenderness, the moistness, of the eye the moment before it is violated). What is particularly disturbing in these three works is the way they conjoin the thematics of the eye with a denial of interiority. The events depicted in these 'blocked' narratives do not lead the reader–viewer to a state of comprehension, to a point of clarification. Their complex achievement hence can not be explained or explained away; they can only be relived, reexperienced, as a perfected, remorseless state of disquietude. Through the force of his reading, Toles gives lie to Durgnat's claim (made in 1974) that Hitchcock is 'a Sade without the courage of his convictions'.[12]

Part III is entitled 'Romance/Sexuality'. The virgule, the short oblique stroke placed between the two terms, is meant to indicate that the appropriate word choice is to be 'chosen [by the reader] to complete the sense of the text'.[13] This, of course, is meant to allude to the different (even contrary) readings of the various interpersonal relations – the possibilities and impossibilities of sexual union – discoverable in Hitchcock's universe.

The first essay in this section, Raymond Bellour's 'Hitchcock – Endgame', could just as easily fit into the section on aesthetics. This is because, for Bellour, Hitchcock's interest in the formation of the (hetero)sexual couple is simply an expression or extension of his interest in the perfection of form. As Hitchcock himself acknowledged, his attraction to form, to pure design, always threatened to reduce his characters and narratives to abstractions – 'algebraic figures' as Truffaut put it during their conversation on *Strangers on a Train* (it is here that Hitchcock famously exclaimed 'Isn't it a fascinating design? One could study it forever').[14] For Bellour, Hitchcock's *Family Plot* (1976) is not so much a reduction as it is a clarification of classical Hollywood narrative patterns into their abstract purity: the union of two, male and female, into one through the formation of a couple. This is not the first time that this has occurred. But whereas *Psycho* exemplifies the absolute violence contained in such a 'sexual' union, Hitchcock's last film presents this convergence in a more relaxed, playful mode (under the sign of eros). This is due in part to the director's willingness to share his perception, the text's enunciation, with a female protagonist, Madame Blanche, who appropriately enough is a medium – even better, a fake clairvoyant.

In Chapter Thirteen, Michael Walker conducts a close analysis of two neglected

Hitchcock works, *Young and Innocent* (1937), one of the last of Hitchcock's British films, and *Stage Fright* (1950), made a decade into the director's Hollywood career. What this analysis reveals is both a remarkable structural similarity between the two works, and an equally important dissimilarity which the author argues is related to each work's understanding of, and engagement with, the issue of sexuality. Whereas *Young and Innocent* is exactly that, a chaste and charming romance (and Walker suggests that the film's title is emblematic of Hitchcock's British period), *Stage Fright* is imbued with a deeper understanding of the workings of sexuality. This knowledge gives the narrative added layers of involution and depth, as is attested by Hitchcock's controversial use of the 'lying flashback'. As Walker demonstrates, this flashback contains a complex, systematically elaborated rhetorical structure which is not evident in Hitchcock's British movies. The author concludes that the 'Hollywood aesthetic' aided the development of Hitchcock as *auteur* because its emphasis on sexuality and exhibition, on style and surface, challenged the director to develop, in ways that he would not otherwise have done, the themes of performance and duplicity, which are Hitchcock's two great concerns.

Contrary to those critics who focus upon Hitchcock's more ironic or tragic works (such as *Blackmail*, *Vertigo* and *Psycho*) and take them to be typical of the whole, Lesley Brill, in Chapter Fourteen, emphasises the centrality of redemptive comedy in Hitchcock's films and compares them, in this respect, to the work of Preston Sturges, another director whose work is typically (and for Brill, erroneously) cast in an ironic vein. Brill argues that the works of both directors centre upon the struggle to achieve love and trust between a man and a woman in an 'imperfect' fallen world, characterised by misunderstanding, confusion, and incipient chaos. In this post–lapsarian world, romance is salvaged through the reclamation of innocence and optimism in a context where the sins of the past have been acknowledged, rational knowledge is repudiated, and the power and caprice of sexual attraction is embraced. In the films of Sturges and Hitchcock, the theologically redemptive aspect of romance is underscored by its miraculous occurrence brought about by a sudden, artfully engineered, change in narrative circumstance that signifies a creative renewal of possibilities. The ironic works of Hitchcock are an exception to this rule: there miracles fail and feigning is false, leading not to rebirth but narrative stasis, and the destruction of romance.

In Chapter Fifteen, Richard Allen characterises Hitchcock's films as 'metaskeptical' narratives that at once assert and subvert the possibility and promise of romance through the ambivalent aspect that Hitchcock bestows upon appearances. These contrary readings, like the duck-rabbit figure in Wittgenstein, are co-extensive, and like the Janus-face are mutually incompatible. Allen argues that this doubleness or duplicity emerges as a strategy of male authorial assertion and control in which the threat of desire is at once acknowledged and denied through strategies of textual disguise that have their correlate in Hitchcock's authorial persona as a dandy-rogue (as identified by Thomas Elsaesser in Chapter One), and which are diegetically figured in the dandies and rogues who populate his works. Allen traces the lineage of the dandy-rogue persona and its implications for authorship into debates in nineteenth-century British letters on masculine self-presentation, specifically the problem of how to differentiate a true masculinity from a performative one, and how to distinguish a true gentleman from one who is tailor-made. For Allen, it is only by understanding this complex legacy of Victorianism that we can begin to grasp the relationship between form, content and authorial persona that form the totality of the 'Hitchcock text'.

This section concludes with Lee Edelman's queer analysis of Hitchcock's *The Birds* (1963), which takes seriously the assault on grammer and syntax found in the director's catchphrase to market the film: '*The Birds* is coming'. According to Edelman, the relentless, mechanistic aggression of the birds functions as a figuration of the ceaseless pulse of the death drive, a *jouissance* which threatens to dispell the coherence of the subject through the intrusion of a sexuality without reserve, a sexuality which threatens to bring an end to the future itself. The disruptive force of these drives comes to signify a form of sexuality that cannot be accomodated within the logic of a 'heterosexualising ideology of reproductive necessity' that attempts to ward off this persistent threat to hearth and home through a rhetoric of familialism and futurity invested in the figure of the child – a child who is menaced within this cultural imaginary (and in *The Birds*) by that which comes to seem *contra naturam*. While the author resists any simple equation or collapse of the birds with the homosexual, he demonstrates how Hitchcock's film captures the hetero-genital logic by which this menace to the social structures of meaning and procreation comes to be attached by default and through disavowal to the overdetermined site of homosexuality. For Edelman then – and in stark contrast to Brill – Hitchcock is not redemptive of the heterosexual romance but a harbinger of its destruction.

The essays in Part IV, which examine the director's work in relationship to politics, culture, and ideology, fall into two groups. The contributions of White and, to some extent, Naremore, assess the ideology of Hitchcock's work by exploring it through the lens of particular critical perspectives: the political discourse of feminist theory, and the 'oppositional' aesthetic of film noir respectively. Corber, Miller and Hark offer a more historically specific analysis of how the ideological contours of Hitchcock's work are shaped by the political and popular culture in which they participate.

In Chapter Seventeen James Naremore considers what, at first glance, might seem to be a plausible aesthetic and ideological context in which to understand Hitchcock's work of the 1940s and 1950s: film noir, the ironic cycle of typically urban crime-melodramas involving angular photography, expressionistic lighting, subjective modes of narration, and a deterministic view of character. *Shadow of A Doubt* (1943), *Notorious* (1946), *Strangers on a Train*, and *The Wrong Man* are all plausibly described as 'noir-like'. Yet, as Naremore argues, Hitchcock's work departs from the noir sensibility, in a number of significant ways. First, unlike the urban-American milieu typical of the genre, Hitchcock's works (with the important exception of *The Wrong Man*) are set in a prosperous, virtually all-white milieu that connotes 'Britishness'. Second, because his films are structured to engineer suspense, they are far less inscrutable than the typically convoluted plots found in noir. Third, unlike the cynical view of romance and the often blatantly misogynistic characteristics of the genre, Hitchcock made romance narratives and fostered audience identification with his heroines. Finally, his films display a consistent historical nostalgia: they are preoccupied with the 'uncanny return of an aristocratic past'. Naremore concludes that Hitchcock is best placed in a broader nineteeth-century noir tradition linked to Poe and the roman noir, on the one hand, and Victorian sensation fiction, on the other, rather than the more narrowly defined parameters conventionally ascribed to the American film noir.

In Chapter Eighteen, Susan White traces the history of feminist analyses of Hitchcock's *Vertigo* (1958) that followed Laura Mulvey's pioneering analysis of the male attributes of the gaze. Her essay explores the critically fertile congruence between a psychoanalytically inflected feminist theory that analyzes the way in which patriarchal culture (Lacan's symbolic order) places women outside the sphere of the knowable, and a film whose heroine, Judy/Madeline, is mysteriously unknowable to the hero, Scottie. She demonstrates how the epistemological problem of feminist theory – is woman always unknowable, does any claim to knowledge of woman succumb to a false essentialism? – becomes cast in feminist criticism of *Vertigo* as the possibility or impossibility of discovering the woman's story in the film. The critical perspectives canvassed by White range from those which view the film as fundamentally complicit in a phallocentric ideology; those who argue that while unknown to the hero, there is a woman's story in the film that is either made available by Hitchcock to the spectator, or can be discerned by the female/feminist viewer (but why, White asks, only to them?); critics who claim that Hitchcock successfully anatomizes the way in which patriarchical culture consigns women to a position of unknownness; and those who argue that the lesson of *Vertigo* is not about knowledge of woman per se, but about the impossibility of understanding in general and the limits of interpretation. For White the ongoing nature of these debates is a testimony to the importance of the issues at hand.

During the course of her discussion, White refers to an essay by Virginia Wright Wexman who takes feminist critics to task for narrowly focusing on the question of sexual difference in *Vertigo* while ignoring the way in the film is informed by more historically specific questions of class and race. This is the point of departure for Robert Corber, who argues that the treatment of the problem of the unknown woman in the film at once reflects and exposes the fear of the invisible subversive that gripped America in the cold-war period, a fear that encompassed not just the homosexual, but also heterosexual women who do not conform to traditional familial norms. For Corber, *Vertigo* portrays Judy's crime less as her implication in the murder of Elster's wife, and more as a crime of passing as the upper-class heroine that she is not. It is this crime which makes her an object of surveillance and punishment both for Scottie and the spectator. At the same time, by shifting our point of view from Scottie to Judy at the end of the film, Hitchcock exposes the structure of this surveillant gaze. Corber argues that *Vertigo* is similarly ambiguous in its portrayal of race. On the one hand, the story of Carlotta exposes the repressed history of the relationship between Anglos and Mexicans, and dramatizes the return of that repressed. On the other hand, the film is nostalgic about the past, and the threat posed by class difference serves as a displaced statement in the film of the threat of racial difference that is more commonly found in Hollywood films.

Toby Miller's essay on Hitchcock's *The 39 Steps* (1935) and the cultural history of its influences and reception represents a relatively new direction in film studies and Hitchcock scholarship. It is one that moves away from the textually-based ideological criticism that seeks to demonstrate how a film conforms to or departs from the Zeitgeist, in favour of plotting the passage of a text through time and analyzing the way in which it accrues meaning from the cultures in which it circulates and, in turn, contributes meaning to those cultures. Miller places Hitchcock's film in the context of the general history of espionage fiction and closely analyses its relationship to John Buchan's 1915 novel. Hannay, the hero of novel and film, epitomises the talented amateur typical of the genre who always transcends his environment and, hailing from the Dominions, also demonstrates the value of Britain's colonies for the project of imperial renewal. However, while Hitchcock's film inherits Buchan's Edwardian masculine complacency and hostility to the masses, Miller argues that Buchan's conservatism is muted by Hitchcock's affinity with Mass Observation – a movement that cast a skeptical eye upon the discourses on and by the elite in favor of capturing the texture of everyday life – and his substitution of gender-play for Buchan's xenophobia.

In the final chapter of the volume, Ina Rae Hark, in a similar methodological vein but with a narrower cultural focus, explores Hitchcock's neglected films *Foreign Correspondent* (1940), *Saboteur* (1942), and *Lifeboat* (1944) as works of anti-fascist propaganda. Hark argues that while Hitchcock undoubtedly set out to make anti-fascist films in conformity with the war effort that would celebrate the capacity of democratic institutions to defeat the fascist menace, this goal is contradicted by his profound skepticism about the capacity of those institutions to function with the efficiency required. In particular, Hark shows in her analysis of these films that while Hitchcock ostensibly embraces in his own film-making practice the mission of a free press to uphold democracy, this mission is undermined by his portrayal of print and audio-visual media as prone to error, manipulation and fascist infiltration. In fact, she points out, Hitchcock's portrayal of the Nazi captain in *Lifeboat* (who is clearly a directorial surrogate), in opposition to the decadent and disorganized American crew members, attests to the fact that Hitchcock envied fascist organization and single mindedness, as critics of the time intimated in their hostile reviews of the film. Ultimately, Hark concludes, Hitchcock advocated democratic goals and fascist methods in these works and thereby complicated, if not undermined, the simplistic goals of anti-fascist propoganda.

*

We have tried in this volume to reflect the diversity of critical positions and methodologies that comprise the field of Hitchcock Studies by publishing essays that build upon a wide array of approaches to his films. While we are aware that we cannot do justice to all aspects of Hitchcock Studies within a single compass, we do regret a certain emphasis placed on the American films to the neglect of the British works (which is perhaps related to the American base of the editors and the majority of its contributors), particularly in the area of the silent films. The level of recognition and analysis that Hitchcock's silent works have received is not in any way comparable to the literature on the sound films. However, with new prints of these films now available (many made to celebrate Hitchcock's centenary) we are certain that these works will finally receive the attention they richly deserve. Given the eclectic nature of this volume it is inevitable that any given reader will discover an entry that is not to his or her taste, but it is our conviction that the combined effect of the whole demonstrates the vitality of Hitchcock scholarship and its continuing centrality to the field of Cinema Studies.

Richard Allen & Sam Ishii-Gonzalès
New York, August 1999

Notes

1 Gilberto Perez, *The Material Ghost: Films and Their Medium*, Baltimore and London: Johns Hopkins University Press, 1998, p. 9.

2 Lindsay Anderson, 'Alfred Hitchcock' in Albert J. LaValley (ed.), *Focus on Hitchcock*, Englewood Cliffs: Prentice-Hall, 1972, p. 48; emphasis added.

3 Donald Spoto, *The Dark Side of Genius: The Life of Alfred Hitchcock*, Boston: Little, Brown and Company, 1983, p. 36.

4 Quoted in Spoto, *The Dark Side of Genius*, pp. 102–3.

5 François Truffaut with Helen G. Scott, *Hitchcock*, revised edition, New York: Touchstone Books, 1985, p. 43.

6 Anderson, 'Alfred Hitchcock', p. 58.

7 Alfred Hitchcock, 'Rear Window', in Albert J. LaValley (ed.), *Focus on Hitchcock*, p. 2.

8 Albert J. LaValley, 'Introduction', *Focus on Hitchcock*, p. 2.

9 Eric Rohmer and Claude Chabrol, *Hitchcock: The First Forty-Four Films*, trans. Stanley Hochman, New York: Frederick Ungar Publishing, 1979, p. 152.

10 See Robert Kapsis, *Hitchcock: The Making of a Reputation*, Chicago: University of Chicago Press, 1992, pp.69–121.

11 Slavoj Žižek, '"In His Bold Gaze My Ruin Is Writ Large"', in Slavoj Žižek (ed.), *Everything You Always Wanted to Know About Lacan (But Were Afraid to Ask Hitchcock)*, London and New York: Verso, 1992, p. 243.

12 Raymond Durgnat, *The Strange Case of Alfred Hitchcock, or the Plain Man's Hitchcock*, Cambridge, MA: MIT Press, p. 55.

13 *Random House Webster's College Dictionary*, New York: Random House, 1997.

14 Truffaut, *Hitchcock*, p. 195.

List of Contributors

Richard Allen is Chair and Associate Professor of Cinema Studies at New York University. He is author of *Projecting Illusion* (1995) and co-editor with Murray Smith of *Film Theory and Philosophy* (1997). He is director of the Hitchcock Centennial Conference (1999) at New York University and is writing a book on Hitchcock's works.

Raymond Bellour is the Director of Research at C.N.R.S., Paris. He is interested in Romantic and contemporary literature as well as the system of text–image relations found in the mediums of photography, video, virtual images, and, of course, the cinema. His publications include *Henri Michaux* (1965), *Le Western* (1966), *L'analyse du film* (1979), *L'Entre-Images* (1990), *L'Entre-Images 2* (1999), and *Jean-Luc Godard: Son+Image 1974-1991* (1992) co-edited with Mary Lea Bandy. In 1991, he participated with Serge Daney in the creation of *Trafic*, a magazine on the cinema.

Lesley Brill teaches Film Studies at Wayne State University in Detroit. His most recent book is *John Huston's Filmmaking* (1997). He is currently working on applying Elias Canetti's *Crowds and Power* to the study of movies.

Paula Marantz Cohen is Professor of Humanities and Director of the Literature Program at Drexel University, where she also teaches courses on film. Her recent books include *The Daughter as Reader: Encounters Between Literature and Life* (1991) and *Alfred Hitchcock and the Legacy of Victorianism* (1995). She is currently completing a book on silent film and American character.

Robert J. Corber teaches American Studies and Queer Studies at Trinity College. His most recent book is *Homosexuality in Cold War America: Resistance and the Crisis of Masculinity* (1997). He is also the author of *In the Name of National Security: Hitchcock, Homophobia, and the Political Construction of Gender in Postwar America* (1993).

Lee Edelman is Professor of English at Tufts University. He is the author of *Transmemberment of Song: Hart Crane's Anatomies of Rhetoric and Desire* (1987), *Homographesis: Essays in Gay Literary and Cultural Theory* (1994), and numerous essays on cultural studies, film, and queer theory. He is currently completing work on two books: *Hollywood's Anal Compulsion* and *No Future: Queer Theory and the Death Drive* which will include the essay that appears in this volume.

Thomas Elsaesser is Professor in the Dept. of Art and Culture at the University of Amsterdam and Chair of Film and Television Studies. From 1972–1991 he taught English, Film and Comparative Literature at the University of East Anglia, England. Books as author and editor include *New German Cinema: A History* (1989), *Early Cinema: Space Frame Narrative* (1990), *Writing for the Medium: Television in Transition* (1994), *A Second Life: German Cinema's First Decades* (1996), *Fassbinder's Germany: History, Identity, Subject* (1996), and *Cinema Futures: Cain, Abel or Cabel?* (1998).

Ina Rae Hark is Director of the Film Studies Program at the University of South Carolina and a full professor in the English Department. She has co-edited *Screening the Male* (1993) and *The Road Movie Book* (1997), and her work on questions of masculinity and of politics in cinema has appeared in *Cinema Journal, Film History, The Journal of Popular Film, Literature/Film Quarterly, South Atlantic Quarterly*, among others.

S. Ishii-Gonzalès is a doctoral candidate in the Dept. of Cinema Studies at New York University. His dissertation will explore the use-value of queer cultural production through an analysis of the works of Jean Genet, Rainer Werner Fassbinder, and Todd Haynes.

Deborah Knight is Associate Professor of Philosophy and Queen's National Scholar at Queen's University, Kingston, Canada. She has published in many areas, including the philosophy of mind and language, the philosophy of literature, film theory, and aesthetics in such journals as *New Literary History, Stanford French Review, Metaphilosophy*, and *The Journal of Aesthetics and Arts Criticism*. She is associate editor of *Philosophy and Literature* and *Film and Philosophy*.

Thomas Leitch is Professor of English and Director of Film Studies at the University of Delaware. He is the author of *Find the Director and Other Hitchcock Games* (1991).

Joe McElhaney recently completed his doctoral thesis in Cinema Studies at New York University. His dissertation is on melodrama and its relationship to the decline of classical narrative cinema in the 1960s. He has taught film history and aesthetics at New York University, Columbia University, Hunter College, and the School of Visual Arts.

George McKnight is Associate Professor of Film Studies in the School for Studies in Art and Culture, Carleton University, Ottawa, Canada. He has written on various aspects of British Cinema including the representation of class in the 1930s, British film genres, wartime documentaries, and television docudramas in the 1980s. Recently, he edited *Agent of Challenge and Defiance: The Films of Ken Loach* (1997).

Toby Miller is an Associate Professor in Cinema Studies at New York University. He is the author of *The Well-Tempered Self: Citizenship, Culture, and the Postmodern Subject* (1993), *Contemporary Australian Television* with Stuart Cunningham (1994), *The Avengers* (1997), *Technologies of Truth: Cultural Citizenship and the Popular Media* (1998), and *Popular Culture and Everyday Life* with Alec McHoul (1998). He has co-edited *SportCult* with Randy Martin (1999), *Film and Theory: An Anthology* (1999) and *A Companion to Film Theory* (1999), both with Robert Stam. He also edits *Journal of Sport and Social Issues*, and is co-editor of *Social Text*.

James Naremore is Chancellor's Professor of Communication and Culture at Indiana University and the author of several books on modern literature and film, including *The Filmguide to Psycho* (1973), *The Magic World of Orson Welles* (1978), *Acting in the Cinema* (1988), *The Films of Vincent Minnelli* (1993), and *More than Night: Film Noir in its Contexts* (1998).

Brigitte Peucker is Professor of German and Film Studies at Yale University. She has published extensively on issues of representation, both literary and cinematic. Her last book *Incorporating Images, Film and the Rival Arts* appeared with Princeton University Press in 1995. She is currently at work on a book on spectatorship.

William Rothman is Professor of Motion Pictures and Director of the Graduate Program in Film Studies at the University of Miami. He is author of *Hitchcock – The Murderous Gaze* (1982), *The "I" of the Camera* (1988), *Documentary Film Classics* (1997), and *Cavell's The*

World Viewed: A Philosophical Perspective on Film (forthcoming) with Marian Keane. He is also the series editor for the Cambridge University Press "Studies in Film" series.

Susan Smith is a Lecturer in Film Studies at the University of Sunderland, England. In 1998 she completed her doctorate on *Cinematic Point of View in the Films of Hitchcock.* In addition to contributing various journal articles on the director's work, she is currently completing her own book on the tonal aspects of Hitchcock's films. She has also recently completed an article on Fritz Lang's *Metropolis* and is currently planning a future project on the role of musical performance in narrative film.

George Toles is a Professor of English and Film Studies at the University of Manitoba. He has written a number of original feature-length screenplays for filmmaker Guy Madden, including *Careful* and *Twilight of the Ice Nymphs.* He has recently completed a book of critical essays on film entitled *Revealing the Image.* It contains a number of essays on Hitchcock.

Michael Walker read physics at University College Oxford, taught film studies at Hounslow Borough College for twenty-three years, took early retirement, and currently teaches part-time at Royal Holloway, University of London. He is on the editorial board of *Movie* and has contributed both to the magazine and to the *Movie* books: *Film Noir*, *The Western*, and the forthcoming volume on unexplored Hitchcock. He has also contributed to *Film Dope*, *Cine-Action*, and *Framework* magazines.

Susan White is Associate Professor in the Department of English at the University of Arizona in Tucson, Arizona. She is the author of *The Cinema of Max Ophuls: Magisterial Vision and the Figure of Woman* (1995), and editor of film for *Arizona Quarterly.*

Peter Wollen is Chair of the Dept. of Film and Television at UCLA. His recent books include *Raiding the Icebox: Reflections on Twentieth Century Culture* (1992) and a third revised and expanded edition of *Signs and Meaning in the Cinema* (1969, 1972, 1998). His film work includes the screenplay (co-written with Mark Peploe) for Michelangelo Antonioni's *The Passenger* (1975), *Riddles of the Sphinx* (1977) co-directed with Laura Mulvey, and *Friendship's Death* (1988) which he wrote and directed solo. Working with Zaha Hadid as designer, he curated *Addressing the Century: 100 Years of Art and Fashion* (1999) at the Hayward Gallery in London.

Slavoj Žižek is a Senior Researcher at the Department of Philosophy, University of Ljubljana, Slovenia, and visiting professor at numerous American universities, including Princeton, Columbia, New School for Social Research, Ann Arbor, and Minneapolis. Among his recent publications: *The Art of the Ridiculous Sublime: On David Lynch's The Lost Highway* (1999), *The Ticklish Subject: The Absent Center of Political Ontology* (1999), *The Plague of Fantasies* (1997), and *An Essay on Schelling and Related Matters* (1997).

PART I
The Figure of the Author

The dandyism of sobriety – Alfred Hitchcock

Chapter 1
The Dandy in Hitchcock

Thomas Elsaesser

Not only every generation, but every critic appropriates his or her own 'Alfred Hitchcock', fashioned in the mirror of the pleasures or uncanny moments one derives from his films. Most scholars have arrived at *their* Hitchcock by paying scrupulous attention to his work, to the individual films, as is quite proper – the more so, since Hitchcock the man was an exceptionally private person. And yet, most are aware of the paradox that this private person also cultivated an exceptionally public persona quite apart, or so it seems, from his work. From very early on in his career he was a star, he knew he was a star, and he dramatised himself as a star.

The question occupying me in this paper is whether in this most self-reflexive of cinematic *œuvres* we do not find a 'portrait of the artist'. Not, of course, of the historical individual – that can be left to the biographers – but of the type of creative being, bridging and maybe even reconciling the rift that in the past, before he became a classic, so often appeared in Hitchcock criticism: between the entertainer and the 'serious artist'. Rather than take the usual route of polarising the two terms, I want to make my tentative answer hinge upon what I consider to be the enigma of Hitchcock's Englishness.

In the critical literature, there is no shortage of coherent images of Hitchcock. No need for me to present them in detail: the Catholic and Jansenist, the artist of the occult forces of light and darkness, the master-technician, the supreme showman, and so on. In Britain, two Hitchcocks dominated the crucial period of revaluation in the 1960s. One, found in the pages of *Sight and Sound*, was characterised by either disdainful or regretful dismissal of the American Hitchcock. The foil for it was a preference, nostalgically tinged, for the craftsman-stylist with an eye for typically English realism or social satire. Polemically opposed to this view was Robin Wood's Hitchcock, who emerged not only as a very serious artist, but one who in his American films had a consistent theme, almost a humanist concern: the therapeutic formation of the couple and the family.[1] Such a notion of Hitchcock the moralist was already anticipated and rejected by Lindsay Anderson when he wrote in 1949: 'Hitchcock has never been a *serious* director. His films are interesting neither for their ideas nor for their characters. None of his early melodramas can be said to carry a message, and when one does appear, as in *Foreign Correspondent*, it is banal in the extreme . . . In the same way, Hitchcock's characterisation has never achieved – or aimed at – anything more than surface verisimilitude.'[2]

Peter Wollen might be said to have developed *his* Hitchcock in opposition to both of these English constructs, apparently leaning more towards seeing him as a director who subverts the morality, the politics and the realism of his sources, in order to exhibit their narrative and structural mechanisms. 'For Hitchcock it is not the problem of loyalty or allegiance which is uppermost, but the mechanisms of spying and pursuit in themselves.'[3] But these mechanisms, as Wollen wisely adds, 'have their own psychological significance. In the end we discover that to be a master-technician in the cinema is to speak a rhetoric which is none other than the rhetoric of the unconscious.'[4] Since then, almost all the major readings of Hitchcock have followed and explored this path, often with spectacular success. The very force and cogency of this success – notably through Raymond Bellour's work, strongly persuading us to accept a definition of the American cinema and of classical narrative remade in the image of Hitchcock – makes me, perversely, want to look for a more limited, historical, more English and more 'ideological' Hitchcock.

I take my cue from a few casual remarks by Raymond Durgnat, who has commented on Hitchcock's affinities with Symbolism and Decadence. Durgnat writes: 'Since the cinema is traditionally associated with the lower social grades, a man who delights in perfectly wrought film form is likely to find himself referred to as a master craftsman, and the full sense of his involvement with aesthetics is missed . . . Hitchcock is as lordly as any Symbolist of *l'art pour l'art* . . . A craftsman whose craft is aesthetics and who takes a deep pleasure in practising it as meticulously as Hitchcock does, is an aesthete.' And Durgnat points to a spiritual affinity with Oscar Wilde, calling Hitchcock 'an epicure of suspense and terror' whose films bring to mind 'titles of the Decadence: *Le Jardin des Supplices, Les Fleurs du Mal*'.[5] It is this cultural sensibility and aesthetic temperament that I want to investigate a little further.

Is Hitchcock an aesthete in his work, and as Durgnat implies, was he a dandy in life? Let me remind you of some typical attitudes that are supposed to make a dandy. A dandy is preoccupied, above all, with style. A dandy makes a cult of clothes and manners. A dandy has an infinite capacity to astound and surprise. A dandy is given to a form of wit which seems to his contemporaries mere cynicism. A dandy must be negative: neither believing in the world of men – virility, sports – nor in the world of women – the earthy, the life-giving, the intuitive, the natural and flowing. A dandy prefers fantasy and beauty over maturity and responsibility, he pursues perfection to the point of perversity. He is, to quote an authoritative study, 'a man dedicated solely to his own perfection through a ritual of taste . . . free of all human commitments that conflict with taste: passion, moralities, ambitions, politics or occupations'.[6] And he despises everything that is vulgar, common, associated with commerce and a mass public.

Now, granted, it is difficult to recognise in this description the familiar and portly figure, dressed in sober business suits; Catholic, devoted husband and father, the son of a grocer; the quiet, private upholder of domestic virtues *par excellence*. It is difficult if not incongruous to discern in the familiar silhouette the traits of a Baudelaire, or Oscar Wilde, or Proust or Diaghilev. Neither does there seem to be any connection, either directly or indirectly, with the British Pre-Raphaelites or the Bloomsbury Group. None of the gregariousness, none of the in-group rituals, but also little of the élitism or the anti-democratic exclusivity of the European aesthetic coteries in literature or the performing arts.

But let us look a little further: sartorial dandyism, the cult of clothes. True, Hitchcock wore sober business suits, but he *always* wore them, in every climate, in his office, on the set, in the Californian summer, in the Swiss Alps or in Marrakesh. As John Russell

Taylor remarks: 'When he was filming he would turn up punctiliously at the Studio every day disguised as an English businessman in the invariable dark suit, white shirt and restrained dark tie. In the 1930s the fact of wearing a suit and tie, even in the suffocating heat of a Los Angeles summer, was not so bizarre as it has since become, but in a world where many of the film-makers affected fancy-dress –De Mille's riding breeches, Sternberg's tropical tea-planter outfit – Hitch's was the fanciest of them all by being the least suitable and probable.'[7] Quite plainly, Hitchcock was applying a most rigorous public gesture: the dandyism of sobriety.

The ritual of manners. It already annoyed Lindsay Anderson that Hitchcock, when he came to London, stayed at a luxury hotel. It smacked to him of Bel Air snobbery, contempt, and a vulgar display of *money*. The point, however, was that Hitchcock *always* stayed at the *same* hotel, in the same suite at Claridges, just as at home, he always had dinner at Chasen's. Affecting a superstitious nature, a fear of crossing the street or driving a car was part of the same public gesture: to make out of the contingencies of existence an absolute and demanding ritual, and thereby to exercise perfect and total control, almost as if to make life his own creation. It is a choice, not so different from, say, Ronald Firbank's, a notable dandy of the 1920s who, after moving to another part of London, decided to retain his gardener, but insisted that the gardener should walk, in a green baize apron and carrying a watering can, from his lodgings along Piccadilly and Regent Street to Firbank's new home in Chelsea.

Hitchcock's daily rituals, which he made known to everyone, are not only a rich man's indulgence of his own convenience, they touch one of the dandy's main philosophical tenets: to make no concessions to nature, at whatever price. Hitchcock's life, which has been seen as that of 'a straightforward middle-class Englishman who happens to be an artistic genius',[8] seems in its particular accentuation, its imperviousness to both change and time, more problematic, more enigmatic than merely the attempt to cling to the values of his native country, out of season, as it were. Nor is it simply the mask of a man whose painful shyness makes him adopt a role that everyone recognises and therefore dismisses: for that, his work is too much obsessed with domination – of who controls whom by the power of the gaze, of fascination and its objects. More pertinent, then, is the suggestion that Hitchcock's lifestyle was a determined protest, the triumph of artifice over accident, a kind of daily victory over chance, in the name of a spirituality dedicating itself to making life imitate art. The revolt against nature, of course, is one of the strongest traditions of European aestheticism and dandyism – from Baudelaire's *Paradis Artificiels*, via Huysman's *À Rebours*, to Oscar Wilde's *The Truth of Masks* and *The Decay of Lying*. From the latter comes the most well-known defence of Hitchcock's use of back projection, process shots and studio sets: 'The more we study art, the less we care for nature. What art really reveals to us is nature's lack of design, her curious crudities, her extraordinary monotony, her absolutely unfinished condition. Nature has good intentions, of course, but as Aristotle once said, she cannot carry them out. When I look at a landscape I cannot help seeing all its defects. It is fortunate for us, however, that nature is so imperfect, as otherwise we should have no art at all. Art is our spirited protest, our gallant attempt to teach nature her proper place.'[9] Hitchcock fully responded to Wilde's challenge when, famously, he said: 'My films are not slices of life. They're slices of cake.'[10]

As in his work, so in his life Hitchcock excelled in turning a cliché inside out. Everyone is agreed that he was a professional, an addict to work. Yet, part of the image of a dandy is that he disdains work. Hitchcock was able to cultivate both images simultaneously: that of perfection and of effortless ease. A film is finished before it is begun: creation takes place elsewhere, in another scene, not in the process of filming. No commentator leaves out the description of Hitchcock on the set, sitting in his director's chair, appearing languid, his mind on something else, or simply looking bored. He made a point of never looking through the camera lens. 'It would be as though I distrusted the cameraman and he was a liar . . . I don't rush the same evening to see "Has it come out?" That would be like going to the local camera shop to see the snaps and make sure that nobody had moved.'[11]

This immobility is another important clue: the true work of the dandy is to expend all his effort on creating about his person the impression of utter stasis. One recalls the sphinx-like profile he presented as his trademark, and in later life, his public appearance was designed to accentuate the statuesqueness of his massive body. Disarmingly, he turned himself into his own monument, aware of his own immortality. Of course, he carried it lightly, like the wax effigy with which he let himself be photographed and which, deep-frozen, appeared among his wife's groceries in the refrigerator. In a typical inversion of a romantic motif – that of the double – Hitchcock rehearsed his own death and lent it the semblance of life.

If his working methods show a disdain for improvisation, his films stand and fall by the degree to which they exhibit the intricacies of their design. While one can interpret this as a need for order, for control (and the domination of recalcitrant material is clearly part of the film-maker's ambition to possess the world and fix it through the gaze), it is equally the case that in the quality and patterning of the scripts, Hitchcock manifested a most exuberant freedom and playfulness, a love of ornament, of which the much-vaunted realistic touches seem only the most obvious manifestations. Artifice, in Hitchcock, controls the shape of the films' dramatic structure, based as it is on always seeking out contrasts, counterpoints, ironies and reversals, thereby also appealing to a powerfully *intellectual* sense of abstract form.

In this regard, Hitchcock is a film-maker's director, and one wonders whether the persuasiveness of a Proppian or Levi-Strauss-inspired analysis of Hitchcock's plots stems in no small measure from the 'musical' or contrapuntal temperament typical of an aesthete's sensibility, at least as much as from the archetypal, mythological nature of the communication set in motion by the cinema generally, considered as mass-art narrative. Paradoxically, this draws attention to a certain modernism in Hitchcock, which has to do with forcing as sharply as possible the line where the sensuous, the concrete quality of film appears as a disguise for the mechanical, the abstract, and *its* sensuality. Gavin Lambert has remarked that 'many scenes and details from his movies could be titled like surrealistic paintings: Human Being Caged by Bird, Cigarette Extinguished in Fried Egg, and . . . Young Man Dressed as his Dead Mother . . .'[12] Rather than relating this aspect of Hitchcock to an approximation of dream-like states, an argument can be made that sees him as a film-maker of ideas, in much the same way as Duchamp was a painter of ideas, and with rather a similar cult of the sterile, of the degradation inherent in matter, as the essence of male desire and its manifestations in art.

If this seems rather fanciful, something like it has nonetheless been implicitly recognised before. Hitchcock's critics, for instance, have often been offended by what appeared to be his obsession with 'effects', his purely external manipulation of fear, suspense and the audience's emotions – which he played, according to the well-known dictum, like other people play the piano. What have been negatively described as 'gimmicks', or tricks are, at the same time, signs of a will towards abstraction, and a part of a modernist's conceptualisation of the artist's material. One of the 'gimmicks' that Hitchcock's realist critics objected to, for instance, was the scene in *39 Steps* (1935), when the woman's scream, upon discovering the body, was in effect substituted by the whistle of a train entering a tunnel. Or, in a similar register, the electronic simulation of bird-cries and wing-beating in *The Birds* (1963), the use of a violin at an abnormally high pitch in *Psycho* (1960), the look of surprise on the face of the real Mr Townsend in *North by Northwest* (1959), which turns out to be due not to the photo that Cary Grant is holding out to him but to the knife in his back. Hitchcock's imagination seizes on occasions, emotions, at the point where within the human element the mechanical becomes visible, undoing thereby the anthropomorphism that the cinema so deceptively simulates.[13] One remembers the scene described to Truffaut, that was to have gone into *North by Northwest*: a discussion between the hero and a foreman as they walk along a Detroit car assembly line. We see a new car being put together, and when it's finally completed and rolls off the end of the line, a man's body pops out. Not only does the mechanical here produce the human, it produces it *ex nihilo*, so to speak, and what it produces is a corpse. The scene has a special status in never having been filmed, and yet many times told: it is in itself a parable of cinema, the making of a Hitchcock film.

The principle at work here is that of negativity, where the human is bounded everywhere and contained by the mechanical, by death and by absence: all metaphors of the cinema at work in defying nature. It can perhaps be best exemplified by repeating Hitchcock's own version of the *MacGuffin*: 'The word MacGuffin comes from a story about two men in an English train, and one says to the other: "What's that package on the baggage rack over your head?" "Oh," he says, "that's a MacGuffin." The first one says, "well, what's a MacGuffin?" "It's an apparatus for trapping lions in the Scottish Highlands." So the other one says, "But there are no lions in the Scottish Highlands!" And he answers, "Then that's no MacGuffin." '[14]

We know that the MacGuffin is the red herring, the thing the characters make much of, but which for the story is irrelevant, and for the audience no more than a bait. But looked at from another aspect, Hitchcock's story of the MacGuffin is the very epitome of a narrative process, the process of negation, of cancelling something out, what in the language of Derrida one might call an 'erasure'. Phrased by Hitchcock as a kind of pseudo-definition, the anecdote confirms, in a most theoretical way, Hitchcock's profound grasp of what he usually puts in rather simpler terms, like 'I'm interested not so much in the stories I tell as in the means of telling them'.[15] The MacGuffin, considered as a structure, turns on a contradiction: 'that's a MacGuffin'/'that's not a MacGuffin'. And it does so by operating a switch of identity and transferring the terms' denotation. The MacGuffin is, in Hitchcock's pure cinema, the 'pure signifier' to which no signified corresponds. Without stretching the point, one might speak here of the logic of transference itself, of the dynamic of substitution and erasure. In a film like *Strangers on a*

Train (1951), this logic can be observed in its most abstract form at the same time as it is firmly embedded in the narrative itself. As critics have remarked, the 'theme' of transference of guilt, the exchange of crime, the *doppelgänger* motif is actually realised in terms of a series of verbal and visual puns, centred on the notion of crossing, crossing over, double-crossing, criss-crossing. Visually, the film opens with feet crossing the frame diagonally, then the shape of a double cross formed by the railway tracks, and finally, the crossing of legs, where the two protagonists accidentally meet. On the verbal level, *Strangers* plays on the moral implication of crossing someone, running across someone, being cross with someone and double-crossing someone: all in all, a remarkable case of 'inner speech', as it was defined by the Russian formalists in the 1920s. Not to forget the crossed tennis rackets on Guy's cigarette lighter, or the audience going cross-eyed during the vital tennis match. This is presumably why the film does not end with Bruno's death on the merry-go-round. By repeating the opening scene in the train, and the opening line, 'Say, aren't you Guy Haines?', the film seems to cancel itself by establishing the diagrammatic abstraction in a kind of double mirror, where the mathematical figures of the double (parallel) and the diagonal cross emerge as the true obsession of the film. As Hitchcock says to Truffaut: 'Isn't it a fascinating design? One could study it forever.'[16] Similarly, an early film, like *Number Seventeen* (1932), much underrated by critics looking for realist touches, is entirely constructed around transfer, switch and substitution in an abstract cancellation of the signified, reminiscent of that other master of pure cinema, Fritz Lang.

This 'conceptual' quality of Hitchcock's imagination, which one might, with perhaps too slight an emphasis on its many implications, describe as a love of paradox, is worth noting, because the issue of Hitchcock's morality has so often been debated. If for Rohmer and Chabrol the master theme is the transference of guilt, if Robin Wood found his therapeutic theme in the moral ambiguities of choices opening up at every turn, if we can find Levi-Straussian antinomies and binary oppositions generating and traversing every text, if the secret of Hitchcock's enunciative process is a principle of alternation, we are clearly dealing with something which in its structural dimension considerably undercuts a specific moral impulse that is supposed to inform the work. Rather, it is the insistence on form itself that constitutes an essential part of Hitchcock's morality.[17]

One evident implication, surely, is that Hitchcock's art is the art of surface, intimately connected with the notion of effect on the one hand, and with the sensibility of the dandy on the other. One might phrase it as itself a paradox: Hitchcock cultivates surface as the true profundity of the cinema, and it would be shallow indeed to call him the moralist of appearance. There is in his films a complete devotion to surface, which should not be mistaken for a mere interest in technique, and it might be more appropriate to say that technique is only the very inadequate name applied to a cinema dedicated to the rule of contiguity and metonymy. Whether it's the accidental brush of feet in *Strangers on a Train*, the crossed trajectories in a hotel lobby of *North by Northwest* ('Paging Mr Kaplan') or the converging paths when Karen Black appears suddenly out of nowhere and forces Bruce Dern to stop in *Family Plot* (1976), in every instance, the narrative is generated out of a veritable 'splicing together': the fortuitous encounter of the unlikely with the improbable. The somewhat facile generalisation that in

Hitchcock evil does not lurk *behind* a door but is there, in broad daylight, and comes out of a blue sky, might be rephrased by saying that montage, in Hitchcock (as in Eisenstein) is the very sign of a categorical refusal to give the cinematic image any kind of transcendental value. And it seems entirely appropriate that film scholars, digging deeper in his films, should discover structures that reveal an ever greater simplicity, where the elements become more mathematical, more musical, more schematic. It is therefore one of the incidental virtues of Raymond Bellour's work that it emphatically brings us back to the surface in Hitchcock, where what we need to know can be grasped by an attention to segmentation, the interplay that arises from the precision with which the film-maker controls, for instance, the size of the shot, the direction of the gaze and the motility of the camera.[18]

By outlining some of Hitchcock's particular characteristics as a film-maker of surface and contiguity, I am suggesting that the chance encounter, the collision of apparently unrelated destinies, as in *North by Northwest* or *Psycho* or *Strangers on a Train*, leads us not necessarily into the realm of moral and metaphysical essences, but also constitutes a denial of essence, an aesthetic delight in what, from a different vantage point, is always a catastrophe: identity as merely the violent suppression of random gestures and exchanges. In Hitchcock, action always takes precedence over character, which is why his narratives offer themselves for structural or morphological analysis.[19]

Such partiality for the contiguous is an important clue to Hitchcock's humour, and more specifically, his irrepressible penchant for playing the practical joker, the perpetrator of countless hoaxes: I shall not attempt to recall here the stories, anecdotes and legends, kept in circulation not least by Hitchcock himself, whose point invariably seems to be to confound a certain naïve literalness with lessons in 'lateral thinking'. There is the story of Hitchcock serving blue food at dinner, because one of his guests had, on a previous occasion, made a crack about the master's devotion to 'cordon bleu' cooking. It would be worthwhile to study in detail the principles underlying Hitchcock's wit, his verbal playfulness, his penchant for epigrams: it relates closely to the predominance of paradox and dramatic irony in his plots, and the principle of erasure through double transfer which I briefly analysed as the structure of the MacGuffin. To give an example of Hitchcock's verbal dandyism, let me cite an anecdote that James Stewart likes to tell about work on the set: 'Hitchcock actually has very little regard for the spoken word .... He pays no attention to the actual words – he's done all that, finished all that months before. He's an absolute villain to script girls and people that have to follow the lines. So when the script girl says to him, "Mr Hitchcock, Mr Stewart didn't say anything like what's in the script," he'd say, "It sounded alright; *grammatically* it was alright." '[20]

The need to startle and to baffle an audience is of course part of any showman's artistic make-up. But the practical joker displays a particularly violent ambiguity: he attracts and holds an audience in order to distance himself the more definitely from any community with it. He recalls, in this guise, Baudelaire's *saltimbanque* – the mountebank, the circus artist, the jester of modernist literature and painting – often a figure of pathos, as he stands apart from the crowd, yet bears the burden of their amusement. To the unconscious disloyalty of the audience corresponds the practical joker's betrayal of his victim's trust. We find, especially in Hitchcock's British films, a number of references to this ambiguous figure: the portrait of the jester, for instance, which plays such an important role in *Blackmail* (1929), or the murderer in the 1930 *Murder!* (playing a circus acrobat) and the 1937 *Young and Innocent* (disguised as a black-face minstrel), both of whom one hesitates to call villains, precisely because the pathos of their costume underlines their separateness and isolation from people enjoying each others' company. Separateness, distance, is the hallmark of the public persona which Hitchcock also created for himself with his television appearances. Not only did he stand apart, there was the manner in which he 'presents' the TV shows, quite different from the personal appearances in the films: the host's presentations of *The Alfred Hitchcock Hour* displayed the more grotesque, clownish, aesthetically aggressive sides of his showmanship, letting these find expression and form in Grand Guignol images of himself with a bloody hatchet buried in his bald pate, or carrying his own head under his arm.

The *saltimbanque*, on the face of it, seems to have little in common with the dandy, especially since we do find quite a number of dandies among the villains in Hitchcock's films. From Ivor Novello in *The Lodger* (1926), Peter Lorre in *The Man Who Knew Too Much* (1934), Robert Walker in *Strangers on a Train*, down to James Mason in *North by Northwest*, Hitchcock's villains are often either sharp dressers or aristocratic aesthetes, often made 'sinister' by stereotypically homosexual traits or hints of sexual perversion.[21] Yet some of Hitchcock's *heroes* are also practical jokers and even aristocratic rogues: Robert Donat in *The 39 Steps*, Cary Grant in the 1941 *Suspicion* (and the 1955 *To Catch a Thief*), not to mention Melanie Daniels who in *The Birds* is introduced as a practical joker.[22]

The sensibility I am trying to sketch for understanding the Hitchcock persona, then, is clearly a composite one: a combination of the aesthete, the rogue and the mountebank. At the same time, it's precisely this somewhat unlikely combination that makes Hitchcock's dandyism specifically English and historically definable. For these attitudes can be seen to occupy, in the literary and artistic culture of the 1920s and 1930s, one side of a dialectic which opposes the values of Victorian and Edwardian public life – social responsibility, maturity, moral and artistic seriousness – with the values of a generation who was in rebellion against identifying art exclusively with seriousness, an attitude they considered philistine, suffocating and inartistic. Instead, they affected and cultivated, out of an equally serious commitment to art, a mode of irresponsibility, playfulness, unseriousness and sexual ambiguity that combined the stance of the Oscar Wilde dandy with a more aggressive brand of schoolboy humour and a wilful immaturity. Reacting to the 'consensus humanism' of Edwardian England, because they saw in the cultural forms of seriousness and responsibility an ideology of power and social hierarchy digging itself in, after the débâcle of the First World War, the dandies of the 1920s and 1930s, according to a popular study of the period, 'shared a sense of humour, a humour developed to abnormal intensity, so that it takes over the psychic and social functions usually performed by the erotic or idealistic aspects of personality'.[23]

This seems a pertinent observation also in relation to Hitchcock: if, however remotely, he belongs to this side of the cultural divide, then it may be possible to see his irony, his verbal wit, the apparent unseriousness and showmanship both in his persona and as it manifests itself in the structure and material of his films, as itself part of a more coherent project – that of a refusal, a rejection, a protest against a specifically English concept of maturity, dominant in the culture in which he grew up. We could then say, without merely stating a paradox, that Hitchcock's cultivated unseriousness has behind it the force of a moral stance. In any direct sense, Hitchcock is not a social critic: his morality resides in the complexity of his dandyism and what it entails ideologically. That it is a morality mediated by a culturally specific gesture of refusal makes the reading of his films in the manner of Robin Wood so problematic, because the values that Wood asserts in Hitchcock (maturity, moral growth, the therapeutic theme) are precisely the values upheld by the inheritors of the grand tradition against which the dandy in Hitchcock is in revolt. On the other hand, a purely formal or structural reading of Hitchcock tends to ignore the extent to which Hitchcock's anti-humanism, his cult of artifice and surface are the result of a moral and historical *parti pris*. That Hitchcock chose the dandy side of the British cultural character – a choice greatly facilitated by his move to Hollywood – shows another irony, for in Hollywood, the *dandy* turned into the *saltimbanque*: he chose a disguise that remarkably looked like it belonged to the other party – that of philistine Victorianism.

It does not seem entirely by chance, then, that one finds most of the English dandies from the 1930s but also after, choose to live a kind of double life: both inside and outside the British Establishment. Many of the writers and artists among them moved into voluntary exile – California, France, Italy. Some of them deliberately betrayed their social class: W. H. Auden, Christopher Isherwood, Stephen Spender siding with the cause of the international proletariat, Oswald Mosley founding the British Fascist Party. Others, in apparently secure and even higher places, chose to betray their country. For among the dandies of the 1930s are Guy Burgess, George Blake, Donald Maclean and Anthony Blunt, all at various times spies or agents for the Soviet Union.

This peculiar complexion of the British dandy may well induce us to look once more at the preponderance of the spy, the traitor, the agent and the double agent in Hitchcock's work. In the image of the saboteur, the secret agent, the man who knew too much, the foreign correspondent, there is always in Hitchcock an emphasis on disguise and *mise-en-scène*. Now, a popular entertainer knows that spy stories will always find their public, but few film-makers have given the thrill of playing double agent quite as consummate an embodiment in film after film as Hitchcock. One may well ask whether the man who in his public persona chose to 'disguise' himself as a dandy and jester did not put into these thrilling villains a little piece of his own creative self, giving us a portrait of the artist not just as *metteur-en-scène*, but as the man who knew too much. Or, putting it slightly differently, the role Hitchcock, throughout his long years in California, pleased himself to perform was not, as many believed, that of unofficial ambassador. Instead, he was the secret agent of an Englishness more devious for being deadpan, in a medium that happily knows loyalty and pays allegiance not to king and country, but to the customer as king: His/Her Majesty, the spectator. However, this loyalty, too, must not be taken altogether at face value. Hitchcock's films – splitting our gaze and dividing our attention, transferring our identity and switching our allegiance – teach us the subtlest and most beguiling form of treason: recognising in the other a part of ourselves. Putting our ordinary selves under erasure, the dandy in Hitchcock makes us rediscover the morality of artifice. With such traitors, who needs royalists . . .

Notes

First published in Italian, in E. Bruno, ed., *Per Alfredo Hitchcock*, 1981; first printed in English: in *The McGuffin* no. 14, November 1994.

1 Robin Wood, *Hitchcock's Films*, London: Studio Vista, 1965, p. 26.
2 Lindsay Anderson, 'Alfred Hitchcock', in Al LaValley (ed.), *Focus on Hitchcock*, Englewood Cliffs: Prentice Hall, 1972, p. 58.
3 Peter Wollen, 'Hitchcock's Vision', in *Cinema* (UK), no. 3, June 1969, p. 2.
4 Wollen, 'Hitchcock's Vision', p. 4.
5 Raymond Durgnat, *The Strange Case of Alfred Hitchcock*, Cambridge, MA: MIT Press, p. 38.
6 Ellen Moers, *The Dandy*, quoted in Martin Green, *Children of the Sun*, New York: Basic Books, 1976, p. 9.
7 John Russell Taylor, *Hitch*, New York: Pantheon Books, 1978, p. 159.
8 Taylor, *Hitch*, p. 159.
9 Oscar Wilde, 'The Decay of Lying', in *Intentions*, London, 1981, p. 1.
10 François Truffaut, *Hitchcock*, New York: Simon and Schuster, 1985, p. 103.
11 Alfred Hitchcock, 'I Wish I Didn't Have to Shoot the Picture', in Al LaValley (ed.), *Focus on Hitchcock*.
12 Quoted in Chris Hodenfield, 'Murder by the Babbling Brook', in *Rolling Stone*, 29 July 1976, p. 26.
13 See, for instance, Peter Noble (ed.), *BFI Index to the Work of Alfred Hitchcock*, London: BFI, 1949, p. 3: 'I aim to give the public good healthy mental shake-ups. Civilisation has become so screening and sheltering that we cannot experience sufficient thrills at first hand. Therefore, to prevent our becoming sluggish and jellified we have to experience them artificially, and the screen is the best medium for this.'
14 Truffaut, *Hitchcock*, p. 138.
15 Quoted in André Bazin, 'Hitchcock vs Hitchcock', in Al LaValley (ed.), *Focus on Hitchcock*, p. 64.
16 Truffaut, *Hitchcock*, p. 195.
17 See Robert Mundy, 'Another Look at Hitchcock', in *Cinema* (UK) no. 6/7, p. 11: 'The view of Hitchcock as a Catholic moralist is untenable when *I Confess* [1953] is compared to *Downhill* [1927]: public school morality is assigned the same significance as Catholic dogma. The situation where guilt is transferred is what appeals to Hitchcock, and this situation is not necessarily charged with any religious significance. Religion is almost a MacGuffin.'
18 Bellour's most famous essay on Hitchcock is his 115-page analysis of *North by Northwest*, 'Le Blocage symbolique', originally in *Communications*, no. 23, Paris, Seuil, 1975. Available in English are his '*The Birds*: Analysis of a Sequence', mimeograph, The BFI Advisory Service, n.d.; 'Hitchcock, the Enunciator', in *Camera Obscura*, no. 1 Fall 1977, pp. 66–91; and 'Psychosis, Neurosis, Perversion', in *Camera Obscura*, no. 3–4, 1979.
19 'His idea of character is rather primitive.' Raymond Chandler, quoted in Al LaValley (ed.), *Focus on Hitchcock*, p. 102.
20 Quoted in Chris Hodenfield, 'Murder by the Babbling Brook', p. 24.

21 One might add Joseph Cotten as Uncle Charlie in *Shadow of a Doubt* (1943) and the Right Honourable Charles Adare in *Under Capricorn* (1949).

22 The suggestion of listing among Hitchcock's dandies one of his female heroines would have to contend, as Ken Mogg, editor of *The McGuffin* has remarked, with a statement flatly contradicting it: ' "Woman," wrote Baudelaire, "is the opposite of the dandy. Therefore she must inspire horror [...] Woman is *natural*, that is to say, abominable." ' *The McGuffin* no. 14, November 1994, p. 1.

23 Martin Green, *Children of the Sun*, p. 13.

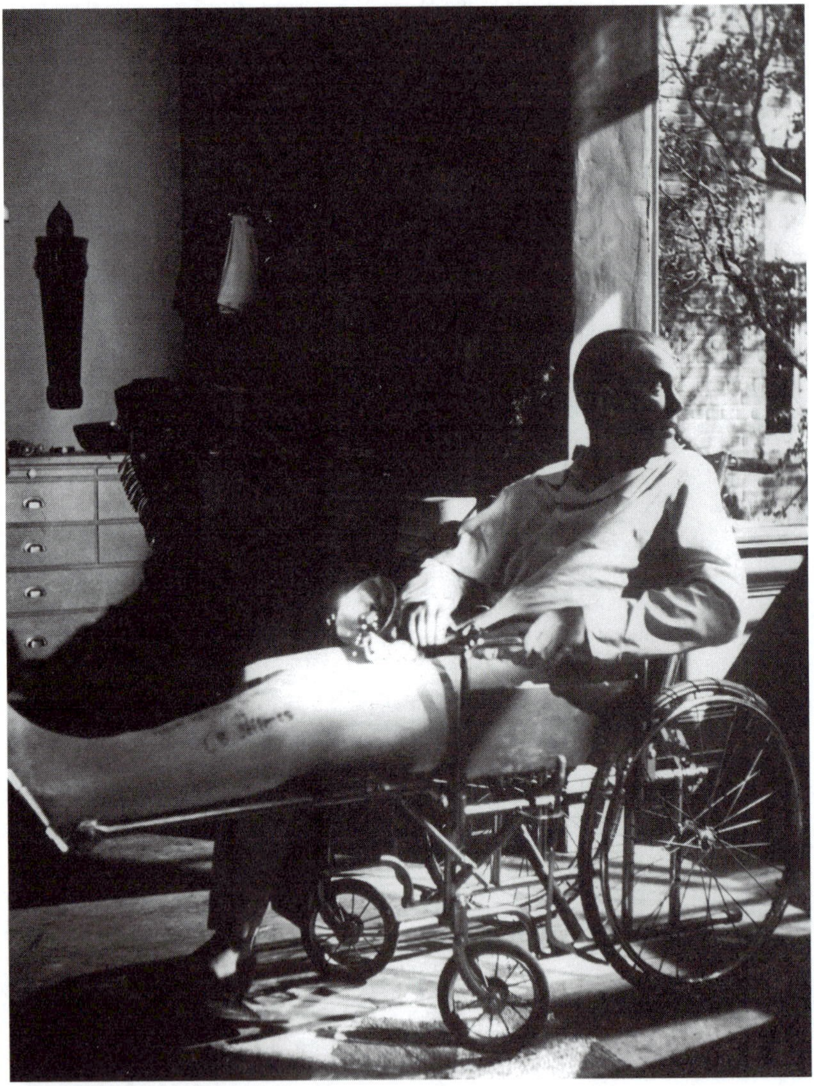

The portrait of a gentleman – Hitchcock's Jamesian classic *Rear Window*

Chapter 2
James, Hitchcock and the Fate of Character

Paula Marantz Cohen

My purpose in comparing Henry James and Alfred Hitchcock is to explore how the form of representation corresponds to the content represented – in this case, literary versus cinematic form as it applies to the idea of character in the world. James and Hitchcock lend themselves to this kind of comparison because they stand in similar positions with respect to the form in which they worked. James began writing novels when the genre was at its peak of influence and popularity; the end of his career coincided with the waning not only of the novel but also of the entire literary tradition of which the novel marked the culmination. Hitchcock entered film as the medium came of age, having thrown off its ties to non-narrative forms of entertainment like vaudeville and the circus; his career followed the development of classical narrative film to its end (if the modernists could speak of the death of the novel, surely we can now speak of the death of narrative film). Henry Nash Smith maintained that Henry James helped bring about 'the liquidation of the nineteenth century'.[1] Alfred Hitchcock, I would maintain, helped bring about the liquidation of the twentieth.

Both James and Hitchcock were large, sedentary men, observers rather than active agents in the world around them. In his autobiographic essay, 'A Small Boy and Others', James recalls being daunted by the rowdiness and physicality of other boys and preferring a quiet life at home in the company of his mother, sister and aunt.[2] He was exempted from military service in the Civil War because of a nonspecific back injury, the kind of vague but suggestive symptom that would plague many of the male protagonists in his fiction and exempt them from a life of action.

Like James, Hitchcock was a social outsider. He was described by schoolmates as 'a lonely fat boy' who stood on the sidelines watching the other boys play.[3] He too was favoured by his mother, grew up in the shadow of a more energetic older brother, and was rejected from military service (in World War I), though less mysteriously than James, on account of his weight.

From these basic affinities, however, the two figures diverge sharply and symmetrically – a divergence that tells a great deal about the medium in which each achieved success.

Henry James was born in New York City into a life of privilege. His paternal grandfather had made the family fortune after emigrating from Ireland, leaving future generations to pursue a life of the mind unencumbered by commercial concerns. James's father, Henry James, Sr., was a towering figure in nineteenth-century intellectual culture: a friend of Emerson and Thoreau, a follower of Swedenborg, and an advocate of progressive educational ideas. He taught his sons to distrust authority and to scorn whatever seemed conventional or routine. Henry's older brother William responded to paternal expectations by shifting his professional focus from art to medicine to philosophy and finally to psychology, where he essentially invented the field in its American form. Henry James, less circuitously, found his means of original achievement in fiction writing.

The genteel and intellectual environment that shaped the novelist could not have been further from the background that produced the film-maker. Born a little more than a half-century after James, Hitchcock grew up in a cockney, Catholic household where money and education were in short supply. His father was a greengrocer and fishmonger, and making a living and going to church seem to have been the family's principal concerns. Hitchcock's salient recollection of growing up (repeatedly recounted to interviewers) involved being sent as punishment by his father to the local police station with a note telling the officer on duty to lock him up. The incident dramatises the difference between James's upbringing, where social authority was distrusted, and Hitchcock's, where it went unquestioned. The differing attitudes would be reflected in the different audiences that each would address through his work.

Although James's earliest stories and reviews brought him a modest degree of success, his style grew more difficult as he gained in experience, and his readership grew accordingly smaller and more select. It was an evolution discernible in the culture at large. When, barely five years after James's death, Hitchcock began making movies, the literary world had become clearly divided into 'high' and 'low': the modernists, writing for an élite coterie, and the popular dime novelists, writing for a large, lower-middle-class market, their work serving increasingly as the basis for movie scenarios. Thus the popular elements of literary culture merged with and were ultimately subsumed by film culture.

Lacking in education and family connections, it seems natural that Hitchcock should be drawn to the popular medium of film, and that he be led there through a visual rather than a literary route. After landing his first job as a researcher for the Henley Telegraph and Cable Company, he quickly found his way into the advertising department. A few years later, at the age of 21, he was hired as a title designer by the newly established British branch of the Famous Players Lasky Company. As he rapidly rose to the position of director, his mind remained, as he put it, 'strictly visual' and indifferent to literary effects. 'I don't like literature that is flowery and where the main attraction is the turn of phrase,' he explained to François Truffaut.[4] He would elaborate on this point in discussing his 1939 adaptation of Daphne du Maurier's novel *Rebecca*: 'The story is old-fashioned; there was a whole school of feminine literature at that period, and though I'm not against it, the fact is that the story is lacking in humor.' The resulting film, he declared, 'was not a Hitchcock picture'.[5] As these remarks suggest, Hitchcock's inclination was to favour humour over sentiment, action over reflection, the visual over the literary, the present over the past. Where James found in the ruminative, 'flowery' aspects of literature a way of reinforcing tendencies cultivated from childhood, Hitchcock embraced film as a means of escaping from such tendencies. Being in control on a movie set and making his cameramen and actors perform difficult manoeuvres and stunts was a way both of getting back at the boys in the schoolyard who played while he looked on and of vicariously putting himself in their place.

But Hitchcock's rejection of literary influence can be seen in formal as well as personal terms. It reflected his appreciation of film as a new narrative form, defined through its difference from literature. This formal appreciation was brought home to him after the box-office failure of *Sabotage*, his 1936 adaptation of Joseph Conrad's *The Secret Agent* and the only adaptation of a classic literary work he would ever attempt. Great literature, he would later explain to Truffaut, 'is someone else's achievement'[6] – and his determination to maintain the distinction between the literary and the cinematic would crop up again and again in their discussion: 'I'm wary of literature. A good book does not necessarily make a good film'; 'I can't read fiction because if I did I would instinctively be asking myself, "Will this make a movie or not?" '; 'What I do is read a story only once, and if I like the basic idea, I just forget all about the book and start to create cinema'; 'When we tell a story in cinema, we should resort to dialogue only when it's impossible to do otherwise.'[7] Such statements express self-conscious support for the integrity of film *as* film – a desire to keep it from contamination by other influences. An analogous loyalty was present for James who wrote numerous essays on the 'architecture of the novel' and the 'house of fiction', and who criticised novelists whose 'baggy monsters' showed an inadequate respect for the shape of their writing. 'The story and the novel, the idea and the form, are the needle and thread,' he explained in his essay 'The Art of Fiction'.[8]

The formal allegiance which each of these figures had to his medium stands behind the reverse direction in which each expatriated himself. For James, America lacked what Lionel Trilling called 'the thick, coarse actuality which the novelist . . . needed for the practice of his craft' and which European culture, with its rich literary tradition and dense social history, offered in abundance.[9] Hitchcock, for his part, felt limited by the cramped facilities and shoestring budgets of the British film industry, and had a 'longing', as Leonard Leff put it, 'for American studios, American craftsmen, and American audiences' – not to mention American money.[10] But Hitchcock's move, while it represented a pursuit of resources in one sense, was also an escape from them in another. For the very lack of cultural and social density that had driven James from America was part of what brought Hitchcock to settle there sixty-five years later and produce his best work.

Movies, as Hitchcock understood very early, were most effective when they made no effort to respect their literary source. This anti-literary bias is compatible with important currents in American thought that had begun to find expression in the nineteenth century. 'I had better never see a book, then to be warped by its attraction clean out of my own orbit, and made a satellite instead of a system,' declared Emerson. 'I did not read books that first summer [at Walden Pond], I hoed beans,' wrote Thoreau. 'A morning-glory at my window satisfies me more than the metaphysics of books,' proclaimed Whitman.[11] These authors were rejecting books, the source and substance of their own livelihood, in favour of more natural and spontaneous forms of expression. They were, in effect, elevating the vitality of American experience over the entrenched customs and traditions of Europe. Film, with its focus on action over words, would be capable of representing the values that nineteenth-century American writers had espoused and identified with their nation. And Hitchcock, with his distaste of 'flowery' language and his avoidance of sources that were part of a 'tradition', would have the conceptual and temperamental resources to realise the potential of film as an American medium.

Hitchcock's British films, from *The Lodger* (1927) with its resonances of Victorian London to *The Lady Vanishes* (1938) with its quirky social types, are linked to a tradition if only because they were made in a culture in which tradition permeated all forms of expression. *Shadow of a Doubt* (1943), with its American setting, is free from the weight of tradition; it shows that depravity could exist even where there was no history of depravity. *Strangers on a Train* (1951), *Rear Window* (1954), the 1956 remake of *The Man Who Knew Too Much*, *Vertigo* (1958), *North by Northwest* (1959) and *Psycho* (1960), all follow in the same mode. They are quintessentially American as well as distinctively Hitchcockian films because they do not rely on assumptions about life or art as these might be produced through a literary tradition or an inherited sense of the past. They are about the immediacy and surprise of experience in action.

If we consider the fundamental difference between literature and film – literature with its loyalties to the historical legacy attached to language, and film with its loyalties to the 'flux of experience' (Emerson's phrase) – we can see why James and Hitchcock would differ in their approach to character. Thus, James uses narrative to *reveal* character, Hitchcock to *create* it in the process of unfolding. One plumbs depths, the other records surfaces. Yet despite this difference in approach, Hitchcock and James follow a similar course of development and arrive at something like the same place. We can see this by comparing the representation of character in James's 1881 novel, *Portrait of a Lady*, and Hitchcock's 1954 film, *Rear Window*. Both works mark a moment of special balance and integration in their respective canons and, when viewed together, reveal basic affinities in the fate of character as it is represented through different media and in different cultural contexts.

Portrait of a Lady is James's best-known and most read novel. James himself called it one of his two 'most proportioned' works, and critics generally see it as an example of the novel form at its best.[12]

Part of what makes *Portrait of a Lady* so representative of its genre is its use of a female character as the guiding consciousness or 'central intelligence' of the work. The use of the female protagonist is bound up with the history of the novel form itself. Economic changes in England and, subsequently, throughout Europe in the seventeenth and eighteenth centuries saw the emergence of a large and affluent middle class. Women from this class, though still confined to domestic space, were liberated from menial household tasks and left free to develop their emotional and imaginative lives – to engage in the kind of anti-utilitarian thinking that could easily be translated into literary style. The first major British novel, Samuel Richardson's *Clarissa*, was, appropriately enough, a novel of letters, since the epistolary form assumed, as the literary critic Ian Watt has pointed out, 'a private and personal relationship . . . which could be carried on without leaving the safety of home'.[13] As the European novel developed into the nineteenth century, it elaborated and refined the personal and domestic attributes of the novel of letters, producing what we tend to call the psychological novel: that penetrating inquiry into the heart and mind of a usually female character as she proceeds, in the wake of obstacles and misunderstandings, to fulfil her destiny in marriage to a man worthy of her. It is a tribute to the influence of the European psychological novel that one can draw a division between American writers like James and Edith Wharton who expatriated themselves in order to be part of this novelistic tradition, and those, like Mark Twain and Herman Melville, who remained in America, and opposed it. The latter, like the less artful dime novelists of the period, can be said to have anticipated the more active, visual and male-oriented attributes of cinema.

But it would be wrong to see Henry James as a conventional practitioner within the European psychological novel. Despite his place in the tradition, he also betrays characteristics that situate him, if not alongside Mark Twain and Edward L. Wheeler (author of the *Deadwood Dick* dime novels), then at least not as squarely with Jane Austen as one might think. James keeps in broad strokes to the form of the European novel, but he also subverts the form by giving his heroines more freedom and by pushing his literary style into new terrain.

James's relationship to the European novel form is seen in the way he presents his heroine to us in *Portrait of a Lady*. In his preface, he explains that he will 'place the centre of the subject in the young woman's own consciousness' and 'show what an "exciting" inward life may do for the person leading it'.[14] This focus on consciousness and inward life is in keeping with standard assumptions about character in European domestic fiction; it assumes that character is 'deep', and it takes advantage of the excavating capacity of words to plumb that depth. But James is not simply content to examine what he describes as 'the fine, full consciousness' of Isabel Archer. He has also set himself the task of having her *act* in the world. 'What,' his narrator in the novel asks, 'was she going to do with herself?'[15] James's object in *Portrait* is to test the effect of experience on formed character – to move the heroine's consciousness from a position of 'being' to one of 'becoming' (to borrow from Emerson again). Heroines from Samuel Richardson's Clarissa Harlowe to Charles Dickens's little Nell were largely reactive, their fine sensibilities vibrating under the pressures that life brought to bear on them. In *Portrait of a Lady*, James wishes to break out of this mould, to use language in the service of something freer and larger than had been possible in the domestic tradition before. He responds to his own question about what Isabel is to do by bringing home his divergence from the tradition in which he is writing: 'With most women one had no occasion to ask it. Most women did with themselves nothing at all; they waited, in attitudes more or less gracefully passive, for a man to come that way and furnish a destiny.' To liberate Isabel from the passive position of 'most women', he engineers a plot that allows for her freedom. Upon her father's death, she is brought to Europe by her aunt where she ingratiates herself with her dying uncle and is left a fortune upon his death. The money, her cousin explains, will 'put wind in her sails';[16] it will give her opportunities that most women of the period, inside or outside of fiction, lacked.

At the same time, however, James is careful to maintain Isabel's freedom within certain gender- and genre-linked conventions. 'I'm not in the least an adventurous spirit. Women are not like men,' Isabel explains to her cousin.[17] Her inclination is not to fight in a war or take a boat down the Amazon, but to marry whom she pleases without consideration of money or status. Her field has been opened, but it remains clearly contained within the limits of the marriage plot.

Rear Window stands with respect to Hitchcock's canon much as *Portrait of a Lady* stands to James's. According to Robin Wood, it is Hitchcock's first masterpiece, and according to Hitchcock himself, it is his greatest example of a 'purely cinematic film'.[18] In keeping with its formal loyalties, *Rear Window* is, in some striking ways, a structural and thematic reversal of James's novel. If the female protagonist in James's novel acts as a filter to experience, examining hidden motives and desires much as the novelist does, the male protagonist in Hitchcock's film is a photographer who records surface reality, much as the film-maker does. L. B. Jefferies (James Stewart) is known by his friends as Jeff, as if to place the intimacy of a first name off limits from the outset. He thrives on following disasters, political uprisings and sports events, and cannot commit to a romantic relationship that might keep him in one place or tethered to one individual. He is all about 'becoming' but has no established or rooted 'being'.

With this conception of character as a point of departure, Hitchcock proceeds to effect change. He incapacitates Jeff with a broken leg, reduces his field of action and vision, and turns him into a facsimile of a woman in much the way that James turns Isabel into a facsimile of a man. Thus, just as James was eager to see how a female consciousness might be tested in the world, Hitchcock shows how a man of action might become a consciousness – might, that is, develop depth. But just as Isabel Archer remains limited by the conventions associated with her sex, L. B. Jefferies remains limited by his. Isabel's drama revolves around a question associated with a domestic plot: who will she marry? Jeff's drama, however, revolves around a question associated with an action plot: how can he prove that the salesman Thorwald (Raymond Burr) murdered his wife? Behind this thematic difference, linked to gender, is a structural difference linked to medium. James, in having Isabel act, continually tells us her motives and desires and keeps us abreast of who she is at every moment, since it is the nature of language to be able to do this. Action in James is really about the rationale for choice. But since film cannot penetrate consciousness in the way language can, it must use surface images to chart the progress of consciousness. And this is what Hitchcock does through the vehicle of the murder that Jeff thinks has happened across the courtyard. The method, as Hitchcock explains it to Truffaut, 'is actually the purest expression of a cinematic idea': 'You have an immobilized man looking out. That's one part of the film. The second part shows what he sees and the third part shows how he reacts.'[19] Looks; sees; reacts – through this visual and dynamic relationship to an extreme experience, Hitchcock is able to chart Jeff's development as an individual with depth and feeling.

The outcomes of both James's novel and Hitchcock's film are compatible with the existential goals they have set for themselves. Isabel begins the novel convinced of her ability to discern the true nature of other people. She ultimately chooses Gilbert Osmond for a husband because she thinks she sees qualities in him that others do not have. But she has not really seen Osmond at all; she has projected her own generous and complex inner life onto him. The antidote to her projection comes from her collision with the world as it 'really' is: depth must find itself checked by surface. To bring home what is at issue, James represents the moment of Isabel's revelation in visual terms: she enters a room and sees her husband sitting while her best friend is standing, and the visual iconography tells her, in a scenic flash, that the two have had an affair. Earlier in the novel, she had been castigated by a practical-minded friend for not being 'enough in contact with reality'.[20] Now, face to face with her husband and his lover, reality is brought home to her with a vengeance. Had Isabel been permitted to choose a husband who coincided with her imaginative expectations (the kind of husband conventionally awarded the heroine in romantic fiction), then her solipsism would have been condoned, her consciousness given no resistance with which to struggle. Instead, the novel means to chasten its heroine: to teach her to be more suspicious of others' motives and to show her how unwieldy reality can be.

Jeff, unlike Isabel, begins the film with no powers of imagination or projection. What so infuriates him about his broken leg is that it leaves him alone and immobilised, and he has no inner resources with which to entertain himself. Marriage, which in the novel constitutes the primary locus of meaning and interest, in the movie seems at first to be the dreariest of last resorts. 'If you don't pull me out of this swamp of boredom,' Jeff warns his boss over the telephone, 'I'm going to do something drastic – I'm gonna get married. Then, I'll never be able to go anywhere.' Spying on his neighbours becomes Jeff's way of filling time, but it is through this occupation that he ultimately learns to feel, and the audience, through his experience, becomes exposed to feelings that might otherwise find no place in a conventional action film.

The scenarios that transpire in the apartments across from Jeff's window are all versions of his 'case', but Thorwald's plot is the most directly matched to his own, its development destined to move in counterpoint to his. When Jeff first sees Thorwald in thrall to a nagging, invalid wife, it is as though he were looking at a film, suitably exaggerated for a mass audience, of what a marriage to his girlfriend Lisa (Grace Kelly) would be like. 'Sometimes it's worse to stay than it is to run,' he comments self-reflexively after Thorwald storms from the apartment. Later, when he begins to suspect Thorwald of murder, his idea seems like simple wish-fulfilment: 'What happens in the Thorwald apartment,' writes Robin Wood, 'represents, in an extreme and hideous form, the fulfillment of Jefferies' desire to be rid of Lisa.'[21] But that desire quickly turns into something else. For the more intent Jeff becomes on proving his murder theory, the more he needs to project himself onto the surface scenarios he has seen; the more, that is, he has to imagine the life of the victim. 'She's an invalid. She needs constant care, and yet no one has been in to see her all day,' he explains, his voice growing shrill and insistent like Mrs Thorwald's had presumably been before her death. A change in sides involves the activation of concern, of discrimination and of empathy. As he pursues Thorwald, he fills himself in, so to speak, until finally, when he confronts his suspect directly, he now occupies the position of immobilised consciousness facing mindless action. He causes the crime to be re-enacted, with himself in the position of the wife and Thorwald in the position of his former self.

While on some level the movie simply takes Jeff from the conventional male position and deposits him in the conventional female position, the change seems to be less about gender and more about larger structural issues. *Rear Window* is a Hitchcock mistaken-identity plot of unusual subtlety and power. We are originally led to believe that Thorwald himself may be the victim of mistaken identity: that Jeff has falsely accused him of murder. But as the viewer becomes more convinced that Jeff is right, more sympathetic with his way of seeing, the mistaken-identity plot shifts to Jeff himself. In solving the murder, he is moving away from a false identification with Thorwald to a true identification of himself (which is really a self-creation) as a character who is not like Thorwald. This movement involves learning to read seemingly insignificant details of relationship as significant, trusting intuition over reason, rejecting conventional, homosocial responses (discounting his detective friend's flip, literal notion of evidence), assuming responsibility and guilt (as he watches his girlfriend being threatened across the courtyard) and, finally, experiencing full vulnerability as he faces Thorwald's attack. Isabel Archer is proven wrong when she marries a man whom she thinks is fine and discriminating but who is in fact cold and mercenary, because James wants Isabel to become cognizant of the world that exists outside her own consciousness. Jeff's lesson goes the other way. He is too much in that outside world, too subject to conventional ideas about how things work; he needs to engage in more projection, not less. In a sense, the outcomes of both the novel and the film represent ways that their creators have of complicating their characters, jolting them out of the complacency bred by the conventional nature of their medium. Isabel is complacent in the richness of her own consciousness, which is presented to us as a function of literary language; Jeff is complacent in the idea that meaning exists on the surface, which is what film is best suited to represent. Jeff's development also parallels Hitchcock's own: he began his career making simple action-suspense films and gradually moved to explore deeper aspects of character and relationship in the 1950s and 1960s. In this context, Mrs Thorwald becomes a symbol of this evolution. She is the circumscribed, emotionally charged novel heroine translated into the surface-oriented, action-disposed medium of film. She is first seen negatively, then reseen and rehabilitated. She is, in other words, the residue of that flowery literary tradition, embodied by Henry James, which Hitchcock claimed to reject, but which he eventually incorporated into his films through the back door – or rear window, as it were.

Portrait of a Lady and *Rear Window* are similar in that both acknowledge an 'outside' to the worlds they depict. Though James centres his novel in his heroine's consciousness, he also makes clear that that consciousness can be forced to revise itself by what lies outside of it. The problem stems from the distinction between what he describes elsewhere as 'the real' and 'the romantic': 'The real represents to my perception the things we cannot possibly *not* know, sooner or later, in one way or another . . . The romantic stands, on the other hand, for the things that, with all the facilities in the world, all the wealth and all the courage and all the wit and all the adventure, we never *can* directly know; the things that can reach us only through the beautiful circuit and subterfuge of our thought and our desire.'[22] Isabel has lived for most of the novel in the realm of the romantic. When she finally 'sees' her husband and her best friend together and realises that they have had an affair, she confronts the real for the first time. By the same token, though Hitchcock depicts a plot based purely on the real – i.e., on images as they appear in the world – he acknowledges that there are aspects to experience that are not accessible to surface representation and teaches his hero to acknowledge this. He ends his film with Jeff facing away from the window, his eyes closed, to suggest that what he sees is not representable through images. Jeff has now entered the world of the romantic.

The two works, which I have just shown to reflect a similar integration of values, though arriving there from different and indeed opposing starting points, must also be placed in the contexts of their creators' respective canons and in the larger cultural contexts in which they were produced. These works represent singular expressions of balance. After them, the relationship between 'inside' and 'outside' that has here achieved equilibrium begins to break down. Hints of what is to come are present in the works themselves. When, at the end of *Portrait*, Isabel confronts the fact of her husband's duplicity and defies his order that she not visit her dying cousin, the novel does not end with what might seem the logical by-product of her action: the decision to end her marriage and strike off on her own. Instead, it sends her back to Rome and to her husband. This return, which many readers have found puzzling and even perverse, connects directly to James's ultimate loyalties not to the visual surface of reality but to the imaginative depths of individual consciousness and the ability of the inner self to engulf and shape reality – the domain, in short, of 'the romantic'. The question of 'what Isabel would do' had launched the novel; now it is posed again, at a new level of difficulty, as Isabel faces the prospect of how to deal with a bad marriage. In this novel, James does not answer the new question; he leaves Isabel 'en l'air', as he puts it. But he returns to answer it in his last completed novel, *The Golden Bowl*, in which the heroine also discovers the duplicity of her husband (again comprehended in visual terms as she 'sees' him return from a weekend with her stepmother). In this novel, the recognition happens not toward the end, as in *Portrait*, but mid way through, and the rest of the story involves recording the heroine's efforts to win back her husband – to assimilate him, so to speak, to her point of view. Could Isabel have done the same? The icily selfish Gilbert Osmond seems like unpromising material – as stubborn a fact of reality as one is likely to find anywhere. But that may be because the novel in which he figures has not yet allowed for the possibility of more difficult kinds of imaginative appropriation. In the later novel, the coordinates have shifted. The heroine's consciousness is so powerful – so really tyrannical – that nothing can stand in its way.

The Golden Bowl is the culmination of a series of novels towards the end of James's career where the heroine's ability to turn a defeat into a victory through force of mind constitutes the fundamental action. James's earlier novels, maintaining their tie to the tradition of the European domestic novel form, had centred on the marriage plot as the structure within which his heroines exercised their imagination. But in the later novels, marriage has either been deconstructed (as in *The Ambassadors* and *The Wings of a Dove*), undergone a radical reformulation (as in *The Golden Bowl*), or been replaced by other human relationships. Thus Maisie Farange, the child heroine of *What Maisie Knew*, turns her relationship with her governess into her source of meaning; Nanda Brookenham, the adolescent heroine in *The Awkward Age* goes off with an 80-year-old grandfather figure; and Fleda Vetch, the marriageable young woman in *The Spoils of Poynton* settles down, not with the 'single man in possession of a large fortune', as it was once universally acknowledged that she should, but with the man's mother. James achieves these transformations through an enlarged faith in the power of language. His later work is increasingly filled with dialogue, but dialogue not in the simple, dramatic sense that we are used to it in plays (it was during this period that James failed miserably writing for the stage), but dialogue cut free from a collision with reality. The characters in these novels speak in fragmented, overdetermined phrases – posing cryptic questions, leaving sentences half-completed or ambiguously worded, giving each other long looks, or 'hanging fire' (a favourite phrase). The idea is that a thought is never complete, that it lies with the 'other', and ultimately falls to the reader, to fill in and stabilise meaning. When, at the end of *The Golden Bowl*, Maggie's father and stepmother have departed for America and she is left alone with her husband, we know that she has achieved something, but it is up to us to determine what. Is this ending a tragedy or a triumph? Has she won her husband through love or fear? What, the novel poses further, is love and commitment? Is it a great expression of sacrifice and loyalty, or is it a crumbling of the will, an erosion of self, an expression of subservience to tyranny? Such questions circulate at the end of the novel but are left unresolved and unresolvable. Meaning does not stop, and one is free to take whatever answer or combination of answers one wants in closing the book. We are in the realm of hypertext here, before the computer was invented.

In Hitchcock's later work, the representation of character is also pushed to a new point. Hitchcock's visual orientation up until the late 1950s had been linked to a notion of realism that demanded that the external world serve as the structuring agent for his character's identity formation. The suspense plot, which often evolved around a case of mistaken identity, was designed to define the protagonist in relation to the identity of the murderer. This is a simple case of definition through opposition in early films like *The 39 Steps* (1936), and becomes, eventually, a purging of undesirable qualities and proclivities as the protagonist learns how *not* to be, as in *Strangers on a Train, Shadow of a Doubt, Rope* (1948) and *I Confess* (1953). Finally, in *Rear Window*, the most developed of these plots, the protagonist learns not only how not to be, but how to be. He acquires a consciousness and becomes a person of feeling and imagination. In all of these films, the surface of reality is never breached. The characters become themselves by living in a world that looks conventionally real.

But Hitchcock's loyalties shift in the late 1950s and early 1960s in a series of films that rely on exaggerated themes and atmospheric effects: *The Wrong Man* (1956) with its hyperdocumentary realism, *Vertigo* with its dream-like imagery and hallucinatory sequences, *Marnie* (1964) with its strange verbal inflections and artificial back projection, *The Birds* (1963) with its science fiction theme and imagery, and *Psycho* with its unorthodox structure (the killing off of the marquee star) and its psychotic main character. In these films, Hitchcock has let go of the need to link his hero's character development to a conventional suspense plot. The suspense no longer pretends to centre on how a man deals with an external event; it now focuses directly on his struggle with an internal one: Manny (*The Wrong Man*) with his emotional passivity, Scottie (*Vertigo*) with his crisis of masculinity; Norman Bates and Mitch (*Psycho* and *The Birds*) with their mother complexes; Rutland (*Marnie*) with his sado-masochism. Hitchcock had represented a mental landscape as early as 1945 in the dream sequence of *Spellbound* (its surrealism showcased by the use of Salvador Dali's set design), only in that film the hero's psychological life was made a function of a larger, more conventional suspense plot. In *Rear Window*, Hitchcock took what he had awkwardly compartmentalised in *Spellbound* and gave it a seamless integration: he made the apartment building across the courtyard from Jeff's window do double duty as the site of suspenseful action and as the representation of Jeff's unconscious. *Rear Window* fulfilled, with maximum efficiency, Erwin Panofsky's edict that 'the price the cinema has to pay for visual storytelling is that both action and inner states of mind, or philosophy, must be spatialized'.[23] But Hitchcock's subsequent films would no longer try to effect this dual spatialisation.

For James, language, used originally to penetrate surfaces, becomes a surface element in its own right, the means of expressing an infinite play of meaning. For Hitchcock, visual surface, used originally to represent external reality, comes to represent the imagined inner life. Both have in different ways 'cut the cable to the real', as James would say, dissolving the distinction between 'inside' and 'outside' that is the binary opposition basic to representation. Truth and fiction, self and other, consciousness and external reality are functions of this opposition; without them a coherent story and sense of character are impossible. Both James and Hitchcock, towards the end of their careers, move toward abstraction.

James's late novels, despite their apparent focus on character, are no longer character studies; they are exercises in the indeterminacy of language. Likewise, Hitchcock's last films, though they still use the skeleton of a suspense plot, are no longer films of suspenseful action but exercises in the permutating design of dynamic images, what some critics have called 'pure cinema'. *Topaz* (1969) is a profusion of locales, plot lines and characters with different nationalities, accents and loyalties, brought together in an intricate but ultimately irrelevant web of intrigue. The film's most memorable moment is the agent Juanita's death, not because of any emotional investment we have come to have in the character but because of the sheer visual brilliance of the scene. In *Frenzy* (1972) the conceits of marriage, food and murder intersect in a witty pattern – 'a crossword puzzle on the lietmotif of murder', in Truffaut's words.[24] In *Family Plot* (1976), the patterning involves the movement from one locale to another, with no sense of settled home or destination, a continual shifting from freedom to constraint as the dynamic coordinates of design. Two thematically gratuitous scenes in the film dramatise this formal structure. One – a clownish struggle in an out-of-control car – is shot at close range, showing arms and legs flailing wildly; it is a framed exhibition of action run amok. The other – an encounter in a cemetery maze – is shot from above and proceeds with stately deliberation: the figures become dynamic extensions of the maze itself.

One is tempted to look at both James and Hitchcock as reflecting an end-of-century malaise that happened to coincide with their own old age. Perhaps it is inevitable that an artist with a long and sustained career should, toward the end of that career, push the limits of his medium to the point where he ceases to function within it. This is the point where innovation merges with exhaustion or, put another way, where it exhausts the resources available to it. Walter Benjamin wrote that each art creates a demand that can only be satisfied with the development of a new art.[25] James, in his literary excesses, can be seen to be pointing toward the birth of a new medium that would reassert the division of character and the world outside of character that he could no longer maintain within the constraints of the novel form. Given that he would, in the words of C. Hartley Grattan, 'strain the English language to its breaking point',[26] it seems fitting that film at its origin should be silent – as if trying to rid itself of the words that had come to overwhelm narrative representation. By replacing words with dynamic images, film began to retrieve the concept of the real that had eroded in late James and in modernist writing in general. But Hitchcock's example shows how film moved to abolish the idea of a communally shared reality as fully as literature had done before it.

Hitchcock died as film, once the pre-eminent form of mass entertainment, began to be superseded by a proliferation of multimedia options. Video games may be the logical extrapolation of Hitchcock's evolution of suspense into pure thrills on the one hand and pure design on the other (*Family Plot*'s ride without brakes and walk through the cemetery maze, respectively). At the same time, these games can be said to reassert a distinction between 'inside' and 'outside' through the addition of a viewer who also controls the game. But as virtual-reality games now loom on the horizon, perhaps we can anticipate another erasure of this distinction. What we see, in short, is a swing back and forth, from delineating to destroying the distinction between internal life and external reality, between self and other, with each spiral shorter in duration and oriented more fully toward movement and surface imagery. Where this will ultimately lead is hard to say, but Hitchcock's career, examined alongside that of his great literary predecessor, gives us the fullest single expression we have of the fate of character, as it is born, lives and dies in conjunction with its medium of expression.

Notes

1 Henry Nash Smith, *Democracy and the Novel*, New York: Oxford University Press, 1978, p. 145.

2 For James's view of his own history see both 'Notes on a Son and Brother' and 'A Small Boy and Others', in F. W. Dupee (ed.), *Henry James: Autobiography*, New York: Criterion Books, 1953. The definitive scholarly biography of James is Leon Edel's *Henry James*, 5 vols., New York: Avon Books, 1953.

3 Donald Spoto, *The Dark Side of Genius: The Life of Alfred Hitchcock*, New York: Ballantine 1983, p. 29. Spoto's tabloidish biography remains the most comprehensive we have.

4 François Truffaut with Helen G. Scott, *Hitchcock*, rev. edn., New York: Touchstone, 1985, p. 316.

5 Truffaut, *Hitchcock*, p. 127

6 Truffaut, *Hitchcock*, p. 71.

7 Truffaut, *Hitchcock*, p. 335; p. 316; p. 71; p. 61.

8 Henry James, 'The Art of Fiction', in Leon Edel (ed.), *Literary Criticism: Essays on Literature*, New York: The Library of America, 1984, p. 60.

9 Lionel Trilling, *Sincerity and Authenticity*, Cambridge, MA: Harvard University Press, 1972, p. 113.

10 Leonard Leff, *Hitchcock and Selznick*, New York: Weidenfeld & Nicolson, 1987, p. 23.

11 Ralph Waldo Emerson, 'The American Scholar' (1837) in *Essays and English Traits*, New York: P. F. Collier & Son, 1909, p. 9. Henry David Thoreau, *Walden*, 1834, rpt. Harper and Rowe, 1961, p. 146. Walt Whitman, *Leaves of Grass*, 1891 edn in *Complete Poetry and Selected Prose and Letters* London: The Nonesuch Press, 1938, p. 43.

12 Henry James, 'Preface to "Portrait of a Lady"', *The Art of the Novel: Critical Prefaces*, New York: Scribner, 1962, p. 52.

13 Ian Watt, *The Rise of the Novel*, Berkeley, CA: University of California Press, 1957, p. 188.

14 James, 'Preface to "Portrait of a Lady"', *The Art of the Novel*, p. 51.

15 Henry James, *The Portrait of a Lady*, New York: Penguin Books, 1982, p. 63.

16 James, *Portrait*, p. 184.

17 James, *Portrait*, p. 151.

18 Robin Wood, *Hitchcock's Films Revisited*, New York: Columbia University Press, 1989, p. 100; Truffaut, *Hitchcock*, p. 214.

19 Truffaut, *Hitchcock*, p. 214.

20 James, *Portrait*, p. 216.
21 Wood, *Hitchcock's Films Revisited*, p. 104.
22 James, 'Preface to "The American"', *The Art of the Novel*, pp. 31–2.
23 Quoted in Roy Huss and Norman Silverstein, *The Film Experience*, New York: Harper and Row, 1968, p. 33.
24 Truffaut, *Hitchcock*, p. 333.
25 Walter Benjamin, *Illuminations*, trans. Harry Zohn, Hannah Arendt (ed.), New York: Schocken Books, 1969, p. 237.
26 C. Hartley Grattan, *The Three Jameses: A Family of Minds*, New York: New York University Press, 1962, p. 209.

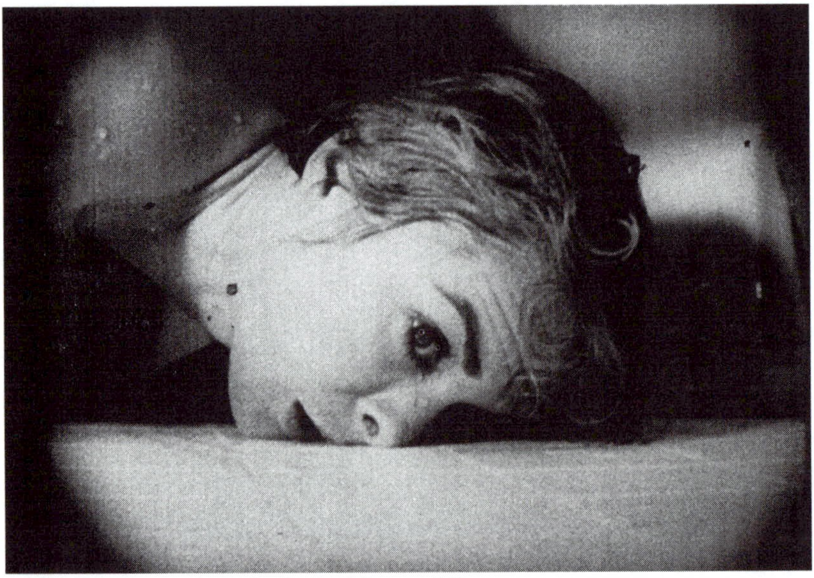

Psycho – 'an allegory about the death of the art of film . . .

Chapter 3
Some Thoughts on Hitchcock's Authorship

William Rothman

When I was asked to contribute an essay to this volume, I expected, and wished, to write something in a celebratory mood. For the fact that we are celebrating the hundredth anniversary of Hitchcock's birth, the fact that we continue to recognise Hitchcock's achievements as a film-maker, is itself something to celebrate. The present piece has turned out to be a somber one. For this, I blame Gus Van Sant, who in any case deserves all the blame anyone might heap on him for making his dreadful version of *Psycho.* Van Sant's actors seem to be going through the motions, to be following a bad script, to be reading lines that do not even seem to have been written for them. An apologist for the postmodern might praise Van Sant for undermining the 'realism' of the original. But aren't we all tired of listening to such nonsense? Hitchcock proudly regarded *Psycho* (1960) as his most powerful demonstration of 'the art of pure cinema', his gift (as he put it to Truffaut) to the film-makers among his viewers. How could a director, especially one not devoid of talent, make a virtually shot-by-shot copy of *Psycho* that is interesting only for being so utterly uninteresting? In *Hitchcock – The Murderous Gaze,* I suggested that *Psycho* declared the death of the art of film as Hitchcock knew it and prophesied the emergence of different, perhaps freer, forms of cinema. The more I dwell on Van Sant's *Psycho,* the more it can seem that cinema itself has now run its course, that the art of film is declaring bankruptcy.

Van Sant's film reminds us – as if we needed reminding – that we are to take with a grain of salt Hitchcock's remarks to the effect that his creative work was finished before filming began, and his remarks to the effect that actors are cattle. It turns out – as if anyone could really have doubted it – that it makes all the difference in the world whether Marion Crane is Janet Leigh or Anne Heche, whether Norman Bates is Anthony Perkins or Vince Vaughn. But it already made a great difference to Hitchcock, when he was storyboarding his scripts, composing his films shot by shot, imagining the world on film before production began, who were to be the inhabitants of that world.

In *Hitchcock – The Murderous Gaze* I wrote somewhat unappreciatively of Janet Leigh as being in Hitchcock's eyes (and mine) an 'ordinary bourgeoise'.[1] Viewing the hapless Anne Heche in Janet Leigh's place, dressed like a clueless nitwit and flailing away in herky-jerky, bird-like movements, helps me to appreciate an important quality Janet Leigh possesses in *Psycho,* a calmness or poise that we might think of as a kind of passivity. This unanxious quality comes out strongly in the shots of her, wide-eyed, driving through the gathering darkness and the rain before arriving at the Bates Motel. Janet Leigh's calm, measured movements manifest themselves as an attunement to, or affinity with, Hitchcock's camera. They match the camera's equally calm, measured movements (for example, when it patiently tracks Marion's every move as she approaches her fateful decision to steal the money). (In *The Wrong Man* (1956), perhaps more than any other Hitchcock film, the camera's movements, as well as the cuts from shot to shot, consistently manifest this unanxious quality. More and more, it might be noted, I have come to regard *The Wrong Man* as one of Hitchcock's greatest achievements.) Marion's calmness, her passivity, is perhaps what makes Norman, with whom the camera identifies in a very different way, feel so superior to her. But perhaps it is also what makes her so threatening to him, as if he could already imagine that she would 'look well, stuffed'.

Vince Vaughn's nervous giggles give away from the outset that he is missing a screw or two. Combined with the fact that he is so hulking and physically imposing, his obvious weirdness makes it inconceivable that any woman worth caring about would willingly accept his invitation to dine with him. These qualities also make it impossible for us to view him, in retrospect, as a mastermind who may be capable of framing his own mother for the perfect murder he has himself committed. Vaughn lacks Tony Perkins's trademark boy-next-door quality, so we are precluded from imagining, as we view him, that behind the mask of the familiar, the ordinary, there is a figure who is not what he seems, one of Hitchcock's sportsmen/artists, a stand-in for Hitchcock himself.

In Hitchcock's films, the figure of the author is an important – perhaps the most important – character. One cannot even accurately relate the story of a Hitchcock film without taking into account the author, or his instrument, the camera. With a few pointless exceptions (Van Sant's Arbogast is reduced to saying, 'If it doesn't jell, it isn't Jell-O,' rather than the immortal line – it's in the pantheon with Emma's 'It's the paprika makes it pink' in *Shadow of a Doubt* (1943) – 'If it doesn't jell, it isn't aspic'; the state trooper's ominously Hitchcockian line 'Did she look like a wrong one to you?' is reduced to the bland 'Did she look like a bad one to you?'), Van Sant's characters speak the same lines as the characters in Hitchcock's film. Often, they mimic their expressions and gestures, too, although there are moments at which they interpolate mannerisms of their own (Vince Vaughn's nervous giggles and screen-shaking masturbating, Anne Heche's jerking movements). Most of the gestures of Hitchcock's camera, however, Van Sant copies without alteration. Or does he? What counts as the *same* gesture of the camera? Indeed, what makes a movement of the camera, or a cut from shot to shot, something that counts as a gesture at all? For a shot cannot be defined purely in terms of formal elements such as lighting or composition or camera angle or camera distance. Indeed, a shot's 'form' cannot be separated from its 'content', the particular things and people, each with distinctive features and qualities, contained within its frame.

It is a central claim of *Hitchcock – The Murderous Gaze* that Hitchcock's films have a *philosophical* dimension. 'Within the world of a Hitchcock film, the nature and relationships of love, murder, sexuality, marriage, and theater are at issue; these are among Hitchcock's constant themes. His treatment of these themes, however, and his understanding of the reasons film keeps returning to them, cannot be separated from his constant concern with the nature of the camera, the act of viewing a film, and filmmaking as a calling.'[2] In demonstrating something about the 'art of pure cinema', as Hitchcock liked to call it, Hitchcock's films are asserting, *declaring*, something about themselves, something about their medium.

In Hitchcock's films the camera performs gestures that have the force of claims, demonstrations, arguments. What a given gesture declares, I argue in *Hitchcock – The Murderous Gaze*, is not an unambiguous answer to the question of what film is. For at the heart of Hitchcock's artistic vision is a sense of film's possessing what seem to be incompatible aspects, irreconcilable tensions or conflicts that crystallise, or crystallise in, an awesome sense of mystery. Understanding, in Hitchcock's films, means acknowledging the limits of understanding, understanding, that there is something all-important – something wonderful? something frightful? – that we cannot understand. Rose, in *The Wrong Man*, understands, when she suddenly breaks into uncontrollable laughter, that Manny, thinking he understands, doesn't really get it at all. And Hitchcock reserves some of his most virtuoso camera gestures for summing up reality's unfathomability, to which, in his view, the medium of film bears a special affinity.

I am thinking, for example, of the immortal moment in *Vertigo* (1958) in which, the Kim Novak character (Judy? Madeleine? Carlotta?) says, 'Can't you see,' and Stewart finally *does* see. This moment at which he overcomes his blindness is summed up in an extraordinary gesture of the camera, a slow dissolve that marks the man looking at himself framed, even as the woman he is viewing frames a woman in her view, a woman who is already framed in a portrait, a woman who is and is not the woman who is looking.

We can turn to an equally profound and moving moment in *The Wrong Man* and find a closely related gesture, as Hitchcock cuts from Manny's mother, praying, to Manny, who seems to be praying, too, then to a shot in which Manny is a shadow in the left foreground, and a painting of Jesus, to whom he is evidently praying, is in the right background, as the camera moves in.

This charged framing/camera movement is followed by the virtuoso passage in which Hitchcock effects an elegiacally slow dissolve from a frontal shot of Manny's face to the real robber, who walks towards the camera until the two faces are perfectly superimposed.

We find a comparable gesture as far back in Hitchcock's work as *The Lodger*.

We can find such gestures in *Psycho*, too. First in the framing of Norman Bates, just before he moves the painting to disclose the fatal peephole.

We find it again in the slow dissolve between the mummified face of Mrs Bates, with its chilling grin of recognition, and the façade of the courthouse. Momentarily, the dissolve superimposes Mrs Bates's empty eye sockets over pillars that present a perfect instance of what in *Hitchcock – The Murderous Gaze* I identify as Hitchcock's '////' motif, one of a set of motifs or signs or symbols – they include what I call 'curtain raisings'; 'eclipses'; 'tunnel shots'; white flashes; frames-within-frames; profile shots; symbolically charged objects (e.g., lamps, staircases, birds); symbolically charged colors (red, white, blue-green, brown) – that recur, at critical moments, in every Hitchcock film.

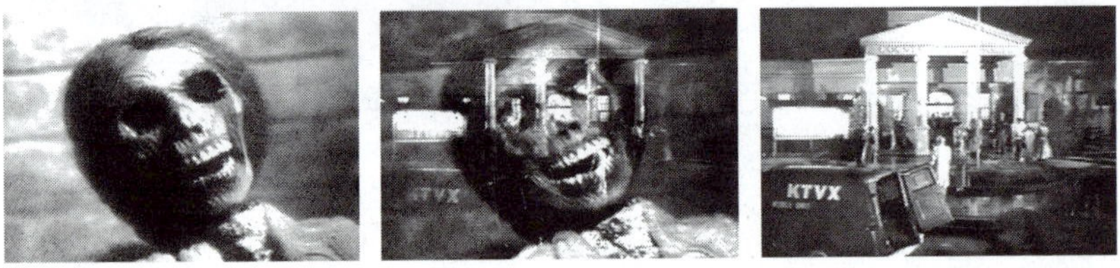

As I demonstrate in *Hitchcock – The Murderous Gaze*, the '////' sign functions, at one level, as an invocation of prison bars, reminding us that the creatures who dwell in the world on film are, within their world, trapped, imprisoned. But they are also imprisoned in another sense, unable to cross the barrier that separates them from us, trapped within the world of the film, a world presided over by the author, Hitchcock. We, too, are barred from crossing that barrier; there are limits to our access to the film's world. Hence the '////' sign also invokes the screen on which all that we view is projected, the barrier-that-is-not-really-a barrier that is the film frame.

Van Sant includes this dissolve in his version. Or does he? Is it the 'same' dissolve as Hitchcock's? For one thing, in recreating Hitchcock's Mrs Bates, Van Sant gives her wild, long hair, like an unkempt hippie's, rather than the 'original' hairstyle, in which the mummy's hair is curled in a tight bun with the spiralling twist shared, uncannily, with Madeleine and Carlotta in *Vertigo*. The spirits of those ghostly Hitchcock women do not possess Van Sant's mummy, so his dissolve is from the outset devoid of the mystery Hitchcock invests in his. And the new courthouse lacks the old one's columns, hence there is no '////' in Van Sant's second shot. The superimposition of one shot stripped of its original significance over another shot likewise devoid of significance turns Hitchcock's complex and profound gesture not into a gesture of Van Sant's own, however altered or diminished in meaning and expressiveness that gesture may be. Rather, Van Sant's dissolve is not meaningful or expressive. It does not have the force of a gesture at all.

What is missing at this moment is missing from every moment of Van Sant's film. Behind the surface of Hitchcock's films, or, rather, on the surface but 'hidden' by being in plain view, are those motifs or signs or symbols, of which the '////' sign is one, whose presence participates crucially in the films' philosophical meditations. At another level, each sign, when it appears in a Hitchcock film, echoes other appearances of the sign in Hitchcock's work. At that level, these Hitchcockian signs, taken together, simply signify that these are Hitchcock films. They function as Hitchcock's signatures, like his name in the credits or his cameo walk-ons.

Any director can make a cameo appearance in his or her films, of course, but only in a Hitchcock film can it be Hitchcock who appears in such a cameo. Only in a Hitchcock film can the cameo serve as Hitchcock's signature. And any director can incorporate any of Hitchcock's signature motifs and use it for its metaphorical or symbolic meaning. I think of a shot in *The 39 Steps* (1935), for example, in which Hitchcock frames Hannay, the suspicious crofter, and Margaret, the crofter's wife, through the slats of a chair at just

the moment at which Hannay's fate seems to be sealed, and what seems a very similar shot in John Stahl's *Imitation of Life* (1934), which frames Louise Beavers through the vertical bars of a staircase, suggesting that to be a black woman in America is to be imprisoned.

The shot in *Imitation of Life* does not, cannot, mean all that the Hitchcock shot means. It does not, cannot, signify Hitchcock's authorship. Thus the entire panoply of Hitchcockian signatures marks a private, or personal, dimension to Hitchcock's films, declaring that they are his creations, not anyone else's.

'Part of *Psycho*'s myth,' I wrote in *Hitchcock – The Murderous Gaze*, 'is that there is no world outside its own, that we are fated to be born, live our alienated lives, and die in the very world in which Norman Bates also dwells.'[3] When we first view Norman/mother, wrapped in a blanket, Hitchcock masks the bottom of the frame. (This is, after all, the point of view of the disgusted guard looking into the prison cell through the peephole in the door.) Hitchcock cuts to a fly on Norman's/mother's hand, then back to what seems a reprise of the previous set-up. However, the mask at the bottom of the frame is now gone. We are now inside the cell, no longer separated from Norman/mother by a window, a screen. Symbolically, the barrier of the movie screen has been breached. But no such transition from outside to inside occurs in Van Sant's version.

Hitchcock's famous shower murder sequence, too, envisions the breaching of the movie-screen barrier. When the frame-within-the-frame of the featureless, translucent shower curtain comes to engulf the frame, it is as if nothing separates this curtain from the screen on which our view is projected. In this shower curtain, the camera's gesture declares, our world and the world of *Psycho* magically come together. Or this gesture declares that there has never been a real barrier separating them. Thus, when Marion Crane's killer theatrically pulls the shower curtain open, it is as if the torn curtain reveals that we, like Marion, are confronting the imminent prospect of our own murder. Again, Van Sant blows it. Unwilling to leave well enough alone, he provides a patterned shower curtain, not a featureless one, so he misses Hitchcock's gesture of effectively merging the shower curtain with the movie screen.

To view the world on film as a 'private island' (to use Marion's term) wherein we can escape the real conditions of our existence is to make the world on film a self-contained universe. This is to make the real world – the world into which we have been born, the world in which we are fated to die – only an image, not the real world at all. It is to be condemned to a condition of death-in-life, as if we, too, were shadows on a screen, not human beings of flesh and blood. *Psycho* is an allegory about the death of the art of film as Hitchcock has known and mastered it – the art of creating self-contained universes on film, private islands, to which viewers can imagine themselves escaping from the real conditions of their existence. 'Marion Crane's dead eye and Norman/mother's final grin prophesy the end of the era of film whose achievement *Psycho* also sums up, and the death of the Hitchcock film', I wrote in *Hitchcock – The Murderous Gaze*. 'In *Psycho*, Hitchcock's camera singles out a human subject *as if for the last time*, then presides over her murder. Marion Crane's death in the shower, mythically, is also our death – the death of the movie viewer – and Hitchcock's death.'[4] In *Psycho*, Hitchcock envisions, in the medium of film, that the movie screen has magically been breached. Like Norman Bates, Hitchcock envisions no possibility of liberation. In *Psycho*, the breaching of the movie-screen barrier does not mean freedom. It means death. That is, it changes nothing, for we are already fated to die. In Hitchcock's dark vision, we *are* condemned to a condition of death-in-life. We are born and die in our 'private traps', as Norman puts it. We scratch and claw but never budge an inch.

Already when I was writing *Hitchcock – The Murderous Gaze*, and increasingly in the years following its publication in 1982, it was the dominant view within academic film study – as within academic criticism in general – that the concept of authorship has been discredited on theoretical grounds. No writing on Hitchcock goes as far as *Hitchcock – The Murderous Gaze* in keeping faith with the idea that he is an '*auteur*' – a master, perhaps even *the* master, of the art of cinema. Yet I still believe in the book, and would scarcely change a word of it if I were publishing it for the first time today.

Hitchcock – The Murderous Gaze is an '*auteurist*' study. But it is also a study of the *conditions* of authorship in the medium of film. Hence it is a study as well of the ontology of film. A premise and conclusion of my book is that Hitchcock's films have a philosophical dimension, as I have suggested. They are thinking seriously about their medium, thinking seriously about themselves, thinking seriously about such matters as the nature and relationships of love, murder, sexuality, marriage and theatre. Thus the book rejects and contests the view, which has long held the status of a dogma within the field of film study but which I am proud to say I have always held in contempt, that some theory or other enables us to rest assured that films *cannot possibly* be thinking, that we know films to be in the repressive grip of ideology, a grip only theory can break.

That Hitchcock's films are philosophically serious is a view I share with Slavoj Žižek, for example, who recognises in them an affinity with the Lacanian theoretical framework his own writing embraces.[5] Žižek views Hitchcock, in effect, *as* a Lacanian. There are Derrideans, too, who have found that Hitchcock's films see eye to eye with them, philosophically. The theory and practice of philosophy that *Hitchcock – The Murderous Gaze* aligns itself with is worked out most fully in the writings of Stanley Cavell. The American movie genres Cavell champions in his indispensable books *Pursuits of Happiness* and *Contesting Tears*, the genres he calls 'the remarriage comedy' and 'the melodrama of the unknown woman', reveal the 'classical' Hollywood cinema to be committed to an Emersonian philosophical project that affirms the reality of human freedom, affirms the possibility, and the necessity, of radical change.[6] Cavell, too, is committed to this project, and in this he understands himself to be representative of the films' audience. However, the despairing Hitchcock who emerges in the pages of *Hitchcock – The Murderous Gaze*, it seems, is anything but an Emersonian.

Hitchcock was a master – some would say *the* master – of the 'art of pure cinema'. But the film medium also mastered him, subjected him to an isolation so extreme as to partake of madness, allowed him no escape. One aspect of Hitchcock's work is its declaration of conditions that must be satisfied by anyone who would master this medium. Another is its confession that Hitchcock, personally, embraced those conditions when he dedicated his life to the films that bear his signatures, the films in which he found his voice. His life's blood is on every frame of his films, as I rather melodramatically put it in *Hitchcock – The Murderous Gaze*.

In Hitchcock's dark vision, our world offers no real possibility of transcendence. Only in art – the art of cinema, perhaps the art of murder – can purity be glimpsed. At one level, Hitchcock's films expose the monstrous perversity of the artist's quest for a purity or perfection that human beings are incapable of living in the world. (*Rear Window* (1954) may be a perfect work of art, but in its purity it is also 'cold and lonely', like the perfect emerald Uncle Charles gives Charlie in *Shadow of a Doubt*.) But Hitchcock's films are also products of such a quest. Insofar as they aspire to an inhuman perfection, they perversely go against the grain of the American genres Cavell studies. And they perversely go against the grain of film itself, as Cavell characterises it in *The World Viewed*. (If the world is impure, how can a film, whose views are of the world, be pure?)

Unlike such American genres as the remarriage comedy or the melodrama of the unknown woman, I argue in '*Vertigo*: The Unknown Woman in Hitchcock', the 'Hitchcock thriller,' as we might call it, is a genre whose features cannot be defined, whose underlying myth cannot even be characterised, apart from relating the role the figure of the author plays within it.[7] Without the villainous Gavin Elster, hence without a Judy implicated in his evil design, *Vertigo* might have been an 'unknown woman' melodrama, not a Hitchcock thriller. For in a sense, it is the Gavin Elster in Hitchcock who declares himself in the signature gestures of the camera through which Hitchcock claims his authorship.

> In the genres Cavell studies, the camera is a machine that transfigures human subjects independently of human intentions. In the Hitchcock thriller, as *Psycho* explicitly declares, the camera is an instrument of taxidermy, not transfiguration: The camera does violence to its subjects, fixes them, and breathes back only the illusion of life into these ghosts. (The camera is an instrument of enlightenment as well for Hitchcock, although its truths are also blinding.) It is this murderous camera, mysteriously attuned to the unknownness of women, that is the instrument of authorship in the Hitchcock thriller, the truest expression of who Hitchcock is.[8]

All the Hitchcockian signatures that *Hitchcock – The Murderous Gaze* identifies – the curtain raisings, eclipses, white flashes, frames-within-frames, profile shots, symbolically charged objects, and so on, that mark *The Lodger* and every Hitchcock film to follow – thus also exclude *Vertigo* from the melodrama of the unknown woman. Hitchcock's signature gestures declare his unwillingness or inability ever to forsake his mark, to absorb himself unconditionally in his characters, to leave his own story untold. But they also reveal Hitchcock's affinity, his *identification*, with the unknown woman in *Vertigo* who desperately longs for existence. As I put it in '*Vertigo*: The Unknown Woman in Hitchcock', 'Hitchcock never gets beyond his own case, his own longing for acknowledgment. Hitchcock *is* the unknown woman, and this, too, separates *Vertigo* from Cavell's genre.'[9]

From a Cavellian perspective, remarriage comedies and melodramas of the unknown woman, which insist on the finiteness of people and things in the world (even as they insist on the unity of the world as a whole, on the fact that the world *is* a whole), affirm truths about the world, and about film, that Hitchcock's art would deny. And yet it is Hitchcock's wish to turn film against its own nature, as Cavell might put it, combined with the medium's stubborn resistance, that creates the tension specific to his films, a tension that enables them to push his view of the medium to its limits. Then perhaps it is my wish, in finding my own philosophical voice by writing about Hitchcock's films, to turn my philosophical way of thinking, aligned with Cavell's, against its own nature, combined with philosophy's stubborn resistance, that creates the tension specific to *Hitchcock – The Murderous Gaze*, a tension that enables me to push my view of Hitchcock, and my view of film criticism, to their limits.

Such limits are reached, for example, in the postscript I wrote when Hitchcock died just as I was completing the body of the book. At his death, I felt moved to write, Hitchcock possessed a secret comparable to Uncles Charles's in *Shadow of a Doubt*:

> Part of what he knew is that America never really understood his films. Society's 'tributes' were denials of the meaning of his work. Surely, the spectacle of America playing tribute to itself on the occasion of his death is a Hitchcockian one. I call it that because it would make a chilling, poignant and funny scene in a Hitchcock film, and because his work can teach us to recognize Hitchcock as its secret author. When Hitchcock authorized the language of his public tributes, and in general appeared to endorse the official view of who he was, in effect he scripted his own obituary, assuring that it would be silent on the meaning of his films. All Hitchcock's public speeches and gestures were also silences. I have no wish to attempt to reconcile the official Hitchcock and the knowing figure who emerges in my book, but to convey how the former may be viewed as the latter's creation, as a perfectly Hitchcockian figure, a projection of Hitchcock's authorship.[10]

In *Hitchcock – The Murderous Gaze*, as I acknowledge in the postscript, I cast myself as the figure who steps forward to answer Hitchcock's call for acknowledgement. I knew full well that by assuming this role I was taking the risk of appearing mad or arrogant or merely foolish. In *Film Quarterly*, Brian Henderson (perhaps not quite sure which of these adjectives best fits the case) called the postscript the single most pretentious piece of film criticism he had ever read (and he had been around). But, as I put it in the postscript, 'I would not have written this book' – I would not have cast myself in this role – 'if I did not believe that I had penetrated some of the secret places in Hitchcock's art.'[11]

In following Hitchcock's films with an unprecedented degree and kind of attention, I knew I was also taking the risk of appearing too self-effacing, as if I were subordinating my own voice to Hitchcock's. In a remark notable for its obtuseness (or, perhaps, its disingenuousness) as well as its mean-spiritedness, Tania Modleski contemptuously dismissed me – but not before appropriating a number of the central ideas of my book – as the ultimate male masochist for bowing so obsequiously to Hitchcock-the-master.[12] But to say this is to altogether miss the thrust of the postscript, its suggestion that a life-and-death struggle for authorship is waged, symbolically, in the readings that comprise the book. This suggestion culminates in the following passage:

> Charlie knows that her uncle secretly authored his own eulogy; she also knows that he arranged for the way she is fated to remember him. When I say that my writing aspires to answer Hitchcock's calls for acknowledgment, I also mean that Hitchcock's films call for writing such as this, even call it forth. If Hitchcock is secret author of his own obituary, my readings are equally projections of his authorship; only they are authorized not by his words but by his silences. The Hitchcock who emerges in these readings could well have written them himself. Yet the Hitchcock for whom I speak, who calls forth my words, is also my creation. I am his character and he is mine; the boundary between my identity and his is unfathomable, like that between Norman Bates and 'mother'. That the voice speaking for Hitchcock's films here is also possessed by them is what is most deeply Hitchcockian about the book, what Hitchcock would have appreciated, I believe, what might have moved him beyond words.[13]

In his invaluable recent book *Hearing Things: Voice and Method in the Writing of Stanley Cavell* (a book that ought to be required reading for every film-studies student),

Timothy Gould appreciates the fact that in my critical work on Hitchcock I make use of my own philosophical sensibility to convert insights gained from Cavell's work into insights of my own. But he feels that in doing so I find myself in troubled waters, philosophically. He cites the following passage from '*Vertigo*: The Unknown Woman in Hitchcock' as revealing what he takes to be a conflict between my critical practice, which views itself as underwritten by Cavell's philosophical writings, and Cavell's own philosophical method.

> Cavell, in his readings of the melodrama of the unknown woman and remarriage comedies alike, aspires to put into his own words what films say to their audience. Speaking in his own philosophical voice and out of his own experience ... he declares himself to be, despite everything, a representative member of that audience ... [R]eading a Hitchcock thriller ... I find myself continually called on to make discoveries, to see things that viewers do not ordinarily see, or to see familiar things in an unfamiliar light, to discover unsuspected connections. The *Vertigo* that emerges ... in this essay is not the film as viewers ordinarily view it (although my reading is meant to account for the common experience, which it interprets as the experience that fails to acknowledge Hitchcock and hence misses his meaning).[14]

According to Gould, I take Cavell's philosophical method 'to be one of putting common experiences – experiences that Cavell shares with an ordinary audience – into Cavell's own words', and that I equate this 'putting in his own words' with speaking 'in his "own philosophical voice", which is evidently taken to be the method by which Cavell manages to evince his own uniqueness and to declare his "representative" membership in a film's audience'.[15]

But in the passage Gould quotes, I do not equate Cavell's procedures *in general* with putting common experiences into Cavell's own words. What I do say is that this is Cavell's approach in writing about these American comedies and melodramas. If he did not view these movies as philosophical, as sustaining a serious philosophical conversation with their – our – culture, he would have written differently about them (or not written about them at all). Nor am I claiming that for Cavell putting one's experiences into one's own words is equivalent *in general* to speaking in one's 'own philosophical voice'. What I say is that in *Pursuits of Happiness* and *Contesting Tears* Cavell puts into his own words what these films are saying to their audience; that he does so by putting his experiences of these films into his own words; and that in so doing he does find himself speaking in his own philosophical voice. Again, if these movies were different, if he (and we) experienced them differently, Cavell would have written differently about them. How Cavell feels these films call upon him to write about them, how they motivate him to speak in his own philosophical voice, is revelatory of what these films are. (Cavell has always embraced the Wittgensteinian philosophical principle that the kinds of things that are said, the kinds of things that can be said, about something provide evidence for understanding the kind of thing it is.)

These facts are also revelatory of who Cavell is. Cavell is a philosopher. He personally has claimed a voice within philosophy, and it is within philosophy, above all, that he has found his voice. Not on every occasion in which he speaks in his own voice does he speak in his philosophical voice. But whenever he speaks in his philosophical voice, he speaks in his own voice, his 'empirical voice', as Gould calls it. Gould allows that Cavell's empirical voice is expressive of his unique existence, but he faults me for believing that Cavell's philosophical voice expresses his unique existence, too. 'This uniqueness of the individual voice is taken [by Rothman] to constitute the uniqueness of Cavell's contribution to philosophy,' Gould suggests, formulating my view in terms I can recognise. But I cannot accept his assertion that, given such a view, 'It seems at best an accident that Cavell – or Cavell's philosophizing – could ever speak for anyone else.'[16] For if Cavell found himself unable to speak for others when speaking in his own philosophical voice, as philosophers must find ways to do, he could not have found his voice within philosophy.

When I suggest that in *Pursuits of Happiness* and *Contesting Tears* Cavell 'declares himself to be, despite everything', a representative member of these films' audience, I do not mean that Cavell declares his representativeness *in spite of* the uniqueness of his voice. My 'despite everything' only alludes to what I take to be Cavell's sense that some might think that his status as a philosopher excludes him from being representative. Cavell does not take himself to be unrepresentative for having a unique voice, for having a unique philosophical voice, for being who he is and not another person. Every human existence, hence every human voice, is unique. For Cavell, as for the American comedies and melodramas he studies, to be unique is to be exemplary of humanity, to be representative. To be representative is to be unique.

Thus in Cavell's account, he, the films and the films' audiences all see eye to eye, philosophically. At times, to be sure, he claims to see things others have not managed to see in these films, or says what others have not said. But he does not believe that this forfeits his claim to representativeness. He does not take the members of the films' audiences, however average or typical, for the most part to be missing the films' meaning. In no way do I reject or contest Cavell's accounts of the films his books study. To be sure, I write differently about Hitchcock's films. But, as I have said, Hitchcock's films, too, are different.

For one thing, Hitchcock's films give prominence to the idea – it is typically expressed by one of Hitchcock's gamesman/artist figures, such as Uncle Charles in *Shadow of a Doubt* – that only exceptional people are capable of opening their eyes. Such people, Charles tells young Charlie in an effort to get her to overcome her blindness, are so different from the mass of 'ordinary' people doomed to sleepwalk through life that it is as if they belong to a higher species. However, the idea also figures in Hitchcock's films that people like Manny in *The Wrong Man*, who are utterly incapable of opening their eyes, are the truly exceptional ones. When Rose suddenly laughs hysterically and accuses Manny of still not recognising that their fates are in the hands of a malignant deity, part of the cruel joke, in her eyes, is that she finds herself married to a man who will never see what she sees, never get the joke.

To open one's eyes takes only a spiritual change, but it is a transformation so profound as to be tantamount to death and rebirth – the kind of spiritual change that is so central to the comedies and melodramas Cavell studies, in which such metamorphoses, at least in principle, are open to all who have the will to change. In *Notorious* (1946) and *North by Northwest* (1959), Cary Grant (who is, not coincidentally, the quintessential male lead of comedies of remarriage) undergoes such a change just in time to allow a 'happy ending'. In *Vertigo*, the man's transformation – poetically, tragically – comes just too late. In Hitchcock's films, what is required is not only the will to change, and not only an acknowledgement that one's control has limits, but also submission to a 'higher power'. In Hitchcock films, the 'higher power' capable of making such miracles happen cannot be separated from the figure of the author, from Hitchcock himself.

'When Rothman accounts for the experience of the audience of a Hitchcock film,' Gould writes, 'he is not accounting for an error or an obscurity that he might himself have shared. He is accounting for a state of blindness toward Hitchcock's words that he himself has been delivered from.'[17] Of course, if I have been delivered from the state of blindness of most of Hitchcock's viewers, that must be a state I once shared with them; were it not for my miraculous deliverance, I, too, would still be blind.

'It is a state of mind that cannot be alleviated by any ordinary act of viewing,' Gould goes on,

> nor by anything that Rothman would be willing to call 'representative.' The viewing of the ordinary American moviegoer is blinded by the most intimate workings of American culture. It is blind from birth – doomed in advance, like one of Hitchcock's 'wrong men.' In Rothman's critical vision, we either give in to the commonplace viewing of a film, or we rise above what is (merely) representative in our viewing and achieve a state in which we are capable of acknowledging Hitchcock's authorship.[18]

But if we have the ability to 'rise above what is (merely) representative in our viewing', if we can 'achieve a state in which we are capable of acknowledging Hitchcock's authorship', we cannot be doomed to blindness. Hitchcock's films call upon their viewers to open their eyes, *Hitchcock – The Murderous Gaze* argues, in the face of Hitchcock's conviction that most, perhaps all, will not heed this call. Who, then, has the ability to acknowledge Hitchcock's authorship? In *Hitchcock – The Murderous Gaze*, I declare that I do. But does that make me unrepresentative of Hitchcock's viewers? What of my readers? If I believed that readers were doomed not to see what I see in Hitchcock's films, I would not have written or published my book, which aspires to expressing in my own words what I see and what I think and feel about what I see, as clearly as is humanly possible.

In the writing of *Hitchcock – The Murderous Gaze*, I declare in the postscript, I step forward, single myself out from the ranks of Hitchcock's audience members, to play a particular role. In principle, any member of Hitchcock's audience could have assumed this role, as any viewer could in principle have discovered the genres Cavell discovers. But no one who was not a representative member of Hitchcock's audience, no one who was not once blind, could have felt called upon to deliver my book's message. What it might be about my 'empirical existence' that provoked and prepared me to find or create my own voice in the writing of *Hitchcock – The Murderous Gaze* is not my book's concern. Its concern is to demonstrate a method that might enable my readers, who are members of Hitchcock's audience, to achieve the 'state necessary to acknowledge Hitchcock's authorship'.

Hitchcock – The Murderous Gaze offers practical instruction in viewing Hitchcock's films, thinking about Hitchcock's films, in ways that acknowledge Hitchcock's authorship. The method the book proposes is simply to follow the 'texts' of the films, and one's own experience of the films, with the degree and kind of attention required to follow one's own thinking. And it undertakes to demonstrate the efficacy of this method simply by 'reading' five representative Hitchcock films.

My readings do not instruct readers how they might make *these* discoveries about Hitchcock's films, of course. They stake my claim to critical insights that are my intuitions, not anyone else's. But these readings do undertake to pay the full tuition for these intuitions, as Emerson might put it, by finding words from our common language, words I can believe in, to account so clearly for my own experiences that readers might turn from these words (accompanied by the frame enlargements I chose to accompany them) to the films and find themselves seeing what I see in them (whether or not they then find themselves willing or able to accept my interpretations of what I see). It was my hope that by reading this book, by following its thinking, readers might learn something useful about making discoveries of their own (about these films, about other Hitchcock films, about films not stamped by Hitchcock's authorship, about works of art in other media). As I put it in the postscript, I wrote *Hitchcock – The Murderous Gaze* for Hitchcock's audience, which 'stands in need of instruction in viewing his films'. It was not 'to claim them for myself that I undertook to speak for Hitchcock's films. It was to free these films from me, to free myself from them, to claim my writing for my own.'[19]

Nonetheless, Gould writes, in a stinging passage,

> [Rothman's] acknowledgments of Hitchcock's meaningfulness and unknownness are presented as exclusively the effects of Rothman's critical insight and, indeed, as exclusively Rothman's. They are not acknowledgments that might allow others to hearken to the same voice, or follow the same path of self-illumination, but are acts of private devotion to a greatness that is at once public and hidden. Rothman takes himself, perhaps rightly, to be going public with such acknowledgments at the risk of sharing Hitchcock's destiny of unknownness.[20]

Although my 'acknowledgments of Hitchcock's meaningfulness and unknownness' are based on my own insights or intuitions, I do not present them as 'exclusively the effects' of my 'critical insight'. By demonstrating that what I claim to see in the films is there to be seen, I make my intuitions, I make my self, intelligible to the reader. On what grounds can Gould claim to know, then, that my writing does not allow readers to 'hearken to the same voice' or to follow their own 'paths of self-illumination'?

The greatness of Hitchcock's work *is* at once public and hidden. This was true when I was writing *Hitchcock – The Murderous Gaze*, and it is no less true today, as the present volume testifies. But the writing of *Hitchcock – The Murderous Gaze* was not an act of private devotion. I wrote the book, and published it, in the hope and expectation that it would be read. That is, I refused to accept that unknownness (however much it had been his fate, however much he had sought it) *was* Hitchcock's 'destiny'. To be sure, in undertaking to help the unknown in Hitchcock become known in all its unknownness, I took the risk that my writing, too, would remain unknown. What writer does not take that risk? What writer does not find that risk not worth taking?

Notes

1 William Rothman, *Hitchcock – The Murderous Gaze*, Cambridge: Harvard University Press, 1982, p. 253.
2 Rothman, *Hitchcock – The Murderous Gaze*, p. 7.
3 Rothman, *Hitchcock – The Murderous Gaze*, p. 255.
4 Rothman, *Hitchcock – The Murderous Gaze*, p. 255.
5 Slavoj Žižek, *Everything You Always Wanted to Know About Lacan (But Were Afraid to Ask Hitchcock)*, London and New York: Verso, 1992.
6 Stanley Cavell, *Pursuits of Happiness: The Hollywood Comedy of Remarriage*, Cambridge: Harvard University Press, 1981; *Contesting Tears: The Hollywood Melodrama of the Unknown Woman*, Chicago and London: The University of Chicago Press, 1996.
7 William Rothman, '*Vertigo*: The Unknown Woman in Hitchcock', *Forum for Psychiatry and the Humanities*, vol. 10, 1987. Reprinted in *Images in our Souls: Cavell, Psychoanalysis and Cinema*, Joseph H. Smith and William Kerrigan (eds), Baltimore: Johns Hopkins University Press, 1987, and in William Rothman, *The 'I' of the Camera: Essays in Film Criticism, History and Aesthetics*, New York and Cambridge: Cambridge University Press, 1989, pp. 152–73.
8 Rothman, *The 'I' of the Camera*, p. 172.
9 Rothman, *The 'I' of the Camera*, p. 172.
10 *Hitchcock – The Murderous Gaze*, p. 343.
11 *Hitchcock – The Murderous Gaze*, p. 346.
12 Tania Modleski, *The Women Who Knew Too Much: Hitchcock and Feminist Theory*, New York and London: Methuen, 1988, pp. 118–20.
13 Rothman, *Hitchcock – The Murderous Gaze*, p. 346.
14 Rothman, *The 'I' of the Camera*, p. 173.
15 Timothy Gould, *Hearing Things: Voice and Method in the Writing of Stanley Cavell*, Chicago and London: The University of Chicago Press, 1998, p. 73.
16 Gould, *Hearing Things*, p. 73.
17 Gould, *Hearing Things*, p. 72–3.
18 Gould, *Hearing Things*, p. 74.
19 Rothman, *Hitchcock – The Murderous Gaze*, p. 347.
20 Gould, *Hearing Things*, p. 74.

Sabotage – the film maker as saboteur

Chapter 4
Disruption, Destruction, Denial: Hitchcock as Saboteur

Susan Smith

Sabotage (1936) begins, somewhat unusually, with the following dictionary definition of its title concept, an extreme close-up of which remains on screen as the film's actual title and Hitchcock's name, among others, are superimposed:

> **să·botage** sà-bo-tarj. Wilful destruction of buildings or machinery with the object of alarming a group of persons or inspiring public uneasiness.

In offering such a detailed explanation of its title at the outset, the film immediately attributes a central significance to the meaning of sabotage, the narrational weighting attached to it here suggesting a preoccupation with the word that extends beyond its overt relevance to the plot.

The full relevance of sabotage to the male point of view within the narrative unfolds through the film's sympathetic depiction of the two main saboteurs, Verloc (Oscar Homolka) and the Professor (William Dewhurst). Their involvement with such subversive political activity is presented, in the first place, as an attempt by them to alleviate and resolve concerns about their position and status within the domestic sphere. For Verloc, it is motivated quite explicitly by his need to meet his own pressing financial commitments as provider for both his wife and her younger brother. This is made clear during his visit to the zoo aquarium when he initially resists an assignment intended to cause 'loss of life', only to accede due to economic imperatives (his agent having already withheld the fee due to him from his previous sabotage of London's electricity supplies). That Verloc's sabotage work functions for him as a way of compensating for his sense of inadequacy in the breadwinner role was also demonstrated earlier when his expectation that he would be well paid for his first job even prompted him to make the magnanimous gesture of offering to refund his own cinema patrons' money (having interrupted their film viewing by cutting off the electricity).

Yet Mrs Verloc's (Sylvia Sydney's) subsequent observation, when serving out the food, that they wouldn't have been able to afford even a lettuce if the electricity hadn't been restored just in time to avert the planned refund of the customers' money, suggests a more counter-productive, self-destructive potential to such sabotage activity. This becomes fully realised later on when Verloc's bombing mission results in the blowing up of his younger brother-in-law, Stevie (Desmond Tester), and his own consequent murder (the ambiguous depiction of which invites Verloc's death to be read, alternatively, as an implied suicide). That such tendencies are not confined to Verloc alone is made clear by the attitude of the bomb-making Professor who, on being surrounded by the police during his visit to Verloc's cinema at the end of the film, responds by blowing up himself, his murdered colleague and the building itself. The increasing way in which such violence becomes turned inwardly upon the family and self thus invites the act of sabotage to be read, on a deeper level, as the expression of an unconscious desire on the part of the male characters to subvert, destroy and obtain release from the oppressiveness of their responsibilities.

The Professor's use of his own living quarters as the site for his bomb-making activities epitomises the way in which this male preoccupation with political sedition serves as a displacement of more deeply held impulses towards domestic rebellion. The oppressiveness of the home for the male characters is articulated through the motif of the cage. The first instance of this occurs after the cinema proprietor's return from his initial act of sabotage when he is shown in the dining room wiping away the traces of his crime from a low-angle, detached camera viewpoint that emphasises the bars of a chair in the foreground.[1] The Professor's bird shop itself functions not only (like Verloc's cinema) as a front for his sabotage activities but also as a human cage for himself, his daughter and granddaughter. Most of all, though, it is the rhetorical image of two birds in a cage, in the form of Verloc's gift to Stevie, that symbolises the entrapping, emotionally constrained nature of the Verlocs' own marriage. By extension, then, it is possible to construe the Professor's euphemistic written reminder to Verloc about when the bomb is due to explode ('DON'T FORGET THE BIRDS WILL SING AT 1.45') as a rather fitting allusion to the way in which such marital tensions will eventually find release in violent form.

Verloc's gesture of giving the caged canaries to Stevie is particularly significant for it is this surrogate son who provides the tenuous, ambivalent link between the married couple. On the one hand, he enables Verloc to exert control over his wife by using acts of kindness towards Stevie as a form of emotional blackmail ('You're terribly good to him ... If you're good to him, you're good to me. You know that,' Mrs Verloc tells her husband with a hint of both puzzlement and resentment). Yet ultimately he forms a kind of (sexual) barrier or impediment between the couple for, as long as Mrs Verloc has Stevie, it is implied, the issue of their having a child of their own is evaded. Verloc's 'inadvertent' blowing up of Stevie can be seen, in this sense, as unconsciously willed, fulfilling a wish to be rid of the surrogate son that his acts of kindness otherwise attempt to deny and repress. His ambivalence towards Stevie is perfectly embodied in his 'generous' gift of the cage of canaries that, in reality, carries a bomb hidden in its tray. Verloc's joking remark that Stevie's double errand (involving delivery of the film tins and bomb package) will 'kill two birds with one stone' accordingly assumes a much deeper level of significance for it refers to how the boy's task enables the male protagonist to carry out not only his official sabotage duties but also an even more private, hidden agenda.

Verloc's suggestion to his wife shortly after Stevie's death ('Perhaps, if we had a kid of our own ... ?') in turn acquires a rationale beyond that of mere insensitivity, for it makes clear how the disposal of the surrogate son represents, for the saboteur, the removal of an obstacle to his relationship with Mrs Verloc and one that paves the way for a child of his own. In practice, though, Verloc's plea for a child in the wake of Stevie's death only serves to bring his anxieties about his masculinity to a crisis point for, in provoking Mrs Verloc's departure from the room in disgust and her subsequent murderous impulses towards him, it finally exposes her previously suppressed revulsion towards him in the most extreme way possible. In view of the parallels invited between the caged birds and the married couple, moreover, Verloc's earlier joke about killing two birds with one stone points to an even deeper desire on his part to rid himself not only of Stevie but of his marriage altogether.

That Stevie binds Mrs Verloc in an entrapping marriage as well was suggested during her visit to Simpson's restaurant when she intimated to Ted (John Loder) that she only entered into the marriage for her brother's sake:

Mrs Verloc: Mr Verloc's very kind to Stevie.
Ted: And that means a lot to Stevie's sister?
Mrs Verloc: It means everything.

Verloc's blowing up of Stevie thus breaks the tacit contract on which their marriage is implicitly founded. The possibility that Mrs Verloc's killing of her husband (in response to Stevie's death) serves, in turn, to release her from such a marriage is qualified severely, however, by the problematic alternatives facing her at the end of the film. Like other female protagonists in Hitchcock's films,[2] Mrs Verloc is confronted with either the threat of imprisonment or entry into a relationship that, despite Ted's ostensibly protective motives in trying to stop her from confessing to murder, ominously seems to require the suppression of her own voice and feelings. Ted's role as a rather problematic romantic alternative for Mrs Verloc is implied all the way through, in fact, via the strong parallels established between himself and Verloc, both of whom not only exploit their public role as a front for more secretive activities but also employ the same strategy of using Stevie as a way of ingratiating themselves into Mrs Verloc's affections. That Verloc's death results in only a rather qualified liberation from Mrs Verloc's point of view is suggested by the cut, immediately afterwards, to a shot of the two birds now singing but still confined in their cage.

Many of the tensions underpinning the Verlocs' relationship are mirrored even more clearly in the Professor's domestic situation. His parallel role as surrogate father towards his granddaughter is shouldered in a much more openly grudging way than Verloc's, as revealed during the following encounter between the two saboteurs at the bird shop:

Professor: There you are. No father, no discipline. What can you expect?
Verloc: Is the little girl's father dead?
Professor: I don't know. Might be. I don't know. Nobody knows. My daughter would like to know too. But there you are. It's her cross and she must bear it. *We all have our cross to bear. Hmm?*

The Professor's desire to be rid of *his* surrogate child is also suggested during the same scene when he admits to having hidden away his granddaughter's toy doll in the cupboard containing the bomb-making substances, only to then nearly drop this stand-in of her along with one of the jars of explosives, his subsequent self-rebuke ('Slap me hard. Grand-dad's been very naughty') thereby constituting a double admission of guilty desire on his part. The daughter's rather more silent display of hostility here towards her father finds release near the end of the film via her condemnation of his latest sabotage mission, while her instruction to him to retrieve the bird cage from Verloc's home effectively sends the Professor, now a figure of rather comic pathos, to his death.

Verloc's remorse over killing Stevie ('I didn't mean any harm to come to the boy') is echoed outside of the text by Hitchcock's own repeated protestations of regret, during interviews, at having allowed the boy to be killed by the bomb (an act which Truffaut, in a shared consensus of uneasiness over the incident, also describes as 'close to an abuse of cinematic power'):[3]

> I made a serious mistake in having the little boy carry the bomb. A character who unknowingly carries a bomb around as if it were an ordinary package is bound to work up great suspense in the audience. The boy was involved in a situation that got him too much sympathy from the audience, so that when the bomb exploded and he was killed, the public was resentful.[4]

The notion of the film-maker of *Sabotage* which the director projects here is, like his surrogate within the narrative, that of a rather uncertain amateur who bungles the task assigned to him and who, in a gesture analogous to Verloc's attempt to wash away the traces of his crime at the beginning of the film, then seeks to absolve himself of this cinematic act of violence. Hitchcock's fear of having betrayed and alienated his audience is also anticipated rather uncannily within the narrative via the display of unrest among Verloc's own cinema-goers over the disruption to their viewing caused by their proprietor's initial wrecking of the city's electricity supplies. At one point, a particularly disgruntled customer even angrily complains: 'I know how the law stands. *You broke a contract.* Therefore, you broke the law.'

Hitchcock's own acknowledgement of the need to retain a bond with his film audience similarly finds voice in Verloc's attempt to appease his customers by offering to refund their money on the grounds that 'It doesn't pay to antagonise the public' (a tactic supported by Mrs Verloc who refers to them flatteringly as 'all regular patrons and good friends'). Yet just as Verloc's subsequent remorse and denial of intent with regard to the bombing episode are undercut by suggestions that his killing of Stevie is unconsciously willed, so Hitchcock's own expressions of regret at having broken contract with his audience together with his tendency to construe the bomb scene as simply a miscalculation on his part are very much challenged by the deliberate, coherent way in which the film's rhetorical strategies serve to implicate the director's film-making approach with the act of sabotage. Indeed, through its opening dictionary definition of sabotage as an act of 'wilful destruction' the film seems at pains to stress its intentions with regard to the bomb explosion right from the outset, while the phrase 'with the object of alarming a group of persons or inspiring public uneasiness' serves as a coded acknowledgement of its wish to disrupt and disquiet its own 'public' by such acts of cinematic subversion. Looking beyond the film itself, this definition of sabotage also effectively becomes a seminal metaphor for the kind of disruptive filmic strategies meted out by Hitchcock's cinema in the future, most radically of all in *Psycho* (1960).

The metafilmic significance of *Sabotage*'s title consequently explains the film's concerted strategy of stressing the disruptive impact of Verloc's activities upon his *own* audiences rather than upon the city's general inhabitants (whose initial response, by contrast, is simply to laugh off the inconvenience). Verloc's initial act of depriving his own audience of light provides a particularly apt analogy for the way in which Hitchcock's films often plunge their own audiences into darkness both literally and metaphorically. One thinks, especially, of the disorientating effect of the train tunnel sequence at the beginning of *Suspicion* and the moment during the opening scene in *Psycho* when the camera makes its transition from the bright, sunny outdoors to inside a Phoenix hotel room. Similarly, at the end of the film it is Verloc's audience which is once again disrupted when the threat of yet another bomb explosion (this time within the cinema itself) forces the police to order the auditorium to be evacuated in the middle of a screening.

This analogy between sabotage and film-making, saboteur and film-maker, is illustrated quite vividly during Verloc's visit to the zoo when, having just expressed reluctance to carry out the bombing mission assigned to him by his chief, he then proceeds to project an imagined scenario of blowing up Piccadilly onto one of the aquarium tanks which effectively becomes transformed (via his subjective point of view) into a movie screen. In doing so, it is as if Verloc is drawn irresistibly, against his conscious wishes, to indulge in a fantasy of power on a scale that even outstrips what actually happens later on and in a way that suggests the cinema proprietor's desire to usurp the role of film-maker. Both Verloc and Hitchcock, it seems, engage in spoken acts of denial that are at odds with their cinematic impulses and aspirations.

Such textual strategies of exposure find concrete embodiment within the narrative in the form of the detectives' surveillance of the Bijou cinema, the effect of which is to undermine Verloc's own attempts to hide self-effacingly in the background. At one point, in fact, Ted even goes so far as to admit to Mrs Verloc the police's belief that 'there's something going on here connected with sabotage'. Mrs Verloc's own earlier gesture of shining a torch into her husband's face during the electricity blackout also hints at *her* desire to expose him (the implication both here and elsewhere being that she knows more about his activities than she is prepared to admit).

The film's other main saboteur is the Professor[5] and it is this figure who, in his role as the bomb-maker 'who makes lovely fireworks', serves to implicate the film-maker with the material source of the sabotage function itself. This is established during Verloc's visit to the Professor's bird shop when the sound of a *cock*erel crowing loudly twice in the backyard, as the Professor takes his visitor to his living quarters at the rear, alludes unmistakably to Hitch*cock*'s own authorial presence in the background and in a way that symbolically proclaims the director's involvement with sabotage as an implied assertion of film-making potency. The Professor's role as Hitchcock's other main agent within the narrative becomes even more evident during the bomb scene itself when this character's written reminder to Verloc ('DON'T FORGET THE BIRDS WILL SING AT 1.45') is appropriated by the film-maker as his own direct, suspense-inducing warning to the viewer (who is then confronted with an extreme close-up of it superimposed across the entire frame of the shot).

But the closest analogy between sabotage and cinema ultimately resides in the way that, when sending Stevie on his fatal errand, Verloc gives him not only the bomb package but also a set of film reels, the very title of which (*Bartholomew the Strangler*) could easily belong to the Hitchcock thriller genre. The materials of sabotage and of cinema therefore become physically and symbolically juxtaposed throughout the bomb scene itself, a link even further suggested by the echoing references to the bomb as 'a parcel of fireworks' and the 'flammable' property of film (making the latter illegal to carry on public transport). And it is the film tins that Ted later discovers amid the bomb wreckage, thereby providing the incriminating clue as to who is responsible (Verloc explicitly, Hitchcock implicitly).

Despite Hitchcock's repeated criticisms of his 'mishandling' of the bomb scene (referring to it during one interview as an instance of 'bad technique' which he 'never repeated'),[6] the episode in fact conforms to his own classic definition of suspense so closely that he may well have had *Sabotage* in mind when coining the hypothetical scenario involving a bomb hidden under a table.[7] What is more, the scene also challenges the director's clearly defined distinction between suspense and surprise for, by subverting and denying the audience's conventional expectations that Stevie will be reprieved at the last moment, it effectively exploits its suspense for shock effect. This need to break the standard safety clause usually taken for granted in an audience's implied contract with a film (based upon a set of generic and narrative conventions) is something that Hitchcock frequently advocated in his interviews, yet often without any acknowledgement of how it might challenge his own rationale for criticising the bomb scene. During one television interview, for example, Hitchcock's ritual claim (that in allowing the bomb to explode in *Sabotage* he went too far) is preceded only moments earlier by the following account of his role as film-maker (in response to the interviewer's reference to him as the 'master of the unexpected'):

> That's only because one's challenged by the audience. They're saying to me 'Show us' and 'I know what's coming next' and I say 'Do you?'. And that's the avoidance of the cliché, automatically. They're expecting the cliché and I have to say 'We cannot have a cliché here!'[8]

Hitchcock's comments about his 'bungling' of the bomb incident in *Sabotage* are particularly curious in view of the fact that they were made *after Psycho*, a film which contains, in the form of the shower murder scene, an arguably even more abrupt, violent killing off of a main character, yet one for which the director displayed no such equivalent remorse. The contradictions embedded within Hitchcock's own interviews and *Sabotage*'s marked divergence from some of these post-production comments both indicate the difficulties and dangers involved in trying to relate textual meanings and effects back to the film-maker. What it suggests, instead, is the relevance to Hitchcock's work of the distinction between 'actual film-maker' and what is often referred to as the 'implied film-maker'. That is to say, between the real individual who physically directed the making of the movie and the agency at work within the text itself; between the Hitchcock existing separately outside of the film and the one implied by it during the viewing process.

Yet the fact that part of this reading of *Sabotage* has involved referring to Hitchcock's authorial presence outside of the text (even if only to define the film's meaning *against* it) suggests the impracticality of dismissing this figure altogether. Hitchcock's importance as a media event in his own right suggests, rather, the need to take into account a *third* version of the film-maker: that of Hitchcock the public persona, as an image constructed largely outside of the films themselves through the interviews, the publicity trailers for the films, the *Alfred Hitchcock Presents* television series, the biographies and so on. This third version of the film-maker sits between the other two in an uneasy tension, with the interviewed Hitchcock's attempt to distance himself critically from the one who actually made the film in 1936 being implicitly challenged and upstaged, in turn, by the film's own construction of the film-maker as saboteur. Verloc's role within the film seems to reflect and embody aspects of all three of these: as uncertain amateur who overreaches himself; as public relations figure conscious of the box-office need to appease his audience; and as the more enigmatic individual who uses both of these personae as a screen for his more serious, subversive preoccupations.

As such, Verloc constitutes a rather complex variation upon George Wilson's notion of 'a given character of a film [who] speaks for and/or somehow stands in for the implied film maker'.[9] Verloc's status as surrogate for the film-maker implied by the film rests upon the fact that, as main agent and perpetrator of the sabotage plot, he enacts within the narrative what the film applies as a strategy towards its own audience, thereby fulfilling the criteria 'of a non-narrating, on-screen character who instructively exemplifies properties of the filmic narration upon which its special quality depends'.[10] This notion of characters acting as surrogates or agents for the implied film-maker is something that had already been alluded to in the title of Hitchcock's preceding film, *Secret Agent* (1936), and is also encouraged, of course, by the title of Joseph Conrad's novel *The Secret Agent* (on which *Sabotage*, not the earlier film, is based). The Professor also embodies elements of all three versions of Hitchcock, in the sense that he 'not only reflects aspects of the implied film maker [i.e. in his role as bomb-maker] but also signals the reflection by bearing a salient resemblance to the actual film maker'[11] (as indeed does Verloc, both characters being linked physically to Hitchcock by their plumpness), while at the end of the film he acts out the public Hitchcock's wish to erase all traces of his involvement with sabotage activity. Hence, in a gesture of denial and punishment that anticipates the director's own subsequent self-recriminations about taking his film-making powers of manipulation too far, the Professor appropriately turns his final act of sabotage symbolically upon Hitchcock's own cinema.

The presence of multiple authorial surrogates in *Sabotage*,[12] each reflecting various notions of Hitchcock, contributes, in turn, to a rather multifaceted notion of the implied film-maker that resists any one-to-one correlation between these two categories. The dispensability of these surrogates (both of whom are killed off by the end of the film) is indicative of the fact that the implied film-maker is more than simply a composite of his narrative counterparts. This is made clear during the bomb scene itself when the manipulation of the viewer through the calculated, unrelenting deployment of a range of suspense strategies produces the sense of a much more practised, wilful, omniscient saboteur than Verloc, the saboteur by proxy, who instead waits nervously and helplessly at home, as much victim as generator of the situation.

The film's deployment of humour and laughter are also crucial in conveying the sense of a superior, independent sensibility at work, able to distance itself from its surrogates and their actions. Thus, the stern reprimand issued by Verloc's employer after the initial sabotage act (namely, that 'When one sets out to put the fear of death into people, it is not helpful to make them laugh') and his subsequent written instruction to Verloc that 'LONDON MUST NOT LAUGH' at the next mission, are themselves given an implied rebuke by the film's insistent strategy of foregrounding diegetic laughter emerging out of the bomb episode. It is, then, the nervous tension caused by the prospect of sending Stevie on his bombing errand that prompts Verloc to make (and laugh at) his own joke about killing two birds with one stone. The bomb explosion itself is followed, furthermore, by an immediate cut to a shot of Ted and Verloc laughing. And, finally, it is while in a distraught state, following the discovery that her brother has been killed, that Mrs Verloc joins in with the children's laughter as they watch the Disney cartoon *Who Killed Cock Robin?* in the cinema auditorium. The timing of such laughter just before and after Stevie's death consequently heightens and complicates the disturbing impact of the act of violence itself by disrupting conventional patterns of tone (while also suggesting that Stevie's death may provide some form of unconscious release for all three adult characters concerned). Although Verloc's own joke about killing two birds with one stone embodies much of this spirit of black humour, there is little evidence to suggest that the character himself is aware of the deeply self-revealing nature of his utterance in the way that we infer the implied film-maker to be.

A rather different use of humour occurs during an earlier encounter in the bird shop between the Professor and a woman who complains about her non-singing canary. This incident in fact provides a comic echo of the film's opening scene of audience unrest by showing yet another disgruntled customer angrily demanding her money back. By letting the audience in on the humour of this particular situation, though (centering upon the Professor's ability to outwit his awkward customer by camouflaging her canary's silence amid the collective whistling of the other birds in the shop), this kind of comic strategy invites us to acknowledge the presence of a more endearing, charismatic authority, one that is able to win over us, the film's own 'customers', through mutual understanding rather than deception. Collectively, then, such moments are crucial in developing a notion of the implied film-maker as a more sophisticated saboteur than his narrative counterparts, one who is able to recognise both the wounding *and* healing power of humour: that is, as a disruptive strategy of sabotage in its own right *and* a way of reaffirming contact with the audience. The newspaper caption, 'COMEDIES IN THE DARK', that is used to describe the impact of the first act of sabotage consequently becomes, contrary to Verloc's employer's use of it as an indication of the mission's failure, a rather apt description of the nature of Hitchcock's own cinema as one wherein humour coexists with and is very much part of the thriller fabric.

The comic interlude at the Professor's bird shop also serves a further crucial purpose for, in highlighting this character's inability to make the recalcitrant canary sing, it effectively undermines the authority of his own subsequent euphemistic warning to Verloc about when the bomb is due to explode ('DON'T FORGET THE BIRDS WILL SING AT 1.45') by implying his lack of real control over the sabotage function. This is typical, moreover, of the way in which the film prevents us elsewhere from simply accepting the characters' fictional autonomy within their film world by allowing questions about narrative agency (what the film's original title referred to as 'The Hidden Power')[13] to be voiced quite explicitly within the dialogue. Such a questioning approach begins right at the outset when the men surveying the electricity station respond to their discovery as follows: 'Sand.' 'Sabotage.' 'Wrecking.' 'Deliberate.' 'What's at the back of it?' 'Who did it?' Similarly, when Ted visits Scotland Yard, he asks his superintendent 'Who's behind it?' to which the latter replies, 'Ah, they're the people that you and I'll never catch. It's the men they employ that we're after.'

This interrogative tendency culminates in the screening of the Disney cartoon sequence *Who Killed Cock Robin?* just prior to Verloc's own murder, the title and chorus line of which encourage us to consider, in advance, who is the real cause of the male protagonist's death. The implication that it is Hitchcock, as director of the film, who is ultimately responsible is given added extra-diegetic force by the film-maker's subsequent criticisms of the bomb scene. Yet if Verloc's death can be construed, on one level, as a punishment for his role in causing the bomb to explode, then it is also a punishment to which Hitchcock seems to subject himself symbolically by using the 'cock' symbolism to link his own name to both murdered bird and male protagonist (as implied by the rhyming play upon Hitch*cock*/*Cock* Robin/Ver*loc*). The *Who Killed Cock Robin?* sequence consequently invites us to read Verloc's subsequent death somewhat ambivalently: that is, as an assertion of authorial power by Hitchcock (who, in killing off the male protagonist, asserts his independence from this surrogate figure) *and* a symbolic act of authorial suicide or self-castration on the film-maker's part (by 'killing off' the 'cock' in 'Hitchcock').[14] The enigmatic nature of the film-maker's persona in this film is ultimately embodied in the mysterious identity of the cartoon killer bird. For what this silhouetted,[15] silent figure depicts so well is a sense of the implied film-maker as a rather elusive, inscrutable agency that cannot be rendered in concrete bodily form like its fictional surrogates but is capable, nonetheless, of intruding into the narratives at certain key moments.

If part of this account of *Sabotage* has involved considering the kind of film-maker and overall filmic properties implied by the text, what, then, of the spectator? Hitchcock's own comments on *Sabotage* during his interviews are additionally interesting for the way they imply a particular notion of the audience and one that finds concrete embodiment within the narrative itself in the form of the 'resentful' members of Verloc's own Bijou cinema who respond to the hijacking of their viewing by angrily demanding their money back. Yet while it is tempting to construe this diegetic audience as a surrogate forerunner of ourselves after the bomb explosion, the very act of rendering such an audience in material, fictionalised form inevitably places it at one remove from the actual spectator who is consequently placed in the position of being able to observe the kind of reactions displayed by such cinemagoers in a more detached way. This critical distance from our ostensible surrogates within the film is heightened by an awareness of how easily Ted is able to manipulate them by confusing them with legal jargon. The prescience and import of one customer's complaint about Verloc breaking contract are also undercut by the heavily bespectacled nature of his appearance and his rigid adherence to the law, both of which imply a short-sightedness and inflexibility about his viewing habits and assumptions that we are thus invited to reject.

Arguably, then, the real purpose of this diegetic display of audience unrest is to provide us with a comic preparation or palliative for the future sabotage of our own expectations during the bomb scene itself. The aforementioned instances of humour elsewhere also imply a more sophisticated, critically detached, good-natured spectator than the kinds foregrounded within the narrative. Unlike Verloc's cinema patrons, furthermore, the film's own audience also has access to a range of suspense strategies both during the bomb scene and elsewhere, all of which provide advance warning of what is about to happen. Indeed, taking such epistemic privileges into account, one is obliged to reconsider whether in fact the film *is* breaking contract with its audience after all, for it does nothing in the bomb scene that conflicts with what has been intimated all along. A more accurate appraisal would be to state that the film's breaking or sabotage of general, pregiven cinematic conventions and taboos constitutes, conversely, a *fulfilment* of the terms and conditions of the contract that it draws up with its own audience as the narrative progresses, one of the clauses of which could be described as 'expect the unexpected'. (According to this approach, then, it is Hitchcock's own subsequent criticisms which effectively break contract with the text.)

This 'avoidance of cliché' (to use Hitchcock's own phrase) is demonstrated not only by the fact that the bomb is allowed to explode but also by the way in which Stevie himself is portrayed. The standard, unquestioning view of him as 'simply an innocent victim of tragic circumstances'[16] effectively conforms to the overall reading of the bomb explosion as the breaking of a cinematic taboo. Yet such a view crucially overlooks the way in which the film's own rhetorical devices seek to qualify and challenge this by hinting at a somewhat more problematic side to the boy's character. This undercutting of the child's role as innocent victim is developed throughout the bomb episode by the consistent association of Stevie with the film *Bartholomew the Strangler* (carried by him along with the bomb package). It begins with Stevie's own admission to Ted, just before leaving the cinema on his fatal errand, that he has watched that same film 'fourteen times', the effect of which is to suggest rather ominous, early signs of the boy's own compulsive absorption with violence (and of a kind presumably directed towards women). This is reinforced by the other characters' tendency to identify Stevie quite directly with the fictional male strangler figure himself (a link also alluded to visually via the 'B' emblem on the boy's school cap). Thus, Ted sends Stevie off on his journey with the words 'Well, so long, Bartholomew', a nomenclature that the male conductor also applies to him when letting him on the bus: 'Well, if it's you, Bartholomew, old fella, you can stay. As long as you promise not to set about me, or any of the passengers.' The fact that it is the conductor's playful recognition of Stevie as the strangler figure that sways him to relax his rules and allow the boy onto the bus is particularly crucial as it points to Stevie's association with such male violence as the underlying cause of his death.

So rather than simply portraying Stevie in such a way as to heighten audience outrage at his death, such an unsentimentalised depiction of him encourages us instead to reassess and readjust our more conventional, predetermined response to the bomb explosion by opening up the possibility of deeper motives on the film's part for seeking to have him killed off. This kind of ironic perspective upon Stevie is also evident during the sequence where the street pedlar brushes the child's teeth and greases his hair before sending him on his way with the observation that he is now 'groomed for stardom'. It is as if, via this moment, the film takes us 'backstage' to see the Desmond Tester character being made up for his big scene and, in doing so, it invites us to draw back from our emotional involvement with Stevie and view him rather more self-consciously as a fictional construction within the narrative.

While I cautioned earlier against simply accepting audiences within the narrative as surrogates for ourselves, Mrs Verloc's position as a spectator watching the Disney cartoon *Who Killed Cock Robin?* does come very close, it seems to me, to capturing the complex nature of the film-viewing experience. Her dual response of initial laughter at the cartoon followed by a sobering realisation of its relevance to her personal situation is particularly analogous to the kind of ambivalent responses induced by Hitchcock's own cinema, where humour often appears to offer some form of relief from the darker aspects of the narrative worlds only to become implicated, retrospectively, within it. The triple nature of her relationship to the cartoon characters also demonstrates, more generally, how the act of spectatorship can involve negotiating a range of (here quite contradictory) subject positions. Initially, the cartoon would appear to present a conventional love triangle analogous to the one between Mrs Verloc (as the Mae West bird caught between two male figures' competing interests), Ted (the romantic hero represented by the Bing Crosby serenader) and Verloc (who, like the killer bird, is often shown hiding in the shadows). But the murder of Cock Robin clearly functions more importantly for Mrs Verloc as a re-enactment and reminder of Stevie's recent death, a possibility further supported by the boy's own associations with birds earlier on in the narrative. As such, the murder scenario relates more aptly to the familial triangle within the film, alluding to the 'father's' killing off of the 'son' as his rival for the 'mother's' affections. Crucially, however, the cartoon murder also prefigures Mrs Verloc's own killing of her husband, with the shooting of the arrow in fact resembling Verloc's fate more closely than Stevie's. As a result, Mrs Verloc can be seen to identify successively with all three figures: namely, as love object, victim of violence (via her empathy with Stevie and his fate) and murderer (the first two being stereotypically 'female', the third 'male'). In the last instance, the cartoon murder would seem to function for Mrs Verloc in a comparable way to Verloc's earlier fantasy of blowing up Piccadilly by enabling an unconscious playing out of previously unacknowledged desires on her part. In Mrs Verloc's case, though, what her shifting responses demonstrate so well (as highlighted by their contrast with the children's more constant, uninhibited forms of laughter) is the importance of the female spectator's own lived experience in understanding a film subject to various forms of appropriation.

In foregrounding issues of both authorship and spectatorship, the *Who Killed Cock Robin?* sequence encapsulates the overall complexity of *Sabotage*'s metafilmic concerns. During the course of this article, I have argued that such concerns hinge upon a series of textual analogies between sabotage and film-making, saboteur and film-maker, the combined effect of which is to highlight a far more subversive aspect to both the film and Hitchcock's implied persona than that allowed for by the director's own post-production comments. Prior to discussing its metafilmic significance, I also argued that the act of sabotage serves as an outlet for the male characters' unconscious desire to gain release from the oppressiveness of their domestic situation and that such impulses become increasingly self-destructive in nature. The film's strategy of linking such male saboteurs to Hitchcock consequently acquires a doubly subversive charge by implicitly relating its concerns with authorship and film-making to problematic aspects of masculinity. Yet while the male characters eventually fall victim to their own violent acts of sabotage, the film's rather more sophisticated strategies of suspense and humour ultimately serve to imply that Hitchcock remains in control of *his* self-inscription as saboteur.

Notes

1 This shot produces what William Rothman refers to as 'Hitchcock's //// sign'. See Rothman, *Hitchcock – the Murderous Gaze*, London: Harvard University Press, 1982, p. 33, and Chapter 3 in this volume, p. 27.

2 Compare Mrs Verloc's situation here with that facing her female counterparts at the end of *Blackmail* (1929) and *Marnie* (1964).

3 François Truffaut, *Hitchcock*, London: Paladin, 1986, p. 145.

4 Truffaut, *Hitchcock*, p. 144.

5 Although derived from Conrad's novel *The Secret Agent* (on which this film is based), the Professor's name had already been used for an earlier Hitchcock villain in *The 39 Steps* (1935) and was later also applied to the leader of the American secret service group in *North by Northwest* (1959).

6 Television interview with Huw Weldon (*Monitor*, 1964).

7 Truffaut, *Hitchcock*, p. 91. In defining suspense according to this bomb scenario, Hitchcock contrasts it with surprise:

> We are now having a very innocent chat. Let us suppose that there is a bomb underneath this table between us. Nothing happens, and then all of a sudden, 'Boom!' There is an explosion. The public is *surprised*, but prior to this surprise, it has seen an absolutely ordinary scene, of no special consequence. Now, let us take a *suspense* situation. The bomb is underneath the table and the public *knows* it, probably because they have seen the anarchist place it there. The public is *aware* that the bomb is going to explode at one o'clock and there is a clock in the decor. The public can see that it is a quarter to one. In these conditions this same innocuous conversation becomes fascinating because the public is participating in the scene. The audience is longing to warn the characters on the screen: 'You shouldn't be talking about such trivial matters. There's a bomb beneath you and it's about to explode!' In the first case we have given the public fifteen seconds of *surprise* at the moment of the explosion. In the second we have provided them with fifteen minutes of *suspense*. The conclusion is that whenever possible the public must be informed. Except when the surprise is a twist, that is, when the unexpected ending is, in itself, the highlight of the story.

8 *Monitor* interview.

9 George M. Wilson, *Narration In Light: Studies in Cinematic Point of View*, Baltimore: Johns Hopkins University Press, 1986, p. 137.

10 Wilson, *Narration In Light*, p. 138.

11 Wilson, *Narration In Light*, p. 138.

12 Note, also, the Hitchcock look-alike who appears briefly during the aborted meeting at Verloc's home.

13 See Donald Spoto, *The Life of Alfred Hitchcock: The Dark Side of Genius*, London: Collins, 1983, p. 157.

14 It is interesting, in this respect, how Hitchcock chose to 'castrate' his own name in real

life by dropping the second syllable (the 'phallic' part) of his surname, leaving just 'Hitch' instead.

15 Hitchcock also used a silhouette or outline of his own figure to mark the beginning of his television shows.

16 Spoto, *The Life of Alfred Hitchcock*, p. 155.

The universally known presenter of television's *Alfred Hitchcock Presents*

Chapter 5
The Outer Circle: Hitchcock on Television

Thomas M. Leitch

> The three premises of the *auteur* theory may be visualized as three concentric circles: the outer circle as technique; the middle circle, personal style; and the inner circle, interior meaning. The corresponding roles of the director may be designated as those of a technician, a stylist, and an *auteur*.[1]

Although Andrew Sarris is too kind to say so, there is a fourth circle outside the three he describes, an even more marginal area occupied by, among others, that darling of *auteur* criticism, Alfred Hitchcock: the director as celebrity. In this shadowy area, directors do not function as *auteurs* of interior meaning or visual stylists or even competent technicians but merely as public personages because they are not working as directors; they are merely lending their name, their prestige and, in Hitchcock's case, their unmistakable image to the projects of others in order to fatten their market.

Hitchcock's contribution to this area, one which raised synergy to an art form a generation before *Star Wars* and Jeffrey Katzenberg, was the licensing of his name beginning in 1955 to a pulp monthly, *Alfred Hitchcock's Mystery Magazine*, and two long-running television series, *Alfred Hitchcock Presents* and its successor *The Alfred Hitchcock Hour*. *Presenting* was exactly what Hitchcock did in each case, signing ghost-written headnotes for each issue of the magazine and each anthology culled from its contents, and appearing at the beginning and end of each television episode to deliver the mordantly witty remarks written for him by James Allardice. Both publishing and television ventures, trading on Hitchcock's celebrity to distinguish new ventures from their competitors, were equally successful in reinforcing that celebrity, establishing Hitchcock's name, portly figure and grave Cockney intonations as household fixtures for a generation of film-goers who might well have been hard-pressed to name another Hollywood director.

The critics who claimed Hitchcock as an *auteur* in the 1960s dismissed his work in publishing and television on the grounds that it was not really work at all. To adapt a remark of Sarris's, a great director has to be at least a director. Sadly, the same neglect has generally met the twenty television segments Hitchcock actually directed: seventeen half-hour episodes of *Alfred Hitchcock Presents* first broadcast on CBS (1955–60) and NBC (1960–2), and three hour-long programs: *I Saw the Whole Thing* (1962), the only episode Hitchcock directed in the three-year run of *The Alfred Hitchcock Hour* (1962–5); *Four O'Clock* (1957), the première episode of the NBC suspense anthology series *Suspi-*

cion; and *Incident at a Corner* (1960), an episode in NBC's dramatic anthology series *Ford Startime*.

The resulting gap between the canonisation of Hitchcock's theatrical films and the neglect of his television films has grown so wide that Jane Sloan's monumental bibliography of Hitchcock lists nothing, apart from titles and production credits of the twenty episodes Hitchcock directed, on Hitchcock's television films. Researchers relying on Sloan's guidance would never know of the slender body of critical work on the television films.[2] When is a director not a director? When he is directing a television program.

There is no mystery about why scholars should have given such short shrift to the 268 half-hour episodes[3] of *Alfred Hitchcock Presents* and the 93 episodes of *The Alfred Hitchcock Hour*. Hitchcock's involvement in both programs, by his own admission, was largely restricted to approving or rejecting synopses of the published stories which served as the series' raw material.[4] He neither directed most of the episodes – that job was farmed out to a stable of veterans and newcomers from John Brahm and Robert Florey to Sydney Pollack and Robert Altman – nor produced them, relegating that task to his long-time assistant Joan Harrison. Instead, his 'palpable presence', as frequent series writer Robert Bloch described it, was most often putative or stipulative, in decisions the creative team headed by Harrison made in anticipation of 'his taste and standards – would "Hitch" like this, would he disagree with that?'[5]

Even when Hitchcock directed an episode, he did not select his own scripts, but allowed Harrison to choose properties she thought he might be especially interested in; he followed the protocols of accelerated television production schedules and diminished television budgets, which prescribed limited camera set-ups, mostly on rudimentary indoor sets, over a three-day production allowance (one day for rehearsals, two for shooting); and he 'never looked through the camera viewfinder, but arrived on the set each day with every shot meticulously sketched out.'[6] The production team for both series, headed by Harrison, associate producer Norman Lloyd and story consultant Gordon Hessler, controlled the production of Hitchcock's episodes so tightly that a disinterested observer would be hard-pressed to find any sign of any Hitchcock touch, either thematic or technical, that distinguished the seventeen episodes of *Alfred Hitchcock Presents* directed by the master of suspense from the 251 that were not.[7]

Perhaps in search of such a Hitchcock touch, the scholars who have turned their attention to Hitchcock's television credits have emphasised their thematic and technical affinities with his feature films. The similarities most often noted are to the series' immediate predecessor, *The Trouble with Harry* (1955), the oh-so-British Vermont comedy of manners and mortality whose tone of civilised comic reserve is cited as the inspiration for Hitchcock's television introductions,[8] and to the series' quintessential successor, *Psycho* (1960), shot in black and white for $800,000 in six weeks by a television crew headed by *Alfred Hitchcock Presents* cinematographer John L. Russell, and described by Hitchcock himself as 'a feature film [made] under the same conditions as a television show'.[9] Such comparisons raise two questions the critics who make them have not pursued. Given the radical differences between *The Trouble with Harry* and *Psycho*, which are virtually the two most disparate films in Hitchcock's entire *œuvre*, how closely can a substantial body of work resemble both of them? And apart from the obvious differences in budget and scale, what thematic and structural differences between

Hitchcock's theatrical and television films are obscured by emphasising their similarities?

This second question is particularly urgent because the television episodes Hitchcock directed differ from his theatrical films in some startling ways. As long ago as 1957, Eric Rohmer and Claude Chabrol identified the leading Hitchcock theme as 'the transfer of guilt'[10] between a criminal and a technically innocent, though morally complicit, double somehow involved in the crime, and later critics from Robin Wood to Tania Modleski have taken this doubling of characters or attitudes as the keynote of their analyses. And it is true that a few of Hitchcock's television episodes illustrate this pattern. *Wet Saturday* (1956), for example, concerns a family who, led by their protective father (Sir Cedric Hardwicke), frame a friend (John Williams) for a murder the daughter of the family has committed in order to keep him from disclosing any possible suspicions of them to the police, and then turn him over to the authorities themselves. Even more dramatically, *The Case of Mr Pelham* (1955) confronts an inoffensive businessman (Tom Ewell) with a spectral twin who takes over his life by persuading his intimates that the real Albert Pelham, who has begun to act uncharacteristically panicky, is an imposter. And *I Saw the Whole Thing*, Hitchcock's sole directorial credit on *The Alfred Hitchcock Hour*, presents John Forsythe as a hit-and-run driver accused of running a stop sign by five witnesses, none of whom, his trial makes clear, actually saw his collision with the motorcyclist his car killed.

Often, however, the doubling of criminal and innocent in Hitchcock's television films is transformed by the fact that no crime is ever committed. *Poison* (1958) preserves the structure of the complicit double but turns the innocent into an alcoholic colonial (James Donald) who is certain a poisonous snake is hiding with him in his bed, and the criminal into the skeptical friend and romantic rival (Wendell Corey) who teases him unmercifully about what he is convinced are delusions until the friend himself is fatally bitten. *Mr Blanchard's Secret* (1956) repeatedly invokes the paranoia of *Rear Window* (1954), but the suspect neighbour on whom inquisitive mystery writer Meg Mundy is spying ends up having nothing to conceal, since Mundy has only imagined first his wife's murder and then her kleptomania. The only criminals in *Breakdown* (1955) – the first episode Hitchcock filmed, though not the first to be broadcast – are the escaped convicts who steal ruthless businessman Joseph Cotten's clothes while he sits paralysed in his car after an accident that will bring him to a police mortuary before anyone notices from a tear running down his cheek that he is still alive. Keenan Wynn's social-climbing vacationer in *Dip in the Pool* (1958) is a cheat, but hardly a criminal, in his plan to recoup his large, misguided wager in the ship's pool by jumping overboard in front of a witness in order to slow the ship down. Nor is any crime committed in *The Crystal Trench* (1959), in which Patricia Owens spurns the gentlemanly advances of James Donald, the mountain climber who failed to retrieve the body of her late husband, killed in a climbing accident, and instead waits forty years for a shifting glacier to uncover her husband's body only to find that the locket he is wearing around his perfectly preserved neck carries the photo of another woman. The schemes of long-time adulteress Audrey Meadows in *Mrs Bixby and the Colonel's Coat* (1960) to accept her lover's final gift, an opulent fur coat, without revealing its source, never come close to criminal activity. A priest's conscience takes the place of the police in *The Horseplayer* (1961) when Claude Rains allows a parishioner who has been successful at the track to place a substantial bet for him and then feels obliged to pray that his horse will not win. *Bang! You're Dead* (1961) puts a loaded revolver into the hands of an unwitting little boy (Billy Mumy) playing cowboy without producing any criminal consequences. Even *Incident at a Corner*, whose action turns on accusations that Vera Miles's grandfather Paul Hartman has been molesting the schoolchildren he sees every day as a crossing guard, ends without a single crime more substantial than defamation of character. Although none of these stories features criminals or crimes worthy of the name, these episodes are not simply detours from the general development of Hitchcock's career. Instead, like the silent films *Easy Virtue* and *The Ring* (both 1927), they show that Hitchcock's lifelong concern with guilt and innocence, betrayal and revelation, need not depend on crime for its effects, and suggest that Hitchcock is only incidentally a director of crime films.

When they do concern crime, Hitchcock's television films take an even more surprising turn. If crime films can focus on criminals, detectives or victims, then Hitchcock's films that deal with crime – as opposed to those like *The Lady Vanishes* (1938) and *Torn Curtain* (1966) that deal with espionage – occupy a special position among other crime films, since they almost always focus on victims – more specifically, on one of three types of victim/agents. First are the essentially innocent heroines who kill the men who attack them or their loved ones, becoming murderous victims in *Blackmail* (1929), *Sabotage* (1963), and *Dial M for Murder* (1954). Second are morally complicit but innocent suspects, as in *The Lodger* (1926), *Young and Innocent* (1937), *Rebecca* (1940), *Spellbound* (1945), *Strangers on a Train* (1951), *I Confess* (1952), *To Catch a Thief* (1955), *North by Northwest* (1959) and *Frenzy* (1972). Third are detective figures forced by their moral loyalties into compromised positions isolated from or opposed to the authorities, as in *Murder!* (1930), *The 39 Steps* (1935), *Shadow of a Doubt* (1943), *Rear Window* (1954), *The Trouble with Harry* (1955), *Vertigo* (1958), *Marnie* (1964) and both versions of *The Man Who Knew Too Much* (1934/1956).[11] The primary focus of Hitchcock's feature films is only rarely on detectives detecting (most of them are too busy eluding the police or the criminals) or on criminals committing crimes. *Banquo's Chair* (1959), however, not only makes John Williams's detective, determined to unmask a killer by confronting him with the actress-assisted 'ghost' of his victim, the star, but concludes with a hint of the supernatural utterly foreign to Hitchcock's features: the news that the actress Williams had engaged arrived too late to play the ghost who extracted the killer's frenzied confession.[12]

More frequently and surprisingly, more than a third of the *Alfred Hitchcock Presents* episodes Hitchcock directed, like a similar proportion of the episodes he did not direct, present a protagonist who is a murderer. In most of these episodes, to be sure, the criminal is presented as an unwilling victim akin to Marion Crane, the thief-heroine of *Psycho*. An enraged Ralph Meeker murders the man his wife (Vera Miles) identifies as her rapist in *Revenge*, the first episode of *Alfred Hitchcock Presents* to air in 1955. In *Back for Christmas* (1956), metallurgist John Williams's well-planned murder of his wife (Isobel Elsom) just before they are due to leave on a trip to California is staged as a well-earned release from her merciless henpecking. In *Wet Saturday* (1956) and *One More Mile to Go* (1957), the victims are never seen, or seen too briefly to generate any sympathy, and the emphasis falls on the problems their murders create for the murderers, whether they are pinning the crime on a family friend in *Wet Saturday* or trying to shake off an exasperatingly helpful patrol officer (Steve Brodie) who seems bent on opening the trunk in which they have stowed their wife's body. And in *Four O'Clock*, the watchmaker (E. G. Marshall) who has painstakingly tested and planted a bomb to destroy his wife (Nancy Kelly) and the man he believes is her lover (Richard Long), switches abruptly from criminal to victim when he is tied up by burglars only a few feet from the bomb. But *The Perfect Crime* (1957) and *Arthur* (1959) both deal with premeditated, successful and unapologetic murderers. In the first case, criminologist Vincent Price is willing to resort to murder to conceal his lapse in judgement that led to an innocent man's death; in the second, confirmed bachelor Laurence Harvey kills the demurely bossy ex-fiancée who has returned from another romance assuming that he will greet her with open arms. In both stories, as in Hitchcock's best-known television episode, *Lamb to the Slaughter* (1958), in which Barbara Bel Geddes greets her policeman husband's announcement that he is leaving her by catatonically beating him to death with a frozen leg of lamb she then cooks and serves to the investigating officers wondering what has become of the weapon, there is every indication that the criminal will get off scot-free, at least until the host obligingly supplies the playfully moralising epilogues.

Hitchcock's alternation between stories that do not involve crime and stories featuring criminal heroes, an alternation which already reflects the duality embodied by *The Trouble with Harry* and *Psycho*, is linked to a more general feature of *Alfred Hitchcock Presents* and *The Alfred Hitchcock Hour*: their emphasis on ironic anecdotes whose effect depends on a single amoral twist more reminiscent of O. Henry than of Poe. Hitchcock's dependence on ironic reversals is typical of his features from *Rich and Strange* (1932) through *Frenzy*, but the use of irony as a structuring principle is less common to the innocent suspects or amateur spies favoured by his theatrical films than to other directors' episodes of *Alfred Hitchcock Presents* and to the conventions of other television melodramas like *The Twilight Zone*. And the frequent suggestion, despite Hitchcock's remark at the end of *Revenge* that 'crime does not pay, even on television. You must have a sponsor,' that the congruence of morality and legality challenged throughout most of his films but reaffirmed at the end of every one but *Psycho* and *The Birds* (1963) – two features produced during the run of the television series – may not be so secure after all gives his television films a subversive edge that is surprising for such commercial projects for such a conservative medium[13] from a director normally so committed to ending every nightmare with a sweet.

Just as the playfully amoral ironist who directed some ten hours of television episodes that reflect less interest in innocent suspects than in criminals is clearly at odds with the humanistic moralism of Robin Wood and Lesley Brill, the disengaged Hitchcock who floats through *Alfred Hitchcock Presents* and *The Alfred Hitchcock Hour* without any professional stake in the programs' success is more broadly inimical to the *auteurism* that first established Hitchcock as an artist worthy of serious attention. Because this outer-circle Hitchcock recalls the disengaged aesthete of Raymond Durgnat, the economic brand name of Robert Kapsis and Thomas Schatz, and the deconstructed trademark of Slavoj Žižek, it is tempting to take his success as a decisive blow against the *politique des auteurs*, with its unfashionable assumption that directors (or any strong individuals in particular) are the authorising forces behind their films. But instead of assuming that

Hitchcock's television work should be consigned to the outermost circle because it is merely commercial or marginal or unauthorised, consider the opposite assumption: that the outer circle can be seen as the inner circle if we postulate that the television episodes Hitchcock directed are as typical of his work, as revealing of his range and his preoccupations, and as constitutive of our image of Hitchcock as his feature films. How would this promotion of the outer circle to the inner circle enlarge or otherwise modify our idea of Hitchcock?

A curiously consistent feature of the episodes that feature successful murderers – Vincent Price in *The Perfect Crime*, Barbara Bel Geddes in *Lamb to the Slaughter*, Laurence Harvey in *Arthur* – is that the epilogues Hitchcock returns to supply at the end of each episode assure us that they were punished after all. Price, who presumably burned his accuser James Gregory's corpse in a pottery kiln, was caught when his cleaning woman knocked over a vase Price was proudly displaying that showed revealing bits of gold teeth; ever since then, Hitchcock confides, other cleaning women have broken vases in emulation of her initiative. Bel Geddes was tripped up when she tried to kill her second husband in the same way as her first, not realising that he had forgotten to plug in the freezer, leaving her would-be murder weapon 'soft as jelly'. And Harvey met 'a very sad end' when he was pecked to death by the epicurean chickens to whom he had fed his ground-up ex-fiancée. After *Wet Saturday* ends with the hint of an impending miscarriage of justice, Hitchcock similarly appears to assure us that the police weren't fooled by the family's frame-up, and the daughter, confronted by the authorities, re-enacted her crime, this time with her placidly scheming father as object: 'Broke a croquet mallet too.' In a technical sense, each of these epilogues, which Hitchcock described as 'a small tolerance' and 'a necessary gesture to morality',[14] preserves the legal sense of right and wrong required by the Motion Picture Production Code, and enacted in the more straightforward terms associated with Hitchcock's theatrical films by the ironic endings of *One More Mile to Go*, in which David Wayne's hapless wife-killer is following the officer with a fatal interest in his blinking tail light to the police station, and *Four O'Clock*, in which the imprisoned watchmaker, not realising that a blown fuse has rendered his bomb harmless, goes mad after watching the bomb tick down to zero hour. But although Hitchcock's epilogues supply endings intended to satisfy the Production Code, taking these endings as seriously as the stories themselves would reverse the force of the stories and render some of them, like *Wet Saturday* and *Lamb to the Slaughter*, literally pointless. The amoral irony that marks so many of Hitchcock's television programs through their unusual interest in criminals and their fondness for climactic reversals as abrupt as punch lines, then, is subject to a further instability generated by the dissonance between the frequently subversive diegesis and its apparently normalising (but in its way even more subversive) frame, or between the two storytelling functions represented by Hitchcock the director and Hitchcock the impresario. The noncommittal amorality of the television episodes brackets the official morality of most of Hitchcock's feature films – in which the heroes and heroines strive mightily, and mostly successfully, to maintain their technical innocence – as parochial. In the same way, Hitchcock's drolly understated introductions and epilogues undermine what might otherwise be the straightforwardly dramatic or suspenseful tone of his television morality plays even as they deliver the moral the audience expects.

In short, the outer-circle Hitchcock of the television films is ironic, aloof, anecdotal, manipulative and fond of witty reversals, even if they make nonsense of the stories that have carefully led up to them. This figure, the oracularly controlling presenter of hundreds of television stories with which he had nothing further to do, no more resembles the postmodern Hitchcock of Žižek than the humanist Hitchcock of Wood. But the figure is well known, indeed far more universally known, than the Hitchcock of the feature films. It is Hitchcock the introducer, Hitchcock the featured cameo, Hitchcock the editor and impresario of *Alfred Hitchcock's Mystery Magazine* and its numberless anthologies, Hitchcock the master of suspense whose iconic image dominates the boxes of video-taped episodes of *Alfred Hitchcock Presents*. This is not Hitchcock the film-maker but Hitchcock the raconteur, Hitchcock the interview subject so memorably displayed in Sidney Gottlieb's recent collection of essays and interviews, Hitchcock the coolly elusive biographical subject, Hitchcock the endlessly available public figure whose private life, armoured by the absence of letters or close friendships outside his protective immediate family, remains a closed book to biographers and fans alike. It is this Hitchcock, not Hitchcock the director, who continues to dominate the popular imagination a hundred years after his birth.

The problem, then, is not to reconcile the outer-circle Hitchcock of the television programs with the inner-circle Hitchcock of *Rear Window* and *Vertigo* and *Psycho*, but rather to reconcile Hitchcock the director with Hitchcock the public figure, a persona much more closely congruent with the host of *Alfred Hitchcock Presents* than with the director of any number of masterpieces of the cinema. It is no coincidence, of course, that the television Hitchcock is so closely akin to the public Hitchcock, since Hitchcock's television image was designed specifically to promote and extend the image the director wished to cultivate. Nor is it surprising that the public Hitchcock, fuelled by the film-maker's tendency towards ironic self-distance, should have continued to exert such a powerful grasp on the popular imagination, since the inevitable tendency of *auteurism*, as of any personal canonisation, is to blur the subtleties and contradictions of its subjects by focusing on a few sharp leading features. What is most surprising is how useful Hitchcock's television work can be in focusing the connection between Hitchcock the director and Hitchcock the public persona. By 'Hitchcock's television work' I mean not only the twenty television episodes directed by Hitchcock but Hitchcock's most notable contribution to *Alfred Hitchcock Presents* and *The Alfred Hitchcock Hour*: his introductions and conclusions to each episode. Hitchcock did not write the scripts for these framing segments, of course, any more than he wrote the scripts for the television programs or the features themselves. Nonetheless, he makes them his own through the nature of his address from within a peculiarly depersonal, yet personalised, space that presents him, quite accurately, as the real star of the show.

Hitchcock's opening monologue for *Revenge* perfectly sets the tone of the whole series to follow:

> Good evening. I'm Alfred Hitchcock. And tonight I am presenting the first in a series of stories of suspense and mystery called, oddly enough, *Alfred Hitchcock Presents*. I shall not act in these stories, but will only make appearances, something in the nature of an accessory before and after the fact, to give the title to those of you who can't read, and

> to tidy up afterwards for those who don't understand the endings. Tonight's playlet is really a sweet little story. It is called *Revenge*. It will follow – oh dear, I see the actors won't be ready for another sixty seconds. However, thanks to our sponsor's remarkable foresight, we have a message that will fit in here nicely.

Allardice's cadences capture all the hallmarks of the public Hitchcock: the ceremonious courtesy, the macabre understatement, the deadpan irony, the deliberately misleading description of the coming episode, unusually shocking even for Hitchcock, as 'a sweet little story', the jesting that does not quite conceal a hint of hostility toward both the sponsor (who retaliates only rarely, for example in the epilogue to *Mrs Bixby and the Colonel's Coat* by projecting an astral noose over Hitchcock's critical head) and the audience. Less widely remarked, but equally remarkable, is the peculiar nature of the space from which Hitchcock, filmed in midshot, delivers this monologue. Anyone who has ever followed the program will recall that it begins, over Charles Gounod's 'Funeral March of a Marionette', with a shot of Hitchcock's famous line drawing of his own profile on a flat screen, filled in by the silhouette of the director advancing from the right.[15] Even after the camera pans to the right to reveal a three-dimensional Hitchcock addressing the camera, however, the space continues to appear flat, with even (though slightly *ombréd*) lighting, no props apart from the top of a chair for the host to lean on, not even a clear horizon line.

Though it may seem natural that the program's host address the audience directly from a two-dimensional space unencumbered by props or other people, the space is sharply marked out from the three-dimensional space of both the ensuing episode and the more realistic space inhabited by the introducers of other dramatic anthologies. When he introduces Hitchcock's *Four O'Clock* in the series *Suspicion*, for example, Dennis O'Keefe addresses the audience from a carefully appointed room filled with clocks to speak about the history of timepieces like the sundial and the clepsydra. A truism of television, as against feature films, is that its world is designed to seem like an extension of the audience's own viewing room, with conflicts kept to an intimate scale and characters projected as visitors in the viewers' homes. In its dimensional cues and its attention to detail, the space of O'Keefe's introduction is apparently continuous with both the space of *Four O'Clock* and the space of the rooms in which audiences are most likely to be watching television; it has a specifically mediating function reflected as well by the text of O'Keefe's introduction, which roots the obsessive hero's determination to murder his wife in his vocation as a watchmaker.[16] O'Keefe approaches Hitchcock's dryly understated tone most closely in his final remark: 'After all, there are difficulties in killing one's wife with a clepsydra.' Even here, however, the irony is rooted in a literal truth that would be shattered if O'Keefe went on to describe *Four O'Clock* as a sweet little story. The mediation of Hitchcock's introduction, by contrast, is structurally ironic; just as the space is starkly discontinuous with the space of both the audience and the story, the tone of Hitchcock's introduction is at odds with both the dramatically suspenseful nature of the story and the audience's likely reaction to a straightforward summary of its events. The leading function of Hitchcock's introduction, then, is not to invite the audience into the story by bridging the gap between their mundane world and the story's melodrama, but to establish a distinctive space outside the story and in some obvious ways superior to it.

This superiority is implicit in the nature of the dramatic anthology, which presents a new story with a new cast every week; only the host remains the same. The innovation of *Alfred Hitchcock Presents* was to elevate the host from a minor functionary subordinate to the events of each week's episode to the program's true star. Week after week, Hitchcock is discovered with a single stylised (often oversized) prop – a paperback book in *Breakdown*, an umbrella in *Mr Blanchard's Secret*, a plaster cast of his own head in *One More Mile to Go*, a park bench and a single tree in *Poison*, a ship's rail and a life preserver labeled 'S. S. Hitchcock' in *Dip in the Pool*, a giant key in *I Saw the Whole Thing* – typically photographed in profile, an object often utterly gratuitous. As Hitchcock says in introducing *Back for Christmas*: 'Tonight's story has nothing whatsoever to do with shrunken heads.' Except for the unusually detailed set of the introduction to *Bang! You're Dead*, which presents Hitchcock as a movie ticket seller, even sets that seem likely to break this pattern return to it in the end, as the camera introducing *Wet Saturday* pans right from a sign reading 'MOVED TO NEW LOCATION' to reveal Hitchcock reclining in a coffin-shaped enclosure about to pour his tea, or from the three-dimensional farmhouse at the beginning of *Arthur* to Hitchcock standing before a flat hexagonal window extolling the virtues of the non-rolling egg and displaying a motivational tool executives have developed for his chickens: a sign reading 'THINK SQUARE'.[17]

One apparent exception is the introduction to *The Crystal Trench*, which presents Hitchcock as a mountain climber on the same set as the central sequence of the story itself. Standing in a path in front of a conspicuously flat painting of a mountainous background, Hitchcock casually saws through a rope in his way, apparently sending his climbing partner below to his death (though the partner returns the favour in the episode's conclusion). When the same flat set appears halfway through the episode, however, it is given the illusion of greater depth by means of several moving figures and a snowstorm, in addition to the musical cue and voice-over narration that seek to immerse the audience in a dramatic climax. Photographed on the same set as his characters, Hitchcock retains his distinctiveness.

As befits a host, Hitchcock nearly always appears alone in these introductions. Even when other people are present, they are kept subordinate to the host. The police officer who writes out a ticket to Hitchcock the supermarket shopper in the introduction to *Lamb to the Slaughter*, the masquerader wearing the front half of a horse's costume in *The Horseplayer*, the three young women on safari who tote the belongings of a pith-helmeted Hitchcock in the introduction to *Banquo's Chair*, the kachina psychiatrist he is consulting at the conclusion of the same episode, even the climbing partner who evidently kills him at the end of *The Crystal Trench* – all of them go about their business without uttering a word. Even the two orderlies who hustle Hitchcock offscreen at the conclusion of *The Case of Mr Pelham* – perhaps the wittiest of all Hitchcock's frames, since it closely echoes the story in doubling him with an imposter, a second Hitchcock who moralises sadly as the Hitchcock who introduced the episode is led off – are allowed only a single line of dialogue between them. When the first Hitchcock protests, 'But I'm Alfred Hitchcock! I am, I can prove it!' one of them tells him, 'Sure, everybody is.'

But if the supporting players in the introductions always remain human props rather than characters, Hitchcock never becomes a character himself. Although he is introduced with deerstalker and meerschaum in the introduction to *The Perfect Crime*, any resemblance to Sherlock Holmes is shattered when he blows soap bubbles through the pipe. Hitchcock is not playing the great detective; he is merely playing at being the great detective, as he impersonated himself in the conclusion to *The Case of Mr Pelham*. Although Hitchcock is evidently institutionalised at the end of *The Case of Mr Pelham*, drowned at the end of *Dip in the Pool*, and killed by a plunge down the mountainside at the end of *The Crystal Trench*, the audience treats these calamities no more seriously than the innumerable fatalities that befall Wile E. Coyote in his relentlessly inept pursuit of Road Runner. Indeed Hitchcock's television persona, with its proclivity for extravagant, telegraphic situations which are presented with comical gravity, more closely resembles a cartoon character than either a character in fictional melodrama or an actual human being. Throughout the series, Hitchcock's most characteristic utterances are those most difficult to take seriously. In the introduction to *Breakdown*, he manages to ridicule the idea of television drama as morality play even as he is inflecting his ridicule with the personality of the unfeeling hero played by Joseph Cotten: 'In each of our stories we strive to teach a lesson or point a little moral. Advice like mother used to give, you know. Walk softly, and carry a big stick. Strike first, and ask questions later.' In introducing *The Case of Mr Pelham*, he departs from his customary pretense of soft-hearted squeamishness while maintaining a broadly ironic tone: 'Good evening. Due to circumstances beyond our control, tragedy will not strike tonight. I'm dreadfully sorry. Perhaps some other time.' He declaims the introduction to *One More Mile to Go*, a story about Anne Boleyn's ghost travelling about carrying its decapitated head, entirely in rhymed verse, and caps the episode with a couplet – 'When your heart stops yearning, keep your tail light burning' – both highly apposite and comically inappropriate. The effect in each case, like the effect of Hitchcock returning at the end of *Lamb to the Slaughter* and *The Perfect Crime* and *Arthur* to offer gravely preposterous reassurances to the audience that the apparently successful miscreants met a condign fate, recalls the odd moments when Warner Bros. cartoon characters break the fourth wall to address the camera directly – except that for Hitchcock, this device is not an occasional subversion of what John Fiske calls the 'essentially realistic medium' of television[18] but his normal mode of address.

More generally, as in his feature-film cameos, Hitchcock never appears in any of the introductions as an actor playing a role; the roles are so transparent that the more specific they are (Hitchcock as safari leader, Hitchcock as Sherlock Holmes), the more clearly the immitigably recognisable Hitchcock persona emerges as an enabling term in the comic incongruity. Each role is designed to present Hitchcock as Hitchcock – or, more accurately, to reveal the host's carefully groomed public personality as the one constant term in a weekly game of charades which is in turn the one constant in a series of ironic melodramas. As prolific series writer Henry Slesar puts it: 'Hitchcock had such a strong identity that he made his show a sort of non-anthology in that he himself was the continuing character'.[19]

Taken together, these distinctive features of Hitchcock's television personality – the exaggerated discontinuity between the privileged host and the program he is hosting, the subordination of all supporting figures to two-dimensional props, the redefinition of acting as self-reflexive dressing up and masquerade as a vehicle for the manufacture of an ironic core personality – show why Hitchcock's position on the programs he introduced is indeed their defining feature. The linchpin of *Alfred Hitchcock Presents* and *The Alfred Hitchcock Hour*, the feature that made them more successful than so many rival anthology programs without a strong personality as continuing host, was clearly Hitchcock himself. But what is Hitchcock, this unlikely star who is never either an actor or a character? In terms of the series' enabling myth, he is the gravely jovial presiding spirit defined only by his ironic distance from the stories he introduces and the outlandish poses from which he comments on them. As a mouthpiece for the monologues written by James Allardice, he is an effect rather than a source of the programs' discourse, a product whose identity is sustained and marketed by others. In Robert Bloch's terms, he is the putative controlling force stipulated by the series' actual producers, the *deus absconditus* of the program who does nothing himself but whose presumed preferences are essential to the success of the enterprise. These contradictory ideas of Hitchcock emphasise the foundational instability of Hitchcock's public persona as something both deliberately self-created by its enterprising director, who modelled his image long before Allardice hit on a formula that would sustain it, and creating in turn the myth of Hitchcock the detached Hollywood director who shapes each project to suit his own desires, Hitchcock the ironic *auteur* who assumes complete control over all his films, Hitchcock the protean creator who is the true power behind the screen. Whenever we attempt to look behind Hitchcock the impresario, we find Hitchcock the creator, and vice versa.

Because Hitchcock has served as the model for so many Hollywood *auteurs* who do not write or produce their own films, however, his unique status as the ironic impresario of a long-running television series raises still more pervasive problems for theories of authorship in and out of Hollywood. The case of Hitchcock shows that a member of Sarris's inner circle can at the same time occupy the outer circle so unapologetically because of his secure position in the inner circle that the two positions can become interchangeable, as the outer circle creates the inner circle that authorises it. Hitchcock's television persona, like his television work in general, reveals the author as a construction whose overdetermined status – Hitchcock the *auteur* is created in the image of Hitchcock the impresario, which is constructed by a commercial industry which is in turn manipulated by Hitchcock the businessman, and a production crew whose decisions are based on their intuitions about Hitchcock the *auteur* – suggests that revisionist theories of authorship that present the author as nothing more than an effect of the apparatus, like the realist theories of representation they are meant to correct, are telling only part of the story.

Notes

I am indebted to the staff of the Museum of Television and Radio in New York for their invaluable help in arranging screenings of the television programs discussed in this essay.

1 Andrew Sarris, 'Notes on the Auteur Theory in 1962', rpt. in Leo Brandy and Marshall Cohen (eds.), *Film Theory and Criticism: Introductory Readings*, 5th ed., New York: Oxford University Press, 1999, p. 517.

2 See Jack Edmund Nolan, 'Hitchcock's TV film', rpt. in Al La Valley (ed.), *Focus on Hitchcock*, Englewood Cliffs: Prentice Hall, 1972, pp. 140–44; Gene D. Phillips, *Alfred Hitchcock*, Boston: Twayne, 1984; and John McCarty and Brian Kelleher, *Alfred*

Hitchcock Presents: An Illustrated Guide to the Ten-Year Television Career of the Master of Suspense, New York: St Martin's, 1985.

3 Some sources that list 266 episodes of the program rather than 268 are counting a three-part story, *I Killed the Count*, which aired on 17, 24, and 31 March 1957 as part of the program's second season, as one three-part episode rather than three. Hitchcock's half-hour television programs, filmed to allow for commercials, actually run for 23 minutes each; his three hour-long programs run between 50 and 52 minutes each.

4 The series' invariable dependence on previously published stories marks the first of several departures from Hitchcock's theatrical films, many of which, from *The Ring* (1927) to *North by Northwest* (1959), were based on original screenplays. See McCarty and Kelleher, pp. 17, 48.

5 McCarty and Kelleher, *Alfred Hitchcock Presents*, p. xii.

6 'Murder in the Living Room: Hitchcock by Hitchcock', Museum of Television and Radio website – http://www.mtr.org/exhibit/hitchck/hitchck4.htm

7 It is eminently in keeping with Hitchcock's journeyman approach to his television work that although he was four times nominated for an Emmy award, twice for directing *The Case of Mr Pelham* (1955) and *Lamb to the Slaughter* (1958) and twice as host of the series, the only director to win an Emmy for the series was Robert Stevens for *The Glass Eye* (1957).

8 See Phillips, *Alfred Hitchcock*, pp. 136, 149, and McCarty and Kelleher, *Alfred Hitchcock Presents*, pp. 9–11.

9 François Trufaut, *Hitchcock*, New York: Simon and Schuster, 1967, p. 211.

10 Eric Rohner and Claude Chabrol, *Hitchcock: The First Forty-Four Films*, trans. Stanley Hochman, New York: Ungar, 1979, p. 11.

11 A special category must be created for *Family Plot* (1976), which doubles its unlikely villains with an equally unlikely pair of investigators.

12 Interestingly, Hitchcock toyed in the mid-1960s with the possibility of directing Sir James Barrie's ghost story *Mary Rose*, but gave it up – 'What bothers me is the ghost,' he told Truffaut (p. 232) – and turned to *Torn Curtain* instead.

13 Phillips points out Hitchcock's daring in beginning his series with a story about a rape followed by a particularly brutal, and misguided, example of vigilante justice (*Alfred Hitchcock*, p. 152).

14 McCarty and Kelleher, *Alfred Hitchcock Presents*, p. 45.

15 *The Alfred Hitchcock Hour* begins slightly differently: an angled shadow of Hitchcock's upper body, turned away from the camera, approaches a rear wall on which Hitchcock's profile has been sketched at eye level; when the shadow has climbed the wall high enough to reach the profile, Hitchcock turns to the left, filling the profile with his facial silhouette. After the initial three-dimensional cue of the angled shadow, however, introductions to *The Alfred Hitchcock Hour* proceed in a similarly two-dimensional space.

16 In all these particulars O'Keefe's introduction follows standard industry practices for dramatic anthology programs. Such introductions are nearly always presented in a shallow three-dimensional space which is meant to imply continuity with the audience's viewing space; when their space is flatter, as in Rod Serling's celebrated introductions to episodes of *The Twilight Zone*, their tone of hushed mystery

emphasises their continuity with the dramatic story that follows. A particularly striking exception to this rule is the introduction to Hitchcock's *Incident at a Corner*, in which an overhead shot of George Peppard haranguing a group of other characters excerpted from the middle of the story is abruptly bracketed by the entrance of Vera Miles before the filmed image, speaking over Peppard's harangue to introduce his character: 'That's the man I'm going to marry.' Miles is speaking in the character of Janey Medwick, who plays Peppard's fiancée in *Incident at a Corner*; yet by commenting directly on the story, and by addressing the camera directly in a natural-seeming pose against a highly stylised spatial view which her presence renders flat and artificial, she simultaneously asserts her identity as the actress Vera Miles. The ambiguity is dissolved by her appearance in the program's brief epilogue, in which she stands next to a new 1960 Ford, which is angled to emphasise the three-dimensional quality of the space, while she announces how proud she is to have appeared in this episode of *Ford Startime Theater* and expresses the hope that the audience will return next week.

17 *Arthur*, in fact, has a double frame, since the opening shot of the episode itself is a track-out from the hero's poultry farm to a shot of Laurence Harvey, in an obvious parody of Hitchcock, addressing the camera with a cheery 'Greetings!', introducing the story he will periodically interrupt and conclude with further on-camera commentary about his success as a murderer.

18 John Fiske, *Television Culture*, London: Methuen, 1987, p. 21.

19 McCarty and Kelleher, *Alfred Hitchcock Presents*, p. 24

PART II
Hitchcock's Aesthetics

'A picture unlike any other I have directed' – *Rope*

Chapter 6
Rope: Three Hypotheses

Peter Wollen

Rope and the English private school system

Alfred Hitchcock's film *Rope* (1948) was based on a play of the same name that he had seen on the stage in London in 1929. Both Hitchcock and the author of the play, Patrick Hamilton, went to private schools characterised by violence, bullying and, in Hamilton's case, homosexuality. Patrick Hamilton was the son of a well-to-do lawyer and, when the family moved to London in 1915, he was sent as a boarder to Colet Court, the preparatory school for St Paul's School. This was a prestigious and well-respected school and his parents never suspected what life there was really like. His earlier school experiences had prepared him for endemic bullying, but in the dormitories at Colet Court there was a new sexual dimension. After lights out, in the words of Hamilton's biographer, Nigel Jones, 'mass masturbation, individual or reciprocal was the order of the day, or night. The ringleaders were the older boys who invited the younger ones to join them in bed behind curtains made from rigged-up sheets. Any resistance was met with intimidation and bullying.'[1] Hamilton was withdrawn from the school after his parents learned of what was happening through the family 'nurse' (a trained child-care provider) in whom Patrick had confided.

In 1918, Hamilton, now 14, was transferred to Westminster School, another highly prestigious institution, where he found, of course, the same homosexual culture. This time Patrick fell in love 'with a pretty boy younger than himself' but, troubled by moral reservations, refrained from any actual sexual advances.[2] In fact, according to the same biographer, Hamilton later discovered that the object of his desire would trade sexual favours for a chocolate bar, but nonetheless he restricted himself to shielding his protégé from bullying by other boys. Alfred Hitchcock showed no such compunctions – he was a bully at school and, while Hamilton felt that he had been scarred for life by the teasing he received as a child, Hitchcock repeatedly subjected actresses, actors and others to elaborate and cruel practical jokes. Hitchcock came from a Catholic shopkeeping family and was sent to a Jesuit school where corporal punishment was carried out as a matter of course. Hitchcock himself vividly recalled the numbness induced by the strap. Hitchcock, however, though terrified, was far from innocent. A fellow student, Robert Goold, recalled how he was bullied by Hitchcock – his arms tied, his trousers pulled down and exploding firecrackers pinned to his underclothes. Afraid of recrimination, he told no one.[3]

Hitchcock's own penchant for practical jokes (often crossing the line into cruel bullying) and his fascination with homosexuality both persisted throughout his life and played a significant role in his work as a film-maker. His practical jokes more than once involved the use of manacles and other forms of restraint, as well as abduction, both of which have a direct bearing on *Rope*, a film which pivots on the acts of abduction and restraint – first when a murder victim is kidnapped leaving the theatre and then, after he has been murdered, crammed into an antique chest tightly secured with rope (hence the title of the film). All this, however, simply sets the scene for a much grislier practical joke – an invitation has been sent to the victim's father to come round and look at some rare books, with an eye to buying them, and, during his visit, to be served a supper which has been laid out on the very same chest. Of course, this idea was originally Patrick Hamilton's but it was one which fit well with Hitchcock's own fantasy life. Ceremonial meals, it should be remembered, were also a particular preoccupation of Hitchcock's – he would invite guests to meals cooked in Paris and delivered to Los Angeles by plane.

According to Patrick Hamilton's brother, Bruce, 'the well-known starting-point of the play [*Rope*] was the famous Leopold-Loeb case in America'.[4] Patrick, however, denied this, claiming that he was unable to 'recall this crime having ever properly reached my consciousness until after *Rope* was written and people began to tell me of it'.[5] At the end of his life he told a younger admirer that *Rope* had been conceived as early as 1922, two years before the Leopold-Loeb murder, in which two young homosexuals, wealthy, gifted and popular, killed Loeb's young cousin, supposedly for the thrill of carrying out a perfect crime. In fact, they bungled it completely and were quickly apprehended. (The story of their crime later provided the basis for another film, Richard Fleischer's *Compulsion*, 1959.) Hamilton himself accepted that his reading of Nietzsche was an important influence on the play, particularly *Thus Spake Zarathustra*, which he read in 1927, indulging himself in fantasies of becoming a superman and warning others with Nietzche's warning, 'Beware lest thou spittest against the wind of the Superman.'[6] His brother Bruce described him as 'obsessed' with Nietzsche. The apposite passage, perhaps, is that in which Nietzsche specifically questions the value of the commandment 'Thou shalt not kill!' and calls on his readers, 'O my brothers, break, break the old tablets!'[7]

Bruce Hamilton, in addition to Leopold-Loeb and Nietzsche, mentions two other sources for his brother's play: 'There had also been in Patrick's mind the dramatic possibilities of having a languid, affected, and seemingly ineffective character coming out with tremendous force at a climactic crisis – as with *The Scarlet Pimpernel* on a slighter level. Lastly, there was the situation of a guest overstaying his welcome at a vital moment – "the man who wouldn't go home", as he put it.'[8] Punctuality, it might be relevant to note, was also a governing obsession of Hitchcock's – he was a man obsessed by train and bus timetables and something of this obsession reappears in *Rope*, once the decision had been made to film in a series of continuous long takes that required the actors to time their performances precisely in order to coincide with the movements of the camera, like passengers arriving at the right time to catch their train. Yet I am still inclined to think that Hamilton's experience of homosexuality and bullying at school was more central to the play, although perhaps more buried.

In Hamilton's play, both the murderers and their victim are undergraduates together at Oxford. Here the allusion is surely to the set of aesthetes and undergraduates gathered around Harold Acton or Osbert Sitwell, a social set immortalised in the novels of Evelyn Waugh. The victim, Ronald Kentley, however, is not an aesthete, but an athlete.

Raglan, one of the guests, asks, 'Isn't that Ronald Kentley, the lad who's so good at sports?' Brandon, the Nietzschean murderer, replies, 'That's right. You don't know him, do you?' to which Raglan responds, 'No. I've never met him, but he wins hurdles, and hundreds of yards, and things like that, doesn't he?'[9] What is being enacted here is the old antipathy between the aesthete and the sportsman, the 'arty' and the 'hearty', as the old parlance has it. Patrick Hamilton never went to university, but, after leaving school, was bent on becoming, first a poet, then a writer of plays and novels, without any further education, except for attendance at a crammer in order to obtain a credential for teaching. It makes sense, however, to project his school experiences on to the more glamorous world of Oxford.

In the film, as written by Arthur Laurents, on the basis of Hume Cronyn's adaptation of Patrick Hamilton's play, the two murderers are explicitly characterised as friends from their days at boarding-school and Rupert Cadell, simply an intellectual mentor in the play, has now become the two young men's former boarding-school housemaster, who describes the murder and the practical joke played on the victim's father as 'the sort of mischief that would have appealed to you in school'. The origin of this phrase seems to be a telling line from the original play spoken when Raglan (transposed into Kenneth for the film) tries to seize the key to the chest from Brandon, who gives his attacker's wrist 'a violent twist', causing Raglan to scream in pain. Raglan protests accusingly to Brandon, 'That's what you used to do to me at school...'[10]

This key reference to the torments of private school stayed the course through a number of versions. Hitchcock first telephoned Hamilton as far back as 1937 to suggest a film version of the play, but it was not until 1944 that he and his producer, Sidney Bernstein, began to consider it a practical project. Three years later, Hamilton was put on the payroll and chauffeured to Elstree Studios every day, at Bernstein's expense, in order to work on an adaptation for film, a script which Bernstein then delivered to Hitchcock in Los Angeles. Hitchcock, presumbably after discussions with Alma Reville, passed Hamilton's version on to his old friend Hume Cronyn and asked Cronyn to produce a prose adaptation, which I would imagine amounted to a detailed treatment. Alma Reville had done this for *The Paradine Case* (1947) and Cronyn did the same for *Under Capricorn* (1949), the films that Hitchcock made immediately before and after *Rope*. Arthur Laurents, a playwright, was then brought in to write a final Americanised dialogue version on the basis of Cronin's treatment, much to Hamilton's indignation. Hamilton felt betrayed and disliked the film intensely. He got blind drunk at the film's launch party in London and cursed Hitchcock ever afterwards. It's as if Hitchcock, the school bully, had found a way of tormenting Hamilton by cheating him out of any pleasure he might have expected to get from the filming of his own work – as if Hamilton were the victim of a particularly clever practical joke.

Rope as an experimental film

Rope was made with a number of camera movements blended into each other without any conventional cuts in order to give the appearance of one continuous shot. The joins were skillfully concealed at moments where the camera ended up with a close-up of a featureless frame – the back of a character's jacket, for instance – which then dissolved into the beginning of the next take, starting on the same featureless frame. Despite

Hitchcock's claim that there were only nine takes of ten minutes each, there were in fact rather more, each of which was rather less long. Only three of them, in fact, lasted over nine minutes. Nonetheless the film was a technical *tour de force* and it is clear that Hitchcock got a perverse thrill from successfully shooting a film without any normal editing at all. When the film was released, Hitchcock described his excitement at making *Rope* to one Favius Friedman, a journalist for *Popular Photography*: 'A long time ago I said that I would like to film in two hours a fictional story that actually happens in two hours. I wanted to do a picture with no time lapses – a picture in which the camera never stops. In *Rope* I got my wish. It was a picture unlike any other I've ever directed. True, I had experimented with a roving camera in isolated sequences in such films as *Spellbound* (1945), *Notorious* (1946) and *The Paradine Case*. But until *Rope* came along, I had been unable to give full rein to my notion that a camera could photograph one complete reel at a time, gobbling up 11 pages of dialogue on each shot, devouring action like a giant steam shovel.'[11]

Hitchcock had a special crane constructed for the camera and employed six sound men, four with booms, and two with microphones placed high above the set. The camera lens was specially modified so that the camera could shoot wide shots and close-ups in the same movement. Movements and timings were plotted out in conjunction with those of the actors and the apartment walls were constructed to slide away on Vaseline-greased rollers and then swing back after the camera had passed through. It was a virtuoso performance, a kind of intricate ballet for moving camera, furniture and performers, all carefully plotted out in advance. At the same time, Hitchcock's aim was to make every camera movement seem completely natural. In his words, 'The audience must never be conscious of it. If an audience became aware that the camera was performing miracles, the end itself will be defeated.'[12] In fact, some viewers – connoisseurs perhaps – are bound to be aware of the camera, particularly after repeated viewings of the film. My own experience has been that watching the camera movements becomes more gripping over time than watching the action. Gradually *Rope* changes into another type of film altogether. Instead of being a polished thriller, it becomes an experimental film, more like Michael Snow's camera-centred *Wavelength* (1966) or *Back and Forth* (1969) than a Hollywood product.

Hitchcock's interest in experimental film had first been piqued during the years in which he frequented the London Film Society. During the 1920s, time spent at The Film Society provided Hitchcock with many of his closest friends and collaborators. One of the two co-founders, Ivor Montagu, edited three of Hitch's early silent pictures, *The Lodger* (1926), *Downhill* (1927) and *Easy Virtue* (1927), and was associate producer of the first *Man Who Knew Too Much* (1934), *The 39 Steps* (1935), *Secret Agent* (1936) and *Sabotage* (1936). Montagu was also a good friend of Eisenstein, with whose theories of montage Hitchcock was very familiar – their influence can be seen, for instance, in the notorious shower murder montage in *Psycho* (1960), itself a kind of miniature experimental film, storyboarded for Hitchcock by Saul Bass. Angus MacPhail was supervisor of screenplays for the Elstree studio where many Hitchcock films were made and later worked on *Spellbound* and on the American version of *The Man Who Knew Too Much* (1956). Hitchcock's wife, Alma Reville wrote *The Constant Nymph* (1933) for Adrian Brunel, who had been Montagu's friend at Cambridge University and his first employer in the film business. Walter Mycroft was head of screenwriting at British International, for whom Hitchcock made ten consecutive pictures – one of which, *Champagne* (1928), was from an original story by Mycroft. The Film Society was the jumping-off point for Hitchcock.

Brunel and Mycroft were both on the Society's Council, as was Sidney Bernstein, a film distributor and theatre proprietor who later became head of Granada Television, Hitchcock's advisor in his relations with David Selznick and, subsequently, his partner in Transatlantic Pictures, which produced both *Rope* and *Under Capricorn.* Among the other members of the Society were many artists and intellectuals involved in the modern movement, as it was then known – among them Roger Fry, the critic, John Maynard Keynes, the patron, Frank Dobson, the sculptor, Augustus John, the painter and E. McKnight Kauffer, the designer, who, at Montagu's suggestion, produced the striking title cards for *The Lodger.* The Film Society showed a number of important experimental films, many of which Hitchcock must have seen and which he often alluded to later in his career. In 1960, he talked knowledgably about Dada and surrealist film in an interview with the Parisian journal *Arts, Lettres, Spectacles,* mentioning Buñuel and Dali's *Un chien andalou* (1928), René Clair's *Entr'Acte* (1924), Epstein's *The Fall of the House of Usher* (1928) and Cocteau's *The Blood of a Poet* (1931). (The Film Society had also shown Duchamp's *Anemic Cinema* (1926) and Léger's *Ballet Mécanique* (1924).) In the commercial cinema, he was enormously influenced by Chaplin's *Woman Of Paris* (1923) and, especially, Murnau's *The Last Laugh* (1924), a silent film shot to be released without a single intertitle. Later, he expressed a critical interest in Robert Montgomery's *Lady in the Lake* (1946), a film shot entirely from the subjective point of view of the protagonist, whom the spectator only sees when he looks in a mirror. He also commented favourably on films by Bergman and Buñuel – *Tristana* (1970), in particular.

One of the the London Film Society's projects was their sponsorship of Len Lye's experimental film *Tusalava* (1928), on Sidney Bernstein's recommendation. Later Hitchcock suggested Lye might collaborate with him by animating the apparent burn-up of the film stock in the projector at the very end of *Secret Agent,* after the runaway train explodes. Sadly, this audacious plan eventually came to nothing. Hitchcock did, however, collaborate with another avant-garde artist, Salvador Dali, on the dream sequence in *Spellbound.* He also experimented with sound – as with the use of the theremin in *Spellbound* and the electronic score for *The Birds* (1963), a film whose art design was inspired by Munch's *The Scream.* Perhaps the strongest experimental influence on Hitchcock came from German silent film – *The Cabinet of Dr Caligari* (1919), Pabst's *Secrets of a Soul* (1926), Dupont's *Variety* (1925), Lang's *M* (1931), all of which he admired, along with *The Last Laugh.* Hitchcock seems to have oscillated between seeing himself as a 100 per cent commercial director and as a frustrated art-film director. In 1938, for instance, he complained that 'the power of universal appeal has been the most retarding force in the motion picture as an art. In the efforts of the maker to appeal to everyone, they have come down to the common simple story with the happy ending; the moment they begin to become imaginative, then they are segregating their audience. Until we get specialized theatres, we shall not be able to do anything else.' Commercial pressure on the cinema, he concluded, had 'gone a long way to destroy it as an art'.[13] Hitchcock the public showman was in constant conflict with Hitchcock the private aesthete.

It is in this context that *Rope* should be viewed – the whole scheme of turning a hit stage play into a cinematic experiment. Hitchcock was clearly proud to quote the observer who described *Rope* as having 'the most revolutionary technique Hollywood has ever seen'.[14] He was quick to point out that the screenplay was 'the first time a scenario was written without time-lapses'.[15] It is as if he felt that, at long last, he was outdoing his master, Friedrich Murnau, and Murnau's own masterpiece, *The Last Laugh*. *Rope* is the ultimate *kammerspielfilm*, unmatched until Fassbinder made *The Bitter Tears of Petra von Kant* (1972). In *Rope* Hitchcock set out to employ the camera as adventurously as Murnau did in *The Last Laugh*, in which, as Kracauer put it, Karl Freund's cinematography 'pans, travels and tilts up and down with a perseverance which not only results in a pictorial narrative of complete fluidity, but also enables the camera to follow the course of events from various viewpoints. The roving camera makes him experience the glory of the uniform as well as the misery of the tenement house, metamorphoses him into the hotel porter, and imbues him with the author's own feelings. He is psychologically ubiquitous.'[16] Yet in *Rope* the spectator is kept at a distance from the drama. Psychologically it is at the opposite pole from another of Hitchcock's experimental films, *Rear Window* (1954).

Hitchcock saw *Rope* as the culmination of a series of earlier experiments with long takes (*Spellbound*, *Notorious* and *The Paradine Case*, with *Under Capricorn* still to come). He justified it by its effect of sustaining 'the mood of the actors',[17] but it is obvious from the account he gave to Favius Friedman, for publication in *Popular Photography*, that his real purpose was to overcome a multitude of technical difficulties and achieve something which had never been done before, stretching designer, cinematographer, grips, prop men and actors to the limit. Strangely, however, Hitchcock's own enthusiasm was lavished principally on the cyclorama. In his account of the film, after describing the flying furniture and the walls sliding on greased rollers, the special camera modification which allowed him to move in from wide shot to shoot the inside of the murder victim's hat with a single, unchanged lens, the special camera dolly created for the picture, the elaborate plotting of every movement and the six overhead mikes operated by six sound men, Hitchcock chose as his finale the 12,000 square foot cyclorama, describing it as 'the most magical of all devices' – 'an exact miniature reproduction of nearly 35 miles of New York sky-line lighted by 8,000 incandescent bulbs and 200 neon signs requiring 150 transformers'.[18] Significantly, Hitchcock denominates this amazing contraption as a 'light organ' and tells how 'by the time the picture went from the setting of the sun in the first reel to the hour of total darkness in the final *dénouement*, the man at the light organ had played a nocturnal Manhattan symphony in light'.[19]

I believe that the 'the man at the light organ' represented Hitchcock's dream image of himself as director, playing the moving picture on his keyboard as an organist might compose and play a fugue. The more direct analogy is with Scriabin whose own experiments with a light organ made such an impression on Eisenstein. Scriabin's music, Eisenstein said, had 'a physiological quality' which he tried to emulate in his own films.[20] Despite some important differences, Eisenstein prefigured Hitchcock in his experiments with montage – in making *The* [doomed] *General Line* (1929), he used what he called 'rhythmic' as opposed to 'metric' montage. By this he meant both the rhythm of '*movement* within the shot' (his italics) and the rhythmic variation of light, as it changed along a scale of tonality.[21] To achieve the right formal rhythm of 'light tonality', the right decrescendo, Hitchcock's still photographer took pictures of the setting sun at five-minute intervals for an hour and forty-five minutes in order to get a continuous effect, not unlike the effect achieved by Michael Snow in *Wavelength*. Like both Eisenstein and Snow, Hitchcock saw light in musical terms. Thus, he described the neon light created by a 'Storage' sign flashing through the window (later emulated in *Vertigo* (1958)) as 'much like the increasing crescendos of an orchestra at the climax of a symphony'.[22]

Hitchcock's musical vision of light takes us back to the earliest experiments of Survage, Eggeling or Lye, attempts to find visual imagery which could be correlated with musical rhythm and tone to give the effect of synaesthesia. In this sense, *Rope* can be seen as falling within an experimental tradition more radical than that of German expressionism or the *kammerspielfilm*. Hitchcock's project as a film-maker, I am convinced, was to have his cake and eat it, to achieve massive popular success while, at the same time, experimenting artistically in ways which were carefully camouflaged, so that they would be perceived only 'physiologically', as Eisenstein put it, by the mass audience. Meanwhile, Hitchcock himself could enjoy his secret pleasure as maestro of the light organ and unacknowledged perpetrator of avant-garde films, working within the conventional feature-film format but carefully hiding his accomplishment from general view. Like a master criminal, Hitchcock left few clues to his master project, preferring to enjoy it in aesthetic solitude.

Mobility and claustrophobia

Hitchcock exulted in the camera movements which dominated *Rope*. He delightedly described the intricate way in which the shoot was carried out like a military operation, every movement plotted on a blackboard and then cued during the take. As a result of this new technique, Hitchcock explained, 'the continuous flow of action meant the eye was occupied constantly. And the elimination of the conventional shifting camera excites the audience by making the picture flow smoother and faster.'[23] Yet at the same time he noted with barely disguised glee that the *cassone*, which was the central focus of the drama, had to be repeatedly moved out of the camera's way by four hefty prop men, while 'all the time the strangled actor that played the youth had to remain inside the chest! Since there were no time lapses or camera cuts in the usual scene, he was inside the chest for a full ten minutes, the shooting of 950 feet of film. After the third take, this actor began to get, well, a little tired. "I hope to God they get it on this take," he said fervently. "Those ten minutes seem like ten hours." '[24] The chest, it goes without saying, was tied up with rope.

In this situation, Hitchcock noted both the extreme deceleration of time and the claustrophobic restraint forced on the young actor. Hitchcock, of course, was particularly given to imposing forms of restraint on his characters – the handcuffs in *The 39 Steps* provide the classic instance. Inevitably, restraint of movement gives cause for claustrophobia – consider, for example, the survivors crammed together in *Lifeboat* (1944) or the wheelchair-bound protagonist unable to leave his confined quarters in *Rear Window*. In this claustrophobic situation L. B. Jefferies (played by James Stewart) finds relief from tedium and enclosure by allowing his gaze to wander compulsively out of the window, just as Hitchcock had compensated for the claustrophobic situation of the characters in *Rope* by the continuous flow of the camera's gaze – and the view through the window of the ever-changing cyclorama. In both films, his aim was to place the spectator in a confined space but, through either continuous camera movements or point-of-view shots, create the effect of a kind of optical mobility. In *Psycho* the viewer is placed within a doubly claustrophobic and static space, first that of the off-highway motel, then that of the shower unit, before being submitted to a rapid burst of changing points of view in the murder montage. As Janet Leigh points out in her book *Psycho, Behind the Scenes of the Classic Thriller,* there were seventy-eight different points of view in Saul Bass's storyboard, which concluded with a shot in which, as Leigh put it in her memoir, 'the camera started on a close-up of the dead eye, then gradually pulled back to include more and more of the tub, the shower, the bathroom, until it was very high (as from a bird's-eye view, a *stuffed* bird's-eye view?)'.[25] In other words, a reverse point-of-view shot, moving outwards into space. Janet Leigh went on to note that this reverse gaze ended as a bird's-eye view – a foretaste of the murderous gaze of *The Birds* and an echo of the taxidermic gaze of the stuffed birds who looked down on Norman's equally claustrophobic office.

I myself was once fortunate to meet Farley Granger, the star of *Strangers on a Train* (1951) as well as *Rope,* and I took the opportunity of asking him why Hitchcock was so fascinated by trains. 'The mixture of claustrophobia with movement,' he replied.[26] In a train, the passenger is both trapped and constantly shifting point of view. Once again, the outward view through the window is crucial. Hitchcock, we know, was obsessed by trains. As a young man he painstakingly memorised routes and timetables, fascinated to the point of obsession by the details of the British railway timetable, which he learned by heart. By the time he was eight, his biographer tells us, he had ridden every train line in London and 'constructed a huge wall-chart showing the positions on each day of virtually every British ship afloat'.[27] This same obsessive quality is evident in Hitchcock's own description of the precise timing of the camera dolly's movements in *Rope,* its scheduled arrival exactly on time at each point in its complex itinerary. Not only are trains themselves traps, confined spaces from which there is no exit while the train is in motion, but the train consists of a series of smaller, more intimate traps – compartments or sleeping cabins or, most private of all, bathrooms. Trains figure prominently in many of Hitchcock's most celebrated films – *Number Seventeen* (1932), *The 39 Steps, Secret Agent, The Lady Vanishes* (1938), *Suspicion* (1941), *Saboteur* (1942), *North by Northwest* (1959). In many of these films there is a tension between the train as claustrophobic space, as trap or potential trap and the train as means of escape. The train is simultaneously, as Freudians might say, a 'good' and a 'bad object'.

'To turn now to pathology,' as Michael Balint put it in his startlingly relevant book, *Thrills and Regressions,* 'one may say that ocnophilia [compulsive clinging] is related to self-effacement, to anxiety-proneness, especially in the form of agoraphobia; whereas philobatism [compulsive thrill-seeking] may lead to a self-contained detachment, to paranoid attitudes, and possibly to claustrophobia.'[28] The second path is clearly the one followed by such typical Hitchcock heroes as Richard Hannay or Roger O. Thornhill. Balint's book begins with a chapter entitled 'Funfairs and Thrills' in which he discusses the special pleasure which people obtain from roller-coaster rides, roundabouts, swings and so on. Thrills in general, Balint points out, are related to giddiness and vertigo, to high speed, to exposed situations, to chases and to unfamiliar or completely new forms of satisfaction, all of which are repeatedly to be found in Hitchcock's films. In situations such as these the philobat enjoys the 'mixture of fear, pleasure and confident hope in face of an external danger, which [according to Balint] constitute the fundamental elements of all *thrills*'.[29] Hitchcock's films are especially like roller-coaster rides in their typical combination of confinement with movement.[30]

The philobat, in fact, sounds exactly like a Hitchcock hero and almost everything Balint mentions is typical of Hitchcock's films. The key element for Hitchcock was the connection between thrill and suspense – what he called 'the time factor', the ever-diminishing period of time left to the hero before impending disaster struck as danger drew ever closer. Suspense, according to Hitchcock, depended on the existence of a threat known to the viewer, as opposed to mystery, where the nature of the threat remained unknown, or shock, where it erupted unexpectedly. Hitchcock himself, though a law-abiding citizen, suffered from a phobia about the police which he traced back to a childhood experience. As a boy he was briefly locked in a police cell, an experience instigated by his parents as a salutory warning against misbehaviour. In *Rope*, as we have seen, the victim is subjected to confinement at the very beginning of the film, while, at the end, it is the perpetrators who are set to be confined, in the classic triad of handcuffs, wagon and cell. Freud, on the other hand, suffered from travel anxiety, particularly in relation to railway trains, which he himself saw as a form of claustrophobia.[31]

Rope brought together two of Hitchcock's favourite literary texts – De Quincey's essay, 'Murder Considered as One of the Fine Arts', which laid the foundations for criminal connoisseurship, and Edgar Allan Poe's *Tales of the Grotesque and Arabesque*, particularly 'The Pit and the Pendulum', which vividly portrayed the terror of confinement. In *Rope*, the dramatic structure is built around mystery if we look at it from the point of view of the dinner guests, but as suspense if seen from the point of view of the murderers, increasingly trapped as Rupert Cadell closes in on them. It is significant that Hitchcock, unlike Patrick Hamilton, showed the strangling itself – one of the changes from the original stageplay that most irritated Hamilton – but this was necessary, from Hitchcock's point of view, in order to avoid mystery and to strengthen suspense. From this point on, there is continuous camera movement until the very end, when the police are summoned and the murderers are about to be put under restraint. This perpetual motion, I would argue, is designed to put the spectator into the room as if on a train, endlessly moving on tracks and yet simultaneously trapped in a confined space, thus creating a kind of claustrophobic travel anxiety. On another level, as we have seen, the confined space is that of the dormitory or basement boiler-room where Hamilton and Hitchcock spent their schooldays. The cyclorama viewed through the window stands in for the outside world – envisaged by the murderers as the welcoming open space, 'the friendly expanses', in which they will be able to travel free from any further danger, while, in fact, at the end of the film, it is from the world outside that retribution finally comes, leaving them with no way out, betrayed and abandoned by the very parent whose loving approval and protection they had so confidently sought.

Notes

1 Nigel Jones, *Through A Glass Darkly: The Life of Patrick Hamilton*, London: Scribners, 1991, p. 48.

2 Jones, *Through A Glass Darkly*, p. 60.
3 Donald Spoto, *The Dark Side of Genius: The Life of Alfred Hitchcock*, New York: Ballantine, 1983, p. 32.
4 Bruce Hamilton, *The Light Went Out*, London: Constable, 1972, p. 55.
5 Patrick Hamilton, cited from 'the preface to the unidentified published version of *Rope*' without further information in Jones, *Through A Glass Darkly*, p. 153.
6 Friedrich Nietzsche, *Man and Superman*, cited in Jones, p. 153.
7 Nietzsche, *The Portable Nietzsche,* New York: Penguin Books, 1959, p. 314.
8 Hamilton, *The Light Went Out*, p. 55.
9 Patrick Hamilton, *Rope*, London: Constable, 1929, p. 21.
10 Hamilton, *Rope*, p. 59.
11 Alfred Hitchcock, 'My Most Exciting Picture', *Popular Photography*, November 1948. Reprinted in Sidney Gottlieb (ed.), *Hitchcock on Hitchcock*, Berkeley and Los Angeles: University of California Press, 1995, p. 275.
12 Hitchcock, 'My Most Exciting Picture', p. 277.
13 Alfred Hitchcock, 'Director's Problems', *The Listener*, 2 February 1938. Cited in Gottlieb, p. 191.
14 Cited from an unfootnoted source in Hitchcock, 'My Most Exciting Picture', p. 276.
15 Hitchcock, 'My Most Exciting Picture', p. 277.
16 Siegfried Kracauer, *From Caligari to Hitler*, Princeton: Princeton University Press, 1947', p. 105.
17 Hitchcock, 'My Most Exciting Picture', p. 275.
18 Hitchcock, 'My Most Exciting Picture', p. 277.
19 Hitchcock, 'My Most Exciting Picture', p. 278.
20 S. M. Eisenstein, 'The Fourth Dimension in Cinema', *S. M. Eisenstein: Writings 1922 1934*, trans. and ed. Richard Taylor, London: BFI, 1998, p. 183.
21 Eisenstein, 'The Fourth Dimension in Cinema', p. 188.
22 Hitchcock, 'My Most Exciting Picture', p. 282.
23 Hitchcock, 'My Most Exciting Picture', p. 284.
24 Hitchcock, 'My Most Exciting Picture', p. 281.
25 Janet Leigh, Psycho: *Behind the Scenes of the Classic Thriller*, New York: Harmony Books, 1995', p. 72.
26 Conversation at the *Aprile Hitchcock* conference in Rome, April 1980, organised by the Assessorato alla Cultura della Regione Lazio and *Filmcritica.*
27 Spoto, *The Dark Side of Genius*', p. 19.
28 Michael Balint, *Thrills and Regressions*, London: Maresfield Library, 1959, p. 136.
29 Balint, *Thrills and Regressions*, p. 23.
30 Hitchcock was quite aware of this. In 'On Style', an interview first published in *Cinema* 1, no. 5, August–September 1963, he observed that, in his own movies, he aimed to create 'the experience of a person on a roller-coaster', which he considered the quintessential cinematic thrill: 'That old roller-coaster angle has been shot ever since silent films – way, way back. I remember when they made a film years ago called *A Ride on a Runaway Train* and they put the camera up front and looked the world in the face. I can go as far as 1912, maybe earlier, maybe 1910, when they used to have a thing in London called "Hale's Tours" . . . and you sat there, and you were taken for a ride on the train.' Gottlieb, p. 292.

31 Freud connected his own travel anxiety with guilt caused by the sexual excitement he associated with trains. See, for instance, his essay on 'Infantile Sexuality', the second of *Three Essays on the Theory of Sexuality* (1905), where he writes that there is a 'compulsive link' between railway travel and sexual thrill which can cause attacks of panic if repressed. 'The combination of fright with mechanical agitation', all too typical of railway travel, can thus cause a 'severe, hysteriform traumatic neurosis'. See Sigmund Freud, *The Standard Edition*, Vol. VII, London: The Hogarth Press, 1953, p. 202.

The fascination with surface subjectivity – *Marnie*

Chapter 7
Touching the Surface: *Marnie*, Melodrama, Modernism

Joe McElhaney

The cinema is necessarily fascination and rape, that is how it acts on people.

Jacques Rivette

What is to be done with *Marnie*? Of Hitchcock's major works, it has always been something of a problem child, more sharply dividing the director's admirers into camps than any of his other films. Released in 1964, it appears at the end of a string of by-now widely acknowledged canonical Hitchcocks: *Vertigo* (1958), *North by Northwest* (1959), *Psycho* (1960) and *The Birds* (1963). Does *Marnie* belong in this group or not? Is it the last great Hitchcock film or the first which represents the period of his decline? How is this film to be historically placed within Hitchcock's body of work?[1]

In an attempt to link Hitchcock's cinema with 'the legacy of Victorianism', Paula Marantz Cohen briefly discusses the degree to which *Marnie* is an example of an important shift which takes place in Hitchcock's cinema in the 1960s. In *Marnie*, Hitchcock is no longer tied to a psychological conception of character so central to a number of his Hollywood films. Instead, he presents the spectator with a world of surface appearances and blatant artificiality in which objects are not related to psychology but 'to a vocabulary about sex and death that can be manipulated to produce new effects'.[2] Marantz Cohen reads this exploration of a cinema of surfaces in *Marnie* as a development out of several of Hitchcock's films of the 1950s in which novelistic and psychological conceptions of 'depth' undergo a gradual transformation. In *Vertigo*, for instance, Madeleine is not so much a character as a 'vehicle for potential identities'. *Vertigo* presents us with a 'surface subjectivity' in which we find 'not the world leading into the mysteries of the individual mind but the individual mind opening out into the chaos of the world'.[3] For Marantz Cohen, *Marnie* takes this tendency towards surface subjectivity to an even higher level. The film does not explore the dialectic of surface/depth in the title character which had been so central in Hitchcock's treatment of female psychology and sexuality in his earlier American work. With Marnie, there is nothing beneath her surface, 'no desire to be sparked; the surface coldness speaks the truth'.[4] In this regard, *Marnie* belongs with the other Hitchcock films of the 1960s in that they 'fail to evoke more than a fleeting sense of the reality of individual character'.[5]

Why the increased dominance of surface subjectivity and non-psychological conceptions of character in *Marnie* and Hitchcock's other 1960s films? And what is the importance of this? Marantz Cohen is not terribly specific aside from touching on certain cultural shifts of the period and the nature of Hitchcock's own internal developments at this time. While her arguments about surface in the film raise some interesting possibilities, there is something insufficient about them. I cite Marantz Cohen's work here for two reasons: first, it is among the more recent examples of the numerous attempts over the last three decades to define the nature of this difficult film; and second, its emphasis on surface in the film, however problematically argued, is nevertheless central to the film's operation. Consequently, I would like to make use of the spaces left open by her arguments and try to construct a more general framework within which this film may be approached. These spaces are primarily historical, the result of *Marnie*'s troubled relationship to the larger developments of narrative cinema in the early 1960s and Hitchcock's attempts to acknowledge these developments.

If *Marnie* is the last great Hitchcock film, it does not achieve this status without an enormous process of struggle. Or, to be more precise, the fascination of the film arises out of observing and uncovering this process of struggle itself. While clearly emerging out of various lines of development in Hitchcock's cinema up through the 1960s, the film also seems to be trying to reach a new level of expressivity and meaning for Hitchcock. In particular, this new level relates to Hitchcock's desire to incorporate into the film certain innovations in European art cinema of the early 1960s, directly following experiments begun on *The Birds* a year earlier.[6] And *Marnie* does, in fact, have some suggestive parallels with Antonioni's *Red Desert*, released the same year (although it is unlikely that Hitchcock was able to see this particular Antonioni film before making *Marnie*). But the incorporation of various aspects of European art cinema into the forms and structures of a Hitchcock thriller produces a certain anxiety on the part of the film which it is not able to resolve.

When *The Birds* opened in France, Jean-André Fieschi noted that it was the first Hitchcock film 'where the tension isn't aimed at solving a mystery, but at elaborating and developing it' and drew links between *The Birds* and the recent work of Alain Resnais.[7] But in *Marnie*, Hitchcock returns to solving a mystery in the manner of a more conventional psychological thriller. Does this immediately result in a more conventional film? There is not a simple response to this. Indeed, the various terms flung at *Marnie* over the years – character study, Gothic melodrama, art film, avant-garde masterpiece, feminist text, misogynist text, old-fashioned woman's film – bear the traces of the perpetually unresolved tension between the film's ambitions and final achievement. To do justice to *Marnie* one must account for the film's scattered and diffuse quality. Writing about it must likewise be a form of struggle in which tracing out these various and sometimes irreconcilable ambitions prevents one from being able to ever firmly define the nature of this elusive Hitchcock work.

It is probably best to acknowledge as quickly as possible a certain mythology surrounding the film which has arisen in the aftermath of Donald Spoto's biography of the director. Hitchcock (rather like Scottie Ferguson in *Vertigo*) allegedly became obsessed with transforming a woman – the film's lead actress, Tippi Hedren – not simply into a star but also into the idealised figure of his romantic dreams. But both the dream of possessing the woman in real life and the dream of transforming the woman into a star collapsed after their personal falling out and the film's critical and financial failure. This financial failure and critical dismissal was not based upon the supposedly modernist strategies of the film but what was perceived to be its old-fashioned nature – its conventional melodramatic scenario with its ties to 'women's fiction' as well as the somewhat archaic look of the film, with its reliance on obvious matte work and rear projections. All of this gave *Marnie* the aura of a slightly stale Hollywood studio product. With both the production and reception of *Marnie*, Hitchcock seemed to suffer both a private and public humiliation, one in which his integrity and relevance as a film artist was called into question.[8]

While I would like to avoid any simplistic reading of the film as one in which Hitchcock's personal obsessions with an actress spill over into the formal excesses of the film, this mythology does have a certain degree of interest and usefulness. What it suggests is that Hitchcock's authorial control on *Marnie* is 'off', unsure of itself and struggling within both the more traditional forms of Hitchcock's cinema and the new forms it is attempting to adapt. This possibly results in the film's resistance to being easily categorised as either modernist or classical. However, in itself this is hardly unusual for a Hitchcock film. As Gilles Deleuze has written of Hitchcock, 'you might equally well say that he's the last of the classic directors, or the first of the moderns'.[9] What is important about *Marnie* is the intensity with which both these classical and modernist impulses are present. It is as though in its extremity the film serves as a heightened example of this key transitional role which Hitchcock plays within the historical development of cinema.

Although Marantz Cohen does not historically contextualise her arguments about the centrality of surface appearances in *Marnie* and how these lead to 'new effects', her positioning of *Marnie* in this way would seem to connect the film with contemporaneous developments in modernist cinema, particularly those of Antonioni. As Sam Rohdie has written on Antonioni's cinema: 'The films will pose a subject (only to compromise it), constitute objects (only to dissolve them), propose stories (only to lose them), but equally, they turn those compromises and losses back towards another solidity . . . a wandering away from narrative to the surface into which it was dissolved, but in such a way that the surface takes on a fascination, becomes a "subject" all its own.'[10]

Does this happen in *Marnie* as well? Do the surfaces ever become a subject of their own? In a way, yes. There is a strong response to surfaces in the film in relation to bodies, faces and objects which, while not without precedent in Hitchcock's work, appear here with a frequency which is unusual. At times, this response creates a powerful desire on the part of the camera to touch these subjects, to get closer and closer, as if to penetrate the essence of what is being filmed and break down a classical system of representation. But this enormous investment in surface intensity also creates a desire on the part of the film to understand and explain what is being shown in ways which are still strongly tied to models derived from classical narrative cinema and, in particular, to psychological conceptions of character.

The production designer on the film, Robert Boyle, has explained the difficulty Hitchcock faced on *Marnie*: 'Hitchcock was trying to get at something you couldn't see. He was trying to tell a story of things that are not at all overt . . . He was trying desperately to really dig into the psyche of this woman.'[11] Within this context, discussing *Marnie* simply as a film of surfaces, in opposition to a psychological cinema, is clearly unacceptable. As Spoto notes, the film has a psychological intimacy to it unusual in

Hitchcock, 'a naked feeling [he] had never allowed in his films before'.[12] At the same time, this knowledge, this 'naked feeling' is also traumatic for the film and causes it to pull back from the full implications of this system. It is this vacillation between surface and psychology, between tactility and knowledge, which dominates the film and seriously complicates attempts to account easily for the nature of the film as a whole.

First let us attempt to situate the film within the nature of Hitchcock's relationship to classical cinema on the one hand and modernist cinema on the other. If Deleuze is correct in historically placing Hitchcock as the last of the great classical film-makers and the first of the modern ones, how does this come about? Deleuze's distinction between classical and modern cinema is well known. The classical cinema of the 'movement–image' which dominates the period prior to World War II is one which strives towards achieving unity between space and movement. In this cinema, time is subordinated to and conquered by movement. The modern cinema of the 'time–image' which comes to dominate after World War II is one in which the 'sensory–motor schema' which defined classical cinema becomes severed. The cinema of the postwar period is no longer classical because movement is defined by its relationship to time, dreams and memory. The protagonists of this cinema no longer enjoy a unity between thought, action and movement as in classical cinema. Instead, they see rather than act, are prey to visions which they cannot control, and consequently often become spectators of their own lives. The emergence of Italian neo-realism in the 1940s – of which Antonioni was such a major figure – was central in establishing this new time–image.

Deleuze argues that Hitchcock's 'special place' in between these classical and modern conceptions of the image is the result of Hitchcock's development of the 'mental image'. The mental image insists upon all actions and perceptions being determined by their relation to *something else* rather than simply existing as autonomous entities within a causal chain of events, as in the classical movement–image.[13] Working out of Charles Peirce's notions of 'thirdness' as central for defining the philosophical tradition of relations, Deleuze argues that it is Hitchcock who introduces relations-through-thirdness into the cinema. There is a 'perpetual tripling' in the structure of Hitchcock's films, with relationships between characters conceived in terms of triangles, with a crucial third partner in the events. Citing Chabrol/Rohmer, he stresses the importance of how crimes in Hitchcock are always being committed in such a way that the criminal 'offers up' her/his crime on behalf of someone else. Marnie and Norman Bates in *Psycho* do not commit crimes (respectively, theft and murder) on their own behalf – both do it 'for' their mothers, resulting in the crime having a triangular structure: Marnie/Strutt/Mrs Edgar or Norman/Marion/Mrs Bates. This tripling likewise spills over into objects, perceptions, affections, creating a cinematic world in which 'all is interpretation, from beginning to end'.[14] Furthermore, characters in Hitchcock (in a manner which anticipates the protagonists of the time–image) are frequently spectators themselves, caught up in the chain of fascination over the relations being represented along with the viewers of the film.

Deleuze claims that it is not the look as such which defines Hitchcock's cinema but how the look assumes a position within the 'tapestry' of Hitchcock's framing of relations. These relations are mental relations and Hitchcock's primary concern is with *the tracing of thought*, the mental image representing the most complex realisation of the cinema's capacity to render thought up to that point in the history of film form. 'It's not a matter of the look,' Deleuze says of the mental image, 'and if the camera's an eye, it's the mind's eye.'[15] For example, when Marnie is first hired at Rutland & Co., she has a brief conversation with another secretary during which the secretary pulls a key out of a purse. This key unlocks a drawer in her desk which contains the safe combination which Marnie wants. Two camera set-ups are employed here through which a sense of the mental image emerges: Marnie's point-of-view shot as we see the secretary's hand reach into the purse, pull out the key and open the drawer, and a slight overhead shot of Marnie looking down.

By cross-cutting between these two set-ups, a dual process of thought tracing emerges, that of Marnie's and that of the spectator observing this. We do not simply look at what Marnie sees through her point-of-view shots by the cross-cutting; this cutting also enables us to observe her thoughts and come to an understanding that the task she is setting for herself is to get her hands on this key in order to read the safe combination in the drawer. At the same time, our own perceptions as spectators are being directly solicited here. The overhead shot of Marnie has a strong authorial feel to it, of something deliberately placed there in order for us to notice it as a shot, as a camera set-up. This is not a mere stylistic flourish but an announcement to the spectator: this is a woman thinking. Furthermore, in the camera set-up which shows the hands of the secretary reaching for her key, the movements of her hands with the key have a slightly artificial quality to them as she pauses first with the key coming out of her purse and then when she opens the drawer. Both gestures are held an 'unnaturally' long time in terms of realist convention. But this extension of time also enables the spectator to read more easily the images and grasp what is going on inside Marnie's mind. These protracted gestures of the secretary's are there for our benefit and not Marnie's. They seem to be addressing us and not her. As Godard has noted, Hitchcock creates films in which the spectator does not simply look at the film, the film also looks back at the spectator.[16]

The task of implicating and involving the spectator in a set of relations at the same time that the characters metaphorically become spectators results in a conception of the image which repeatedly seems to be examining its own operations, not simply classical narrative films but also films which are *about* the process of classical narrative cinema. In this regard, Hitchcock anticipates many of the concerns of the postwar modern cinema of the time–image. The French new wave (all of whom were committed to Hitchcock's work) were likewise concerned with the implications of the mental image. But they were committed to it in order to construct a definite break with the classical movement–image, severing the mental image's ties to action or character: 'What Hitchcock had wanted to avoid, a crisis of the traditional action–image, would nevertheless happen in his wake, and in part as a result of his innovations.'[17]

However, there is also something else going on here. I referred to the hand movements of the secretary as being held an unnaturally long time and ascribed these entirely to their narrative function and to their relationship to the mental image. I am struck, however, by the poised, almost ritualistic quality to these hand movements and to the fetishistic impact of the opening of the leather purse and the tiny key held in the secretary's hand. These shots seem to be a bit overdetermined, exerting a tactile fascination which slightly oversteps their function within the narrative. Rather than observing a simple action here, we seem to be in a world in which these actions are transformed into, as Deleuze phrases it, 'symbolic acts that have a purely mental existence'.[18] Granted, Hitchcock's cinema is full of such moments as this one in *Marnie*. As a technical and stylistic *tour de force*, this sequence would seem to be rather minor in comparison with that other great key shot in Hitchcock, the elaborate craning movement in *Notorious* (1946) from the top of the stairs of Alex Sebastian's home down to Alicia's closed hand, holding the key to the wine cellar. But the impact of this moment in *Marnie* derives not simply from the execution of the sequence itself as from how it fits within the film's larger structure of meaning. And it is this structure of meaning which is central in the film's struggle to bring forth a different kind of Hitchcock film.

> The close-up modifies the drama by the impact of proximity. Pain is within reach. If I stretch out my arm I touch you, and that is intimacy. I can count the eye-lashes of this suffering. I would be able to taste the tears. Never before has a face turned to mine in that way. Ever closer it presses against me, and I follow it face to face. It's not even true that there is air between us; I consume it. It is in me like a sacrament. Maximum visual acuity.
>
> Jean Epstein

Deleuze refers to a tactile cinema which emerges out of the collapse of the classical movement–image. In this cinema, the hand 'relinquishes its prehensile and motor functions to content itself with pure touching'.[19] The ultimate example of this cinema for Deleuze (and he does not mention Hitchcock at all here) is Robert Bresson's, in which the hand often replaces the face in terms of affects and becomes a mode of perception itself. In this cinema of tactility, the optical function is doubled through the hand's newly discovered powers of perception. The hand itself now becomes a kind of eye.[20] *Marnie* is not *Pickpocket* (1959). Unlike Bresson's film, it does not systematically and structurally orchestrate the relationship between the hand and the eye, between seeing and touching. But this tactility is nevertheless there in the film, imbedded within its narrative and psychological conflicts. *Marnie* demonstrates a desire to break through certain classical narrative conventions and to enter a realm of 'pure touching' in which the hand both feels and sees.

In the midst of a montage sequence on board the honeymoon cruise ship in *Marnie*, Mark Rutland describes to Marnie an object in Africa which, to the naked eye, appears to be a flower. It is not until one reaches out and touches this object that one is able to perceive that the flower is in fact a conglomeration of tiny insects gathered together in the shape of a flower as a form of protection from the forces of nature. This brief monologue (almost tossed away by the film) is nevertheless crucial for understanding the relationship between touching and looking which structures much of *Marnie*. The desire to touch another human being who does not want to be touched animates the system of looking and perceiving which always determined Hitchcock's cinema. But here this system is taken to another level in the manner in which it is integrated within the narrative and thematic content of the film. In *Marnie*, the relationship of the look – that of the camera, of the characters, of the spectators – to desire has seldom been as intense as it is here because it now introduces touch, the presence of a hand against an object, another human being, an animal (and Marnie's physical response to her horse,

Forio, is far more intimate and sexual than with any human being in the film) as the culmination of the chain of desire and of the process of perception.

Central here is a sequence which takes place about ten minutes into the film. In this sequence Marnie and her mother, Mrs Edgar, have a conversation in Mrs Edgar's kitchen. This conversation centres around the possibility of Mrs Edgar's neighbours, Mrs Cotton and her young daughter Jessie (a rival for Marnie's affections for her mother), moving in. The sequence is brief but powerful. Before discussing its importance and effectiveness within the context of the film as a whole it is necessary to describe it in some detail.

As the sequence begins, it is initially composed of a rather mundane medium two-shot of the women, followed by a frontal medium close-up of Marnie as she cracks pecans sitting at the table, alternating with two medium close-ups of her mother (one from her front, the other from her side) standing as she pours syrup. Mrs Edgar detects Marnie's jealousy of Jessie and begins to chide her for it. This emotional rupture results in the editing configuration suddenly being broken as the camera position on Marnie shifts from the front to her side and moves in closer as she looks up at her mother and asks, 'Why don't you love me, Mama? I've often wondered why you don't. Why you never give me one part of the love you give Jessie.' We now return to the shot of her mother taken from the side but she now appears rather vulnerable in the shot, standing at the far right of the composition, unable to answer Marnie's question, in opposition to her daughter who sits centre frame. Mrs Edgar moves towards a salt shaker on the table and there is a cut to a close-up of Marnie's hand touching her mother's and uttering the word, 'Mama'. Mrs Edgar pulls her hand away as the camera pans up to her horrified face. A cut returns us to a medium two-shot as Marnie asks, 'Why do you always move away from me. Why? What's wrong with me?' 'Nothin',' the mother says, 'there's nothin' wrong with ya.' 'No, you've always thought that, haven't you? Always.' A cut returns us to the centred close-up of Marnie looking at her mother as she continues accusing her mother of not loving her, detailing all the things she has done to make her mother love her. But this time the close-up on Marnie is an almost imperceptibly slow tracking shot into her, while the reverse shots of her mother which periodically interrupt those of Marnie's outburst, are still taken from the same slightly off-centre position. Marnie's accusations build in intensity until Mrs Edgar's hand enters the space of Marnie's close-up, slapping her. This is followed by a cut to Marnie's hand hitting the bowl of pecans, knocking them to the floor.

It is difficult to describe on paper the emotional quality of this scene. In the rigour of construction and emphasis on looking it is recognisably Hitchcockian. But it has an emotional intensity of a particular kind which is rare in this director's work. (The final sequence of the film, also set in Mrs Edgar's home, has a similar quality.) The centred close-ups of Marnie accusing her mother of insufficiently loving her just slightly avoid being direct addresses into the camera. Nevertheless, there is (to borrow a phrase from Spoto) a naked emotional feeling at work here, so naked that, like Mrs Edgar, one feels the impulse to recoil from what we are witnessing. Marnie is centred in the composition and is on the offensive but is seated and seems diminished in the shot; Mrs Edgar is standing but is shoved to the far right of the shot, finding it difficult to move. The close-up of the two women's hands touching breaks this particular tension but creates another more acute one, establishing the problematics of touch as a motif which will recur throughout the film, a touch which can only be expressed in an indirect fashion. Mrs Edgar cannot touch her daughter's hand as an expression of love but she can use the same hand to slap Marnie's face, as Marnie's hand simultaneously hits the bowl of pecans intended for a pie for Jessie.

Perhaps the shot which contains the greatest emotional volatility and potential violence here is the close-up of Marnie's hand touching her mother's. In this sequence so strongly built around close-ups of the faces of the two women and in which the activities of their hands are devoted to banal and mechanical domestic duties (cracking pecans, pouring syrup), this close-up carries such an emotional weight because the hands are now suddenly being called upon to carry an expressive function, stopping the action, so to speak. This expressive function is something that Mrs Edgar refuses, and she must give her hand a more precise function, slapping the accusing face of her daughter, restoring both the hand and the face to their 'proper' functions. What this sequence makes clear is that Marnie's projection of herself in the world outside of her mother's home, as an unavailable object of desire, is an unconscious response to this situation with her mother. Since her mother will not touch her, will not love her, then she will move in a world in which no one – particularly no man – will be able to touch her. Out of this arises Marnie's (and the film's) drive towards a world of surfaces, a drive which is nevertheless intimately related to the need to unmask surfaces, to touch what is beneath the seductive and remote exterior.

But does this sequence lend itself to a reading which would claim it for a modernist cinema of tactility? In spite of the emphasis on touching here and the almost Bressonian power of the close-up of Marnie's hand reaching out to her mother's, probably not. The sequence has a hysterical theatricality, the feeling of something carefully written and performed, which links it strongly with the world of melodrama. Melodrama was vital to the formation of Hitchcock's cinema. His pursuit of 'pure cinema' found in the genres of melodrama a set of codes, iconographies, narrative structures, character types, through which his particular concerns with exploring the formal possibilities of cinema could be articulated. In the espionage and detective thriller, the Gothic woman-centred melodrama and the horror film, there is a fascination with looking and voyeurism, with complex and shifting issues of point of view and focalisation, a fascination which Hitchcock was able to integrate into the broader concerns of his cinema of mental relations. Nevertheless, the melodramatic tone of this sequence from *Marnie* is still rare for Hitchcock.

Peter Brooks has written of melodrama that it 'handles its feelings and ideas virtually as plastic entities, visual and tactile models held out for all to see and handle'.[21] Recall the famous scene in Hitchcock's Gothic melodrama *Rebecca* (1940) in which Mrs Danvers takes the heroine on a tour of Rebecca's closets, inviting her to insert her hand under the folds of Rebecca's lingerie and rub her face against the sleeve of a fur coat. *Marnie*'s concern with tactility, then, is perhaps as much a late development out of a particular tradition of melodrama as it is a response to European art cinema. But in *Marnie*, instead of simply filming and representing this desire for tactility – as in *Rebecca* – Hitchcock is intent upon his entire film-making apparatus being called upon to simulate this desire. Melodrama in *Marnie* is made use of and then passed through, as it were, the form's logic of tactility pushed to such a degree that genre conventions are almost beside the point. As Raymond Durgnat has written, often in this film 'the melodrama is merely a symbol, a symptom, a mask'.[22]

The most extreme and violent instance of touch within the film occurs almost immediately after Mark's description of the African insects: the rape scene. This rape scene was vital to Hitchcock's conception of the film. It had to be there. Marnie's original screenwriter, Evan Hunter, refused to write the sequence, finding it unmotivated and fearing that Mark would completely lose audience sympathy as a result.[23] Hunter was replaced by Jay Presson Allen. One of the interesting things about this sequence, however, is that Mark does not seem to lose this audience sympathy. (Robin Wood rhapsodises over the rape as 'one of the purest treatments of sexual intercourse the cinema has given us'.[24]) Various reasons for this come to mind: the star persona of Sean Connery is so completely bound up with him as a charismatic romantic and sexual figure that Marnie's refusal to have sex with him threatens to render her in somewhat unsympathetic terms instead (what 'normal' heterosexual woman would not want to sleep with James Bond?); and after the rape, the film very quickly works to restore Mark to his place as a romantic male protagonist, substitute psychotherapist for Marnie, and detective figure for the unravelling of the central narrative enigma.[25] Furthermore, it is hardly unprecedented in melodrama for an ostensibly sympathetic male figure to rape a woman, provided the woman is his wife and that she, within the logic of the film, 'deserves' this violent act performed against her: *Gone with the Wind* (1939) and *The Foxes of Harrow* (1947) are two examples of Hollywood films in which the hero feels compelled to rape the sexually recalcitrant heroine/wife. But even more crucial than these reasons, I think, are those which relate back to both how this rape scene functions within the film's structure of touch, as well as how the sequence itself is formally organised.

According to Raymond Bellour, Hitchcock's authorial presence in *Marnie* (and elsewhere in his work) is largely connected with power. Mark and Strutt are 'nothing but doubles' of Hitchcock, 'the first among all his doubles, a matrix which allows their generation'.[26] This desire for power as expressed through the camera – particularly in relation to the looks directed towards Marnie by Mark, Strutt and Hitchcock in his cameo appearance – is unquestionably there, as Bellour argues. In fact, Hitchcock's desire to articulate this relation between power and desire in *Marnie* is unusually forceful. But I would argue that there is no other Hitchcock film in which the camera's look directed towards the desirable female protagonist is *less* mediated through the look of a strong, desiring male protagonist. In spite of Bellour's contention that in the opening moments of *Marnie*, Strutt and Mark function as doubles for Hitchcock (and if Strutt is a double for Hitchcock he is a most unpleasant one), the overwhelming impression generated by these moments is that of Marnie being presented to us and to the camera largely free of a strong male character as a secondary figure in terms of the look. The looks directed towards Marnie by Strutt and Mark are continually being superseded by Hitchcock's camera. While these men may look at Marnie – and Mark is given a number of point-of-view shots of her later in the film – Hitchcock continually reserves the greatest moments of intensity for looking at Marnie for his own camera, divorced from or strongly intervening in the look generated by the male characters.

In the first sequence of the film in which we see Mark and Strutt, the look which the two men possess is wholly an operation of the mind in relation to memory: Strutt's fetishistic inventory of her features, Mark's reduction of her to 'the brunette with the legs'. In his cameo, Hitchcock looks briefly at Marnie as she passes through the hall, reserving the first look at her within the diegetic world of the film for himself, suggesting a privileging of his and the camera's look over the other male characters. Indeed, throughout this opening as we see Marnie on the train platform, in the hotel room as she unpacks and exchanges identities, rinsing the black dye out of her hair, etc., we are being brought into spaces for looking at Marnie which are denied Mark or Strutt (even if their descriptions prepare us for it), highly private spaces in which the texture of objects – the yellow leather purse, the tweed suit, the jet-black hair, the pink nail polish, the gold metal case holding her plastic identity cards – are clearly meant to serve as displaced extensions of Marnie's body and in which our eyes are invited to metaphorically touch these objects. In the second sequence of the film, as Strutt recites his inventory of Marnie's features to the detectives, he looks off into space and gestures with his hands, as though somehow language, sight and memory are inadequate for the full articulation of his desire for Marnie; he must somehow ritualistically re-enact the gesture of touch which he was never able to realise when she was under his employ. All of this sets up a powerful environment in which the look generates the desire for touch, to get even closer to the object of desire. But this look in itself is also determined by an indecisiveness, moments of possession of Marnie by the camera alternating with moments in which that look by the camera is broken off: it pulls back, it looks away (the pan away from Marnie's face during the rape scene to a porthole, for example), it delegates the look to someone else, as though it realises it cannot go any further or get any closer.

The opening shot of the film encapsulates this position for the camera in *Marnie*: an extremely close shot of a yellow purse, tightly held in Marnie's arm against a green tweed jacket, the camera moving along behind her, the two movements at one, until she picks up speed and the camera recedes until she is further away on the platform and the camera sees her in long shot, remote and unapproachable. Pascal Bonitzer has described the movement from further away to close up as Hitchcock's most characteristic device, a passage from the large picture to the small, from environment to object.[27] However, we often get the reverse of this in *Marnie*: the camera now immediately wants to be as close as possible, to get inside the woman both physically (to touch, to penetrate) and mentally, to convey her psychological state, that something which cannot be seen. The role of enunciator (as Bellour calls it) that Hitchcock traditionally reserves for himself is threatened by this reversed conception of movement in that this role was always predicated on a slight and ironic distance from the chain of desire which he sets into motion as the enunciator. Now Hitchcock's camera seems even more caught up in the chain of desire than his characters, more than Mark (too insufficiently realised as a character) or Strutt (too unsympathetic, too much of a heavy to generate spectator identification).

The most important character in possession of the look in the film is not Mark but Marnie. But this creates a problem for the film. Stojan Pelko has referred to 'the long chain of Hitchcock's female characters who persistently oscillate between presence and absence'. Pelko writes: 'Each and every one of them owes her status of simulacrum to the very cinematographic disposition that is capable, with a single stroke, of replacing presence with absence . . . '[28] This female character is both object of the look and bearer of it. As bearer of the look she may even possess this look to an intense degree and be subject to visions, a look at once acute (in that she sees more deeply into the abyss than the male characters often do) and myopic (in that this also limits her ability to see relations, the larger picture of things). It is this space for seeing relations (the Deleuzian notion of thirdness) which is reserved for the spectator and for Hitchcock as authorising agent. In *Marnie*, on the other hand, the acuteness of the heroine's vision is too internalised. She 'sees' in her red flashes and her recurring nightmares but does not know, does not understand, nor do we – until the end – as spectators. She is not drawn by her visions but subject to them. They become problems to be deciphered. So that when her vision is at its most acute, it does not take us closer into the heart of relations which make up the film but instead becomes an enigma, something which freezes the chain of relations.

There is a split in the film between these moments of vision Marnie has and the more mundane tracing of her thoughts through the point-of-view shot, most often centring around the theft of money and changing of identities. These point-of-view shots are rather banal in their intensity in comparison to what is clearly troubling Marnie. Marnie's looks in the film raise two separate questions in relation to the narrative. The first and most urgent of these is: What is wrong with Marnie? – a question which the film delays in answering. The other – Will she get caught stealing the money? – more directly animates the film and creates narrative suspense. But it is clear that Marnie's stealing is a symptom of something, the source of which she does not know or understand, so that Marnie's look and her activities which animate the narrative (and supply her with goals in the tradition of characters in classical narratives) are nevertheless contaminated with her enigmatic visions. In other words, both of these looks, which are at the centre of *Marnie*'s operation, intensify the sense of displacement which runs throughout the film and to the sense that Hitchcock is attempting to render visible what is, in cinematic terms, invisible. This something which can't be seen is a mind which records and observes but does not understand and does not even primarily wish to understand, but merely to act upon a set of unconscious desires. The operation of the mental image, so vital to the *pleasure* of Hitchcock's cinema, is present in a 'neurotic' state here. The pleasures to be had by observing mental processes is secondary in *Marnie* to the recording of a mental state which is blocked, unable to process. As a result, vision itself here often becomes a kind of surface in its own right, as in the red flashes which fill the screen whenever Marnie sees the color red or the crude backwards and forwards zooms when she tries to steal money from the Rutland safe after the death of Forio, devices which simultaneously seem to bring the image closer to us and push it away.[29]

Throughout the film, however, there is a powerful need for Hitchcock's camera to possess Marnie, to offer her up as something which cannot only be viewed but physically touched as well. This provides the spectator with a strong sense of intimacy in relation to the character, but it is an intimacy tinged with a certain amount of discomfort or embarrassment in that the relationship with the protagonist is inevitably an imaginary one. We are being pulled into a network of desire which we know, on some level, to be impossible. Hitchcock's cinema is replete with moments in which the camera cannot seem to get close enough to what it is filming, particularly if it is filming a woman. Two examples from the opposite ends of death and desire in this fixation with proximity: the opening shot of the first 'true' Hitchcock film, *The Lodger* (1926), in which the face of a woman in the process of being murdered is placed almost directly on the lens of the camera; and the first shot of Lisa Fremont in *Rear Window* (1954), slowly and seductively moving into the camera as though to make love to it.

However in *Marnie*, through a combination of the repetition of these kinds of examples and the way in which tactility emerges as a thematic thread, this emphasis on proximity and touch becomes a governing principle of the film. During the first kiss between Mark and Marnie in his office during the thunderstorm, the camera comes in to a close two-shot of the couple and then, as if to confound all expectations, the camera executes an even tighter slow zoom into them, obliterating everything but eyes, noses and mouths. This close-up has obvious correspondences with the love scene in *The Lodger*, with the extended kiss in *Notorious* (1946), and the first kiss between L. B. Jefferies and Lisa in *Rear Window*. But in an even more extreme way in this sequence from *Marnie*, Hitchcock's camera is almost refusing to acknowledge boundaries between the actors, the camera and the spectator. These tactile-like images in which flesh seems to cover the frame are not so much returning a look to the spectator as they are returning a touch, the faces almost seeming to brush against the camera and across the imagination of the viewer.[30]

In spite of such volatile moments as the kiss and the rape, Hitchcock was unhappy with the film's failure to adequately define Mark Rutland as a character. In particular, he was disappointed with the film's inadequacy in documenting that the fundamental nature of Mark's obsession with Marnie had to do with a fetish – an attraction to a woman because she is a criminal. Indeed, throughout the film, Mark's desires for Marnie, and his declaration of love for her as they are driving on the highway, are somewhat hazily defined and motivated, quite the opposite of the treatment of Scottie's attraction for Madeleine in *Vertigo*, which is very precisely articulated. But one could argue that this does not really matter because Hitchcock's camera is the primary desiring subject in *Marnie* and has, in effect, *replaced* the male protagonist who is now reduced to being a kind of supporting player. It is not Mark alone who is penetrating Marnie during the rape scene. This sequence acquires its force not simply from the dramatic event itself but by the specific cinematic properties at work here. As Marnie is lowered onto the bed, the camera position suggests not only Mark's point of view as he brings himself toward her body, but the camera here also appears to be attempting to penetrate Marnie. This, of course, it ultimately cannot do. It must pan away to the visual metaphor of the porthole before actually making physical contact with her.

Chris Marker has written that the 360-degree tracking shot in the hotel room in *Vertigo* ('the most magical camera movement in the history of cinema') should be seen as a substitute for the moment of sexual union between Scottie and Judy which Hitchcock, for reasons of censorship, cannot show.[31] By the time of *Marnie*, this language of metaphor is increasingly inadequate for Hitchcock. He must get even closer and the camera must begin to assume a more literal function. In this regard, the rape scene from *Marnie* stands somewhere in between the *Vertigo* tracking shot and the strangulation and rape scene in *Frenzy* (1972). In the rape and murder sequence from *Frenzy*, all attempts at seduction of the viewer are gone. No spectacular camera movements, no luxurious lighting, no glamorous movie stars. We are in a drab, straightforward universe in which all touch is violence (significantly here, murder by strangulation), all sex is rape, and human beings are reduced to a set of animal-like instincts and behaviour. (The film's repeated insistence on the linking of food, sex and human beings is expressed here by the rape and murder taking place in the midst of the woman's lunch break, with the murderer finishing his victim's half-eaten apple after killing her.) This sequence from *Frenzy* may be read as, in some ways, a negative and bitter response to the rape sequence in *Marnie*. What began as a gradual breakdown of the cinematic language of metaphor in the 1964 film in favour of a cinema which points towards the affective possibilities of touch are violently forsaken, in the 1972 film, in favour of a crushing and nihilistic literal-mindedness.

This rapist/murderer from *Frenzy* (why recall the character's name?) is far removed from Mark Rutland in terms of sympathy. To return, then, to the rape sequence from *Marnie*, another possible reason why Mark does not seem to lose audience sympathy after the rape relates to the question of thirdness so central to Hitchcock. Mark is not a mere aggressor in his relationship with Marnie during the rape. His relationship with her *duplicates* Marnie's relationship with her mother, with Mark assuming Marnie's role and Marnie assuming her mother's. He is not simply Marnie's antagonist nor her romantic opposite, but a kind of double of her in relation to the film's motif of touch and desire: Mark wants to touch Marnie who wants to touch her mother.

There are, however, two characters in the film who represent the final points of this chain of touch and desire, characters at the opposite ends of Marnie's two families, her biological family and the one she marries in to. First, there is Mark's sister-in-law Lil who creates a crucial third element in the chain of desire in the Mark/Marnie marriage: Lil desires Mark and touches him – aggressively kissing him on the mouth as he departs for his honeymoon – but cannot possess him sexually. When Marnie is brought to the Rutland estate for the first time, Lil even pretends that her wrist is sprained, preventing her from pouring the tea and forcing Marnie to do it instead – an act of subterfuge which allows her to more boldly take Marnie in with her eyes. Lil's look throughout the film has the potential for powers of acuteness, something which Marnie seems to instinctively realise. At their first meeting in the film, in the Rutland office, Lil's point-of-view shot as she looks at Marnie is one in which Marnie's head turns away, refusing to make eye contact with her, a gesture she repeats throughout the film. Lil's look at Marnie is one connected to pure knowledge unrelated to sexual desire – a desire for Marnie, at any rate – and is motivated by the need to unmask Marnie, to reveal the truth under the surface appearance of her rival for Mark's affections. This is what Marnie seems to instinctively realise about Lil. She avoids her glance because it is not one that she has any power over. Lil immediately understands where the source of Marnie's power comes from – her appearance. (Her first question to Mark after meeting Marnie: 'Who's the dish?') But Lil's potential function in regard to uncovering the truth behind Marnie's appearance is never systematically followed through in the film. Instead, she uncovers information about which we are already familiar: Marnie's relationship with Strutt, the fact that Marnie has a mother in Baltimore.

Second, there is Mrs Edgar who freely touches Jessie, the child who becomes the third party in relation to the chain of desire within the space of Mrs Edgar's home. But even more crucial here is Mrs Edgar's former profession – prostitute, a woman who, as Mark phrases it near the end of the film, 'makes her living from the touch of men'. The central narrative enigmas of the film (Why does Marnie steal? Why is she sexually unresponsive? And what does her past life with her mother have to do with this?) are derived from this world of her childhood in which 'the touch of men' was a central fact of her life with her mother: significantly, a recurring enigmatic image in Marnie's nightmares as an adult is of a disembodied man's hand knocking against a window pane. It is the touch of someone other than her mother – the sailor who puts his hands on the young Marnie when she is having a nightmare – which traumatises her and leads to the confused hysteria and murder of the sailor with a poker by Marnie's own hands which sets into motion the central psychological conflicts of the film.

But however thematically valid this resolution is in terms of the motif of touch, it also raises another problem in terms of reading the film too easily as belonging to a modernist cinema of tactility. The resolution to *Marnie* is one which explains the source of Marnie's neurosis in terms of a repressed traumatic childhood memory. There is an attempt to tie up loose ends and provide a tentative hope for a possible cure for Marnie. This resolution may contain its own internal contradictions and ambivalences; and the final moments of the film have a vague tapering-off effect rather than a sense of a firm conclusion. But the need for this more traditional melodramatic resolution in which appearances are uncovered and explanations offered is still present. This more traditional resolution would seem to mark a regression, a movement away from the art-cinema-influenced ambiguous ending of *The Birds* the year before. Fassbinder has commented on this ending: 'I just couldn't make a film like Hitchcock's *Marnie* as *Marnie* is told, because I don't have the courage for such naïveté, simply to make such a film and then at the end to give such an explanation. I don't have that something which is a natural part of courage, but maybe some day I will have it, and then I'll be just like Hollywood.'[32] Fassbinder's own melodramas of the 1970s, produced within a firmly alternative film-making practice, consistently resist the kind of 'happy ending' which Hitchcock imposes on himself here. However much Hitchcock's work anticipates and then overlaps with the modern cinema of the postwar period through his development of the mental image, a film like *Marnie* makes it clear that his manner of thinking as a film-maker is still deeply entrenched in the pre-war period's conception of (as Deleuze puts it) 'the ideal of knowledge as harmonious totality, which sustains this classical representation'.[33] Hitchcock's desire for possession and control of his camera reaches a peak of intensity in *Marnie*. But it is also a possession bound up with loss – loss of the female star, loss of public interest in his latest work and, most damaging of all for Hitchcock, loss of a firm sense of control over the final result.

In *Red Desert* (which David Bordwell has termed an 'antilyrical melodrama'[34]), Antonioni, like Hitchcock, presents us with a heroine, Guiliana (Monica Vitti), who is mentally disturbed. Like Marnie, the experience with colours is often troubling for her and they become a sign of her mental instability. Also like Marnie, Giuliana is both strongly drawn to (and sometimes recoils from) the sense of touch. The film partly explains that Guiliana's mental condition was activated by a car accident but it is also clear that her problems run much deeper than that. What they are precisely is something which the film never attempts to locate, at least not within the conventional terms of melodrama to which *Marnie* is indebted. But like *Marnie*, the film holds out a tentative possibility at the end that the heroine will cope, will survive her mental ordeal. There is a moment early in the film when Giuliana is standing on the street and a newspaper drifts down from somewhere above her. As it begins to reach the ground, she holds it down with her foot and we observe the oddly fascinating sight of Monica Vitti's high-heeled shoe pressed against this newspaper before she lets it go. Rohdie writes of this sequence: 'For a moment, the narrative is halted as the paper descends along the wall bringing forward in its movement the sense of that movement itself, the effect of it on the colour and texture of the wall, the feel of the air, and then the narrative returns . . .'[35]

There is a similar moment in *Marnie*, after she checks an old suitcase, which contains the objects of her identity as Marion Holland, into a locker at a bus station. She takes the key over to a heating vent and drops it through, which we see in close-up, the tip of her high-heeled shoe delicately shoving the key down the vent until it disappears: four shots alternating between Marnie moving across the station floor, her gloved hand holding the key, her point-of-view shot of the vent and finally the key being dropped down. In *Red Desert*, we have a moment in which the narrative (such as it is) is suspended in favour of a moment of purely formal contemplation; in *Marnie*, we have a moment which serves a narrative function but which, in the organisation of shots, carries a fascination which cannot simply be reduced to that narrative function. These shots in *Marnie* are both classically economical in the narrative information they convey but also overdetermined in their fetishistic response to details – the gloved hand, the key, the high-heeled shoe – and in the fragmentation of Marnie's body in this brief journey from the locker to the vent. (In one of Godard's recent episodes of *Histoires du cinéma*, he extracts this shot of Marnie's shoe with the key out of its narrative context, slows it down and freezes it, allowing the latent abstraction of this moment to come forward.)

At moments such as these, Hitchcock and the European art cinema of the period come face to face. But Hitchcock must finally explain in a way that Antonioni does not. The abstraction of the moment involving the newspaper is part of a much larger system at work in *Red Desert* of exploring the elusive relationship between narrative and form, between surfaces and what may potentially lie beneath them. In Antonioni, stories, motivations, psychology, are ultimately swallowed up by the space and form of the film itself. Hitchcock's cinema implies such a possibility. But most of his films must come back around to narrativising and explaining. The reasons for these differences are complex, the result of a network of historical and cultural forces which have gone into making Hitchcock and Antonioni the kinds of film-makers they are. Fundamental, in the case of Hitchcock, are his ties to classical narrative cinema, to Hollywood and to the logic of melodrama, which always insists upon the need to explain and provide meaning, to reinforce and underline, to offer abundance rather than absence, a world in which surfaces must finally reveal. But in *Marnie* these revelations, while present, no longer seem completely adequate to the issues which the film has raised. It is almost as though this tactile world being offered up to us acquires such a fascination that no narrative explanation can possibly locate that fascination.

Durgnat has written that Antonioni and Hitchcock are 'like two rivers arising from the same range of mountains'. Antonioni leads us to 'the enigmas of experience' and away from 'the chatter of false explanation', while Hitchcock 'conjures up our nightmares only to shunt our minds into complacencies of conformism and unreality'.[36] This isn't quite right either, but it is indicative of a certain attitude towards the supposed inadequacies of Hitchcock's cinema during the period in which his later films were produced. (Durgnat's book on the director, excerpts of which began appearing in the late 1960s, was published in 1974.) This inadequacy towards his film-making practice was something which Hitchcock himself felt acutely. Two years after making *Marnie*, he saw *Blow-Up*. His response to the writer Howard Fast: 'My God, Howard! I've just seen Antonioni's *Blow-Up* (1966). These Italian directors are a century ahead of me in terms of technique! What have I been doing all this time?'[37] Hitchcock feels the pull, the attraction of this new conception of the image which he sees in the work of Antonioni and others, is aware of this development and is no doubt fascinated by it as he must clearly recognise its relationship to his own work. He wants to claim some part of this cinema for himself, not simply because it is fashionable but because he is entitled to do so. But he remains a film-maker perpetually on the dividing line between the pre-war classical cinema and the postwar modernist cinema in spite of himself.

All of this touching in *Marnie*, all these hands grasping at something – perhaps just the symptom of a man fascinated by a beautiful but unattainable actress. But why not also read those hands as reaching out towards something else – the postwar art cinema, a world equally unattainable to Hitchcock and which fascinates him even more?

Notes

1 Robert E. Kapsis has provided a detailed account of *Marnie*'s rehabilitation (which has occured primarily through *auteurist*, feminist and psychoanalytic writings) since the film's original release in *Hitchcock: The Making of a Reputation,* The University of Chicago Press, 1992. A certain skepticism persists, however. Slavoj Žižek, for example, classifies *Marnie* as belonging to what he designates as the fifth and final period of Hitchcock's career, a period of 'disintegration'. In Žižek, ed., *Everything You Always Wanted to Know About Lacan (But Were Afraid to Ask Hitchcock)*, London and New York: Verso, 1992, p. 5.

2 Paula Marantz Cohen, *Alfred Hitchcock and the Legacy of Victorianism*, Lexington, KT: The University Press of Kentucky, 1995, p. 154.

3 Marantz Cohen, *Alfred Hitchcock*, p. 153.This is similar to an argument made by Eric Rohmer and Claude Chabrol in relation to *Rear Window*: 'Everything happens as though they were projections of the voyeur's thoughts – or desires; he never will be able to find in them more than he had put there, more than he hopes for or is waiting for. On the facing wall, separated from him by the space of the courtyard, the strange silhouettes are like so many shadows in a new version of Plato's cave.' In *Hitchcock*, trans. Stanley Hochman, New York: Frederick Ungar Publishing Co. 1988, pp. 125–6. Originally published in French in 1957 by Éditions Universitaires.

4 Marantz Cohen, *Alfred Hitchcock*, p. 154.

5 Ibid.

6 The lack of a resolution at the end of *The Birds* is an obvious sign of this influence; the absence of a non-diegetic score is another. The release of *Marnie* came in the aftermath of a number of events around which Hitchcock was indeed being taken seriously as an

artist: the 1963 Museum of Modern Art retrospective, the choice of *The Birds* as the opening-night feature of the Cannes Film Festival, and an accelerating body of *auteurist* writings on Hitchcock which placed him at the forefront of the development of cinema. Truffaut's interview book with Hitchcock, published in 1967, was a culminating moment. See chapter three of Kapsis, 'Reshaping a Legend', pp. 69–121. Kapsis writes that prior to shooting *The Birds*, Hitchcock screened a number of European art films by Godard, Antonioni and Ingmar Bergman, p. 78. This incorporation of certain aspects of European art cinema into his work was hardly new to Hitchcock. At the beginning of his career in the 1920s, Hitchcock attempted to make use of various modernist developments in cinema of the period, particularly certain methods of Soviet montage and Weimar cinema. The most detailed account of this is available in Tom Ryall, *Alfred Hitchcock and the British Cinema*, London & Atlantic Highlands, NJ, 1996. Originally published in 1986 by Croom Helm Ltd.

7 Jean-Louis Comolli, *et al.*, 'The Misfortunes of *Muriel*', trans. Diana Matias, in *Cahiers du cinéma, The 1960s*, Jim Hillier, (ed.), Cambridge, MA: Harvard University Press, 1986, p. 73. Originally published in *Cahiers du cinéma* 149, November 1963.

8 François Truffaut writes that 'Hitchcock was never the same after *Marnie*' and ascribes this entirely to his falling out with Hedren. In François Truffaut, *Hitchcock*, rev. edn, with the collaboration of Helen Scott, New York: Simon and Schuster, 1984, p. 107.

9 Gilles Deleuze, *Negotiations*, trans. Martin Johghlin, New York: Columbia University Press, 1995, p. 55. Originally published in French as *Pourparlers*, Paris: Les Éditions de Minuit, 1990.

10 Sam Rohdie, *Antonioni*, London: BFI Publishing, 1990, p. 3.

11 Kapsis, *Hitchcock*, p. 129.

12 Donald Spoto, *The Dark Side of Genius*, New York: Little, Brown and Company, 1983, p. 508.

13 Deleuze, *Cinema 1: The Movement–Image*, trans. Hugh Tomlinson and Barbara Habberjam, Minneapolis: University of Minnesota Press, 1986, p. 201. Deleuze's approach to Hitchcock forms part of a tradition of French writing on this film-maker and owes a good deal to André Bazin's review of *Rear Window*, much of the Rohmer/Chabrol book, and to Jean Douchet's essay on *Psycho*.

14 Deleuze, *Cinema 1: The Movement–Image*, p. 200. While not citing Deleuze, Mladen Dolar, writing against the standard approach to the supposed structure of doubling in *Shadow of a Doubt* (1943), points out that in this film 'every duality is based on a third'. 'Hitchcock's Objects', in Žižek, p. 33.

15 Deleuze, *Negotiations*, p. 54.

16 Serge Daney, 'Godard Makes [His]tories, Interview with Serge Daney', in *Jean-Luc Godard: Son + Image*, Raymond Bellour and Mary Lea Bandy (eds), New York: The Museum of Modern Art, 1992, p. 164. Interview originally published in *Libération*, 26 December 1988.

17 Deleuze, *Cinema 1: The Movement–Image*, p. 205.

18 Deleuze, *Negotiations*, p. 54.

19 Deleuze, *Cinema 2: The Time–Image*, trans. Hugh Tomlinson and Robert Galeta, Minneapolis: University of Minnesota Press, 1989, p. 12.

20 Deleuze, *Cinema 2: The Time–Image*, p. 13.

21 Peter Brooks, *The Melodramatic Imagination*, New York: Columbia University Press, 1984, p. 41.

22 Raymond Durgnat, *The Strange Case of Alfred Hitchcock*, Cambridge, MA: The MIT Press, 1974, p. 363.

23 Spoto, *The Dark Side of Genius*, p. 497.

24 Robin Wood, *Hitchcock's Films Revisited*, New York: Columbia University Press, 1989, p. 189.

25 Mark's character combines several archetypal male characters out of melodrama: the sinister husband/lover figure, the doctor affecting a cure for the neurotic heroine, and the detective figure who uncovers the mystery and 'saves' the heroine. Durgnat's chapter on *Marnie* in his study of Hitchcock is very illuminating in tracing the cultural, generic and historical matter at work in the film. While aware of the film's debts to melodramatic conventions, he also compares *Marnie*'s ambitions with those of European art cinema. Arguing that the film's 'relationship to experience is that of the detective-story rather than the soul-fight', he nevertheless insists upon the film's 'intellectual intricacy' as being closer to the work of Bergman, Luis Buñuel and Bresson than that of Douglas Sirk (p. 368).

26 Raymond Bellour, 'Hitchcock the Enunciator', trans. Bertrand August and Hilary Radner, *Camera Obscura 2*, Fall 1977, p. 73.

27 Pascal Bonitzer, 'Notorious', in *Everything You Always Wanted to Know About Lacan (But Were Afraid to Ask Hitchcock)*, ed. Žižek, p. 153.

28 Stojan Pelko, '*Punctum Caecum*, or, Of Insight and Blindness', in Žižek, p. 115.

29 Mary Ann Doane has written that the look of the female protagonist in melodrama is often tied to a 'crisis of vision'. She writes of the woman's film that its 'narrative structure produces an insistence upon situating the woman as agent of the gaze, as investigator in charge of the epistemological trajectory of the text, as one for whom the "secret beyond the door" is really at stake'. 'The Woman's Film: Possession and Address', in Christine Gledhill (ed.), *Home is Where the Heart Is,* London: BFI, 1987, p. 286. In *Marnie,* however, Marnie herself is a highly problematic figure as an agent of the gaze,and the role of investigator for the epistemological trajectory of the text is split between a male figure, Mark, and a female, Lil. This partly results in a film in which many of the structures and elements of melodrama are present but so displaced and rearranged that a sense of melodramatic urgency is somewhat off-balance.

30 Spoto writes about the production of *Marnie*: '[Hitchcock] gave Robert Burks unusual instructions about photographing [Hedren's] face – the camera was to come as close as possible, the lenses were almost to make love to her.' (p. 500). These instructions to Burks evoke Hitchcock's description of the effect he was aiming for in the kiss between Ingrid Bergman and Cary Grant in *Notorious.* He told François Truffaut that the public, 'represented by the camera, was the third party to this embrace'. In Truffaut, *Hitchcock,* pp. 261-2. When Peter Bogdanovich asked Hitchcock whose point of view was being represented in the lovemaking scenes of *Marnie,* Hitchcock replied, 'I think they're in my point of view, really.' In Bogdanovich, *Who the Devil Made It,* New York: Ballantine Books, 1997, p. 538.

31 Chris Marker, 'A Free Replay (notes on *Vertigo*)', in *Projections 4 1/2*, John Boorman and

Walter Donohue (eds.), London/Boston: Faber & Faber, 1995, p. 124. While there are important thematic relationships between *Vertigo* and *Marnie*, it is significant that in *Vertigo* the act of touch is something which is frequently elided. Sexual penetration is completely secondary to Scottie's obsession with Madeleine, which is initially generated by her physical and emotional distance from him. In *Vertigo*, Hitchcock is still within the realm of love/obsession/fetishism as ideas, mental states, something bound up with looking rather than touching.

32 Wilfried Wiegand, 'Interview with Rainer Werner Fassbinder', in *Fassbinder*, New York: Tandam Press, 1981, p. 90.

33 Deleuze, *Cinema 2: The Time–Image*, p. 210.

34 David Bordwell, *On the History of Film Style*, Cambridge, MA, and London: Harvard University Press, 1997, p. 248.

35 Rohdie, p.159. Various claims for *Marnie* as a latent modernist text have been put forth in the years since its release. Jacques Rivette has said that in the midst of shooting *L'amour fou* (1968), he and the cast and crew went to see *Marnie* again. Rivette says that 'not only did we have the feeling that Hitchcock had already filmed the whole subject of *L'amour fou* and beyond, but afterwards this vision of *Marnie* integrated itself into the film for us'. In 'Time Overflowing', interview with Rivette by Jacques Aumont, Jean-Louis Comolli, Jean Narboni, and Sylvie Pierre, *Rivette: Texts and Interviews*, ed. Jonathan Rosenbaum, trans. Amy Gateff, London: BFI, 1977, p. 12. In Michele Piso's essay on *Marnie*, she compares the film's visual style to Mondrian, Bresson and Antonioni. 'Mark's Marnie', in *A Hitchcock Reader*, Marshall Deutelbaum and Leland Poague (eds.), Ames: Iowa State University Press, 1986, p. 292. I am also reminded of the occasional screenings *Marnie* received at the Collective for Living Cinema in New York in the early 1980s, often introduced by the avant-garde film-maker Warren Sonbert. Sonbert would insist upon *Marnie*'s formal audacity, arguing that the film was more avant-garde than anything by Antonioni. Sonbert's 1983 film *A Woman's Touch* is, in fact, a partial reworking of *Marnie*.

36 Durgnat, *The Strange Case of Alfred Hitchcock*, p. 31.

37 Spoto, *The Dark Side of Genius*, p. 525. Hitchcock and Howard Fast collaborated on a script for a film to be called *Kaleidoscope*. Rejected by the executives at Universal, *Kaleidoscope* was to be Hitchcock's boldest attempt to make a film influenced by alternative film-making practices of the period.

Impure suspense – Cary Grant and Ingrid Bergman in *Notorious*

Chapter 8
Suspense and Its Master

Deborah Knight and George McKnight

When Hitchcock was asked about suspense – which was often – he would tell a story that contrasts two scenarios. The first has the audience watching as some event unfolds, only to be surprised by an unanticipated outcome. The second keeps everything else the same, except that the audience knows in advance what had previously been concealed. Hitchcock says that the first scenario produces shock, but it cannot produce suspense because the audience lacks the information necessary to anticipate the unwelcome eventuality. If a group of people is sitting at a table and a bomb unexpectedly goes off, we experience shock. But if we know that they are unaware of the bomb ticking away underneath their table, we will be caught in the grip of suspense. In 1948, Hitchcock said that if you tell everything to the audience, making sure that they know more than the characters do about the fictional situation, 'they'll work like the devil for you because they know what fate is facing the poor actors'.[1] The same idea was reiterated to Truffaut when Hitchcock remarked: 'In the usual form of suspense it is indispensable that the public be made perfectly aware of all the facts involved.'[2] 'As far as I'm concerned,' he said in 1948, 'you have suspense when you let the audience play God.'[3]

Nevertheless, Hitchcock's films do not always conform well with theories that purport to capture what is basic to suspense. How, one might reasonably ask, could a basic theory of suspense fail to accommodate suspense's boldest classical master? Equally noteworthy, many signature moments in Hitchcock's films do not correspond to his own pronouncement that the audience should know everything about the situation in which characters find themselves. This lack of fit between basic theories of suspense and Hitchcock's work, as well as the tendency for his own work to depart from the maxim that best describes what Hitchcock himself calls the 'usual form,' is the starting point for our investigation of Hitchcockian suspense. We first establish what a basic theory of film suspense would look like, and compare Hitchcock's practice to that prototype. In the second part, we look specifically at four variations of Hitchcockian suspense in *Notorious* (1946), *Strangers on a Train* (1951), *Psycho* (1960) and *Vertigo* (1958).

Suspense: assumptions and theories

The basic structure of suspense involves an arc of events with a recognisable 'initiating event' that frames the development of plot action over time and leads towards a resolution of the problem that got the sequence underway.[4] This pattern differs from two others, the curiosity structure and the surprise structure.[5] Curiosity structures, most typically mysteries or plots revolving around an enigma, tend to be backward-looking, since what motivates plot action is the discovery of something that has already taken place. Curiosity plots suppress crucial information, but make that suppression central to the unfolding of the story. Surprise structures also suppress key information – for instance, that there is a bomb under the table – but for an entirely different dramatic effect, since the suppressed information is not hinted at until it bursts into view. Of course, these structures can overlap, so we find suspense, curiosity and surprise structures in, for instance, *Spellbound* (1945), *North By Northwest* (1959) and *Marnie* (1964), not to mention *The 39 Steps* (1935) and *Psycho*.

Suspense relies upon the audience's strong sense of uncertainty about how events will play out. This focused uncertainty allows the audience to imagine different possible outcomes that could impact positively or negatively on the characters. And the audience has to care which outcome obtains. The requirement of keen audience interest is why suspense is often associated with notions such as hope and fear. Typically, spectators hope that the central character will fare well in a situation where they fear that things will go badly. But Hitchcock denies that fear is necessarily a component of suspense, and cites as an example the switchboard operator in *Easy Virtue* (1927), who eavesdrops on a marriage proposal. Clearly, this example is intended to generalise, to cover cases in which it is the spectator, rather than a character within the fiction, who is caught up in the unfolding action. Hitchcock insists that the operator feels suspense, though there is no danger or threat in this scenario. Suspense that is keyed to how a limited episode resolves itself Hitchcock describes as situational, and he contrasts it with the sort of prospective suspense 'that makes the public ask itself, "What will happen next?".'[6]

Hitchcock's point is important. Suspense that lacks any real peril turns out to be a feature of many films, for instance romantic comedies. The worst thing that could befall the protagonists of most romantic comedies is that they fail to recognise that they are destined to be together. And often the device that Hitchcock associates with suspense's 'usual form' is exploited in such films, since the audience knows full well that the protagonists are perfect for each other, even though this is just what the characters themselves have to find out.

But we don't usually conjure up images of plots with happy endings when we think about suspense. It is more common to think of ones that foreground the potential for unhappy endings, and which expose their central protagonists to the threat of imminent danger: for example, action films and innocent-on-the-run thrillers and the female Gothic. Not surprisingly, these are genres Hitchcock favoured. And though Hitchcock distinguished between situational suspense, where we worry about how some present situation will resolve itself, and cases where we worry instead about what will happen next, it is actually a very fine distinction to make, especially since suspense is not merely a macro feature of narratives, governing a single arc between beginning and conclusion, but is also a basic component of individual sequences within an unfolding narrative – and as such can be found in films that one would not standardly think of as suspense films.

How do our imaginative projections work with respect to the unfolding of suspense stories? Factors such as audiences' expectations concerning genre and star personae play their role, and Hitchcock made use of both. Hans J. Wulff argues that the experience of suspense relies on the spectator's recognition of specific future-directed narrative cues called *cataphors*.[7] A cataphor is an advance reference signalling some event or action that could occur later in the story. Cataphors take many forms. Hitchcock excelled at creating object cataphors. The bomb under the table, provided the audience knows it is there, is just such an object cataphor. And the bomb illustrates Wulff's point that cataphors can sometimes encourage us to imagine future events that do not in fact happen. We will feel suspense whether or not the bomb goes off. Hitchcock's most memorable object cataphors have prominent roles in his films: think of Guy's lighter in *Strangers on a Train*, the key to the wine cellar in *Notorious*, or the $40,000 that Marion Crane steals in *Psycho*. But not all cataphors are objects. Some are stylistic. Consider *Vertigo*'s insistence on downward-looking shots that show Scottie's experience of the film's title disorder.[8] There are also thematic cataphors, such as the threat of discovery for Hitchcock's innocents on the run. This thematic cataphor directs our imagining of how situations play out every time, for instance, we think that Hannay will be recognised and turned over to the police in *The 39 Steps*.

Suspense cataphors operate both situationally and prospectively. From the moment Alicia takes the key from her husband's key ring, we know she is at risk and we worry on her behalf not only with respect to individual scenes but also how each scene will impact future action. The same is true for thematic cataphors. For instance, in *North by Northwest*, Thornhill is made drunk and forced to drive a car down a particularly treacherous road by villains who want him dead. The cataphor here is the possible death of the innocent protagonist. Even though Hitchcock plays the scene for comedy, the audience has little trouble imagining the grisly fate that seems to await Thornhill. During this scene, the suspense is situational. But because Hitchcock's cataphors reveal the internal logic of his suspense films, it is not surprising that what seemed to be merely situational has a progressive aspect to it. Though Thornhill survives his drive, we have nevertheless imagined the possibility that he would be killed, and the rest of the film gives us good reason to continue to imagine that he might wind up dead. Indeed, in one of Hitchcock's best moments of comic irony, Thornhill is 'shot to death' by Eve Kendall.

Cataphors help to frame our understanding of the dangers that threaten protagonists under conditions of uncertainty. But recognising the role of cataphors does not amount to a theory of suspense. Dolf Zillman and Noël Carroll have each produced accounts of what is basic to film suspense.[9] Whatever it is that keeps us caught up in the grip of suspense, both argue that it is not because we 'identify' with fictional characters caught in perilous circumstances. Their rejection of the concept of 'identification' needs some explanation, since it is a concept frequently used by people to explain their emotional responses to fictions, and indeed is a term that Hitchcock himself uses from time to time. Zillman's and Carroll's argument is that identification involves some sort of peculiar psychological 'merging' between spectators and characters. They doubt that such merging occurs – if it did, it would cause spectators to have the same feelings in suspenseful situations as the characters with whom they identify. Yet as Carroll has long argued – and Zillman agrees – an audience can feel intense suspense even when the characters on whose behalf the suspense is felt are quite oblivious to the perils facing them. The sort of relationship suspense requires is one in which spectators observe the fictional events from a position not identical to that of any of the characters. And since suspense is not, in fact, an experience available for God, Hitchcock's comment that 'you should let the audience "play God" ' only makes sense understood in this way. According to Zillman, the witnessing relationship is fundamentally empathetic. He argues that the audience's 'appraisal of conditions threatening protagonists and the immediate empathic reaction to their plight are essential contributors' to the experience of suspense.[10] Carroll's view is closely related, since he believes that suspense follows from a profound sense of moral empathy between audience and protagonists.

Zillman argues that suspense 'features sympathetic, liked protagonists in apparent peril, frequently so and in a major way'.[11] Hitchcock does not accept Zillman's point. In the Truffaut interview, he acknowledges that in the 'classical situation' of suspense – for instance, when there is a bomb under the table – suspense could be generated even if the characters in question were gangsters or villains.[12] While the degree of suspense might depend on the intensity of the audience's allegiance to the characters under threat, that does not preclude suspense in cases where those at risk are not particularly well liked by the audience.

Carroll maintains that our pro-dispositions toward characters 'are at root moral'.[13] Action in suspense films will 'point to two logically opposed outcomes whose opposition is made salient (to the point of preoccupying the audience's attention), and where one of the alternative outcomes is morally correct but improbable (although alive) or at least no more probable than its alternative, while the other outcome is morally incorrect or evil, but probable'.[14] We experience suspense because of our assessment of the morality of the two possible outcomes combined with our rating of their relative probability, where one outcome will be understood to be morally correct and the other incorrect. Not only does suspense depend upon the clear structuring of alternatives, it links the morality of the possible outcomes to their relative probability in a precise fashion: the morally correct outcome must seem comparatively less probable than the morally incorrect one.[15]

One of Carroll's examples of a suspenseful situation features our heroine tied to a log, at risk of being sliced in two at the sawmill. The logically opposed outcomes, obviously, are these: 'the heroine will either be torn apart by the buzzsaw, or she will not be'.[16] Hitchcock imagined this very scenario in 1949 as 'the legendary, though now sadly obsolete, circular bandsaw approaching the bound and gagged heroine'. But Hitchcock tells us more than Carroll about the way in which such a scenario works – at least in its 'classical' presentation. He writes: 'The saw will never reach its intended target. The plot may, and indeed should, indicate that the heroine's rescue is totally impossible. But deep in the subconscious mind of the spectator is the certainty, engendered by attendance at similar dramatic works, that the totally impossible will occur. The hero, though we have just been made aware that he lies unconscious at the bottom of a pit, surrounded by rattlesnakes, boiling oil, and the smell of bitter almonds, will appear in time to reverse the action of the saw and trap the villain. Or the saw will break down. Or it will appear that the villain has carelessly neglected to sharpen it – or, if it is an electric saw, to pay his electric bill.'[17]

While Carroll's theory insists that in any specific suspenseful situation there is one governing question, Hitchcock's description of the various ways in which the scene might play out shows how important two additional factors are in our experience of suspense fictions. One is the expectation of good fortune in the face of overwhelmingly bad circumstances which is largely based on our past experience with similar narratives. The second concerns the alternative ways in which an evil outcome might be prevented, since part of the suspense is in the audience's expectation that one or another of these will come to pass. But the resolution to a suspenseful episode may not itself be based on the principles of suspense. The resolution can instead be based on surprise: the villain's failure to pay his electricity bill may be something we only learn about when the power goes off in the sawmill.

The heroine tied to the log – or for that matter tied to the train tracks or abducted by a giant ape – is one of the most basic examples of suspense because the moral nature of the characters is never in question and the morality operative within the fiction is one that is both clear and congruent with the morality we take to obtain in our own experience. The heroine is good and virtuous, the villain loathsome and despicable, and the heroine's apparent fate is not only clearly immoral but cruel and vicious as well. Both Zillman's and Carroll's theories generalise from fictions where there is little ambiguity concerning whether our protagonists are (in Zillman's phrase) likeable, and whether the risks they run are both seriously threatening and unwarranted. The modification Carroll introduces is that our assessment of whether any outcome is morally correct or incorrect is constructed by the film. We do not simply map our own moral views onto the film, but make our judgements within the moral framework of the film's unfolding action. Thus Carroll is better able than Zillman to explain why we might feel suspense on behalf of certain protagonists – for instance criminals in caper films – who ordinarily would not be thought of as 'ethically upstanding', but who within the film have recognisable 'virtues' such as daring or ingenuity.[18] Still, even Carroll doesn't go as far as Hitchcock in acknowledging that suspense can be experienced even for 'bad guys', and even when what seems likely to happen is that they are about to get their just desserts.

A synthesis of Zillman's and Carroll's positions characterises one quite common prototype of suspense. Nevertheless, this prototype is a special case, best suited to popular and predominantly action-driven entertainments.[19] And while Hitchcock prided himself as a popular film-maker, and regularly made films that were action driven, the basic theories of either Zillman or Carroll do not wholly account for suspense in Hitchcock's films. The first departure from the prototype suspense situation is that (contra Zillman) Hitchcock often employs protagonists whom the audience may not like and might in fact actively dislike, doubt or otherwise feel suspicious about, or who (contra Carroll) do not always make up in 'virtues' what they lack in morally appropriate behaviour. Often in Hitchcock's films our relationship to the central protagonist – or, more frequently, to the pair of central protagonists – is complex, and thus not just a case of liking. The second departure is that the moral world of so many Hitchcock films is supremely ironic. This does not invalidate Carroll's notion that the film creates the moral situation against which we recognise certain characters or actions as moral and others as immoral. But it certainly complicates that process, and suggests that intratextual morality is not a condition that transparently determines our allegiance to specific characters or our assessment of particular actions.

An additional feature of Hitchcock's film-making, previously noted, is that Hitchcock departs from his own maxim that, in prototypical suspense situations, the audience should be 'made perfectly aware of all the facts involved'. This departure has ramifications for Zillman's and Carroll's accounts of suspense, since arguably the audience would need to be perfectly aware of all the facts in order reliably to know which characters to like, feel sympathetically towards or trust. The audience would also have to be aware of all the facts in order, reliably, to understand which outcomes should be construed as morally correct and morally incorrect within the moral horizon of the fiction – at least if that moral horizon is ironic or ambiguous. Making the audience perfectly aware of all the facts seems to capture very well the transparency condition that we have just mentioned. But Hitchcock's films do not always make the audience perfectly aware. In Hitchcock's films, suspense can be generated when the audience knows less than the characters, as well as when the director knows more than the audience. Yet such situations do not seem to be prototypical

Hitchcock regularly violates the transparency requirement of prototypical suspense by complicating our engagement with his films. Often he presents us with information or with situations which are incomplete or ambiguous and thus open to conflicting interpretations. And we may not always immediately realise that the situation we are watching is opaque in this way. Spectators initially believe they understand what they are watching, only later to discover new information that forces them to reassess what they had previously understood. For instance, whatever Marion Crane's anxieties about stealing $40,000 and being on the run, she has no particular reason to distrust Norman Bates. And although Hitchcock gives us independent reason to worry about Bates and his interest in Marion, our anxieties on her behalf cannot lead us to foresee her fate. In *Vertigo*, Scottie initially has no reason to doubt Gavin Elster, and neither do we. But for us, as for Scottie, even tentatively accepting Elster's story about his wife's mysterious possession by the dead Carlotta Valdez means operating within a dangerously restricted understanding of the real situation. Conversely, both audience and protagonist may know they know very little about the situation they find themselves caught up in – a situation best exemplified by Hitchcock's innocents on the run including Hannay and Roger Thornhill. This means that, like the innocent protagonist, we might misrecognise or misjudge the motives of those who wish to help.

We may be aligned with a central character who wishes to trust someone whom they – and we – have reason to doubt, thus causing us to worry on their behalf about the reliability of that other character. Consider Hitchcock's female Gothics: in *Rebecca* (1940), we are uncertain both about Max's moral position with respect to his new wife and about his role in the death of his first wife, while in *Suspicion* (1941), we might well distrust Johnnie's motives to the very end. Even when the central characters' moral positions and motives for action seem relatively straightforward, Hitchcock frequently introduces reasons for second thoughts: an example would be L. B. Jefferies's voyeurism in *Rear Window* (1954) (itself the predominant cataphor of the film), or the change in our moral alignment with Scottie as he becomes progressively more obsessed with Judy in *Vertigo*. Or we may feel sympathetically towards characters whose motives are not transparent either to us or to others around them and whom we also have reason not to trust, such as we experience with respect to Eve Kendall in *North by Northwest* and John 'the Cat' Robie in *To Catch a Thief* (1955). In early films, the question of whether a character should be trusted is usually a problem internal to the fiction, so in *The 39 Steps*, Pamela doesn't trust Hannay, though we know he is not the murderer she believes him to be. But in later films, it is not always clear whether we should feel confidence in

Hitchcock's central characters including Uncle Charlie in *Shadow of a Doubt* (1943), John Ballantine in *Spellbound*, both Alicia and Devlin in *Notorious*, Guy in *Strangers on a Train*, Marion Crane in *Psycho* and Marnie. While uncertainty about the fate of characters is central to suspense, Hitchcock often adds to this a deep uncertainty about characters' motives and intentions. And this means that we cannot be sure just how they will act in critical situations, and thus we cannot even be confident that their actions will be morally correct.

While the prototype theory of suspense nicely describes a major range of mostly mass suspense fictions, Hitchcock's practice departs from the prototype in recognisable ways. In the second part of this chapter, we will look at the use of suspense in four of his films. We start with *Notorious* as perhaps the best example from Hitchcock's *œuvre* of pure suspense, and thus as the film which comes closest to matching the prototype. We then turn to *Strangers* because Carroll believes it to be a challenge to his general theory of suspense. We examine the challenge *Strangers* poses and whether Carroll is right. Suspense is the overarching narrative structure of both *Notorious* and *Strangers*. But Hitchcock uses suspense for other purposes, notably in the service of other narrative ends, and we discuss two of these other ends with respect to *Psycho* and *Vertigo*.

Hitchcock and the practices of suspense

Pure suspense is the sort Hitchcock described in 1948, where the audience knows what the characters do not, namely, the fate facing them. Of course, *Notorious* is an imperfect example of pure suspense because our initial relationship with both Alicia Huberman and Devlin is problematic. Though we learn quickly enough what Devlin already knows, that Alicia is politically untainted by her father's Naziism, her life has, as she says, 'gone to pot' as a result, and she is marked in the film as someone who is assumed to be 'first, last, and always not a lady' – an attitude which Devlin with icy sarcasm attributes to the agents who have dreamt up the plot of using her as a mole to discover secrets about Nazi activities in Brazil. While we may not be, strictly speaking, uncertain about Alicia's or Devlin's motivations, we realise that he is severely compromised by his commitment to his job and his pronounced jealousy of Alex Sebastian, and that Alicia is increasingly endangered by his inability to act. And given that we have Cary Grant and Ingrid Bergman in the film's central roles, our primary interest is to know how things will come right in the end. So the governing question for this film could well be: 'Will Devlin rescue Alicia, or not?' – itself only a variation of: 'Will Devlin admit he loves Alicia, or not?' And as is characteristic of suspense narratives, both these questions are marked by an implicit intensifier: will he do it *in time*?

The elements that make suspense work in *Notorious* include our understanding of the intertwined generic conventions that direct the plot, our recognition of salient cataphors, the constant reiteration in the film's dialogue of its main suspense thematics, and a carefully constructed shift in narrative alignment that eventually permits the audience to know quite clearly the fate of the central characters. Up to the grand party at the Sebastians' mansion, the spy thriller is set against the developing romance between Alicia and Devlin. But with the grand party, the female Gothic comes to the fore, and with it the focus of suspense on the fate of the investigating woman.

The dramatic structure of the grand party builds across a series of smaller episodes which emphasise the risk Alicia is running and encourage us to expect that she will be caught, and caught directly, by Alex. Point-of-view shots are a stylistic cataphor during the party, with Alex often shown watching Alicia and Devlin from across the room, and Alicia and Devlin recognising that they are being watched. The risk to Alicia is magnified because the atmosphere is fraught with Alex's (and Devlin's) sexual jealousy. Alex is not initially concerned that his wife is a spy – he doesn't suspect – but that she is in love with Devlin; and both Alicia and Devlin know that Alex's jealousy is a threat to them and their plans. Two intertwined lines of suspense play out during the party: the suspense we feel on Alicia's behalf in case Alex catches her in the act of spying on him, and the suspense we feel in case Alex finds out what we already know, that his jealousy of Devlin is justified.

The uncertainty during the party sequence is whether Devlin and Alicia will be discovered, both as spies and as lovers. Initially, suspense is developed through object cataphors: the key, which Alicia passes to Devlin in the hand she holds out for him to kiss, and the rapidly diminishing supply of champagne. Devlin actually voices the worry that the champagne will run out, so we cannot fail to anticipate that Alex will find his key is missing. Once Devlin and Alicia are in the winecellar, the likelihood that Alex will catch them increases. Dialogue and cross-cutting intensify our suspense. Alicia announces that she is terrified and draws attention to how slowly they are cleaning up the broken bottle of 'vintage sand' that Devlin has fortuitously knocked over. This is cross-cut with the party upstairs. As the butler searches out Alex to suggest they will need more wine, Hitchcock begins to put in place the conditions he will exploit later for a crucial shift in narrative alignment from Alicia to Alex.

Alicia and Devlin are not, as it turns out, caught spying in the winecellar. But just as they go out through the garden door, they realise that Alex has seen them. What the party sequence has encouraged us to imagine is that Alicia will be caught directly by Alex in her role as an agent. Not only do we expect that she will be caught spying, but that she will know she has been caught. As Devlin kisses Alicia, their romance – however ironically it has been represented and however hopeless Devlin appears – comes back into the open. Whatever Devlin's private motivation, his public motivation is to take Alex's mind away from the winecellar and, with luck, create a plausible alibi to explain why Alicia and he have been found together, alone, away from the party. Though the kiss is in part an act put on to distract Alex's attention, it reveals to Alex the truth about Devlin and Alicia. So in a sense we have been right to anticipate that Alex will catch Alicia directly. With Alex observing Devlin kissing her, she has certainly been caught.

When Alex goes a second time to the cellar, he finds what we have expected him to, that his key is missing. From this point, his behaviour towards Alicia changes dramatically because he recognises that there are graver perils in view. At this point, the shift in narrative alignment occurs, positioning us with Alex rather than with Alicia. As a result, we witness Alex's discovery that the winecellar key is back on his keyring though we are not shown Alicia putting it there. And when Alex wakes his mother with the confession that he is married to an American agent, we discover precisely the fate that awaits Alicia. The shift from Alicia to Alex is chilling since it puts in place the conditions of pure suspense. We know Alicia's fate, because we hear the plot ourselves. But the shift in narrative alignment tells us something that arguably we didn't quite expect when the party sequence began. What we expected, what seemed most likely, and what Alicia's new, active role indicated was possible, was that she would be caught in the act and she would know she was caught. Indeed, she has been caught, but she does not know. The shift in narrative alignment from Alicia to Alex only emphasises the degree to which she is totally unaware of what Alex has learned.

Notorious, then, is as straightforward an example as we will find of a Hitchcockian suspense narrative deliberately constructed so that its final and most dramatic sequences play out with the audience fully apprised of the fate awaiting Alicia. And while our hero is not 'unconscious at the bottom of a pit, surrounded by rattlesnakes, boiling oil, and the smell of bitter almonds', he might as well be, given his persistent refusal to do anything to extricate Alicia from her exploitation by the American intelligence agents. But Devlin's last-minute decision to visit the Sebastians' mansion leads to Alicia's rescue, thus finally delivering the romantic conclusion that the beginning of the film had encouraged us to hope for.

In contrast to *Notorious*, *Strangers on a Train* is a test for the prototypical account of suspense. *Strangers* does not fit well with Zillman's theory that suspense hinges on the audience's concern for likeable protagonists. Indeed, the initial meeting between Guy and Bruno effectively blocks any easy audience sympathy for Guy, who passively allows Bruno to impose on his time and demand his attention. But, as has already been argued, Zillman's requirement of a likeable protagonist is unnecessary, since suspense can still be felt even if protagonists are less than sympathetic, and, indeed, suspense can be felt even for other characters, including villains, given appropriate circumstances.

But what about the audience's relationship to the antagonist, Bruno? Zillman suggests, plausibly enough, that such a relationship is governed by counter-empathy – exactly the reverse of the relationship that holds between audience and protagonist. In short, we should experience strong negative feelings toward Bruno and hope that his plans do not succeed. Yet Truffaut himself remarked that Robert Walker as Bruno is 'undoubtedly more attractive' than Farley Granger as Guy,[20] and noted Hitchcock scholar Robin Wood believes that there are scenes in *Strangers* where audience sympathy is with Bruno. Indeed, talking about the scene where Bruno drops Guy's lighter into a sewer – the lighter with which Bruno intends to implicate Guy in the brutal murder of Guy's wife, Miriam (a murder Bruno, in fact, has committed) – Wood asks: 'who hasn't *wanted* Bruno to reach the lighter?'[21] The scene with the lighter is located in a larger chain of events which includes Guy's attempt to race through a tennis match and elude the police who have him under surveillance in order to stop Bruno's plan. The macro question here would be: will Bruno succeed in framing Guy, or not? But this question does not mean that we are rooting for Bruno. While Truffaut probably only means that Bruno is an interesting villain, Wood is claiming that the audience feels suspense on his behalf and hopes he will get the lighter back. If Wood is right, this poses a problem for Carroll because the audience would be hoping for an immoral outcome. But we aren't compelled to agree with Wood, and it isn't clear that Carroll needs to give up on his theory in this instance.

The scene itself occurs quite unexpectedly. Bruno is bumped by a passer-by and the lighter falls straight into a sewer grate. Being mostly concerned with the emotional response of suspense, the prototypical theory does not say very much about the narratological aspects of suspense, chief among which is the drawing out of incidents where our interest in knowing how things will be resolved borders on fascination. But the drawing out of suspenseful events in order to maximise our concern is a Hitchcock specialty. So Guy's tennis match – which itself is dragging out against Guy's hopes for a quick victory – has been cross-cut with Bruno's trip to Metcalfe to frame Guy. Hitchcock continues this cross-cutting as Bruno attempts to retrieve the lighter. Carroll, who is quite aware of the narratology of suspense, has talked about the devices commonly used to stretch out the period of our suspenseful uncertainty. He mentions an example also favoured by Hitchcock: a clock ticking off the moments leading up to disaster. Bruno's fingers reaching slowly towards the small object that is his only means of controlling Guy serve an identical function.

This episode is really not a counterexample to Carroll's theory, since the micro question, 'Will Bruno retrieve the lighter from the sewer, or won't he?' does not mean we are supporting Bruno. A more serious challenge occurs if we find that suspense can be experienced even in situations where the morally correct outcome does not seem to be at risk. And Carroll acknowledges that a second episode from *Strangers* may be just such a situation. Bruno has fantasised a contract between himself and Guy such that each will 'do' a murder desired by the other. Thus, Bruno has killed Guy's estranged wife to clear the way for Guy's marriage to Anne, Senator Morton's daughter, and has demanded in exchange that Guy kill his father. The scene Carroll has in mind follows a night-time phone conversation between Bruno and Guy, in which Guy announces, 'I've decided to do what you want. I'll make that little visit to your father.' Perhaps we might fear that Guy is actually planning to kill Mr Anthony. But that is unlikely, especially since Guy has just confessed the whole wretched mess to his fiancée, Anne. Nevertheless, Guy's visit to Mr Anthony's house is suspenseful. This is emphasised by the near-*noir* lighting and the canted angles of the shots, not to mention that Guy takes along the gun Bruno has given him to kill his father. Like the lighter, the gun is a significant object cataphor in *Strangers*, but in this sequence, our anticipation about what Guy is doing with the gun may well be mistaken. If we take the question prompted by this cataphor to be, 'Will Guy kill Mr. Anthony, or not?' we will experience suspense – but we will have framed the wrong question, since Guy has no intention of harming Bruno's father.

What this scene demonstrates is that various projected versions of how things will work out are possible in films like *Strangers* where we do not have a straightforwardly empathetic relationship with our protagonist. Still, the main suspense-related emotion that we feel, arguably, is also the paradigm one: uncertainty. Even Carroll describes himself as bewildered.[22] We aren't sure what Guy plans to do, and have reason to worry that whatever it is, it might not go well. Significantly, this is a scene that runs against Hitchcock's dictum that in the usual cases the audience should know more about the circumstances than the characters, since clearly the audience knows less than either Guy or Hitchcock. But this sequence shows an important limitation in Carroll's version of the prototypical suspense theory. We may well feel suspense as Guy approaches and enters Mr Anthony's house, even though we don't for a second believe he's there to kill Mr Anthony, and thus do not feel that there is any obviously immoral outcome that could arise. Indeed, it is striking that Hitchcock uses suspense to aid of surprise in this sequence, since we have little reason to anticipate that it will be Bruno, not his father, whom Guy discovers in the master bedroom.

Of course, Carroll's theory of suspense based on moral empathy cannot exhaust the field, and we want to consider briefly an important case that moves us beyond Carroll's account. It is exemplified by those like Truffaut, Wood and Hitchcock himself – in other words, by film-makers, critics and scholars whose interest is not primarily at the level of empathetic regard for characters considered as if they were people. As Peter Vorderer observes, suspense can 'develop out of an interest in the progress of the story (*qua* story) and not out of an interest in the protagonist's well-being (the story as apparent reality)'.[23] Spectators are not restricted to viewing the film from one position alone, either for the story *qua* story or for the story *qua* reality. Our response can incorporate both perspectives, and just such a non-singularist account of spectator involvement with suspense fictions might explain Wood's idea that we hope Bruno in fact gets the lighter out of the drain. We do not hope this because we empathise with Bruno and hope his mad schemes succeed, but we do hope that the plot will arrive at a confrontation between protagonist and antagonist, and for Bruno to lose the lighter now might make such a confrontation impossible.

We turn now to two films in which suspense operates quite differently: *Psycho* and *Vertigo*. *Notorious* does exemplify Hitchcock's notion that suspense depends upon the audience knowing the fate facing the characters. *Strangers* also foregrounds Bruno's machinations. *Psycho* and *Vertigo*, by contrast, not only exploit our uncertainty about the fates of the characters, but the uncertainty of what we could reliably claim to know about the characters and the situations in which they find themselves.

Psycho is a lesson in the construction of suspense through cataphors, but unlike *Notorious* and *Strangers*, the opening sequence of *Psycho* presents us with cataphors that direct our attention away from, rather than towards, the events that will in fact take place. Cataphors can be used this way because they only signal *possible* future developments in the plot. Wulff argues that Hitchcock intentionally uses Marion Crane's theft of $40,000 as a misleading cataphor, and adds that it is later dropped 'for no reason'.[24] The theft and Marion's drive from Arizona to California raise all sorts of questions for a first-time viewer about what her boss will do when he discovers the theft, about whether the highway patrolman suspects that Marion has committed the theft, about how Sam will respond. First-time viewers might even hope that Marion will come to her senses and decide to make things right with her boss and his client. Wulff thinks that we are misled by Marion's theft, since it has directed us away from what eventually happens to Marion at the Bates Motel.

We agree with Wulff that the shower murder could not be anticipated from the events that precede it in the opening sequences of *Psycho*. That is only to state the obvious, since the shock of the shower murder is only partly its graphic brutality and extraordinary editing; what makes this murder of a female character so difficult to accept is that it is the murder of the only central character with whom we have any ongoing narrative alignment. And whatever our sense that Marion has violated the moral order, let alone the law, this is not necessarily enough for us to lose sympathy with her, especially when, after her sandwich in Norman's sitting room, she decides to do the right thing. But Wulff is wrong to think of the stolen money as a *deliberately misleading* cataphor. Rather,

Psycho is explicitly concerned with what happens when the completely unexpected intervenes in an otherwise fairly predictable course of events. Marion, reacting to the frustration of having to wait – seemingly interminably – for Sam to dig himself out from under financial obligations to his dead father and his ex-wife, for a moment thinks that the $40,000 could be converted into a realisable future with the man she wants to marry. The film gives us no reason to believe this could work out. That Marion should be stabbed to death in the shower at the Bates Motel minutes after deciding to do the morally correct thing is one of this dark film's many ironies. But we have not been *misled*; rather, we have been confronted with something that is virtually unthinkable in the construction of mainstream narratives. *Psycho* is about behaviour that is beyond expectation and common-sense comprehension. Suspense, in the beginning sequence of *Psycho*, is used in the service of shock, and shock is what Hitchcock uses to figure the unthinkable.

This brings us to the conclusion of *Vertigo*, which has something of the effect of shock, but in which Hitchcock uses suspense in the service of tragedy. The object cataphors in *Vertigo* are easy to list, and include staircases and stepladders, bouquets of flowers, Madeleine's outfits and hairstyle and, of course, the necklace that finally proves to Scottie that Judy and Madeleine are, at least in some sense, the same person. *Vertigo* is replete with stylistic cataphors as well, notably the visual cataphor of downwardness and descent, established right at the beginning of the film as Scottie clings desperately to the gutter of the roof from which his fellow police officer falls, and this stylistic marker recurs throughout the film as a figure for the fate of both Madeleine/Judy and, metaphorically, for Scottie himself.

But if *Vertigo* is a tragedy, it doesn't initally look that way. It seems to be a mystery focused on discovering what has happened to the enigmatic Madeleine. The possibility of tragedy occurs later and involves another one of Hitchcock's signature shifts in narrative alignment. But this one works quite differently from the one we have discussed in regard to *Notorious*. There, we became aligned with Alex, but this hardly required feeling sympathetically towards him (certainly not, since during this shift he plans Alicia's death). Nor did it alter our allegiance to Alicia. From the moment we observe Judy draft the letter that confesses her role in Gavin Elster's plot, the conditions are in place for a shift in our sympathy from Scottie to Judy. However peculiar Scottie's obsession with Madeleine has been – and Midge's reaction has given us some sense of this – we have accepted what he has imagined to be his role as her protector. And however disturbing Scottie's next obsession with the woman who reminds him of Madeleine, this has been naturalised because of his psychological breakdown upon having – or so he believed – witnessed Madeleine's death. Even though Judy destroys the confessional letter, the audience learns about her complicity in Elster's scheme as well as her equally obsessive love for Scottie. At this point, we know what Scottie does not yet know: Judy's true identity. Scottie does not discover who Judy is until she puts on Carlotta's necklace. But here we recognise what Judy does not, that Scottie has discovered her secret.

So when Scottie insists on taking Judy out for dinner, we have reason to doubt his motives. And when they arrive again at the church, our feeling of suspense is linked to our fear on Judy's behalf. As Scottie forces Judy inexorably up the steps of the belltower, commenting on the sentimental mistake she has made by keeping Carlotta's necklace, he pries the truth out of her about her role in Elster's wife's death. Not only does Scottie learn how Elster killed his wife, he finds out that Judy had been Elster's lover. And he guesses correctly that Elster had 'made Judy over' into Madeleine, a transformation eerily repeated by Scottie himself, one that involved not only making Judy look like Elster's wife, but creating a personality and manner that – as the audience has already seen for itself – is so very different from Judy's own.

The most important cataphor in *Vertigo* is a thematic one which, when we recognise it, helps us to understand the essentially tragic structure of the film. The additional cataphor is Madeleine, the object of Scottie's obsession. Scottie believed that Madeleine was the woman he pulled out of the bay and the woman who fell from the belltower to her death. What Scottie now knows is that Madeleine was never anything more than a fiction, a performance in an elaborate plot calculated to make him the unwitting alibi for murder. And in the last moments of the film, Judy again has become the perfect incarnation of Madeleine, not simply in terms of clothing and hair, but right down to speech and intonation. It is the insistence of the repeated cataphoric elements that tells us with such certainty that we know the fate facing Scottie and Judy. Indeed, once they emerge out through the trap door and stand beside the bell, their fate is sealed by the narrative causality of the film's most insistent cataphors: the stylistic motifs of descent, and the fictional/real figure of Judy as Madeleine. Judy's fate must be the fate Scottie believed to have befallen Madeleine, and Scottie's fate is to be complicit in the death now of a second woman, Judy, whom he understood as imperfectly as he understood the character of Madeleine when Judy played her. Just as inexorably as Scottie forces Judy to the height from which she falls, the suspense of *Vertigo* moves us inevitably toward Judy's death. Superficially, her death seems completely accidental – she is frightened by the unexpected apparition of a nun. But it is the culmination of the plot's tragic structure.

It is striking that Hitchcock only once made a film with the lyrical quality and tragic structure of *Vertigo*, and that after *Vertigo*'s middling results at the box office he returned to the bright/dark comedy/irony of *North by Northwest*. But perhaps it is more striking still that Hitchcock understood the close connection between suspense and tragedy so well that he could use suspense in the service of a tragic plot. After all, his earliest descriptions of suspense called for the audience to be given all the facts and, in a sense, to play God. This is remarkably close to the classical definition of tragedy, where what the audience in fact did know was the fate of the characters. *Vertigo* is, arguably, one of those rare things, a legitimate contemporary tragedy. While Hitchcock does not have the service of a Greek chorus, the question of the characters' fates is already implicit in the logic of the film's central cataphors.

Suspense is the operative logic of Hitchcock's films. Zillman and Carroll try to capture the logic of suspense, and there is much to recommend their work as basic theories. But Hitchcock requires something more. His vision is scarcely prototypical. It involves a complex mix of the main master genres of narrative: comedy, tragedy, romance and irony – in each case inflected by ordinary genres such as the spy thriller or the psychological thriller, and indeed often by more than one of these. And a corollary of this is just how regularly Hitchcock's films begin as one thing and then are transformed into something else – and always something more sinister. *Psycho* might be the paradigm example, but there are many more. Often these beginnings seem benign, as we find with the innocents on the run but also with films as different from one another as *Rebecca*, *Strangers on a Train* and *Rear Window*. But the benign beginning turns, sometimes quickly (*Strangers*) and sometimes more slowly (*Rebecca*, *Rear Window*), placing the protagonists at great risk. And the risk involved is often, as we have indicated, tied to fundamental uncertainties about characters' motivations and reliability.

Hitchcock regularly intermingles the basic narrative structures we discussed at the beginning: suspense, curiosity and surprise. Clearly, curiosity and surprise structures are central to Hitchcock's style of suspense, which so often develops in relation to a clear and pressing mystery, and is intensified by the periodic interpolation of shock or surprise elements. Also central is Hitchcock's cinematic self-consciousness. As Truffaut remarked, his films have a preciseness of stylisation that is almost diagrammatic.[25] Object cataphors are one obvious aspect of this cinematic self-consciousness, but so too are stylistic and thematic cataphors. Cataphors are not merely forward-looking cues; they ground and govern the logic of suspense in Hitchcock's films. So, to return for a moment to *Strangers*, it is obvious that Bruno must recover the lighter from the sewer. When Guy absently lends Bruno the lighter in the film's first scene, Bruno notes that its inscription, 'A to G', reveals Guy's relationship with Anne, which in turn shows why Guy is anxious to be divorced from Miriam. If found at the scene of the murder, it would not only implicate Guy but provide a motive for the murder as well. And it is only when the lighter falls from Bruno's hand after he is killed that the police realise Guy has been telling the truth all along.

Suspense depends upon highly specific advance references. These references encourage audience interest in the future developments of the plot and the fate facing the characters. To understand Hitchcockian suspense, we must recognise what Hitchcock recognised: the power of a narrative dramaturgy unrelentingly developed through cataphors.

Notes

A previous version of this paper was delivered to the American Society for Aesthetics Pacific Division (May 1999). We particularly wish to thank Allan Casebier and Noël Carroll for their comments. This research was supported by the Social Sciences and Humanities Research Council of Canada.

1 Hitchcock, 'Let 'Em Play God', *Hitchcock on Hitchcock: Selected Writings and Interviews*, Sidney Gottlieb, (ed.), Berkeley: University of California Press, 1995, p. 113.
2 François Truffaut, *Hitchcock*, London: Secker & Warburg, 1968, p. 58.
3 Hitchcock, 'Let 'Em Play God,' p. 113.
4 William F. Brewer, 'The Nature of Narrative Suspense and the Problem of Rereading', *Suspense: Conceptualizations, Theoretical Analyses, and Empirical Explorations*, Peter Vorderer *et al.* (eds.), New Jersey: Lawrence Erlbaum Associates, 1996, pp. 107–27.
5 Brewer, 'The Nature of Narrative Suspense', pp. 111–14.
6 Truffaut, *Hitchcock*, p. 58.
7 Hans J. Wulff, 'Suspense and the Influence of Cataphora on Viewers' Expectations', *Suspense: Conceptualizations, Theoretical Analyses, and Empirical Explorations*, pp. 1–17.
8 On the pattern of descent in Hitchcock's films, see Lesley Brill, *The Hitchcock Romance: Love and Irony in Hitchcock's Films*, Princeton: Princeton University Press, 1988.

9 Dolf Zillman, 'The Psychology of Suspense in Dramatic Exposition', *Suspense: Conceptualizations, Theoretical Analyses, and Empirical Explorations*, pp. 199–231; Noël Carroll, 'The Paradox of Suspense', *Suspense: Conceptualizations, Theoretical Analyses, and Empirical Explorations*, pp. 71–91.
10 Zillman, 'The Psychology of Suspense in Dramatic Exposition', p. 215.
11 Zillman, 'The Psychology of Suspense in Dramatic Exposition', p. 209.
12 Truffaut, *Hitchcock*, p. 58.
13 Carroll, 'The Paradox of Suspense', p. 80.
14 Carroll, 'The Paradox of Suspense', p. 78. Carroll presents this material in the form of a philosophical argument with numbered propositions. We have eliminated the numbers. A very similar definition of suspense was provided by Carroll in 'Toward a Theory of Film Suspense', *Theorizing the Moving Image*, New York: Cambridge University Press, 1996, p. 138. Carroll has also developed this theory in his *The Philosophy of Horror*, New York: Routledge, 1990.
15 Noël Carroll, 'Toward a Theory of Film Suspense', p. 101.
16 Carroll, 'The Paradox of Suspense', p. 76.
17 Alfred Hitchcock, 'The Enjoyment of Fear', *Hitchcock on Hitchcock*, pp. 117–18.
18 Carroll, 'The Paradox of Suspense', p. 78.
19 A point made generally also by Peter Vorderer, 'Toward a Psychological Theory of Suspense', *Suspense: Conceptualizations, Theoretical Analyses, and Empirical Explorations*, pp. 233–54.
20 Truffaut, *Hitchcock*, p. 166.
21 Robin Wood, *Hitchcock's Films,* New York: A. S. Barnes and Co., 1977 [1966], p. 65.
22 Carroll, 'Toward a Theory of Film Suspense', p. 117.
23 Vorderer, 'Toward a Psychological Theory of Suspense', p. 240.
24 Wulff, 'Suspense and the Influence of Cataphora', p. 14.
25 Truffaut, *Hitchcock*, p. 165.

The Birds – the maternal superego and the modern American family

Chapter 9
The Hitchcockian Blot

Slavoj Žižek

The phallic anamorphosis

Oral, anal, phallic

In *Foreign Correspondent* (1940), there is a short scene that exemplifies what might be called the elementary cell, the basic matrix of the Hitchcockian procedure. In pursuit of the kidnappers of a diplomat, the hero finds himself in an idyllic Dutch countryside with fields of tulips and windmills. All of a sudden he notices that one of the mills rotates against the direction of the wind. Here we have the effect of what Lacan calls the *point de capiton* (the quilting point) in its purest: a perfectly 'natural' and 'familiar' situation is denatured, becomes 'uncanny', loaded with horror and threatening possibilities, as soon as we add to it a small supplementary feature, a detail that 'does not belong', that sticks out, is 'out of place', does not make any sense within the frame of the idyllic scene. This 'pure' signifier without signified stirs the germination of a supplementary, metaphorical meaning for all other elements: the same situations, the same events that, till then, have been perceived as perfectly ordinary acquire an air of strangeness. Suddenly we enter the realm of double meaning, everything seems to contain some hidden meaning that is to be interpreted by the Hitchcockian hero, 'the man who knows too much'. The horror is thus internalised, it reposes on the *gaze* of him who 'knows too much'.[1]

Hitchcock is often reproached for his 'phallocentrism'; although meant as criticism, this designation is quite adequate – on condition that we locate the phallic dimension precisely in this supplementary feature that 'sticks out'. To explain, let us articulate three successive ways of presenting an event on-screen, three ways that correspond to the succession of 'oral', 'anal' and 'phallic' stages in the subject's libidinal economy.

The 'oral' stage is, so to speak, the zero degree of film-making: we simply shoot an event and as spectators we 'devour it with our eyes'; the montage has no function in organising narrative tensions. Its prototype is the silent, slapstick film. The effect of 'naturalness', of direct 'rendering of reality', is, of course, false: even at this stage, a certain 'choice' is at work, part of reality is enframed and extracted from the space–time continuum. What we see is the result of a certain 'manipulation', the succession of shots partakes of a *metonymical* movement. We see only parts, fragments of a never-shown whole, which is why we are already caught in a dialectic of seen and unseen, of the field (enframed by the camera) and its outside, giving rise to the desire to see what is not shown. For all that, we remain captive of the illusion that we witness a homogeneous continuity of action registered by the 'neutral' camera.

In the 'anal' stage montage enters. It cuts up, fragments, multiplies the action; the illusion of homogeneous continuity is forever lost. Montage can combine elements of a wholly heterogeneous nature and thus create new *metaphorical* meaning having nothing whatsoever to do with the 'literal' value of its component parts (compare Eisenstein's concept of 'intellectual montage'). The exemplary display of what montage can achieve at the level of traditional narration is, of course, the case of 'parallel montage': we show in alternation two interconnected courses of action, transforming the linear deployment of events into the horizontal coexistence of two lines of action, thus creating an additional tension between the two. Let us take, for example, a scene depicting the isolated home of a rich family encircled by a gang of robbers preparing to attack it; the scene gains enormously in effectiveness if we contrast the idyllic everyday life within the house with the threatening preparations of the criminals outside: if we show in alternation the happy family at dinner, the boisterousness of the children, father's benevolent reprimands, etc., and the 'sadistic' smile of a robber, another checking his knife or gun, a third already grasping the house's balustrade . . .

In what would the passage to the 'phallic' stage consist? In other words, how would Hitchcock shoot the same scene? The first thing to remark is that the content of this scene does not lend itself to Hitchcockian suspense insofar as it rests upon a simple counterpoint of idyllic interior and threatening exterior. We should therefore transpose this 'flat', horizontal doubling of the action onto a *vertical* level: the menacing horror should not be placed *outside, next to* the idyllic interior, but well *within* it, more precisely: *under* it, as its 'repressed' underside. Let us imagine, for example, the same happy family dinner shown from the point of view of a rich uncle, their invited guest. In the midst of dinner, the guest (and together with him ourselves, the public) suddenly 'sees too much', observes what he was not supposed to notice, some incongruous detail arousing in him a suspicion that the hosts plan to poison him in order to inherit his fortune. Such a 'surplus knowledge' has, so to speak, an abyssal effect on the perspective of the host (and ours with it): the action is in a way *redoubled in itself,* endlessly reflected in itself as in a double mirror play. The most common, everyday events are suddenly loaded with terrifying undertones, 'everything becomes suspicious': the kind mistress of the house asking if we feel well after dinner wants perhaps to learn if the poison has already taken effect; the children who run around in innocent joy are perhaps excited because the parents have hinted that they would soon be able to afford a luxurious voyage . . . things appear in a totally different light, although they stay the same.

Such a 'vertical' doubling entails a radical change in the libidinal economy: the 'true' action is repressed, internalised, subjectivised, i.e., presented in the form of the subject's desires, hallucinations, suspicions, obsessions, feelings of guilt. What we actually see becomes nothing but a deceptive surface beneath which swarms an undergrowth of perverse and obscene implications, the domain of what is *prohibited*. The more we find ourselves in total ambiguity, not knowing where 'reality' ends and 'hallucination' (i.e., desire) begins, the more menacing this domain appears. Incomparably more threatening than the savage cries of the enemy is his calm and cold gaze, or – to transpose the same inversion into the field of sexuality – incomparably more exciting than the openly provocative brunette is the cold blonde who, as Hitchcock reminds us, knows how to do many things once we find ourselves alone with her in the back seat of a taxi. What is crucial here is this inversion by means of which silence begins to function as the most horrifying menace, where the appearance of a cold indifference promises the most passionate pleasures – in short, where the prohibition against passing over into action opens up the space of a hallucinatory desire that, once set off, cannot be satisfied by any 'reality' whatsoever.

But what has this inversion to do with the 'phallic' stage? 'Phallic' is precisely the detail that 'does not fit', that 'sticks out' from the idyllic surface scene and denatures it, renders it uncanny. It is the point of *anamorphosis* in a picture: the element that, when reviewed straightforwardly, remains a meaningless stain, but which, as soon as we look at the picture from a precisely determined lateral perspective, all of a sudden acquires well-known contours. Lacan's constant point of reference is Holbein's *Ambassadors*:[2] at the bottom of the picture, under the figures of the two ambassadors, a viewer catches sight of an amorphous, extended, 'erected' spot. It is only when, on the very threshold of the room in which the picture is exposed, the visitor casts a final lateral glance at it that this spot acquires the contours of a skull, disclosing thus the true meaning of the picture – the nullity of all terrestrial goods, objects of art and knowledge that fill out the rest of the picture. This is the way Lacan defines the phallic signifier, as a 'signifier without signified' which, as such, renders possible the effects of the signified: the 'phallic' element of a picture is a meaningless stain that 'denatures' it, rendering all its constituents 'suspicious', and thus opens up the abyss of the search for a meaning – nothing is what it seems to be, everything is to be interpreted, everything is supposed to possess some supplementary meaning. The ground of the established, familiar signification opens up; we find ourselves in a realm of total ambiguity, but this very lack propels us to produce ever new 'hidden meanings': it is a driving force of endless compulsion. The oscillation between lack and surplus meaning constitutes the proper dimension of subjectivity. In other words, it is by means of the 'phallic' spot that the observed picture is subjectivised: this paradoxical point undermines our position as 'neutral', objective observer, pinning us to the observed object itself. This is the point at which the observer is already included, inscribed in the observed scene – in a way, it is the point from which the picture itself looks back at us.[3]

The blot as the gaze of the other

The finale of *Rear Window* (1954) demonstrates perfectly how the fascinating object that drives the interpretative movement is ultimately the gaze itself: this interpretative movement is suspended when Jeff's (James Stewart's) gaze, inspecting what goes on in the mysterious apartment across the yard, meets the gaze of the other (the murderer). At this point, Jeff loses his position as neutral, distant observer and is caught up in the affair, i.e., he becomes part of what he observed. More precisely, he is forced to confront the question of his own desire: what does he really want from this affair? This *Che vuoi?* is literally pronounced during the final confrontation between him and the perplexed murderer who asks him again and again: 'Who are you? What do you want from me?' The whole final scene, in which the murderer approaches as Jeff attempts desperately to stop him by the dazzle of flashbulbs, is shot in a remarkable, totally 'unrealistic' way. Where we would expect rapid movement, an intense, swift clash, we get hindered, slowed-down, protracted movement, as if the 'normal' rhythm of events had undergone a kind of anamorphotic deformation. This renders perfectly the immobilising, crippling effect the fantasy object has upon the subject: from the interpretative movement induced by the ambiguous register of symptoms, we have passed over to the register of fantasy, the inert presence of which suspends the movement of interpretation.

Where does this power of fascination come from? Why does the neighbour who killed his wife function for the hero as the object of his desire? There is only one answer possible: *the neighbour realizes Jeff's desire*. The hero's desire is to elude the sexual relation at any price, i.e., to get rid of the unfortunate Grace Kelly. What happens on *this side* of the window, in the hero's apartment – the amorous misadventures of Stewart and Kelly – is by no means a simple subplot, an amusing diversion with no bearing on the central motif on the film, but on the contrary, its very centre of gravity. Jeff's (and our) fascination with what goes on in the other apartment functions to make Jeff (and us) overlook the crucial importance of what goes on on this side of the window, in the very place from which he looks. *Rear Window* is ultimately the story of a subject who eludes a sexual relation by transforming his effective impotence into power by means of the gaze, by means of secret observation: he 'regresses' to an infantile curiosity in order to shirk his responsibility towards the beautiful woman who offers herself to him (the film is at this point very unequivocal – note the scene where Grace Kelly changes into a transparent nightgown). What we encounter here is, again, one of Hitchcock's fundamental 'complexes', the interconnection of the gaze and the couple power/impotence. In this respect, *Rear Window* reads like an ironic reversal of Bentham's 'Panopticon' as exploited by Foucault. For Bentham, the horrifying efficacy of the Panopticon is due to the fact that the subjects (prisoners, patients, schoolboys, factory workers) can never know for sure if they are actually observed from the all-seeing central control tower – this very uncertainty intensifies the feeling of menace, of the impossibility of escape from the gaze of the Other. In *Rear Window*, the inhabitants of the apartments across the yard are actually observed all the time by Stewart's watchful eye, but far from being terrorised, they simply ignore it and go on with their daily business. On the contrary, it is Stewart himself, the centre of the Panopticon, its all-pervasive eye, who is terrorised, constantly looking out the window, anxious not to miss some crucial detail. Why?

The rear window is essentially a fantasy window (the phantasmatic value of the window in painting has already been pointed out by Lacan): incapable of motivating himself to action, Jeff puts off indefinitely the (sexual) act, and what he sees through the window are precisely *fantasy figurations of what could happen to him and Grace Kelly*. They could become happy newlyweds; he could abandon Grace Kelly, who would then become an eccentric artist or lead a desperate, secluded life like Miss Lonely Hearts; they could spend their time together like the ordinary couple with a small dog, yielding to an everyday routine that barely conceals their underlying despair; or, finally, he could *kill* her. In short, the meaning of what the hero perceives beyond the window depends on his actual situation this side of the window: he has just to 'look through the window' to see on display a multitude of imaginary solutions to his actual impasse.

Careful attention to the film's soundtrack, especially if we approach *Rear Window* in retrospect, on the basis of Hitchcock's subsequent films, also reveals unmistakably the agency that hinders the hero's 'normal' sexual relation: the *maternal superego* embodied in a *voix acousmatique*, a free-floating voice that is not assigned to any bearer. Michel

Chion has already drawn attention to a peculiarity of the film's soundtrack, more precisely, its background sounds: we hear a diversity of voices to which we are always able to assign bearers, i.e., emitters. All *except one*, the voice of an unidentified soprano practicing scales and generally emerging just in time to prevent the fulfillment of sexual union between Stewart and Kelly. This mysterious voice does not originate from a person living on the other side of the courtyard, visible through the window, so the camera never shows the singer: the voice remains *acousmatique* and uncannily close to us, as if its origins were within us.[4] It is on account of this feature that *Rear Window* announces *The Man Who Knew Too Much* (1956), *Psycho* (1960) and *The Birds* (1963): this voice transmutes first into the awkwardly pathetic song by means of which Doris Day reaches her kidnapped son (the famous '*Que será será*'), then into the voice of the dead mother taking possession of Norman Bates, until it finally dissolves into the chaotic croaking of the birds.

The tracking shot

The standard Hitchcockian *formal* procedure for isolating the stain, this remainder of the real that 'sticks out', is, of course, his famous tracking shot. Its logic can be grasped only if we take into account the whole range of variations to which this procedure is submitted. Let us begin with a scene from *The Birds* in which the hero's mother, peering into a room that has been ravaged by the birds, sees a pajama-clad body with its eyes torn out. The camera first shows us the entire body; we then expect it to track forward slowly into the fascinating detail, the bloody sockets of the missing eyes. But Hitchcock instead gives us an *inversion* of the process we expect: instead of slowing down, he drastically *speeds up*; with two abrupt cuts, each bringing us closer to the subject, he quickly shows us the corpse's head. The subversive effect of these quickly advancing shots is created by the way in which they frustrate us even as they indulge our desire to view the terrifying object more closely: we approach it too quickly, skipping over the 'time for understanding', the pause needed to 'digest', to integrate the brute perception of the object.

Unlike the usual tracking shot that endows the object-blot with a particular weight by slowing down the 'normal' speed and by *deferring* the approach, here the object is 'missed' precisely insofar as we approach it precipitously, too quickly. Thus, if the usual tracking short is obsessional, forcing us to fix on a detail that is made to function as a blot because of the slow motion of the tracking, the precipitous approach to the object reveals its own hysterical basis: we 'miss' the object because of the speed, because this object is already empty in itself, hollow – it cannot be evoked other than 'too slowly' or 'too swiftly', because in its 'proper time' it is nothing. So delay and precipitousness are two modes of capturing the object-cause of desire, object small *a*, the 'nothingness' of pure seeming. We thereby touch upon the *objectal* dimension of the Hitchcockian 'blot' or 'stain': the signifying dimension of the blot, its effect of doubling meaning, of conferring on every element of the image a supplementary meaning that makes the interpretative movement work. None of this should blind us to its other aspect, however, that of an inert, opaque object that must drop out or sink for any symbolic reality to emerge. In other words, the Hitchcockian tracking shot that produces the blot in an idyllic picture is achieved as though to illustrate the Lacanian thesis: 'The field of reality rests upon the extraction of the object *a*, which nevertheless frames it.'[5] Or, to quote Jacques-Alain Miller's precise commentary:

> We understand that the covert setting aside of the object as real conditions the stabilization of reality, as 'a bit of reality'. But if the object *a* is absent, how can it still frame reality?

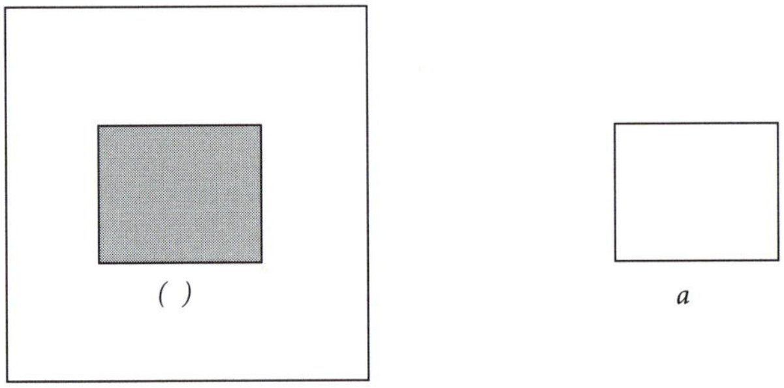

> It is precisely *because* the object *a* is removed from the field of reality that it frames it. If I withdraw from the surface of this picture the piece I represent by a shaded square, I get what we might call a frame: a frame for a hole, but also a frame for the rest of the surface. Such a frame could be created by any window. So object *a* is such a surface fragment, and it is its subtraction from reality that frames it. The subject, as barred subject – as want-of-being – is this hole. As being, it is nothing but the subtracted bit. Whence the equivalency of the subject and object *a*.[6]

We can read Miller's schema as the schema of the Hitchcockian tracking shot: from an overall view of reality, we advance toward the blot that provides it with its frame (the shaded square). The advance of the Hitchcockian tracking shot is reminiscent of the structure of a Moebius strip: by moving away from the side of reality, we find ourselves suddenly alongside the real whose extraction constitutes reality. Here the process inverts the dialectic of montage: there it was a matter of producing, through the discontinuity of the cuts, the continuity of a new signification, of a new diegetic reality, linking the disconnected fragments, whereas here the continual advance itself produces an effect of banking, of racial discontinuity, by showing us the heterogeneous element that must remain an inert, nonsensical 'blot' if the rest of the picture is to acquire the consistency of a symbolic reality.

Whence we could return to the succession of 'anal' and 'phallic' stages in the organisation of filmic material: if montage is the 'anal' process *par excellence*, the Hitchcockian tracking shot represents the point at which the 'anal' economy becomes 'phallic'. Montage entails the production of a supplementary, metaphorical signification that emerges from the juxtaposition of connected fragments, and, as Lacan emphasised in *The Four Fundamental Concepts of Psycho-Analysis*, metaphor is, in its libidinal economy, an eminently anal process: we give something (shit) to fill out the nothing, that is, to make up for what we do not have.[7] In addition to montage within the framework of traditional narration (as typified by 'parallel montage') we have a whole series of 'excessive' strategies that are designed to subvert the linear movement of traditional narration (Eisenstein's 'intellectual montage', Welles's 'inner montage', and the antimontage of Rossellini, who tried to forgo any manipulation of the material and allow for the emergence of the signification from the 'miracle' of fortuitous encounters). All such processes are only variations and reversals within the same field of the montage, whereas Hitchcock, with his tracking shorts, changes the field itself: in place of montage – the creation of a new metaphoric continuity by the combination of discontinuous fragments – he introduces a radical discontinuity, the shifting from reality to the real, produced by the very continuous movement of the tracking shot. That is, the tracking movement can be described as a moving from an overall view of reality to its point of anamorphosis. To return to Holbein's *Ambassadors*, the Hitchcockian tracking shot would advance from the total area of the picture toward the erected, 'phallic' element in the background that must fall away, remain simply a demented stain – the skull, the inert fantasy-object as the 'impossible' equivalent of the subject itself ($\$\diamond a$), and it is no accident that we find this same object in several instances in Hitchcock's own work (*Under Capricorn* (1949), *Psycho*). In Hitchcock this real object, the blot, the terminal point of the tracking shot, can assume two principal forms: either the gaze of the other insofar as our position as spectator is already inscribed within the film – i.e., the point from which the picture itself gazes at us (the eye sockets in the skull, not to mention the most celebrated of Hitchcock's tracking shots, the shot into the drummer's blinking eyes in *Young and Innocent* (1937)) – or the Hitchcockian object *per excellence*, the nonspecularisable object of exchange, the 'piece of the real' that circulates from one subject to another, embodying and guaranteeing the structural network of symbolic exchanges between them (the most famous example: the long tracking shot in *Notorious* (1946), from the overall view of the entrance hall down to the key in Ingrid Bergman's hand).

We can categorise Hitchcock's tracking shots, however, without reference to the nature of their terminal object, that is, based on variations in the formal process itself. In addition to the zero degree of tracking (which moves from the overall view of reality to its real point of anamorphosis), we have at least three other variants in Hitchcock:

- The precipitous, 'hystericised' tracking shot: see the example from *The Birds* analysed above, in which the camera draws into the blot too quickly, through jump-cuts.
- The reverse tracking shot, which begins at the uncanny detail and pulls back to the overall view of reality: witness the long shot in *Shadow of a Doubt* (1943) that starts with the hand of Teresa Wright holding the ring given her by her murdering uncle, and pulls back and up to the overall view of the library reading room in which she appears as nothing but a small dot in the centre of the frame; or the famous reverse tracking shot in *Frenzy* (1972).
- Last, the paradox of the 'immobile tracking shot', in which the camera does not move: the shift from reality to the real is accomplished by the intrusion into the frame of a heterogeneous object. For an example, we can return to *The Birds*, in which such a shift is achieved during one long, fixed shot. A fire caused by a cigarette butt dropped into some gasoline breaks out in the small town threatened by the birds. After a series of short and 'dynamic' close-ups and medium shots that draw us immediately into

the action, the camera pulls back and up and we are given an overall shot of the entire town taken from high above. In the first instant we read this overall shot as an 'objective', 'epic' panorama shot, separating us from the immediate drama going on down below and enabling us to disengage ourselves from the action. This distancing at first produces a certain 'pacifying' effect; it allows us to view the action from what might be called a 'metalinguistic' distance. Then, suddenly, a bird enters the frame from the right, as if coming from behind the camera and thus from behind our own backs, and then three birds, and finally an entire flock. The same shot takes on a totally different aspect, it undergoes a radical *subjectivisation*: the camera's elevated eye ceases to be that of a neutral, 'objective' onlooker gazing down upon a panoramic landscape and suddenly becomes the subjective and threatening gaze of the birds as they zero in on their prey.[8]

The maternal superego

Why do the birds attack?

What we must bear in mind is the libidinal content of this Hitchcockian stain: although its logic is phallic, it announces an agency that perturbs and hinders the rule of the Name-of-the-Father – in other words, the stain materialises the *maternal superego*. To prove it, let us return to the last of the above-mentioned cases: that of *The Birds*. Why do they attack? Robin Wood suggests three possible readings of this inexplicable, 'irrational' act by which the idyllic, daily life of a small northern California town is derailed: 'cosmological', 'ecological', 'familial'.[9]

According to the first, 'cosmological' reading, the attack of the birds can be viewed as embodying Hitchcock's vision of the universe, of the (human) cosmos as system – peaceful on the surface, ordinary in its course – that can be upset at any time, that can be thrown into chaos by the intervention of pure chance. Its order is always deceiving; at any moment some ineffable terror can emerge, some traumatic reality erupt to disturb the symbolic circuit. Such a reading can be supported by references to many other Hitchcock films, including the most sombre of them, *The Wrong Man* (1956), in which the mistaken identification of the hero as a thief, which happens purely by chance, turns his daily life into a hell of humiliation and costs his wife her sanity – the entering into play of the theological dimension in Hitchcock's work, the vision of a cruel, arbitrary and impenetrable God who can bring down catastrophe at any moment.

For the second, 'ecological' reading, the film's title could have been *Birds of the World, Unite!*: in this reading, the birds function as a condensation of exploited nature that finally rises up against man's heedless exploitation. In support of this interpretation, we can cite the fact that Hitchcock selected his attacking birds almost exclusively from species known for their gentle, nonaggressive nature: sparrows, seagulls, a few crows.

The third reading sees the key to the film in the intersubjective relations between the main characters (Melanie, Mitch and his mother), which are far from being merely an insignificant sideline to the 'true' plot, the attack of the birds: the attacking birds only 'embody' a fundamental discord, a disturbance, a derailment in those relations. The pertinence of this interpretation emerges if we consider *The Birds* within the context of

Hitchcock's earlier (and later) films; in other words, to play on one of Lacan's homophonies, if we are to take the films seriously, we can only do so if we take them serially.[10]

In writing of Poe's 'The Purloined Letter', Lacan makes reference to a game of logic: we take a random series of 0s and 1s – 100101100, for example – and as soon as the series is articulated into linked triads (100, 001, 010, etc.), rules of succession will emerge (a triad with 0 at the end cannot be followed by a triad that has 1 as its middle term, and so on).[11] The same is true of Hitchcock's films: if we consider them as a whole we have an accidental, random series, but as soon as we separate them into linked triads (and exclude those films that are not part of the 'Hitchcockian universe', the 'exceptions', the results of various compromises), each triad can then be seen to be linked by some theme, some common structuring principle. For example, take the following five films: *The Wrong Man*, *Vertigo* (1958), *North by Northwest* (1959), *Psycho* and *The Birds*: no single theme can be found to link all the films in such a series, yet such themes can be found if we consider them in groups of three. The first triad concerns 'false identity': in *The Wrong Man*, the hero is wrongly identified as the burglar; in *Vertigo* the hero is mistaken about the identity of the false Madeleine; in *North by Northwest* Soviet spies mistakenly identify the film's hero as the mysterious CIA agent 'George Kaplan'. As for the great trilogy *Vertigo*, *North by Northwest* and *Psycho*, it is very tempting to regard these three key Hitchcock films as the articulation of three different versions of filling the gap in the other. Their formal problem is the same: the relationship between a lack and a factor (a person) that tries to compensate for it. In *Vertigo*, the hero attempts to compensate for the absence of the woman he loves, an apparent suicide, on a level that is literally *imaginary*: he tries, by means of dress, hairstyle and so forth, to recreate the image of the lost woman. In *North by Northwest*, we are on the *symbolic* level: we are dealing with an empty name, the name of a nonexistent person ('Kaplan'), a signifier without a bearer, which becomes attached to the hero out of sheer chance. In *Psycho*, finally, we reach the level of the *real*: Norman Bates, who dresses in his mother's clothes, speaks with her voice, etc., wants neither to resuscitate her image nor act in her name; he wants to take her place in the real – evidence of a psychotic state.

If the middle triad, therefore, is that of the 'empty place', the final one is in its turn united around the motif of the *maternal superego*: the heroes of these three films are fatherless, they have a mother who is 'strong', who is 'possessive', who disturbs the 'normal' sexual relationship. At the very beginning of *North by Northwest* the film's hero, Roger Thornhill (Cary Grant), is shown with his scornful, mocking mother, and it is not difficult to guess why he is four times divorced; in *Psycho*, Norman Bates (Anthony Perkins) is directly controlled by the voice of his dead mother, which instructs him to kill any woman to whom he is sexually attracted; in the case of the mother of Mitch Brenner (Rod Taylor), hero of *The Birds*, mocking disdain is replaced by a zealous concern for her son's fate, a concern that is perhaps even more effective in blocking any lasting relationship he might have with a woman.

There is another trait common to these three films: from one film to the next, the figure of a threat in the shape of birds assumes greater prominence. In *North by Northwest* we have what is perhaps the most famous Hitchcockian scene, the attack by the plane – a steel bird – that pursues the hero across a flat, sun-baked landscape; in *Psycho*, Norman's room is filled with stuffed mounted birds, and even the body of his mummified mother reminds us of a stuffed bird; in *The Birds*, after the (metaphorical) steel bird and the (metonymic) stuffed birds, we finally have the actual live birds attacking the town.

The decisive thing is to perceive the link between the two traits: the terrifying figure of the birds is actually the embodiment in the real of a discord, an unresolved tension in intersubjective relations. In the film, the birds are like the plague in Oedipus's Thebes: they are the incarnation of a fundamental disorder in family relationships – the father is absent, the paternal function (the function of pacifying law, the Name-of-the-Father) is suspended and that vacuum is filled by the 'irrational' maternal superego, arbitrary, wicked, blocking 'normal' sexual relationship (only possible under the sign of the paternal metaphor). The dead end *The Birds* is really about is, of course, that of the modern American family: the deficient paternal ego-ideal makes the law 'regress' toward a ferocious maternal superego, affecting sexual enjoyment – the decisive trait of the libidinal structure of 'pathological narcissism': 'Their unconscious impressions of the mother are so overblown and so heavily influenced by aggressive impulses, and the quality of her care is so little attuned to the child's needs, that in the child's fantasies the mother appears as a devouring bird.'[12]

From the Oedipal journey to the 'pathological narcissist'

How should we locate this figuration of the maternal superego in the totality of Hitchcock's work? The three main stages of Hitchcock's career can be conceived precisely as three variations on the theme of the impossibility of the sexual relationship. Let us begin with the first Hitchcockian classic, *The 39 Steps* (1935): all the animated action of the film should not deceive us for a minute – its function is ultimately just to put the love couple to the test and thus render possible their final reunion. It is on account of this feature that *The 39 Steps* starts the series of Hitchcock's English films of the second half of the 1930s, all of which, with the exception of the last (*Jamaica Inn* (1939)), relate the same story of the *initiation of an amorous couple*. They are all stories of a couple tied (sometimes literally: note the role of handcuffs in *The 39 Steps*) by accident and then maturing through a series of ordeals. All these films are thus actually variations on the fundamental motif of the bourgeois ideology of marriage, gaining its first and perhaps noblest expression in Mozart's *Magic Flute*. The parallel could here be expanded to details: the mysterious woman who charges the hero with his mission (the stranger killed in Hannay's apartment in *The 39 Steps*; the nice old lady who vanishes in the film of the same title), is she not a kind of reincarnation of the 'Queen of the Night'? The black Monostatos, is he not reincarnated in the murderous drummer with blackened face in *Young and Innocent*? In *The Lady Vanishes* (1938), the hero attracts the attention of his future love by playing what? A flute, of course!

The innocence lost on this voyage of initiation is best presented in the remarkable figure of Mr Memory, whose number in the music hall opens and closes the film. He is a man who 'remembers everything', a personification of pure automatism and, at the same time, the absolute ethic of the signifier (in the film's final scene, he answers Hannay's question 'What are "the thirty-nine-steps"?', although he knows the answer could cost him his life – he is simply obliged to honour his public engagement, to answer any question whatsoever). There is something of the fairy tale in this figure of a Good Dwarf who must die in order that the liaison of the amorous couple finally be established. Mr

Memory embodies a pure, asexual gapless knowledge, a signifying chain that works absolutely automatically, without any traumatic stumbling block hindering its course. What we must be careful about is the precise moment of his death: he dies after answering the question 'What are "the thirty-nine steps"?', i.e., after revealing the MacGuffin, the secret propelling the story. By disclosing it to the public in the music hall (which stands here for the big Other of common opinion), he delivers Hannay from the awkward position of 'persecuted persecutor'. The two circles (that of the police chasing Hannay and that of Hannay himself in pursuit of the real culprit) rejoin, Hannay is exonerated in the eyes of the big Other, and the real culprits are unmasked. At this point, the story could end since it was sustained solely by this intermediary state, by Hannay's ambiguous position *vis-à-vis* the big Other: guilty in the eyes of the big Other, he is at the same time on the track of the real culprits.

It is this position of the 'persecuted persecutor' that already displays the motif of the 'transference of guilt': Hannay is falsely accused, the guilt is transferred onto him – but whose guilt is it? The guilt of the *obscene*, '*anal' father* personified by the mysterious leader of the spy network. At the film's end, we witness *two* consecutive deaths: first the leader of the spy ring kills Mr Memory, then the police, this instrument of the big Other, shoot down the leader, who falls from his theatre box onto the podium (this is an exemplary place of denouement in Hitchcock's films: *Murder* (1930), *Stage Fright* (1950), *I Confess* (1953)). Mr Memory and the leader of the spy ring represent the two sides of the same pre-Oedipal conjunction: the Good Dwarf with his gapless undivided knowledge, and the mean 'anal father', the master who pulls the strings of this knowledge-automaton, a father who exhibits in an obscene way his shortened little finger – an ironic allusion to his castration. (We encounter a homologous split in Robert Rossen's *The Hustler* (1961), on the relationship between the professional billiard player, an incarnation of the pure ethic of the game (Jackie Gleason), and his corrupt boss (George C. Scott).) The story begins with an act of 'interpellation' that subjectivises the hero, i.e., it constitutes him as desiring by evoking the MacGuffin, the object-cause of his desire (the message of the 'Queen of the Night', the mysterious stranger who is slaughtered in Hannay's apartment). The Oedipal voyage in pursuit of the father, which constitutes the bulk of the film, ends with the 'anal' father's death. By means of his death, he can assume his place as metaphor, as the Name-of-the-Father, thus rendering possible the amorous couple's final reunion, their 'normal' sexual relation which, according to Lacan, can take place only under the sign of the paternal metaphor.

In addition to Hannay and Pamela in *The 39 Steps*, couples tied by chance and reunited through ordeal are Ashenden and Elsa in *The Secret Agent* (1936), Robert and Erica in *Young and Innocent*, Gilbert and Iris in *The Lady Vanishes* – with the notable exception of *Sabotage* (1936), where the triangle of Sylvia, her criminal husband Verloc and the detective Ted foreshadows the conjuncture characteristic of Hitchcock's next stage (the Selznick period). Here, the story is, as a rule, narrated from the point of view of a woman divided between two men, the elderly figure of a villain (her father or her aged husband, embodying one of the typical Hitchcockian figures, that of a villain who is aware of the evil in himself and who strives after his own destruction) and the younger, somewhat insipid 'good guy' whom she chooses at the end.[13] In addition to Sylvia, Verloc and Ted in *Sabotage*, the main cases of such triangles are Carol Fisher, divided between loyalty to her pro-Nazi father and love for the young American journalist, in *Foreign Correspondent*; Charlie, divided between her murderous uncle of the same name and the detective Jack, in *Shadow of a Doubt*; and, of course, Alicia, divided between her aged husband Sebastian and Devlin, in *Notorious*. (The notable exception here is *Under Capricorn*, where the heroine resists the charm of a young seducer and returns to her aged, criminal husband after confessing that the crime her husband was convicted for was her own.) The third stage again shifts the accent to the male hero to whom the maternal superego blocks access, thus prohibiting a 'normal' sexual relation (from Bruno in *Strangers on a Train* (1951) to the 'necktie murderer' in *Frenzy*).

Where should we look for the wider frame of reference enabling us to confer a kind of theoretical consistency on this succession of the three forms of (the impossibility of) sexual relationship? Here, we are tempted to venture a somewhat quick 'sociological' answer by invoking the three successive forms of the libidinal structure of the subject exhibited in capitalist society during the past century: the 'autonomous' individual of the Protestant ethic, the heteronomous 'organisation man', and the type gaining predominance today, the 'pathological narcissist'. The crucial thing to emphasise here is that the so-called 'decline of the Protestant ethic' and the appearance of the 'organisation man', i.e., the replacement of the ethic of individual responsibility by the ethic of the heteronomous individual, oriented toward others, leaves intact the underlying frame of the ego–ideal. It is merely its contents that change: the ego-ideal becomes 'externalised' as the expectations of the social group to which the individual belongs. The source of moral satisfaction is no longer the feeling that we resisted the pressure of our milieu and remained true to ourselves (i.e., to our paternal ego-ideal), but rather the feeling of loyalty to the group. The subject looks at himself through the eyes of the group, he strives to merit its love and esteem.

The third stage, the arrival of the 'pathological narcissist', breaks precisely with this underlying frame of the ego–ideal common to the first two forms. Instead of the integration of a symbolic *law*, we have a multitude of *rules* to follow – rules of accommodation telling us 'how to succeed'. The narcissistic subject knows only the 'rules of the (social) game' enabling him to manipulate others; social relations constitute for him a playing field in which he assumes 'roles', not proper symbolic mandates; he stays clear of any kind of binding commitment that would imply a proper symbolic identification. He is a radical *conformist* who paradoxically experiences himself as an *outlaw*. All this is, of course, already a commonplace of social psychology; what usually goes unnoticed, however, is that this disintegration of the ego–ideal entails the installation of a 'maternal' superego that does not prohibit enjoyment but, on the contrary, imposes it and punishes 'social failure' in a far more cruel and severe way, through an unbearable and self-destructive anxiety. All the babble about the 'decline of paternal authority' merely conceals the resurgence of this incomparably more oppressive agency. Today's 'permissive' society is certainly not less 'repressive' than the epoch of the 'organisation man', that obsessive servant of the bureaucratic institution; the sole difference lies in the fact that in a 'society that demands submission to the rules of social intercourse but refuses to ground those rules in a code of moral conduct',[14] i.e., in the ego–ideal, the social demand assumes the form of a harsh, punitive superego.

We could also approach 'pathological narcissism' on the basis of Saul Kripke's criticism of the theory of descriptions, i.e., from his premise that the meaning of a name (proper or of a natural kind) can never be reduced to a set of descriptive features that characterise the object denoted by it. The name always functions as a 'rigid designator', referring to the same object even if all properties contained in its meaning prove false.[15] Needless to say, the Kripkian notion of the 'rigid designator' overlaps perfectly with the Lacanian notion of the 'master signifier', i.e., of a signifier that does not denote some positive property of the object but establishes, by means of its own act of enunciation, a new intersubjective relation between speaker and hearer. If, for example, I tell somebody 'You are my master', I confer upon him a certain symbolic 'mandate' that is not contained in the set of his positive properties but results from the very performative force of my utterance, and I create thereby a new symbolic reality, that of a master–disciple relationship between the two of us, within which each of us assumes a certain commitment. The paradox of the 'pathological narcissist' is, however, that *for him, language does indeed function according to the theory of descriptions*: the meaning of words is reduced to the positive features of the denoted object, above all those that concern his narcissistic interests. Let us exemplify this apropos of the eternally tedious feminine question: 'Why do you love me?' In love proper, this question is, of course, unanswerable (which is why woman ask it in the first place), i.e., the only appropriate answer is 'Because there is something in you more than yourself, some indefinite X that attracts me, but that cannot be pinned down to any positive quality'. In other words, if we answer it with a catalogue of positive properties ('I love you because of the shape of your breasts, because of the way you smile'), this is at best a mocking imitation of love proper. The 'pathological narcissist' is, on the other hand, somebody who *is* able to answer such a question by enumerating a definite list of properties: for him, the idea that love is a commitment transcending an attachment to a series of qualities that could gratify his wishes is simply beyond comprehension.[16] And the way to hystericise the 'pathological narcissist' is precisely to force upon him some symbolic mandate that cannot be grounded in its properties. Such a confrontation brings about the hysterical question, 'Why am I what you are saying that I am?' Think of Roger O. Thornhill in Hitchcock's *North by Northwest*, a pure 'pathological narcissist' if ever there was one, who all of a sudden, without any apparent reason, finds himself pinned to the signifier 'Kaplan'; the shock of this encounter derails his narcissistic economy and opens up to him the road of gradual access to 'normal' sexual relations under the sign of the Name-of-the-Father (which is why *North by Northwest* is a variation of the formula of *The 39 Steps*).[17]

We can now see how the three versions of the impossibility of sexual relationship in Hitchcock's films refer to these three types of libidinal economy. The couple's initiating voyage, with its obstacles stirring the desire of reunification, is firmly grounded in the classical ideology of the 'autonomous' subject strengthened through ordeal; the resigned paternal figure of Hitchcock's next stage evokes the decline of this 'autonomous' subject to whom is opposed the victorious, insipid 'heteronomous' hero; and finally, it is not difficult to recognise in the typical Hitchcockian hero of the 1950s and 1960s the features of the 'pathological narcissist' dominated by the obscene figure of the maternal superego. Hitchcock is thus staging again and again the vicissitudes of the family in late-capitalist society; the real 'secret' of his films is ultimately always the family secret, its tenebrous reverse.

A mental experiment: *The Birds* without birds

Although Hitchcock's birds do give body to the agency of the maternal superego, the essential thing is nevertheless *not* to seize upon the link between the two traits we have noted – the appearance of the ferocious assailant birds, the blockage of 'normal' sexual relations by the intervention of the maternal superego – as a sign relationship, as a correlative between a 'symbol' and its 'signification'. The birds do not 'signify' the maternal superego, they do not 'symbolise' blocked sexual relations, the 'possessive' mother, and so on; they are, rather, the making present in the real, the objectivisation, the incarnation of the fact that, on the symbolising level, something 'has not worked out', in short, the objectivisation–positivisation of a *failed* symbolisation. In the terrifying presence of the attacking birds, a certain lack, a certain failure assumes positive existence. At first glance, this distinction may appear factitious, vague; that is why we shall try to explicate it by means of a fairly elementary test question: how might the film have been constructed if the birds were to function *in fact* as the 'symbol' of blocked sexual relations?

The answer is simple: first, we must imagine *The Birds* as a film *without birds*. We would then have a typically American drama about a family in which the son goes from one woman to another because he is unable to free himself from the pressure exerted by a possessive mother, a drama similar to dozens of others that have appeared on American stages and screens, particularly in the 1950s: the tragedy of a son playing with the chaos of his sexual life for what was in those days referred to as the mother's inability to 'live her own life', to 'expend her vital energy', and the mother's emotional breakdown when some woman finally manages to take away her son, all seasoned with a touch of 'psychoanalytic' salt à la Eugene O'Neill or Tennessee Williams and acted, if possible, in a psychologistic, Actors' Studio style – the common ground of the American theatre at mid-century.

Next, in such a drama we must imagine the appearance from time to time, particularly at crucial moments of emotional intrigue (the son's first encounter with his future wife, the mother's breakdown, etc.), of birds – in the background, as part of the ambience: the opening scene (the meeting of Mitch and Melanie in the pet shop, the purchase of the lovebirds) could perhaps remain as it is; and, after the emotion-charged scene of conflict between mother and son, when the sorrowing mother withdraws to the seacoast, we might hear the cawing of birds. In such a film, the birds, even though or, rather, *because* they do not play a direct role in the development of the story, would be 'symbols', they would 'symbolise' the tragic necessity of the mother's renunciation, her helplessness, or whatever – and everyone would know what the birds signified, everyone would clearly recognise that the film was depicting an emotional drama of a son facing up to a possessive mother who is trying to transfer onto him the price of her own failure, and the 'symbolic' role of the birds would be indicated by the title, which would remain unchanged: *The Birds*.

Now, what did Hitchcock do? In his film, the birds are not 'symbols' at all, they play a direct part in the story as something inexplicable, as something outside the rational chain of events, as a *lawless* impossible real. The diegetic action of the film is so influenced by the birds that their massive presence completely overshadows the domestic drama: the drama – literally – *loses its significance*. The 'spontaneous' spectator does not perceive *The Birds* as a domestic family drama in which the role of the birds is 'symbolic' of intersubjective relationships and tensions; the accent is put totally on the traumatic attacks by the birds, and, within that framework, the emotional intrigue is mere pretext, part of the undifferentiated tissue of everyday incidents of which the first half of the film is made up, so that, against the background, the weird, inexplicable fury of the birds can be made to stand out even more strongly. Thus the birds, far from functioning as a 'symbol' whose 'signification' can be detected, on the contrary *block*, *mask*, by their massive presence, the film's 'signification', their function being to make us *forget*, during their vertiginous and dazzling attacks, with what, in the end, we are dealing: the triangle of a mother, her son and the woman he loves. If the 'spontaneous' spectator had been supposed to perceive the film's 'signification' easily, then the birds should quite simply have been *left out*.

There is a key detail that supports our reading; at the very end of the film, Mitch's mother 'accepts' Melanie as her son's wife, gives her consent, and abandons her superego role (as indicated by the fleeting smile she and Melanie exchange in the car). And that is why, at that moment, they are all able to leave the property that is being threatened by the birds: the birds are no longer needed, their role is finished. The end of the film – the last shot of the car driving away surrounded by hordes of calm birds – is for that reason wholly coherent and not at all the result of some kind of 'compromise'; the fact that Hitchcock himself spread the rumour that he would have preferred another ending (the car arriving at a Golden Gate Bridge totally blackened by the birds perched on it) and was forced to accede to studio pressure, is just another of the many myths fomented by the director, who was at pains to dissimulate what was really at stake in his work.

It is clear, therefore, why *The Birds* – according to François Regnault[18] – is the film that closes the Hitchcockian system: the birds, the ultimate incarnation in Hitchcock of the bad object, are the counterpart of the reign of maternal law, and it is precisely this conjunction of the bad object of fascination and the maternal law that defines the kernel of the Hitchcockian fantasy.

Notes

1 From this perspective, the denouement of *Dial M for Murder* (1954) is extremely interesting insofar as it *reverses* the usual situation of Hitchcock's films: 'the man who knew too much' is not the hero foreboding some terrifying secret behind the idyllic surface, but *the murderer himself*. That is to say, the inspector traps the murderous husband of Grace Kelly through a certain surplus knowledge – the murderer is caught knowing something that it would not be possible for him to know if he were innocent (the hiding place of the other key to his apartment). The irony of the denouement is that what provokes the downfall of the murderer is precisely his quick and clever reasoning. If he had been just a little bit more slow-witted, i.e., if, after the key in his jacket had failed to open the door to his apartment, he had been unable to deduce quickly what must have happened, he would have been forever safe from the hand of justice. In the way he sets the trap for the murderer, the inspector acts like a real Lacanian analyst: the crucial ingredient of his success is not his ability to 'penetrate the other', to understand him, to adapt to his reasoning, but rather his capacity to take into account the structuring role of a certain object that circulates among the subjects and

entangles them in a network that they cannot dominate – the key in *Dial M for Murder* (and in *Notorious*), the letter in Edgar Allan Poe's 'The Purloined Letter', etc.

2 Cf., for example, Lacan, *The Four Fundamental Concepts of Psycho-Analysis*, London: Hogarth Press, 1977, p. 92.

3 We must be attentive to the diversity of the ways this motif of the 'uncanny' detail is at work in Hitchcock's films. Note just five of its variations:

- *Rope* (1948): here, we have the spot *first* (the traumatic act of murder) and *then* the idyllic everyday situation (the party) constructed to conceal it;
- *The Man Who Knew Too Much*: in a short scene in which the hero (James Stewart) makes his way to the taxidermist Ambrose Chappell, the street the hero traverses is depicted as charged with a sinister atmosphere. In fact things are precisely what they seem to be (the street is just an ordinary suburban London street, etc.), so that the only 'stain' in the picture is *the hero himself*, his suspicious gaze that sees threats everywhere;
- *The Trouble with Harry* (1955): a 'stain' (a body) smears the idyllic Vermont countryside, but instead of provoking traumatic reactions, people who stumble upon it merely treat it as a minor inconvenience and pursue their daily affairs;
- *Shadow of a Doubt*: the 'stain' here is uncle Charlie, the film's central character, a pathological murderer who rejoins his sister's family in a small American town. In the eyes of the townsfolk, he is a friendly, rich benefactor; it is only his niece Charlie who 'knows too much' and sees him as he is. Why? The answer is found in the identity of their names: the two of them constitute two parts of the same personality (like Marion and Norman in *Psycho*, where the identity is indicated by the fact that the two names reflect each other in an inverted form);
- And finally *The Birds*, where – in what is surely Hitchcock's final irony – the 'unnatural' element that disturbs everyday life is the birds, i.e., *nature itself*.

4 Cf. Michel Choin, 'Le quatrième côte', in *Cahiers du cinéma* 356, 1984, pp. 6–7.

5 Jacques Lacan, *Écrits*, Paris: Seuil, 1966, p. 554.

6 Jacques-Alain Miller, 'Montré à Premontré', in *Analytica* 37, 1984, pp. 28–9.

7 'The anal level is the locus of metaphor – one object for another, give the faeces in place of the phallus', Lacan, *The Four Fundamental Concepts of Psycho-Analysis*, p. 104.

8 This scene, creating as it does a phantasmatic effect, also illustrates the thesis that the subject is not necessarily inscribed in the phantasmatic scene as observer, but can also be one of the objects observed. The birds' subjective view of the town creates a menacing effect, even though our view – the camera's view – is that of the birds and not that of their prey, because we are inscribed in the scene as inhabitants of the town, i.e., we identify with the menaced inhabitants.

9 Robin Wood, *Hitchcock's Films*, New York: A. S. Barnes and Co., 1977, p. 116.

10 Jacques Lacan, *Le séminaire, livre XX: Encore*, Paris: Seuil, 1975, p. 23.

11 Lacan, *Écrits*, pp. 54–9.

12 Christopher Lasch, *The Culture of Narcissism*, London: Abacus, 1980, p. 176.

13 Here it is crucial to grasp the logic of the connection between the woman's perspective and the figure of the resigned, impotent master. Lacan's answer to Freud's famous question '*Was will das Weib*? What does the (hysterical) woman want?' is: *a master, but one whom she could dominate*. The perfect figuration of this hysterical fantasy is

Charlotte Brontë's *Jane Eyre* where, at the end of the novel, the heroine is happily married to the blinded, helpless father-like figure (*Rebecca*, of course, belongs to the same tradition).

14 Lasch, *The Culture of Narcissism*, p. 12.

15 Cf. Saul Kripke, *Naming and Necessity*, Cambridge, MA: Harvard University Press, 1972.

16 It is against the background of this problem that we could perhaps locate the lesson to be drawn from Stanley Cavell's *Pursuits of Happiness: The Hollywood Comedies of Remarriage* (Cambridge, MA: Harvard University Press, 1981), namely a version of the Hegelian theory of repetition in history: the only proper marriage is the second one. First we marry the other *qua* our narcissistic complement; it is only when his/her delusive charm fades that we can engage in marriage as an attachment to the other beyond his/her imaginary properties.

17 It is because *North by Northwest* repeats the logic of the Oedipal journey that it offers us a kind of spectral analysis of the function of the father, dividing it into three figures: Roger Thornhill's *imaginary* father (the UN diplomat stabbed in the hall of the General Assembly), his *symbolic* father (the CIA 'Professor' who invented the *name* 'Kaplan' to which Thornhill is tied), and his *real* father (i.e., the resigned, perverse villain Van Damm).

18 Cf. François Regnault, 'Système formel d'Hitchcock', in *Cahiers du cinéma*, hors-série 8.

This essay was originally published in Slavoj Žižek, *Looking Awry: An Introduction to Jacques Lacan through Popular Culture*, Cambridge, MA: MIT Press.

The Christ-like feet of the 'artful' corpse in *The Trouble With Harry*

Chapter 10
The Cut of Representation: Painting and Sculpture in Hitchcock

Brigitte Peucker

In 1974, having concluded his address before the Film Society of Lincoln Center with a quotation from Thomas de Quincey's essay, 'Murder as One of the Fine Arts', Hitchcock added a brief footnote to his speech: 'As you can see, the best way to do it is with scissors.'[1] Hitchcock refers, in this typically macabre moment, not only to the infamous murder weapon in *Dial M for Murder* (1954), but to the art of film editing or cutting *per se*, and to the fragmented image of the human body in the cinematic frame. Knowingly or unknowingly, Hitchcock alludes to a pervasive concern in the body of his films with fragmentation, castration and dismemberment.

In this chapter, I will relate the practice and figuration of dismemberment in Hitchcock's films to images and representational strategies familiar to us from the visual arts. Hitchcock's films, so narrative oriented, so intent on the twists and turns of plot, mask a continuous preoccupation with the stasis of sculpture and painting, suggestive of and displaced by the death around which every Hitchcock plot inevitably turns. In many instances, it is the body of the woman that is fragmented or dismembered, conflated with the 'dead' space of the pictorial or with the sculptural fragment, and most intimately bound up with the uncanny and paradoxical capacity of cinema both to fragment the body and to animate it. But often the body of the fragmented woman is mirrored in that of a male counterpart. Suffice it to add, for the moment, that in 1927 Hitchcock chose to send a Christmas card to his friends depicting the famous caricature of himself in profile: the card was a jigsaw puzzle, meant to be taken to pieces and then reassembled.[2]

This essay opens with a discussion of the relation between bodies and their conversion into works of art, both still lifes and sculpture; it begins, that is, by considering the movement between the real and representation. It moves on to examine a moment of painterly doubling, linking it to the Janus-face and to specularity, and then to look at instances of 'decapitation' figured through portraits and portrait busts.[3] All of these concerns are inspired by Louis Marin's work on Caravaggio's 'Head of Medusa', and set the scene for a more direct application of Marin's reading to an analysis of the painterly and sculptural concerns in *Vertigo* (1958) with which the essay concludes.[4] Not surprisingly, Ovid's *narrative* of Medusa is particularly useful as a foil for Hitchcock's work because it resonates thematically with his films, with issues of fragmentation (Perseus severed Medusa's head from her body), the death-bringing power of the gaze (Medusa's gaze turned men to stone), and the castration that this threat figures.[5]

More particularly, however, as Marin reads it, Caravaggio's *painting* of Medusa's head has representational strategies in common with Hitchcock's films: a reliance on doubling, mirroring and contradiction, such as the both/and of ambiguous gendering. Caravaggio's painting does not simply represent Medusa's decapitated head, as Marin points out, but is a 'decapitation' of another kind.[6] This essay suggests that a 'metaphysics of representation', like the one that Marin locates in Caravaggio's painting, is centrally operative in the films of Hitchcock, and provides a schema within which to locate a persistent recycling of the images, themes and strategies discussed below.

Natures mortes, trophies and mummies

Still-life paintings in Hitchcock seem incidental, remote from the action, and their connection to the body – fragmented or whole – may initially appear oblique. Detectives in Hitchcock films look at still lifes in puzzlement, as though the solution to a mystery lies there. If Detective Benson is fascinated by a cubist still life for a brief 'out of action' moment in *Suspicion* (1941), this is, as Stephen Heath has suggested, a fleeting escape from a scene dominated by the portrait of General MacLaidlaw.[7] But the alternative space that Benson's diegetic excursion creates is a fragmented female space of fruits and flowers. A cubist rendering in the manner of Picasso, this still life embodies a 'fractured' image, produced by the multiple planar surfaces by means of which its objects are rendered.[8] Speaking more generally, we can say that in Hitchcock's films character and spectator attention is drawn to still lifes not only as the space of the feminine, but because these paintings embody an uncanny contradiction. No matter that their subject is organic, was once living: still lifes are *natures mortes* – dead nature – their flowers and fruit killed off into and fixed within the space of representation.

In *Rear Window* (1954), we find a still life of fruit and flowers over Jefferies's fireplace, occupying the place where a portrait so often hangs in Hitchcock. This painting, in front of which another detective pauses as though it contained a clue, features the natural as food, specifically as fruit, which stands in for the body of the mother. Although Western culture tends generally to connect Mother Nature to her bounty, we can also turn to psychoanalytic theory for several accounts that more specifically link the maternal body part to food. As Tania Modleski mentions in her discussion of Jefferies, Lacan contends that the mirror stage is preceded by an earlier phase dominated by the fantasy of the 'body-in-pieces', an autoerotic phase that antedates the formation of the ego.[9] In this earlier stage, the infant connects the satisfaction of its need for nourishment with the breast that supplies it. As Freud tells it, sucking is more than a means of satisfaction; it is eroticised and becomes pleasurable. Thus, the infant's satisfaction is linked to a constellation of 'partial' objects, such as the breast and the mouth.[10] While the actual means of satisfaction is the mother's milk, the breast – the source of pleasure – emerges as the fantasmatic object of desire. No sooner has the breast become an object, however, then this object is 'lost' as the infant learns that the breast belongs to the body of the mother.[11] At this stage of development, the maternal imago is fragmented into part objects to be incorporated – in this instance ingested – identified with, or destroyed. In a telling instance of *Rear Window*'s black humour, Stella's fascinated musings about cutting up bodies take place just as Jefferies is cutting up his breakfast.

This is not the only Hitchcock film to link the corpse with food, creating the distinct suggestion of cannibalism that *Frenzy* (1972) will repeatedly reinforce. As the spectator becomes aware, Kent, the 'Garden of England', is also the place where the bodies of women are dumped by the greengrocer/sex murderer with a particular fondness for his mum. In this film, the detective's wife has taken a gourmet-cooking class featuring the preparation of body parts such as fish heads and pigs' trotters, body parts connected to the fragmented bodies of women whose corpses are scattered about the countryside. As Modleski points out, in serving the detective these dishes, his wife repeatedly 'forces him to partake of a symbolic feast of the corpse'.[12]

It is in *The Trouble With Harry* (1955), a more benign predecessor of *Frenzy*, that food and the corpse are most obviously linked to art.[13] The signifying chain that links them is both on the surface and circuitous: connected by the theme of preservation, food, the female body, the corpse and visual representation are conjoined. Sam Marlowe's paintings – among them semi-abstract still lifes and landscapes, as well as a Modigliani-like female portrait – are for sale alongside jugs of cider at a farm stand. Further, Sam barters his paintings for groceries, thus reinforcing the connection between works of art and fruit. Women in this film are also repeatedly connected with fruit as nourishment; they offer men lemonade, blueberry muffins and elderberry wine. Hitchcock ironically alludes to Eve's offer of the apple, of course, but the connection runs deeper: when the captain refers to Miss Gravely as 'preserves that have to be opened someday', fruit and the female body are equated. Like Miss Gravely, the autumnal landscape is overripe: it is as though the corpse's blood stains the leaves of the sugar maples crimson.[14] When Mrs Rogers suggests ironically that her husband's corpse should be 'stuffed and put in a glass case', this body is rendered an *objet d'art*. While sketching in the woods, Sam comes across Harry's corpse and makes a pastel of him, commemorating his (dead) face in a portrait. Of course there are displacements here: the corpse of this film is not that of a mother, but of a father, a father by law. But the narrative takes care to point out that another father, Mr Gravely, has been killed by a harvester, 'harvested', that is, by a mechanical Grim Reaper that treats him like a food crop. As Lesley Brill points out, Harry's body, too, is repeatedly 'planted and harvested'.[15] Harry is connected, then, with Mother Nature's seasonal cycle; he is further feminised by being a man whose wife, in the parlance of the film, 'didn't let him in'.

In *The Trouble With Harry*, the corpse is Žižek's Hitchcockian blot, the 'remainder of the real', 'the detail that "does not fit", that "sticks out" from the idyllic surface scene and denatures it, renders it uncanny'.[16] As Žižek suggests elsewhere, the cool detachment, if not to say disregard, with which the characters treat Harry's corpse in their midst, reveals an 'obsessional neutralization of an underlying traumatic complex'.[17] The characters of this film cannot come to terms with the real: Harry's body must be recovered within the realm of the symbolic before its death can be acknowledged. Its representation in art has a similar effect. Harry's corpse is first casually sketched by Sam, who records it as part of the natural scene that he has chosen to depict. Later, Harry's 'death's head' is portraitised: now, it must be 'covered over' by representation, just as the corpse must finally be acknowledged in the rituals of a conventional burial. Consequently, during a verbal parody of psychoanalytically tinged art criticism performed for the deputy, Sam transforms the portrait from that of a death's head into that of a sleeping man.

In simultaneously retouching the portrait and performing a verbal sleight-of-hand in which obfuscation masks as exposure, the artist as film-maker 'disposes' of the corpse, covers it over with representation. For the film's spectators, of course, Harry's corpse already exists in the symbolic – but not only because we see it in the images of a film. The many shots of Harry's foreshortened body, complete with feet 'sticking out' – the full body rendered with a close-up of the feet rather than the head – are far from suggesting the 'artless bluntness' attributed to them by Brill.[18] They are 'artful', indeed, doubly situated within the symbolic: this is the famous angle from which Mantegna painted his dead Christ. A final irony lies here: historically, this image has been thought shocking because it represents Christ too realistically, as a corpse. Feet 'sticking out' like those of Christ, Harry's artful corpse – as blot – is the final image of the film.

One body is laid to rest, another must be brought to life. As the Captain puts it, Miss Gravely is a 'well-preserved woman' as well as a jar of preserves to be tasted, but Miss 'Gravely' is also in some sense a corpse. A Galatea in a minor key, she is revivified or 'renovated', as Marlowe puts it, brought to life by the artist as a Pygmalion who cuts her hair and does her make-up: his 'art' is performed directly on her body. When she later enters the Captain's house, she will encounter another Galatea there: a large figurehead from the captain's ship, 'a fine figure of a woman' with prominent breasts and a red dress. The Pygmalion–Galatea relation of *Vertigo*, though trivialised in *The Trouble With Harry*, is fleshed out in this sequence: the 'painted' Miss Gravely is raised from the dead, she is the statue (figurehead) come to life. And like that statue she is also sexualised. A benign version of the scarlet woman, Miss Gravely wears its metaphorical red dress; presumably the preserves the Captain has in mind are strawberry. When Marlowe decides finally to barter his paintings (now headed for the Modern Museum), he will receive in exchange two boxes of strawberries each month for Mrs Rogers. For himself – to be shared with her – he requests a double bed.

Sometimes in Hitchcock, bodies remain too relentlessly within the material world, and the real of the corpse is inadequately subsumed by the symbolic. In these scenes, they are often featured as material representations, as sculpture rather than as painting. Like *The Trouble With Harry*, *The Man Who Knew Too Much* (1956) presents representational issues in a comic light, diverting the spectator from the awareness that, in this film, body parts are preserved to become sculptural and fetishistic objects of display. The fragmented body is introduced in a joke by the James Stewart character, a surgeon who recites a catalogue of the body parts that have financed the vacation upon which he and his family have embarked: one patient's appendix, another's gall bladder, the triplets produced in the womb of yet another. The film suggests that someone who thinks about fragmented bodies in terms of profit (a figuration of the film-maker as surgeon) deserves the experience that Stewart has in this film.

During the course of the film, Stewart mistakenly enters a taxidermist's establishment that has the look of an artist's studio and the atmosphere of a mortuary. As he wanders about in search of his son's kidnappers, the surgeon is terrorised by the fierce-looking stuffed animals and animal heads on display – a fitting punishment for one so inured to dismemberment as to think of gall bladders and appendixes primarily as separable from their owner. Displaced from the human onto the animal, the body's fragmentation is countered by the preservation of its parts, the taxidermist's stuffed and mounted trophy heads. And it is supplemented by the action of the camera as a 'chasseur d'images'[19] that stalks and 'shoots' its prey, as though it were the rifle that had killed them off. If the camera is hunter and gun, its aim, like that of the taxidermist, is to preserve the body.

Taxidermy is Norman Bates's hobby, too; he likes 'stuffing things', as the spectator of *Psycho* (1960) is only too well aware.[20] Beaks open, wings arrested in flight, the stuffed birds that decorate Norman's parlour are now objects of display. Stuffed birds on perches can be found among arrangements of dried or artificial flowers as well, constituting three-dimensional still lifes, more *natures mortes*, whose lighting emphasises their sculptural status. Other images in *Psycho* underline its preoccupation with death, art and objecthood: when Lila enters the mother's bedroom, her eyes stray to a bronze sculpture of Dürer's praying hands, at once image and object, body parts ironically displayed in a clichéd quotation of high culture. But it is the preserved corpse of the mother that has the most in common with the stuffed birds. As André Bazin has so famously said with regard to the photographic image: 'If the plastic arts were put under psychoanalysis, embalming the dead might turn out to be the fundamental factor in their creation. The process might reveal that at the origin of painting and sculpture there lies a mummy complex.'[21] Norman's macabre 'mummy', both body and image, like the birds, gruesomely tropes the camera's capacity to 'embalm time'.[22]

Near the sarcophagus, Bazin goes on to report concerning Egyptian burial practices, terracotta statuettes were placed to stand in for the mummies, lest they after all suffer the depredations of time.[23] It is our awareness of the vulnerable interior of the body, placed within its all too penetrable shell, that must be magically denied by the 'idealized carapace' of the statue, a protective shell that also functions as a crypt or a tomb.[24] We can bring this sense of the sculpture as a figured 'container' for the body – like the anthropomorphic Egyptian sarcophagus that contains the body[25] – to bear on two different yet related images in and around Hitchcock's work: one of these is an anecdote involving the making of *Spellbound* (1945), the other occurs in *North by Northwest* (1959). Famous for its dream sequence based on drawings by Salvador Dali, *Spellbound* contains only an attenuated form of the sequence originally planned; its best-known image is that of a woman using scissors to cut drapes covered with huge eyes, an image obviously inspired by *Un chien andalou* (1928). Combining images of castration with images of theatre, this figuration is a variant on the idea of film-maker as surgeon. Interestingly, Hitchcock claims that other images in the dream sequence as conceived by Dali were too excessive even for him, complaining to Truffaut that 'Dali had some strange ideas: he wanted a statue to crack like a shell falling apart, with ants crawling all over it, and underneath, there would be Ingrid Bergman, covered by ants! It just wasn't possible.'[26]

When, in *North by Northwest*, Eva Marie Saint is called a 'little piece of sculpture' for which the villain 'must have paid plenty' at an art auction, the implication of the remark is rather different. But when, at the end of the film, a statue with which Eva's character has become identified is dropped, breaks into pieces, and reveals hidden microfilm – pointing, as Stanley Cavell also supposes, to 'the present film'[27] – something more is at stake. If, in one sense, the statue in *North by Northwest* can be said to generate the film, then the fate of this statue demonstrates that the female body must be shattered, fragmented, in order to produce it. In both instances – in the case of the 'impossible' image in *Spellbound* that Hitchcock, in the kind of evasive conversational move typical of him, attributes to Dali, and in the case of *North by Northwest* – the statue functions as carapace. Somewhat shockingly, the cracked statue of *Spellbound* would have opened to reveal Ingrid Bergman as a corpse, already covered with ants, thus exposing the real of the body after the 'shell' of representation cracks. In *North by Northwest*, on the other hand, the statue connected with Eva Marie Saint is opened in order to give birth to the film. But the contradiction governing these two examples is only a seeming contradiction. At some level, the female corpse and the film function simultaneously as opposites and equivalents.

The Janus-face

In conversation with Truffaut, Hitchcock speaks of making the same film over and over, comparing himself to the painter Rouault in the bargain. 'Not that I'm comparing myself to him,' Hitchcock says in a typical disclaimer, 'but old Rouault was content with judges, clowns, a few women, and Christ on a Cross . . . That constituted his life's work.'[28] It is in Rouault's work, interestingly, that the paintings of Mrs Anthony, Bruno's mother (*Strangers on a Train*, 1951), find their inspiration. Bruno claims that his mother paints because it soothes her nerves; despite the fact that his remark parodies Freud's connection of neurosis with the production of art, it is meant to be taken seriously. Mrs Anthony's portrait of her husband gains sympathy from her son, since it represents his father as a king who exerts despotic control over wife and son alike: Hitchcock's double allusion to Oedipus and *Hamlet* is not lost on us. Another portrait of a father as a representative of the patriarchal order, this painting resembles those of General MacLaidlaw (*Suspicion*) and Mr Brenner, the dead father in *The Birds* (1963). But in this instance, too, visual representation is coterminous with the space of death, for Mrs Anthony's portrait of Bruno's father places him under the sign of death in the eyes of their son.

The space of painting can be occupied by male figures in Hitchcock, especially the sexually ambiguous males in whom, as in the case of Bruno or Norman, incestuous desires and a murderous psychosis reside. An early case in point may be found in *The Lodger* (1926), where doubling is suggested both in the form of an incestuous desire for the dead sister, and its hints that the lodger and the Avenger may be one and the same. When Ivor Novello's feminised lodger looks at portraits of blonde women, women who resemble his sister, he also sees himself. William Rothman has called our attention to a frame in the film that includes both the lodger and the female portrait.[29] This frame initially suggests that the painting is behind him, but when the lodger begins to move, it becomes clear that he is moving toward the portrait, and that the mirror behind him reflects both. In a sense, the lodger is positioned between two mirrors – that of the portrait in front of him, and that of the mirror behind him. He is located within a specular space that is the mirror of art.

The issue of male and female doubling within the context of painterly representation takes a suggestive form in *Blackmail* (1929). This film tells the story of the near seduction of a young woman, Alice, who is lured into the apartment of an artist to 'see his etchings'. Playfully and under the artist's direction, Alice picks up his palette and brush and almost accidentally places a mark upon an empty canvas. She is then encouraged by the artist to 'draw something', as if in order to recuperate the transgressive mark, and paints a female head around it, transforming the mark into its mouth. Taking up the brush himself, the artist and would-be seducer hastily sketches the outline of a naked female body under this head, a body complete with breasts, but lacking genitalia; thus both man and woman create a composite portrait, a work that is genuinely heterogeneous. Soon, stabbing and killing the artist in defense of her virtue, Alice brandishes the knife as she has brandished the paintbrush, and becomes the prey of a blackmailer. In an ironic reversal typical of Hitchcock, the blackmailer meets his end in a chase sequence that begins in the sculpture gallery of the British Museum and the woman goes free.

Punctuating the narrative of this film is yet another portrait, that of a jester, rendered as though 'shot from below', who points an accusing finger at his beholder. The first of its diegetic beholders is Alice herself, once before and once after the stabbing, when she slashes the painting, as though to enact at the level of representation what she has done in the domain of the real. Its second beholder in the film is her fiancé, a policeman whose image in the form of a photograph exerts its authority on the wall of Alice's bedroom. Investigating the crime, her fiancé is mocked by the portrait in the apartment that is both the scene of a murder and of a more intimate transgression. In yet another instance in which a detective examines a painting in search of knowledge, the fiancé also looks twice at the portrait of the jester, once while fetishistically holding something that will prove to be Alice's glove.

Not surprisingly, the portrait of the mocking jester has been read as a self-representation of Hitchcock,[30] the jester/film-maker as both prankster and truth-teller. We see both portraits again at the end of the film, in Scotland Yard, when the jester's mocking laugh will function as yet another commentary on the ironies of the plot. This time, they are being carried by someone whose shape is possibly that of Hitchcock himself: carried back to back under his arm, they form a 'two-sided' painting. The surprising doubling that we see in this composite, 'two-sided' painting plays upon the two-sided Janus-face.[31] In *Blackmail*, the significance of this relation is underscored by being revealed in the moment of a Hitchcock cameo, as though in humorous acknowledgement that the Janus-face[32] was usually represented in the profile and relief typical of actual cameos.

Mocking and accusatory, the jester with his pointing finger seems the representative of a carnivalesque inversion of the law. The painting of the woman, now on its reverse side was, as we recall, created around a circular mark naturalised as a mouth, around a vacancy that marks the site of castration. This act of recuperation – an act that turns the wound of castration into the organ of speech and therefore marks it as phallic – is performed by Alice. The artist, on the other hand, avoids the problem altogether by resorting to a convention of representation that simply eliminates all genitalia from his drawing of the nude. But both man and woman are complicit in a rendering that makes ambiguous the 'castration' of the female body, and hence undermines the binarism of male and female. Alice's conversion of the mark of absence into a mouth allows us to read the mouth both as the organ of speech and as *vagina dentata*, just as the absence of genitalia on the male artist's nude can be read both as a representation of castration and as an avoidance of the issue.

The relation of the images that constitute the 'two sides' suggests a Janus-face, two profiles gazing in opposing directions, at once opposites and doubles: in this case, the male and female aspects of an ambiguous gendering that is both and neither. Does the gaze of the jester as artist, in an ironic echo of the gaze of Medusa, have the power to fix the female body in the death that is painting, much as Medusa's gaze renders men statues? In some sense, the position of the two paintings on opposite sides of the canvas suggests that the gaze and the laughter of the jester are connected with the female body whose 'castration' is simultaneously covered over and manifest. I will return to their relation below; for now it should be noted that the spaces of the two paintings are made permeable to one another by means of the slash in the canvas that Alice has made with the knife, creating an opening in the canvas reminiscent of the eye-shaped hole we see in *Psycho*.

In this later film, Norman Bates lifts a painting representing the familiar subject matter of 'Susannah and the Elders' in order, similarly, to spy upon the naked Marion in her shower bath.[33] This painting of the bathing female body with its male voyeurs both 'doubles' the events of the narrative and serves as a screen of sorts that 'covers' Norman's peephole. Modelled upon the eye, the peephole has jagged edges that suggest a torn canvas as well as the organ of sight. In a sense, then, we can say that this painting, when 'slashed', provides Norman's deadly gaze access to the naked Marion. As Bellour has suggested, the 'pressure of the doubling process that underlies all of [Hitchcock's] films' is operative in a doubling that links Norman (already doubled, as both Norman and mother) to Marion.[34] We can surely say, then, that the slashed, two-sided painting of *Blackmail* opens up a space for the merger of jester and female figure, as well. In *Blackmail*, the female portrait, product of a man and a woman, is a self-portrait that represents the two sides of the composite body.

We can read the figure of the Janus-face, with its two profiles emerging from one head, as a variant of the specular relation – the mirror portrait – that links Caravaggio to his representation of Medusa. Not surprisingly, the Janus-face is a figure for the dialectic. Like 'Head of Medusa', it is also a 'decapitation', and is rarely, if ever, represented on a body. The gazes that look outward from its head are the inverse of the 'opposing' gazes of a figure and its mirror reflection, and of the gazes of 'doubles' at one another. These seemingly opposite – but essentially equivalent – doublings relate to the way in which the female figure, when read as castrated and powerless, is an image the male thus fears may reflect his own condition, and is in this instance an image of the castrated self, a mirroring based upon equivalence. But when the woman is read as castrating and powerful – as Medusa – the defensive strategy such a reading engenders turns the castrating and murderous gaze against itself.

Herein lies one aspect of the appropriateness of Marin's reading of Medusa as a paradigm for specular relations in Hitchcock. Just as the castrating gaze of Medusa is defended against and mirrored by Perseus's bronze shield that turns the deadly gaze upon its reflection, thus leading to her death and decapitation, so in Hitchcock's films the camera is trained upon the castrating woman, at once absorbing her power and fragmenting, even destroying, her by means of it. As Marin shows, Caravaggio's portrait of Medusa is, interestingly, also a self-portrait: 'The painter, after all, not only disguises himself as Medusa; he also cross-dresses as a Gorgon, a woman, or at least the head of a woman.'[35] In the case of this painting, the female portrait is also the image that the male artist sees in the mirror. In Hitchcock's films this form of specularity is of central significance: when the man looks at female portraits and still lifes, he hopes that he will not find himself mirrored there.

Decapitations: cut-outs and busts

Blackmail's best-known image does not include either of the portraits I have discussed. Most frequently cited is the image of the mammoth Egyptian-style stone head next to which the blackmailer, a tiny figure by contrast, slithers down a rope in the British Museum. This is not a serious decapitation: the stone head is smiling even though, like justice itself in this film, it is blind. Likewise in ironic jest, the Mount Rushmore sequence in *North by Northwest* juxtaposes the gigantic, impassive presidential heads of stone with specks of human figures moving across them, figures for whom this is also the setting of a life-and-death struggle. These heads, representations of power and authority though they may be, are also decapitations: they are portrait busts, heads separated from the bodies to which they belong. Where, we ask, is the Medusa who has turned these men to stone? And why, like Medusa herself, have they been beheaded?

In *Rebecca* (1940), the nameless heroine, the second Mrs de Winter, is tricked by the housekeeper into dressing as the woman-in-white in one of the full-length family portraits that hang in the gallery. Appearing at a fancy-dress ball in this costume, it is not the woman of the portrait whom the second wife evokes for her spectators, but Rebecca, the first wife, whose Gothic presence haunts this film with a supernatural power. It is not the ancestral portrait that is brought to life, in other words, but the dead Rebecca who had worn this same costume to an earlier ball. We never see Rebecca: her body is only conjured up for the spectator by the fetishistic garments that hid – or didn't quite hide – it. Yet the lady of the portrait and Maxim de Winter's two wives, enclosed in the folds of identical dresses, faces framed by identical hats, are virtually indistinguishable. Or perhaps we should say that they *would* be indistinguishable were it not for their faces: in some sense, then, their faces resemble cut-outs, separable from their bodies in identical, paper-doll dresses,[36] the result of some ghastly decapitation. Recalling that the head of the hybrid female portrait in *Blackmail* was 'executed' by Alice, while the body was sketched by the male artist, we realise that this head, too, is not of a piece with the body.

In *Vertigo*, the female head in another painting made by a woman has the uncanny look of a cut-out. Midge, the artist, has copied the body of a woman, Carlotta Valdes, from a painting that hangs in the Legion of Honor museum. But on Carlotta's body, Midge has painted her own head, perhaps in an effort to suggest to Scottie, the James Stewart character with whom she is in love, that she herself would be an adequate substitute for the inaccessible woman linked in his imagination with the woman in the painting. The shock value of Midge's painting, even for today's spectator, is difficult to account for when one considers how accustomed we now are to similar effects created in modernist painting. Indeed, Midge is a fashion designer who works in a studio full of examples of abstract painting and sculpture, among them a brassière, mounted on a free-standing wire bust, that she describes as working on the principle of the cantilever bridge. When Midge tells Scottie that she has 'gone back to her first love, painting' (it was Hitchcock's, too),[37] Scottie asks whether she is painting a still life. 'Not exactly,' she replies, and in the irony of her reply lies a partial explanation for the shock that her painting occasions in us, since the unnatural conjunction of body and head has rendered her painting a decapitation. It is transgressive and uncanny because it violates an order whose linchpin is the wholeness of the body. Notwithstanding the presence of the brassière-bust nearby (the breast as as partial object recalling other still lifes to mind), this portrait may be *morte*, but it is no still life.

In *Vertigo*, this scene with its flaunting of fragmented and modernist works of art figures the ambiguity created in the film by its multiplicity of perspectives, the splitting of point of view that finds its visual analogue in the fragmentation of the female body. This fragmented body is displayed not only in the doubled portrait, with its 'portrait bust' head, but in the sculptural model of the brassière. Like the breast for which the brassière stands in – and as in the portrait 'bust' that it ironically figures – the head is separated from the body on which it belongs. The fact that this portrait is the work of a female artist, and that she has superimposed upon the portrait her own head complete with the spectacles that signify her access to the gaze, contributes to the sense of 'unnaturalness' that we perceive in the painting. Midge's self-portrait represents her as Medusa, and her deadly gaze out of the canvas is death-bringing. Midge claims to have made the painting for Scottie – 'I thought I might give it to you,' she says – but the extreme reaction of *this* detective tells her that she has been foolish indeed to confront him with what is a mirror image of his own castration.[38] Subsequently, this painting, like the one in *Blackmail*, is 'wounded': when Midge defaces her portrait with a paintbrush, she is both committing self-mutilation and striking out at another.

More obviously than *The Trouble With Harry*, *Vertigo* echoes the story of Pygmalion, the sculptor who fell in love with his own creation, Galatea. Since Pygmalion is at once father and husband to Galatea, Ovid's story narrativises incest, 'the relation in which same mates with same',[39] and inverts the narrative of *Psycho* in which a son fashions his mother into a sculpture. A film about a female portrait 'brought to life', *Vertigo* also tells the tale of a body rigidified into a statue. The Galatea with whom Scottie becomes obsessed is first presented to the spectator as an image: at Ernie's restaurant, 'Madeleine' (or the character Judy who impersonates her) is briefly framed by the tracking camera in a composition that has a painting at its centre. Moving in on her from behind, the camera lingers on her motionless body, surrounded by the draperies of stole and dress, and focuses on the marmoreal whiteness of her naked back and neck. When, from the point of view of Scottie, the camera centres 'Madeleine' within the frame of a doorway, she begins to move, creating the effect of a sculpture not quite fully brought to life, her movements interspersed with static shots that present her face in profile, in cameo-like relief.[40]

Later, for the benefit of Scottie's gaze, Madeleine/Judy enacts a series of silent performances in spaces that further promote the connection of her living body with painting and sculpture. One of these spaces is the graveyard, where we see her posed in long shot, resembling, in her grey suit, graveyard statuary among the tombstones. Madeleine has 'died into art', it is suggested, her unmoving body positioned as though it were a funerary sculpture next to the grave and headstone of Carlotta Valdes. The museum, of course, is the cultural edifice in which the exchange between 'real' body and image is finalised. From his vantage point in an antechamber, Scottie surveys Madeleine seated still as a statue before a female portrait. Madeleine's trance-like look at Carlotta simulates a mystical communication with the image, effected through the gaze.

Scottie is an apt interpreter of Madeleine's pantomime: twice the camera's motion, standing in for Scottie's glance, traces a connection between the 'real' and the represented, focusing first on the bouquet lying next to Madeleine, and then on an identical one in the portrait. Next it fixes on the whorl into which Madeleine's hair is sculpted in order to point to that same figure in the painting. This whorl – a visual analogue for the snakes that replace Medusa's hair – is the figure for vertigo. Although Madeleine is seated before the painting as its beholder, the scene implies that for Scottie, at least, her space is continuous with it. If Madeleine can be said to collapse into the portrait of Carlotta, a moment refigured by her 'death', then Judy under Scottie's direction later brings the painting to life again. After she 'dies', Madeleine is figured in Scottie's dream as Carlotta's animated portrait, an animation that paradoxically stresses her death rather than the portrait's coming to life. Repeatedly in this film, then, the experience of vertigo is connected to the perceptual shift that accompanies the collapse into the two-dimensionality of the image, as well as the reverse movement from flatness into the three-dimensional. I will return to this movement below.

Between the death of Judy's 'Madeleine' and her re-creation by Scottie in the role of Pygmalion, Scottie suffers from extreme melancholia, an intense unwillingness to separate from the loved object. Scottie's dream during his illness suggests that he has not withdrawn his libido from Madeleine, but has withdrawn it into his own ego instead. He sees himself in the graveyard where Madeleine had once posed, and substitutes his body for hers in the dream's final image, the corpse that has landed on the roof. For the head of Madeleine that fixes his attention when he first sees her, the dream substitutes Scottie's own head in yet another instance of doubling, of 'same' figured as 'same'. Like Medusa's, Scottie's head, too, is a decapitation: it exists in the dream as a fragment, detached from his body, a fetish that is both a sign of castration and a defense against it. Like the head of Medusa on the shield of Perseus, the function of this fetishistic head is apotropaic: it wards off what it conjures up.

Perseus, we are told, captures Medusa's image as a reflection in the mirror of his shield. Like Hitchcock, Perseus uses a 'ruse of representation',[41] the mirror. When Caravaggio gazes into the mirror he sees his own reflection, a reflection that provides the features for the portrait of the severed head of Medusa – the 'head of a transvestite'[42] – that he is painting directly on an actual shield. Here other ambiguities are produced. As Marin points out, the support of Caravaggio's painting, the shield, is convex, but the painting itself looks concave.[43] The movement of the eye from background to foreground and back again that these antithetical optical effects invite has its analogue in the visual effect of vertigo engendered by the approach and retreat – the simultaneous tracking out and zooming in – of Hitchcock's camera. The problem of vertigo, or of what Marin refers to as the problem of the convex mirror and its effects, is the problem of ambiguity or hesitation – of the both/and of male and female, life and death – transposed to the field of vision. The motif of decapitation in painting – the use of self-portraits of painters for heads of personnages, say, in history painting – suggests acts of artistic self-disguise.[44] The decapitation that Midge performs in her portrait, therefore, is deeply self-revelatory for Hitchcock. We might look to the photograph of Hitchcock holding a wax model of his own head at Madame Tussaud's wax museum for an ironic commentary on this reading.[45]

The shield of Perseus

There is yet another kind of doubling that warrants investigation in Hitchcock's films, a doubling that can also be explored by means of Caravaggio's painting. For the moment, let us turn to a space within *Strangers on a Train*, a space that announces the self-consciousness of the filmic text by means of a theatricality revealed through a direct gaze into the camera by a character (Bruno) in the film.[46] It occurs during the tennis championship as Bruno sits staring directly into the camera, in marked contrast to the other spectators, whose heads follow the ball back and forth in synchronised engrossment in the action. It is this image in which Žižek anchors his claim that the stain in Hitchcock 'ultimately coincides with the threatening gaze of the other'.[47] Bruno's motionless head – indeed, his 'motionless gaze', as Žižek puts it – creates the effect of 'sticking out like a strange body and thus disturbing the harmony of the image by introducing a threatening dimension'.[48] This is precisely an example of 'the picture looking back at us':[49] accentuated by the other heads turning in unison, Bruno's pronounced lack of movement reinforces his placement within a different kind of space, what one might call a 'painterly' space within the cinematic frame. Midge's gaze out of her self-portrait constitutes a similar moment in *Vertigo*, and here, too, Žižek's formulation, oddly reminiscent of traditional aesthetics, serves us well: her cut-out head 'disturbs the harmony' of the image.

The first picture that 'looks at us' forcefully in Hitchcock is that of the jester in *Blackmail*. As I indicated above, Alice is the first diegetic spectator to look at the painting. But the mocking image of the jester is only retrospectively suggested to be from Alice's point of view: initially, its look is directly at the spectator. The gaze out of the frame is followed by one of Hitchcock's signature reverse tracking shots, 'one that begins at the uncanny detail'[50] – in this case, in the eye of the jester, stressing the power of the gaze – and then rapidly tracks out to reveal the rest of the painting. What interests us here is that the camera's movement can be read both as the jester's approaching gaze, and as the retreating movement of the spectator. Jester and spectator are bound together in that 'double' motion.

Hitchcock's version of what Michael Fried describes as a self-conscious 'theatricality'[51] in painting reinforces themes of mirroring and doubling, since the character's gaze *at* the camera and 'out of the film'[52] engages both camera and spectator with the direct gaze of the character. In effect, a 'theatrical' painting removes the 'fourth wall' that separates the spectator from the space of the painting.

In addition to Midge's portrait, two other important moments in *Vertigo* feature the direct gaze out of the frame. One occurs after Scottie, who has pursued Judy into her apartment and persuaded her to have dinner with him, leaves Judy alone, initiating the flashback that reveals the events surrounding Madeleine's death to have been duplicitous. Marian Keane has read Judy's direct look *out* of the frame as a look *into* the camera. For Keane, this is the turning point of *Vertigo*, a direct declaration of the camera's presence, a look that 'acknowledges Hitchcock and us'.[53] Here she draws on the work of Rothman (and ultimately Cavell) for whom the direct gaze into the camera, restricted to a very few characters, 'confronts' the camera.[54] The characters to whom this is permitted, claims Rothman, 'seem to have access to the views that make up the film itself, as if they shared Hitchcock's position as author or our position as viewers', though he goes on to declare these characters 'signifiers of Hitchcock's authorship and our own acts of viewing'.[55] What Judy sees when she first looks into the camera, Keane does not say, though she speculates that 'what she views there will be, in part, a figure for Hitchcock's camera, an embodiment of its gaze'.[56] What Keane does not mention is that, at this particular moment, Judy's direct gaze into the camera – and hence at the spectator – is something more: the next shot reveals Judy to be looking into a mirror on her wall. The camera gazes at Judy out of the mirror.

If Hitchcock's films, like Caravaggio's painting, suggest that representation is 'a cutting blade', a cut that 'severs the story from the subject who tells it while also severing the scene from those who look at it and produce it as a scene'[57] – severing it from author and spectator alike – then the mirroring relation such as we find in Hitchcock does not always allow the blade to cut completely. In the sequence of *Vertigo* under discussion, Judy gazing into the mirror sees her own image, a ghostly double that is also Scottie/Hitchcock, as well as the gaze of the camera that records her own gaze doubled back upon itself. But what of the gaze of the spectator? With the first shot we are brought into the space of representation by the force of Judy's direct, threatening gaze that similarly draws our own gaze into the frame. But the next shot, the shot that reveals Judy to have been looking into a mirror, retrospectively interpellates that mirror as a 'fourth wall', a shield between ourselves and the threatening gaze, reflecting the gaze back onto itself.

Later on, in the bell tower, when the re-created Madeleine/Judy looks directly into the camera again, editing procedures suggest that the ghostly nun was the object of her look. But that uncanny figure is only retrospectively the object of her gaze. At the moment of her first, direct look, it is the spectator who is is object, though we will momentarily be collapsed into that ghostly figure of death. This is the moment of the 'cut' in Hitchcock: a hesitation, a gap is introduced between one object of the gaze and its replacement. Here the direct gaze of Hitchcock's Medusa, as we might now put it, unlike the indirect gaze of Caravaggio's, fleetingly brings the spectator into the space of representation, rather than separating us from the scene. But if Medusa's gaze turns us to stone, renders us statues, it also introduces the statue – double of the cadaver – as a shield between ourselves and our death.[58]

Notes

1 Donald Spoto, *The Dark Side of Genius: The Life of Alfred Hitchcock*, New York: Ballantine Books, 1983, pp. 563–4.

2 Marshall Deutelbaum and Leland Poague, 'Hitchcock in Britain', *A Hitchcock Reader*, Marshall Deutelbaum and Leland Poague (eds.), Ames: Iowa State University Press, 1986, p. 64.

3 Drawing upon the work of Hélène Cixous, Tania Modleski suggests that 'decapitation', as opposed to castration, is 'what is at stake for the female – in cinema, as elsewhere'. See *The Women Who Knew Too Much: Hitchcock and Feminist Theory*, New York and London: Routledge, 1988, p. 20.

4 Marin also has a profound interest in decapitations. Louis Marin, 'Et in Arcana hoc', *To Destroy Painting*, trans. Mette Hjort Chicago: University of Chicago Press, 1995, pp. 95–169. Although my work draws directly on that of Marin, I have also read with

interest an essay by Catriona MacLeod called 'Floating Heads: Portrait Busts in Classical Weimar', forthcoming in *Unwrapping Goethe's Weimar*, Burhard Henke, Susanne Kord and Simon Richter (eds.), and her references to Medusa in *Embodying Ambiguity: Androgeny and Aesthetics from Winckelmann to Keller*, Detroit: Wayne State University Press, 1998. This essay was also inspired by the title of a book by Paul Coates: *The Gorgon's Gaze: German Cinema, Expressionism, and the Image of Horror*, Cambridge, UK: Cambridge University Press, 1991.

5 Marin, *To Destroy Painting*, pp. 145–9. Marin refers to and elaborates upon Freud's 'Medusa's Head', in which Freud links decapitation to castration, and the terror of Medusa to terror at the sight of the mother's genitals.

6 Marin, *To Destroy Painting*, p. 112.

7 Stephen Heath, 'Narrative Space', *Questions of Cinema*, Bloomington: Indiana University Press, pp. 23–4. See also Diane Waldman's reading of this still life in 'The Childish, the Insane, the Ugly: The Representation of Modern Art in Popular Films and Fiction of the Forties', *Wide Angle* 5, no. 2, 1982, p. 55.

8 It is a female space because of the way in which the fruit ('Nature's bounty', the nurturing maternal body) and the flowers (which are connected, among other things, to the metaphor of female 'deflowering') both function to connote conventional tropes of the feminine. I might add that this particular painting, with its fragmentation of space, serves to double the connotative value of the still life.

9 Modleski, *The Women Who Knew Too Much*, p. 80.

10 Jean Laplanche, 'The Ego and the Vital Order', *Life and Death in Psychoanalysis*, trans. and ed. Jeffrey Mehlman, Baltimore: Johns Hopkins University Press, 1976, p. 76.

11 Jean Laplanche, 'The Order of Life and the Genesis of Human Sexuality', *Life and Death in Psychoanalysis*, pp. 19–20.

12 Modleski, *The Women Who Knew Too Much*, p. 109. In her chapter on *Frenzy*, Modleski is concerned with the question of the pollution that the ingested corpse engenders. It seems apparent that Peter Greenaway's *The Cook, The Thief, His Wife, and Her Lover* is indebted to *Frenzy*.

13 I thank Richard Allen for pointing me in the direction of this film, and thank him as well for his close reading of this chapter and for sound advice that helped to shape it.

14 Using Hitchcock's words, Pascal Bonitzer refers to the 'stain' in Žižek's sense in this film as a 'drop of blood' in the 'clear waters' of a stream. See 'Hitchcockian Suspense', *Everything You Always Wanted to Know About Lacan (But Were Afraid To Ask Hitchcock)*, Slavoj Žižek (ed.), London and New York: Verso, 1992, p. 22.

15 Lesley Brill, *The Hitchcock Romance: Love and Irony in Hitchcock's Films*, Princeton, NJ: Princeton University Prerss, 1988, p. 285.

16 Slavoj Žižek, 'The Hitchcockian Blot', *Looking Awry: An Introduction to Lacan Through Popular Culture*, Cambridge, MA: MIT Press, 1991, pp. 90–93. (The article is reproduced in this volume: see Chapter 7.)

17 Žižek, 'The Real and Its Vicissitudes', *Looking Awry*, p. 26. This is a far cry from the prelapsarian innocence accorded to the characters of this film by Brill, *The Hitchcock Romance*, p. 284.

18 Brill, *The Hitchcock Romance*, p. 289.

19 James Lastra, 'From the Captured Moment to the Cinematic Image: A Transformation

in Pictorial Order', *The Image in Dispute: Art and Cinema in the Age of Photography*, Dudley Andrew (ed.), Austin: University of Texas Press, 1997, p. 276.

20 As Rothman points out, Norman's hobby is 'analogous to Hitchcock's hobby, fixing the human subject with a camera', *Hitchcock – The Murderous Gaze*, Cambridge, MA: Harvard University Press, 1982, p. 279.

21 André Bazin, 'The Ontology of the Photographic Image', *What is Cinema?*, vol. 1, ed. and trans. Hugh Gray, Berkeley and Los Angeles: University of California Press, 1967, p. 9.

22 Richard Allen, 'Avian Metaphor in *The Birds*', *Hitchcock Annual* (1997–8), pp. 58–9, makes the following connection between the birds and Bates's mummy: 'this "stuffed bird" ' was created by the act of "stuffing a bird" in the sense that combines both a sexual act – the implied incest between Norman and his mother – and the act of killing'.

23 Bazin, 'Ontology of the Photographic Image', p. 9.

24 Kenneth Gross, *The Dream of the Moving Statue*, Ithaca: Cornell University Press, 1992, p. 19.

25 Gross, *The Dream of the Moving Statue*, p. 23.

26 François Truffaut with Helen G. Scott, *Hitchcock*, rev. edn, New York: Simon and Schuster, 1983, p. 165.

27 Stanley Cavell, '*North by Northwest*,' *A Hitchcock Reader*, p. 263.

28 François Truffaut with Helen G. Scott, *Hitchcock*, p. 319.

29 Rothman, *Hitchcock – The Murderous Gaze*, p. 19.

30 Maurice Yacowar, *Hitchcock's British Films*, Hamden, Ct: Archon, 1977, p. 111.

31 One critic suggests that Hitchcock's interest in the double may have been influenced by Murnau's *Der Januskopf* (1920), now lost. See Theodore Price, *Hitchcock and Homosexuality*, Metuchen, NJ and London: Scarecrow Press, 1992, pp. 202, 220.

32 Sir William Smith, *Smaller Classical Dictionary*, rev. edn, New York: E. P. Dutton, 1958, p. 163.

33 One of the paintings in *The Lodger* is interesting with respect to its classical subject matter: it is of a woman tied to the stake, an image of martyrdom.

34 Raymond Bellour, 'Psychosis, Neurosis, Perversion', *A Hitchcock Reader*, pp. 328–9.

35 Marin, *To Destroy Painting*, p. 143.

36 In her seminal article on visual pleasure, Laura Mulvey refers to the focus on one body part or fragment in a film as endowing it with the visual quality of a 'cut out'. See 'Visual Pleasure and Narrative Cinema', *Narrative, Apparatus, Ideology*, Philip Rosen (ed.), New York: Columbia University Press, 1986, p. 203.

37 Spoto, *The Dark Side of Genius*, pp. 38ff.

38 Modleski suggests that it is as if Scottie were continually confronted with the fact that 'he resembles her in ways intolerable to contemplate'. See *The Women Who Knew Too Much*, p. 92.

39 J. Hillis Miller, *Versions of Pygmalion*, Cambridge, MA: Harvard University Press, 1990, p. 11.

40 Robin Wood, 'Male Desire, Male Anxiety: The Essential Hitchcock', *A Hitchcock Reader*, p. 228.

41 Marin, *To Destroy Painting*, p. 117.

42 Marin, *To Destroy Painting*, p. 143.

43 Marin, *To Destroy Painting*, p. 126.

44 Marin, *To Destroy Painting*, p. 133.

45 Bruno Villien, *Hitchcock*, Marseille: Rivages, 1985, p. 7.

46 See Brigitte Peucker, *Incorporating Images: Film and the Rival Arts*, Princeton, NJ: Princeton University Press, 1995, p. 69.

47 Žižek, 'Pornography, Nostalgia, Montage', *Looking Awry*, p. 116.

48 Žižek, 'Pornography, Nostalgia, Montage', p. 116.

49 Žižek, 'The Hitchcockian Blot', p. 91.

50 Žižek, 'The Hitchcockian Blot,' p. 96.

51 Michael Fried, *Absorption and Theatricality: Painting and the Beholder in the Age of Diderot,* Berkeley and Los Angeles: University of California Press, 1980), pp. 100–3. See also Richard Wollheim, 'The Spectator in the Picture: Friedrich, Manet, Hals', *Painting as an Art,* London: Thames & Hudson, 1987, pp. 101–85. We might look to Manet's *Bar at the Folies Bergère* as an example of 'theatrical' painting. Posed in front of a mirror, Manet's barmaid looks directly out of the picture. But where is the painting's beholder, who is surely male? Does he face her directly, and does her body therefore block his reflection in the mirror? Or is he present in the scene, reflected in the mirror's surface because he is standing at an angle, looking at her awry? Has he entered, or is he prevented from entering the space of the picture?

52 For an overview of 'the look back' in the cinema, see Wheeler Winston Dixon, *It Looks at You: The Returned Gaze of Cinema*, Albany: State University of New York Press, 1995.

53 Marian E. Keane, 'A Closer Look at Scopophilia: Mulvey, Hitchcock, and *Vertigo*', *A Hitchcock Reader*, p. 234.

54 Rothman, following Cavell, suggests that some of Hitchcock's characters 'seem to possess the power to confront – hence also to avoid – the camera's gaze', *Hitchcock – The Murderous Gaze*, p. 60.

55 Rothman, *Hitchcock – The Murderous Gaze*, p. 60.

56 Keane, 'A Closer Look at Scopophilia', p. 235.

57 Marin, *To Destroy Painting*, p. 143.

58 Gross sees the 'statue as an archaic double for the cadaver', *The Dream of the Moving Statue*, p. 19.

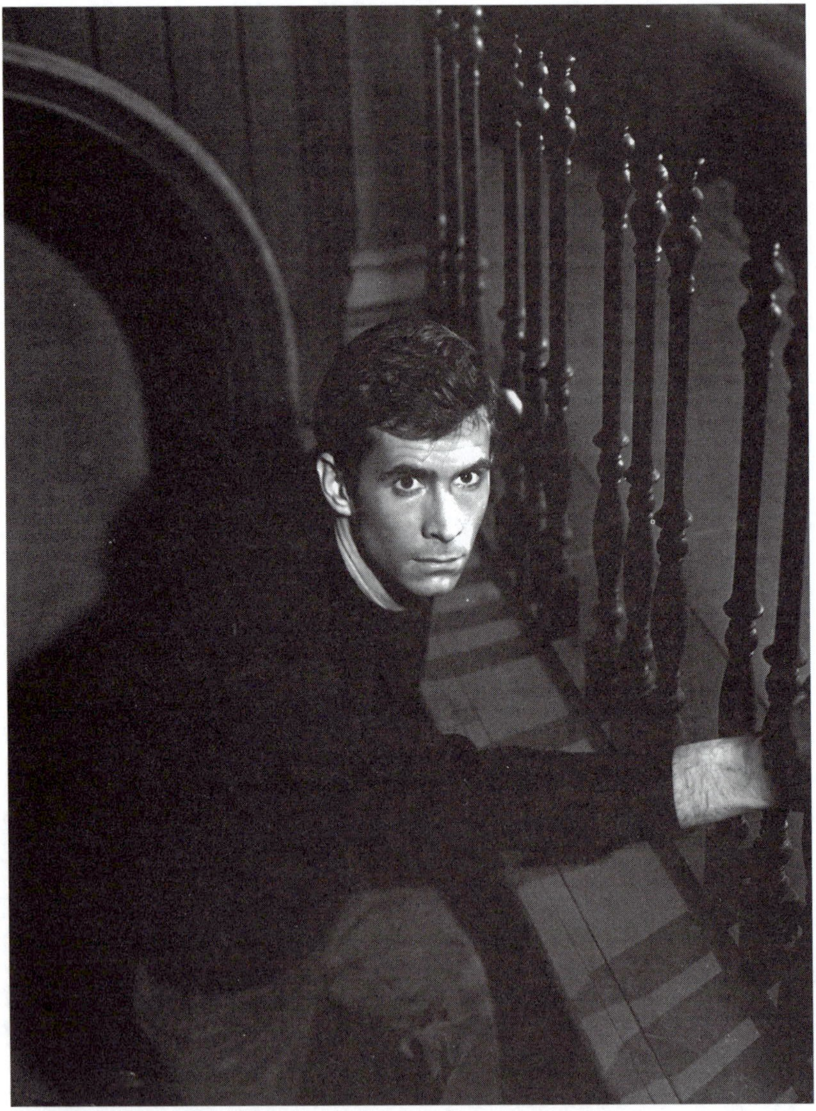

At the centre of the narrative – the awful emptiness of eyes. Anthony Perkins as Norman Bates in *Psycho*

Chapter 11
'If Thine Eye Offend Thee . . .': *Psycho* and the Art of Infection

George Toles

Once all the narrative surprises of Alfred Hitchcock's *Psycho* (1960) have been discovered and its more obvious emotional provocations understood, I find that the most potent sources of my uneasiness while viewing it are still unaccounted for. Discomfort with this work is, in my experience, an endlessly renewable response; it is like a slowly spreading stain in the memory. The film feels as stifled and stifling as the indecipherable mind of its protagonist, Norman Bates. Not only does *Psycho* contain no point of release for the viewer – it also remains unclear what precisely the viewer expects (or needs) to be released *from*. *Psycho* offers a number of gestures of release – a snarling tow chain craning a vehicle out of a swamp, Marion's slowly upraised arm as she sits in the tub after the shower stabbing – which turn out to be no release at all. In the latter episode, for example, Hitchcock caresses us, in the dying woman's presence, with a hope of recovery, then immediately crushes it out as Marion extends her arm beseechingly *to us* (why don't you *do* something?), clutches the shower curtain and collapses to the floor. Marion's gesture to save herself answers our felt need, then instantly turns that need against us. Part of Hitchcock's complex achievement in the film is gradually to deprive us of our sense of what 'safe ground' looks like or feels like.

Psycho properly belongs in the company of such works as Edgar Allan Poe's 'Berenice' and Georges Bataille's *Histoire de l'œil*. These narratives, in addition to achieving their respective forms of pornographic intensity by impersonally rendered shocks, also attach the same obsessive significance to the *eye* as metaphor. Metaphor rather than object: the eye asserts its value and power chiefly through its 'migration toward other objects', as Roland Barthes has suggested in his essay on Bataille's *Histoire*.[1] The true content of the narratives has much less to do with the fate of characters than with the fate of an image – the eye – as it undergoes repeated metamorphoses. Perhaps because the eye seems to represent identity simultaneously at its point of fullest concentration and maximum vulnerability, it naturally functions, in works so deeply concerned with aggression, as the principal locus of metaphoric transformation and exchange. The eye, after all, is the ultimate goal for any act of violation; it is the luminous outward sign of the private soul one wishes to smudge with depravity. But the eye is also profoundly linked with repression, and here it becomes threatening to the violator as well. Everything from the realm of experience that has proved damaging to the self, that has inflicted psychic wounds, has been channelled through the eye. Inevitably, the eye will be the vehicle of recurrence.

In Poe's 'Berenice', there is an effort to limit the eye's potency by treating it as though it were inexpressive to the point of blankness. 'The eyes [of Berenice] were lifeless, and lustreless, and seemingly pupilless, and I shrank involuntarily from their glassy stare to the contemplation of the thin and shrunken lips.'[2] The narrator flees from the overwhelmingly oppressive presence of the eye, persuading himself in the process that the eye cannot see whatever it is that the narrator himself is afraid to see, that is, what he is struggling to repress. In his desire to avoid Berenice's gaze, however, he begins to fix his attention on her mouth, which instantly acquires the characteristics of a substitute eye. The mouth becomes an organ of intellection, whose teeth are oddly endowed with the eye's 'sensitive and sentient power'. As Daniel Hoffman has pointed out, Poe requires us to consider, perhaps for the first time, the ways in which 'mouth and eye resemble each other. Each is an orifice of the body, surrounded by lips or lids which seem to open and close by a will of their own. Each is lubricated by a fluid of its own origin, and each leads inward . . . toward the mysterious interior of the living creature.'[3] The eye and mouth also take on the attributes of the 'opening' that most frightens the narrator (and, in all likelihood, the author as well), and that forms the content of his repression: the vaginal orifice. The mind has made the latter unthinkable by confusing its properties with the mouth's. The vagina, too, is furnished with teeth that demand to be removed ('long, narrow, and excessively white, with the pale lips writhing about them'). In 'Berenice' the eye's transformations can be construed entirely as an effort to block the passage of forbidden material to the conscious mind. With the sort of hideously perverse logic that we encounter in Poe's most distressing tales, the eye must turn into the thing it dreads in order to be spared the sight of it.

Georges Bataille's *Histoire de l'œil* may appear, at first, to offer a less suitable analogue for the workings of *Psycho* than Poe's 'Berenice'. Hitchcock resembles Poe in his relentless preoccupation with repressed material. The spread of a massive, buried hurt or wound seems, as in Poe, to paralyse Hitchcock's narrative from within, finally rendering all of its wary, questing-for-order surface activity beside the point. Bataille, by contrast, foregrounds his horror, coolly displays it in a naked state, and plays with it at close range, like an intimate. The sordid and vicious so fully define the surface action of *Histoire* that the reader can't easily feel that this surface is potentially a screen for something worse. Bataille's story, nevertheless, strikes me as blocked in much the same way that Poe's and Hitchcock's are. His central overdetermined image – the eye, once again – feels like the only solid thing, the only living variable in a world of copulating phantoms. (The characters dwell in 'a world so frail that mere breath might have changed us into light'.)[4] Eyes and their metaphoric substitutes – eggs, a saucer of milk, a bull's testicle – are visually 'there' for us in a way that nothing else is. Bataille imagines a world in which the eye, divorced from a specific personality and body, can pursue a life of pure objecthood, witnessing with pristine detachment acts of staggering vileness. Even when the eye becomes the focus of these acts (to be caressed, licked, pissed upon, punctured), it somehow always seems to float free in the end, aloof and intact. Bataille's repeated emphasis on the slicing and spilling open of eyes has the quality of a magician's demonstration: however mutilated the ceremonial object appears to be, it is perfectly restored in an instant. Though continually assaulted, the 'eye' of the narrative can never go blind.

Punishment inflicted on the eye is not only a means of severing someone's ties with the world (as in the case of Oedipus); it can also be a way of reducing one's consciousness to the status of an object, so that one must learn to deal with consciousness entirely in object terms. The torture of the eye can mark a refusal of inwardness. One can't get past the literal eye, Bataille insists. Nothing stands behind it. Bataille's psychic strategy is to make his inner world so ossified and remote that no living experience, no emotionalised thread of memory can adhere to it. When Bataille addresses us in what we are meant to accept as his own voice in the final section of *Histoire de l'œil*, he disturbs us more thoroughly than at any point in his previous litanies of the monstrous. He recounts memories of his childhood – an utterly frozen landscape – as though they belonged to someone else. His hideous family ordeals are assigned the same value, and given precisely the same sheen of obscenity, as the events of the preceding narrative. Bataille's language refuses at every point to possess what it touches: it is truly a dead language. One finds it almost inconceivable that it could have been formed from the inside, that a life could speak through it.

Tonally, Bataille's endeavour to empty himself through indifference approximates (in function and effect) the austere, insulating wit of Hitchcock's *Psycho*. The best account of Bataille's attraction to the possibilities of indifference occurs in a passage from his study of Manet's paintings: 'Manet's was *supreme indifference*, effortless and stinging; it scandalized but never deigned to take notice of the shock it produced ... The stuff indifference is made of – we might say its intensity – is necessarily manifested when it enters actively into play. It often happens that indifference is revealed as a vital force, or the vehicle of a force otherwise held in check, which finds an outlet through indifference.'[5] Bataille's *Histoire* aspires to show us the paradoxical vitality of an indifference without limits. This indifference might be said to commence at that hypothetical point in the life of an endless scream when the sound is so customary that it is no longer worthy of notice. Personal pain is generally regarded as the one area of experience to which insensibility cannot extend. If, like Bataille's forever entranced character, Marcelle, we were to become so lost to our feelings that we had no way of 'telling one situation from another', we would still be alive to the shock of physical torment. It is this last bastion of aliveness that Bataille desires to level out. What *Histoire*'s narrator reports are agonies without personal dimensions, sensations that mimic those of misery but that somehow exist in a flat, becalmed state. By granting pain a significance, by making any form of emotional concession to it, we only increase its power over us. Let us rather do life the appropriate disservice of denying to all of it the force of a lasting impression. Indifference alone rescues us from the humiliation of engagement.

Wit is Hitchcock's less conspicuous means of announcing *his* indifference, his refusal to be engaged or soiled by his transactions with suffering. The persistent presence of wit in *Psycho* should not be mistaken, in the calmness of its operations, for a mitigation of brutality. *Psycho*'s wit is hard and deeply ingrown; it stays well below the surface of action, strangely unavailable (on a first viewing) to characters and audience alike. It is only with Norman's final speech that the director's mode of joking seems to merge with the awareness of a figure within the film's world. When the mysteriously mocking voice of 'Mrs Bates' at last reaches us, we cannot avoid the feeling that in its ironically 'vacant' depravity it is the one voice we have heard that genuinely expresses the film's tone: 'It is sad when a mother has to speak the words that condemn her own son.' Bataille once wrote that 'decent people have gelded eyes. That's why they fear lewdness.' Mrs Bates, whose sockets are both full and hollow, directly scrutinises us (the viewers) with the gelded eyes of decency. She speaks quietly to us of a mother's duty to put an end to a bad son while we are confounded by the sight of her effortlessly inhabiting the lost son's body. (Yet another case of a character's gaze turning into the image it is forbidden to see.)

One is not really permitted to go anywhere with this image, or with the speech that accompanies it. Everything about them is sealed in, like the dead eye 'soaked with tears of urine' that peers out of Simone's womb near the close of *Histoire*. We are almost beyond the language of 'implications' here. Mrs Bates's speech, imposed on Norman's rigid features, is offered as the impenetrable punch line of the joke that is *Psycho*. In the widest possible sense, we are left in the dark.

For Hitchcock, who is as sedate and comfortable in his chair as Mrs Bates is in hers, wit always has the right to assert its innocence. It provides the inner life with a means of guarding itself absolutely in the very act of unveiling. Wit opens a place for the self to stand, composed and invulnerable, at a vast remove from any sense of pain that could damage it or spoil its game. Wit allows one to punish to one's heart's content, in the manner of Mrs Bates, and yet remain blameless. It is the public guarantee that a crime or sin (regardless of appearances) has not quite been committed. The underlying content of art that compulsively seeks out some form of 'joke container' for the expression of disorder may be understood as 'the holding back from things', a phrase Sanford Schwartz has recently applied to the early paintings of de Chirico. 'The pictures are about waiting, keeping oneself clean and untouched. The undercoating of nightmarish dread in them comes from someone who fears making a certain move.'[6]

The fear of making a move is pervasive in Hitchcock's work, but it achieves special prominence in *Psycho*, where neither the characters nor the imagery seem to possess any alternative to immobility. Perhaps it is the complete dissociation of authorial self from an imagery that is struggling to express it that gives to *Psycho*, 'Berenice' and *Histoire de l'œil* their 'infected' character. The normal poetic activity of making metaphors becomes precarious in these works because images have somehow lost the capacity for internal growth. An image cannot build beyond itself, provoking new connections with the 'world at large' when it is entirely cut off from the impulse, desire or need that called it into being. Instead of widening its range of associations, it can only replicate itself obsessively, craving the origin that is denied it, futilely attempting to burrow inward. The artist can neither separate himself from his dominant image nor see it plainly enough to penetrate it. Art that lacks all mobility, as this art does, can only fester in the place where it's stuck – and hence communicates by infection, spreading the mess that can't be gotten rid of to whatever it touches. Bataille, Poe and Hitchcock cannot – in the works we're examining – give their oppressive metaphors any outward, public meaning except that of shock; but they are equally blocked from carrying the 'eye' image inside. It is the interior, above all, from which this image is in flight. Like Scottie Ferguson, standing traumatised at the edge of the Mission Bell Tower in the final shot of Hitchcock's *Vertigo* (1958), unable to take a single step forward or back, these narratives can only articulate the hopeless stasis that has engendered them.

Having made some progress in establishing the nature of the metaphor we are concerned with, I will try to show how it operates in the shower-murder sequence of *Psycho*.

Once more we are confronted with a narrative situation in which a vicious, morally appalling act (murder this time), that would seem to demand our full emotional engagement, is subordinated to an eye's encounter with visual analogues. Why are we encouraged to notice, while Marion Crane is being stabbed, that the shower rose, Marion's screaming mouth and finally the drain into which her blood flows all correspond, at some level, to the victim's congealed eye? In a culminating extreme close-up, this eye contemplates us with the alert fixity of death, while a false tear, formed by a drop of shower water on Marion's face, announces that emotion (of any kind) has no further part to play here. The tear might as well be a fly: nothing is but what is. Why does Hitchcock linger so long over this image, and why does the match cut between the drain and the corpse's eye seem so conclusively to define the imaginative centre of the film?

Oddly enough, Marion does not appear to lose her place in the world of *Psycho* after being brutally slain. Instead, one has the feeling that she has at long last *found* her proper relationship to that world. When Hitchcock's camera seems to emerge from the darkness within the drain *through* Marion's eye, and then eases back further to reveal her twisted head insensibly pressed against the floor, the camera comes as close as it ever will to caressing the object placed in front of it. We are being invited – before we have had any chance to recover our equilibrium – to participate in the camera's eerie calm by looking at things in the ways that the camera instructs us. How *evenly* dead this girl is. How perfectly and compliantly she harmonises with the other blank surfaces in her environment. Turbulence has surprisingly given way to an order, a settled view, that nothing can put a stop to.

The camera elects to remain in a room that is temporarily deprived of any human presence. Its purpose in doing so is to tranquilise this setting by invoking an aesthetic response to it. The fearful disarrangement of the bathroom space that horror has just visited is not simply curtailed, it is denied. By the time Norman rushes into the motel room, discovers the body and turns away from it in panicky disbelief, his response is already disproportionate to ours. His anxiety subtly registers as an overreaction. Norman's agitated gestures fly in the face of the hypnotic stillness and order that the gliding camera of the previous scene proposed as normative, reasonable.

For a number of years now, the standard means of justifying the shower murder to viewers who find it repellent has been V. F. Perkins's argument that Hitchcock's skilful montage succeeds in 'aestheticizing' its cruelty.[7] After all, we never actually see the knife penetrating Marion's flesh; we are only required to imagine it. Clearly this line of defense needs to be re-examined. There seems to be an underlying assumption that an aesthetic effect automatically acts as a cleansing agent, or as a guarantee of moral discretion in the creative process. But as we have seen in the case of 'Berenice' and *Histoire de l'œil*, even the most unsavoury, abhorrent imagery can be made to yield a powerful aesthetic impression.

Before drawing any conclusions about the formal lucidity of Hitchcock's conception of the shower sequence, one would do well to consider the massive weight that this episode achieves within the total narrative structure. In Robert Bloch's potboiler novel, from which *Psycho* was adapted, Marion's death – far from being the central action in the plot – is matter-of-factly reported in a single, terse sentence. If it is appropriate to point out that Bloch made nothing of an event that Hitchcock responded to with astonishing imaginative intensity, it is also appropriate to inquire why Hitchcock made so much of it. Does it seem either dramatically feasible or fitting that a female protagonist whose status in the narrative never rises above that of pitiable victim should be disposed of in so extravagant, prolonged and visually intoxicating a fashion? Is Marion's shabby, useless death a proper occasion for a virtuoso set piece? Surely an abbreviated, less conspicuously artful presentation would honour the victim more, if the *meaning* (in human terms) of what transpired figured at all in the artist's calculations.

The consequence of Hitchcock's aestheticised rendering is, instead, to enlarge the minutiae, in the manner of a pornographer prowling around flailing torsos, seeking out details to close in on. Hitchcock wants to make the act of slicing wholly *legible*, as opposed to merely visible. To show the knife piercing flesh might cause the viewer to avert his gaze. Hitchcock designs the stabbing to be as salaciously riveting as possible. We are meant – in fact, positively encouraged – to *see it all*, both what he shows and what he refrains from showing. The blanks that his editing leaves can only be filled in one way. Marion's degradation is increased immeasurably by our awareness that nothing in the moment-to-moment scrutiny of her ordeal is random or accidental. The entire murder feels densely inhabited by the director himself. What are we to make of his calm determination to extract a kind of classical shapeliness and beauty from this broad, unbeautiful pour of chaos?

It is impossible to understand the vision that *Psycho* as a whole is expressing in any terms other than those used in the shower sequence. But, as I hope to have demonstrated, Marion's murder refuses to accommodate any of the humanised or aesthetically dignified meanings one would be inclined to project onto it. I am sure that Hitchcock was not trying to deceive us when he said that the shower sequence had *no* meaning, as far as he was concerned. He placed it in that strangely aseptic realm of 'pure cinema', where images, like poems, should not mean but be. For an image simply 'to be', in Hitchcock's terms, it must be acknowledged as something with no depth – the screened image is both literally and ontologically flat. As Garrett Stewart has suggested in his essay on Keaton's *Sherlock Jr.* (1924), the most formidable illusion of movie space is that we seem to be looking into a frame 'past which is recess and perspective'.[8] Hitchcock's style is predicated on the belief that the *surface* of a screened image is absolute. It never yields to anything 'within'. The only interior it has is supplied by the mind of the spectator.

For Hitchcock the passage of material from life to the cinema involves an immediate (and total) subtraction of unmanageable elements. Film is not a medium for introspection. Disordered activity of any sort has no place there. Hitchcock conceives the act of building a patterned sequence of images as a means of asserting control over a 'problem' without ever being required to *examine* it. In designing a series of shots, the mind can limit itself to lateral motion. There is no need to 'look down', to probe past the image surface. One can always substitute further complications of formal arrangement for the distasteful messiness of analysing one's position. Joseph Stefano, the screenwriter of *Psycho*, memorably described Hitchcock directing a nude model in the shower sequence. He stood on a platform above the shower in his dark business suit, 'a model of rectitude and composure. One sensed that Alfred Hitchcock does not stand in front of naked women, and that he has precisely this feeling about himself, so that for him she was not naked, and that was that.'[9]

Arranging a composition for the camera is the way to demonstrate that its content is manageable. And the only level on which this content has to be seen and accounted for is the level of form. It is possible, therefore, for Hitchcock to work in the very midst of his obsessive fears and unacceptable desires, yet not be confronted by them. His negotiations with obsession are never carried on from the inside. He has only to 'frame' his anxiety, flatten it into an image, for it to be held in place. Viewers, of course, as he well knows, will very likely 'dirty' themselves as they imagine the experience that he has at no point felt obliged to touch. They cannot keep the images at a regulated distance (and thus handle them with the proper delicacy) because they did not control the process that brought them into being. Control, as always for Hitchcock, is to be understood here as the ability not to internalise. However much he may be stirred by his proximity to the extremes of sadism in the shower killing, he is persuaded that the search for visual order is a permanent safeguard against fixation, and that he can endlessly brood upon the separate details of the action while keeping his perceptions chaste. Hitchcock's decision to link the 'eye' throughout the shower sequence with as many other ovals as possible derives from his conviction that any painful subject can be stabilised if one locates a point of concentration apart from the 'thing itself'. There is invariably something distinct from the business of suffering to claim one's attention.

But eyes and eye surrogates, as the examples of Poe and Bataille make clear, are never safe resting places. In fact, the three Hitchcock films that seem to me the purest (and most extreme) embodiments of his imaginative concerns (*Rear Window* (1954), *Vertigo* and *Psycho*) make an affliction of the eye their ascendant theme. *Vertigo*'s credits present us with a mask-like female face in which only the nervously moving eyes betray any distress. The camera then proceeds to move into one of these eyes, passing mysteriously through the pupil and coming out 'behind' it – thus marking a path to which Hitchcock will return in *Psycho*. Only in the latter he reverses his direction, as the dark drain 'proposes' a withdrawal from an eye that is dead. Interestingly, all of the eyes that matter in *Psycho* are counterparts of this dead eye – cruel, staring or frozen, they seem to hold only one expression. And eventually we discover that this single, ominous look, forever resurfacing like a figure in a nightmare, has belonged from the outset to Norman Bates.

Earlier, I suggested that Norman's voice at the end of *Psycho* is the only authentic voice we hear in the film. He is simultaneously revealed – at that instant when he finally meets the camera's gaze and looks directly at us – as possessing the only acceptable pair of eyes. The man whose stare has become an awful and limitless conjunction of emptiness is *Psycho*'s one true seer. The hobby of this seer, one recalls, was taxidermy, which allowed him to conduct studies of birds to find out how eyes 'die' (or, as in his mother's case, fail to die – transformed into living wounds that the son must try to heal). The film as a whole is equally concerned with the process by which eyes surrender their identity (or life) to Norman. By a spectacular feat of absorption, Norman ultimately manages to contain the entire world of the film in his pitiless glare.

Psycho's next-to-last image is a dissolve of Norman's face into the mummified features of his mother; for a moment he seems to peer through the empty sockets in which his eyes are now imaginatively sealed. The dissolves could continue almost indefinitely, however, because Hitchcock's key imagery in the film is nearly all constructed on the same principle: Mr Lowery's accusing glance that launches Marion's flight by car; the policeman's sunglasses looming gigantically over her as she wakens from sleep; Marion, throughout her nocturnal journey, peering toward us anxiously from behind the wheel of her car as we share her thoughts. (At one point, when imagining Cassidy's threat to replace his stolen money 'with her fine, soft flesh', she smiles in close-up, and her expression hauntingly duplicates Norman's final, mocking look.) Following Marion's introduction to Norman, we are shown the silent company of stuffed night birds that 'watch' Norman in his parlour, one of whose wings are extended so that it appears forever in passage toward its prey; when Marion has left the parlour, we see Norman's eye, in mammoth close-up, intently fixed upon his hidden peephole – a large, dark, circular gouge in the wall with a single point of light at the centre. (The hole–eye linkage clearly prepares us for the comparison of eye and drain.) And as the shower sequence commences, there is a close-up of a toilet bowl flushing down a torn scrap of paper that Marion doesn't wish anyone to see. By this juncture, as we have already observed, the eye is fully available for complex metamorphic exchanges with other objects. The toilet bowl, like the drain, is yet another visual sign for the eye evacuating its contents.

Once Marion is dead, and Norman sets about eliminating all traces of her presence, two additional eye metaphors emerge. Thus Hitchcock completes the series that began with Norman at his peephole by circling back to him and, in effect, showing how Marion's eye has resolved itself into his. There is an overhead close-up of the circular rim and black interior of Norman's pail as first his bloodied cleaning rags and then the mop with which he has cleaned the sides of the tub are thrust into it. Here, and in the more potent image that soon follows – the top of Marion's car forming a ghostly white spot in the middle of an encircling swamp – the hollow eye of the drain is replaced by more clotted and retentive ovals: eyes filling up rather than emptying, but only with unwanted things. Norman contrives to make whatever disturbs him disappear from sight, but instead, like the vehicle suspended in the swamp, the objects of his anxiety look back at him.

Norman relates to his field of vision as though it were somehow interchangeable with the field of consciousness. (In this respect, he resembles Hitchcock.) The successful manipulation of perception is taken to mean that the mind is under equally strict direction. Life, for Norman, has gradually been reduced to an endless tidying up of his barely manageable visual space. His is forever devising fresh hiding places for his mother's (and his own) garbage. Anything that his mother judges depraved (i.e., anything provoking strong desires in Norman – and mother always knows) must be dropped from the perceptual frame. 'Out of sight, out of mind' is the chief article of faith in the Bates household. If one thinks about it carefully, one realises that the dramatic situation in *Psycho* literally dictates that Norman and his 'mother' can never see the same things at the same time and never see them in the same way. They are constantly vying for possession of the same visual field; whoever 'sees' at a given moment is empowered to make an interpretation, but the meaning of the visual field alters radically as control of it shifts back and forth. The question that I feel is necessary to consider is, where does Norman's vision go, where does his knowledge and desire hide during those intervals when he is not permitted to absorb what his eyes perceive?

Norman's extreme but eminently logical solution to his impossible filial bind is to learn how to see and do the things that are forbidden to him without actually seeing anything. That is to say, the fact of his presence and involvement in acts that are literally unthinkable for him is 'dropped from the frame'. As his mother blindly wields the knife, Norman's eyes are somewhere else, trying to stay focused on what is decent. It is doubly imperative then that he do a thorough cleaning job when 'something bad' happens because he must expunge the event from both public *and* personal view. As Norman desperately suppresses his own powers of vision, he comes to believe that the work of seeing has been taken over by the inert forms that fill his landscape. His closed world has truly become a beast with a thousand eyes, whose sole end is to keep him under surveillance.

Norman's perception is restricted to the order he manages to maintain within his frame. Beyond that increasingly close-at-hand point where order ceases, he encounters a blank wall. But the various 'holes' he has filled for the sake of order – the swamp, the fruit cellar, the parlour with its mounted birds, his mother's corpse – have sprouted eyes whose awareness is rooted in that ugly disorder Norman has gone to such pains to eradicate. The blank space where Norman's vision tapers off is the place where theirs begins: 'they' can see further because 'they' can see into things. And because Norman's carefully limited outer world has become hopelessly confused with his inner world, he expresses any form of looking as a violation. As he tells Marion in his parlour, he knows what it feels like to have 'cruel eyes' studying him. His survival, however, depends on his ability to keep the perception of this undifferentiated other split off from his own. He cannot allow himself to imagine, even for a moment, what it is those alien, impenetrable eyes might know about him.

This aspect of Norman's predicament helps to explain the omnipresence of mirrors and reflections in *Psycho*. Beginning with Marion's decision to steal $40,000, which she arrives at while looking at herself in the mirror, almost every interior scene prominently features a mirror that doubles as a character's image, but that *no one* turns to face. In Marion's case, as James Naremore points out in his valuable *Filmguide to Psycho*, the ability to confront her own image is lost after the theft.[10] This is one of the many ways in which Marion's surrender to her 'nameless urge' serves to draw her ineluctably into Norman's frame of reference. After Marion is repeatedly shown attended by reflections of herself that she does not acknowledge (in the bathroom of the used car lot, at the motel registration desk and in the motel room itself), the pattern is given a sudden, disquieting twist. While Marion is stationed in profile beside the motel's dresser mirror, Norman stands in for the reflection in the following series of shots. In Hitchcock's shot–countershot cutting between Norman and Marion, we notice that the profile views of the two facing figures are perfectly symmetrical. Norman occupies the extreme right-hand side of an imbalanced frame, Marion the extreme left-hand side in alternate shots: mirror images.

Norman's imprisonment in the midst of steadily more ominous reflections is shadowed forth in Marion's situation at the motel. In the world of *Psycho*, whenever one picture of the self cracks or is denied recognition, another more dangerous image must form in its place. Inside the crack, so to speak. Marion refuses to look at herself, so Norman will look for her. He will reflect her life by making it into a likeness of his own, although he doesn't understand (any more than she does) what this will entail. Once this life mirroring has commenced, it proceeds on a number of levels. Norman seems to stand in for Sam Loomis, Marion's lover, as well as for her (the physical resemblance of the two men has been noted by many critics). The last, frustratingly inconclusive meeting of the two lovers is replayed in a more sombre key by Norman and Marion.

Sam Loomis, who is not strong enough to act upon his love (or whose love is not strong enough to require action), gives way to an even weaker Norman, whose emotional energies have been strangled and for whom 'falling in love' can only mean what it means to Scottie Ferguson in *Vertigo*: falling into the void at one's centre. Norman's eye for beauty is really an incurable appetite for nothingness. And yet strength of a certain kind exists in Norman. He is sufficiently strong to punish a *desire* for love that has no right to assert itself (mother says so) and nowhere to go. Unlike Sam, he will carry things through to an end point; if Marion can only threaten and confuse him as an image of love, she can be made to reflect him in some other way that will allow for a completing action.

Marion had stolen the money, as she sees it, because she chose to stake everything on love. She flees by car through the night, driving, she imagines, toward her love, but at some point in her journey passes 'through the looking glass' and ends up facing Norman instead, a ghastly inversion of that love. Then Hitchcock, having revealed the things that prevent love from becoming what it wants to be in the world of this film, discloses what is left for it to become. 'On the right hand could slide the left glove,' as Robert Graves wrote in his poem 'The Terraced Valley'. 'Neat over-under.'

Norman's 'courtship' of Marion revives, in ghostly fashion, many of the gestures, conversational topics and objects of attention present in *Psycho*'s opening love scene – whatever filled the intervals between Sam and Marion's dispirited, unsatisfying embraces. The meal that Marion 'didn't touch' in the hotel (and that Mrs Bates wouldn't permit her to touch in the intimate precincts of her household) is finally completed with Norman in the motel parlour. Both Sam and Norman are given a moment where they throw open a window in response to the felt pressure of Marion's presence – Sam, out of discomfort with her talk of marriage; Norman, in his embarrassment at being alone with Marion in her bedroom. (The sudden, rasping sound of the venetian blinds as Sam jerks them up matches the sound and motion of the shower curtain being torn open.) Marion counters Sam's suggestion that they leave the hotel together by pointing out that he hasn't got his shoes on. These are the joking terms of their final separation. Sam remains behind, and we last observe him standing motionless, staring down at his stockinged feet. Just before Norman leaves Marion's motel room to go up to the house to arrange for their private supper, he registers his guilty delight at her acceptance of his invitation by stammering instructions to get herself settled 'and – and take off your wet shoes'. The removal of her shoes will serve to hold her there in the bedroom until his return – that is to say, in this particular bedroom, the site of all his secret erotic investigations. For Norman, requesting a woman to take off any article of apparel signals a daring advance in intimacy; the mention of shoes is his nervous, shorthand approach to 'Why don't you slip into something more comfortable – and revealing?'.

Later, in the parlour, Norman picks up the thread of Sam's earlier talk about 'traps'. Sam had described his life as a confinement within the 'tiny back room' of his hardware store. (After Marion's death, Hitchcock provides a long-shot view of Sam at his desk in this room, from a camera positioned in the main doorway of the store. This shot neatly matches the hallway perspective of Norman seated at the kitchen table of the Bates's mansion directly before the shower scene. The mammoth interior of this house visually dwarfs him; the only spaces that he feels free to occupy in his own person are 'out of the way' rooms behind the main living area.) Sam had also complained to Marion about having constantly to 'sweat for people who aren't there'. In the parlour scene, Norman vastly extends the scope of Sam's plight. 'We scratch and claw, but only at the air, only at each other. And for all of it, we never budge an inch.' There is no distinction to be made between 'the air' and 'each other'. We want the world to at least double itself for us when seen through eyes of love, but it remains intractably single (whatever our delusions to the contrary). We are always much 'further out' than others think, to paraphrase a line of British poet Stevie Smith, 'And not waving but drowning.' The only movements we make that are truly answered are those we see in our mirrors. And this, too, is empty space; we are forever thrown back on ourselves, possessors of nothing.

The only fully spontaneous moment Sam and Marion have together – one in which Marion's desperation is as much in evidence as her attachment to her lover – occurs when she runs towards Sam for an extended embrace in front of the large screen of a closed venetian blind. The next time Marion is placed before such a screen, it has become a shower curtain. Now it is Norman who is coming toward *her*, to be joined with Marion in a different kind of embrace. Touching and caressing have, of course, been the subtracted element in Norman's halting variation on Marion's assignation with Sam. He has only managed to touch her nakedness with his eye. At last he presents himself to her without barriers – on her side of the curtain-screen – and enacts his 'violent feeling' for her in the only way possible for him.

From Marion's standpoint, the shower (prior to the attack) is both a moral cleansing and an act of self-restoration. Afterwards, she will once again be able to meet her own gaze in the mirror. But as we have seen, Norman has replaced the image she turned away from. Having lost sight of herself once, while in the grip of compulsion, she is denied any chance to find her way back. In the course of her journey to Bates's motel, she has had to escape from one distrustful, accusing face after another. 'Who are you and what are you doing?' is the unspoken question in every conversation. And Marion could not begin to formulate an answer. Everything conspires to turn her world inside out. In this condition, she at last lights upon the sympathetic image of Norman Bates, someone whose look she is not afraid of. He offers to keep her company in the darkness. As she listens to him divulge the story of his barren life, he becomes more troubling, but at the same time she begins to recognise herself in his tormented presence (or thinks she does). She sees him as the instrument of her salvation: 'This could be *my* life; I must not let it be.' Having reached this understanding, Marion turns away from Norman, just as she withdrew from the uncomfortable figure regarding her in her mirror at home. But she is forced to confront this dim, hovering reflection one more time in the shower episode.

In Hitchcock's exceptionally demanding metaphoric scheme, where the eye is the faculty for 'unseeing' and mirrors are present only so that they can be avoided, the shower murder, as I've previously argued, is the point of greatest metaphoric blockage, and consequently, greatest pressure for release. It is the place where Hitchcock, like Bataille and

Poe (but equally like Norman and Marion), can neither separate himself from the image, nor see it plainly enough to penetrate it. Hitchcock goes to such extreme lengths to create the impression that Norman and Marion and Marion and Sam mirror each other because the world of *Psycho* is traumatically fixated; it has no capacity for enlargement. Everything in it seems to be formed at the point of rupture in Norman's vision – the blocked passage between his public self and 'lost' private self. This is the point at which *nothing* can ever be seen or taken in. In his brilliant study of metamorphosis in literature, *The Gaping Pig*, Irving Massey suggests that 'trauma, like art, develops at the point where imitation replaces action . . . We mimic what we cannot fight off.'[11] The shocks in *Psycho* all seem to erupt from within, as they do in dreams, where characters form and reform under the pressure of a single image, and where all movement leads to the same place. ('And for all of it, we never budge an inch.')

I have already compared the shower curtain to the screen of the venetian blind in the hotel room. (And recall that Hitchcock's camera, anticipating Norman's shadow slowly advancing behind the curtain, introduced itself in *Psycho* by entering like a phantom behind the venetian blind and probing the dark opening of an eye-like window. This first descent into a vacant eye is the action that brings the film's world into focus.) The curtain also invites comparison with a mirror. Norman's dark silhouette serves as a mirror for Marion when she whirls to face it because all the unresolved elements in her experience seem to converge in it with hallucinatory force: the car windshield wiper making 'knife strokes' against the rain; the policeman's huge, disembodied head in dark glasses startling her awake that morning; the swooping owl in Norman's parlour; Norman's visible desire for her; his anxious, lonely eyes suddenly turning rigid and glowering as he leaned forward in his chair; her fear of being captured and exposed; and ultimately, ending at the place where she (and the film) began, her own body lying motionless (on a bed/bathroom floor), eyes fixed upon a man looming over her: Sam/Norman. Marion's recognition – that this death is meant for her and not anyone else, that all her confused strivings have been directed to this goal, which imitates her life and which she fends off like a traumatic recollection – solves nothing, of course. It simply places her squarely on the hopeless ground she is doomed to occupy: 'Now I know where I am.' This is more than the viewer can say as the film's action comes to a dream-like halt with the death of its apparent subject, and then – inexplicably – continues.

When Hitchcock's camera finally relinquishes its hold on Marion, after fully expressing its fascination with her immobility, it moves out of the bathroom and over to Marion's night table, where her stolen money lies in a newspaper. The camera registers uncertainty about what its subject should now be; it does not appear to know what it's looking for. This is an uncertainty shared by all of *Psycho*'s remaining characters.[12] Once Marion's theft, her guilt and the money itself have been eliminated as concerns of the film, Hitchcock contrives to keep the subject of *Psycho* physically absent and morally indefinable. It is pushed out of everyone's reach. No one, including Norman, is in possession of what is withheld. To the extent that it can be identified at all, *Psycho*'s 'issue' becomes the silhouette behind the curtain – an image poised to shatter at the eye's moment of contact with it, like the double reflection that startles Marion's sister Lila during her search of Mrs Bates's bedroom. (As Lila turns to accost the woman behind her, what she discovers is her own distraught face in the looking glass.) *Psycho*'s missing subject is perhaps best described as a figure glimpsed but never quite seen: a dim outline in a lighted upstairs window; the spectral imprint of a rigidly coiled form on a mattress. On a first viewing, we chiefly feel it as a threat of recurrence that is under no one's control.

The various subjective filters through which the search for answers is carried forward (Arbogast, Lila, Sam) seem to know less and less about the quality of dread that fills the air. Our only link with these characters is the act of searching, but they are only able to search for things that we know are not there. (Marion rolled up in a curtain; the money rolled up in newspaper.) They futilely retrace each other's steps and imitate each other's actions, without ever having the sense of what their eyes need to connect with. In effect, they are all the same character, existing only to pass through the rooms of the motel and house, exposing themselves to the disturbing features of a landscape that will never be made clear. This composite searcher belongs to the 'inside world' as surely as Norman Bates does. From Norman's side of the mirror, it is the strangers' search which poses the danger of uncontrollable repetition: it is the shadow of *his* trauma that seems to draw nearer with Arbogast's and Lila's furtive movements through his domain. They are closing off his mental exits, sealing him in. The only place for him to hide from the object of his dread is within the object itself: 'Hold me, mother; hold me tight. I'm afraid to go to sleep.' As long as mother is there to protect him, the dark places can't be opened. To quote Massey once again, trauma 'may be a thought that has never been killed, that has never been set off from the self'.[13] Norman's murders are attempts to eliminate a thought that must not take form. Killing is, paradoxically, the deepest place of forgetting.

It remains to inquire why so many of the films made by Hitchcock in this period place the problems opposing the characters so fully in the realm of mind, but out of the mind's reach. Hitchcock's customary starting point in a film project was a situation in which *outer* circumstances had somehow passed out of one's control. The emphasis shifted decisively in *Vertigo*, where inner circumstances become the unmanageable factor. As anyone who has studied Hitchcock's style is aware, the basic building block in his narrative structures is always the 'reacting look' of his characters. Major scenes are typically conceived as an intricate juxtaposition of glances with various objects and figures to which the perceiver has a clearly defined emotional relation. Hitchcock generates suspense by uniting the viewer's gaze with a character who, for some reason, is prevented from seeing his situation whole. Characters are menaced either by details they've failed to see or by the sheer mass of what they do see. The audience generally has no difficulty in reading a character's look because they know what to make of the objects set before them; they understand why the character finds those things important.

In *Vertigo* Hitchcock is no longer dealing with 'transparent' reactions. The precise nature of Scottie Ferguson's relationship to what he sees is in doubt from the beginning. *How* his eye sees becomes vastly more important than the information it is given to process. His perceptions reflect a mounting internal strain and distortion; there has been a poisoning at the source. The camera in *Vertigo* repeatedly performs hypnotic circling movements around its subjects so that everything comes to be seen in the light of Scottie's disorder. Circling also defines Scottie's problematic visual relationship with the objects that seriously engage him: they form a vortex for the eye. He stands helpless under their spell. For example, Scottie discovers that he is in love with Madeleine as he stares himself into a haunted state. Being in love means not being able to look away, being so utterly lost to the properties of one image that no other is in any meaningful sense visually alive. Whatever is associated with the beloved is hyperfetishised – which is to say, rendered static, immutable. If Madeleine would return his love, she can only prove the genuineness of her feeling for him by remaining forever the same, exactly as he first saw her.

Scottie has been immobilised by a profound emotional shock in the film's opening scene (a policeman attempting to rescue him as he hangs suspended from the side of a building, loses his balance and plunges to his death). Scottie attempts to free himself from this trauma by exchanging his fear for what he takes to be love, but the only form of love he is open to is one that will reproduce or imitate the conditions of that original shock. He requires a love that will not participate in the dangerous flux of reality – that will stay frozen, suspended, at a fixed distance. The cure for vertigo, he believes, is to make something in his world stand perfectly still. There is no need to question his own immobility in the presence of one who is compelled to share it. Naturally, a love with trauma at its base must eventually find its way back to that trauma. Both of Madeleine's declarations of love to Scottie are quickly followed by the sight of her falling from the tower of the Mission Dolores. Madeleine's plunge to annihilation is at once an absolute barrier to love and its only possible expression. The vision of her descent possesses Scottie completely. The real reasons for Scottie's continual resubjection to the image that blinds and paralyses him are not those manufactured in the external plot. What numbs the viewer, finally, in *Vertigo* is that all of its mysterious occurrences seem called into being by a terrible inner necessity. To meet the demands of Scottie's love, Madeleine must literally fall through the hole of his gaze. It is only there, where love empties itself and dies, that he is able to see her.

In *The Birds* (1963) it might appear that Hitchcock has returned to the realm of purely external aggression, but an examination of its structure reveals that the terms of inquiry are a further elaboration of those in *Vertigo* and *Psycho*. Once again, and in a most daring manner, Hitchcock effects a strange separation between his characters and a subject that resists formulation, perhaps even widening the gap that we feel in *Psycho*. As so many critics complained at the time of *The Birds*'s release, the painstakingly elaborated network of psychological relationships that is Hitchcock's primary focus for roughly the first half of the film has only the most tenuous pertinence to the bird invasions that dominate the second half. The latter seem to function more as an interruption than as an extension of the film's thematic concerns. Furthermore, one is not convinced that the birds have any role to play in the elucidation or working through of the characters' difficulties. They appear to be there for their own sake, and Hitchcock consistently baffles our efforts to make anything of them.

I would argue that, like the 'dead eye' in *Psycho*, the birds are a metaphor caught in transit – one that can only repeat itself because it has no capacity for growth or conversion. The birds are the 'forgotten' image in Hitchcock's world, the shadow behind the curtain ('so vacillating and indistinct an outline') that cannot quite be seen for what it is or truly named. For that reason it is empowered to translate everything (at any moment) into its own dark language. Only once in the course of the film does Hitchcock provide us with direct visual evidence of the worst that the birds can do: in a lake of silence, the camera executes three harrowing jump-cut moves toward the corpse of Dan Fawcett, whose pecked-out eyes have become rings of blood. The 'shock that has no end' is the secret quarry of *The Birds*. By the end of the film, each of the surviving principal female characters – Melanie, Lydia, and Cathy – has been steeped in a trauma that she will never be able to decipher. The child, Cathy, is obliged to stand by a window and watch, stunned, as the protector who had just pushed her to safety behind the door is swiftly mutilated. Lydia, upon her discovery of Dan Fawcett's corpse, rushes from his house in a daze and struggles, for what seems an eternity, to find a word or a scream that can be fitted to what she has beheld. No sound will come forth, and thereafter her main activity in the film is to listlessly survey the contents of her household, waiting for them to resume their former connection to her, or hoping perhaps to stare them back into some form of sense. Melanie, who is subjected to a long, tremendously savage attack near the film's conclusion, offers us, as one of her last gestures, a 'clawing of the empty air' in front of her in a desperate attempt to stave off a horror she can still see. *The Birds*, then, is also about the process of being caught in spaces from which there can be no mental advance.

In *Psycho* Hitchcock's camera can never complete its search for 'Norman Bates' because from the very outset it is so firmly fused with the object of its quest. The camera eye, in effect, is seeking to uncover itself, recalling once more the moment when Lila is trapped between the two facing mirrors in the Bates's mansion. It is in this sense that *Psycho* demands consideration as a *personal* film. Both the proclivities and areas of withdrawal in Norman's mode of vision – in fact, his whole strategy of structured avoidance – faithfully reproduce Hitchcock's own method of screening the world, where exposure is always an act of concealment. The landscape of *Psycho* is one that no one inside the film knows how to look at, and the camera merely reinforces the characters' arrested gaze. In no other Hitchcock film does the camera close in on so many objects that refuse to disclose their significance. The nearest thing to a penetration of the interior is Lila's exploration of the Bates's house, but here, as before, whatever the inquiring eye approaches seems instantly to escape what it designates. Moreover, like the front door of the Bates's dwelling, which appears to move toward Lila as soon as it looms into view, the space seems sentient, as though a living thought were trying to remember itself through these objects (the bronzed hands; the flower-patterned sink; the imprint of the bed; Norman's dolls and stuffed animals; and the untitled book that Lila prepares to open as the scene ends). Lila's function in this episode is like that of the silent menial at the close of Poe's 'Berenice', who merely points at the objects that need to be seen until they are recognised and can 'freeze' the eye that knows them. But in *Psycho* there is no final shock of recognition. Everything we have witnessed in the film ultimately appears to have been pulled through the hollow sockets into which Norman's face dissolves in the last scene. In the strikingly simplified visual field of *Psycho's* conclusion, there is only a rigid form against a blank screen. The psychiatrist's explanation that has just ended has no more to do with what we now see than Marion's money had to do with her as she lay on the bathroom floor, her eye firmly fixed on nothing. All movement has subsided except for that of the steadily advancing camera. When Norman meets its gaze, the camera halts, as though transfixed by its own reflection. The image dissolves to reveal a half-submerged object, coated with filth, rising toward us from the swamp; and here *Psycho* ends.

Notes

This essay was originally published in *New Literary History* 15, no. 3 (Spring 1984).

1 Roland Barthes, 'The Metaphor of the Eye', in *Critical Essays*, trans. Richard Howard, Evanston: Northwestern UP, 1972, p. 239. See also Roland Kuhn, 'The Attempted Murder of a Prostitute', in *Existence, A New Dimension in Psychiatry and Psychology*, Rollo May, Ernst Angel, and Henri F. Ellenbarger (eds.), New York: Basic Books, 1958, pp. 365–425.

2 Edgar Allan Poe, 'Berenice', in *The Complete Tales and Poems*, New York: Modern Library, 1965, p. 645.

3 Daniel Hoffman, *Poe Poe Poe Poe Poe Poe Poe*, New York: Doubleday, 1973, pp. 234–35.

4 Georges Bataille, *Story of the Eye*, trans. Joachim Neugraschel, New York: Urizen Books, 1977, p. 56.

5 Georges Bataille, *Manet*, trans. Austryn Wainhouse and James Emmons, New York: Skira, 1955, p. 82.

6 Sanford Schwartz, 'Reflections: The Mystery and Melancholy of a Career', *The New Yorker*, 28 June 1982, p. 93.

7 V. F. Perkins, *Film as Film*, Harmondsworth, UK: Penguin Books, 1972, p. 108.

8 Garrett Stewart, 'Keaton Through the Looking Glass', *The Georgia Review*, 33, summer 1979, p. 365.

9 John Russell Taylor, *Hitch: The Life and Times of Alfred Hitchcock*, New York: Pantheon Books, 1978, p. 256.

10 James Naremore, *Filmguide to Psycho*, Bloomington: Indiana UP, 1973, p. 36.

11 Irving Massey. *The Gaping Pig: Literature and Metamorphosis*, Berkeley; U of California P, 1976, p. 8.

12 For a discussion of a similar search in Poe's 'The Purloined Letter', see Jacques Lacan, 'Seminar on "The Purloined Letter"', *Yale French Studies*, No. 41, 1972, pp. 38–72.

13 See Massey, *Gaping Pig*, p. 6.

PART III
Sexuality/Romance

A radical testament. Hitchcock's last film – *Family Plot*

Chapter 12
Hitchcock – Endgame

Raymond Bellour

> 'You're a Capricorn, aren't you?'
> 'No, I'm a Leo.'
> 'That's what I thought.'

Hitchcock has always had a passion for telling two stories at once. At least two, chosen among many (in *The Trouble with Harry* (1955), for example, there are as many storylines as there are possible murderers of the unfortunate Harry), which often give the impression that they can be reduced to one as soon as a man and a woman are left alone – two stories which end in a marriage really only makes one story. If *Psycho* (1960) was a moment of film trauma, crossing the line of classical Hollywood cinema and still haunting both what remains of American cinema, and avant-garde and postmodern consciousness, it is because this 'process' (to borrow Roussel's definition) appears through the film in all its unequivocal cruelty. One story intersects with another; the body of the neurotic (the woman) is offered up, in a motel, to the blows of the psychotic (the man) in such a way that the reasons behind this odyssey are eventually seen to come undone; the true nature of the cinema-mechanism, as divined by Hitchcock, becomes clear: irrepressible perversion, fetishism and voyeurism, bound up with an inescapable obsession with sexual difference.

The peculiar force of *Family Plot* (1976), coming after three heavy, awkward films (*Torn Curtain* (1966), *Topaz* (1969), and the mildly caricatural *Frenzy* (1972)), lies in its reworking, with the ethereal grace of a gesture rendered purer by virtue of being Hitchcock's last, of this process of two stories, which is taken to the point where it touches on the abstract madness associated with the cult of the image, the subjective, social (historic) conditions which are peculiar to both this madness and this worship. This film is not (or not only) a 'family plot', but also both a scheming plot and the story of a family – as though the true nature of sex, like that of suspense cannot be disassociated, for Hitchcock, from this 'story' which gives rise to all other stories.

Seeing, first and foremost seeing. *Pretending that you can see.* Allowing someone else to see by whatever subterfugeis necessary, so strong is his or her desire to see. Madame Blanche, in a trance, a false trance, lets Julia Rainbird catch a glimpse of exactly what she wants to see. ('Someone is here, not closely, not willingly, I feel her holding back. What's the trouble, Henry?') So much so that when Miss Rainbird takes over the scene, giving the necessary information, Madame Blanche knows how to continue to 'see' and provides the old lady with what she needs so that the message is finally complete, readable, shared between the two women and the third-party viewer. Forty years ago, Miss Rainbird decided to take an illegitimate child away from her sister Harriet and get rid of it in order to preserve the family honour. Now, close to death, haunted night and day by the image of her sister who comes to reproach her for her action, she wants to find the child, whose trace has been lost, in order to give him back the family name and make him the heir of her substantial fortune. Rather than going to a private detective, Julia Rainbird chooses, for $10,000, to entrust Madame Blanche with the inquiry, in the interests of confidence and discretion, but especially because of the gift of seeing bestowed on Blanche, the existence of which she has just proved by offering to tell the old woman's story of which she already seems certain thanks to the voice which emanates from within her.

For Blanche, throughout this opening scene, talks to a being whom she addresses with her quiet, fluty voice and who answers her with a hoarse voice, a man's voice, incongruous in her frail body. It is 'Henry' (this is the name of the voice) who makes contact with the sister, allowing Blanche to orchestrate the surreal exchange between the two women, one loving, the other dead. 'Henry' is also the one who dictates to Julia Rainbird the conditions according to which she may, thanks to Blanche, find the child. He becomes the power which allows Blanche to be the one who sees, to recount what she sees and to thus engender the film, to elucidate its vision and all that it entails. Through the voice of this *énonciatrice*, which thus enters the strategy of the *mise-en-scène*, 'Henry' becomes the background *énonciateur*; his *mise-en-scène* depends on Blanche's invention of it, just as she herself has been invented. 'Henry' reminds us, then, that if Hitchcock delegates to a woman, more clearly than ever before, his powers of vision, of knowledge and his ability to stimulate one by means of the other – in order, perhaps, to recognise that after having occupied, for so long and so ferociously the position of object, woman can finally manage to occupy the position of subject – in the end he repossesses all the power he seems to grant to her as he is reborn from within her body as a voice. *Henry*, abbreviated to *Harry* or *Hal* is also the name of the devil, whose prop is woman. It seems only fitting that Hitchcock should at last represent the *mise-en-scène* as the devil's share, giving his long-standing tendency to grant himself the powers of a god as tormented by morality as he was obsessed with sex.

The sequence which follows this opening scene clearly shows what is at stake. We see, on the one hand, Blanche's boyfriend, taxi-driver George – who she is trying to convince, more or less successfully, to play detective – attempting to take credit for his share of 'Henry's' predictions to the clients which are based, in part, on the information he supplies. George thus places his faith on the side of reality, a reality no supernatural enunciation can do without. This reality, on the other hand, cannot be too absolute because it drifts wherever the enunciations upon which it depends take it; this reality can only become the story through the free play of its elements. Moreover, this splitting of the knowledge–power matrix between man and woman is clearly both sexual and symbolic. The dialogue which surrounds the Rainbird affair and the mysterious child-heir, is focused on the sexual feats which George may, or may not, be able to perform that night (Hitchcock delighted in the art of salacious dialogue which he takes almost to its limit in this instance as he compares sex with the pleasures of the theatre: 'You don't have to worry about my performance tonight, honey. As a matter of fact, on this very evening, you're going to see a standing ovation.') The coveted sum of $10,000 could well enable Blanche and George to get married at last.

At this moment the story suddenly branches off, as George brakes sharply to avoid hitting a woman crossing the road: the camera takes advantage of the wide high-angle shot to focus on the woman, following her for a while with not so much as a thought for either Blanche or George, or their film. The viewer clearly presumes that this diversion is not unwarranted, and that the second, nascent plot is related to the enigma posited in the first. But this plot is dependent on a sequence of facts which appear autonomous, detached from their introduction. Fifteen minutes of the film are long enough for George's investigations to bear fruit; the couple who feature in the second plot must, in turn, take to the trail in an attempt to throw some light on the motives of Blanche and George. The two plots have no choice but to converge. The man of the second couple is, of course, Edward Shoebridge, the illegitimate child, hiding behind the pseudonym Arthur Adamson. Yet the two plots remain parallel, existing, strangely, back to back insofar as the motivations of the first couple (Blanche and George) seem to have no link whatsoever with the activity of the second couple (Arthur/Eddie and Fran). Unless the enigma is not, or not only, where we expect to find it, but is, like the purloined letter, so visible as to be rendered invisible.

All is clear as far as the first story is concerned, up to and including the realist and vulgar clairvoyance; except perhaps the impression of belief which it instils in its victims, and thus in the viewer who is positioned as both judge and judged. All is clear, as well, as far as the second story is concerned, but then the order of temporal succession begins to deteriorate, to decompose. The present of the second story irrupts in the present of the first story which is diverted during the long bifurcated sequence that introduces the second: the man and woman who we stumble across are high-flying crooks, as gloriously professional as George and Blanche are hopelessly amateur. Thus we see them, at the end of a faultless itinerary, exchange a politician for his ransom, a collector's diamond. The past, on the other hand, is unearthed by George's investigation and its consequences: at the age of twenty, Eddie Shoebridge, who was entrusted, by the Rainbird's driver, to the care of an unassuming couple who adopted him, and who gets rid of his foster parents by coldly setting fire to their house. He finally manages to pass himself off as dead in the fire (a plaque erected in the cemetery just a little too late corroborates this) and reappears with the name of Arthur Adamson, respected jeweller. The intervention of Blanche and George must, therefore, in the eyes of Arthur and Fran, be justified as much (or more) by the present as by the past, causing the cinema-mechanism to go slightly berserk and for the threads of the two stories to become entwined, knotted, even though they do not seem to belong to the same narrative tapestry.

An improbable sequence provides just such an opportunity for this union. George is going to the church to meet Reverend Wood, Bishop of St Anselme, whose name came back to Julia as a result of the elements of 'Henry's' investigation transmitted to her by Blanche (the Bishop was the one who baptised the bastard, and who undertook to watch over him). At the very moment when George is trying to find a way of meeting the clergyman, who is in the middle of conducting Mass, a woman walks into the church and collapses not far from the Bishop, who, followed by his assistant, rushes to her aid. His assistant, while leaning over the Bishop, plunges a syringe into his shoulder, and, supporting him with the help of the woman, who is now on her feet again, carries him down the central aisle to the stupefaction of the horrified congregation who can only watch, finally, from the church entrance, like so many powerless spectators, as the car carrying the kidnapped Bishop turns the street corner.

As far as Arthur and Fran are concerned, then, George seems to be in a position to know something which they have planned in the utmost secrecy. They recognise in him, as soon as they see him in the church, an informed witness of their *mise-en-scène*. Indeed Fran is thinking of the *mise-en-scène*, of which they are also the victims, as they speed along in the car with the unconscious Bishop: after a long discussion, she ends up convincing Arthur that extrasensory perception (Blanche's powers, in other words) can be the only explanation for such an unlikely coincidence. In the same way, we come back to the *mise-en-scène* as soon as we try, in the course of the film, to understand our surprise as we see how the threads of this double plot are being woven together. Hitchcock had always been aware that the greatest risk his films ran was that the 'main characters sometimes tend to become mere figures'.[1] Real male and female bodies tend to disappear under the pressure both of the plot's logic and of the abstract drives which this logic inscribes within the film. The strength of *Family Plot* stems from the fact that it takes this risk as its subject. By refusing, from the first, to believe in the characters, believing instead, and making us believe, in their schematisation, by giving way to the dizzying heights of an abstraction centred on the body (especially on the bodies of the two couples), *Family Plot* is transformed into a radical film, a testament, like Lang's final *Mabuse* (1960). We touch the moment where the work, carried along on its own myth, has nothing left to lose, thanks to the situations and fantasies haunting it, which have been enacted so many times before.

Hitchcock's *œuvre* wins the freedom to simultaneously lay its cards on the table and hide them from us, announcing its programme in advance without renouncing any of the means by which it can still seduce and frighten. This presupposes a ludic consent, a kind of exacerbated distance which the eternal accomplice, the viewer, is asked to share, in order that they be reminded, all the more freely, of all those past films where, so often before, they have already witnessed these woven threads.

But what of the common link between the two plots that joins them together while they retain an autonomy which would be caricatural (like the actors are on purpose) if it weren't for our impression that this forced characteristic contained within it an excess of meaning, whose mimed truths are being transmitted to us? The singularity of the two couples comes from their parallel existence: they do not lead a mutually dependent existence, where one element of the first couple helps make up the second couple, and where there is a third element which exists in excess as the madness of desire. In *Psycho*, we have Marion and Sam on the one hand, and Marion and Norman on the other, with the mother as/in excess. In *Shadow of a Doubt* (1943) we find the same pattern: Charlie-the-Niece and the detective/Charlie-the-Niece and Charlie-the-Uncle/the 'joyous' widows killed by the uncle. Here there is no such pattern, only two couples who mirror each other. The chic couple united in their criminal transgression by an enigmatic pact – with neither depth nor history: pure algebra. ('We move as one, everything together, nothing held back.') But we find, between the man and the woman the usual dividing line which places the former on the side of murder and psychosis: Eddie is the one who killed his parents, Fran rebels when it is time to kill George, and especially Blanche. In any case, each couple is bound (even as they are divided like Eddie and Fran) by the ties which bind sex to sin and to death.

This is what Hitchcock, who never tires of it, takes to its burlesque, incandescent extreme in the scene where George and Blanche find themselves hurtling down a mountain road in a car whose accelerator is blocked and whose brakes have been tampered with. The sequence is beyond description. But the more George, who is at the wheel, scorns all reality, by mastering the damaged car on a road transformed into a theatre or a dream scenario, the more Blanche clings onto him, in the throes of a fit of hysteria which renders this scene one of the most sublimely erotic and absurd in the history of cinema. In the same way, a (parodic) model of aggression comes from the woman (the opposite of masculine psychotic desire, here displaced, disguised). When the car, having finally left the road, rolls over and stops on its side, George's face is deformed, in close-up, by Blanche's foot. An effective way of demonstrating that if the man, in the other couple, is the one who kills and who wants to kill Blanche – because she knows too much about the secret of his birth and the (sexual) sin committed by his mother which serves as the primal scene – the woman always poses a sexual threat to the man, and by extension, any love or sex scene is only ever the other side of a murder scene. We have already heard an echo of this at the end of the long sequence between Eddie and Fran after the branching-off of the film. Fran wants to know where the diamond is; Eddie has hidden it 'where everybody can see it'. He adds, as she again tries to convince him to tell her where it is, 'you'll have to torture me first'. And she concludes, as she is already waiting for him in the bedroom, 'Oh, I intend to, in a few minutes.'

For the diamond could well reflect everything: death, sex, reflected light, which all gather in the eye of the viewer, as if through the lens of a camera, through the vision of the *mise-en-scène*, the vision of whatsoever becomes its intercessor. At the end of the film, Blanche, helped by George, deceives her abductors by trapping them in the secret room where they keep their victims. First comes the compliment: 'Blanche, you faked that brilliantly, you are still a champ.' But it would be even better if they found the diamonds. Blanche surpasses herself. She goes into a trance and heads straight for the chandelier, where Eddie has hung them, and where we see them again, as Blanche sees them, very close up, gleaming. She is thus allowed a second compliment: 'Blanche, you did it, you are psychic.'

The look she gives the viewer in the last shot of the film just before the credits roll against a background shot of the diamonds, comes full circle back to the crystal ball in which her face appears, eyes closed, during the opening credits of the film, and from which she emerges, in order to tell us and Julia Rainbird, in her man-woman voice, what she has seen and what she sees. From the diamond to the eye, from one couple to the other, from the seer to the hidden hypnotist – the enunciator who manipulates her – the *mise-en-scène* is, indeed, this power to see. Ludic, ironic, terribly logical. It is crystallised in the light which sex gives out, which is gathered, folded, unfolded throughout the discourse, the two plots and their improbable links, a light which never stops gleaming until, through the diamond and through Blanche's vision, the story is condensed and seems clarified from all angles, just as Blanche becomes 'a real psychic'. The mechanism's logic lies in the family plot(s). Henceforth everything leads from the dark light of the mother's sinful body to the pure light of the diamond, which leads it back through the obsession of the murderous son and all that this entails: this film which we see thanks to Blanche's eye modulated by Hitchcock's. As Michel Foucault said, 'The family is the quartz in the mechanism of sexuality.'

Notes

This text first appeared in the catalogue of *Le dernière Œuvre*, 'Cinéma et littérature 10', CRAC de Valence, 1992, Françoise Calvez and Raymond Bellour (eds.). A modified version, from which this translation is drawn, appeared in *Trafic* 26, pp. 97–102 (summer 1998). The text is translated by Hannah Thompson.

1 François Truffaut with Helen G. Scott, *Hitchcock*, rev. edn, New York: Touchstone Books, 1985, p. 198.

Jane Wyman greets Marlene Dietrich on her arrival at Associated British Studios, Elstree, for the filming of *Stage Fright* – a Hollywood British movie

Chapter 13
The Stolen Raincoat and the Bloodstained Dress: *Young and Innocent* and *Stage Fright*

Michael Walker

In the enormous amount of published material on Hitchcock, *Young and Innocent* (1937) and *Stage Fright* (1950) are two works that have been relatively sketchily covered.[1] Among the comedy thrillers of his 1930s British films, *Young and Innocent* has tended to be overshadowed by *The 39 Steps* (1935) and *The Lady Vanishes* (1938). The first of the films Hitchcock made under his late 1940s deal with Warner Bros., *Stage Fright* has usually been seen as a minor work.[2] Nevertheless, there are for each film a couple of articles which are enthusiastic.[3] My project here is to expand on the insights in these articles by looking at the films in the context of the development of Hitchcock as *auteur*. Beginning with a structural comparison of the two films, I want then to look at key differences between them as a way of highlighting the effect of Hollywood on Hitchcock's work. Whereas *Young and Innocent* belongs firmly to his British period, *Stage Fright* was made in England after almost ten years in Hollywood. It was produced by Warner Bros., but made at the ABPC studio in Elstree. Although Warner Bros. had by this stage a 37½ per cent interest in ABPC,[4] Hitchcock's deal gave him 'unprecedented freedom in his choice of material, cast and writers'.[5] In practice this meant that, although he imported two Hollywood stars, Marlene Dietrich and Jane Wyman, for box-office reasons, the film was in other respects a British production: made at a British studio and with a British cast and crew.

Structural parallels

To the best of my knowledge, no one has pointed out these two films' close structural links. First, the characters. At the heart of each film is a young, naïve heroine and her relationship with her father. In *Young and Innocent*, Erica (Nova Pilbeam) is only eighteen but, with her mother (presumably) dead, she has assumed the maternal role in the family: she has four younger brothers and sits at the dinner table at the opposite end to Colonel Burgoyne (Percy Marmont), the local Chief Constable. In *Stage Fright*, Eve (Jane Wyman) is an only child, and although – as a drama student at RADA – she lives with her mother, Mrs Gill (Sybil Thorndike) in London, she has a much closer relationship with her father, Commodore Gill (Alastair Sim), who, separated from his wife, has retreated to a coastal cottage. During the narrative, he moves back to London in order to help Eve with her investigation.

In each film, there is a 'falsely accused hero'[6] whom the heroine seeks to help. He is accused of murder, a murder which stems from his past relationship with a famous star, in both cases an older woman. In *Young and Innocent*, Robert Tisdall (Derrick de Marney) is accused of murdering Christine Clay (Pamela Carme), a movie star, with whom he is suspected of having had a sexual relationship (Robert denies it). He meets Erica for the first time when under arrest (she administers first aid when he faints); the narrative then brings them together while he's on the run. As the Chief Constable's daughter, Erica is understandably reluctant at first to help him evade the law, but he quite quickly wins her support. In *Stage Fright*, Jonathan Cooper (Richard Todd) is only apparently falsely accused, since we discover at the end of the film that he did commit the murder at the beginning. But, through the device of the 'lying flashback', the film convinces us until this point that he is falsely accused: in other words, structurally he is the equivalent figure to Robert. Here, the murder was of the husband of a famous actress/singer, Charlotte Inwood (Marlene Dietrich), and, far from denying the past sexual relationship, Jonathan insists on it. But Eve is already in love with him when the film starts, and so has no hesitation in helping him.

In each film, the 'hero' (in quotes because Jonathan is a false hero) is thus between a young, innocent woman (the heroine) and an older, more glamorous and sophisticated woman, who functions structurally like a *femme fatale*. But *Stage Fright*, mindful of Jonathan's guilt, includes another man for the heroine: 'Ordinary' Smith (Michael Wilding), a detective inspector investigating the murder case. As part of her plan to help Jonathan, Eve befriends Smith, but then finds herself falling in love with him: he is the figure she goes off with at the end. Although there is a trace of this character in *Young and Innocent*'s Inspector Kent (John Longden) – the Scotland Yard detective who interrogates Robert and seems to resent Erica's sympathy for him – the important link is with Erica's father. Colonel Burgoyne and Smith are both policemen who are threatened by the heroine's illegal activities (helping a fugitive from justice). At the end of *Young and Innocent*, Erica smilingly presides over her father finally signalling his approval of Robert. Both films thus end with the transgressive heroine reconciled with the law.

There are also minor character links. In *Young and Innocent*, Erica's Aunt Margaret (Mary Clare) is like a bossy, interfering mother-figure: she is highly suspicious of Erica's relationship with Robert and is the person who 'reports them' to Colonel Burgoyne. By contrast, Mrs Gill is scatty but obliging, taking in her stride the way young men turn up at the house to visit Eve when Eve herself is elsewhere. Each film also includes a working-class helper, and here the benevolent figure is Old Will the china-mender (Edward Rigby) in *Young and Innocent*, who joins forces with Robert and Erica in their hunt to track down the real murderer. By contrast, Nellie, Charlotte's maid (Kay Walsh) in *Stage Fright* has to be handsomely bribed before she agrees to help; in her case, by making it possible for Eve to act as Charlotte's maid for a few days. But here, too, the narrative function of the helper is similar: convinced by Jonathan's story, Eve wants to find evidence that will reveal Charlotte as the murderer.

The narrative. Each film begins with an unseen murder. In *Young and Innocent* it arises out of the opening row between Christine and her ex-husband Guy (George Curzon), who refuses to accept her 'Reno divorce' and who is extremely jealous of her relationship with Robert (sneeringly referred to as one of her 'boys'). In the second scene, Robert finds Christine's body (on the beach) and, as he runs to get help, two young women see him and subsequently claim to the police that he was 'running away'. *Stage Fright* begins in Eve's car with Jonathan narrating his 'lying flashback'. This starts after the murder, which Jonathan says Charlotte committed: she arrived at his apartment in a bloodstained dress to seek his help. As Jonathan then went to Charlotte's house to get her a clean dress, again we see the 'hero' next to the body, and again he was spotted by a young woman (Nellie) and was seen 'running away'. In *Young and Innocent*, the equivalent of the bloodstained dress (an incriminating item of clothing) is the raincoat belt which the police insist was used to strangle Christine: Robert can't prove that it isn't his, because his own raincoat has been stolen.

Each 'hero' then escapes from the police. As he's being taken to court to be remanded in custody, Robert slips away, using his lawyer's reading glasses as a disguise. He meets Erica again when her car runs out of petrol and pays for it to be refilled. Assuming that, if he can find his raincoat, he can clear himself, he wants Erica to take him to Tom's Hat, the drivers' café where it was stolen. But, still uncertain of him, she leaves him in a deserted old mill to hide out. He falls asleep. The key points of this narrative are then echoed in *Stage Fright*: the escape from the police, getting a lift from the heroine in her car and being taken to a hideout – in this case, Eve's father's coastal cottage – where Jonathan promptly falls asleep. Here the incriminating item of clothing has remained with the 'hero' and, as Jonathan sleeps, Commodore Gill examines it. He realises that the blood has in fact been smeared on the dress but, believing Jonathan's story, assumes Charlotte did this. He wants to take the dress to the police. However, when Eve wakes Jonathan and tells him her father's suspicions, he instantly burns the dress. Although, in retrospect, this is an act which should have raised Eve's and Gill's doubts about him, they continue to believe his story, and discuss ways of getting evidence against Charlotte.

Each heroine then returns home. Erica goes back to her family for lunch, and learns that the three shillings Robert spent on the petrol was all the money he had on him. As her brothers fantasise about him dying of starvation, she becomes guilt-ridden, and returns to the mill with three shillings and some bread and cheese. She now listens sympathetically to Robert's story and, when two policemen interrupt them, she escapes with him. Eve returns to London, where her plan is to visit Charlotte and have it out with her. The police on the door stop her entering, so she follows Detective Inspector Smith to the pub where he goes for lunch, and contrives to meet him.

We are now about thirty minutes into each film: this is the end of the first act (all the major characters have been introduced) and Hitchcock signals the structural importance of this point by having a lunch scene. Erica does not in fact eat any lunch, but when she takes Robert the bread and cheese (his lunch), this signals an important shift: henceforth, she will be with him rather than her family. Eve, too, does not eat any lunch, but Smith's sandwich is the equivalent of Robert's snack and, although she has no way yet of knowing this, Eve has also made an important shift: she has now met the film's true hero and it is only a matter of time before she falls in love with him.

Each heroine then begins her investigation by seeking assistance from working-class figure(s) in a crowded café/pub. In *Young and Innocent*, Erica questions the patrons of Tom's Hat about Robert's raincoat, receiving information which eventually leads to the helper, Old Will, who now has the coat. In *Stage Fright*, Eve returns to the pub and bribes Nellie, the helper, in order to take over Nellie's role for a few days. In these scenes, the heroine is in an environment which is alien to her and she is playing a part which carries a degree of risk. In both cases, the working-class characters are highly suspicious of her motives, and in *Young and Innocent* this even leads to a fight breaking out among the men in the café.

At this point, the close parallels between the two films break down. However, they return towards the end of the second act, beginning with the 'hero's' second escape from the police (Robert, when he and Erica are stopped by a policeman who recognises them both; Jonathan, when he escapes – thanks to Eve – from Charlotte's dressing-room). Accordingly, only the material in the middle of Act Two is substantially different. In *Young and Innocent*, all this material is in one scene: the birthday party of Felicity, Erica's young niece, presided over by Aunt Margaret, Felicity's mother. Erica had forgotten about Felicity's birthday, with the result that her calling in to see her aunt, which she had intended to be casual, becomes increasingly complicated as first she and then Robert are drawn into the party and subjected to a robust interrogation about their relationship. Eventually, Uncle Basil (Basil Radford), discerning their plight, blindfolds his wife during a game of blind man's bluff so that the couple can make a getaway.

In *Stage Fright*, there are four 'narrative segments' in place of this one.[7]

1 Eve at her mother's trying out her working-class disguise as Doris, Nellie's fictional cousin;
2 her first scene as Doris at Charlotte's, when she contrives to avoid Smith – who has come with a colleague to question Charlotte – and meets both Charlotte and Freddie Williams (Hector MacGregor), Charlotte's manager;
3 the scene when Smith comes to Mrs Gill's to tea, which also marks the point at which Gill returns to London
4 Charlotte on stage at the theatre and her meeting with Jonathan in her dressing-room.

Gill is also present in the theatre for this last segment, and Eve is present during all of them, except for a brief scene between Charlotte and Freddie at the end of 2. (For the equivalent scene between Charlotte and Jonathan at the end of 4, Eve is present in that she eavesdrops.)

It is not difficult to account for these structural differences between the films. First, the whole of the children's party scene from *Young and Innocent* has been condensed into the tea scene in *Stage Fright*. Both scenes function as the introduction of the heroine's new young man to her parents/parent-figures in a suitably bourgeois setting, with the important difference that Robert must necessarily be evasive about his true identity, which seems highly suspicious, whereas Smith displays his impeccable bourgeois credentials by charming Mrs Gill with small talk and playing a wistful tune on the piano. The links show once more the structural sophistication of Hitchcock's narratives: just as we had a lunch scene at the end of Act One, we now have an afternoon tea scene in the middle of Act Two (in *Young and Innocent*, because of the children, ice cream replaces tea, but it's still teatime). Second, since in *Stage Fright* the glamorous star is not only still very much alive, but also the murder suspect, scenes are included which (a) enable her to display her talents, and (b) further the narrative requirement to keep her looking suspicious. Finally, the scene in which Eve first tries out her disguise as Doris, complete with her mother's reading glasses and a cigarette, is an echo of Robert's first escape from the police in his improvised disguise in *Young and Innocent*: in both cases, the borrowed spectacles render the wearer almost blind.

During this act, there is an equivalent structuring principle operating in both films: the heroine is acting illegally and doing her best to help someone suspected of being a murderer. Eventually, in Act Three, her transgressions catch up with her: Erica's actions take her father to the brink of resignation; Smith finds that the woman he has fallen in love with has been both using and deceiving him (specifically, about her role as Doris Tinsdale, whom she knows he is very anxious to question). But, before this happens, three parallel developments occur: the heroine is confronted with the problem of her conflict of loyalties, she and the hero realise that they are in love and, crucially, the incriminating item of clothing is reintroduced – in a displaced form.

The first of these developments occurs at the end of Act Two, immediately after the scene which brings the narratives back into parallel: the 'hero's' second escape from the police. After the policeman has recognised them both, Erica follows Robert's wishes and drives her car away, but the encounter has made her realise what she's doing. This releases an extraordinary semi-hysterical speech which expresses her conflict: on the one hand she imagines herself getting ten years as an accessory and then what will happen to the boys; on the other, she feels that she must now keep going and urges the car to go faster. The speech brilliantly captures her predicament, and the melodramatic excess – she'll go to jail; the family will fall apart – serves to ironise her anxiety: the speech is also moving and funny. That night, they hide the car in a railway goods yard. By now, the conflicting pressures on Erica have made her almost unable to speak, but in Robert's attempts to cheer her up and in their gentle gestures of concern for each other, we can see that they are in love. It's a touching, tender scene, which gains in intensity from its (very British) understatement.

In *Stage Fright*, the equivalent scene occurs when Eve and her father return home after Jonathan's escape from the theatre and find him in the house with Mrs Gill. In his dressing-room scene with Charlotte, Jonathan learnt to his dismay that she was no longer especially interested in him, and so he turns once more to Eve for help and sympathy. But, as he embraces her, Eve looks at the piano which Smith had played that afternoon. The wistful tune, reprised non-diegetically on the soundtrack, now becomes the film's love theme, signalling that Eve's thoughts are of Smith. She permits Jonathan to hide out in her house, but she is emotionally detaching herself from him. Although we have here the same structural point as in *Young and Innocent* – the heroine divided between her 'falsely accused boyfriend' and a representative of the law – Eve's dividedness is weighted differently from Erica's. Because she is now less emotionally involved with the 'falsely accused' figure, there is not as strong a sense of an inner conflict.

This also means that the ensuing love scene between Eve and Smith lacks the traumatic sense of its equivalent in *Young and Innocent*. It occurs the next day, as the two of them travel in a taxi to a garden party where Charlotte will be singing. At the start of the drive, Eve sets out to try and shift Smith's suspicions from Jonathan to Charlotte. But, as the drive continues, the piano love theme transforms the mood and, as they gaze at each other, both lose track of what they're saying. Again, this is an extremely fine scene, beautifully capturing the moment when a couple find that they're falling in love and all the other priorities simply fade away.

The reintroduction – in a displaced form – of the incriminating item of clothing happens in both films shortly afterwards. Robert tracks down Old Will in a doss-house and, as the local police are once more alerted, drags him off in the car. They discover that Will does indeed have the coat, but it lacks a belt: in other words, it could well have been Robert's belt which was used to strangle Christine. (In fact, it was. Here the crucial item of clothing has been divided: the fact that the raincoat is beltless further incriminates Robert.) Then, as they drive into some old mine workings, the ground gives way and the car starts to sink, almost taking Erica down into the mines, before Robert and Will haul her out. The police now catch up with them and, although Robert and Will contrive to escape, Erica runs back into their arms.

The ground giving way under Erica is her traumatic moment. It may be seen, psychically, as the wrath of the father threatening her for what she's been doing. As many critics have noted,[8] Hitchcock's films are full of such oneiric moments, translating the psychic fears and fantasies of the characters into actual events. Erica comes very close to serious or even fatal injury at this point, and even though she is saved, she loses her car, the vehicle which has enabled her to keep escaping from the police and roaming freely with Robert. We can thus understand her sudden flight from Robert back to the police: she's frightened. But, when Colonel Burgoyne summons her to his study to explain her behaviour, she continues to insist on Robert's innocence. It's at this point that her father shows her his letter of resignation and sends her to her room. After Erica has cried herself to sleep, we then have another oneiric moment: Robert climbs in the window, exactly as if she's dreamed him up. Since all seems lost, Robert says he's going to give himself up and insist that he forced Erica into accompanying him: in other words, he appears here as her protector, another feature which suggests the wish-fulfilment of a dream. But he then realises that the box of matches the police found in the raincoat pocket is a clue: it directs them to the Grand Hotel for the film's climax.

In place of the lower-class environments of the doss-house and the old mine workings, the equivalent developments in *Stage Fright* occur during a middle-class garden party. In the doss-house, the middle-class Robert was the intruder; at the garden party, the working-class Nellie is the intruder. She arrives to demand more money from Eve, which obliges Eve to summon her father. But Gill then devises a plan. Having first ensured that Eve and Smith are in Charlotte's audience, he obtains a doll, smears its dress with his own blood and sends a boy scout, holding the doll, up to Charlotte as she sings on stage. The displaced version of the incriminating item of clothing is thus here integrated into the action. Gill's assumption is that Charlotte will react to the sight of the doll so as to give herself away and that Smith will witness this. But, although Charlotte is upset by the doll, it is Eve who is exposed: Freddie Williams calls to her from the stage to come and help Charlotte, addressing her as Doris. Eve is thus obliged to walk away from Smith revealed as his deceiver.

In contrast to Erica's nightmarish experience in the mines, Eve's equivalent 'traumatic' moment is handled more realistically; it's her acute embarrassment at being caught out that is conveyed. But she, too, is now obliged to explain her conduct to the policeman whose will she has apparently thwarted. In this case, the scene is preceded by one with 'the hero' upstairs in her bedroom, where the question of him giving himself up is raised (unlike Robert, Jonathan is reluctant). And here the scene with the policeman downstairs involves a lot more explanation: not just about Eve's impersonation and the business with the doll, but also about her relationship with Jonathan. However, she manages to convince Smith that, even though she still believes Jonathan is innocent, Smith is now the man she loves. Mrs Gill and Gill then enter the room to further the development of the plot: the former to reveal inadvertently to Smith that Jonathan is hiding upstairs; the latter to propose a way of forcing Charlotte's hand: pretending that she has the original bloodstained dress, Eve will try blackmailing Charlotte while the police listen in. This directs the key characters to the theatre for this film's climax.

The settings for the climactic scenes are quite different: in *Young and Innocent*, a crowded hotel dance floor and its environs; in *Stage Fright*, an empty West End theatre. But the purpose of each is to find/expose and then apprehend the true murderer, and the characters are much the same: the heroine and her father; the hero (Robert; Smith); the falsely accused murderer (Robert; Charlotte) and the actual murderer (Guy; Jonathan). The scene in *Young and Innocent* also includes Old Will, but even his role is paralleled in *Stage Fright*. In order to sit in the hotel's tearoom with Erica, Will wears a hired dress suit; in her role as Doris, Eve is in a similar class-based disguise. (In that Eve is standing in for Nellie, she combines the two roles – heroine and helper – into one.) Finally, both suspects are entertainers.

The scenes have further similarities. In each, the hero takes a back seat: it is the heroine who carries the main burden of finding/exposing the suspect. In *Young and Innocent*, we now have the famous 145-foot crane over the dancers to show Guy, the band's drummer – like the rest of the musicians, in black-face – in close-up as he twitches; the facial tic that will enable Will to identify him. This tell us that Erica and Will have come to the right place. Guy now becomes as much the focus of the scene as those two. He recognises Will, which exacerbates his twitching; during a break, he sees the police, including Colonel Burgoyne, arriving at the hotel (in fact, summoned to pick up Erica), which makes him feel even more nervous, and he ends by breaking down completely, collapsing on the dance floor. By now, Robert has given himself up and Erica has been reclaimed by her father, but – echoing her first aid on Robert in her first scene – she goes to help. Her solicitousness thus takes her to the villain who, the moment he comes to, confesses what he did with the raincoat belt: 'I twisted it round her neck and choked the life out of her.'

In *Stage Fright* the scene is more elaborate, because it has two stages: (a) Eve as Doris going through her fake blackmail routine and forcing Charlotte to confess and (b) the arrival of Jonathan, under arrest, and his third escape from the police. Even now, Eve still believes him innocent – and so disbelieves Charlotte's confession – and she follows him into the depths of the theatre; here, the heroine's solicitousness puts her life in danger. But Eve still, in effect, resolves the case: Charlotte's confession provides the police with the evidence they needed, and when Eve realises that Jonathan is the murderer (her father calls out to warn her), she contrives to lead him to a place where she'll be safe and he can be caught. It's at this point that Hitchcock includes another version of the sense of encirclement by the police Guy experienced in *Young and Innocent*: trapped in the theatre's orchestra pit, and then on the stage, whichever way Jonathan looks, he sees police blocking his escape.

The crucial feature that connects and distinguishes these two films is the role of the heroine: structurally the central figure, she does most of the work in carrying the investigation and the narrative forward. Investing such power in a heroine is, of course, rare, and we might anticipate strategies to 'contain' it, i.e. seek to control its potentially subversive elements. In the context of *film noir*, I have already discussed the ways in which films typically 'manage' the role of a 'seeker heroine'.[9] *Stage Fright* follows the pattern: the motive (to help her 'falsely accused' boyfriend); the background 'supervision' of a male authority figure (her father, later Smith); the use of masquerade (her role as Doris), and the fact that her primary object of investigation is another woman (Charlotte). All of these factors – as well as the fact that she's mistaken in her faith in Jonathan – serve to limit Eve's transgression: it does not go too far. In *Young and Innocent*, the investigation is shared more between Erica and Robert, but the absence of a supportive male authority figure, and the fact that their quest goes beyond the circumscribed world considered suitable for a heroine (e.g. the Tom's Hat scene) means that Erica is more vulnerable and exposed than Eve. Her transgression is also the greater: it is against her whole family upbringing. Accordingly, although all is resolved by the end, *Young and Innocent* has served to raise more of an ideological disturbance than *Stage Fright*. Nevertheless, the very fact that *Stage Fright* has a seeker heroine whose actions are crucial to the solving of the plot is in itself progressive.

It is beyond the scope of this article to consider the implications of the remarkable structural parallels between these two films. In due course, as more work is done on Hitchcock's narratives, it will no doubt be possible to perceive his meta-narratives, i.e. those narrative patterns which may be discerned across a range of his films. I am convinced that most of his films may be grouped with others in the structural manner that I have indicated here. As the patterns arising from the juxtapositions are brought to light, we will then be able to explore the implications.

Young and Innocent: Englishness and class

Critics have often commented on one of the key differences between Hitchcock's British and American movies: that the former are much more concerned with 'class'. Robin Wood has already noted this feature in *Young and Innocent*,[10] but I would like to add some more comments. First, the film shows English society of the period as absurdly class-conscious and hierarchical. Twice middle-class intrusions into working-class environments lead to violence (the fist fight prompted by Erica asking questions in Tom's Hat) or threatened violence (Robert in the doss-house, where someone calls out 'Go on Will, bash his mug in'). Because Will is little more than a tramp, Erica says that the police will never believe his evidence (that he was given the raincoat by someone other than Robert) and, when Will comes out of the shop in his dress suit, a policeman immediately accosts him ('Well if it isn't Cinderella . . . I've been watching you for the last half hour'), as if a working-class character in formal bourgeois attire must necessarily be up to no good. In addition, there is a short scene in the magistrate's court prior to Robert's intended appearance in which a working-class husband is bound over to keep the peace for six months. As the man leaves the court, his wife identifies the 'old pal' that he's about to visit as 'the King's Arms': in other words, it is implied that his wayward behaviour is linked to drink, a familiar middle-class perception about the 'unruly' working class.

But the film is also humorous at the expense of the upper middle-class lifestyle, especially the antics of Aunt Margaret during the children's party. She and her husband seem to be engaged in subtle marital games-playing: she barks orders to him, telling him to get the crackers; he takes calculated revenge by handing them out to the children literally on top of her, so that she is buried under excited children. Her interest in Erica and Robert's relationship is obviously prurient: she is persuaded into wearing the blindfold by Robert saying 'You can try and catch me', and she's delighted when she thinks that she has caught Robert and most disappointed when it turns out to be her husband. That she has to be blindfolded (another of Basil's cunning ploys) in order for Erica and Robert to escape is a comment on her power as bourgeois matriarch, a power which one can trace in Hitchcock's films from Mrs Whittaker (Violet Farebrother) in *Easy Virtue* (1927) to Lydia Brenner (Jessica Tandy) in *The Birds* (1963).

Erica's family, although similarly upper middle-class (both families have several servants), is more sympathetically viewed. Her father is basically a decent man, and her brothers behave in the first meal scene in a way which argues for a non-repressive upbringing: they rag one another, joke with their father and he handles himself with a surprising equanimity when the youngest suddenly displays a rat he has shot. Here it's Erica who seems to be the bossy figure. Nevertheless, we attribute most of her abrupt attempts to regulate her brothers' conduct as arising from nervousness about her recent encounter with Robert, especially when the conversation switches to discuss his escape. However, in the second (subdued) meal scene we also see the brothers' more sensitive side. (This dinner scene completes the film's structure of bourgeois family meal scenes: it occurs in the middle of Act Three.) Colonel Burgoyne is now conspicuous by his absence; we shortly discover that he's in his study, writing his letter of resignation. Erica's brothers obviously know that she's been on the run with a suspected murderer but, far from wanting to criticise her behaviour, they are quietly supportive: one gives her an encouraging smile, and the eldest is on the point of reaching out to touch her when middle-class inhibitions awkwardly intervene.

Hitchcock introduces this scene with a shot which is framed around Colonel Burgoyne's empty chair, a visual statement of the effect of Erica's transgressive behaviour: she has displaced her father from the meal table, and threatens to displace him from his job. The empty chair here is an echo of the empty magistrate's chair in the courtroom, which was a consequence of Robert's initial escape. In other words, just as Robert disrupted the court proceedings, bringing them to a sudden halt, so Erica disrupts the bourgeois home, threatening the power of the father. In this case, however, the disruption is only temporary. The film's final line is Erica saying to her father, 'Don't you think we ought to ask Mr Tisdall to dinner?' Colonel Burgoyne will be restored to his position at the head of the table, and Robert will now be incorporated into the family: indeed, one can imagine him getting on extremely well with Erica's brothers. Not only will the bourgeois family survive, it will be enriched by another member.

With its focus on Nova Pilbeam's delightful smile, there is no doubt that this is one of Hitchcock's most optimistic endings. The ending of *Stage Fright* is very different. Here the father is indeed displaced: we see or hear nothing more of Gill after his (in context, rather reckless) warning to Eve to come away from Jonathan. And here the murderer is not merely apprehended, but rather brutally killed (falling under a descending safety curtain). As Smith turns Eve's head away from this sight and then leads her off down a theatre corridor, even the final reprise of the love theme on the soundtrack is muted, as if the film can't really commit itself to seeing the ending as uplifting. There are quite a few Hitchcock films which end with the heroine 'going off with' a policeman (*Blackmail*, 1929; *Sabotage*, 1936; *Jamaica Inn*, 1939; *Shadow of a Doubt*, 1942; and *Notorious*, 1946), and in almost every case the ending seems in important respects unresolved or uneasy. The crucial difference between the typical endings of these films, including *Stage Fright* and that of *Young and Innocent*, is that the policeman in the former is in a position of moral superiority: either the heroine herself has killed someone (*Blackmail* and *Sabotage*) or he himself has been proved right about the guilt of the charismatic villain who has just been killed. Only *Notorious* breaks this pattern, and shares with *Young and Innocent* a very different ending, in which the policeman finds that he's been mistaken: he's chastened. Accordingly, we should not see the ending of *Young and Innocent* as 'simply' about the restoration of the father, but, rather, about the formation of a renewed family unit, with the father now aware of his failings.

Overall, *Young and Innocent* is a highly enjoyable film, with the humour, sense of pace and gallery of British eccentrics so typical of Hitchcock's best 1930s movies. It also has a freshness and charm that is extremely engaging. Above all, although made during the spring, it is a summer film. Most of its action takes place on one long day, which begins in the police station at dawn (we hear a cock crow), with the blinds being raised as a prelude to the meeting of the hero and heroine, and ends with the muted love scene in the goods yard. Throughout the day, Erica and Robert travel everywhere in her rickety open-top convertible, and as they drive across southern England, the bird songs, the sunny weather and even the length of the daylight hours contribute to the mood of optimism. The chasteness of their romance is also part of the film's charm: the innocence of a youthful love affair that doesn't even get to its first kiss. George Perry has claimed that this was Hitchcock's favourite of his British films.[11] It is not hard to see why.

Stage Fright: A Hollywood British movie

The title *Young and Innocent* is emblematic of the flavour of Hitchcock's British work. As soon as he went to Hollywood, his focus shifted. Even though many of his early Hollywood films are set in England, from the heroine's point of view, they deal, rather, with loss of innocence. Sexuality is important to some of his British films (*Blackmail* in particular), but it is infused into the fabric of most of his Hollywood ones. In *Young and Innocent*, we don't really believe that Robert had an affair with Christine: he, too, seems an innocent. In *Stage Fright*, Jonathan is far from innocent: here we assume he did have an affair, and certainly he killed on Charlotte's account.

We can see something of the shift if we look at some of the key ways in which *Stage Fright* differs from *Young and Innocent*. The most obvious is the 'lying flashback'. In fact, because some of Jonathan's story must be true – Nellie did see him running away and the police did come after him (Eve saw them) – this is clearly an unsatisfactory term. I would propose a solution by linking this sequence with those in *Rashomon* (Akira Kurosawa, 1950), where we see four different versions of a rape and killing. What we have in both instances is a visualisation of someone's *account* of a past event. Of course, it was highly unusual in 1949 that a duplicitous account should be visualised, especially in a mainstream film. (The art cinema was granted more leeway: one wonders how many of those who criticised Hitchcock here then went on to praise Kurosawa.) Even today, the device is sufficiently unusual in a mainstream film to cause something of a stir, as critical reaction to *The Usual Suspects* (Bryan Singer, 1995) attests.

Obviously, the very idea of opening a film with a duplicitous account in itself signals a different attitude towards the audience from that in the earlier British movies: it's much more radical. The implications of beginning the film this way have in fact already been discussed by Kristin Thompson. In her article, she argues that the account is by no means merely a trick to fool the audience, but rather 'the determining device of the whole film's structure of motivating devices. It determines the lies and the theatrical metaphor.'[12] This leads her into a detailed consideration not only of the way duplicity is structured into most of the film's relationships, but also of the repeated role-playing and references to theatre in the film, which thereby emerges as a highly self-conscious work, repeatedly foregrounding these elements. I am in agreement with her argument, and my comments should be seen as complementary.

I want to look at some of the details in the opening scenes of Jonathan's account in order to consider the 'textual procedures' involved: the elements selected for attention and the way these are presented. It is at this textual level that I would maintain that *Stage Fright* shows a different aesthetic from Hitchcock's earlier British work. First, a general point about the account: its rhetoric. Since there is no voice-over, everything hinges on the images and dialogue, and it is important that, when we review the film, we can see that it makes sense that Jonathan is telling the story in this particular way. For example, in the opening shot, the camera cranes with him down the stairs so that, as he opens the door, he's confronted with a distraught woman (Charlotte, but her face is at first unseen) who whips open her coat like a flasher to reveal an enormous bloodstain on her dress: the one he himself would later be responsible for. (At the end of the film, Jonathan tells Eve that, although Charlotte's dress was slightly spattered with blood – i.e. she was there when the murder took place – he then went on to smear it with more blood – his own? – in order to make Eve believe his story.) On reviewing, we can thus see that Jonathan is telling his story to Eve with himself in the distraught role: the person who comes, with a bloodstained dress as a guarantee of authenticity, to a lover to seek his/her help. The first words Charlotte speaks, which we read as a measure of her uncertainty over whether Jonathan loves her enough to help, are thus really showing Jonathan's anxiety about Eve's feelings for him: 'You love me; say that you love me; you do love me don't you?' At the end of this section of Jonathan's story, his own words to Charlotte are then designed to cue the response he wants from Eve: 'I'd do anything for you, you know that.'

In other words, Jonathan is cleverly telling his story so that Eve will pick up the parallel he wants: just as he 'saved' Charlotte, so Eve will save him. This also accounts for the particular way Hitchcock films the opening shot in the 'flashback': the crane is designed to have the bloodstain as its visual focus – it heads inexorably towards it. By contrast, when Jonathan descends the same stairs later – and we know that the police are outside – Hitchcock uses the familiar track and reverse of his Hollywood movies: point-of-view track forward with the moving character/reverse angle track back in front of the character. Now, Hitchcock uses this technique when he wishes us to identify with a character's apprehension about what he or she is doing/heading towards. At the beginning of Jonathan's account, Hitchcock wants us to be shocked into sharing his point of view. By the time we get to this later point in Jonathan's story, the rhetoric has shifted: Hitchcock now encourages us to identify with him.

The second scene in Jonathan's story (his visit to Charlotte's house to get her a clean dress) offers an illuminating parallel to the second scene in *Young and Innocent*. When Robert finds Christine's body, the scene is relatively straightforward. He's concerned when he discovers that it's the body of a woman he knows, and the young women irrationally accuse him of running away (in that case, why did he come back?), but the main purpose of the scene would seem to be to make Robert look guilty at the expense of making his accusers look stupid. The equivalent scene in *Stage Fright* is much more complex, with a number of links to other scenes in the movie.

A crucial point about the scene is that the husband's body lies next to the bed, but the bed itself is not shown – we only catch a glimpse of a corner of it, in extreme long shot, in the point-of-view shot of Nellie discovering the body and turning to see Jonathan. Now, this is most unusual for Hitchcock's bedroom scenes: consider the emphasis on the bed in Rebecca's bedroom or Mrs Paradine's in *The Paradine Case* (1947). However, in a number of shots, we see – as if in place of the bed – the chaise longue Charlotte will later lounge on as she tells her own duplicitous story to the police. The chaise longue, in turn, is echoed in the contoured couches on stage for her number 'The Laziest Girl in Town': again Charlotte lounges seductively on them. As for the bed, it is most prominent in the one scene when she and Freddie are alone together: Charlotte stands with it behind her as Freddie moves forward to kiss her.

These details suggest, first, that whereas Freddie has (probably) been admitted into Charlotte's bed, Jonathan has not. However, this does not mean that she and Jonathan did not have an affair, as the emphasis on the chaise longue makes clear. But there are two conflicting ways of reading the film's use of the various 'couches'. If we take the words in the song 'The Laziest Girl in Town' (who was so lazy, she couldn't be bothered with lovers) as referring to Charlotte herself, then we may conclude that she was bored with Jonathan. As she talks to the police, her gesture of leaning her head back on the chaise longue closely anticipates her movements during her stage number. What she tells the police is that, when her husband came home from New York, Jonathan had still wanted to see her ('He wouldn't let me alone') but she had refused. The link with the number could thus be held to support her story. But the words of the song may well be deceptive: perhaps Charlotte enjoys having lots of lovers. If so, her gesture with the police may be read differently: she is leaning back in delicious remembrance of how Jonathan wouldn't leave her alone. (Dietrich's marvellously theatrical playing of the scene at least hints at this possibility.)

As Jonathan is busy trying to make the murder look like the consequence of an interrupted burglary – smashing the glass on the French window; emptying the desk drawers – his attention is caught by a publicity photograph of Charlotte with six male dancers in top hats and tails flanking her. Hitchcock cuts to frame her and the dancer on her left: Jonathan himself. It's over this shot that Nellie's scream is heard, interrupting his reverie. This is a brilliant example of condensation. First, Hitchcock is being ironic at Jonathan's expense: Jonathan sees only the two of them, whereas the photograph, from Charlotte's point of view, shows her surrounded by admiring men (they are looking at her; she's looking at the camera). Second, having Nellie discover the body at this moment comments on the outcome of his admiring look in the photograph: he has killed on Charlotte's account. Third, the timing of the scream identifies the guilty couple. Fourth, it's as if Nellie is screaming *at* the couple in the photograph: as if the very idea of them as a couple was ludicrous.

My argument about these two opening scenes is that, first, they are packed with textual and narrative information and that this is typical of the film overall. The way Hitchcock films the scenes, the details he selects for emphasis, the relationship of the textual elements to those in other scenes, the structuring point that the scenes are not 'the truth' but someone's carefully crafted story – all these point to a highly worked-out complexity to the film. While such complexity is certainly there in some of Hitchcock's British films, it is much more developed in the vast majority of his Hollywood ones. Second, the elements which these opening scenes set in play – the deceptive bloodstain on the dress; the change of clothing; the body in the bedroom; the bed/couch polarity; the innocent photograph which becomes sinister in context – are crucial to the concerns of the film as they will subsequently be developed: issues of performance, sexuality and duplicity. Again, such a laying out of a density of concerns at the beginning of a film is more typical of Hitchcock's Hollywood work.

A final point about the film overall is the casting. In his Hollywood films, Hitchcock frequently shows an acute awareness of the effect of casting a particular star in a particular role: here, he makes excellent use of Dietrich's star persona, with its flamboyant theatricality and sense of irony. Indeed, most of the film's wonderful humour – another of its little-appreciated virtues – stems from Dietrich as star and Sybil Thorndike as character actress.

The stolen raincoat and the bloodstained dress

I would like to elaborate on the key differences between the films by looking in more detail at the incriminating items of clothing in order to see what the parallels and contrasts between them suggest. This takes us back to the opening murders and what lies behind them. First, through its connection to murder, each item is 'sexualised'. Hitchcock's murders incline to the 'sexually perverse', and one can imagine Guy taking perverse pleasure in strangling Christine with her alleged lover's raincoat belt. (Indeed, one senses that this 'pleasure' is registered in his manic laughter when he finally confesses to Erica what he did with the belt.) However, Guy then gave the raincoat itself to a tramp. This is a most curious way of disposing of an incriminating item of clothing – as if Guy felt unable to destroy it, but nevertheless sought to 'repress' it by hiding it in the film's social underclass. But the raincoat is also a 'guilty secret' for Will himself, since people assume that he stole it. Hence he wears it under his outer tramp's clothes, so that his possession of such a 'middle-class' garment cannot be seen.

The strangeness of this scenario forces us to read the fate of the raincoat in symbolic terms, as a register of the guilt of the murderer, as guilt which never goes away, but remains dormant in the film's 'repressed'. Even the (false) guilt of Will 'hiding' the real guilt of Guy suggests the raincoat as an embodiment of a repressed memory. At the deepest level of this symbolic repression is the box of matches in the raincoat pocket – the very item which will serve to lead Guy's accusers to him. The moment when Guy sees Will in a dress suit in the hotel ballroom is thus 'the return of the repressed'. As Guy looks at Will, Hitchcock shows that he recognises him by dissolving, briefly, to Will in his tramp's clothes, presenting him as Guy's guilt image. But the fact that Will is wearing a dress suit also points to the symbolic operation here: it's as if Guy is presented with an oneiric image which has accumulated, in its 'return', other material associated with the murder; in particular, Christine's class status as glamorous movie star (which Guy also resented and so sought to 'repress'). (There's no evidence that he would be aware of the other crucial point: that Will is sitting with Erica, Robert's 'new romance'.)

In *Stage Fright*, the opening murder was obviously Oedipal: Charlotte is an older woman, and Jonathan killed her husband (structurally a father-figure) in order to take sexual possession of her. In this case, the incriminating item of clothing bears testament to the sexuality of the *motive* for the murder. The blood which originally spattered on Charlotte's dress was her husband's, and it would have served, forensically, to incriminate both her and Jonathan. But, far from getting rid of the dress, as he said he would, Jonathan went on to smear it with more blood, like a hysterical projection of his own guilt on to Charlotte. Indeed, Jonathan's act also serves the function – as in a neurotic symptom – of revealing the very guilt he is seeking to deny. Then, in his flight from the police, the one thing he takes with him is the dress, as if he could not bear to be parted with it. It's as if the dress has become a fetish object, not in the Freudian sense, but in that discussed by Gaylyn Studlar in her work on the 'masochistic aesthetic': 'Most children . . . use transitional objects to ease the separation from the mother. If the child cannot accommodate itself to this separation, the transitional object may be retained and lead to fetishism . . . Wulff concludes that the fetish "represents a substitute for the mother's breast and the mother's body"'.[13] (It is highly relevant that Studlar has developed her theories particularly in relation to Marlene Dietrich in her films with Josef von Sternberg.[14])

At the end of Jonathan's duplicitous account, the dress begins to exert its (perverse) power over other characters. As Eve commits herself to helping him, Jonathan signals his gratefulness by clasping her hand, shown in a close-up which places their hands over the bloodstain. It's as if their pact is sealed with the blood on the dress. The establishing shot of Gill's cottage then occurs over a dissolve from this close-up, a dissolve which precisely superimposes the bloodstain on to the cottage, as if contaminating it with its associations. As Jonathan then sleeps, Gill looks at himself in a mirror while holding the dress in front of him. It's at this point that he speaks of the dress as a 'costume' in the melodramatic play that he is imagining them to be in;[15] he then goes on to examine the bloodstain and declares that the dress is a clue. Gill, too, has now become fascinated by the dress, a fascination which will lead him eventually to cut his own hand in order to reincarnate the bloodstain in miniature on the doll.

The apparition of the boy scout and bloody doll confronting Charlotte on the stage parallels the image of Old Will seen by Guy at the climax of *Young and Innocent*. Again this suggests the return of the repressed, and again the outcome is that the person giving a public performance is unable to continue. Equally, again the guilt image is complex, incorporating a condensation of material. Early in the film, Jonathan interrupted Eve on the RADA stage; here it's as if the boy scout – mobilised by Gill on Jonathan's behalf – stands in for Jonathan himself, threatening Charlotte with exposure. But Charlotte has just come from her husband's funeral, so the boy scout could also be seen as like his ghost. Equally, the doll itself is suggestive, like an image of violated femininity. Is it an image of Charlotte herself? Although we know very little of Charlotte's relationship with her husband, she is delighted to be rid of him. Is the doll reminding her of how he treated her?

A further point about the incriminating items is that they seem to acquire a mysterious power. In *Young and Innocent*, although the police have the belt, the raincoat is elusive. The quest for it is marked by violence (the Tom's Hat scene) and Robert has to go into the 'depths' of the doss-house to retrieve it. Its discovery on Old Will is then followed immediately by the accident in the mine, as if it carried a curse. In *Stage Fright*, the item is destroyed but then reincarnated, as if it had a life of its own, and both the necessity to compete for the doll (the shooting match) and the blood Gill cuts from his own hand suggest a ritual involving symbolic sacrifice. The doll then shows its power by causing Charlotte to dry up on stage. However, when each item then passes into the hands of the law, there is a shift in the way it functions. The raincoat now delivers its secret (the box of matches) and, as Smith holds the doll, aural flashbacks tell us that he now realises what's been going on: it's as if the doll enables him to 'see'. Finally, the item is crucial to the film's final confessions: Guy's guilt image of Will, oscillating between the actual image of Will in a dress suit and the memory image of him in his tramp's clothing, stands in for the raincoat; Eve forces Charlotte to confess by 'explaining' about the bloody doll and convincing her that she has the dress. And the confessions themselves at last clarify the hitherto uncertain relationship between the item and the murder.

Clearly what we have here are 'overdetermined' objects; the product of a condensation of each film's concerns. In *Young and Innocent*, these are primarily to do with class. Not only has Guy sought to repress the sign of his guilt into the film's underclass but, when it returns in the image of Will in a dress suit, Guy is in black-face, as if seeking to hide himself in this class. Although the associations of blackface would normally be to do with race (the racist idea of whites caricaturing 'black behaviour'), I would argue that the dominant idea here is much more to do with class. One of the structural oppositions within the film is middle-class cleanliness versus working-class dirt. The houses of the Burgoynes and Aunt Margaret are both spotlessly clean (the rat being produced at the lunch table is disturbing primarily because it threatens this); the working-class figures are for the most part dirty. Accordingly, when the black make-up is wiped off Guy, it's as if the 'dirt' is being removed to reveal the middle-class murderer. One might even take this further: an iconic image of 'dirt' on the face of a working-class figure is coal dust on a miner. Given that the quest for the raincoat took in the old mines, and that the coat itself actually went down with the car into the depths of the mine, one could argue that this association, too, has a place in the film's unconscious.

In *Stage Fright*, the underlying concerns are more to do with sexuality. While class as an issue is certainly present in the film, it is – apart from Nellie – subordinated to a much more developed theme: that of role-playing. Eve *pretends* to be working-class. But the issue of sex is paramount, and the dress focuses this: that the item is a woman's dress rather than a man's raincoat inevitably 'sexualises' it, and it also carries the 'stain' of an Oedipal murder. Moreover, when Jonathan brings the dress to Eve, is he using it to say not just 'look, Charlotte is a murderer', but also 'I was her lover' (and here's her dress to prove it). The dress is thus eroticised in a way quite foreign to Robert's raincoat. The

Oedipal trace to *Stage Fright* then continues in that, although the son-figure destroys the dress, another father-figure reincarnates it. On this occasion, we actually see the blood-letting involved and, given that this scene closely parallels the climax of *Young and Innocent*, we could argue that the 'dirt' motif of the earlier movie has been replaced here by a 'blood' motif: symbolically switching from a signifier of 'class' to one of 'sex and murder'. The power that these items seem to possess – so that they come to seem like magical objects – is thus an expression of the force of the psychoanalytical discourses operating through them. As, in their different ways they keep 'returning' into the films' narratives, they confront the suspects with their guilt and force them into their confessions.

Despite the richness of these psychoanalytical discourses, my argument overall is that, in comparison to *Stage Fright*, *Young and Innocent* lacks 'narrative texture', the complex interweaving of elements one typically finds in Hitchcock's best work. This, I would maintain, is what fundamentally distinguishes his Hollywood from his British period. In returning to England to make *Stage Fright*, he reintroduced much of the humour and many of the thematic elements of his earlier British films, but he combined these with a Hollywood aesthetic.

Notes

I would like to acknowledge the stimulating feedback provided by Stephen Blumenthal and Natasha Broad in the drafting of this chapter.

1 Jane Sloan, *Alfred Hitchcock: The Definitive Filmography*, Berkeley: University of California Press, 1995, contains details of most of the published material on Hitchcock up to 1994.

2 In his article, '*Stage Fright*: The Knowing Performance', *Film Criticism*, 9(2), winter 1984/85, pp. 41–50. Richard Abel begins by considering the critical consensus on the film.

3 For *Young and Innocent*, I would cite the chapter on the film in Maurice Yacowar's *Hitchcock's British Films*, Hamden, CT: Archon Books, 1997, pp. 216–31, and especially the discussion of the film in Chapter 2 in Lesley Brill's *The Hitchcock Romance: Love and Irony in Hitchcock's Films*, Princeton, NJ: Princeton University Press, 1988. For *Stage Fright*, I would cite Abel's article and especially 'Duplicitous narration and *Stage Fright*' in Kristin Thompson, *Breaking the Glass Armour: Neoformalist Film Analysis*, Princeton, NJ: Princeton University Press, 1988, chapter 5.

4 Margaret Dickinson and Sarah Street, *Cinema and State: The Film Industry and the British Government 1927–84*, London: BFI, 1985, p. 102.

5 Donald Spoto, *The Dark Side of Genius: The Life of Alfred Hitchcock*, London: Frederick Muller, 1988, p. 314.

6 The prevalence of this figure in Hitchcock's work is discussed in Robin Wood, *Hitchcock's Films Revisited*, New York: Columbia University Press, 1989, chapter 11.

7 Here I am using Richard Abel's useful structural breakdown of *Stage Fright*, in which he divides the film into thirteen 'narrative segments' (pp. 42–3). The segments in question correspond to his nos. 5–8.

8 An early formulation in English is in Peter Wollen, 'Hitchcock's Vision' (*Cinema*

magazine, Cambridge, June 1969): Hitchcock's films 'speak a rhetoric which is none other than a rhetoric of the unconscious, the world which surges up beneath the thin protection offered us by civilization' (p. 3). With specific reference to Hitchcock's British films, in the introduction to Charles Barr (ed.), *All our Yesterdays: 90 Years of British Cinema,* London: BFI, 1986, Barr writes: 'Increasingly, Hitchcock makes a point of showing us characters asleep or otherwise unconscious, at significant stages of the narrative, as if to convey all the more strongly the oneiric, subjective logic of the action (*The 39 Steps, Young and Innocent, The Lady Vanishes*)' (p. 20).

9 Michael Walker, Introduction (especially pp. 19–20) and *Phantom Lady* (especially pp. 113–15) in Ian Cameron (ed.), *The Movie Book of Film Noir*, London: Studio Vista, 1992.

10 Robin Wood, *Hitchcock's Films Revisited*, pp. 283–7.

11 George Perry had said this in a number of his books – e.g. *The Films of Alfred Hitchcock,* London: Studio Vista, 1965, p. 61 – but does not give a source.

12 Thompson, *Breaking the Glass Armour*, p. 151.

13 Gaylyn Studlar, 'Masochism and the Perverse Pleasures of the Cinema' in Bill Nichols (ed.), *Movies and Methods II,* California: University of California Press, 1985, p. 613.

14 Gaylyn Studlar, *In the Realm of Pleasure: Von Sternberg, Dietrich and the Masochistic Aesthetic,* Illinois: University of Illinois Press, 1988.

15 This is one of the many theatrical metaphors in the film discussed by Thompson, *Breaking the Glass Armour*, pp. 151–8.

Mr and Mrs Smith – Hitchcock's screwball comedy

Chapter 14
Redemptive Comedy in the Films of Alfred Hitchcock and Preston Sturges: 'Are Snakes Necessary?'[1]

Lesley Brill

Nearly sixty years after its release, Hitchcock's 1941 screwball comedy *Mr and Mrs Smith* strikes most viewers as an anomaly in its director's career. (*The Trouble with Harry* (1955) has screwball tendencies, but it too is regarded as a detour.) Preston Sturges's screwball *tour de force* of the same year, *The Lady Eve*, on the other hand, may reasonably be taken as typifying its director's film-making. The movies share more than their year of release, as do their directors. Their plots concern marriages all but lost, then restored. Their titles suggest universality: Mr and Mrs Everyman, and Eve, the progenitor of all humankind. Sturges, a screenwriter metamorphosed, was relatively new to the Hollywood director's folding chair; as was Hitchcock, an experienced movie-maker, but in California for only a year. Each, in fact, was releasing just his third Hollywood film. Born less than a year apart, they shared a European background. However different the specifics of their upbringings were (in many respects they could scarcely have been less alike), both directors brought a cosmopolitan viewpoint to their films and an outsider's freshness and amused scepticism to their observations of the culture and folkways of the United States.

Both were autodidacts and tinkerers, curious and technically inventive. As a teenager, Hitchcock took some courses in engineering and navigation; his understanding of the technicalities of cinematography and his innovations in filming are well known.[2] Sturges was a professional inventor and engineer. Each had an abiding interest in food and wine, Hitchcock as a connoisseur and Sturges as the owner of a fashionable restaurant. Notwithstanding his recent arrival in Hollywood, Hitchcock was already among the best-known and paid American directors, a status that Sturges would soon achieve.[3] A *New York Sun* ad for *Christmas in July* (1940) linked Sturges with Hitchcock (and John Ford): 'Alfred Hitchcock For Suspense! John Ford For Drama! Now . . . Just for Fun – PRESTON STURGES!'[4]

A genealogy of one of Hitchcock's most famous images, the bloodstained water that twists down the drain at the end of Marion's murder in *Psycho* (1960), runs through Sturges. Hitchcock's camera follows the water into the drain from which it pulls back, now twisting itself, to reveal that it is also emerging from the unmoving eye of the dead woman. Two years earlier the titles of Hitchcock's *Vertigo* (1958) spiralled out of the eye of another woman, probably Madeleine–Judy. Now let us go back another ten years, to Sturges's 1948 *Unfaithfully Yours*. As the orchestra conductor slips into his paranoid fantasies of cuckoldry and revenge, the camera tracks toward his face, continues to an extreme close-up of his eyes, and then goes without a cut into the pupil of his left eye and the darkness of his brain, where the schemes of his afflicted imagination are taking shape. Sturges's shot itself recalls the long track to the drummer's eyes at the end of Hitchcock's *Young and Innocent* (1937) and the close-ups of Gregory Peck's eyes before psychoanalytic flashbacks in *Spellbound* (1945). The addition of swirling water to this image in *Psycho* is anticipated in *Unfaithfully Yours* by Sturges's double-printing of draining water over the conductor's face when he kills himself during a trial of Russian roulette in his third jealous fantasy. That shot too has a Hitchcockian forebear, the multiple printing of a similar shot over the heroine's face as she loses consciousness in *The Lady Vanishes* (1938).

Visual and thematic echoes rebound among Hitchcock's first *The Man Who Knew Too Much* (1934), *Unfaithfully Yours* and the second version of *The Man Who Knew Too Much* (1956). The later two films expand the concert of the first into elaborately photographed representations of orchestras in performance. In all three, cymbals are emphasised, and in the later two Hitchcock and Sturges literally orchestrate their opening credits. Symbolically, the orchestra in each of the three films functions similarly. In the Hitchcock pictures it models artistic and social harmony. Sturges varies that theme with the idea of 'vulgarity', which in *Unfaithfully Yours* evolves from the conductor's snobbish judgement of other people into his recognition of shared human weakness; and therefore shared responsiveness to musical (and, explicitly, cinematic) embodiments of love and its attendant insecurities.

Both versions of *The Man Who Knew Too Much* and *Unfaithfully Yours* set the practised perfection of art against the recalcitrance of ordinary reality. This theme appears embryonically in the first *The Man Who Knew Too Much* in the nearly slapstick fight in the chapel and the police barrage at the end of the film. For Sturges fourteen years later, there is no 'nearly' about the slapstick. The perfection of the melodramatic dreams engendered in the concert hall contrasts emphatically with the intransigence of the material world when Sir Alfred attempts to realise his fantasies in his apartment. Similar comic encounters with the obstinate reality of Moroccan chicken and English taxidermy obstruct the professionally accomplished Dr McKenna in Hitchcock's second *The Man Who Knew Too Much*.

All three films further converge in the emphasis they accord to ideas and images of time, a dimension that joins ideal artistic worlds with social–political ones. 'The regulation of time,' wrote Elias Canetti, 'is the primary attribute of all government.'[5] Similarly, the embodiment of time lies at the centre of art, especially the arts of music and storytelling, which are joined with particular intimacy in narrative films. For both versions of *The Man Who Knew Too Much* (as for many other Hitchcock films) time is of the essence. Musical performances, assassination attempts and plot climaxes occur simultaneously. In the second *The Man Who Knew Too Much* they do so twice, first in the Albert Hall, then in the embassy with Doris Day's overwrought '*Que sera sera*'. In *Unfaithfully Yours*, Sir Alfred's murderous, self-sacrificing and suicidal imaginings unfold in synchronisation with the varying moods of the music he conducts.

Between Sturges's third film, *The Lady Eve*, and Hitchcock's forty-fifth, *Vertigo*, there is a remarkable connection. In each, a man falls in love twice, with women he believes to be different but who are, as Mugsy insists in Sturges's movie, 'the same dame'. The outcomes of the plots of the two films differ, but the stakes remain similar: the recovery of a love into which characters have suddenly fallen and which they have grievously lost. At their visual and kinetic centres both Hitchcock's and Sturges's films have images and acts of falling: in love (both); from a rooftop, in a terrifying nightmare, from a kitchen step-stool (*Vertigo*); over Jean's ankle, off a chair, over a couch and then a coffee table, into the mud, over Jean's ankle again (*The Lady Eve*); in love again, with the same woman once more, and thence down to bliss (*The Lady Eve*) or agony (*Vertigo*).

Behind the similarities noted thus far between Hitchcock and Sturges, one might argue, loom more cogent differences. Where Sturges's movies are amusingly zany, Hitchcock's are ominously bizarre. Hitchcock finds strange darkness lurking behind the light of ordinary little days; his humour frequently leans towards the pessimistic or ironic. Sturges inflates everyday misunderstandings and clumsiness into harmless slapstick. Though both were among the small group of directors who were also media stars, the trajectories of their careers diverged wildly. Hitchcock's endured through fifty-three feature films over fifty-one years that spanned the evolution of cinema from silent film through early talkies, the technical mastery of black-and-white sound film in the great Hollywood studios of the 1940s, the domination of colour, a liaison with 3-D and the standardisation of wide-screen. As his fame grew decade by decade, Hitchcock developed his famous television shows, became a major stockholder in a giant entertainment company, and eventually achieved the popular status of an adjective. His long ascent contrasts with the meteoric appearance and extinguishing of Sturges's directorial star. Although Sturges had a decade of screenwriting experience preceded by an apprenticeship of the same duration in the New York theatre, eleven of his twelve movies appeared between 1940 and 1948, eight of them between 1940 and 1943. After *The Beautiful Blond from Bashful Bend* (1948), his career as a writer–director effectively ended.

Are likenesses between Hitchcock and Sturges, then, remarkable chiefly for framing fundamental differences? I think not. Not only do their films have profound congruences, but their thematic and stylistic affinities draw our attention to aspects of their directors' work that are underappreciated or misinterpreted. The sources of their similarities – a shared era, milieu, industrial situation; kindred talents and sensibilities; perhaps even direct influence on each other – must be matters of supposition. Inventiveness in artists springs from exceptionally complete and thoughtful assimilation of cultural heritage and nurture. Witness Shakespeare, the least apologetic of plagiarists and the most original of dramatists. And, as it happens, one of the pre-eminent influences on both Sturges and Hitchcock.

Arguments for the affinities between the movies of the two directors arise from the works themselves. Let me scan the most significant lines of convergence. The films of both Hitchcock and Sturges often pivot on trust or mistrust between female and male protagonists – a common enough issue in movies, but one that is both especially pervasive in Sturges and Hitchcock and that raises religious harmonies in both.

Male leads in Sturges and Hitchcock tend to be boyishly impulsive; leading women are usually somewhat more sophisticated and self-possessed. This pattern persists even when the man is significantly older than the woman. For Hitchcock's pictures, such characterisation is more marked in his American movies than his British ones. He often complicates it by revealing apparently naïve or weak heroines to be as shrewd as their male opposites and emotionally stronger. The innocent men of Hitchcock's films include heroes from the New World who are contrasted with more worldly wise British or European heroines or antagonists: Hannay in *The 39 Steps* (1935), Johnny Jones in *Foreign Correspondent* (1940), and Mark in *Dial M for Murder* (1954) are obvious examples. But if such heroes prove innocent and vulnerable, they nonetheless prevail; while besieged heroines discover in themselves acuteness and strength. In effect, heroines' strengths and heroes' weaknesses move them together.

Intricately intertwined with questions of trust between men and women are plots that stress miracles and faith and their realistic sublimations: improbabilities and unconditional romantic love, respectively. Technologically updated *dei ex machinae* illustrate this tendency in Hitchcock, as does such cinematic razzle-dazzle as that which gets Eve and Roger Thornhill off a cliff face and into a honeymoon berth at the end of *North by Northwest* (1959). The extravagant improbabilities that wrap up Sturges's *The Palm Beach Story* (1942) and *The Sin of Harold Diddlebock* (1946) are good examples of the same tendency. The title of *The Miracle of Morgan's Creek* (1944) and its modernised retelling of the Christmas story point towards its religious analogues.

Hitchcock and Sturges were superb writers, though Hitchcock always worked with at least one collaborator and Sturges preferred to write with no help other than a typist. Both were virtuosos in setting comic–romantic story elements against the pull of tragic–ironic ones. This tension is praised in Hitchcock as suspense; in Sturges it is casually attributed, less accurately, to quirky originality. Both, in practise, were 'masters of suspense' – that is, of managing the energizing tensions between conflicting genres. Ray Cywinski observes that French commentators on Sturges have repeatedly characterised his films as constructed of a '*mélange des genres*', and he asserts that Sturges exhibits a 'conscious disregard for genre expectations'.[6] I suggest that Sturges does not so much disregard such expectations as create pressure by clashing them against each other. 'What kind of a story,' he makes us wonder, 'is this going to turn out to be?' The romantic aspect of romantic comedy, furthermore, intrinsically raises the kind of suspense characteristic of Hitchcock's and Sturges's movies, because the structure of romance favours the sort of serial adventures familiar from *The Odyssey* to *The Adventures of Baron Von Münchausen*. Unlike 'pure comedy', romance incorporates genuine suffering and even death, which it generally then turns to redemptive ends, albeit in conclusions that may inspire mixed emotional responses. Nonetheless, one need not forgo joy and laughter just because, as Sturges once said, one is 'living in contemplation of death'.[7]

Lively and precise as screenwriters, neither Hitchcock nor Sturges ever forgot that motion pictures must move; their films rarely stall into talking heads. More specifically, motion up and down has special importance, in part because both directors use vertical movement to figure forth symbolic falls from, and/or recoveries of, happiness and self-realisation. In Hitchcock's films, as I have argued elsewhere, the ratio of downward movement to actions of ascent signals the dominance of ironic or romantic modes.[8] Patterns of motion in Sturges's pictures are more complicated, but they often signify in much the same way. Realistic sublimations of the myth of the loss of Eden and the recovery of grace are particularly marked in *The Lady Eve* with its numerous falls, but systematic use of motion up and down of both camera and characters occurs in most of Sturges's other movies also. *The Sin of Harold Diddlebock*, for example, begins by screening the athletic falls and rise to glory of the protagonist at the end of Lloyd's *The Freshman* (1925) and then proceeds to refigure such movements in the movie that follows with Diddlebock's firing twenty years later, his descent into a basement bar, ascent to improbable riches, and his struggle to avoid falling again – literally to the street far below a skyscraper's ledge from which he dangles by a leash attached to a circus lion named Jackie. The repeated fainting fits and sprawling through fences and railings that Norval undergoes in *The Miracle of Morgan's Creek* similarly precede his triumphant elevation at the end of the film.

The most distinctive feature of Sturges's films is the humour and, in particular, the comic brilliance of minor characters. Although less obtrusive, Hitchcock's humour, even in his grimmest films, is rarely absent for long. His fondness for quirky incidental characters, like the 'okey-dokey' inn-keeper in *The Paradine Case* (1947), reminds one of Sturges, as do the innkeeper and his wife in *The 39 Steps* (1955), Charters and Caldicott in *The Lady Vanishes*, Herb in *Shadow of a Doubt* (1943), Hitchcock's daughter Patricia as Chubby (!) in *Stage Fright* (1950) and as Caroline in *Psycho*, the charwoman in *Marnie* (1964), and so on. Hitchcock's cameo appearances more often than not take a similar humorous shape, from the child-beleaguered subway rider in *Blackmail* (1929) or the director's photograph on a weight-reduction product advertisement in *Lifeboat* (1944) to the frustrated man who misses the bus at the beginning of *North by Northwest.*

The pain, or threat of pain, in much of Hitchcock's humour is well known. The same quality in Sturges's movies is almost equally common and accounts for his frequent classification as a satirist, a label that largely mistakes him. Sturges's movies, like Hitchcock's, contain a good deal of incidental satire; but again like Hitchcock's movies, they focus much more on specific actions and on characters as individuals than on the social stereotypes that satire generally deals in. In particular, as I will argue, the emphasis in his films on romantic love, amorous misfortunes and redemptive plot outcomes does not square with the acerbity we usually associate with the label 'satirist'. Cywinski calls Sturges's humour 'cynical, absurd, ironical and oftentimes cruel' and notes that 'satire, though ostensibly concerned with changing the follies it exposes, usually ends up taking a stance of detached superiority and disdainful or laughing pessimism'.[9]

Sturges and Hitchcock exhibit something close to an obsession with acting, lying, and other forms of pretense, benignant or malign. Eccentric versions of backstage romance recur throughout Hitchcock's career from his first film, *The Pleasure Garden* (1927), which begins with images of a line of chorines, to his last, *Family Plot* (1976), with Blanche's closing, complicit wink at the audience – Hitchcock's final directorial gesture. Sturges comes closest to a backstage romance with *Unfaithfully Yours*, but virtually all his movies require extended performances of their characters – most obviously Jean as Lady Sidwich in *The Lady Eve* and the '4-F' Woodrow Truesmith as a decorated marine in *Hail the Conquering Hero* (1944). Emblems and actions of performance in the pictures of Hitchcock and Sturges often reinforce their self-reflexivity – that is, their tendency to muse on their status as works of art.

The most revealing overlap between the movies of Hitchcock and Sturges, and the focus of the rest of this essay, concerns the struggle for trust, love and understanding between a man and a woman that preoccupies many of their films and that is present in virtually all of them. In Hitchcock's movies, its importance is frequently displaced early in the film by the 'MacGuffin', an object or goal that propels the main characters into a world of adventures and that brings them into contact with each other – and that thereby leads to the love story that becomes the central concern of the film. In Sturges's movies, the conflicts and accommodations between hero and heroine are often explicitly central, but he too has his MacGuffins: the unknown identity of the biological author of Trudy's pregnancy, for example, and consequent legal ambiguities in *The Miracle of Morgan's Creek*. When the thematic focus begins elsewhere in Sturges's films, however – the question of comedy versus grim realism in *Sullivan's Travels* (1941), for example – the secondary concern with the relationship between the male and the female protagonist does not usually move to the thematic centre of the film.

Between 1940 and 1948, the years during which Sturges was making movies in Hollywood, Hitchcock completed eleven films. Nine of them are very much concerned with the attempts of their heroines and heroes to afford each other trust, mutual aid and love. Particularly striking is the frequency with which their plots turn on declarations of trust or, in movies that have ironic or tragic outcomes, discoveries of betrayal. Whatever their outcomes, Hitchcock's reiterated explorations of faith between men and women constitute one of the defining concerns of his career – both during the decade of film-making that he shared with Sturges and throughout the rest of his career.

In his films of the 1940s (to bracket for a moment longer the part of Hitchcock's career that corresponds in time with Sturges's), romantic faith is variously realised and arrives at diverse conclusions. De Winter's confession to his young wife in *Rebecca* (1940) gives her true partnership in their marriage at last; his belated trust in her, as much as the revelation that frees him from legal jeopardy, leads to the happy ending of their story. The comic irony at the end of *Mr and Mrs Smith* devolves from the principals' rediscovery of their suitability and need for each other. Critics diverge about *Suspicion* (1941), but no one disputes that the degree and justification of Lina's confidence in her feckless husband is a crucial issue. *Saboteur* (1942) returns to a simpler pattern, with Barry's attempts to convince Priscilla of his innocent devotion to his country and his tangential courtship of her taking the same path as his attempt to clear his name. *Shadow of a Doubt* and *The Paradine Case* each have doubled resolutions in which one male–female relationship comes to tragic conclusion (Charlie and Young Charlie, Keane and Mrs Paradine) while a second (Young Charlie and Jack, Keane and his wife) re-establishes bonds of love and trust. In the two films that Hitchcock made with Ingrid Bergman during the period of Sturges, *Spellbound* and *Notorious* (1946), distrust occasioned by a devastating past threatens to undo the fragile bonds of sudden, intense romantic love. Balantyne must put himself into the hands of his lover/psychiatrist – who bears the suggestive name of Constance – in order to cure the amnesia that threatens to deprive him of both her and his freedom. 'Why won't you trust me, Dev?' asks Alicia, midway through *Notorious*. Alicia's life and the happiness of both protagonists depend upon Dev's finding the confidence to trust the woman with whom he is in love.

Across Hitchcock's career as a whole, happy endings to the love stories in his movies occur more frequently than most commentators remember, but such conclusions are by no means simply the rule. Even in those films that end equivocally or tragically, however, the issue of trust remains crucial. The mutual loyalty that Alice and Frank lack at the beginning of *Blackmail* they achieve at the end, but at great cost. In *Frenzy* (1972), Barbara, like Daisy in *The Lodger* (1926) and Erica in *Young and Innocent*, believes in her lover against all evidence. Nevertheless, she is raped and murdered, as is Blaney's sympathetic ex-wife. Ironic but far from tragic, *Rich and Strange* (1932) takes its married couple through crises of confidence as eventful as their round-the-world cruise. Home again, the wife can hardly trust her husband, for he has amply proved that he does not merit it. Instead she accepts his needy weakness and recommits herself to her marriage on that decent but uninspiring basis.

In most of Sturges's movies, and in many of Hitchcock's, distrust is inevitable in the fundamental structure of relations between women and men. *The Lady Eve* and *The Miracle of Morgan's Creek* pointedly clarify the myth underlying that distrust and the promise that it can be overcome: to wit, the fall from Eden and the prospect of eventual forgiveness and redemption. Hopsie's year up the Amazon casts him in the role of another Adam, ripe to follow another Eve into sinful knowledge and expulsion from Paradise. The terrible lesson Jean-as-Eve teaches him confirms the fated disappointments of postlapsarian adult love, all instances of which derive from humankind's first infidelity, committed with the serpent by the original Eve.

But such an interpretation is partial; it does not account for Jean's humane epigram, 'The best ones [girls] aren't as good as you probably think they are and the bad ones aren't as bad, not nearly as bad.' Nor does it account for the recovery of the couple's love.

Hopsie is naïve rather than innocent. The Amazon is an illusion of life without the complications of adult love in a fallen world. A viewer more alert than the hero will notice the leave-taking Mugsy offers his native companion, a farewell of mixed sentiment, dismissal and evasion. Hardly a snapshot from Eden. 'As for the earthly paradise,' Northrop Frye remarks, 'according to Christian doctrine it was, but it cannot now be; consequently in romance, the paradisiac is frequently a deceitful illusion . . .'[10] Hopsie needs to recognise that a corrupt world stains everyone. People can be redeemed, however, by love. Such redemption consists of a reawakening and nurturing of innocence that can flourish within the knowledge of sin. Hopsie must come to a truer understanding of himself, women and life. As regards love, all women have pasts and all men are, as Harry says, 'sucker sapiens'. Wisdom is to be found in acknowledging that one is a sucker, a 'poor fish'.

Faith, the radical basis of trust, believes the impossible. 'Oh, you still don't understand,' exclaims Jean at the end of *The Lady Eve*. In truth, however, Hopsie understands exactly what he needs to: 'I don't want to understand, I don't want to know . . . All I know is I adore you . . .' The luckiest and best of Hitchcock's characters might well say the same to each other. In Hitchcock's films, 'knowing' is frequently untrustworthy and destructive, and faith leads both to deeper understanding and redemption from loss and error. Love needs no reasons; indeed, it *cannot* have sufficient cause.

To love and accept love, one must know human weakness, including one's own; and one must believe in forgiveness. Theologically, such knowledge begins with the story of Adam and Eve and ends with eternal salvation. Psychologically, in Sturges's movies and other romances, including Hitchcock's, it is figured forth in lovers' comprehension of a shared past and their shared faith in the future. Whether their past occurs historically, as in the growing up together of Trudy and Norval in *The Miracle of Morgan's Creek*, or is created together, as in *The Lady Eve*, doesn't much matter. Hopsie attempts to imagine an ideal past with Jean and then with Eve. To both (that is to her twice), he declaims, 'You seem to go way back ... you're a little girl ...' His bland ideal of childish innocence shatters, however, first on Jean's true past as the daughter of a card-sharp and then on the oceanic sexual experience of The Lady Eve. Jean, who already partly knows what it means to have a past, will come to a deeper understanding. Although she intends 'to be what he [Hopsie] thinks I am', thereby collaborating in her lover's creation of an innocent girlhood, she also tells her father, 'I'm not your daughter for free, you know.' She is threatening Harry, but the bill for her past will come to her and Hopsie.

In their two abortive courtships, Hopsie and Jean create a truly mutual past for themselves: first as a hustler at cards and a rich, guileless scientist; then as a noble Englishwoman and a parvenu American. What they learn from all their pasts – those that they try to make up or to erase and those that they create together – leads to one conclusion, the necessity for forgiveness. The next-to-last thing they do is to ask each other for forgiveness. That makes possible their last action, their admission that they are married, for better or for worse.

Mr and Mrs Smith achieve precisely the same understanding by the end of Hitchcock's film. Like the protagonists in Sturges's comedy of remarriage, they finally go beyond rational knowledge and the law to love and mercy. At the same time, more than coincidentally, both pairs acknowledge their intense sexual attraction, what Jean calls 'this awful yen for each other'. Snakes and sex are both necessary.

Generally speaking, Hitchcock's heroines and heroes must experience weakness or badness in order to offer and accept forgiveness and love. In romantic comedies like *The Farmer's Wife* (1928), *To Catch a Thief* (1955) and *Family Plot*, the lovers' lapses are funny, their sins no worse than venial. For films, the predominant modes of which are irony or melodrama, like *Easy Virtue* (1927), *The Secret Agent* (1936) or *The Birds* (1963), past sins and present failings loom larger and more dangerous. Even in *The Trouble with Harry*, Hitchcock's filmic working out of the hypothesis, 'Suppose that people could be truly innocent', forgiving the past and granting faith to a lover who requires it find expression in the courtship of Miss Gravely and Captain Wiles. When the unforgiving logic of tragedy dominates in *Vertigo* or *Topaz* (1969), weakness and evil are too persistent to overcome. Love fails.

Among Hitchcock's works, those with the most explicit religious conceptions include *I Confess* (1953) and *The Wrong Man* (1956). The setting and plot of *I Confess* and its cutting and camera work liken Father Logan to Christ. Since his ordeal parallels Christ's passion, his confrontations with weakness, including his own, dominate the film. The influence of past errors is deflected largely onto the now-married girlfriend of his youth, who remembers an Edenic garden in which she and Logan spent a night only to be expelled by the film's serpentine villain. For her as well as for Logan, triumph follows from faith in the possibility of present forgiveness and the acceptance and transcendence of weakness.

Generally taken at face value as an exercise in *cinéma verité*, *The Wrong Man* invokes the most important prefiguration in the Old Testament of Christ's suffering, Job. The relief of Manny's ordeal, however, does not turn on his Jobian tenacity but on a Christian miracle portrayed with the conspicuous cinematic virtuosity of the longest lap-dissolve in Hitchcock's career. While he prays to a portrait of Christ, Manny's image is gradually replaced by that of a second man who will be recognised as the perpetrator of the crime for which Manny stands accused. As his given names Christopher Emanuel suggest, the protagonist of *The Wrong Man*, like his counterpart in *I Confess*, evokes Christ; and like the surname of the couple in *Mr and Mrs Smith*, the name which everyone calls him, 'Manny', encourages us to think of him as humankind typified. The title of *The Wrong Man* also hints at its Christian heritage, for Jesus's conviction and sentence was imposed on the wrongest possible man.

Other Hitchcock films, more intermittently, draw on their director's Christian upbringing. Hitchcock stages a scarcely disguised crucifixion from which the Lodger is rescued at the climax of that film. Forty-two years later, Scottie assumes a similar posture on a mission's bell tower. At the conclusions of his last silent film, *The Manxman* (1928), and his first sound film, *Blackmail*, Hitchcock sends fallen couples to wander the world with the sobering knowledge of their own faithlessness. Less sombrely, *Shadow of a Doubt* ends with its couple standing before a church contemplating the inseparability of good and evil in the world. An Eve whose perception of life has been forever complicated walks through alternating shadow and light at the ambivalent end of *Stage Fright*. In *North by Northwest*, another Eve is rescued from an enemy called Van Damm by a man whose name recalls Christ crucified with his crown of thorns on a hill. Ingrid Bergman looks down on a statue of Christ as she flies into Rio in *Notorious* and her (fictional) husband describes her in *Under Capricorn* (1949) as 'a holy blessed angel' who would ride 'at a fence like it had the Kingdom of Heaven on the other side'. At the end of *Marnie*, a man who bears the comforting Christian name of Mark stands beside a woman whose superficial sophistication must yield to deeper knowledge of her fundamental weakness – a dark truth, however, from which hope can flow.

For Sturges also the truth, however difficult or dismaying, creates hope. In the redemptive films of both directors, as in Christian belief, a fall (like The Fall) ultimately leads to rapture; along with sorrow it brings the possibility of redemption. Relations between women and men recapitulate the myth of Eve's infidelity with the serpent, Adam's complicity, and their discovery together of shame, grief and the promise of forgiveness and salvation. As Adam exclaims in *Paradise Lost*, when he learns that 'the Serpent [must suffer] now his capital bruise' and that 'then the Earth/Shall all be Paradise, far happier place/Than this Eden . . .' (XII, ll. 463–5),

> . . . full of doubt I stand
> Whether I should repent me now of sin
> By mee done and occasioned, or rejoyce
> Much more that much more good thereof shall spring . . .
>
> (XII, ll. 473-6)[11]

The story of humankind ultimately reaches a comic conclusion. On the secular level, for the heroes and heroines of the kind of romantic comedies that Sturges and Hitchcock favoured, the tribulations into which human weaknesses plunge their lovers eventually sweeten their happiness. They achieve again, more gratefully and with more self-understanding, the love and trust that they first stumble upon as a gift, then lose painfully, and finally recover.

As Christian doctrine understands it, the world is corrupt and humanity, even in its best exemplars, enfeebled and besotted. Happy endings require that grace and mercy supersede justice and that miracles displace dire causality. Stories with such outcomes are called comedies. Despite film scholars' focus on his tragic and ironic works, Hitchcock may be judged by the majority of his movies to be a predominantly comic film-maker. Sturges, despite the attempts of many critics to dismiss his happy endings, is almost always one.[12]

Among Sturges's films, none exemplifies better than *The Miracle of Morgan's Creek* the wonder that propels his plots and their congeniality to a Christian understanding. The course of true love in Morgan's Creek never does run smooth. Figured as a series of crashes, clashes, bumps, falls, mistakes and misunderstandings, it leads to jail and a fugitive life for the stammering Norval and to an equivocal pregnancy for his beloved Trudy – whose name, however, iterates her essential faithfulness. As the title promises, miracles of new life and forgiveness subtend the unforgiving surface of chaos and human law. The swing of the plot up to its wildly improbable outcome begins with Sturges's reworking of the Christmas story – the moment when, in Christian cosmology, human fate turns decisively. Lest we miss the significance of the country house, Christmas tree, cow in the living room, old Jewish man bearing a gift, and unaccountably pregnant woman, Trudy's father steers us toward the relevant association by urging her to 'have more confidence in the Almighty', and by reminding her, 'It's almost Christmas. Where was He born? In a cow shed.' The spectacular improbabilities of the denouement follow in quick succession: the birth of sextuplets, the involvement of the Governor, the celebration of Trudy as a pattern of constancy and motherhood, the ecstatic admiration of the nations of the world, the despair of totalitarian dictators, amnesty for Norval, his commissioning in the National Guard, and, most importantly, his recognition as Trudy's true husband and her children's father. As one of my students argued, a repressive paternal policeman and his reign of law are replaced by a forgiving father and a reign of love.[13]

If the astonishing outcomes of most of Sturges's other pictures do not summon Christian tradition so explicitly, they are scarcely less miraculous. *Christmas in July* ends with a practical joke turning, against all odds, into actuality. A collocation of convenient circumstance and Jean's quick action brings *The Lady Eve* to its happiest of conclusions. *Sullivan's Travels* rescues its hero and faith in comedy itself with Sullivan's 'death', post-mortem confession to his own murder, and 'resurrection'. *The Palm Beach Story* restores the marriage of its central couple and marries off the left-over characters by reanimating that *semper virens* of comic devices, two sets of identical, interchangeable twins. *Hail the Conquering Hero* solves its tangled webs with a miracle of enthusiastic forgiveness; while *The Sin of Harold Diddlebock* – whatever his sin may be – is washed clean in his middle-aged crisis, fruitful descent into the underworld of bars, horse races and circuses and re-emergence with a fortune, a loud suit and a beautiful wife. The trusting ending of *Unfaithfully Yours* declares its kinship with other comedies of miracles, faith and errors set straight. In the effective *coup de grâce* for Sturges's career as a writer–director, *The Beautiful Blond from Bashful Bend*, the wretched Baserman brothers return from the dead and Freddie is pardoned by the court so that she can marry her devoted if frequently tempted lover Blackie. Even the apparently unlucky end of *The Great McGinty* (1940) springs the hero from jail, leaves his wife and her children with a drawerful of cash, and allows him to brawl happily ever after in Mexico with his boss, The Boss.

For Hitchcock, the exceedingly fortunate or miraculous circumstance – often realised as a last-minute rescue – and its evil twin the catastrophically unlucky coincidence, have always had an essential place. Examples are so frequent that reviewers periodically complained about incredibility during Hitchcock's career and the director counterattacked with his own complaints about 'our friends the plausibilists'. Recall some instances taken from Hitchcock films of various periods and types: the nick-of-time capture of the 'red-handed' Avenger in *The Lodger*, the ship that delays sinking long enough in *Rich and Strange* to allow the rescue of the protagonists and the rebirth of their marriage; the saving *deus ex machina* of a last-minute fighter plane attack in *The Secret Agent*, the manic confession of 'The Drummer Man' that saves Robert in *Young and Innocent*, the patently manipulated fall of Uncle Charlie in front of an oncoming train in *Shadow of a Doubt*, the happy coincidence that sets *The Wrong Man* right, and the amazing last-second marksmanship of the state trooper in *North by Northwest*. In most of these sequences conspicuous, even intrusive, technical virtuosity highlights the implausibility. Hitchcock seeks out resolving miracles, and draws attention to the technical wonders that make their representation possible. His stylistic practice suggests that accepting such marvels is essential to both our responsiveness to his art and our belief in the ultimate justice of life. As creators of romantic narratives have always done, Hitchcock declares, 'It is required/You do awake your faith' (*The Winter's Tale*, V. iii. 93–4).

When Hitchcock's films end in catastrophe or bitterness, they do so because the miracles fail. As his movies approach tragedy, such failures seem inevitable. The epiphany that Norman catalyses for Marion in *Psycho* leads not to new life but death. Arbogast ascends to find not truth but, like Marion, a flashing knife; the car that is retrieved from the swamp carries only useless money and a corpse. The Hitchcock of *Blackmail*, *Rope* (1948), *Strangers on a Train* (1951), *Vertigo*, *Psycho* – that is, the ironic or tragic Hitchcock – has been disproportionately attended to by academic critics. *Chacun à son goût*. But we should remember that Hitchcock's creative taste repeatedly brought him back to comedy and romance, and that in all his films faith and miracles of salvation – whether achieved, partly achieved or missed entirely – are at issue. The outcomes and generic modalities of his movies vary widely, the central themes much less.

Like Hitchcock, Sturges is always conscious that love may languish and miracles miss. The distinctive genius of Sturges's comedy, like Hitchcock's storytelling in all genres, comes from the energy with which he raises the dark side of his themes, the daring with which he balances between loss and redemption, disaster and triumph, cynicism and faith, genuine suffering and comic anxiety. *Christmas in July*, *Sullivan's Travels* and *Hail the Conquering Hero* all have distressing first endings which second conclusions reverse. Harold Diddlebock's recklessness and vulnerability are so alarming that only Harold Lloyd, the scariest daredevil comedian of the silent era, seems right for the role. Cuckolding of elderly husbands by young wives is a venerable comic subject, but the sympathy accorded Sir Alfred in *Unfaithfully Yours* and his relative youth carries that film close to the pathos of bitter sexual jealousy.

Because art can be seen as a miracle of creation and as an occasion for belief in what is impossible, self-reflexivity in the movies of Sturges and Hitchcock has close thematic ties to the faith and wonders of comic romances and, perforce, to their negations in tragedy or irony. A movie meditates on itself as a work of art in one or both of two ways: by the representation of other art or by an emphasis on its own artfulness that renders its audience conscious not only of what is represented but also of the means of representation. In Hitchcock's films, examples of plays, role-playing and other deceptions, musical performances, magic, carnival acts, fashion shows, courtroom theatrics, other films and assorted other creations are so numerous that to list them would practically duplicate his filmography. Self-reflexivity is also implicit in the conspicuous displays of technical virtuosity that support the marvellous turning points of Hitchcock's plots.

Virtually all of Sturges's comedies depend on play-acting and other forms of performance. McGinty adopts various pretenses, including, at first, his marriage. (The turning of his public-relations marriage into a real one recalls Hitchcock, who puts men and women together for expediency or under duress, then shows them falling in love.) Most of the action of *Christmas in July* develops from a faked telegram; and *The Lady Eve*, *Sullivan's Travels* and *The Palm Beach Story* feature adoption by one or more characters of false identities. *Hail the Conquering Hero* has its protagonist, however unwillingly, living a lie; and Harold Diddlebock, like a comic Dr Jekyll, temporarily turns into his own opposite. Sir Alfred's fantasies cast him in three roles quite impossible for him to play in reality, as the last section of *Unfaithfully Yours* demonstrates. Finally, *The Beautiful Blond from Bashful Bend* unfolds a series of tricks, pretenses and the adoption, again, of a false identity. Sturges's comedies present human beings as achieving their purposes and discovering their identities through the feignings of art or artful feignings.

A similar case could be made for the outcomes of pretense in Hitchcock, with an important qualification: the transformative power of art and its analogues lead to truth only in the Hitchcock films which develop predominantly as romantic comedies. In his more ironic works, feigning is fundamentally false and lies do not miraculously turn into the truth. The hopeless stasis of an ironic world renders real transformations impossible; and love, the most critical of human metamorphoses, ends not in rebirth but miscarriage or abortion.

Although threats of such outcomes arise in Sturges's comedies, all of them finally resolve happily – keeping in mind that the depth and resonance of Sturges's understanding of people and their world make what he shows as human good fortune a complicated matter indeed. In his films, as in Hitchcock's comic romances, self-reflexive elements are firmly allied with the fortunate faults of the protagonists and with the miracles of happy coincidence through which everything that falls must rise. Art and other kinds of pretending constitute, in a comic–romantic world, both a way to represent the redeeming metamorphoses of human life and the substance of such transformations. The perfections of art and the blamelessness of romantic comedy may be the greater part of whatever happy innocence humans achieve. *Sullivan's Travels* makes this understanding of life and art the main point of its parable. Imaginative re-creations of the world of innocence re-enact the original creation of an unspoiled universe. The capacity of art to imitate benignant creativity leads to its self-reflexive celebration in the cinema of Hitchcock and Sturges and in the comic romances of their predecessors and successors.

For some readers, my assertion that the films of Hitchcock and Sturges share central concerns and structures will remain unconvincing. My argument that romance and optimistic comedy have predominant importance in their work, moreover, articulates a distinctly minority understanding. Commentators, whatever their methodological orientation, take Hitchcock to be an ironic and superbly skilled manipulator of audience expectations whose works generally set forth a threatening vision of the world and of human vulnerability. Sturges, as I have noted, is often regarded as an acerbic satirist, the happy endings of whose films are either deliberately implausible or serve as aesthetically gratuitous pap for the emotional gratification of vulgar masses. Neither of these views seems to me to account for the predominant energies of the majority of Hitchcock's movies and nearly all of Sturges's. From my discussion, I hope that a richer understanding of both directors may emerge, an understanding more in alignment with the totality of Sturges's and Hitchcock's careers. In particular, the stylistic and thematic affinities between their movies and their incorporation of Christian myth and doctrine suggest that the two directors share deep aesthetic and sentimental predispositions.

Their explorations of love, faith, wonder and their antagonists and opposites hardly make Hitchcock and Sturges unique among film-makers; but as is often the case with dominant artists, common myths and archetypes appear in their works with unusual clarity. Although Rohmer and Chabrol labelled Hitchcock a Catholic director half a century ago, they did not so much argue as assert that opinion, and the Christian warp of Hitchcock's tapestry has been neglected by most explicators. Sturges's pictures are coloured with many of the same hues. Religious analogies and references have been remarked in *The Miracle of Morgan's Creek*, but significant Christian thematics and narrative configurations underlie most of his other films as well.

Unable to reconcile themselves to Sturges's optimism, critics frequently dismiss the endings of his films as deliberately unbelievable or as abdications of artistic integrity in favour of Hollywood's presumed financial interest in happy outcomes. Hitchcock's more optimistic films, one might note, have received similar treatment from those who amplify ironic undertones at the expense of a dominant comic key. We do better to take the films as they present themselves, to accept the truth of their feignings rather than to try to outsmart them. Without discounting the application of contemporary intellectual preoccupations to Hitchcock's and Sturges's movies, I am convinced that we miss something central if we fail to acknowledge their deep concern with faith and betrayal, weakness and despair, redemption and hope. We will remain uncomprehending of much of what moves us most deeply if we ignore, in particular, the broadly Christian conceptions that their movies repeatedly approach, allude to, and sometimes quite specifically invoke.

Notes

1 *Are Snakes Necessary?* is the book that Hopsie (Henry Fonda) reads in the dining room of the liner he boards at the beginning of *The Lady Eve*. As James Palmer pointed out to me, the title of this fictional book probably alludes to the popular 1929 work by James Thurber and E. B. White, *Is Sex Necessary? or Why You Feel the Way You Do*.

2 Regarding Hitchcock's technical education, see John Russell Taylor, *Hitch*, New York:

Berkeley, 1980, p. 11, and Donald Spoto, *The Dark Side of Genius*, Boston and Toronto: Little, Brown, and Company, 1983, pp. 35–6.

3 By 1944, Sturges was the highest-paid director at Paramount and, in 1947, the IRS listed him as the third highest-paid salaried worker in the US. See Andrew Dickos, *Intrepid Laughter: Preston Sturges and the Movies,* Metuchen, NJ, and London: The Scarecrow Press, 1985, p. 40, and James Curtis, *Between Flops: A Biography of Preston Sturges,* (New York and London: Harcourt Brace Jovanovich, 1982), p. 244.

4 Curtis, *Between Flops*, Plate 14.

5 Elias Canetti, *Crowds and Power*, trans. Carol Stewart, New York: Farrar, Straus and Giroux, 1962, p. 397. Originally published as *Masse und Macht*, Hamburg, 1960.

6 Ray Cywinski, *Preston Sturges: A Guide to References and Resources,* Boston: G. K. Hall & Co., 1984, p. 19.

7 Sturges is quoted in Curtis, *Between Flops*, p. 136.

8 Lesley Brill, *The Hitchcock Romance*, Princeton: Princeton University Press, 1988, pp. 202–3.

9 Cywinski, *Preston Sturges*, pp. 18, 32.

10 Northrop Frye, *The Secular Scripture*, Cambridge, MA and London: Harvard University Press, 1976, p. 98.

11 Quotations from *Paradise Lost* are taken from Merritt Y. Hughes (ed.), *John Milton Complete Poems and Major Prose*, New York: The Odyssey Press, 1957.

12 Cywinski cites many critics and scholars who regard the endings of Sturges's movies sceptically. He also champions one version of such a view. Sturges, he writes, 'mocks the notion of the rosy Hollywood ending' (p. 32). His 'miraculous endings may suggest a deeper and darker ambivalence toward success ... The resolutions, far from being standard commercial cop-outs as some critics aver, may actually testify to the opposite – a part of Sturges that believes ultimate success is impossible, or at least very fleeting' (p. 27). Among early critics who wrote at length on Sturges, Manny Farber and W. S. Poster offer a more complex understanding of Sturges and his endings, but they call his humour 'mean' and classify him as a satirist in 'Preston Sturges: Success in Movies', first published in *Film Culture*, 1962, and reprinted in Farber, *Negative Space,* New York: Praeger, 1971. James Agee, in several reviews of Sturges films reprinted in *Agee on Film* New York: Grosset and Dunlop, 1958), has admiring if ambivalent responses to the director, but finally regards his work as deeply informed by cynicism. The inclusion of Sturges among the directors discussed in Bazin's *Le cinéma de la cruauté* [cruelty], François Truffaut (ed.) Paris: Flammarion, 1975, speaks for itself. Gerald Mast, in *The Comic Mind: Comedy and the Movies,* (Chicago and London: University of Chicago Press, 1973) discusses Sturges at length, but eventually, as Cywinski notes, he 'retreats to the familiar denunciation of Sturges's "miraculous" ' endings. 'Such endings', Mast asserts, 'are cop-outs'. (Cywinski, p. 104). More recently, Scott Siegel and Barbara Siegel, in *American Film Comedy*, New York: Prentice Hall, 1994), p. 267, declare that Sturges's 'humor was cynical, sometimes savage, SATIRE that usually undercut Hollywood conventions and expectations ...' and that he 'often gave his audiences illogical happy endings ...'. James Harvey, in *Romantic Comedy in Hollywood from Lubitsch to Sturges,* New York: Alfred A. Knopf, 1987, p. 370, remains among those who find much of Sturges's comedy 'coldly brilliant', but he is inclined to accept the endings of his films at

face value. As he says of *The Lady Eve's* conclusion, 'Its final effect is not only exhilarating but positively good-natured.' A notable dissenter to those who read the endings of Sturges's movies against the grain and who regard him as a cynical satirist is Stanley Cavell, whose 1978 *New Literary History* essay on *The Lady Eve* became a chapter in *Pursuits of Happiness: The Hollywood Comedy of Remarriage,* Cambridge, MA and London: Harvard University Press, 1981.

13 Jeremy Dunckel, 'Norval Jones, the New Papa', unpublished essay.

The Lodger – Ivor Novello's duplicitous masculinity

Chapter 15
Hitchcock, or The Pleasures of Metaskepticism

Richard Allen

> Each time they kissed, there was the thrill of love . . . The threat of murder! –
> – poster for *Suspicion* (1941)

The anatomy of metaskepticism

In a significant revisionist work of recent years that runs decidedly counter to the dominant stream of Hitchcock scholarship that links Hitchcockian artifice to irony, Lesley Brill has argued that Hitchcock's stylistic self-consciousness contributes to rather than subverts the romance narratives that are his central preoccupation. For Brill, Hitchcock's insistence on artifice, surface and masquerade are part and parcel of the fairy-tale romance 'where the ordinary constraints of rational law are loosened' in plots characterised by 'lucky co-incidence', a 'high degree of conventionality' and 'artificiality'.[1] Hitchcock's male characters are flawed and his female characters may be duplicitous or deceiving, but this fallen condition of human beings is precisely what defines and makes possible the miracle of romance, emblematised for Brill by the magical match on action at the end of *North by Northwest* (1959), that allows Roger Thornhill (Cary Grant) to pull Eve Kendell (Eve Marie Saint) from the face of Mount Rushmore and extinction straight into the nuptial bed as the comically phallic Twentieth Century Ltd. rattles into a tunnel. To be sure, Brill argues, Hitchcock made some deeply pessimistic works such as *Blackmail* (1930), *Vertigo* (1958) and *Psycho* (1960), but their significance has been grossly overstated, and as a result, the body of Hitchcock's work has been largely misunderstood.

Brill offers a valuable corrective to those critics who conceive of Hitchcock primarily as an ironist, not simply because he identifies the centrality of the romance narrative in Hitchcock's works but because he offers an account of the place of irony within them through the category of the mixed romance. Brill's analysis of the mixed romance is developed from the literary theory of Northrop Frye where romance and irony are conceived as contrasting narrative archetypes that can conjoin in any text. In romance, the formation of the heterosexual couple is emplotted within a narrative universe where time cycles and rejuvenates; in irony, the possibility of romance is blocked by deceit, deception and evil, and narrative time is entropic; in the mixed romance, the two processes are uneasily juxtaposed producing 'perfusive formal tension'.[2] Searching for a way to exemplify how romance and irony can combine in Hitchcock, Brill points to an early moment in *Rear Window* (1954) where the spectator views a negative close-up of the image of a female model in Jefferies (James Stewart's) apartment and then a positive image of the same photograph on the cover of a fashion magazine. Jefferies can obviously become the stay-at-home fashion photographer that Lisa Freemont (Grace Kelly) wants him to become and thereby acknowledge, so to speak, her positive image, yet this is something he resists. In a way he cannot fully acknowledge, he also wants to efface her presence in his life. 'These images,' Brill writes, 'are at once identical and opposite to each other. Irreconcilably different, they reflect the same reality and are also, in a way, mutually defining . . . For Hitchcock's ironic films in general, this pair of images serves as a pattern for the way in which opposites refuse to stay in unequivocal opposition but implicate each other and complicate audience responses'.[3]

Brill's insight here is fundamental my own argument, yet, in the context of a book that insists on the significance of romance over irony in the films of Hitchcock, it is an insight that fails to be redeemed. Brill privileges the romance narrative in Hitchcock in a manner that ultimately distorts his overall understanding of Hitchcock's work and, as we shall see, his interpretation of individual films. I contend that it is the admixture of romance and irony inscribed in a double aspect Hitchcock bestows upon appearances or upon what the audience perceives (like the positive and negative of the photograph), and not the romance narrative *per se*, that is the defining feature of Hitchcock's work. I call this double aspect 'metaskepticism' in order to evoke the sense in which Hitchcock at once affirms the reality of appearances and affirms the 'fiction' of romance appearances serve to sustain, yet, at the same time, calls into question the reality of appearances, and by doing so undermines the 'fiction' of romance by exposing its fictiveness – its illusory quality. The metaskeptical character of Hitchcock's romance narrative is crafted in relationship to the figuration of a duplicitous masculinity within the romance narrative, a masculinity at once threatening and alluring. This duplicitous masculinity is embodied in Hitchcock's dandies and rogues whose ambivalent allure lies in the way that their identity is constituted by their potentially deceptive surface appearance.

The connection I am seeking to establish between Hitchcock's narration and Hitchcock's presentation of masculinity is crystallised most succinctly in two works: *The Lodger* (1926), Hitchcock's third film made in England, and *Suspicion* (1941), the fourth film he made after coming to the United States. Both texts are adaptations of novels in which the central male characters are unambiguously murderers: the first, a 1913 novel, *The Lodger*, by Marie Belloc Lowndes, based on the case of Jack the Ripper; the second, a murder mystery, *Before the Fact*, by Francis Iles. In the Lowndes novel, the villain conforms to the nineteenth-century stereotype of the aristocratic dandy whose self-consciously contrived and controlled performance of masculinity is an index of sexual perversity and predation. In the Iles novel, the villain conforms to the stereotype of the socially irresponsible rogue male, his gentlemanly persona (more middle class and twentieth century) is a self-serving masquerade, a mask to be assumed at will. Hitchcock's strategy of adaptation is to portray the villain as a falsely accused or 'wrong man' hero, while maintaining the connotation of villainy, and to thereby transform these murder mysteries into 'mixed romances'. In this way Hitchcock renders character psychology and motivation ambiguous. It becomes difficult to distinguish the true from the false gentleman or the man who passes as a gentleman, the romantic lead, from the sexual predator, and the lure of the romantic hero for the heroine stems from this ambivalence. Hitchcock sustains the connotation of villainy, or a predatory masculinity, by deploying modernist strategies of representation, which, in the case of *Suspicion*, are grafted upon classic Hollywood strategies of narration. The rhetoric of visual expressionism Hitchcock learned from German cinema of the 1920s casts a layer of malevolence – possibly paranoid, possibly not – upon the appearance of the male lead; his use of visual symbolism, metaphor and montage, learned from the Soviet directors, inserts a layer of commentative meaning upon narrative events that is unavailable to the characters within the fiction.

In *The Lodger*, a mysterious man, the lodger, played by Ivor Novello, with the aristocratic mannerisms and sartorial air of a dandy, appears suddenly at the house of the blonde middle-class heroine. His remarkable appearance there coincides with the time and place of a series of brutal murders of blonde women, of 'golden curls', by 'the Avenger', and with the moment when the virginal golden-curled heroine Daisy must decide whether to say 'yes' to the bland, wooden, straight cop, Joe, who is her suitor and is already, peremptorily, installed in the family kitchen as the narrative begins. The lodger's appearance announces or enacts the central conundrum of the film: is the lodger really the Avenger? Slim, ethereal and phallically rigid in form, the Lodger appears at the door of the Bunting's house (door no 13!) like Nosferatu the vampire, shrouded in mist, his face covered by a muffler, just as the gaslights within the house mysteriously go off. When Daisy's mother opens the door she recoils in shock at what she sees, and the audience responds with her, for the lodger has the uncanny appearance that we have been led by the narrative to believe belongs to the Avenger.[4] The Lodger's actions continue to cast suspicion. He exhibits a curious fascination and repulsion towards the pictures of golden-curled women on his bedroom wall. He anxiously paces his room.

He mysteriously enters and leaves the house at the moment another murder is committed, and his room contains a map of the murders. At the same time, the Lodger soon becomes the object of Daisy's affection and assumes the role of romantic hero and rival to Joe. Furthermore, the Lodger's own story, that he has turned detective after witnessing the death of his sister at the Avenger's hands, that we learn late in the story, does seem vindicated by the arrest of a suspect at the end of the film. Yet, at every point in the narrative Hitchcock's metaskeptical narration sustains our uncertainty about the Lodger's motivation. Even the flashback in which the Lodger reveals his motivation is ambiguously staged to suggest that he could be concealing his own role in his sister's murder. Since William Rothman has provided a brilliant and exhaustive analysis of *The Lodger*'s textual ambiguity, three scenes will serve as illustration.

When Daisy brings the Lodger his breakfast, and for the first time they are in close proximity, we see the Lodger in close-up pick up a knife from the breakfast table; a shot that is followed by a close-up profile of the Lodger that, as Rothman notes, precludes access to the character's interiority.[5] But we also see a gleam of light on the Lodger's teeth, as his mouth is frozen slightly open. Beneath the controlled, opaque mask-like veneer, the shot suggests, may lie a chaotic murderous desire. It turns out that the Lodger uses the knife, innocently, to flick an unsightly speck (of food?) from Daisy's clothing, but even this gesture is ambiguous given the Lodger's intense preoccupation with the image of the feminine. A title card announces their next encounter. 'One evening, a few days later, the Lodger made himself agreeable': Daisy and the Lodger play chess in front of a fireplace whose rainbow arch, as Brill argues, links them in romance.[6] But as Daisy reaches to pick up a chess piece we see that the Lodger, unknown to her, has picked up a poker which is poised in the frame close to her head. We imagine, as Rothman remarks, a frightful continuation of the gesture.[7] At this moment, Hitchcock cuts to Joe's arrival at the house – he has just been put on the Avenger case – and when we return to the couple, the Lodger is stoking a raging fire with his poker. He puts the poker down and impulsively reaches to caress Daisy's hair. 'Beautiful, golden hair,' he asserts – and they look into each other's eyes before they and the camera nervously pull back. In the final scene of the film, after the Lodger has been exonerated and the real murderer has ostensibly been caught, the couple embrace on the staircase of the Lodger's mansion, but outside the window a neon sign flashes 'Tonight Golden Girls', a sign whose earlier display in the film signalled both the promise of the dance revue, the promise of romance and incipient murder.

Brill warns against exaggerating the 'mildly ironic suggestions of tarnish' on the hero of the Lodger for it will render the central themes of the film 'incoherent'. 'To equate the Avenger with the hero', he writes, 'asks us to forget that the former is a madman who has killed innocent young women and that the latter is the grieving brother of one of its victims.'[8] But in contesting a reductively ironic interpretation of the film – 'the Lodger is really no different from the Avenger' – Brill minimises the force of the irony whose presence he wishes to acknowledge and he thus misunderstands the character of romance in Hitchcock. The Lodger's attraction for Daisy clearly consists in what sets him apart from 'the average Joe', and what sets him apart from Joe places him in proximity with the Avenger. The heroine's desire for a romantic hero, a true gentleman, contains within it a desire for that which lurks beneath the gentleman's benign exterior. In expressionist works such as *The Cabinet of Dr Caligari* (1919) or *Nosferatu* (1922), the self-annihilating force of the heroine's yet to be experienced passion is externally objectified in the uncanny image of the predatory vampire. In *The Lodger*, the figure of the predatory vampire is contained in the figure of the dandy–hero whose gentlemanly aspect at once suggests and conceals a predatory aspect that is connoted through Hitchcock's expressionist visual style. The Hitchcock romance is defined by the way in which the encounter with a dark self-annihilating desire is promised in and through conventional appearances that appear to negate it.

Suspicion, made in 1941 soon after Hitchcock arrived in Hollywood, opens with his favourite romantic scenario: the accidental encounter on a train where, in an instant, chance becomes necessity, strangers become lovers. In this case, Johnnie (Cary Grant), bumps into the virginal Lina (Joan Fontaine) who is rather beyond marrying age and threatened with spinsterhood. Her eyes, as Mark Crispin Miller describes them, 'are overglazed by the wide, bright lenses of her spectacles, across which a dense and luminous reflection of the passing landscape streams like water', a visual metaphor for her 'clouded vision'.[9] Lina is clearly a figure who is ripe for deception, and she immediately falls in love precipitously, head over heels, with the ne'er-do-well Johnnie. Why does she fall in love with him? Because she is in love with the idea of being in love. She knows Johnnie is a rogue; indeed his roguish freedom from social constraints defines for her his desirability (as in *To Catch a Thief*, a later Grant vehicle). Immediately, Lina is passively complicit in a touch of roguery when, at the film's opening, Johnnie impudently takes a stamp from her purse to make up his first-class fare (he only has a third-class ticket), in an act that transgresses both sexual and class boundaries. Lina believes that if she brings Johnnie into her world, the horizons of that world will be infinitely expanded and that, simultaneously, he will be reformed and domesticated. The opportunity presents itself moments when they meet at a hunt. But doubts about Johnnie's motivations cloud her ideal and are crystallised after the hunt in a scene which defines both the concerns of the film and Hitchcock's cinema as a whole.

Johnnie lures Lina out of the stuffy family domicile for a trip to church with a bunch of admirers, but before they enter, he whisks her away from the party (and from behind a policeman's back!) to a hilltop where, after an abrupt ellipsis, we see them struggling in long shot as nature's wild wind billows around them. 'What do you think I was trying to do? Kill you?' Johnnie asks. 'Nothing less than murder could justify such violent self-defense! Look at you ... Oh, I'm just beginning to understand. You thought I was going to kiss you, didn't you.' But what really happened on the hilltop? Perhaps what

occurred was a romantic embrace, sharply curtailed by Lina's paranoid fear of the ego-threatening character of her own sexuality, projected onto an essentially innocent Johnnie. After all, moments later, overhearing Lina's father General Mc*Laidlaw* speak of her approvingly as 'not the marrying sort', Lina, in a self-conscious, performative act, kisses Johnnie on the lips as if to instantly undo the thought, and her previous moments of defensiveness, reciprocating Johnnie's opening gambit. However, the way the viewer perceives the event does not unambiguously support this interpretation, an interpretation which, after all, is essentially that of Johnnie's, whom we already know to be a liar. The long shot is evasive, concealing as much as its reveals, and from where the spectator is placed it supports the worry that Johnnie actually harbours rapacious, murderous intentions. Johnnie believes that Lina perceives his actions to be an assault; in this he is undoubtedly right. But what do we see? Are we seeing Johnnie's actions as Lina perceives them to be or are we really seeing an assault? Hitchcock's expressionist visual style, in the framework of a 'wrong man' plot that poses the question of the hero's criminality, forces the spectator into diametrically opposed interpretations of what he sees, and these turn on the question of whether romantic love harbours a murderous or self-annihilating desire.

This ambiguity is both sustained and intensified as Lina plunges into romance to escape her stifling family. The threat posed to Lina by Johnnie's profligate and predatory sexuality is mainly articulated by his insatiable appetite for acquiring and spending other people's money, although the film intimates that he has an affair with the maid.[10] Lina's fears about the marriage are expressed through the *mise-en-scène* of the family home where the hallway doubles as a gigantic spider's web, with Johnnie the predatory spider at its centre. According to the psychological logic of the narrative this image of predation is the negative reflection of Lina's idealisation of Johnnie, of her refusal to see him for what he is, and of her self-deceiving belief that she can reform him. It is also the positive reflection of her unconscious; that is, an unacknowledged, desire to be stalked and captured. Yet, the spider's web also reflects a reality – Johnnie is a predator, and portends the deaths that are to follow.

Lina's suspicion of Johnnie's murderous intent is precipitated by the death of her father.[11] On the one hand, this suspicion is represented as a paranoid fantasy triggered by a word game in which she pictures Beaky (as a surrogate for herself) being thrown by Johnnie from a clifftop that she found threatening in a previous drive with Johnnie, and which she subsequently believes is the location of an actual murder attempt. According to this psychological logic, Lina's fears are groundless: Johnnie is bad with money and maybe with women, but the fears that he is a murderer are a hysterical delusion precipitated by the death of her father that intensifies the anxiety she feels about her sexuality. If she can be cured of these delusions, and if Johnnie could make more of an effort to reform his ways, the romance can be retrieved; such, at least, is the promise of the film's happy ending. On the other hand, Lina's nightmare may be real. Beaky does die and circumstantial evidence implicates Johnnie. Furthermore, it seems that Johnnie is trying to poison Lina: he has been reading up on murders committed with undetectable poisons and he climbs the Gothic staircase to Lina's bedroom carrying a glass of milk that seems ominously illuminated with the poison that Lina believes it to contain.

Feeling her life is threatened, Lina decides to leave, and as Johnnie drives her along the cliff road where she earlier imagined him killing his friend, the car door flies open and, in a montage of shots, we see what is possibly an attempt by Johnnie to prevent her falling out of the car, but what is equally plausibly the action of pushing her out which she is struggling to resist. This scene reproduces exactly the ambiguity that characterised their earlier struggle on the heath outside the church. Lina believes he pushed, he claims he pulled, but Lina is persuaded to give him one last chance. Returning to the car, Johnnie performs a U-turn and they drive back towards their home with their backs to their camera. As the romantic music swells, Johnnie coils his arm around Lina in a romantic embrace. But is this a romantic embrace or the snake-like coil of death? The visual metaphor of the snake-like coil of Johnnie's arm returns us to the images of natural predation that have recurred through the film.

The question posed in both *The Lodger* and *Suspicion*, as in all Hitchcock's work, is the enigma of the wrong man – is the hero a criminal? – and it is a question that turns on deciphering the gentleman's appearance. Straightforwardly, the promise of the hero is that of the *gentle*man and not a sexual predator. But the Lodger's gentlemanly presence is that of the aristocratic dandy whose austerely refined exterior connotes a perverse core concealed beneath it. In *Suspicion,* Johnnie is what in late nineteenth-century England was called a 'gent', he is a lower-class man masquerading as a gentlemen. Furthermore, *Suspicion* draws brilliantly upon Cary Grant's own persona – the transformation of Archie Leach, the cockney lad, into 'Cary Grant', the romantic hero who always seems to contain Leach under his skin.[12] This gentlemanly surface, this class passing, at once reveals and conceals the (desired) secret of something less polished, lending an ambiguity to Lina's desire. Overtly, she wants to redeem the diamond in or from the rough; covertly she desires a rough diamond. Actual sexual predation is incompatible with romance and the gender complementarity it serves to sustain. The standard popular romance narrative works to resolve the tension between love and desire by idealising love as the culmination or realisation of female desire and by domesticating the rogue. In effect the 'gent' turns out to be a gentleman after all. Hitchcock's narration refuses to simply endorse this fiction, it refuses to domesticate romance.

To summarise: I have used the term 'metaskepticism' to define the manner in which Hitchcock's films are governed by a point of view that at once embraces a romance plot, and with the sense of hope, futurity, redemption and personal transformation that go with it, and ironically undercuts that romance plot with the suggestion that encrypted in love are dark desires for and of annihilation, of both the self and the human. The idea of metaskepticism attempts to capture the way in which the simultaneous assertion and subversion of romance in Hitchcock's work turns upon the ambivalent aspect that is bestowed upon appearances, and the contradictory conclusions the spectator is invited to draw on the basis of what they see. These two aspects of the Hitchcock narrative coexist rather like the two aspects of a duck–rabbit figure, a single figure that we can see in two incompatible objects that are nonetheless coextensive, although in the case of Hitchcock's metaskeptical narrative, the two aspects of the figure are opposites, like the famous drawing of Freud's face within which you can see the figure of a naked woman, or, to draw a slightly different analogy, like the form of the Janus-face where the aspect seen and the aspect hidden are polar opposites.

Hitchcock's narration poses two distinct, though related, questions which are of a philosophical character. The first is the question of establishing truth on the basis of what we see, when appearances are deceptive. Hitchcock doesn't simply propose that appearances are deceptive and cannot form a reliable basis for knowledge in the manner of the skeptic. Instead, he proposes alternative, mutually compatible interpretations of the same impression. The second question addresses the difficulty of establishing the intentions of another, in particular, the romantic intentions of the individual – how can we know for sure the heart of another? Again, it is not simply that Hitchcock presents us with the difficulty of knowing the intentions of another, but he presents us with the worst-case scenario: that love, the acknowledgement of another, harbours its reverse, a dark, annihilating predatory desire. These two questions are united by the fact that the answer to the second turns on the problem of deciphering appearance, the problem which defines the first. Specifically, the answer to the second question turns upon deciphering the appearance of the male. Hitchcock is not concerned to resolve the dilemma; his point is to stage it. The clothing of the dandy–rogue in the film, reduplicated as it were in the clothing of the conventional romance narrative, acts as a lure that at once reveals and conceals its opposite, the 'repressed' of Freudian vocabulary, that which is both desired and detested. Hitchcock's narration exposes the deceptive character of appearances and the fictive nature of romance that conceals predatory desire. Yet, by asserting simultaneously the reality of appearances and of the fiction of romance, his films suggest the way in which it is a concealed self-annihilating or predatory desire that renders romance possible. For this desire functions as the concealed lure upon which the romantic fantasy is sustained – immanent, but never actualised. The actual emergence of this desire would explode the fantasy of romance; its concealment enables it to take place.[13]

A genealogy of metaskepticism

Metaskepticism as a self-conscious aesthetic strategy has at least one origin in romanticism of the later Regency period (*c.*1820) – specifically in the work of Keats – that figures male ambivalence about sexual desire and asserts the triumph of a form of masculine authorship in which the idea of romance is articulated in plots of self-conscious hermeneutic complexity that display authorial brilliance and ensure authorial immortality. In subsequent years, the relationship between desire and masculinity is explicitly posed as a problem for the man of letters whose currency is romance, who writes for and under the public gaze, and largely for the approbation of an audience of female readers. Victorian writers from Carlyle to Pater struggled to discriminate an authentic masculinity of the man of letters from the dandy, with whom the man of letters became associated in the postromantic era, whose masculinity is a narcissistic masquerade, a false lure, that signals not gentlemanly integrity but dissolution, and in the case of the dandy, effeminacy. Hitchcock arrives at a historical moment, when, after Wilde, the distinction between the dandy and gentleman has collapsed, and gentlemanliness can become in English culture the very sign of its opposite, as the careers of Burgess, Philby and Blunt attest. Hitchcock's career becomes marked by the self-conscious, ludic cultivation of an artistic persona characterised by 'passing' as a gentleman, and by films that obsessively explore the lure of appearances to entice the critic and, most of all, to entertain the spectator.

In another important recent Hitchcock study, Paula Marantz Cohen argues that Hitchcock's cinema is concerned with coming to terms with the Victorian legacy of separate gender spheres that was at once inscribed within and challenged by the nineteenth-century novel with its predominately female readership.[14] The Victorian system of gender roles pits a philistine, masculine public sphere of self-control, autonomy, self-assurance and unselfconscious goal-oriented action against a feminine domestic sphere of imagination, self-doubt, emotional yearning and self–other dependency. Cohen argues that Hitchcock's career unfolds as an attempt to inflect the impersonal, action-centred masculine plots to which cinema was attracted, on account of its form and ownership, towards an exploration of the depth psychology associated with the feminine. This aspiration was realised most fully once Hitchcock arrived in America and collaborated with Selznik who was deeply schooled in the nineteenth-century novel. It reaches an apex in John Michael Hayes's narratives of gender complementary of the 1950s – *Rear Window* and *The Man Who Knew Too Much* – where the distant and deficient heterosexual male (in both cases James Stewart) is tutored in feeling by the female character who also acts in a way to rectify his blindness and mistakes. It is as if Hitchcock, in moving to America at the end of the 1930s, at once enacts and anticipates the 'feminization' of British culture in the postwar period, that involved, at once, an increased role for middle-class women in the public sphere and the embrace of American popular culture.

Cohen is undoubtedly right to identify the fundamental legacy of Victorianism in Hitchcock's work as the separation of gender spheres. Furthermore, her identification of a dialectic of gender complementarity in Hitchcock's work begins to suggest the significance of Hitchcock's collaboration with writers, including Alma Reville, in the genesis of his narratives. However, Cohen ignores the fact that the threat posed by the idea of the feminine to masculine self-identity had long been a source of worry to the man who identified himself as, or with, the artist. It is a worry that has its roots deep in the nineteenth century. In Cohen's narrative of Hitchcockian authorship, Hitchcock begins by inhabiting a conventional Victorian masculinity, producing static, one dimensional, masculine-centred, action plots, and then moves towards embracing a conception of 'character' associated with the feminine that challenges orthodox gender roles. I would suggest, in contrast, that Hitchcock's conception of masculinity is already inscribed with an anxiety over masculine sexuality, an anxiety over the 'feminine' in man that is evident in his earliest works, such as *The Lodger* and *Murder!* (1930), and that engenders the metaskeptical text. The process that Cohen accurately identifies supervenes upon textual metaskepticism, producing more complex characterisations and a revision of masculinity, especially through the John Michael Hayes–James Stewart collaboration, but it fails to disturb the underlying dialectic of Hitchcock's work and the ambivalent allure of 'deviant' masculinities within it, an allure that is marked by surface rather than depth, and by a certain refusal of character.

It is certainly arbitrary to locate a single author who originates the complex relationship between the masculinity and textual metaskepticism in Hitchcock's work, and yet one finds a striking prefiguration of the Hitchcock text and the male anxiety that lurks beneath it in John Keats's *Eve of St Agnes* and its genesis, about which we now understand a great deal.[15] This poem portrays the ritual that follows the legend of St Agnes, who, condemned to be raped before her execution, had her virginity miraculously preserved. On the Eve of St Agnes, young virgins enter into a trance to imagine their future husbands. In Keats's poem, the romantic vision of Madeline, the young heroine, is answered by the arrival of the hero, Porphyro, the man of her dreams, who seduces her with food and music, makes passionate love to her, and joins her in taking flight 'with happy speed' across the southern moors to make a home together. Keats's poem has been construed by many critics as an affirmation of romantic love, and romance is indeed plainly realised.[16]

However, as Jack Stillinger has taught us, this romance has a dark side. Porphyro appears as a peeping Tom who hides 'in a closet, of such privacy/That he might see her beauty unespied,/And win perhaps that night a peerless bride' (165–7), before she is fully conscious. When he finally takes her she is in an agitated trance, eyes open, yet within 'the blisses of her dream' (301) and when the act is over she feels the 'bitter chill' of St. Agnes's Eve, the 'frost wind' and the 'icèd gust' which suggest that the dead world that surrounds her has now invaded her room. But the fault is not all, or not unambiguously, Porphyro's. He may in one aspect appear to be a rapist, but in another sense his actions result from Madeline's own self-deception: 'hoodwinked with faery fancy' (70) she is all too willing to buy into the old wives' tales of St Agnes's Eve when 'Young virgins might have visions of delight/And soft adorings from their loves receive' (47–8). The ritual requires that she must look neither 'behind nor sideways' (53), but as Stillinger notes, 'the real point is that if she did look behind, she would discover Porphyro, and then "the charm" would be "fled" for a more immediate reason.'[17] Madeline is therefore self-deceived and the rude encounter with Porphyro results from her foolishness.

The point of Stillinger's commentary is not to suggest that Keat's text is, after all, skeptical of romantic love, but rather to point to the complexity and indeterminacy of the text. It leaves character motivation opaque in favour of a layering of ambiguity that centres on the deceptive character of appearances, just as in the Hitchcock's works we have been examining. Does the romantic hero fulfil the heroine's wish for romance or is he cut out for this role by a heroine who deceives herself about reality? Daisy in *The Lodger* and Lina in *Suspicion* are both possibly 'self-hoodwinked' dreamers. Like Madeline, Lina's vision is clouded (as I have already noted), a condition that often afflicts Hitchcock's heroines. Conversely, the Lodger and Johnnie Aysgarth, like Porphyro, have a threatening demonic quality, and in both cases the demonic quality is inscribed through an atmosphere and *mise-en-scène* that connotes a predatory vampirism. I have already noted the Lodger's mysterious appearance at the house and his ethereal presence. Johnnie also takes on the appearance of a figure of death when, dressed in a black suit, he delivers the message of the death of Lina's father. These could be clothes of mourning, but, as we have seen, perhaps Lina is not so foolish in conflating the message with the messenger. Elsewhere, he 'materialises' in Lina's presence in a manner that is less suggestive of a human and more of a supernatural or demonic presence.[18] This vampirism can be traced back from the influence of Murnau's *Nosferatu* on Hitchcock back through the nineteenth-century Gothic tradition to Romanticism itself. Indeed Porphyro himself emerges out of 'the bitter chill' in *The Eve of St Agnes*, to prey upon a sleeping woman who has called him there.

As Stillinger notes, Keats was anxious about his own sexuality, an anxiety he connects to Keats's ambivalent portrayal of Porphyro. 'When I am among Women I have evil thoughts,' Keats wrote, and he describes these thoughts elsewhere as 'goatish winnyish lustful love'.[19] Keats was also, because of his lowly class background, extremely sensitive to being slighted.[20] Recently, James Chandler has recast the question of Keats's self-anxiety as a narrative of masculine self-definition through poetic predation or, to use Keats's own term, 'smoking', an activity that implies an understanding that at once incorporates, transcends and discards its object. In an imaginative reconstruction of the intellectual origins of the poem, Chandler traces the way that Keats's 'Eve' brings about a self-conscious transformation of an earlier poem on the myth of Cupid and Psyche by the Irish poet Mary Tighe. Tighe's version of the myth sentimentalises it: 'she reduces the allegory to a set of communicable representations of Psyche's narrative situation . . . And she does so, it would seem precisely to make it possible at various points in the story to 'sympathize' with Psyche.'[21] Keats version of the myth becomes 'superior' to Tighe's because the psychology is rendered opaque, layered with a deliberate ambiguity that renders it less easily 'smokable'.

It is not hard to see in Chandler's narrative of Keat's poetic career of one upmanship – out of which emerges the poet as hero, self-conscious of his place in history – the narrative of the ambitious Alfred Hitchcock. Hitchcock, like Keats, came from a lowly, cockney background, was sensitive to slight and delivered it in return, was uncomfortable with his sexuality, and demonstrated great ambition at a young age.[22] Hitchcock was utterly dependent upon writers to provide him with psychological depth and motivation, and they attest, again and again, to Hitchcock's lack of affinity to character.[23] Yet Hitchcock was notoriously reticent in acknowledging the contribution of writers to his projects – consistent character motivation and plausible character psychology – which he disguised or 'smoked' within a commentative, self-conscious, metaskeptical narration, with its elaborate visual design and formal set pieces. It is not that Hitchcock ignores character psychology. In fact, Cohen has emphasised that it is central to his evolution as an artist. Rather, in Hitchcock's films the elaboration of character psychology is consistently subordinated to the assertion and elaboration of textual metaskepticism, whose opacity renders the text alluring and inexhaustible, and bestows fame on Hitchcock not as the author of the story but the maker of the film.

I have developed, by analogy, a connection between Keats's authorship in the first decades of the nineteenth century and Hitchcock's authorship in the first decades of the twentieth century, because I believe it illuminates some of the motivation for Hitchcock's textual metaskepticism. However, Hitchcock's distinctive form of self-representation as an author is manifest not simply in a textual metaskepticism, but in his direct projection of a distinctive authorial persona. Hitchcock's performance of the author behind the text comes at the end of a century of reflection upon the role of the man of letters in Victorian culture. From Thomas Carlyle (a contemporary of Keats) to Walter Pater, the problem for the male arbiters of taste and decorum of the newly enfranchised middle class of Victorian England was how to square masculinity, specifically the Victorian middle-class idea of the gentleman, with the popular association of the writer and the artwork with a degenerate form of masculine self-display – that of the dandy and effeminate aristocrat.

The association between writer and dandy did not arise immediately. The Romantic poets, with the important exception of Byron, were not of the aristocracy, nor did they partake in the aristocracy of taste that defined dandyism. Indeed, in certain respects the romantic temperament seems antithetical to the sensibility of the original dandies. For Beau Brummell, the original dandy, self-presentation in and to aristocratic society was his sole concern, together with acute sensitivity to another's lapse in taste, which would be met by a lacerating cut. According to Ellen Moers, Brummell's wardrobe was quite conventional, distinguished mainly by Brummell's scrupulous cleanliness and poise, and he was free of romantic attachments of any kind.[24] Such austere narcissism scarcely seems to square with the romantic imagination. However, subsequent dandies such as the Count d'Orsay were associated with sexual scandal, and the caricature of the dandy as effete womaniser was sealed by the publication of Edward Bulwer's dandy novel, *Pelham* (1828). Partly through the notoriety of Byron, who scandalised the public with, among other things, a rumored affair with his half-sister, the figure of the romantic poet became conflated with the idea of the effeminate dandy aristocrat in the practical imagination of the newly enfranchised middle class. Both were tarred with the same brush of unmanliness. For the emerging voices of that class, represented in *Frazer's* magazine, defining a form of masculinity that did not exhibit the effeminacy of a feckless aristocracy became something of a preoccupation.[25] In a review of Bulwer's novel *Pelham*, William Maginn concluded, 'There are gentlemen of two sorts; the natural and the tailor made.'[26] However, the problem was how to distinguish between the two, especially when the gentleman concerned was the writer called upon to stage his self in the public eye. If gentlemanliness was not a mere surface appearance but a natural essence, how was this essence to be manifest and distinguished from the interiorised selfhood that defined the feminine sphere in the nineteenth century? If gentlemanliness was a matter of self-presentation, how was the gentleman to be distinguished from the dandy and rescued from a self-display that was deemed effeminate?

In his fantastic tract on clothing, *Sartor Resartus* (1832), Thomas Carlyle is drawn to satirise the vanity of the 'dandiacal body' that exists solely for self-display, and to contrast this body with that of his prophet hero Teufelsdröckh.[27] As James Eli Adams points out in his fine study of Victorian masculinities, *Dandies and Desert Saints*, Teufelsdröckh is characterised as a 'disembodied subjectivity' of impenetrable 'savage' depth and gravity.[28] Yet since this dormant savage spirit always threatens to erupt and dissipate, Carlyle imagines another hero, George Fox, heroically stitching a one-piece suit of leather as a way of renouncing the advice of his elders to 'drink beer and dance with the girls' and to contain his 'temple of immensity'.[29] The inner spirit that defines masculinity yet threatens to be dissipated must be contained and concealed within an ascetic regime of sartorial discipline. For Carlyle, therefore, the clothing makes the man in a way that seems to threaten the desired distinction between the natural and the tailored gentleman. Indeed both the dandy and hero are compared by Carlyle to the artist and their masculinity to works of art.

Later in the century, Walter Pater defined gentlemanliness in a manner that acknowledged the lure, the fiction upon which it depends, and prepared the ground for Oscar Wilde and Alfred Hitchcock. As Adams demonstrates, for Pater, in *Marius the Epicurean*, gentlemanliness becomes a mask of reserve that, as a mask, exerts the fascination for something, something unreserved that is hidden from view.[30] Furthermore, he shows how 'the appeal of that reserve mirrors the appeal that Pater discovers in art'.[31] Pater suggests that the traditional subject matter in Leonardo's art becomes 'a cryptic language for fancies all his own' which intimates 'something far beyond the outward gesture or circumstance'.[32] But it is crucial to the command, the lure, of both the gentleman and the artwork, that the secret, while it is recognised, remains hidden. Oscar Wilde's flamboyant theatricalisation of both gentlemanliness and his art – a theatricalisation that harboured scandalous ideas of indolence and decadence without straying beyond the boundaries of bourgeois propriety and convention – amplified but did not transgress Pater's logic of conformity. Wilde also made explicit the fact that the artist–dandy could succeed in a modern consumer culture by self-conscious management of his persona in the public eye, until he allowed his secret to be exposed.

Hitchcock's persona is a self-conscious, ludic performance of Victorian English gentlemanliness that combines the austerity of Pater with the self-publicity of Wilde. If we wish, we can suspect, along with Donald Spoto, that beneath the masquerade of conformity lurks the same deep anxieties about sexuality that haunted Keats and Carlyle. However, it is not necessary to literalise the secret in this way in order to recognise that Hitchcock's masquerade of Victorian masculinity is designed to harbour a secret about what lies beneath the appearance, and he cannily recognised the power that this shared secret could exert upon the audience. The lure was only intensified by its transposition in time (second half of the twentieth century) and place (England to America), and its scope was enhanced beyond Wilde's wildest dreams through Hitchcock's canny manipulation of the mass media. Hitchcock's art operates within the traditional vocabulary of the (mass-cultural) romance narrative, yet secretes in this narrative, through his stylistic self-consciousness, a sense of something hidden. Hitchcock is perhaps the most successful example of the aesthete as commercial artist, the cult film-maker with a universal following.

As Thomas Elsaesser has noted in his suggestive essay on 'The Dandy in Hitchcock', Hitchcock's ludic conservatism emerges at a precise historical moment.[33] The First World War did not simply kill a lot of young British men; it challenged Edwardian complacency and self-righteous masculinity. A central manifestation of this reaction to Edwardian masculine values of sport, spartanism, service and self-denial, was an efflorescence of Wildean dandyism that germinated in the corridors of Eton and Oxford and was epitomised by such figures as Harold Acton and Brian Howard, who, as Martin Green writes, 'saw themselves as originators of a new "aesthetic" phase in English high culture, to be characterised by ornament, brilliancy, playfulness, and youthfulness, and by a turning of the back on the old forms of seriousness and power'.[34] In Green's account, the more rambunctious rogue type is allied with the dandy in this act of rebellion: 'The rogue', he writes, 'is often coarse, rough, brutal, and careless. He is like the Dandy, however, in his conscious enjoyment of his own style and in his rebellion against mature and responsible morality. Sexually, he is as much the narcissist as the dandy is, but "typically" the rogue is heterosexual, the dandy homosexual.'[35] Yet, as Green also argues, while these rogues and dandies where rebels, they were also sons of the establishment and adopted establishment conventions and inhabited positions of authority. This divided identity – pillar of the establishment and rebel against it; gentleman, yet rogue and dandy – is vividly articulated in the espionage careers of Philby, Burgess and Blunt.

Elsaesser is correct, it seems to me, in locating Hitchcock as part of this cultural formation and finding in it a source for Hitchcock's authorial persona as well as his lifelong fascination with dandies and rogues. As an avid theater-goer and member of the élite film society, he undoubtedly absorbed this sensibility of revolt through style as the 'new dandies' came down from Oxford to London in the mid-1920s. Of course, as a lower middle-class cockney Catholic, Hitchcock was a class apart from these sons of the establishment. In this sense, like Dickens before him, Hitchcock began as a gent rather than an authentic dandy or rogue – that is, he was an upwardly mobile working-class lad self-consciously playing at being a gentlemen, although by the time he comes to America the class distinction is erased. However, Elsaesser does not address Hitchcock's attitude to homosexuality; that is, the importance of the *distinction* between dandy and rogue masculinities that emerged in post-Wildean English culture for Hitchcock's work.

Central to the Edwardian reception of Oscar Wilde was, of course, Wilde's revelation as a homosexual. After Wilde, the dandy–aesthete, as popularly perceived, was not simply an effeminate seducer; he was potentially queer in the homophobic sense of the term 'perverted'. The stereotype becomes consolidated in America of the late 1940s and early 1950s in the context of cold-war psychiatry and, as Robin Wood points out, Brandon in *Rope* (1948) and Bruno in *Strangers on a Train* (1951), conform to the homophobic stereotype of the 'murderous gay', the homosexual as perverted psychopath.[36] However, while Hitchcock's mobilisation of this stereotype is evidence of a superficial conservatism, it is reductive to regard it simply as a manifestation of post-Wildean homophobia. Rather, this stereotype should be understood in the light of the way that the idea of homosexuality as perversion enters into the long history of Victorian masculinity I have briefly sketched. For the point is not that Hitchcock represents homosexuals as criminals, but rather that he uses these characters to stage the performance of a gentlemanliness beneath which the darkest secrets are harboured. The fact that what lies beneath the surface is rumoured to be 'homosexual perversion' only intensifies the lure. Many of Hitchcock's dandies do not suggest homosexuals, even when they are psychopathic murderers such as Uncle Charlie in *Shadow of a Doubt*, Rusk in *Frenzy* (1972) and Arthur Adamson in *Family Plot* (1976). Furthermore, in every case, both where homosexuality is suggested and where it is not, Hitchcock's dandies are attractive to women and their allure usually contrasts with the anodyne 'straight' men (usually cops) against whom they are defined. It is significant, in the context of my argument, that Hitchcock employed actors who were known or rumoured to be homosexual since he presumably believed that homosexual actors have the capacity to bring to their acting a self-conscious sense of performativity and to project their masculinity as a lure or a mask.[37]

I have identified the copresence of romance and irony, of the ideal of love and of a self-annihilating and predatory desire, as the key feature of Hitchcock's work. I suggested the way in which this copresence is inscribed in a double aspect that is accorded to appearances through Hitchcock's deployment of an expressionist, commentative, visual style. This doubling of the text is centred on a depiction of masculinity in the figure or the rogue and the dandy whose conventional gentlemanly exterior disguises the darker allure of a predatory desire, whose concealed presence is evoked by Hitchcock's visual style. The genesis of the metaskeptical text lies not simply in male anxiety over the fact of sexual desire, but in the anxiety of the male author who places himself on display through the text and in the public eye. The staging of masculinity as a lure in the text is thus reproduced in Hitchcock's staging of his own masculinity as a lure outside and alongside the text. Hitchcock positions himself, as Elsaesser asserts, as a rogue–dandy. The metaskeptical text thereby encompasses not simply Hitchcock's narration but his authorial persona as well. And the authorial persona brings us back to the essentially ludic quality of Hitchcock's cinema, his appeal as an entertainer, which tends to be lost by the critic who focuses, as I have done, on the more serious films in his canon.[38]

Notes

It is my pleasure to acknowledge the many people who have contributed to this paper and made it better than it would otherwise have been. Sam Ishii-Gonzalès, my co-editor, commented upon many drafts with wisdom and good humour. My editors at *October*, Annette Michelson and Malcolm Turvey, provided sound editorial advice. Roland Chambers gave me the term 'metaskepticism.' A version of this paper was delivered as the Critical Inquiry lecture at the University of Chicago, where I received invaluable suggestions from James Chandler, Tom Gunning, and Miriam Hansen. This essay was originally published in *October* 89 (Summer 1999).

1 Lesley Brill, *The Hitchcock Romance*, Princeton NJ: Princeton University Press, 1988, p. 6.
2 See Northrop Frye, *The Anatomy of Criticism,* Princeton NJ: Princeton University Press, 1957, pp. 186–205, 223–9; Brill, *Hitchcock Romance*, pp. 71–4.
3 Brill, *Hitchcock Romance*, pp. 73–4.
4 This scene quotes a moment from Weine's *Cabinet of Dr Caligari* (1919) when the heroine of the film visits the mysterious Dr Caligari and first spies the uncanny, phallic, monstrous body of his 'assistant' Cesare. Overall, though, the main influence on *The Lodger* is undoubtedly Murnau's film *Nosferatu* (1922).
5 Rothman writes: 'It is characteristic of Hitchcock to frame a figure in profile at the moment of his or her most complete abstraction and absorption in an imagined scene to which we have no access. In such a profile shot, the camera frames its subject in a way that does not allow that figure's interiority to be penetrated', *Hitchcock – The Murderous Gaze*, Cambridge: Harvard University Press, 1982, p. 22.
6 Brill, *The Hitchcock Romance*, p. 88.
7 Rothman, *Hitchcock –The Murderous Gaze*, p. 24. Rothman also notes in a footnote that the sequence of shots leading to the framing of the poker against Daisy's head suggests a kind of zoom (or tracking shot) in to Daisy's golden curls. This underscores their significance as a privileged object or lure in the narrative world that Slavoj Žižek has called the 'Hitchcockian blot'.
8 Brill, *The Hitchcock Romance*, p. 92.
9 Mark Crispin Miller, 'Hitchcock's Suspicions and Suspicion', in *Boxed In*, Evanston, IL: Northwestern University Press, 1988, p. 242.
10 See Miller, 'Hitchcock's Suspicions', p. 270.
11 In Frances Isles's *Before The Fact* from which *Suspicion* is adapted, Johnnie's need for money leads him to murder the General in the hope of an inheritance; to concoct a business scheme using the money of his friend, Beaky Thwaite, only to do away with him; and finally to plan to murder Lina for her life insurance. As Miller argues, in Hitchcock's version of events Johnnie is not literally but symbolically responsible for the General's death. Lina unconsciously feels responsible for her father's death by marrying Johnnie and projects that responsibility onto Johnnie whom she then

suspects of murderous intentions towards her. See Miller, 'Hitchcock's Suspicions', pp. 266–7.

12 On Grant's star persona, see David Thompson's fine appreciation in *A Biographical Dictionary of the Cinema*, London: Secker & Warburg, 1975, pp. 236–8; and Graham McCann's *Cary Grant: A Class Apart*, New York: Columbia University Press, 1996, pp. 52–80. McCann, as opposed to Thompson, fails to appreciate Grant's work for Hitchcock.

13 This is the aspect of Hitchcock's work that has lent it so readily to Lacanian analysis and which Slavoj Žižek and other Lacanians have in turn illuminated. See, for example, the essays in Slavoj Žižek (ed.), *Everything You Wanted to Know about Lacan But Were Afraid to Ask Hitchcock*, New York: Verso, 1992.

14 Paula Marantz Cohen, *Alfred Hitchcock: The Legacy of Victorianism*, Lexington, KT: University of Kentucky Press, 1995.

15 I owe a great debt to James Chandler who first suggested to me the significance of Keats for Hitchcock.

16 It should be noted that by centring the narrative on Madeline's fantasy, Keats's poem is not typical of his work, which is usually narrated from the standpoint of a male hero who idealises, and is correlatively deceived by women, such as the hero of *Lamia*. But the division in Keats's work corresponds to the division in Hitchcock's *œuvre* two between male-centred romance narratives such as *The 39 Steps* (1933) and *North by Northwest* (1959) and female-centred romance narratives such as *Suspicion*.

17 Jack Stillinger, 'The Hoodwinking of Madeline: Skepticism in the Eve of St Agnes', in Allan Danzig (ed.), *Twentieth Century Interpretations of the Eve of St Agnes*, Englewood Cliffs, NJ: Prentice Hall, 1971, p. 65.

18 Hitchcock evokes the sense that Grant suddenly 'materialises' like a predatory vampire by having the actor suddenly step into the frame in close proximity to Lina with his back to the camera. Male characters 'pop up' from off-screen space in this fashion in many Hitchcock films, including Uncle Charlie in *Shadow of A Doubt* and Rusk in *Frenzy*.

19 See Stillinger, 'Hoodwinking', p. 62.

20 For a detailed examination of this aspect of Keats's biography see Christopher Ricks, *Keats and Embarrassment*, Oxford: The Clarendon Press, 1974.

21 James Chandler, *England In 1819: The Politics of Literary Culture and the Case of Romantic Historicism*, Chicago: University of Chicago Press, 1988, p. 404.

22 Hitchcock's formation as an individual and artist receives a detailed and thoughtful treatment in Donald Spoto's biography *The Dark Side of Genius: The Life of Alfred Hitchcock*, Boston: Little, Brown, and Company, 1983, pp. 5–44.

23 Brian Moore, writer of the ill-fated *Torn Curtain* (1966), provides an extreme statement of this: 'He had absolutely no conception of character – even of two dimensional figures in a story', Moore reported to Spoto. See Spoto, *Dark Side of Genius*, p. 488.

24 Ellen Moers, *The Dandy: Brummell to Beerbohm*, New York: The Viking Press, 1960, p. 31.

25 *Frazer's* magazine was founded in 1830 as the mouthpiece of the new middle class that sought to challenge the political irresponsibility and social and literary exclusivism of Regency aristocracy. It was the first to publish the text of Thomas Carlyle's *Sartor Resartus*.

26 Quoted in Moers, *The Dandy*, p. 174.

27 Thomas Carlyle, *Sartor Resartus, Collected Works of Thomas Carlyle*, New York: Greystone Press, 1832, pp. 139–47.

28 James Eli Adams, *Dandies and Desert Saints: Styles of Victorian Masculinity*, Ithaca: Cornell University Press, 1995, p. 32.

29 Carlyle, *Collected Works*, p. 108. See also Herbert Sussman, *Victorian Masculinities*, New York: Cambridge University Press, 1995, pp. 28–9.

30 Adams, appropriately enough, calls his study a 'genealogy of the closet' after the pioneering work of Eve Kosofsky Sedgwick. See her *Epistemology of the Closet*, Berkeley and Los Angeles: University of California Press, 1990.

31 Adams, *Dandies and Desert Saints*, p. 195.

32 Walter Pater, *The Renaissance: Studies in Art and Poetry*, Donald L. Hill (ed.), Berkeley and Los Angeles: University of California Press, 1980, pp. 93, 97. Quoted in Adams, *Dandies and Desert Saints*, p. 195.

33 Thomas Elsaesser, 'The Dandy in Hitchcock', *The McGuffin*, no. 14, November 1994. Reprinted in this volume, see Chapter 1, p. 3.

34 Martin Green, *Children of the Sun*, New York: Basic Books, 1976, p. 14.

35 Green, *Children of the Sun*, p. 12.

36 See Robin Wood, *Hitchcock's Films Revisited*, New York: Columbia University Press, 1989, pp. 336–57.

37 Examples of such actors include: Ivor Novello (*The Lodger*); Farley Granger (who plays a homosexual in *Rope*, and the ultra straight Guy in *Strangers on a Train*); Montgomery Clift (*I Confess* – Hitchcock also wanted him for *Rope*); Anthony Perkins (*Psycho*); and even Cary Grant himself, who was rumoured to be homosexual, although the rumour is hotly contested.

38 The best analysis of the ludic intent underlying Hitchcock's work is Thomas Leitch, *Find the Director and other Hitchcock Games*, Athens: University of Georgia Press, 1991.

Filled with the force of the death drive – *The Birds*

Chapter 16
Hitchcock's Future

Lee Edelman

In an article timed to coincide with the ritual of affective displacement enshrined as Mother's Day in the United States, Sylvia Ann Hewlett and Cornel West, proving the left as observant as the right in its celebration of this hallowed day in the calendar of state religion, announced in 1998 their intention to launch a campaign promoting a 'Parent's Bill of Rights', a series of proposals designed, as they put it, to 'strengthen marriage and give greater electoral clout to mothers and fathers'. In order to achieve that visionary end, they sounded the following hortatory call, performing in the process – and with a heartfelt sincerity untroubled (or should I say unredeemed?) by a twinge of ironic self-consciousness – the mandatory profession of faith in the gospel of sentimental futurism that is the lowest common denomination of our universal creed:

> It is time to join together and acknowledge that the work that parents do is indispensable – that by nourishing those small bodies and growing those small souls, they create the store of social and human capital that is so essential to the health and wealth of our nation.
>
> Simply put, by creating the conditions that allow parents to cherish their children, we will ensure our collective future.[1]

Ignore for a moment what demands to be called the trans*parency* of this appeal: ignore, that is, how quickly the spiritualising vision of parents 'nourishing and growing . . . small bodies and . . . small souls' gives way to a rhetoric affirming instead the decidedly more pragmatic (because politically imperative) investment in the 'human capital . . . essential to the health and wealth of our nation'; ignore, by so doing, how the passage renominates human 'souls' as 'capital' without yielding the fillip of Dickensian pathos that prompts us to 'cherish' these 'capital'-ised humans ('small' but, like the economy in our current usage, capable of being grown) precisely insofar as they come to embody this thereby humanised 'capital'; ignore all this and one's eyes might still pop to discover that only political intervention will *allow*, and the verb is crucial here, 'parents to cherish their children' so as to 'ensure our collective future' – or to ensure, what comes to the same in the faith that properly fathers us all, that our present will always be mortgaged to a fantasmatic future in the name of the political 'capital' that those children will thus have become.

Near enough to the surface to trouble its status as merely implicit, but sufficiently buried to protect it from every attempt at explicitation, a globally destructive, child-hating force is posited in these lines – a force so strong as to *disallow* parents the occasion to cherish their children, so profound in its virulence to the species as to put into doubt 'our collective future' – and posited the better to animate a familial organisation mommified to distract us from how badly it's been mummified. No need to trick out that force in the flamboyant drabness of the paedophile, whose fault, as 'everyone' knows, defaults, *faut de mieux*, to a fear of grown women – and thus, whatever the sex of his object, condemns him to, and for, a failure to penetrate the charmed circle of heterosexual desire. No need to call it names, with the vulgar bluntness of the homophobe whose language all too often is not the bluntest object at hand: unnamed, this force can carry both the signature of the crime expressly named as *not* to be named among Christians and an alibi that lets it refute such a signature, lest anyone try to decipher it, as having been forged by someone else. To be sure, the stigmatised other *in general* poses a threat to the idea of the future – the threat, more precisely, of contaminating that future, of violently appropriating it toward the realisation of what seem unendurable ends; but one *in particular* is stigmatised as threatening the end of the future itself. That *one* remains always available to embody the force, which need never be specified, prohibiting America's parents, for example, from being able to cherish their children, since that *one*, as we know, interferes in the privileged reproduction of familialism by stealing, seducing, proselytising, in short, by *adult*erating those children and putting in doubt the structuring fantasy that ensures 'our collective future'.

Elsewhere I have proposed that this child-aversive, future-negating force, answering so well to the inspiriting needs of a moribund familialism, be thought as *sinthome*-osexuality, a term by which I identify the knot that joins the symbolic subject's defense against the 'stupid' or meaningless *jouissance* of the Lacanian *sinthome* to the abjection of a homosexuality made to figure a fatal break in the life-sustaining circuit of meaning-production. The *sinthome*, as Lacan evokes it in the difficult last phase of his career, designates a locus of enjoyment beyond the logic of interpretation, and thus beyond the logic of the symptom and its cure. It refers to the specific mode of *jouissance* that constitutes the subject, marking the subject as insistently, and as randomly, as a fingerprint and defining it no longer as subject of desire, but as subject of the drive. For the subject of desire now registers as a symptomatic misprision of the *sinthomatic* engagement with the pursuit of *jouissance* played out on the far side of meaning in the ceaseless pulse of the drive. Where the symptom sustains the subject's relation to the reproduction of meaning, sustaining as well the fantasy of eventually realising meaning's plenitude through investment in the principle of reproductive futurity, the *sinthome*, through its link to the drive, unravels every fantasy by which the subject means. And since, as Bruce Fink puts it, 'the drives always seek a form of satisfaction that, from a Freudian or traditional moralistic standpoint, is considered perverse', the *sinthome* that drives the subject, that renders him subject of the drive, engages, on a figural level, the discourse of homosexuality, especially insofar as homosexuality is conceived in terms of access to enjoyment at the expense of a social future; to quote Bruce Fink once more: 'What the drives seek is not heterosexual genital reproductive sexuality, but a partial object that provides jouissance.'[2] *Sinthome*-osexuality, then, would mean by figuring a *threat* to meaning insofar as meaning is invested in reproduction's promise of coming – in a future always necessarily deferred – into the presence that reconciles meaning with being, the impossible beyond of the signifier on which any ject's cathexis of the signifying system depends. As the shadow of death that would put out the light of heterosexual reproduction, however, *sinthome*-osexuality functions, perversely, as a life-support system of sorts for familial ideology to the extent that it allows the familial pledge of futurity to represent itself as always about to expire. Nor can any *sinthome*-osexual hope to escape the coils of the twisted fate that ropes him into embodying this denial of futurity, this fatality to meaning's survival in the figure of the child, simply by virtue of being, or having been, someone's child himself.

On 12 October 1998, the evening of the death of Matthew Shepard, a 21-year-old gay student at the University of Wyoming who had been picked up under false pretenses by two straight men in a Laramie bar and then taken in the dark to a deserted spot where he was savagely beaten and pistol-whipped and then tied to a wooden fence and abandoned to the frigid temperatures of the night – temperatures from which he would not be rescued until, already comatose, he was discovered some eighteen hours later by a bicyclist who initially mistook the limp, bloody body lashed to the post for a scarecrow; on that evening of Matthew Shepard's death a hospital spokesman, 'voice choked with emotion', made the following statement to the press: 'Matthew's mother said to me, "Please tell everybody who's listening to go home and give your kids a hug and don't let a day go by without telling them you love them."'[3] The words of a grieving mother, widely reported on the news, produced a mimetic outpouring of grief from people across the country just as they had from the spokesman whose own voice choked as he announced them. But those words, which even on the occasion of a gay man's murder defined the proper mourners as those who had children to go home and hug, specified the mourning it encouraged as mourning for the threat to familial futurity – a threat that might, for many, take the form of Matthew Shepard's death, but a threat that must also, for others, take the form of Matthew Shepard's *life*.[4]

Thus even at his funeral, where solemn mourners came to pray at the bier of a mother's slain child, others gathered with signs to condemn a 'lifestyle' that made Matthew Shepard, for them, a dangerous bird of prey. The *New York Times* cited speculation that the symbolic significance for the killers of leaving the body strung up on a fence might have had something to do with 'the Old West practice of nailing a dead coyote to a ranch fence as a warning to future intruders'.[5] The bicyclist who mistook him for a scarecrow, then, would not have been far from the mark; for his killers, by posing Shepard's body this way, could be understood to be crowing about the lengths to which they were ready to go to scare away birds of his feather: birds that may seem to be more or less tame – flighty, to be sure, and prone to a narcissistic preening of their plumage; amusing enough when confined to the space of a popular film like *The Birdcage* or when, outside the movies, caged in the ghettos that make them ethnographically visible (and for certain tourists, punitively so) or in the closets that enact a pervasive desire to make them all disappear – but birds that the *cognoscenti* perceive as never harmless at all.[6] For whatever apparent difference in species may dupe the untrained eye, inveterate birdwatchers always discern the tell-tale mark that proves each one a chicken-hawk first and last.

In an atmosphere all atwitter with the sound of cries that echo between those who watch and those who hunt such birds, what matter who killed Cock Robin? The logic of *sinthome*-osexuality justifies that violent fate in advance by contending that what such a cock had been robbing was always, in some sense, a cradle. And that cradle must endlessly rock, of course, even if the rhythm to which it rocks beats out, with every blow delivered to a Matthew Shepard's skull, a counterpoint to the melody's resonant hymn to the meaning of life. That meaning, continuously affirmed as it is both in and as cultural narrative, never can rest secure insofar as it never, quite simply, can rest. The compulsive need for such repetition, for the regular drumbeat with which it proceeds to pound into our heads (and not always, though not infrequently, by pounding in a Matthew Shepard's) that the cradle bears both the meaning of futurity and the futurity of meaning, testifies to something that always exceeds the meaning it means to affirm: to a death drive that carries, on full-fledged wings, into the inner sanctum of meaning that is the reproductive mandate, the burden of that negativising force that *sinthome-osexuality* names.

Only the dumbest of clucks would expect such a story about the stories by which familial ideology seems constantly to take its own pulse to find a prominent place among cultural narratives valued for parroting the regulatory fantasy of reproductive futurism. Why, after all, would a social structure that sells that ideology as the linchpin of its survival foul its own nest with texts that explore how the fact of this iterative parroting – automatic and machine-like as it is – speaks, regardless of intention or will, to the structuring mechanism of a death drive propelling its life-affirming thematics? Yet such a text might just *feather* the nest it seems ordained to foul if the tensions of form and content it describes are projected, in reverse, onto it: if, that is, its efforts to dismantle the large-scale thematics of futurism are themselves viewed as ill-considered themes in a work that rewards our attention by means of its technical achievement alone, or else if its apparent threat to the logic of reproductive ideology can plausibly be made to serve the cause of naturalising futurity. And where better to look for that *rara avis* among privileged cultural narratives – for the text that could teach us how to read the relentless reproduction of reproductive ideology – than to Alfred Hitchcock's *The Birds* (1963), a film whose defenders have frequently had recourse to each of these strategies of evasion.

Hitchcock himself, for example, interpreted the film as a triumph of technique, immodestly declaring it, on just that ground, 'probably the most prodigious job ever done'.[7] But while insisting on the technical difficulties the film both posed and overcame, thus celebrating it for its masterful demonstration of formal and artisanal skills, Hitchcock continued to defend, if tepidly, what critics dismissed as its vapid thematics by pitching the film as an admonition to those who would violate nature: 'Basically, in *The Birds*, what you have is a kind of an overall sketchy theme of everyone taking nature for granted,' he explained before offering his own interpretation of the film: 'Don't mess about or tamper with nature.'[8] If something in this reading sticks in one's craw, it's not simply the simplification (baited with the lifeless, but often effective, worm of a ponderous didacticism), but also, and more pressingly, the clear contradiction between this would-be embrace of the natural, on the one hand, and the significance attached to the technical manipulation of reality by the camera, on the other. Neither in theme nor in visual practice does *The Birds* sing Mother Nature's praise; nor do mothers and children receive from the film the extorted tribute that sentimentality would grant them as 'their due'. *The Birds*, to the contrary, comes to roost, with a skittish and volatile energy, on a perch from which it proceeds to brood on the abyss at once opened and, thematically, filled, by a force that is *contra naturam*: the force of the death drive as figured and displaced by *sinthome*-osexuality.

Like swallows returning to Capistrano, critics of Hitchcock's film return to the question its characters repeatedly pose: what do the bird attacks mean? 'What do you suppose made it do *that*?' wonders Melanie Daniels ('Tippi' Hedren) after the first gull gashes her head; 'What's the matter with *all* the birds?' asks Lydia Brenner (Jessica Tandy) in the wake of the full-scale assault on the children at her daughter's birthday party; 'Why are they doing this, the birds?' young Cathy (Veronica Cartwright) plaintively inquires of her brother, Mitch (Rod Taylor), echoing, in the process, the challenge hurled at Melanie by a frantically overwrought mother following a massive bird attack on the centre of Bodega Bay: 'Why are they doing this? Why are they *doing* this?' Why, we might ask, ask why? Robin Wood wrote some years ago that 'the film itself is quite insistent that either the birds can't be explained or that the explanation is unknown';[9] and he went on to observe, quite properly, that the birds 'are a concrete embodiment of the arbitrary and the unpredictable, of whatever makes human life and human relations precarious, a reminder of the fragility and instability that cannot be ignored or evaded and, beyond that, of the possibility that life is meaningless and absurd'.[10] This largely persuasive account of the film, to which I will return, rightly resists the impulse to localise the meaning of the attacks, but in doing so it refuses as well to localise the contexts within which this very refusal of meaning takes place. The narrative that raises meaninglessness as a possibility, after all, necessarily inflects the particular meaning of meaninglessness itself; by deploying some figure, as here the birds, for the 'possibility that life is meaningless', the text will always gesture toward some *specific* threat to meaning against which, by deploying that figure, the text will attempt to defend.

Though Wood, then, may be right to note that the birds embody 'whatever makes human life and human relations precarious', there is something else that he needs to note: they come from San Francisco; or, at any rate, it's in San Francisco that we first see them flit through the air. And another thing: they seem to display a strong predilection for children. When Mrs Bundy (Ethel Griffies), the butch and tweedy bird-lover who knows the perfect time for The Tides – conveniently making her entrance just as Melanie, talking to her father by phone, is reporting the schoolhouse attack – dismisses out of hand the idea that the birds could have mounted such a raid, she turns to Melanie and demands of her with unconcealed condescension: 'What do you think they were after, Miss ...?' 'Daniels,' Melanie informs her, before delivering her icily calm response: 'I think they were after the children.' 'For what purpose?' Mrs Bundy presses; and Melanie, after a pause fully worthy of the governess in James's *The Turn of the Screw*, accepts the challenge and rises to it, enunciating clearly: 'To kill them.' To be sure, the objects of avian violence most gruesomely visualised in Hitchcock's film – Dan Fawcett, Annie Hayworth and Melanie Daniels herself – are not exactly spring chickens; but the threat of the birds achieves its most vividly iconic representation in the two crucial scenes where they single out young children to attack.

That their first all-out assault, their first joint action, disrupts the party in honour of Cathy's eleventh birthday (which occasion gave Mitch – who passed it on, unwittingly, to Melanie – the idea of presenting Cathy with a pair of lovebirds as a gift) suggests the extent to which the birds take aim at the social structures of meaning such festivities enact and secure: take aim, that is, not only at children and the sacralisation of childhood, but also at the very organisation of meaning around ritualised elaborations of subjectivity constrained to reinforce the heterosexualising ideology of reproductive necessity.[11] Like Bruno Anthony (Robert Walker) in *Strangers on a Train* (1951), who punctures the balloon of cuteness that hangs like a halo above one annoying child and has no compunction about casually tossing a second and even more troublesome tot to what might have been his death, the birds beset the children with an unconstrained aggression that mirrors and displaces the aggression adults prohibit, aggressively, in children. Indeed, when Cathy, blindfolded to play her part in blind man's buff, suffers the first glancing blow from a bird, she assumes without hesitation that another child has struck her and calls out, more in pique than in pain, 'Hey, no touching allowed!' As dozens of birds then swoop down with hoarse cries, inducing a sort of echoing screech in the children who panic and run, the film implies that the ravaging birds are too like the children to like them too much, or to like them as more than the objects of their murderous desire.

The film insists on this aggressive echoing (and this echoing aggression) in the relation between children and birds from the opening sequence in San Francisco. Since the audience gets its first chance to feast on the face of Hitchcock's star, his newest discovery, 'Tippi' Hedren, when she turns toward the camera in response to what critics conventionally call a 'wolf-whistle', it's significant that the source of that whistle is less a sheep than a lamb in wolf's clothing, a cheeky young boy whose age we might put, to hazard a guess, at eleven. Melanie, expecting to confront some loutish lothario as she wheels about angrily, flashes a smile of relief and surprise when she sees that her would-be cock of the walk is no more than a featherweight bantam. Charmed by his boyish bravado, the crowing of a youngster sufficiently cocky at eleven to augur with absolute certainty a full-fledged prick by twenty-one, Melanie, refusing to see the incipience of that straight male sense of entitlement for which, in only a matter of minutes, she'll seek to clip Mitch Brenner's wings, responds to this sexually freighted call by hearing its amorous coo in the key of a prepubescent chirp. Her smile acquits the act of what she grasped as its aggression (about which, though prepared to squawk, she wasn't really ruffled) when she thought it the sonorous panting of one more accustomed to wearing long pants.

No sooner has her face lit up – her anger defused, her defenses let down – at the vision of the child, than Melanie hears the whistle return, multiplied a hundred times over, but coming from somewhere else.[12] A cut to Melanie's point of view now gives us the sky in long shot and in it a virtual cloud of gulls whose calls seem to mock the boy's whistle as, birds of a feather, neither sowing nor reaping, they noisily cruise San Francisco. In reverse shot that cloud crosses Melanie's face, her joy in the boy eclipsed by the grating cries of the circling gulls, their harsh and guttural echo stripping the whistle of its charm, as if their taunt were targeting both the woman and the boy, or targeting, instead, what the film had allowed them jointly to perform: a pantomime of the displacement of erotic tension into the child who gives that tension meaning, and relieves it of all taint, by reading the constitutive friction – the violent aggression – inherent in eros as the agency that calls forth meaning and the child in a single blow, breeding thereby a happy heterosexual economy in which the child means 'meaning' for adults whose lives can only ever hope to attain it insofar as they consent to participate in the labour of giving (it) birth.[13]

This sequence, then, like an egg, contains the film in embryonic form, with Melanie caught between a libidinal energy redeemed through the figure of the child, the heterosexualised version of eros traditionally served sunny side up, and the disarticulation that scrambles it in the figure of the birds: the arbitrary, future-negating force of a brutal and mindless drive. It may be the boy in this scene who whistles, but through him, and through its investment in him, we can hear the whole heterosexual symbolic whistling past the graveyard. And just as the boy's sweet tweet is cheapened by the echoing cheep of the birds, so the reassuring meaning of heterosexuality as the assurance of meaning itself confronts in the birds a resistance, call it *sinthome*-osexuality, that fully intends to wipe the satisfied smile off Melanie's face. By yoking her thus to the birds through the boy, this sequence might well be construed as the egg from which Melanie's story emerges, but this scene, however primal within the logic of the film, refers to a moment *outside* the film and marks, as would an umbilicus, a distinctly non-avian origin that Hitchcock reproduces here to generate *The Birds.*

Donald Spoto recounts the moment this opening sequence so clearly recalls, the moment when Hitchcock first noticed the blonde he thereafter took under his wing: 'one morning ... Hitchcock and Alma [his wife] were watching the NBC network's *Today* show. He saw a commercial featuring an attractive, elegant blond [sic] who passed across the screen and smiled, turning amiably in response to a little boy's wolf-whistle ... That morning, he told his agents to find out who she was, and that afternoon an appointment was made for her.'[14] In fact the commercial, hawking a diet drink meant to account for the backward glances, bespeaking another kind of hunger, bestowed on her by the men Hedren passes as she walks along the street, resolves itself more pointedly than Spoto's rendering suggests. For Hedren, holding a bag of groceries as she pauses to admire the fashions adorning the mannequins in a window-display, stands with her back to the camera when the sound of the 'wolf-whistle' indicates that *she's* on display herself. She starts to turn, but before we can catch a glimpse of her expression, the camera cuts to an insert of the whistle's unlikely source: a boy, to be sure, as Spoto notes, eleven years old, more or less, but crucially – and this Spoto doesn't report – the boy represents *her son.* Sitting in the car (like Melanie's, a convertible) where his mother had left him to await her return, the child gets his mother's attention by offering the tribute of a man, then deflects the ramifications thereof by flashing the grin of a boy. Hedren's broad smile in response to the joke allows her and her son and the viewer to bask in the innocent glow of the child, ignoring the fact that he stands in the place of the numerous men whose heads Hedren turned as she passed them just moments before.

And since no head turned with more interest than Hitchcock's, his response might be said to enact exemplarily the logic of desire anticipated by the narrative frame the commercial constructs: a logic wherein the permissible (because 'innocent') whistle of the child takes the place of explicitly sexual energies (understood as more threatening, unstable and aggressive) that the commercial nonetheless, and at the same time, undertakes to promote and inflame. Hitchcock, a model spectator here, in more than one sense of that phrase, identifies with and reproduces, the youngster's bold trill of desire; like the boy, he too responds to the vision of Hedren by sounding a call. But when, in *The Birds*, he introduces his star by reconstructing the scene, or a version of the scene, that first introduced her to him, he completes it by inserting immediately thereafter the eponymous figures of the film. Not that they haven't been heard from already: the film threads their cries through the audio track from before, one might say, its beginning: a visual fade-out separates the opening credits from the narrative proper, but the clamour of the birds persists as a bridge of sound between the two. When the film fades in again (through the blue-green filter that announces its dominant tones), the sights and sounds of San Francisco command our full attention. The bird calls, though continuous, become mere background to the scene until, in the wake of Melanie's affirmation of the child – which is also an affirmation of his capacity to neutralise the threat inherent in heterosexuality *as* sexuality – the gulls parrot back the boy's whistle as materialised agents of sexual threat.

If they bring out, in the process, what the child as ideological construct redeems by repressing – the relentlessness of erotic drive that the cuteness, and the social utility, of the child as a cultural product would mask; if they bring out, that is, the overpowering force of Hitchcockian compulsion that rehearses, without its saving grace, the child's expectant grace-note, then they also embody the process of bringing or coming out *per se*, shedding invisibility here and demanding, having always been present before, to be recognised, to be seen. Like Marion, the librarian, in *The Music Man*, another blonde whose path to the promise of heterosexual relationality depends upon the purifying cuteness of a child, Melanie Daniels might well exclaim: 'There were birds/In the sky/ But I never saw them winging/No, I never saw them at all/'Till there was you'[15] – words equally apt if imagined as marking the moment of recognition attained by a second blonde Marion, one whose road to heterosexual bliss dead-ended when she mistook for the innocence of a child, and interpreted as redemptive, the wounded-sparrow twitchiness she encountered in Norman Bates. More hawk than sparrow, Norman Bates himself deconstructed the avian analysis to which he famously gave voice: 'I think only birds look well stuffed because, well, because they're kind of passive to begin with.' But *The Birds* explicitly portrays the revenge (visualising in the process the fantasmatic threat) of those construed as passive, by depicting the activist militancy that attends their act of coming out.[16]

One might, to be sure, object that Hitchcock's preferred cinematic strategy, a distinguishing feature of his camera's keen epistemological investigations, consists of just this bringing out of a latency, some would call it a queerness, inhabiting things that otherwise tend to pass without remark: a pair of scissors, a household key, a dangling piece of rope.[17] As figured by *The Birds*, however, this coming out, though seized on as the seed for various interpretations of what exactly it means, refuses the promise of meaning condensed in the seed that is the child; nor would it be flying too far afield to suggest that precisely by coming out the birds give the bird to the fantasy of heterosexual reproduction as the guarantor of futurity that divorces heterosexual sex from mechanistic drive. What Judith Butler identifies as the 'heterosexual matrix' may tempt us, with Susan Lurie, to approach the birds as phallic part-objects, or else, with Slavoj Žižek, as embodiments of maternal superego; by resisting the hetero-genital logic, the either/or that such readings suppose, we might find ourselves in a position, however, to kill those two birds with one stone by arguing that the birds in Hitchcock's film, by fucking up or fucking with the matrix of heterosexual mating, desublimate the reproductive rites of heterosexual lovebirds about which, as about the products of which, they don't give a flying fuck.[18]

Let me pause, though, to make something perfectly clear: my point is not that the birds represent, or ought to be seen to signify, homosexuality or same-sex desire; nor is Hitchcock's film, as I read it, intending an allegory of gay coming-out. Insofar as the birds express what I call *sinthome*-osexuality, which dissociates heterosexuality from the death drive that shatters the egg of meaning on which the symbolic endlessly broods, it would, in fact, be more accurate to say that the meaning of homosexuality remains intimately bound to what the film so memorably figures in the birds: the unnatural access to *jouissance* that comes out with their attacks, the target of which, the compulsory fantasy of an always impending future that only a fruitful heterosexual coupling manages to assure, Hitchcock evokes and refuses at once in the catchphrase he cannily devised to sell the film: '*The Birds* is coming'.[19]

Affirming though it does the imminence, the narrative covenant, of futurity – of something, as Wordsworth put it, 'evermore about to be' – this slogan suggests, as well, the sort of coming without reserve that would expend itself improvidently, thus wasting all hope of futurity and refuting the tranquil faith in an order of narrative intelligibility that Hamlet, for instance, defers to when he forbears from deferring his fate: 'Not a whit, we defy augury. There is a special providence in the fall of a sparrow. If it be now, 'tis not to come; if it be not to come, it will be now; if it be not now, yet it will come. The readiness is all' (V.ii. 220–4). The falling sparrows of Hitchcock's film – and the film will specify sparrows as the birds that fall from the Brenner's chimney like a living stream of dirt or waste turning meaning into shit – decline, in their present progressive coming, indicative of their coming out, to 'be not to come', in Shakespeare's phrase, since coming becomes their being.[20] Exposing the latent impropriety informing the structures of the proper, embedding grammatical violation in the very logic of grammar itself, '*The Birds* is coming' anticipates the film's libidinal economy by confounding the anticipation of simple syntactic or narrative sense. The slogan fucks with the copula, meaning that meaning comes apart, thus advertising the threat of *The Birds* to the narrative teleology of the subject who only comes into being at the *expense* of *jouissance*, at the cost of the violent involuntarity, the pulsive pressure of a coming in the throes of which, as subject of meaning no less than as meaningful subject, she or he comes apart too.[21] Trenching as it does on this trench in the subject that *jouissance* hollows out, the slogan alludes to a fissure that sunders the syntax of social reality as the slogan itself seems to sunder the rightful agreement of subject and predicate. 'Coming' thus comes into conflict with the subject's predication of a future to come, and *The Birds*, as the site of this conflict, no less than the birds that flesh it out, claws at our faith in the future, at the generative grammar of generation, by coming at the force of the death drive instead, in the clenched, mechanistic grip of which, though we come, we come to nothing: or come, which may come to the same in the end, to a place like Bodega Bay.

What a perfect spot for a pair of lovebirds to build their little nest. Defined, as if allegorically, in opposition to San Francisco, the sophisticated urban centre described by Cathy, quoting her brother Mitch, as 'an anthill at the foot of a bridge', Bodega Bay might stand for the concept of natural beauty as such were it not for the fact that its natural settings have the peculiar habit of metamorphosing into unnatural studio sets. Time and again, and at pivotal moments, its vistas get flattened into painted backdrops, obviously artificial, as when, for example, Melanie crosses the lake to deliver her gift of lovebirds to Cathy at the Brenner farm, or when she and Mitch share their thoughts and a drink on a sandy hill before the birds begin their attack at Cathy's party, or when she and Annie, having opened the door to find a dead gull on the porch, stare up at the light of the moon that should have kept it from losing its way, or when Melanie, observing a single bird descending toward the schoolhouse, turns to follow its course with her gaze and discovers the playground behind her completely overrun with crows. Each of these instances also involves an avian annunciation, a descent from on high that does not bring glad tidings or the promise of miraculous conception; instead, boding ill for Bodega Bay and all whose abode it is, the birds expose the misconception on which its reality rests: the misconception that conception itself can assure the endurance, by enacting the truth, of the symbolic organisation of meaning, can reinforce the non-contingency of social structuration by affirming the logic of the other as anchoring reality in meaning's plenitude.

For our governing politics of futurity, the only politics we're permitted to know, organises and administers an apparently self-regulating economy of sentimentality in which futurity comes to signify access to the plenitude of meaning simultaneously promised and prohibited by the fact of our formation as subjects of the signifier. As a figure for the supplementarity, for the logic of restitution or compensation that sustains our participation in the perpetual deferrals that language compels, the future holds out the hope of a final undoing of the fragmentation, the originary fracture, the primal lack that effects our constitution as subjects; and it offers that hope by mobilising a fantasy of temporal reversal, as if the future were pledged to make good the loss it can only repeat. But in this sense we might observe, as well, following Paul de Man's reading of Walter Benjamin on history, that the future as such only ever engages temporality in the mode of figuration since the future stands in the place of a linguistic, and not a temporal, destiny: 'The dimension of futurity,' as de Man insists, 'is not temporal but is the correlative of the figural pattern and the disjunctive power which Benjamin locates in the structure of language.'[22] That structure, as de Man interprets it, necessitates the perpetual motion of what he calls 'a wandering, an *errance*', and 'this motion, this errancy of language which never reaches the mark', is nothing other, for Benjamin, than history itself, generating, in a phrase from de Man, 'this illusion of life that is only an afterlife'.[23]

The violent reduction of reality to this status as illusion, the consequence for de Man of history viewed as a rhetoric, as a poetics, rather than as the dialectic of meaning's temporal realisation, bears down upon Bodega Bay in the figure of the birds. Not that I wish to identify the birds with the ceaseless mobility of the signifier, as if Hamlet, when asked by Polonius to tell him what he was reading, meant to say 'Birds, birds, birds' when he answered 'Words, words, words'; but I do want to call attention to the fact that Hitchcock's birds, in the obdurate specificity of their material embodiment, resist, both within and without the film, hermeneutic determination by carrying, in the figural atmosphere through which they wing their way, the force of a poetics never fully contained by a hermeneutic claim, at least where 'poetics', to quote de Man, is construed 'as formal procedure considered independently of its semantic function'.[24] Expressing this surplus of form or style that inhabits and exceeds (and hence threatens to confound) the imperative to generate meaning, the birds may persistently beat against, but can nonetheless only fly through and not from, the medium of meaning in which they come to mean its degeneration. Our obligatory faith in the 'realness' of reality may render it as natural and as needful as the air we breathe, but the excess that the birds connote, like the iteration and accumulation of heterosexualising narratives – social and political narratives no less than literary or aesthetic ones – bespeaks a drive that eludes all efforts to formulate its meaning insofar as that drive would itself inform every meaningful formulation.[25] The formal insistence of the drive thus has the effect of *deforming* meaning while coming to mean *as deformation* insofar as it shows how the absolute privilege accorded the 'semantic function' serves as the dominant mechanism for maintaining the collective 'illusion of life'. Performing the unintelligibility of this formal mechanism or drive, the birds usher in the collapse of an ideologically naturalised reality into the various artificial props that collaborate to maintain it.

If this appears to impose on *The Birds* a weight of linguistic implication beneath which it too seems bound to collapse, then perhaps it is wise to bear in mind that Melanie, as she proudly announces to Mitch, is herself a student enrolled in a course in 'General Semantics' at Berkeley. Even more to the point, the film begins as she's heading toward Davidson's Pet Shop where she expects to find a myna bird she has ordered as a gift for her aunt – a practical joke of a gift, we soon learn, since the aim is to shock her 'straightlaced' aunt by teaching the bird a few 'four-letter words' that Melanie has picked up at school. The myna bird, in narrative terms, will prove to be a red herring, but only because it undergoes a symbolic exchange with the lovebirds in the aftermath of the exchange of words between Melanie and Mitch. And like the myna bird whose place they take, the lovebirds – which are, significantly, themselves a variety of parrot – are made to signify the signifying potential inherent in the 'natural'; they reflect, that is, the human will to make the world answer to, and in, the voice of the subjects addressing it. By doing so they confirm *as* natural the order of meaning itself, which coincides conveniently, though not by mere coincidence, with the heterosexual logic that renders the world and the subject intelligible through their relation to each other.

It should come as no surprise, therefore, that the lovebirds most successfully perform the naturalisation of human meaning at the moment when the film personifies them, strategically, as children. I refer, of course, to the sequence in which, as Melanie travels the Pacific Coast Highway *en route* to Bodega Bay, the wheels of her sportscar squealing as she takes each turn in the road too fast, the camera cuts to a close-up of the lovebirds beside her in their cage, their bodies tilting left and right each time the car rounds a curve. Always earning the laugh it solicits, this moment adduces the lovebirds in the connotative plumage of their smallness and dependency to read them, in the same way that Melanie earlier read the whistling boy, as 'cute'. But the ideological labour of cuteness, though it falls most often to the smallest, imposes no insubstantial burden in a culture where cuteness performs a general misrecognition of sexuality (which always implicitly endangers ideals of sociality and communal enjoyment) as, at least in the dominant form of reproductive heterosexual relations, securing the collective reality it otherwise threatens to destroy.[26] Visually framed as children, and thus as figures for the irresistible charm of a heterosexual romantic ideology that regularly translates adults into children to explain (which is also to say, to elide) how children themselves are produced (similar in this to Cupid, who, despite his involvement with Psyche, we represent as pre-pubescent), the lovebirds, shadowed by the myna bird whose narrative place they take, are thereby made to speak the truth of a 'General Semantics': for they mean here as figures of meaning – of, more precisely, the domestication, the colonisation, of the world by meaning – insofar as their cuteness both echoes and reinforces the meaningfulness of the child about which even the dumbest animals are 'naturally' able to speak.

How then could the lovebirds, wedded by name both to each other and to the task of naturalising the reality heterosexual meaningfulness constructs, anticipate the violence with which their fine-feathered friends will divorce themselves – unexpectedly, out of the blue – from the nature they are made persistently, if also unnaturally, to mean? How else but with the eruption, or let us say rather, the coming out, of something *contra naturam* always implicit in them from the start, something we might discern, for instance, in Cathy's blurted-out question – camouflaged only in part by the calculated alibi of cuteness – demanding that the lovebirds speak their mandated meaning louder still: 'Is there a man and a woman? I can't tell which is which.' Melanie, to whom she directs this question, deflects it with an awkward laugh and a rather dismissive, 'Well, I suppose.' But what if her supposition were wrong? Or what if, more disturbing still, her answer were *literally* true: what if the structuring principle, the world-making logic, of heterosexual meaningfulness were merely a supposition, merely a *positing*, as de Man would say, and not, therefore, imbued with the referential necessity of a 'meaning' since, as de Man himself reminds us, 'language posits and language means . . . but language cannot posit meaning'?[27]

Cathy's question can *only* mean, paradoxical though this may be, by casting a shadow of doubt on the subjectifying principle of meaning itself – the principle sounded, for example, in the whistle with which the boy and the film both identify sexual difference as self-evident. No birdbrain, Cathy must understand that the lovebirds, in their sameness, their apparent interchangeability, resist or suggest a resistance to, the homogenising universalism of this heterosexual dispensation. Perhaps we might hear in her question, then, an unintentional echo of Proust, whose narrator in *Sodom and Gomorrah* remarks, while watching Charlus and Jupien strike poses in an effort to manoeuvre their mutual cruise into a somewhat more intimate docking, 'one might have thought of them as a pair of birds, the male and the female, the male seeking to advance, the female – Jupien – no longer giving any sign of response to this stratagem, but regarding her new friend without surprise . . . and contenting herself with preening her feathers'.[28] For these two birds, anatomically indistinguishable as they are, 'male' and 'female' refer to positions, like top and bottom, that one must posit, not fixed biological destinies self-evidently meaningful from the start; yet their preening positional presence – partly peacock, partly vulture – hovers lightly in the atmosphere that Cathy's query, despite itself, makes heavy for a moment, since her question, simply cuckoo when asked of a heterosexual pairing, parrots what everyone wonders where same-sex couples are concerned, the meaning of all such couplings being coupled to the meaning that heterosexuality both determines and confirms.

If these lovebirds, as in the molting season ('a particularly dangerous time'), are imagined, with Cathy's question, to drop their beads and their feathers at once, as what could they come out in the collective fantasy life of America circa 1963 but members of that reprobated, predatory hoard who, looking like scavenging crows in the standard dark raincoats of their tribe, loiter in public parks and school playgrounds waiting until the moment is ripe to pick up some innocent kid for the peck that everyone, even the pecker himself, would perceive as the kiss of death? Birds of ill omen condemned to fruitless matings on the wing, these raptors who famously feed on the young that they cannot produce themselves are labelled as degenerate for this antipathy to generation, this preference, instead, for a *jouissance* indifferent to social survival. Not that the scene at the schoolhouse, perhaps the most famous in the film, is meant to 'mean' allegorically a scenario such as this. The crows, unlike the myna bird, resist the demand that they speak to us; no stool pigeons, they won't talk. As they fly in the face of meaning, though, they do so on wings unable to shed the meanings with which they're feathered, wings that beat to the steady, monotonous rhythm of the drive ('Don't they ever stop migrating?') and reduce the hope of futurity to the mechanics of repetition, the promise of reproduction to the constant coming of *jouissance*, as if to affirm the value, above all else, of a bird in the hand.

Whatever else we may learn by going to school at Hitchcock's schoolhouse, then, we must surely be struck by the structure of this brilliantly realised scene of instruction – struck, that is, by the strictness with which, in a masterstroke, Hitchcock constructs it by restricting the play of his camera to patterns of formal repetition. To be sure, throughout his career in film, he will generate spectatorial anxiety by rhythmically cutting between people or things that are certain to spark an explosion, sometimes literally, when their paths converge; this sequence, though, seems to allegorise that pattern of repetition by producing a sort of rhyme between the director's formal practice here (increasing the level of tension by cutting repeatedly from shots of Melanie – framed in ever tighter close-up – to shots of the birds as they gather on the jungle gym behind her) and his narrative representation (visualising the notion of increase through the multiplication of the crows). As the cigarette, from which Melanie takes her deep, occasional drags, burns down, like the lighted fuse of a bomb, time and hope and futurity all going up, as it seems, in its smoke, more and more birds, indistinguishable one from the other, like clones, alight, producing a visual antitype to the reproductive future that the children – figures of increase themselves turned, suddenly, songbirds here – both signify and assure.

Heard but not seen, the children triangulate Melanie's relation to the crows as they lend their voices to a score that serves, in no small part, to underscore the cumulative formal insistence on repetition in this scene. Their verse perversely veers from sense to nonsense, shuttling back and forth, with no clear narrative trajectory, from sketches that seem to focus on failed heterosexual domesticity ('I married my wife in the month of June'; 'She combed her hair but once a year'; 'With every stroke she shed a tear'; 'I asked my wife to wash the floor'; 'She gave me my hat and showed me the door') to incremental repetitions of various meaningless sounds ('Ristle-tee, rostle-tee, now, now, now' 'Ristle-tee, rostle-tee, hey donny dossle-tee, rustical-quality, ristle-tee, rossle-tee, now, now, now'). The song's formula (better: its lack thereof) serves to make it, in principle, endless – verses repeat out of order, nonsense syllables expand and contract – and for just that reason it has the effect of marking time in this scene: of measuring and protracting the deferral of Melanie's mission to the schoolhouse (she has come to take Cathy home and thus to put Lydia's mind at ease) and to identify such deferral with temporality itself. The order of narrative futurity for which the children have come to stand thus stands, with this song, exposed as bound to a structure of repetition – a structure that, as the formal support of the meaningfulness of reality, resists domestication by the meaning that it bears, despite being made to bear the meaning of domestic reproduction. Its excess, however, precisely as form, as what's always unaccounted for in meaning's domestic economy, betrays – like the children's song, or the crows – the intractable force of a drive that breaks, again and again, like the waves in which the bird attacks seem to come, against and within the reality that meaning means to erect. Perhaps, then, we shouldn't be too surprised when Melanie turns and discovers the crows, massed as if to interpret Kant's mathematical sublime, and Hitchcock frames her reaction-shot against a crudely painted background, evoking with this the derealisation effected by the birds as they bring out the repetition compulsion, the meaninglessness of the drive, that symbolic reality closets in itself and projects onto *sinthome*-osexuals made to figure *jouissance*.

Out to get the children, then, by coming and coming out, the birds, when they flock from their playground perch, seem to darken the sky like a stain, emerging, as Hitchcock shoots the attack, as if from the school itself to suggest the unacknowledged ghosts that inhabit the social machine. As horrified youngsters shriek and flail, racing to return to the shelter they still think their parents and home will provide, the birds bear down with talon and beak, pecking and scratching at eyes and skin, clearly out for blood. 'Ristle-tee, rostle-tee, now, now, now' comes back with a vengeance here, unpacked, in these fierce wingéd chariots not content to hover near, as the full-fledged force of the death drive that its dull repetition bespeaks. Calling attention to this particular scene at a pivotal moment in his career-long critical ambivalence about *The Birds*, Robin Wood saw it as localising the larger 'weakness' of the film in 'the perfunctory treatment of the children ... Hitchcock's notable failure to respond to the notion of renewed potential they and the school might have represented, his reduction of the concepts of education and childhood – the human future – to the automatic reiteration of an inane jingle.'[29] Distorted though this reading is by its own automatic reiteration of the ideological jingle that always seems to top our culture's charts (anticipating the pop-timistic credo belted out by Whitney Houston – 'I believe that children are our future' – in what we might as well adopt as our national anthem right now and be done with it), Wood's observation picks up, nonetheless, on something that all other critics ignore: Hitchcock's deliberate reduction of childhood, education, collective reality and thus the future itself, to the status of mere machinery, automatic reiterations – which is to say their reduction to the status of the drive.[30]

If the bird attacks, as many note, seem coloured by desire, enacting as sexual aggression the experience of sexuality itself, then they locate the place where sexuality and the death drive come together, exposing what Jean Laplanche calls 'a kind of antilife as sexuality, frenetic enjoyment [*jouissance*], the negative, the repetition compulsion'.[31] In doing so they testify to what regimes of normativity, of sexual meaningfulness, disavow: the antisocial bent of sexuality as such, acknowledged – and then as pathology – only in those who are bent themselves. 'Sexuality in the context of family and procreation has natural limits,' claims Alan Keyes, conservative radio talk-show host and occasional candidate for the Republican presidential nomination: 'It has built into it constraints, responsibility, discipline and so forth.' 'Restraint,' by contrast, according to Keyes, 'goes counter to the whole idea of sexuality that's involved in homosexuality itself, which is to say sexuality freed from constraint, freed from convention, freed from the context and limitations of procreation.'[32] Dissociating reproductive pleasure from the shock of *jouissance*, the joys of procreation from the 'violent liveness' of what, after Lauren Berlant, we should understand as 'live sex',[33] Keyes, defending the comic-book version of heterosexuality (to be sure, the only version that we've ever been given to read), posits sexuality as hetero to normative heterosexual practice, linking access to 'frenetic enjoyment', the loss of control in *jouissance*, to a homosexuality constructed as *sinthome*-osexuality. For sexuality as such now bears the *sinthome*'s unbearably meaningless mark.

Thus the birds in their coming lay waste to the world condensed in Bodega Bay since they, like the 'homosexual generation' seen as 'driven and driving' in a book that was published in 1965, 'so hate the world that will not accept them that they, in turn, will accept nothing but the destruction of that world'.[34] 'Driven and driving': a perfect description of the family at the end of the film. In a landscape that pulses with volatile birds, they pack themselves into Melanie's car still clinging, albeit desperately, to hope, that thing with feathers, in the form of the lovebirds that Cathy refuses to leave behind: hope, that is, for the future – for the *reproductive* future – that Cathy and the lovebirds together ought normally to guarantee. It may be just such a future that the family, driven from their domestic security by the drive that propels the birds, is driving toward at the end; but the film concludes inconclusively with an image of driving or drive alone while the soundtrack supplies, in Hitchcock's words, a 'monotonous low hum ... a strange artificial sound, which in the language of the birds might be saying, "We're not ready to attack yet, but we're getting ready. We're like an engine that's purring and we may start off at any moment." '[35]

Were we to ask, with other critics, at what this Hitchcockian engine is driving, we might be torn between reading the birds, with Wood, as 'a concrete embodiment of the arbitrary and unpredictable', or with Žižek as 'the incarnation of a fundamental disorder in family relations'; but these alternatives, as I hope to have argued, come together in the film as they come together in the logic of heterosexual familialism as well. For Hitchcock's anatomy of 'family relations', especially as Žižek depicts it, should seem uncomfortably predictable: 'the father is absent, the paternal function ... is suspended and that vacuum is filled by the "irrational" maternal superego, arbitrary, wicked, blocking "normal" sexual relationship'.[36] Like the momism as which it will not come out, this reading, promoted by the film itself, blames the mother for the bird attacks precisely insofar as it would blame her as well for the sexual abnormality of her son. We haven't, apparently, come too far from the pop psychology being hawked at the time the film was being made – a psychology epitomised in the following rehearsal of that era's received ideas: 'Kinsey has given us a brutal picture of the homosexual's mother, listing, (a) her overpossessive love of him during his infancy and early childhood, and (b) her underlying hatred of his wife, no matter how wise, devoted, and long-suffering the latter may be.'[37] This mass-market version of gay etiology might afford some interpretative purchase on the film – allowing us at last to make sense of the ascot Mitch wears beneath his sweater and letting us catch the full force of her drift when Annie wistfully muses out loud, 'Maybe there's never been anything between Mitch and *any* girl' – but the birds don't alight in Hitchcock's film because Mitch is light in the loafers.[38] They come because coming is what they do, arbitrarily and unpredictably, like the homosexuals Keyes condemns for promoting 'a paradigm of human sexuality divorced from family and procreation, and engaged in solely for the sake of . . . sensual pleasure and gratification'.[39] They come, that is, to trace a connection, as directly as the crow flies, between 'disorder in the family' and the rupture, the radical loss of familiarity, unleashed by *jouissance*. It's not that the birds *mean* homosexuality, but that homosexuality necessarily shapes the ways in which the birds mean for a culture that assigns it the negativising burden of sexuality itself: sexuality, that is, as *sinthome*, as always *sinthome*-osexuality, sexuality as that force that threatens to leave futurity *foutú*. In the 'monotonous low hum', the 'artificial' sound with which Hitchcock ends the film, we hear, if not the siren song, then the bird call of futurity. The engine revs; the machine purrs on; the family drives through danger. Somewhere, someone else will be savagely beaten and left to die – sacrificed to a future whose beat goes on, like a pulse or a heart – and another corpse will be left like a makeshift scarecrow to scare off the birds that, as scary as anything Hitchcock conceived, beat their wings and keep on coming.

Notes

1 Sylvia Ann Hewlett and Cornel West, 'For Mothers, It's No Paradise', *The Boston Sunday Globe*, 10 May 1998, C7. My quarrel with this article, I want to make clear, is not a quarrel with the particular suggestions offered for improving the lives of underpaid working women and mothers; it is a quarrel, instead, with the ideology the authors invoke in order to naturalise and promote those suggestions.

2 Bruce Fink, *A Clinical Introduction to Lacanian Psychoanalysis: Theory and Technique*, Cambridge, MA: Harvard University Press, 1997, p. 211.

3 'Murder Charges Planned in Beating Death of Gay Student', 12 October 1998, CNN Interactive, *http://www/cnn.com/US/9810/12/wyoming.attack.03.*

4 It is worth noting, in this context, that less than two weeks after Shepard's murder, the *New York Times* reported on an effort in Fort Collins, Colorado (where the hospital in which Shepard died was located) to list sexual orientation as a protected category in its anti-discrimination ordinance. The article included the following sentence describing one of the responses provoked by the distribution of materials supporting that addition to the law: ' "I was handing out stickers on a parade route, and one boy held out his hand for one," recalled Bob Lenk, spokesman for the group promoting the ordinance change. 'His mother said, "You put that on him and I'll break your arm." ' James Brooke, 'Anti-Bias Effort Roils City Where Gay Man Died', *New York Times*, 28 October 1998, A16.

5 James Brooke, 'Gay Man Dies from Attack, Fanning Outrage and Debate', *New York Times*, 13 October 1998 late edition, p. A17.

6 Consider, for example, the following passage, which appeared in 'i.e.', an on-line web magazine published by the Family Research Council the same month that Matthew Shepard was killed: 'Homosexuality is not merely about a harmless personal preference. It is about a lifestyle that involves having sex with another person of the same gender. More often than anyone would like to admit, it's about promiscuity – and even violence. It is about unnatural, unsafe, and unhealthy behavior.' Laurel L. Cornell,

'Coming Out of Homosexuality: What's This All About', October 1998, http://www.frc.org/ie/ie98j.html.

7 Alfred Hitchcock, 'It's a Bird, It's a Plane, It's . . . *The Birds*', originally published in *Take One* 1, no. 10, 1968, pp. 6–7; reprinted in *Hitchcock on Hitchcock*, Sidney Gottlieb (ed.), Berkeley: University of California Press, 1995, p. 315.

8 Alfred Hitchcock, interviewed in 'Just One Hitch', also cited by Camille Paglia, *The Birds* London: BFI: 1998, p. 88.

9 Robin Wood, 'The Birds', in *Hitchcock's Films Revisited,* New York: Columbia University Press, 1989, p. 153.

10 Wood, 'The Birds', p. 154.

11 That birthday celebrations are, in general, marked by this ideology of reproductive necessity finds telling reinforcement from a casual sentence that appeared, in a wholly unrelated context, in the pages of the *New York Times*. Evoking the genocidal terror enforced in Cambodia by Pol Pot's Khmer Rouge, an article on Cambodian photography during the years of that brutal dictatorship begins by distinguishing between the photographic record left by that regime and the uses to which photography is normally put in the social relations of the Western world: 'There are no wedding pictures here. No babies. No birthdays' (Seth Mydans, 'Khmer Rouge Photography: Smiles Were Rare', *New York Times*, Sunday, 24 January 1999, section 4, p. 5). The trajectory evoked is precisely that of the organising (and heterosexually insistent) narrative logic that shapes the connection for us between meaning and subjectivity. While the fact that Cathy's eleventh birthday might, then, be construed as marking the onset of sexual maturation (a possibility that would be reinforced by her desire for lovebirds as a gift), my point is not that this birthday *in particular* asserts the elaboration of subjectivity in relation to a reproductive imperative, but rather that birthday rituals as such reinforce the indissociability of subjectivity from an investment in the necessity of reproduction.

12 The vision of the child here is heartening, of course, not only because it substitutes the 'innocent' child for the 'lecherous' adult, thus purging heterosexuality of the messiness of sex through a form of metaleptic reversal in which cause is replaced by effect, but also because the child, though displacing the heterosexual male adult, is reassuringly heterosexualised even at the moment of this displacement.

13 In the so-called final version of the script, Annie Hayworth, when she admits to Melanie her own unhappy history with Mitch, delivers a speech, not included in the film, that evokes her commitment to the children she teaches in Bodega Bay, describing them as the source of meaning in her life, indeed, as her *raison d'être*: 'I'll go into that classroom on Monday morning, and I'll look out at twenty-five upturned little faces, and each of them will be saying, "Yes, tell me. Yes, please give me what you have." [pause] And I'll give them what I have. I haven't got very much, but I'll give them every ounce of it. To me, that's very important. It makes me want to stay alive for a long long time.' (*The Birds*, script by Evan Hunter, 26 January 1962, shot sequence 202.)

14 Donald Spoto, *The Dark Side of Genius: The Life of Alfred Hitchcock,* New York: Ballantine Books, 1983, p. 474.

15 *The Music Man*, words and lyrics by Meredith Wilson, opened on Broadway in 1957 and was released as a film in 1962.

16 Mrs Bundy, echoing Norman Bates, says to Melanie in The Tides: 'Birds are not aggressive creatures, Miss. They bring beauty to the world.' This might call to mind a similar assessment of another type of airy creature: 'Oh Mary, it takes a fairy to make something pretty,' as Emory announces in Malcolm Crowley's play, *The Boys in the Band.*

17 See under 'bird' in the Random House *Dictionary of the English Language*, 2nd edn, unabridged, definition 4: '*Slang.* a person, esp. one having some peculiarity: *He's a queer bird*'.

18 Judith Butler, *Gender Trouble: Feminism and the Subversion of Identity*, New York: Routledge, 1990, pp. 5, 35–78, and 151 n. 6; Susan Lurie, 'The Construction of the "Castrated" Woman in Psychoanalysis and Cinema', *Discourse*, no. 4, winter 1981, pp. 52–74; Slavoj Žižek, 'Les Oiseaux: Le surmoi maternel', in *Tout ce que vous avez toujours voulu savoir sur Lacan sans jamais oser le demander à Hitchcock*, Slavoj Žižek (ed.), Paris: Navarin Éditeur, 1988, pp. 197–207. Both Lurie's and Žižek's articles are powerfully important interventions in the critical debate around *The Birds.* My point is not to diminish their value, but to locate the heterosexualising binarism on which the effort to read the filmic text so frequently founders.

19 Evan Hunter, the screenwriter for *The Birds*, recalls what happened when Hitchcock announced his promotional slogan to the advertising staff at Universal:

> 'Gentlemen,' he said, 'here's how we'll announce the movie. Are you ready?'
>
> There was a moment of suspenseful silence, the master at work. Spreading his hands wide in the air, Hitch said, '*The Birds* is coming!'
>
> It was pure genius. A seemingly ungrammatical catchphrase that combined humor and suspense.
>
> One of Universal's young advertising Turks said, 'Excuse me, Mr Hitchcock, sir?'
>
> Hitch turned to him.
>
> 'Don't you mean "The birds *are* coming", sir?'
>
> *Me and Hitch,* Boston: Faber & Faber, 1997, pp. 76–7

20 Falling from the chimney like dirt or shit, like parodic reversals of Santa Claus with his less desublimated gifts, these birds enact Hitchcock's charged but phobic fantasy about uncleanliness and waste. The salesman in The Tides will excoriate birds in general as 'messy' creatures and the metalepsis that reads the birds, the source of waste that drops from the sky, as a trope of waste themselves (dropping out of the sky and into visibility in the film), is central to Hitchcock's text. Spoofing *The Birds* in *High Anxiety* (1977), Mel Brooks understood this intuitively as he graphically depicted the plague of birds as producing a plague of shit. Hitchcock, of course, could never bear to contemplate a vision of filth other than metaphorically – and the moment in *The Birds* when that violation of order and cleanliness is figured most effectively is the famous shot where Hitchcock, in close-up, shows us the finger of Melanie's glove stained with a drop of dark blood. This horror of uncleanliness, however, appears throughout the film, as in Lydia's obsessive desire to maintain the semblance of domestic order, for example, or in the song sung by the schoolchildren that centres on the uncleanliness of the nameless 'wife' who 'combed her hair but once a year'. For a fuller consideration of

Hitchcock's relation to questions of waste and anality, see my essays 'Piss Elegant: Freud, Hitchcock, and the Micturating Penis', *GLQ: A Journal of Lesbian and Gay Studies*, 2, nos. 1–2, 1995, pp. 149–77 and '*Rear Window*'s Glasshole', in *Out-Takes: Essays on Queer Theory and Film*, Ellis Hanson (ed.), Durham: Duke University Press, 1999, pp. 72–96.

21 That notion of coming as coming apart will be represented most clearly in the fate of Melanie Daniels who suffers her psychological breakdown, her dissociation from symbolic meaning, as a result of her decision to remain in Bodega Bay for Cathy's party. Perhaps, in this context, it is useful to recall the words with which Cathy appealed to Melanie to join her at the party: 'Oh, won't you come? Won't you please come?'

22 Paul de Man, 'Conclusion: Walter Benjamin's "The Task of the Translator" ', in *The Resistance to Theory*, Minneapolis: University of Minnesota Press, 1986, p. 92.

23 De Man, 'Conclusion', p. 92.

24 Paul de Man, *The Rhetoric of Romanticism*, New York: Columbia University Press, 1984, p. 268.

25 My use of the term 'heterosexualising' does not intend to suggest that these narratives, in any simple, unmediated way, produce the heterosexual desire within which particular subjects locate the specificity of their erotic investments; rather, I want to argue that these narratives produce heterosexuality as the dominant mode of ideological self-recognition *for heterosexual and non-heterosexual subjects alike.* They set forth the logic that enables the subject to imagine its own reality, affording a social trajectory that polices the possibilities for alternative experiences, by establishing a narrative template that articulates reality as the arena for a mandatory movement toward the subject's 'realisation', a movement that both presupposes and procures a fundamental allegiance to futurity.

26 For a superb and profoundly influential analysis of the anti-communalism of eros, see Leo Bersani's *Homos*, Cambridge, MA: Harvard University Press, 1995, esp. pp. 151–81.

27 Paul de Man, 'Shelley Disfigured', in *The Rhetoric of Romanticism*, p. 117.

28 Marcel Proust, *In Search of Lost Time*, volume IV, trans. C. Scott Moncrieff and Terence Kilmartin, revised by D. J. Enright, New York: The Modern Library, 1993, p. 8.

29 Robin Wood, 'Retrospective,' in *A Hitchcock Reader*, Marshall Deutelbaum and Leland Poague (eds.), Ames, Iowa: Iowa State University Press, 1986, pp. 39–40.

30 It is surely not insignificant that this sequence ends after Melanie and Cathy, having rescued a girl knocked down by savage crows, lead her to the shelter of an unlocked automobile. Cars and driving have been, and will be, a recurrent image in the film – the image, as I will go on to suggest, of the persistence of drive itself. One might also consider how the editing of this sequence alludes to Eisenstein's famous montage of the Odessa Steps in *Potemkin*, which also manipulates its audience by depicting a threat to an infant or child.

31 Jean Laplanche, *Life and Death in Psychoanalysis*, trans. Jeffrey Mehlman, Baltimore: Johns Hopkins University Press, 1985, p. 124.

32 Alan Keyes, *The Alan Keyes Show*, radio transcript from Friday, 10 July 1998, http://alankeyes.com/071098.html.

33 Lauren Berlant, *The Queen of America Goes to Washington City*, Durham: Duke University Press, 1997, p. 73.

34 Ken Worthy, *The Homosexual Generation*, New York: L. S. Publications, Inc., 1965, p. 184.

35 François Truffaut, *Hitchcock*, rev. edn, New York: Simon and Schuster, 1985, p. 297.

36 Slavoj Žižek, *Looking Awry: An Introduction to Jacques Lacan through Popular Culture*, Cambridge, MA: MIT Press, 1991, p. 99.

37 Worthy, *The Homosexual Generation*, p. 44.

38 Not only for his eagle-eye where sartorial style is concerned, but also for his exemplary insights into Hitchcock's style more generally, I am delighted to express deep gratitude for my ongoing conversations with D. A. Miller.

39 Keyes, *The Alan Keyes Show*, 10 July 1998.

PART IV
Culture, Politics, Ideology

Shadow of a Doubt – Teresa Wright in Hitchcock's noir with a difference

Chapter 17
Hitchcock at the Margins of *Noir*

James Naremore

The discourse on *film noir* belongs largely to 'postmodernist' culture, but it seems preoccupied with 'modernist' values, particularly in a series of Hollywood thrillers or bloody melodramas from the 1940s and 1950s. The pictures it names are a heterogeneous group, dealing with everything from hard-boiled detectives (*The Maltese Falcon*, 1941) to bourgeois women in distress (*Caught*, 1949), from love on the run (*Gun Crazy*, 1949) to foreign intrigue (*The Mask of Dimitrios*, 1944), from costume melodrama (*Reign of Terror*, 1949) to western adventure (*Pursued*, 1947), and from sleek eroticism (*Gilda*, 1946) to naturalistic social satire (*Sweet Smell of Success*, 1957). Even so, we can make a few generalisations about them. Considered generically, they involve what Jean-Paul Sartre called 'extreme situations' and are usually located in a realistic realm to one side of Gothic horror and dystopian science fiction. Stylistically, they tend to be associated with angular photography, subjective modes of narration, and an approximately Freudian or deterministic view of character. Commercially, they blur the distinction between violent melodramas and art movies.

Why, then, does the literature on *film noir* have so little to say about Alfred Hitchcock? Much of his work would seem at first glance to belong somewhere within the broad category I've just described, and yet Alain Silver and Elizabeth Ward's *Film Noir: An Encyclopedic Reference to the American Style* gives detailed treatment only to *Notorious* (1946), *Shadow of a Doubt* (1943), *Strangers on a Train* (1951) and *The Wrong Man* (1957).[1] Patrick Brion's lavishly illustrated coffee-table reference, *Le film noir*, includes all of these plus *Rebecca* (1940), *Suspicion* (1941), *Vertigo* (1958) and, in more qualified fashion, *North by Northwest* (1959).[2] (If the last, why not virtually everything else?) Critical studies of *noir*, with the notable exception of Foster Hirsch's *Film Noir: The Dark Side of the Screen*, usually mention Hitchcock briefly or in passing, and writings on Hitchcock as an *auteur* seldom deploy the idea of *noir*. Slavoj Žižek's brilliant essay, 'In His Bold Gaze My Ruin is Writ Large', even goes so far as to argue that 'Hitchcock's universe is ultimately incompatible with that of the *film noir*'.[3] Few critics would take such a radical position, but even when they acknowledge Hitchcock's importance to the so-called *noir* movement or genre, they often describe him as *sui generis* or a 'strange case'.

This tendency can be traced back to the very origins of critical writing on American *film noir*. The French cineastes who created the category (which has less to do with a body of artifacts than with a set of values that determine how certain films will be read) recognised from the beginning that Hitchcock was one of its practitioners, but they spoke about him in qualified or tangential ways. Consider, for example, Nino Frank, the Parisian critic who is often regarded as the first person to apply the term '*noir*' to

American movies. Frank's influential essay on the topic, originally published in a 1946 issue of *L'Écran français*, is chiefly concerned with a series of 'criminal adventures' released in France slightly after World War II: *The Maltese Falcon*, *Double Indemnity* (1944), *Laura* (1944) and *Murder, My Sweet* (1944). In the course of the essay, Frank observes parenthetically that Hitchcock's *Suspicion* belongs at least technically in the same group as the others; it, too, is a literary adaptation, inspired by an 'admirable novel by Francis Iles', and it emphasises criminal psychology rather than mystery or detection. In Frank's opinion, however, *Suspicion* is an 'absolute failure'.[4] Apparently Frank was in agreement with Billy Wilder, who, just prior to the release of *Double Indemnity*, had publicly declared his intention to 'out-Hitchcock Hitchcock'.

Raymond Borde and Étienne Chaumeton's groundbreaking historical study, *Panorama du film noir americain (1941–53)*, makes a roughly similar argument, situating Hitchcock at the borders of 'true' Hollywood *noir*, which Borde and Chaumeton regard as a quasi-surrealistic form determined by an American social and cultural context. Hitchcock's pre-war British films (particularly *The 39 Steps*, 1933; *Sabotage*, 1936; and *Jamaica Inn*, 1939) strike Borde and Chaumeton as a 'feeble' influence on the American style.[5] In their view, *Rebecca* and *Suspicion* are formative pictures in an emerging *noir* series, but *Spellbound* (1945), which takes a somewhat clinical approach to psychoanalysis, is closer in spirit to a social-problem picture like Anatole Litvak's *Snake Pit* (1948). *Shadow of a Doubt*, on the other hand, is a 'major work', helping to shape a new, distinctively American style of dark movies about attractive killers and morally ambiguous protagonists. After the war, during what Borde and Chaumeton describe as the 'grand epoch' of *noir* (1946–8), three of Hitchcock's productions – *Notorious*, *The Paradine Case* (1947) and *Rope* (1948) – can be termed *noir* 'in different degrees'.[6] The most *noir*-like of these pictures, Borde and Chaumeton argue, is *Notorious*, a powerfully oneiric and erotic melodrama (not unlike Charles Vidor's *Gilda*) which demonstrates an acute sense of the surreal quality in such ordinary objects as a wine bottle, a door key and a coffee cup. Next in line is *The Paradine Case*, a 'good documentary about English justice', distinguished mainly by its ironic courtroom scenes, which are worthy of comparison with Carl Dreyer's *Joan of Arc* (1928), Mervyn LeRoy's *They Won't Forget* (1937), and Orson Welles's *Lady from Shanghai* (1948). As for *Rope*, Borde and Chaumeton say that it belongs in company with other dark films chiefly by virtue of its emphasis on 'gratuitous crime', 'criminal psychology' and 'spellbinding sadism'.[7] They also note that in the last, 'decadent' phase of the *noir* cycle (1949–50), Hitchcock produced *Under Capricorn* (1949), a darkly psychological costume picture blending the technical experiments of *Rope* with the Gothic romanticism of his early films with Selznick. At the end of the period, however, he directed a 'masterpiece', *Strangers on a Train*, based on a *roman noir* by Patricia Highsmith. In this film, according to Borde and Chaumeton, 'all the essential elements of the *noir* genre [oniericism, Gothicism, eroticism, ambiguity and cruelty] are met with again, mixed in an original cocktail that doesn't lack humor'.[8]

Borde and Chaumeton's influential commentary may account for the fact that in subsequent writings about *noir*, *Shadow of a Doubt*, *Notorious* and *Strangers on a Train* are the most frequently cited pictures by Hitchcock. Given the particular values that Borde and Chaumeton emphasise, however, there seems no good reason why we can't describe virtually every Hitchcock movie, or any reasonably 'adult' picture about murder or criminal adventure produced in America from the late 1930s until the present day, as a *film noir*. In *Panorama* and most other places, '*noir*' is simply the name for modernist, European-influenced crime stories that convey some degree of scepticism toward established institutions, and that involve subjective narration, psychologically 'deep' views of character and an eroticised treatment of violence. Hitchcock was manifestly important to the history of such a form. His pre-Hollywood thrillers have something in common with the German-expressionist crime cinema of the 1920s and the surrealist-inspired French *films noirs* of the 1930s; his American career begins at almost the same moment as the so-called classic or historical period of Hollywood *noir*; one of his close associates, Joan Harrison, was the producer of Robert Siodmak's *Phantom Lady* (1944) and other canonical *films noirs* of the 1940s; and several of the 'original' American movies in the category, including *The Maltese Falcon* and *Double Indemnity*, were explicitly compared to his British work by contemporary reviewers. More importantly, we can find a great many of Hitchcock's signature themes or motifs in what we usually regard as 'true' *films noirs*. The wrong-man plot, for example, is central to *The Blue Dahlia* (1946) and *The Big Clock* (1948), and the rear-window motif can be seen in *Pushover* (1954) and *Killer's Kiss* (1946). Notice also that several of Hitchcock's most memorable characters are anticipated by definitive examples of the *film noir*: Mark Macpherson in Otto Preminger's *Laura* (1944), like John 'Scottie' Ferguson in *Vertigo*, is a hard-headed detective of Scottish ancestry who is haunted by the image of an aristocratic woman; Ralph Hughes in Joseph H. Lewis's *My Name Is Julia Ross* (1945), like Bruno Anthony in *Strangers on a Train*, is a psychopathic killer who is excessively attached to his dotty mother; and Al Roberts in Edgar G. Ulmer's *Detour* (1945), like Marion Crane in *Psycho* (1960), is an obsessive-compulsive who drives by night across an American wasteland, ultimately encountering violence and death in a cheap motel.

In my own view, the two most impressive Hollywood directors in the 1940s and 1950s were Hitchcock and Orson Welles, who seemed equally attuned to a *noir*ish repertory of situations and images. As many critics have observed, the inquisitive camera movements at the openings of *Rebecca* and *Citizen Kane* (1941) echo one another, as do the closing shots of the burning 'R' and the burning 'Rosebud'. (Here we might remember that Welles adapted both *The 39 Steps* and *Rebecca* on the radio in 1938, and that David Selznick wanted the movie version of the DuMaurier novel to resemble the Welles broadcast.) Welles's production of *Journey Into Fear* is influenced by Hitchcock's espionage movies of the 1930s, particularly in its clever blending of comedy and menace, and his production of *The Stranger* (1946), despite its political theme, is influenced by *Shadow of a Doubt*. Welles experimented with the wrong-man or 'exchange-of-guilt' story on several occasions, most notably in *The Trial* (1962) and *The Lady from Shanghai*, both of which also contain a good many absurdist jokes reminiscent of Hitchcock (as when Michael O'Hara escapes from his trial for murder by walking out of the courtroom among the jurors). Last but not least, *Touch of Evil* (1958) anticipates *Psycho* in many ways, especially in the motel scenes between Janet Leigh and Dennis Weaver.

If both Hitchcock and Welles are not totally subsumed under the rubric of *film noir*, that is partly because of the different questions we ask when we study individual films or artists as opposed to signifying systems, and partly because of the way the name of the author functions in relation to the name of the genre. We should recall that American *film noir* became important to international film criticism during the heyday of the French *auteurist* movement, when new-wave productions were often based on *série-noire* thrillers, and when the best writing about movies attempted to reveal a surplus of personal meaning. In the case of Welles, whose reputation was founded on unorthodox projects such as *Citizen Kane* and *The Magnificent Ambersons* (1942), it was quite easy to show that individual style transcended generic formulas. Hitchcock, however, was another matter. Despite the fact that he made a variety of films during his long career, few major directors have been so exclusively connected with a specific type of movie. (C. B. DeMille was known for biblical epics, John Ford for westerns and Vincente Minnelli for musicals, but even these figures were not completely synonymous with a genre.) Thus Hitchcock became one of the great tests of the *auteur* theory and a kind of genre unto himself. A paradoxical figure, he was described as the 'master of suspense' who used formulas as a mere pretext; as the Hollywood professional who, in the words of Gilles Deleuze, appeared 'at the juncture of the two cinemas, the classic that he perfects and the modern that he prepares'; and as the *noir* director who was somehow an exception to the rule.

And yet Hitchcock's off-centre position in the pantheon of *noir* can't be explained entirely on the basis of *auteurist* reception or the reluctance of certain critics to see him in relation to the cultural, industrial and historical trends of his day. There are, I would suggest, intrinsic qualities of subject matter, tone and style that make his films appear slightly alien to the *noir* universe – especially when we think of *noir* as a phenomenon produced by Hollywood in the 1940s and 1950s. If we define *noir* in terms of a prototypical series of crime pictures from the rather narrow historical context of post-World War II Hollywood, we can use the concept as a kind of foil, bringing certain distinctive qualities of Hitchcock's 'world' into bold relief. By way of illustration, let me devote the remainder of this essay to a discussion of four aspects of Hitchcock's work that seem to me to constitute some of his most specific and least '*noir*-like' traits.

Britishness

The idea of *film noir* can be traced back to the French poetic–realist cinema of the 1930s, and more particularly to French intellectual culture of the *avant-guerre*. In the years immediately after World War II, however, French critics strongly associated *noir* with the hard-boiled or 'tabloid–realist' school of American literature. Most of the Hollywood pictures they admired featured tough-guy protagonists in business suits who moved fairly comfortably among the proletariat and the urban underworld. (This is true even of *Laura*, in which Dana Andrews's working-class policeman is vividly contrasted with Clifton Webb's Park Avenue aesthete.) Hitchcock never explored such materials, nor did he deal with the theme of existential angst that French critics sometimes extrapolated from Bogart thrillers. At one point he attempted to hire Dashiell Hammett as screenwriter for *Strangers on a Train*, and he eventually offered the job to Raymond Chandler; but he found Chandler's work so disappointing that he rewrote the entire film in collaboration with a woman screenwriter, Cenzie Ormond. Although he sometimes used seamy, low-rent settings (as in parts of *Shadow of a Doubt*, *The Wrong Man* and *Psycho*), most of his films took place in a prosperous, virtually all-white milieu that was characterised, at least outwardly, by a feeling of whimsy, sophistication and good manners – in other words, by qualities that the typical American associated with upper-class 'Britishness'.

Despite or perhaps because of his Cockney origins, Hitchcock's carefully constructed public image was almost a parody of British reserve. His first American work was done under contract with David Selznick, an Anglophile producer whose studio was modelled on the homes of the WASP aristocracy, and at the end of his career he became 'Sir Alfred' when he was knighted by Queen Elizabeth. Hitchcock often satirised the gentry by placing comments about them in the mouths of charming rogues – nowhere more so than in *Rebecca*, in which Jack Favell, a suave scoundrel who makes his living as a 'motor-car salesman', climbs into the back seat of Maxim de Winter's limousine, munches a chicken leg with one hand and smokes a cigarette with the other, and speculates on what it would be like to 'live comfortably without working'. (Later, Favell accuses DeWinter and the other leaders of the community of behaving like a 'trades union'.) In both the Selznick period and afterward, however, Hitchcock's distinctive 'world' looked polite and relatively well-to-do, if only because he repeatedly used actors who spoke with cultivated British or mid-Atlantic accents (Laurence Olivier, George Sanders, Cary Grant, Claude Rains, Louis Calhern, Charles Laughton, Ray Milland, Grace Kelly, Cedric Hardwick, John Forsythe, Edmund Gwynne, James Mason, Leo G. Carrol, John Williams, etc.). By the same token, a great many of his Hollywood pictures were set in Britain, and in several cases he required American stars to imitate English characters: see, for example, Gregory Peck's awkward impersonation of a barrister in *The Paradine Case* (Hitchcock had wanted to cast Olivier or Ronald Colman) and Jane Wyman's only slightly more convincing portrayal of a RADA student who works as a lady's maid in *Stage Fright*.

The rather ersatz, postcard view of England we find in Hitchcock's American features is in one sense quite typical of Hollywood's A-budget productions in the classic period, and is no doubt a symptom of both American fantasy and Beverly Hills snobbery. To some extent, it has less to do with Hitchcock himself than with the industry in which he worked, and with the commercial value of promoting the director as an English eccentric. It must be emphasised, however, that 'Britishness' had great dramatic advantages for Hitchcock, enabling him to intensify one of his most important effects: the feeling of repressed anxiety or violence breaking through a well-ordered surface. Notice also that Hitchcock's rather mannered and artificial settings, which create what he liked to call a 'counterpoint' between the civilised and the sordid, tend to reverse the priorities of hard-boiled *film noir*. In Chandleresque classics such as *The Big Sleep* (1946) or *Murder, My Sweet*, we always sense a fascination with 'the dark side of town'. The world in these films is *manifestly* corrupt, pervaded by Baudelairian decadence, expressionist gloom and *nostalgie de la boue*. In Hitchcock, by contrast, the world is often calm and well lit, and when we glimpse the gutter it has terror but no romantic fascination.

All this may help to explain why, on the few occasions when Hitchcock uses the outward paraphernalia of the hard-boiled thriller, he works against our expectations of the genre. The early scenes of *Shadow of a Doubt* show a dreary rented room and an urban alleyway; but the film soon changes its locale, becoming the study of a patrician killer who visits a polite family in small-town America. The first half of *Psycho* offers a virtual survey of *noir* settings, including a cheap hotel, an insurance office, a used-car lot, a nocturnal drive and a neon-lit motel; but the second half looks more like a cross between a provincial melodrama and a James Whale horror movie. Even more remarkable is *The Wrong Man*, one of the most underrated and least 'British' of Hitchcock's films. Like *Call Northside 777* (1948) and several other police-procedurals from the 1940s and 1950s, this picture is photographed at the actual scene of a 'true crime', and it contains many stylistic or iconographic features we associate with classical *noir*: black-and-white film stock; night-for-night exteriors; deep-focus perspectives; radical camera angles; cops and criminals who wear overcoats and snap-brim hats; a sleek Manhattan nightclub where people dance the rhumba; a seedy police station; a courtroom; a dilapidated rooming house; a psychiatrist's office, etc. And yet Hitchcock subtly undermines or deflates all the hard-boiled conventions he employs. As Jean-Luc Godard remarks in his superb commentary on *The Wrong Man* (one of the longest critical essays Godard ever wrote), Manny Balestero's lawyer only 'play[s] at being the Perry Mason of Stanley Gardner's novels', and Manny himself suffers from 'semi-inertia and [a] taste for playing – like the bourgeois family in *Shadow of a Doubt* – the detective of thrillerdom'. The police and the frightened women at Manny's insurance company may think they inhabit a *film noir*, but they are obviously wrong. Even though Manny fits one of the stereotypical images of the Hollywood gangster (an Italian-American musician who works in a nightclub), he is in fact an idealised and curiously passive paterfamilias who has exceedingly regular habits. The true terror of the film arises not from violence in the 'naked city', but from an ever-present economic anxiety that helps to determine an undramatic madness at the core of Manny's family life. One of the chief ironies of *The Wrong Man*, as Renata Salecl has observed, lies in the fact that the criminal atmosphere and the documentary treatment of justice are little more than catalysts for a deeper trauma – a depression that afflicts Rose Balestero from the beginning of the film, and that ultimately overtakes her completely.[10] As Godard puts it, *The Wrong Man* differs from the usual Hitchcock suspense story in that 'what one was afraid of happening does not finally happen'.[11] What *does* happen, however, is equally terrible to contemplate. A title card at the end of the picture assures us that Rose has recovered, but we never see her restored to health. *The Wrong Man* is less about crime and punishment than about the breakdown of a fragile, lower middle-class marriage under the pressure of debt and patriarchy, and the slow descent of one of its members into an unglamorous, psychological darkness. One of the bleakest movies ever produced in Hollywood, it leaves us with a far more downbeat impression than the usual *film noir*.

Suspense and classical form

Borde and Chaumeton define *film noir* on the basis of affective qualities that 'disorient' the spectator and remove the 'psychological guideposts' of classic narrative. Hitchcock deals in these qualities (eroticism, perverse violence, moral ambiguity, etc.), but, as everyone recognises, the overriding aim of most of his pictures is to create suspense. As a result, he depends more upon clarity than upon disorientation. Compared to his work, *films noirs* such as *The Big Sleep*, *The Lady from Shanghai*, *The Big Heat* (1953), *Gun Crazy* and *Kiss Me Deadly* (1955) seem murky, confusing and not at all suspenseful; indeed the *film noir* is usually admired by critics precisely because it dispenses with logical coherence, elevating 'mood' or 'tone' over plot. The very term '*noir*', as David Bordwell has pointed out, functions to describe 'patterns of nonconformity' within the classical system, chief among them a tendency to complicate the spatial, temporal and moral coordinates of narrative.[12] Hitchcock does not quite fit this model, or at least his nonconformity manifests itself in different ways. For all his interest in absurd or improbable situations, he never devalues classical narrative and never allows what Roland Barthes called the semic, cultural and symbolic codes to predominate over the hermeneutic and proaeratic. 'I am against virtuosity for its own sake,' he tells Truffaut during their interview. 'The beauty of image and movement, the rhythm and the effects – everything must be subordinated to the purpose.'[13] And the 'purpose' is usually a feeling of anxious waiting, which is created by a lucid, relentless logic of narrative exposition.

Hitchcock's images are composed with the directness and simplicity of a storyboard or a cartoon, and their sequential organisation is intended to lead the audience step by step through the action, providing exactly the information that will condition their response. For example, the American remake of *The Man Who Knew Too Much* (1956) goes to elaborate lengths to prepare viewers for the climactic Albert Hall sequence: at the end of the credits it shows a set of cymbals and announces that musical instruments are going to change a family's life; later it shows the villains listening *twice* to a recording in which a crucial passage of music is punctuated by a crash of cymbals; and finally, at the concert, it pans across a sheet of music and stops on the single note that will be played by the cymbalist. Recalling the film in his interview with Truffaut, Hitchcock comments that 'ideally, for that scene to have maximum effect, all of the viewers should be able to read a musical score'. He also describes the great pains he took to establish key points: 'In the audience,' he remarks, 'there are probably many people who don't even know what cymbals are, and so it was necessary not only to show them but even to spell the word. It was also important that the public be able not only to recognize the sound of the cymbals but to anticipate it in their minds. Knowing what to expect, they wait for it to happen'.[14]

At every juncture, the audience in a Hitchcock film is made keenly aware of the various possibilities or logical paths of the narrative. 'I've often found,' he tells Truffaut, 'that a suspense situation is weakened because the action is not sufficiently clear. For instance, if two actors should happen to be wearing similar suits, the viewer can't tell one from the other; if the location is not clearly established, the viewer may be wondering where the action is taking place ... So it's important to be explicit, to clarify constantly'.[15] It follows from this concern that the 'look' of a Hitchcock picture is less shadowy and prone to optical distortions than the prototypical examples of Hollywood *noir*. Significantly, Hitchcock was one of the first directors of murder stories to experiment with colour, a medium that makes expressionist lighting less necessary; and in his black-and-white films he often stages horrific situations in broad daylight or in bright interiors without dramatically cast shadows. Except for a few shots in *Strangers on a Train* and *The Wrong Man*, he avoids the extreme wide-angle, deep-focus perspectives or bizarrely out-of-kilter compositions that are typical of a director like Orson Welles or a photographer like John Alton. By the same token, he makes relatively few films involving flashbacks (*Spellbound*, *I Confess* (1952), *Stage Fright* (1950) and *Marnie* (1964) are the chief examples), and the emotional texture of his most popular work is more like a thrill ride or a slowly rising anxiety than a poetic–realist meditation on the dark past. Perhaps most importantly, his American work seldom bears the marks of poverty. Not until *Psycho* did he produce a film in the B-picture style often associated (accurately or not) with the *noir* sensibility. On the contrary, he made his reputation in Hollywood as a director of high-end productions – glamorous, star-filled movies that were manufactured as solidly, cleanly and expensively as a Rolls-Royce.

Because of his desire to play games of suspense, Hitchcock is concerned with symmetrical design, straightforward narrative logic and classical editing. Even when he makes a supposedly authentic *film noir* such as *Strangers on a Train*, he remains committed to classical *découpage*, and the total effect is less a repudiation of the dominant Hollywood style than a triumphant illustration of its fundamental tenants. How appropriate that the chief formal device of *Strangers*, a film in which the motif of the 'double' is so obvious, is parallel editing. The spectacular climax involves exactly the kind of suspenseful cross-cutting that was first perfected by D. W. Griffith – although Hitchcock intensifies the power of the technique with an elaborate pattern of visual or graphic conflicts worthy of Eisenstein. First we see a close shot of Guy Haines, dressed in sporting whites and violently swinging a tennis racquet on a grassy, sunlit playing field; then we see a close shot of Bruno Anthony, dressed in a grey business suit and trying to retrieve a lost cigarette lighter from the shadowy recesses of a city storm drain. Each character is racing against the clock, but the motions of Guy's arm are large and sweeping, whereas the movements of Bruno's hand are small and measured. The most unorthodox element of this brilliant sequence lies not in its form, but in Hitchcock's sly willingness to reveal that everything is in one sense pointless, founded on a formal technique or a trick. At the end of each character's desperate effort to achieve a goal – after Guy has won the tennis match and Bruno has retrieved the lighter – the audience realises that its anxiety has been slightly in excess of the real situation. Despite all the urgency of the scenes we have been watching, a great deal of time remains left on the clock. Bruno can't plant the incriminating evidence against Guy until the sun goes down, so he has to sit and wait for an hour or two at an empty carnival while Guy rushes to meet him.

Woman and mass culture

The American *film noir* is for the most part a masculine form of entertainment, built on a kind of ambivalence about sexual romance to which Hitchcock has a complex, dissonant and in some ways contradictory relationship. To make this point clear, I need to elaborate somewhat, first by emphasising that most of the films initially described as *noir* were shaped not only by male-oriented adventure fiction, but also by a longstanding misogynist ideology that developed within high modernism, and that often expressed itself through cultural debates over Hollywood. In *After the Great Divide* (1986), Andreas Huyssen convincingly argues that one of the salient characteristics of modernist art during the first half of the twentieth century was a hostility toward a sleek, Americanised, and supposedly 'feminine' mass culture. The male modernists who voiced this attitude were speaking not about proletarian literature or residual folk art, but about lending libraries, best-sellers, books-of-the-month, radio programs, Hollywood movies and all the products of the capitalist culture industries, which they repeatedly portrayed as appealing to shallow female consumers. As Huyssen observes, intellectual attacks on mechanically reproduced kitsch inevitably mingled with a misogynist discourse 'which time and again openly states its contempt for women and for the masses and which had Nietzsche as its most eloquent and influential representative'.[16]

Huyssen's argument needs to be qualified on two counts. First, some of the high modernists were feminists; and second, 'mass culture', which often functioned as modernism's debased 'other', was increasingly inflected by modernist aesthetics. Nowhere was the modernist influence on mass-produced art more evident than in pulp writers such as Hammett and Chandler, the 'fathers' of the *roman noir*, who were immediately recognised as literary innovators working in a popular field. Significantly, the hard-boiled school of detective fiction appeared at virtually the same moment as Ernest Hemingway's early short stories, and it was sponsored and praised by vanguard literary intellectuals. *Black Mask* magazine was partly owned by H. L. Mencken, America's leading 'man of letters' in the 1920s, who was an important commentator on Nietzsche and who later helped to launch the career of James M. Cain in *The American Mercury*. Edmund Wilson, the major American critic of the 1930s and the author of a famous book on high modernism (*Axel's Castle*), was a great booster of Hammett, Cain and the 'the boys in the back room'. Wilson's enthusiasm was hardly surprising, because the best of the pulp authors saw themselves as proponents of authentic culture and were explicitly critical of the feminine masses. For example, Raymond Chandler's literary manifesto, 'The Simple Art of Murder', was an attack on best-selling British novelists Agatha Christie and Dorothy Sayers, together with their supposedly female readers, who enjoyed a type of fiction that seemed to Chandler like 'a cup of luke-warm consomme at a spinsterish tea room'. Such gendered assaults on capitalism, Main Street America and the women consumers of pop culture were fairly typical in 'tough' fiction, and they were not greatly different from the ones we find in an overtly high-modernist and distinctly *noir*-like novel such as Nathanael West's *Miss Lonelyhearts*, which symbolises the voice of the public in the form of a vapid, sentimental and totally imaginary woman author of a newspaper advice column.

Similar attitudes can be found in the 1940s and 1950s cycle of films derived from the hard-boiled writers. These films are filled with techniques associated with modern art (expressionist lighting, dynamic camera angles, non-linear narratives, dream sequences, etc.), and, in keeping with the ideological agenda I've been describing, they openly criticise certain aspects of industrial modernity. As Mike Davis has pointed out in *City of Quartz* (1990), many of the classic *films noirs* can be understood as a deliberate reaction by intellectuals and European émigrés against Hollywood itself – particularly against the movie moguls, southern California power-brokers, and real-estate salesmen who promoted visions of a sunny utopia for the masses. In the classic *film noir*, however, the consumers and emblems of what Orson Welles called the 'bright, guilty world' usually turn out to be seductive females. One thinks of Phyllis Dietrichson, the black widow in *Double Indemnity*, who wears vulgar ankle bracelets and lacquered hair, and who plans murder in a supermarket; or of Elsa Bannister, the *femme fatale* in *The Lady from Shanghai*, who looks like a synthetic Hollywood pin-up, and who lures men to their death by singing a pop tune in a soft-focus close-up; or even of certain bit players, such as the silly but attractive hat-check girl in *In a Lonely Place*, who tells Bogart the story of the latest best-seller. These women are threatening to the somewhat proletarian male hero not simply because they are desirable, but because they represent capitalism – to love them or even to become romantically involved with them is to 'sell out', compromising one's values at the level of both sex and money.

Hitchcock does not fully participate in this attitude, even though he is a modernist director working in the popular arena. On the one hand, he has a rigorous, quasi-scientific temperament, and his films are strongly influenced by vanguard European art (especially by German expressionism, French surrealism and Soviet montage). By the 1940s, he had fully attained his reputation as a 'master', a term that connotes phallic power and control. But on the other hand, when he came to America the tone of his work changed, and he was accused by intellectuals of becoming slick and Hollywoodish. (This opinion was voiced by several British reviewers, and by such distinguished American critics as James Agee and Stanley Kauffman; it is also a minor theme in Raymond Durgnat's 1977 book on Hitchcock.) His early pictures in California (except for *Shadow of a Doubt*) lacked an 'authentic' social milieu and, to make matters worse, he was a practitioner of the female Gothic – a director who, in collaboration with Selznick, specialised in glossy, romantic, 'women's pictures'.

Again and again, Hitchcock invited his audience to identify with the point of view of women, and in films such as *Rebecca*, as Tania Modleski has observed, his adaptation of a 'feminine' best-seller constitutes 'a challenge to the male spectator's identity'.[17] Even in *The Paradine Case* (scripted by Selznick, with assistance from Hitchcock's wife, Alma Reville), in which we encounter a true *femme fatale*, the emotional or psychological effect is different from a hard-boiled detective story. Mrs Paradine is a remote beauty (Alida Valli) who coldly rejects the attentions of an infatuated investigator–barrister (Gregory Peck), but who suffers from her own *amour fou* in the form of a passionate attachment to a beautiful, rather androgynous groom on her blind husband's estate (Louis Jourdan). In many ways the scenario develops in *noir*-like fashion, so that the barrister's fascination with his treacherous client makes him seem ineffectual and masochistic, in vivid contrast to the sadistic old judge (Charles Laughton) who presides over the trial. Significantly, however, both the judge and the barrister have bourgeois marriages in which their wives play utterly subordinate roles. Mrs Paradine comes from a different world and is a different kind of wife; by openly voicing her sexual desire in a crowded courtroom, she not only humiliates the barrister but also threatens the social hierarchy of the film. 'My only comfort,' she says to her defender as she admits to a crime that will send her to the gallows, 'is in the hatred and contempt I feel for you.'

Perhaps because Hitchcock required his audience to identify with women, his complex manipulations of scopic and narrative pleasure, which reveal the underlying mechanisms of the 'sadistic gaze', have been crucial to the development of radical psychoanalytic theory, chiefly through Laura Mulvey's groundbreaking essays of the 1970s and 1980s.[18] Notice also that on the level of heterosexual romance, his work as a whole is open to quite un-*noir*-like interpretations – as in the first edition of Robin Wood's *Hitchcock's Films* (1965), which puts great emphasis on the moral or 'therapeutic' quality of Hitchcock's love stories, and in some parts of Raymond Durgnat's *The Strange Case of Alfred Hitchcock*, which points out that all but one or two of Hitchcock's movies can be seen as 'New Comedies'.[19] Durgnat's suggestion is greatly reinforced in the excellent studies of Hitchcock by Lesley Brill and Stanley Cavell, who view the director not in the context of dark thrillers, but in the context of utopian romance.[20]

Hitchcock celebrates the romantic union to a degree seldom found in *film noir*, where the threat of sexual relationships is palpable and in one sense deeply political. He nevertheless treats romance with an undercurrent of dark irony, and it is impossible to say with any certainty whether his repeated use of the woman's point of view was a product of his personal inclination or his commercial calculations. Throughout his career he had a tendency to represent female subjectivity on the screen; but from Selznick, and perhaps also from the dominant intellectual discourse of the 1930s and 1940s, he arrived at the conclusion that the audience for classic Hollywood entertainment was chiefly female, and that box-office success depended on satisfying women consumers. He says as much during his interview with Truffaut, at a point when the two men are engaged in a protracted debate over whether or not sex on the screen should be implicit (as in Hitchcock) or explicit (as in the *film noir*):

> FT: [M]y guess is that this is one aspect of your pictures that's probably more satisfying to the feminine viewers than to the male audience.
>
> AH: I'd like to point out that it's generally the woman who has the final say on which picture a couple is going to see. In fact, it's generally the woman who will decide, later on, whether it was a good or a bad picture.[21]

In an earlier encounter with André Bazin, Hitchcock seemed almost resentful of the female audience, who – according to him – lacked a taste for dark humour. Here is Bazin's summary of remarks by Hitchcock (mediated by an interpreter) on the set of *To Catch a Thief*: 'Hollywood films are made for women; it is toward their sentimental taste that scenarios are directed because it is they who account for the bulk of the box-office receipts. In England films are still made for men, but that is also why so many studios close down'.[22] Later in the same discussion, Hitchcock returned to the theme: 'Hitchcock appeared to me to be somewhat conventionally concerned with correcting [the] criticism of being commercial by affirming that it was easy to make an 'artistic' film but the real difficulty lay in making a good commercial film ... Such as it was, the sense of his first self-criticism was unequivocal and the necessity of renouncing adult, masculine humor in order to satisfy American producers was presented as exquisite torture'.[23]

Notice, too, that Hitchcock's films reveal a contempt for certain females – especially for rich American matrons such as the ones played by Gladys Cooper in *Rebecca*, Constance Collier in *Rope* and Marion Lorne in *Strangers on a Train*. (The charmingly witty exception is Jessie Royce Landis in *To Catch a Thief* (1955) and *North by Northwest*. (1959)) Moreover, the closer he comes to the prototypical atmosphere of American *film noir*, the more he treats women with derision. When Bruno Anthony almost strangles a society lady in *Strangers on a Train*, there is a distinct cruelty in the way Hitchcock lingers on a close-up of the woman's face, inviting us to laugh. Earlier in the film, we identify with Bruno as he reaches out to strangle Guy Haines's promiscuous wife, Miriam (Laura Elliott), who loves vulgar amusements and is almost a symbol of woman as mass culture. These two sorts of female – one rich and the other cheap – also have peripheral but significant roles to play in *Shadow of a Doubt*, Hitchcock's most 'American' project of the 1940s, and a film in which the *noir*-like connection between women and capitalist mass culture is somewhat more clear. Homicidal maniac Charlie Oakley is not simply a momma's boy who murders out of an Oedipal compulsion; he is also on some level a rebel against modernity – a Luciferian aesthete or dandy who is keenly aware that his sister has moved down in the world by marrying a bank clerk. Using his considerable charm and vaguely aristocratic manner, Oakley preys upon the rich widows of Santa Rosa, California, meanwhile forming a perverse bond with his niece and namesake, a vibrant young woman who lives a life of quiet desperation among 'ordinary' folk. In a local restaurant, where a barmaid lingers over the table and comments that she would 'kill' for an expensive ring, Uncle Charlie tells niece Charlie that the houses in her neighbourhood are façades to conceal 'swine'. We are supposed to be horrified when the madman drops his mask, but the film also makes his critique of an idealised, Norman Rockwell community seem at least partly valid. Throughout *Shadow of a Doubt*, Hitchcock depicts the American town as a petit-bourgeois matriarchy, filled with timid, emasculated males like Joe Newton and his next-door neighbour Herbie Hawkins. He makes us admire and identify with niece Charlie, who represents the town, but he also suggests that she is a spiritual double for the villain, and that she has too little control over her destiny to become a true heroine. The ostensible happy ending leaves her shaken and depressed, standing outside a local church with her prospective bridegroom, about to be fully integrated into the community. Off-screen, we hear a priest delivering a hypocritical eulogy for her murderous relative. The modern world, represented by women, has won, but the victory seems hollow.

Nostalgia

In *Shadow of a Doubt*, Charlie Oakley suffers from a kind of delusional nostalgia for a nineteenth-century *belle époque*, signified by the elegant ballroom dancers and the 'Merry Widow' waltz during the credit sequence. A similar memory of a bygone world can also be found in other films we describe as *noir*; indeed, according to Paul Schrader, who wrote one of the most influential commentaries on the topic, the 'overriding' themes of such films include 'loss, nostalgia' and 'fear of the future'.[24] But the sense of pastness in Hollywood's dark cinema of the 1940s and 1950s usually has more to do with personal than with historical time. *Noir* protagonists such as Swede in *The Killers* (1946), Jeff Bailey in *Out of the Past* (1947) or Nancy Blair in *The Locket* (1946) don't feel the loss of an older society; they suffer instead from dark memories that are fully situated within what Vivian Sobchack calls the *noir* 'chronotope'.[25] Charlie Oakley may resemble these characters in his quasi-Freudian compulsion to repeat his past, but his specific nostalgia has historical dimensions, pointing to a nineteenth-century, hierarchical society. Hence the thematic structure of *Shadow of a Doubt* is somewhat less like a typical *film noir* than like Welles's *Magnificent Ambersons* (a quality intensified by the coincidence that Joseph Cotten stars in both pictures).

There are, to be sure, several examples of *noir* 'costume' movies or nineteenth-century melodramas (among them *Gaslight* (1944), *Doctor Jekyll and Mr Hyde* (1941) and *The Spiral Staircase* (1946), but such films tend to be exceptions to the rule. More significantly, they rarely mix images of the modern and the historical past. In Hitchcock, by contrast, the entire meaning or emotional effect often depends upon a strategic use of certain familiar cultural codes of the nineteenth century alongside images of the present day. Perhaps because of his European background, but more probably because he collaborated so often with Selznick, his early American films seem preoccupied with sharp contrasts between the old world and the new. The baronial mansions in *Rebecca*, *Suspicion* and *The Paradine Case* become virtual characters, symbolising a mixture of patriarchal oppression and passionate romance, and they strongly affect the modern-day people who inhabit them. Notice also that the historical past remains an important feature in some of Hitchcock's later work. In *Psycho*, for example, the surreal juxtaposition of a Gothic mansion and a motel is central to the meaning of the narrative, and it tends to upset our usual expectations of *noir* iconography.

The Hitchcock film in which historical imagery figures most prominently is *Vertigo*, which resembles both a conventional private-eye melodrama and a surrealist ghost story on the order of Selznick's *Portrait of Jennie* (1948). Significantly, *Vertigo*'s many unsatisfactory imitations, including *Obsession* (1976), *Body Double* (1984), *Final Analysis* (1992) and *Basic Instinct* (1992), are closer in spirit to the classic *film noir* precisely because they omit the theme of the old world. Compared to these films, *Vertigo* seems more like a mixture of Dashiell Hammett and Edgar Allan Poe. It tells a story of a solitary urban investigator at the fringe of the middle class who is fascinated by a rich, duplicitous woman; but it soon becomes preoccupied with historical romance, necrophilia and the uncanny return of an aristocratic past – a past belonging to what Eric Hobsbawm has called the 'Age of Capital', when bourgeois patriarchy was in the ascendency, when Hollywood did not exist, and when men had 'the power and the freedom', as one character says, to cast their unwanted women aside. Ultimately, its images of contemporary San Francisco give way to a pre-modernist setting, and the spirit of Poe dominates the film. Madeleine Elster, for example, seems to echo Madeleine Usher, the woman who rises from the grave at the end of Poe's *Fall of the House of Usher*. (The difference, and what most infuriates Scottie Ferguson, is that Madeline is only pretending to be a ghost; much to his frustration, she also assumes the guise of a mass-cultural, American type named Judy Barton, who comes from Kansas.) The last lines of one of Poe's most famous poems, 'Annabel Lee', might almost serve as an epigraph to *Vertigo*: 'And so, all the night-tide, I lie down by the side/Of my darling, my darling, my life and my bride,/In her sepulchre there by the sea – /In her tomb by the side of the sea'. An equally good epigraph would be a line from Poe's essay, 'The Philosophy of Composition,' which argues that the most 'poetic' theme in art is 'the death of a beautiful woman'.

Vertigo is exemplary of Hitchcock in many ways, and its historical nostalgia seems to me to blend with most of the other qualities I've discussed in this essay, enabling me to draw my argument to a conclusion. Notice, for example, that even though *Vertigo* stars an icon of 'American-ness' (James Stewart), it is chiefly about the central character's ironic, painful longing for an old, vaguely British world of refinement and power. (Gavin Elster, played by the British actor Tom Helmore, represents that world, and his rich, exceptionally masculine office is filled with nineteenth-century paintings of sailing ships.) The film is almost completely lacking suspense (and even Hitchcockian comedy), but it remains pellucidly clear in execution, sharply aware that the classic Hollywood narrative requires the end of the story to answer the beginning – indeed one might say that it gives us closure with a vengeance. It offers a photographic expressionism and a bizarre dream sequence, but it seldom looks *noir*-like, partly because it experiments with a colour photography that dispenses with cast shadows, and partly because it is shot in the glamorous, big-budget, 'Hollywood' manner. It deals with a private eye and a duplicitous woman, but at crucial junctures it shows the world from the woman's point of view, and it retains a feeling of old-fashioned, passionate romanticism even when it makes us sharply aware of the protagonist's neurosis and perversity.

Vertigo was, of course, based on a French novel, and it was the French who taught us to appreciate not only the American *film noir*, but also Hitchcock and Edgar Allan Poe. If we consider Hitchcock's entire career in this light, we can see that he functions as a kind of transitional figure in a tradition that the French helped to create. As I've tried to indicate, he has an obvious affinity with the Hollywood directors of *film noir*, but he is also quite similar to Poe, who might be regarded as the progenitor of the *roman noir*. Like Poe, Hitchcock takes a quasi-scientific approach to his work; like Poe, he specialises in horror and the irrational; and like Poe, he is an aesthete who appeals to a popular or mass audience. In fact, all the 'Hitchcockian' qualities I've listed can be explained in terms of the director's middle position between the nineteenth and twentieth centuries – a position that reveals certain links between Europe and America, between Poe and Hollywood and between aestheticism and modernism. Another way of making the same point would be to say that Hitchcock's work tends to show its roots in the ur-surrealist romantics and the early films of D. W. Griffith, even while it reveals the darker side of twentieth-century art. In the last analysis, therefore, one could argue that Hitchcock is central to the larger, more broadly cultural history of *noir*, or to the long tradition of what the Victorians called 'sensation fiction'. He seems marginal only in a somewhat parochial context, when we consider him in relation to the American *film noir*'s Hollywood manifestations in the 1940s and 1950s.

Notes

1 Alain Silver and Elizabeth Ward (eds), *Film Noir: An Encyclopedic Reference to the American Style*, rev. edn., Woodstock: Overlook Press, 1992.
2 Patrick Brion, *Le film noir*, Paris: Editions de la martinière, 1992.
3 Foster Hirsch, *Film Noir: The Dark Side of the Screen*, New York: A. S. Barnes, 1981; Slavoj Žižek, 'In His Bold Gaze My Ruin is Writ Large', in Slavoj Žižek (ed.), *Everything You Always Wanted to Know About Lacan (But Were Afraid to Ask Hitchcock)*, London: Verso, 1992, p. 258.
4 Nino Frank, 'Un nouveau genre "policier": L'aventure criminelle', *L'Écran français* 61, 28 August 1946, p. 14. My translation.
5 Raymond Borde and Etienne Chaumeton, *Panorama du film noir americain, 1941–53*, Paris: Editions du Minuit, 1955, p. 27. My translation.
6 Borde and Chaumeton, *Panorama*, p. 90. My translation.
7 Borde and Chaumeton, *Panorama*, pp. 90–1. My translation.
8 Borde and Chaumeton, *Panorama*, p. 129. My translation.
9 Jean-Luc Godard, *Godard on Godard*, trans., Tom Milne, New York: Viking Press, 1972, pp. 54 & 48.

10 Renata Salecl, 'The Right Man and the Wrong Woman', in Slavoj Žižek (ed.), *Everything You Always Wanted to Ask Lacan*, pp. 185–94.

11 Godard, *Godard on Godard*, p. 51.

12 David Bordwell, Janet Staiger and Kristin Thompson, *The Classical Hollywood Cinema*, New York: Columbia University Press, 1985, p. 74.

13 Francois Truffaut, *Hitchcock*, rev. ed., New York: Simon and Schuster, 1985, p. 68.

14 Truffaut, *Hitchcock*, p. 63.

15 Truffaut, *Hitchcock*, p. 63.

16 Andreas Huyssen, *After the Great Divide*, Bloomington: Indiana University Press, 1986, p. 49.

17 Tania Modleski, *The Women Who Knew Too Much: Hitchcock and Feminist Theory*, New York and London: Methuen, 1988, p. 55.

18 Laura Mulvey, *Visual and Other Pleasures*, Bloomington: Indiana University Press, 1989.

19 Robin Wood, *Hitchcock's Films Revisited*, New York: Columbia University Press, 1989; Raymond Durgnat, *The Strange Case of Alfred Hitchcock*, Cambridge, MA: MIT Press, 1974.

20 Lesley Brill, *The Hitchcock Romance*, Princeton: Princeton University Press, 1988; Stanley Cavell, 'North By Northwest' in Marshall Deutelbaum and Leland Poague (eds), *A Hitchcock Reader*, Ames: Iowa State University Press, 1986, pp. 249–61.

21 Truffaut, *Hitchcock*, p. 168.

22 André Bazin, 'Hitchcock vs. Hitchcock', in Albert LaValley (ed.), *Focus on Hitchcock*, Englewood Cliffs: Prentice Hall, 1972, p. 65.

23 Bazin, 'Hitchcock vs. Hitchcock', pp. 65–6.

24 Paul Schrader, 'Notes on Film Noir', in Alain Silver and James Ursini (eds), *Film Noir Reader*, New York: Limelight Editions, 1966, p. 58.

25 Vivian Sobchack, 'Lounge Time: Postwar Crisis and the Chronotope of Film Noir', in Nick Browne (ed.), *Refiguring American Film Genres: History and Theory*, Berkeley: University of California Press, 1998, pp. 129–70.

Women and men; reality and knowledge – Kim Novak in the continuously provocative *Vertigo*

Chapter 18
Vertigo and Problems of Knowledge in Feminist Film Theory

Susan White

Like Roger Thornhill in *North by Northwest* (1959), Alfred Hitchcock's *Vertigo* (1958) has played various roles in the past twenty-odd years of its career as an object of criticism. Among feminist theorists, with whom this chapter is largely concerned, the film has been described as a tale of male aggression and visual control; as a map of the female Oedipal trajectory; as a deconstruction of the male construction of femininity and of masculinity itself; as a stripping bare of the mechanisms of directorial, Hollywood studio and colonial oppression; and as a place where textual meanings play out in an infinite regress of self-reflexivity. The film's radical take on problems of representation and sexuality, not to mention its moving portrayal of love and loss, evokes deeply felt responses from its analysts. Whether they see it as a film that sustains traditional heterosexual male and female roles, or as fundamentally questioning those roles, critics have sought in *Vertigo* a proving ground for a complex array of theories on the ontology, psychology and epistemology of cinema in its relation to gender, history and the aesthetic realm.

According to much of the recent writing on *Vertigo*, the film speaks to us of failures: 'the necessary failure of criticism',[1] the impossibility of representation, and the perhaps equally necessary failure of love and desiring relationships, particularly, though not uniquely, heterosexual ones. There are also those who would challenge the language of failure and assert that it is possible and necessary to recognise how *Vertigo* 'opens a space' for such vexed entities as feminine agency and historical oppressions.[2] In feminist theory, questions of knowledge (epistemology) have been closely linked to issues of vision and desire, and the history of feminist commentary on that linkage can certainly be traced in the abundant essays on the film. The debate over what we can learn from *Vertigo* often focuses explicitly on questions of knowledge. What, for example, can 'man' know of his 'other', woman? Must the object of desire be posited as outside knowledge, mysteriously unknowable? What can a work of art tell us about the historical 'reality' it seems to invoke? Obviously a Lacanian will answer those questions differently than will a Marxist historian. Among the films that deal with the complexities of knowledge and desire, *Vertigo* is unusual in its capacity to provoke debate on problems of *being*: what does it mean to say that something or someone is 'real'? – a comment that is often made about various characters in the film even by theorists who usually avoid such bold referentiality. In this chapter I will address some of these issues by outlining how feminist critics of *Vertigo* have navigated the film's seemingly contradictory imperatives about the possibilities and ethics of knowledge, representation and gender relations. I will also, to some degree, position these 'navigations' in the larger context of feminist film theory's historical transformations. Finally, I will comment on the irony that a film 'about' the failure of representation has come to be regarded by many as one of the most adequate representations of a particular social reality.

Laura Mulvey was the first theorist to place 'the woman' in *Vertigo* explicitly within the circuit of male knowledge and visual control.[3] For Mulvey, *Vertigo* enacts the typical male strategies of denial and aggression found in all 'classic Hollywood films'. As every theoretically inclined film student knows, Mulvey describes James Stewart's Scottie as an embodiment of the 'active gaze' of the male spectator who initially enacts the investigative side of voyeurism by following and interrogating 'Madeleine'. By means of these persecutory interrogations, Scottie ultimately triumphs over his vertigo. Male 'curiosity wins through' and the woman is 'punished' in the second half of the film.[4] Scottie continues the cycle of abuse begun by Gavin Elster when the former reconstructs and redestroys the woman as fetish object, the representation of 'lack' or 'castration'.[5] Although it seems to exemplify what she sees as the rigidly dichotomised pattern of male voyeurism and scopophilia, and although her political emphasis in the essay is on leaving behind the context of Hollywood-style cinema to seek more verdant possibilities for the female spectator in experimental cinema, Mulvey finds redeeming value for feminism in *Vertigo* because the film turns the viewer's psychological processes back on 'him'self:

> The Hitchcock hero ... has all the attributes of the patriarchal super-ego. Hence the spectator, lulled into a false sense of security by the apparent legality of his surrogate, sees through his look and finds himself exposed as complicit, caught in the moral ambiguity of looking.[6]

Mulvey's *Vertigo* can at best function as a kind of *moral* mirror for the (male) spectator, who expects to be flattered and reassured by his identification with a super-ego figure but meets with an unpleasant reflection. The film presumably arouses discomfort and guilt, as well as erotic pleasure, in the male spectator because it illustrates how women are ultimately made to suffer for men's visual and narrative pleasure. He sees himself in the unappealing role of oppressor of women, complicit with an oppressive desiring machine. For Mulvey, then, *Vertigo's* limited virtue is that it may induce self-knowledge in the male spectator, who identifies with a protagonist made uncomfortably aware of his identification with an immoral power structure.

The problems with Mulvey's formulation have been pored over with great exegetical intensity. First, even if we agree that the film is likely to induce such self-knowledge on the part of the male spectator, if we adhere to the terms of Mulvey's Lacanianism, self-awareness through mirroring remains an 'imaginary' function and not socially efficacious. And, more crucially, as feminist critics have observed in innumerable contexts, according to Mulvey's model we can have no knowledge at all of 'the woman' herself, either as spectator or as referent: her desire does not figure in classic Hollywood cinema except in 'transvestite'[7] terms and her existence is entirely occulted or constructed as absence – '*La femme n'existe pas*', as Lacan notoriously intoned.[8]

Mulvey's placement of 'woman' outside the boundaries of representation had an almost hypnotically powerful effect on feminist film theorists, who struggled for years to theorise their sense that feminine subjectivity and desire are indeed expressed in mainstream cinema, however indirectly or incompletely. Indeed, these critics, like other theorists of mass culture, began to move away *en masse*, if with some difficulty, from the view that popular texts express only dominant ideologies. Critics including Claire Johnston posited that female desire and subjectivity could erupt into the 'gaps' and 'fissures' of the film text, presented as a site of rupture and contradiction.[9] Others saw the female spectator herself as the locus of ideological subversion in her capacity to read against the grain of the classic narrative films Mulvey had described as 'cut to the measure' of male desire. Debate raged concerning the kind of viewing position 'woman' could take with respect to mainstream cinema.

Tania Modleski and Teresa De Lauretis are among those who played a pivotal role in challenging and complicating Mulvey's theoretical matrix for the representation of women in film. Perhaps not incidentally, both authors chose Hitchcock's films as a particularly crucial setting for the analysis of female subjectivity and the representation of women. Modleski's work on *Rebecca* (1940), for example, laid the groundwork for further work on the representation of the persistence of female pre-Oedipal desire in film.[10] (I will return to her work on *Vertigo* below.) Teresa De Lauretis's influential book, *Alice Doesn't*, focused in part on the way that 'feminine' narrative structures, specifically, a 'divided or double desire' that is both heterosexual and homosexual (as in *Rebecca* and *Vertigo*) are proffered and then negated by 'either the massive destruction or the territorialization of women' in the films.[11] But although De Lauretis focuses on the revolutionary potential of the female Oedipal complex and challenges the binarism of Mulvey's view of mainstream cinema as 'illusionistic' and alternative feminist cinema as destructive of illusion, her guarded assessment of Hitchcock's films' representation of female experience does not radically diverge from Mulvey's account of Hitchcock's films.

Karen Hollinger's essay on feminist theory and *Vertigo* systematises and extends Modleski's and De Lauretis's discussions of the narrative elements of Hitchcock's cinema as expressive of 'the female Oedipal drama'.[12] Although she draws heavily on De Lauretis's earlier insights, Hollinger's tone (like Modleski's) reflects a new emphasis in feminist theory regarding the possibility of retrieving a 'female gaze' or female stories in classic cinema. By extrapolating De Lauretis's view that the narrative strand of the film (as opposed to the visual track) is a locus where female desire can work itself out, Hollinger attempts to move feminist film theory from its task of exposing 'the discursive strategies which locate and characterise woman as absence, lack, or destructive negativity' to a more 'positive' view of the structuring power of feminine sexuality itself.[13] In so doing, Hollinger finesses the caution shown by De Lauretis towards the project of female subject-formation. She cites *Vertigo* as a film in which female desire *is* 'narratively' present through the working out of the female Oedipal drama, in which the female infant's fixation on the mother as primary object of desire (Madeleine's obsession with 'Carlotta') is displaced by her 'seduction' into acceptance of male-defined femininity (represented by Madeleine's idealised beauty). Hollinger salvages the image track from its domination by the 'male gaze' when she hypothesises that the powerful maternal presence that haunts *Vertigo* is not banished but becomes a form of (masochistically) pleasurable visual identification with female icons (a phenomenon Modleski had already observed in her reading of *Rebecca*).

Hollinger's emphasis on showing how we might see woman as a positive structuring force in *Vertigo* has its pay-off. More than had any other critic up to that point, she examined the role of female spectatorial surrogates in *Vertigo* as possible points of identification for women. Thus Madeleine represents one important facet of the female spectator's Oedipal dilemma in that (under Scottie's direction) she must 'sever herself from all connections with the mother'[14] in order to secure the male gaze. Even though Madeleine's story of possession by Carlotta is fictitious, it is a fiction that (according to this argument) accurately reflects female ambivalence towards that primordial attachment to the mother.

Midge is also singled out by Hollinger as 'representative of the female spectator' in that, like the women viewing the film, she watches Scottie's every move and tries to understand his obsession with Madeleine. But Midge's lack of ideal feminine traits, her 'boyishness' and, paradoxically, her 'motherliness', make the spectator's identification an uncomfortable one: her inability to incite or at least to hold male desire, demonstrated in the scene where she caricatures Carlotta's portrait, 'illustrates', for Hollinger, 'the incompatibility of male desire with female individuality'.[15] When Midge walks down the long asylum corridor and exits from the film, leaving the institutionalised Scottie to his Mozart and spider webs, 'the female spectator finds herself without a female character with whom she can identify'.[16] She must identify with Scottie's longing for Madeleine until Judy jumps into the fray and breaks the visual link between Scottie and the spectator through the infamous device of the flashback that reveals her role in the Elster plot. But, as with Midge, identification with Judy is 'uneasy' – in this case, not because she is unfeminine, but because she is 'vulgar' and 'cheap'. Still, despite the uneasiness with which one might identify with her, crucially, for Hollinger, Judy is 'represented as a real woman',[17] rather than a fantasy one: female spectators will presumably respond to Judy as reflecting something of their own everyday, 'real' experience, just as they see in Midge something of their own striving for 'individuality'. Thus Hollinger postulates that we can 'know' something about female desire by watching Hollywood cinema, and presumes a certain knowledge of the psychology of the female spectator who identifies with the women on screen. From being a film in which femininity functions only as a repressed organising principle, *Vertigo* is becoming an exemplary site of female self-recognition. But this 'positive' project produces another set of problems for feminist critics when they seek to define just what a 'real' woman or a particular spectatorial practice may have been, historically speaking, when so much of feminist theory 'places the real beyond the reach of phenomenal appearance'.[18]

Many critics will turn to discourse theory as a way out of the difficulty of locating the 'real', but the political objectives of feminism seem to demand a continual reassessment of how lived experience may be represented in cinema. Tania Modleski, for example, is, like Hollinger, impatient with those who regard realist representation in cinema as necessarily dominated by a monolithic patriarchy. Modleski posits the intervention of feminine subjectivity as an active textual force. Rather than seeing women as semiotically disabled by patriarchy (although she does recount the ways in which Hitchcock's heroines are made to doubt their vision), Modleski claims that women (critics, film characters, film-makers) are better positioned than men to critique patriarchy – an approach that contradicts Mulvey's view that 'realist representation can only be ideologically complicit'.[19] Modleski finds theoretical backing for her position in Jameson's *The Political Unconscious*:

> According to Jameson . . . consciousness on the part of the oppressed classes, expressed 'initially, in the unarticulated form of rage, helplessness, victimisation, oppression by a common enemy', generates a 'mirror image of class solidarity among the ruling groups . . . This suggests . . . that the *truth* of ruling-class consciousness . . . is to be found in working-class consciousness'. Similarly, in Hitchcock, the 'truth' of patriarchal consciousness lies in feminist consciousness and depends precisely on the depiction of victimised women found so often in his films.[20]

The notion of the proletariat as the bearer of knowledge is, of course, traditional in Marxist theory. But this proletariat would not necessarily be the enunciator of its own knowledge – it's just a mirror; ergo the need for a vanguard party, and so forth. Jameson and Modleski both place women and other 'oppressed' people in a position of privilege with respect to truth, but Modleski changes the status of Jameson's political 'unconscious' when she says that women consciously know the truth of patriarchy, as if patriarchy or the ruling class had a single truth, or that women somehow see the same reality when they look at patriarchy. This is obviously an essentialist position, which Modleski is using polemically. Indeed, *Vertigo* encourages such essentialism in its representation of characters like Judy and Midge who are as women very different, but who both seem to have a grasp of the 'truth' that eludes Scottie. In *Vertigo* the kind of blindness that comes from what Doane would call overidentification with the maternal body can be readily described as a male problem and a male fantasy.[21] Like Midge herself, Modleski paints the picture of the Hitchcockian 'knowing woman', often a wearer of glasses, with extraordinary conviction: Midge *does* know more and suffers for her knowledge.

The mid-1980s saw another, more fully developed materialist–historicist and feminist reading of *Vertigo* that challenged the psychoanalytic framework of feminist film theory. Virginia Wright Wexman's 1986 essay, 'The Critic as Consumer: Film Study in the University, *Vertigo*, and the Film Canon', seeks to place the film's representation of women and its possible reception in a historical context not previously examined. In this essay Wexman takes to task the critics who, like William Rothman, assert *Vertigo's* status as 'pure cinema' (cinema that allegorises its own operations) noting that they rationalise the hegemonic functions served by particular cinematic institutions at work in the film.[22] The appeal to Gramsci's notion of hegemony is part of Wexman's attempt to articulate an 'outside' of capitalist patriarchy that would be knowable rather than an unknown and mystified entity. As a materialist feminist, Wexman expresses strong discontentment with the work of (psychoanalytic) feminist critics who, like Mulvey, theorise *Vertigo* as a film that enacts the objectification and fetishisation of 'woman', since these critics do not take into account the effect that the increasingly powerful positions occupied by white bourgeois intellectual women has on the vested interests of their critical stances. For these critics, according to Wexman, 'woman' is white, middle- or upper-class, a reflection of themselves – someone we 'know' as an extrapolation from 'our' self-knowledge as privileged subjects of speech.

This argument (which has affinities in the work of bell hooks and other critics of colour, and is implicit in De Lauretis's 'woman' – 'women' distinction asserts that the positions of power in which academic feminist critics find themselves produce 'methodological constraints that prevent it from addressing broader and more historically specific issues of class, race and economics'.[23] Feminist critics are, in effect, blinded by their own class position, and thus do not occupy the 'standpoint' from which the historical truths of the narrative can emerge. Their knowledge is limited by their class and race privilege. For Wexman, a more materialist approach than that of psychoanalytic and other 'idealist' critics would involve grounding Hitchcock's allegory of the creation of the star (Judy as Madeleine) not simply in the directorial drive towards controlling his leading ladies but in the industry-wide phenomenon of manipulation and control of the female star. The reading of *Vertigo* as simply recreating the director's relationships with his female stars, according to Wexman, 'shifts the focus of discussion away from the meaning inherent in the star's *own presence*' (my emphasis).[24] Wexman would move away from allegorical readings of the general cinematic processes reflected in the film to looking at the meaning 'inherent' in the bodily presence of the star herself. The evidence that Wexman adduces to support her reading is appealing: she goes on to detail just how Kim Novak was held hostage in her dressing-room by the producers at Columbia, constantly watched and allowed to eat only food specially prepared for her (this 'fat Pollack', as she was termed). But what philosophical or interpretive strategy leads Wexman to say that particular meanings are 'inherent' in a material presence such as Novak's? As a materialist historian, Wexman must see meaning as historical rather than inherent. That it may reflect a philosophically indefensible position makes Wexman's comment the more fascinating as continuing evidence of the kind of anxiety over the 'real' woman's body *Vertigo* seems to draw out of its commentators.

Wexman's approach to reading *Vertigo* – materialist in that she investigates the events and economic relationships as they influenced the making of the film (a materialism she sees as occluded in other readings by the self-interest of bourgeois feminism) – would also recognise how the film's 'buried references to issues of class and race were contained during the fifties as part of a nationalist ideology that defined American society in terms of its ability to achieve world dominance'.[25] When Gavin Elster 'speaks nostalgically of "the old San Francisco" when men had "freedom and power"', we are indeed hard-pressed not to read this as a harking back to the good old days of unselfconscious US power-mongering on the international scene. For the ultimate trope of this desire to dominate lies not merely in the film's discourse about a man both yearning for and visually persecuting a woman, but in the oppositions set into play between the upper-class setting of the desired woman (Madeleine is clearly aristocratic) and the lower-class background of the 'real' woman, Judy. This class difference seems to have been 'unspeakable' for the formalist critics of both schools that Wexman criticises. And even more 'unspeakable' is the question of racial or ethnic opposition: in Scottie's nightmare, Wexman writes, he sees Elster not with the 'patrician' Madeleine, but with the darkly ambiguous Carlotta. 'In the nightmare, Carlotta represents what ultimately terrorises Scottie, and the fears that Carlotta arouses in him are more *culturally specific* than either Hitchcock or his feminist critics are in a position to acknowledge' (my emphasis).[26] The 'culturally specific' here takes the shape of that menacing, unformalisable entity – Carlotta – a metonym for the dark, densely material and densely 'historical' past of the perky and gum-snapping Judy.

Wexman's reading is part of a general effort to recognise how and to what degree feminist criticism 'is complicitous with the institution within which it seeks its space'.[27] Such challenges are politically crucial, for as Gayatri Spivak has said, academic feminists continually risk performing 'the lie of constituting a truth of global sisterhood where the mesmerizing model remains male and female sparring partners ... who are the chief protagonists in that European [and American] contest'.[28] But my objections to Wexman's reasoning are several. Not least, it is ironic that, in the name of recognising repressed subjectivities, Wexman here reiterates Mulvey's sense of a blockage in vision and knowledge for women, in this case not because of their status as oppressed but because of their complicity with institutions of oppression. As is the case for Modleski, for Wexman only the underclass can know the 'truth', but white women seem to have lost their claim to being an underclass as more dramatic stories of oppression come to the fore. In her scrupulousness about making claims for a 'global sisterhood', Wexman dramatically excludes white women not just from 'speaking' the stories of Third World women, but from being able to hear those stories. And despite my appreciation of this reading of the film and its welcome introduction of issues of race and class into discussions of the film (for she's right, they were occluded) I continue to wonder how Wexman, a white, feminist, academic critic, conceptualises her own ability to recognise the historical specificities in question. Why is she not, like the feminist critical establishment she confronts, 'blinded' by her own position? Obviously she has produced a paradox.

To pose the problem more broadly, if truth cannot be a product of privilege, what happens when this kind of historical resurrection of the ethnically marginal becomes 'mainstream' in academia and the stuff of tenure, raises and promotion? The 'truth' of history must then change, it seems. As an earlier version of this essay indicates,[29] I am enough of a de Manian to think that all critical positions produce some kind of blindness, and to agree with Wexman that we must try to find positions from which to discover those blindnesses. But that does not mean that any position is necessarily one of blindness, even if it is that of a professor at a major American university. Locating the working-class woman's voice or the Hispanic mistress's voice in *Vertigo* has obvious value, as do queer readings of the film. It may very often be politically important to displace white women's authority in readings of films like *Vertigo* in order to consider who else may be 'speaking'. But this is in fact a political move and not about a relationship to 'truth'. Or, rather, to situate, for example, the 'Hispanic' woman in the place of a repressed historical specificity is also part of the way a 'colonial power' may construct its 'regime of "truth" '.[30] Race and class are not 'unspeakable' but the way they are spoken is always about power and desire – and there is no guarantee that any particular voice can speak transcendent truth.[31]

Another small irony in the annals of criticism is that Wexman's confidence in *Vertigo's* ability to say something about the conditions of the oppressed is greater than her confidence in (white, middle-class) feminists. This is quite a change of pace from Mulvey's position, or even Modleski's (who is annoyed by Robin Wood's desire to 'save Hitchcock for feminism'[32] – to put the *auteur* and his films over the needs of the feminism itself). For Wexman, *Vertigo* does contain the cries of the oppressed and she believes those cries can be heard, although she does not articulate a theory about what makes such hearing possible at this time. I would like to move to discuss various other critics who have recently shown confidence in the powers of Hitchcock's films to articulate criticism of gendered social relationships. In order to introduce these new works, I must return to Tania Modleski's reading of *Vertigo* and to psychoanalytic assessments of the film.

While she does not consider in depth the kinds of ethnic and class oppressions that Wexman does, Modleski takes her critique of Mulvey's paradigm even farther than an assertion of the existence of female Oedipal patterns in the *Vertigo*. Where Mulvey saw *Vertigo* as 'constructing' a male spectatorial position, Modleski sees the film as 'deconstructing' that position, and even humorously commenting on men's tendency to construct women as fantasy objects. According to this powerful and persuasive reading of masculinity in *Vertigo*, Hitchcock's ambivalent fascination and Scottie's identification with the 'mother–daughter dyad', in which the mother constitutes the ghostly, unknown figure the daughter risks becoming, represents a *masculine* fear of and fascination with immersion in the maternal rather than primarily a feminine problem. This male complex expresses itself in Hitchcock's films first as captivation by mother-obsessed women, (including Iris in *The Lady Vanishes*)[33] and then as an overtly masculine concern, as in *Psycho* (1960) (Norman does not identify with a woman who identifies with her 'mother', but becomes mother himself). Modleski's insistence that Scottie is not in fact an icon of control and lawful masculinity but is suffering in his feminine identification reflects a wider shift in emphasis among feminist film critics from regarding masculinity as emblematic of power and control to a focus on the panic that underlies the male need to assert dominance over women.[34] Even as she reifies female spectatorial responses, Modleski breaks down gender binarism as she draws out the implications of female 'bisexuality' for male spectators of the film:

> [I]t is possible to see the film as soliciting a masculine bisexual identification because of the way the male character oscillates between a fascination with the woman's desire and a sadistic attempt to gain control over her, to possess her.[35]

Modleski emphasises the violence with which the film character or perhaps its director seek to reassert the control destabilised in *Vertigo* by the spectacle of female bisexuality, as evidenced in the daughter's continued investment in the ghostly mother.

Why is this bisexuality so threatening? Modleski tells us that this is because the woman's bisexuality reminds the man of his own (menacing and alluring) bisexual nature. Just as the Stewart character in *Rear Window* is immobilised and in that way can be identified with a victimised female invalid whose murder he is investigating, *Vertigo*'s Stewart is in a position of enforced passivity – he suffers from his painful identification with femininity, his own potential, even actual femininity. At the beginning of the film, while he watches Midge draw a brassière designed on the principle of the cantilever bridge (a double gesture of demystifying the woman's constructed body and alluding to the mystery of Madeleine, who will jump into the Bay near the bridge), Scottie, too, is wearing 'female' undergarments – a corset. By the mid-point of the film, Scottie has become almost completely identified not just with Madeleine but with the 'sad' Carlotta: like her he wanders the streets looking for a lost loved one. In *Vertigo*, according to Hollinger and Modleski, the male subject investigates, adores, abhors, merges with, and finally *abjects* (in the Kristevan sense) the feminine.[36] And, as we have seen, this feminine entity's threat emanates largely from the fact that it defines 'unknowability' for patriarchy, according to the psychoanalytic model.

In the context of *Vertigo*'s solicitation of bisexual desire, a recent work by Robert Samuels, *Hitchcock's Bi-Textuality*, describes the film and Hitchcock's work in general as uncannily 'knowledgeable' about gender, and uses Hitchcock to unseat the position of woman as the cultural 'other'.[37] In this intriguing book these films seem to possess a critical consciousness – whether it is an authorial intent or unconscious behind the critique is beyond my powers of analysis – that is able literally to 'correct' the insights of Lacan and Derrida on sexuality and language. Samuels's methodology combines Lacan's 'theory of ethics' with recent theories of feminine subjectivity and bisexuality. 'Bi-textuality', Samuels's neologism for a textual process that occurs in Hitchcock's films, is described as a kind of return of the repressed feminine subject. The 'bi-textual', Samuels claims, radically alters the terms of earlier discussions of Hitchcockian bisexuality, although he seems to have found his original inspiration in Modleski's work. Samuels wants to go much further than 'saving Hitchcock for feminism'. He views Hitchcock's works as profound philosophical statements that offer an often surprisingly (to me) specific corrective to certain psychoanalytic formulations concerning women. Lacan's 'error' should sound familiar: it lies in his equation of 'the female form with the Real that cannot be symbolised', his placement of this 'female subject in a position of unknowability'.[38] Samuels counters this error with a rereading of Freud: just as Freud posited a fundamental ground of bisexuality for every subject, we can affirm a form of universal bi-textuality that is repressed through different modes of representation yet returns in unconscious aspects of textuality (dreams, wordplay, jokes, and symbolism).

It is the fact that woman as 'object (a) is placed in the position of being the lost product of the signifying chain . . . and takes on the appearance of representing the lost Real'[39] that opens her up for abuses in the real, because (as we have seen) 'men identify with the loss of language and discourse that they project onto women'.[40] *Vertigo* is a prime example of such displaced identifications.

For Samuels, Hitchcock's women reassert themselves from the 'edge of the Symbolic' and struggle against their consignment to the real. Samuels's tropes for feminine resistance have a deconstructive flavour, often functioning through a kind of writing associated with the 'bi-textual presence of absence', such as Rebecca's grapheme, 'R', the black lines on white or red ink on white that mark the 'feminine insistence on writing and lack' in *Spellbound*, *Marnie* and so forth. Men are threatened by these forms of writing because '[w]riting makes the absence of the Thing present, just as in Freud's theory, the vagina makes the absence of the phallus present for man'.[41] Hitchcock's women contest their linguistic castration by choosing to 'reinterpret master signifiers' or attempting, often at their peril, 'to establish a new form of discourse, something like a structured multiplicity or bi-textuality'.[42] Samuels's critique of Lacan is that the latter does not discern the 'misrecognition' involved in putting woman in the place of a real that is both threatening and beckoning, for this 'transformation of the [originary] bisexual object to a feminised form occurs through the [erroneous] equation of the original Thing with the mother'.[43] Lacan is not sufficiently critical or perhaps deconstructive of the culture that performs this transformation. According to Samuels's reading of Freud, via Lee Edelman, because the child's first sight of sexual intercourse, the 'primal scene' occurs (if not literally then structurally) before any awareness of sexual difference, the 'originary object' is actually not the mother, but 'a bi-sexual organ that marks a continuity between masculinity and femininity'.[44] Thus, 'the horror of the Real is fundamentally a horror of the lack of sexual orientation' for both Hitchcock[45] and the sexual subject in general.

With respect to the textual operations of *Vertigo*, it is in Judy's look at the camera and in her wearing of Carlotta's necklace that Samuels finds 'Hitchcock's own desire to resist completely killing off and effacing the original *Real Thing*' (Samuels's emphasis).[46] This resistance to effacing the woman reflects Scottie's and the spectators sense of guilt at having 'murdered' the Real with the Symbolic – that is, through representation. Samuels's appeal to the Lacanian 'Real' has affinities with the 'real' woman of feminism only insofar as she is positioned as unrecoverable, mystified, and unknowable. Madeleine, as an emblem of loss and male projection, is a more likely candidate than is Judy or Midge to stand in for this 'Real'. But Samuels relates 'real' and 'Real' if only to deconstruct the conflation of real or even fantasy women with the original object. *Vertigo* is thus a warning to us all about linking real women with the Real. If we stop such linkages, become aware of the male projections involved, then 'real' women will suffer less.

> An ethics of the Real can only be an ethics based on unconscious bisexual and multi-textual desire. For it is only on the level of our heterogeneous desire that we acknowledge the Real that we continue to negate and avoid. Hitchcock's films offer us an opportunity to witness this effacement and return of our unconscious desire.[47]

We have come a long way from Mulvey's reluctant acknowledgment of *Vertigo*'s 'subversive' potential, but I wonder how significant it is that Samuels has created a kind of abyssal structure in the retreat to the originary bisexual object, where the bisexual itself takes the place of the Real as object of horror. In fact, Samuels acknowledges this possibility repeatedly, characterising the bisexual whirlpool of *Psycho*, for example, as the projection of Hitchcock's 'most profound cultural fears and desires'.[48] In response to this political question, Samuels proposes an 'ethics of reading' whereby cultural workers would seek to make others aware of the ways in which the Real becomes 'equated with feminine and queer subjects', or projected onto debased Others (including racial others) under patriarchy. But if the 'primal scene' is always one of bisexual horror, and representation is the murder of the Real, I'm not sure how exactly we are to emerge from this dilemma and find our way into the utopia of heterogeneous desire that Samuels describes. Would not bisexuality and queerness acquire the abject qualities now in part focused on femininity? Still, Samuels's reading of Lacan at least seems to tender the possibility of using psychoanalysis to the political purpose of tracing just how particular groups become historically linked to the horror associated with the Real.

The kind of infinite regress or abyssal structure that I find potentially problematic in

Samuels's discussion of bi-textuality (because he doesn't seem to anticipate that it may be a problem) is embraced as an inevitable textual process in the deconstructive readings of *Vertigo*, particularly Deborah Linderman's. Like most of the critics who have written in Modleski's wake, Linderman sees as pivotal Modleski's view that Hitchcock's films are 'characterised by a deep and pervasive "ambivalence" about femininity', which renders his identification with the woman both alluring and intolerable. Linderman emphasises, however, that she does not share Modleski's 'characterological' approach to Hitchcock's film:

> My own notion, in the reading that follows, is not only that Scottie 'identifies' with or 'resembles' Madeleine, which are after all psychological positions, but rather that the dynamic of the whole textual system that is *Vertigo* struggles against the collapse of sexual difference, a collapse that the diegesis that limits and conditions this system essays to avert.[49]

Focusing, in the style of Raymond Bellour's scrupulous attention to textual processes, on the film's textual system 'as a set of self-reflecting mirrors', Linderman identifies her purpose as a feminist one – 'to understand how the binarism upheld by the manifest diegesis, victim/victimiser, results from a deadly male aggressivity directed by the latter against the former in the effort to uphold phallic transcendence'.[50] Cavell's insight that the 'unknown woman' film's 'failed structure of deferral', linked to the diphasic structure of human sexuality (humans come to sexual awareness, repress that awareness and go through a latency period), produces repetitions at the textual level is independently confirmed by Linderman's description of how the film's 'tripartite structure' is 'absorbed into a basically diphasic narrative' . . . 'whereby, according to the deorginating principle of the *Nachträglichkeit*, a "second" scenario retroactively constitutes the oracular meaning of a "first" '.[51]

The 'meaning' Linderman traces in Scottie's vertigo has repercussions at the level of the discursive system of the film, which she characterises as 'vertiginous'. The struggle 'against the collapse of sexual difference' (a collapse that would result in reversion to Samuels's originary bisexual object?) of course fails. Linderman returns to Scottie's dream to elucidate one moment of that collapse, which ultimately pulls the spectator into its operations. Linderman shows here why it is important to avoid seeing Scottie in characterological rather than textual terms:

> The point here is that while the dream is in part Scottie's – it is 'about' the fragility of barriers, his feminization (he is spoken by Madeleine), the contagion of her death wish/fear – it is also the *text*'s dream, its mode of organizing its own latencies . . . [N]ot one of the internal dream shots is matched to his gaze and there is no intervention of that gaze in the segment. Replaying images that Scottie has not seen, the dream expressly solicits me, my point of view and my subjectivity; in a salutary way, it is my dream, a *mise-en-scène* of cinema itself.[52]

Like Modleski, Linderman follows the post-Mulveyan tendency to strip Scottie's 'male gaze' of the all-powerful status it enjoyed at least briefly in 1975, and, like many critics, she sees the film as an allegory for its reception by the spectator. But even Linderman seeks a 'point of balance' in the film's seemingly infinite regress of vertiginous structures:

> Is there a point of balance? It would seem to be Midge. In the first place, she is psychologized as 'sensible' ... In the second place, she designs 'cantilever bras' according to the principle of the suspension bridge ... In this connection, we might see Midge as a surrogate for Hitchcock. In a *small* way, Midge equilibrizes, she counteracts the vertigo ... she restores limit.[53]

For Linderman, although Midge is ideologically '*under*positioned by the text' and 'stands outside its spiralling economy of power and victimization',[54] the character so often associated with the spectator figure is a point of equilibrium. This (Linderman notes) is in contrast to the Kim Novak-as-Judy character who, as Hitchcock and Truffaut salaciously discuss in a boyish exchange, does not seem to wear a bra. Thus, Linderman notes, 'Midge, it would seem, designs the foundations that Kim Novak doesn't wear'.[55] I appreciate the wit of Linderman's conclusion and, indeed, the elegance of her argument overall, but it is interesting that *despite her bias against characterological studies* she in fact makes a textual error in order to place Midge in a subject position. Midge does not design bras but is drawing a picture of one designed by an aircraft engineer 'in his spare time'. Midge is a witness rather than a designer in this narrative. In the place where many critics seek a point of contact with the real – in Judy, or in the moment where Judy puts on the necklace that will link her to the 'real' story about what happened to Madeleine, what Linderman calls 'the moment of Scottie's epiphany' – Linderman sees the film as revealing 'the hermeneutic as a spurious anchorage'. Samuels's faith in the hermeneutic, in the 'ethics of reading' and interpretation he outlines in his book, is not, it seems, shared by Linderman. It is thus doubly interesting to me that she seeks, at least momentarily, anchorage in the figure of Midge.

In an overview of deconstructive readings of *Vertigo*, Christopher Morris categorises both Linderman's essay and my essay 'Allegory and Referentiality' as analyses that explore 'the film's gender ambiguity in the context of larger epistemological concerns'.[56] The debate on *Vertigo*, for Morris, exemplifies '[t]he crisis in feminist studies outlined in Judith Butler's *Gender Troubles*'. He formulates Butler's fundamental question in this way: 'whether the exposure of arbitrary patriarchal structures of representation can proceed without the reinscription of a hermeneutics of essentialism'.[57]

Morris goes on to document the film's 'pursuit of tenability', which can be traced in the words of critics as in the actions of characters. Like other deconstructive critics, Morris sees the project of finding any 'referent, ground, foundation, or "signified presence"'[58] in the film as necessarily failing. Morris follows the course of arbitrary and misleading signifiers in the film, as well as the 'undecidability of its characters, political narrative, and ending, all of which suggest the illusion of tenable hermeneutic "points of view" on art and life'. Morris includes his essay with my own in the downward eddy of deconstructive readings:

> Of course, as White has shown, when such criticism [Mulvey, Modleski, *et al.*] goes on to identify Hitchcock's position with the essentialist idea of woman as victim, it

> presupposes a 'single dominating reality' in history; instead she sees *Vertigo* as illustrating de Man's very different idea that history, understood as 'the telling of the story of the generation of a text', is itself produced by allegory. White's use of de Man here at first seems very apt; the idea that history is nothing other than allegory seems patent in the way Pop Liebl's oral history innocently rehearses as it unconsciously betrays western master narratives that mask patriarchy and oppression, as seen above. Where White's position seems less tenable, however, is in her elision of de Man's observation that these allegories tell of the unreadability of history's text and are themselves subject to second (or third) deconstruction, in a potentially endless series. In other words, de Man's argument implies that criticism could deconstruct an allegory like Pop Liebl's – in the manner of Foucault, Greenblatt, or Spivak – only at the cost of committing the same mistake again. And in fact, this is what has occurred in White's analysis (and is in the process of occurring in my own). Doubts of the readability of even feminist, new historicist, or post-colonial interpretations of history arise during the articulation of White's essay and mine.[59]

My 'elision' of de Man's most radically deconstructive implications – for indeed such an elision takes place – speaks of my divided loyalties to the political agenda of feminist theory and the epistemic project of deconstructivism. 'Despite her demonstration of the allegory of criticism, White's ultimate recourse to essentialism is also suggested by her view that a different feminist line of analysis (born of the work of Chodorow, Scheman, and Spivak) might indeed capture in the film a tenable "maternal realm" that is not an "object of knowing".'[60] Like Scottie and Hitchcock's other protagonists I succumb to the 'pursuit of the tenable amid monuments or portentous signifiers that come to disclose, after all, only its absence'.[61] Instead of the Golden Gate Bridge or Mt. Rushmore, we are faced with Hitchcock's films as monuments of our cultural history, and I finally join those critics who look for 'meaning' in those films.

Feminist deconstructivists' move away from an essentialist ontology of 'woman' (however much they may fail in this project) and their adherence to what Richard Allen and Murray Smith have termed 'epistemic atheism' has been a frustrating aporia for many critics.[62] Such epistemic atheism, in the context of this essay, reflects a lack of belief in the referential power of language and images. Feminist theorists' focus on textual processes at the expense of articulating a positive model of female spectatorship – building a referential bridge to real women – seems, to Laura Hinton (the last critic of *Vertigo* I will cite), to be a futile and self-defeating gesture. Hinton stands opposed to Hollinger's, Linderman's and White's 'subversion of signification' in *Vertigo* because they 'sustain the source or abyss, of a Hitchcockian hermeneutic hoax, one that frames the spectator as well as Scottie'. Our readings 'leave no space for women', but 'erode the possibility of a feminist critique by inviting but then frustrating female agency'.[63] Although she acknowledges the frame-within-a-frame structure of *Vertigo*, Hinton also seeks to construct in the film a female subject/spectator who is not a spectre: Midge and Judy are 'live' women, and in which the female spectator has a firmer ground upon which to stand than 'the rigors of hermeneutics' have offered.[64] She locates that ground in women's 'viewing experience', but how is that experience to be articulated except through a hermeneutic practice such as her own?

We can see that Morris and Hinton continue the oscillation between an 'untenable' essentialism and a politically ineffective anti-essentialism characteristic of *Vertigo* criticism and of feminist theory in general. Jennifer Hammett has also recognised and described feminist film theory's characteristic oscillation:

> For the last twenty years, feminist film theorists have struggled to reconcile the supposedly determining force of ideology with the possibility of social change. Despite the recent shift to an emergent historicism, feminist film theorists continue to affirm representation's role in barring our access to the real, a commitment which limits the avenues of change they are able to imagine. Having conceived of the problem as epistemological – having to do with our cognitive relations to the real – they seek epistemological solutions; if ideology governs the representation of the real, then it is necessary to get outside of representation, to a more immediate epistemic relation to the real, in order to escape ideology.[65]

Hammett suggests that we need to challenge the very notion that 'epistemology matters by suggesting that the fact that we cannot get outside representation is without consequences'.[66] Hammett's claims are large – she is urging feminist theorists 'to abandon the project of epistemology, if the goal of epistemology is to make general claims about the nature and sources of true knowledge'.[67] Not representation but representations are what is problematic:

> To the extent that the struggle is over ideas – that is, over representations – what is needed is not a feminist position *vis-à-vis* representation, but feminist representations.[68]

If everything takes place on the 'discursive' level, the playing field is even. No one has access to something called the 'real' or the 'referent'. I think that this is correct, insofar as it works on the drawing board – it's not inconsistent with the deconstructivist's view of language – it's just that we'll stop obsessing over the abysses. But anguish over representations, especially as they are linked to desire, continues to dominate our culture. The sense that *someone* has privileged access to the real, that they should have that access, that their access to it is threatening, that I will never recover the object lost to the real, that a part of me has been amputated (like Midge's head on Carlotta's body) and abjected into the real – these are visions haunting all of us.

The resurgence of the problem of the woman as material being is considered with great insight and precision in Judith Butler's *Bodies That Matter* (1993).[69] Indeed, her opening remarks uncannily echo the terms of problems I have sketched regarding criticism of *Vertigo*.

> Theorizing from the ruins of the Logos invites the following question: 'What about the materiality of the body?' Actually, in the recent past, the question was repeatedly formulated to me this way: 'What about the materiality of the body, *Judy*?' I took it that the addition of 'Judy' was an effort to dislodge me from the more formal 'Judith' and to recall me to a bodily life that could not be theorized ... Perhaps this was an effort to

> recall me to an apparently evacuated femininity, the one that was constituted at that moment in the mid-50s when the figure of Judy Garland inadvertently produced a string of 'Judys' whose later appropriations and derailments could not have been predicted.[70]

Butler's previous writings on gender and sexuality as 'performative' and 'constructed' inspired her interlocutors to bring her back to a material self, one who, like our Judy in *Vertigo*, is clearly the product of a history of representations, but who also seems to be something more. Butler uses the figure of 'Judy' as a means of opening a book-length discussion of the philosophical problem of the exclusion of the body and matter from the domain of intelligibility. Any social system that produces sexed subjects through injunction 'requires and institutes a "constitutive outside" – the unspeakable, the unviable, the nonnarrativizable that secures and, hence, fails to secure the very borders of materiality'.[71] Like Samuels, Butler sees a critical rethinking of the relationship of the feminine and the 'Real' in psychoanalytic discourse as a crucial step in making the 'constitutive exclusions' that govern desire and language less oppressive, in essence to achieve what Hammett recommends. We cannot yet eliminate the problem of representation because we have not yet figured out how to disarm constitutive exclusions. Fear, desire and economic interest are all factors in their construction, their repression and their return to us in eroticised or nightmare form. *Vertigo*'s drama of exclusion excites our desire to know more. Perhaps these discussions of the film can help us to broaden what we conceive of as representable and teach us to manage our knowledge and the power and vulnerabilities it brings.

Notes

I am very grateful for editorial help with this essay from Richard Allen, Susan Z. Bernstein, Peter Fenves, Hilary Radner and Michael Trosset. David Dym provided valuable computer know-how.

1 Christopher Morris, 'Feminism, Deconstruction, and the Pursuit of the Tenable in *Vertigo*', *Hitchcock Annual* (1996–7), p. 4.

2 Tania Modleski, *The Women Who Knew Too Much: Hitchcock and Feminist Theory*, New York and London: Methuen, 1988, p. 87.

3 See Laura Mulvey, 'Visual Pleasure and Narrative Cinema', *Screen* 16 no. 3, 1975, pp. 6–18; reprinted in *Screen* Editors (ed.), *The Sexual Subject: A Screen Reader in Sexuality*, London: Routledge, 1992, pp. 22–33. Subsequent references are to the latter text.

4 Mulvey, 'Visual Pleasure', p. 32.

5 Elster is positioned as Lacan's 'subject supposed to know', or as the 'Other of the Other'. See Slavoj Žižek, *Looking Awry: An Introduction to Jacques Lacan through Popular Culture*, Cambridge, MA: MIT Press, 1991, p. 81. Žižek compares Judy, as sublime object transformed, to the graceful octopus of the depths turning into a 'disgusting lump of slime' when pulled from the water. Thus the idealised other may return as horror, and to 'embody the Thing' always entails mortal danger for women (p. 84).

6 Mulvey, 'Visual Pleasure', p. 32.

7 For an early discussion of the female spectator as 'transvestite', see Laura Mulvey, 'Afterthoughts on "Visual Pleasure and Narrative Cinema" inspired by *Duel in the Sun*', in *Visual and Other Pleasures*, London: Macmillan, 1989, pp. 29–39.

8 William Rothman and Stanley Cavell also consider crucial the woman's relationship to knowledge. See William Rothman, 'Vertigo: The Unknown Woman in Hitchcock', in Joseph H. Smith and William Kerrigan (eds), *Images in Our Souls: Cavell, Psychoanalysis, and Cinema*, Baltimore: Johns Hopkins UP, 1987, pp. 64–81, and Stanley Cavell, 'Psychoanalysis and Cinema: The Melodrama of the Unknown Woman,' *Images in Our Souls*, pp. 11–43. Rothman asks whether *Vertigo* can be considered an instance of a new (sub)genre delineated by Cavell, the 'unknown woman' film, in which women, like Judy, remain 'unacknowledged' or misrecognised by the men they love. For Cavell, this misrecognition reflects the 'villainous potential in maleness', which he locates in a particular interpretation of the 'problem of other minds' (Do other minds exist? Can I know what they know?) Radical scepticism concerning other minds is, Cavell claims, a specifically masculine province with its root cause in a man's inability (before DNA testing) to know whether or not his child is his own. Although he finds 'vulgar' the notion that any, reified form of difference can be located 'in some fixed way women know that men don't', Cavell seems to claim that women can 'know' maternity in a way that men cannot know paternity, and that broader epistemological consequences follow from this knowledge (p. 31). For Rothman, *Vertigo* is a 'melodrama of the unknown woman' insofar as Judy apprehends her condition 'more deeply than do the men in her world' and possesses a 'deeper vision, intelligence, and depth of feeling' than do these men (p. 78), but the film ultimately diverges from the unknown-woman genre in that it is Hitchcock's affinity, his identification with the unknown woman desperately longing for existence, rather than the woman herself, who dominates the film (p. 79). Cavell's complex, delicately hedged essentialism and his experiments in crossing gender boundaries through identification, like Rothman's dramatic auteurism, seem to me to sentimentalise male acknowledgment of the victimised woman. Interestingly, Modleski finds Hitchcock's identification with the unknown woman to be a more radical gesture than does Rothman.

9 See, for example, Pam Cook and Claire Johnston, 'The Place of Woman in the Cinema of Raoul Walsh', in Constance Penley, (ed.) *Feminism and Film Theory*, New York: Routledge, 1988, p. 35.

10 Tania Modleski, 'Never to be Thirty-Six Years Old: *Rebecca* as Female Oedipal Drama', *Wide Angle* 5, no. 1, 1982, pp. 34–41. Mary Ann Doane's *The Desire to Desire: The Woman's Film of the 1940s*, Bloomington: Indiana University Press, 1987, also significantly contributes to feminist Hitchcock studies in its chapter on *Caught* and *Rebecca* (pp. 155–75), but reflects an even more pessimistic view on the impasses of female spectatorship than does De Lauretis's work. See further comments on Doane's relation to Modleski below.

11 Teresa De Lauretis, *Alice Doesn't: Feminism, Semiotics, Cinema*, Bloomington: Indiana University Press, 1984, p. 155.

12 Karen Hollinger, 'The Look, Narrativity, and the Female Spectator in *Vertigo*', *Journal of Film and Video* 39, no. 4, Fall 1987, p. 22.

13 Mary Ann Doane, Patricia Mellencamp and Linda Williams (eds.), *Re-Vision: Essays in*

Feminist Film Criticism, Frederick, Maryland: University Publications of America, 1984, p. 11.

14 Hollinger, 'The Look', p. 23.

15 Hollinger, 'The Look', p. 24.

16 Hollinger, 'The Look', p. 24.

17 Hollinger, 'The Look', p. 25.

18 Christine Gledhill, 'Developments in Feminist Film Criticism', in *Re-Vision: Essays in Feminist Film Criticism*, p. 26.

19 Christine Gledhill, 'Developments in Feminist Film Criticism', in *Re-Vision: Essays in Feminist Film Criticism*, Frederick, Maryland: University Publications of America, 1984, p. 41.

20 Modleski, *The Women Who Knew Too Much*, p. 4. Modleski is quoting Frederic Jameson, *The Political Unconscious: Narrative as a Socially Symbolic Act*, Ithaca: Cornell University Press, 1981, pp. 289–90.

21 Modleski (*The Women Who Knew Too Much*, p. 8) explicitly rebuts Doane's 'nihilistic' view that 'the preoedipal relationship with the mother [i]s the source of insurmountable difficulties for the female spectator' in that her closeness to the female body, her overidentification with the woman's onscreen image, 'prevents the woman from assuming a position similar to the man's in relation to signifying systems' (Modleski cites Doane, 'Film and the Masquerade: Theorising the Female Spectator', *Screen* 23, nos. 3–4, September–October 1982, p. 79). While for Doane there is something really crippling for women in the relationship they are assigned *vis-à-vis* systems of signification, for Modleski these are male fictions about women's incapacities.

22 Virginia Wright Wexman, 'The Critic as Consumer: Film Study in the University, Vertigo, and the Film Canon', *Film Quarterly* 39: 3 (Spring 1986), p. 34. For Rothman's discussion of Hitchcock's cinema as allegorical, see William Rothman, *Hitchcock – The Murderous Gaze*, Cambridge: Harvard University Press, 1982.

23 Wexman, 'The Critic as Consumer', p. 34. For de Lauretis's 'woman–women' distinction, see Teresa de Lauretis, *Alice Doesn't: Feminism, Semiotics, Cinema,* Bloomington: Indiana University Press, 1984, p. 5.

24 Wexman, 'The Critic as Consumer', p. 34.

25 Wexman, 'The Critic as Consumer', p. 38.

26 Wexman, 'The Critic as Consumer', p. 38.

27 Gayatri Chakravorty Spivak, 'Imperialism and Sexual Difference', *Oxford Literary Review*, 8, no. 25, 1986, p. 225.

28 Gayatri Chakravorty Spivak, 'Imperialism and Sexual Difference', *Oxford Literary Review*, 8, no. 25, 1986, p. 226.

29 Susan White, 'Allegory and Referentiality: Vertigo and Feminist Film Criticism', *MLN* 106, no. 5, 1991, pp. 910–32.

30 Homi K. Bhabha, 'The Other Question: The Stereotype and Colonial Discourse', in *The Sexual Subject: A Screen Reader in Sexuality* (London and New York: Routledge, 1992), p. 313.

31 Robert Corber approaches the problem of historical representation in *Vertigo* somewhat differently than does Wexman. In ' "There Are Many Such Stories": *Vertigo* and the Repression of Historical Knowledge', a chapter in *In the Name of National*

Security: Hitchcock, Homophobia, and the Political Construction of Gender in Postwar America, Durham, North Carolina: Duke University Press, 1993. Corber describes the film as enacting a complex set of displacements regarding its *critique* of historical repression and its *participation* in historical repression. Carlotta's story is romanticised as a result of exclusion from official history. This romanticisation is part of what prevents Scottie from seeing 'the connection between her experiences and those of the other women in the film' (p. 158). Thus he 'remains blind' (p. 159) to his own participation in the ongoing racism and misogyny of San Francisco. The film 'not only thematizes the consequences of the repression of historical knowledge but enacts them as well' (p. 159) in encouraging the spectator to romanticise the Scottie–Madeleine relationship. I will return to Corber's essay below.

32 Robin Wood's response to Modleski is in *Hitchcock's Films Revisited*, New York: Columbia University Press, 1989, p. 375.

33 Patrice Petro, 'Rematerializing the Vanishing "Lady": Feminism, Hitchcock, and Interpretation' in *A Hitchcock Reader*, Marshall Deutelbaum and Leland Poague (eds.), Ames, Iowa: Iowa State University Press, 1986, pp. 141–52.

34 In an essay that I consider at some length elsewhere, Marian Keane also critiques Mulvey's view that Scottie is in control of the narrative and points to Jimmy Stewart's capacity for 'suffering' before the camera as a trait Hitchcock knew well how to use. Although I disagree with her comments on Freud, like Stanley Cavell and William Rothman, Keane shows great sensitivity to Hitchcock's use of the actor. For my discussion of Keane's essay, 'A Closer Look at Scopophilia: Mulvey, Hitchcock, and *Vertigo*', in *A Hitchcock Reader* (pp. 231–48) see Susan White, 'Allegory and Referentiality: *Vertigo* and Feminist Criticism', *MLN* 106(5), 1991, pp. 310–32. This essay is to some extent a revision of 'Allegory and Referentiality'.

35 Modleski, *The Women Who Knew Too Much*, p. 99.

36 See Julia Kristeva, *Powers of Horror: An Essay on Abjection*, trans. Leon S. Roudiez, New York: Columbia University Press, 1982, for her discussion of how the 'throwing off' (abjecting) of both mother and child takes place even before complete (psychological and physical) separation has occurred (p. 23).

37 Like Samuels, Corber demonstrates confidence in Hitchcock's understanding of the specific oppression of 'deviant' sexualities. See also Corber's essay in this volume, Chapter 19, p. 281 (which I had not read when this book went to press). In 'There Are Many Such Stories', Corber sees Scottie as responding to the social stigmatisation of 'men who remained single as perverts who suffered from an arrested sexual development' (p. 161). While Samuels sees Hitchcock as correcting the theoretical shortcomings of Jacques Lacan, Corber describes Hitchcock as critical of the Beat generation's racism and misogyny: 'In suggesting that the Beats did not go far enough in rejecting middle-class values, Hitchcock was unusually bold' (p. 160). Scottie's social rebellion against his role as officer of the law produced in him, Corber claims, a fear of his own potential homosexuality, because he continues to interpret his wish to resign from the law according to the 'homophobic categories of the dominant discourse of rebellion' (p. 173), the discourse of the Beats. Because he is so afraid of being homosexual, Scottie overplays his 'lawful' role as detective with Madeleine. This will lead to Scottie repressing what he *knows* – that Elster is plotting to murder his wife

(p. 174). Hitchcock's radical view of history critiques the misogyny and homophobia that the Beats retain as a vestige of their middle-class status: 'The film, then, exposes the homophobic categories of the official narrative of male development as a mechanism for maintaining the economic prosperity and political stability of the 1950s' (p. 174).

38 Samuels, *Hitchcock's Bi-textuality*, p. 81.

39 Samuels, *Hitchcock's Bi-textuality*, p. 29.

40 Samuels, *Hitchcock's Bi-textuality*, p. 42. Samuels does, however, correct Mulvey's reading of the gaze in Lacan: it is not fundamentally a tool of aggression but a locus of vulnerability: 'By reversing Mulvey's interpretation, I will articulate how Lacan's notion of the "gaze" offers a valuable tool for resistant forms of feminine representation. For Lacan, the gaze is precisely that part of the visual world that refuses to be controlled or mastered. In its structure, the gaze proves masculine castration and not, as Mulvey argues, the control of the visual field. I believe that Mulvey's reading is an ideological one that does not take into account the true nature of unconscious and bi-textual desire' (p. 3). Although I agree with Samuels's reading of Lacan, one needs to keep in mind not simply that the (male) gaze is deluded when it asserts itself as powerful/phallic, but also that this projection of power has been backed up by aggression linked to 'male' looking. Mark cannot master the world through his camera in *Peeping Tom*, but he makes a convincing show of mastering the women he stabs to death with his tripod.

41 Samuels, *Hitchcock's Bi-textuality*, p. 30. Samuels's linking of feminity to writing in these films is I think, a significant contribution to feminist studies of Hitchcock.

42 Samuels, *Hitchcock's Bi-textuality*, p. 42.

43 Samuels, *Hitchcock's Bi-textuality*, p. 83.

44 Samuels, *Hitchcock's Bi-textuality*, p. 82.

45 Samuels, *Hitchcock's Bi-textuality*, p. 26.

46 Samuels, *Hitchcock's Bi-textuality*, p. 79.

47 Samuels, *Hitchcock's Bi-textuality*, p. 11.

48 Samuels, *Hitchcock's Bi-textuality*, p. 147.

49 Deborah Linderman, 'The Mise-en-Abime in Hitchcock's *Vertigo*', *Cinema Journal* 30, no. 4, 1991, p. 52.

50 Linderman, 'The Mise-en-Abime in Hitchcock's *Vertigo*', p. 53.

51 Linderman, 'The Mise-en-Abime in Hitchcock's *Vertigo*', p. 55.

52 Linderman, 'The Mise-en-Abime in Hitchcock's *Vertigo*', p. 65.

53 Linderman, 'The Mise-en-Abime in Hitchcock's *Vertigo*', p. 70.

54 Linderman, 'The Mise-en-Abime in Hitchcock's *Vertigo*', p. 70.

55 Linderman, 'The Mise-en-Abime in Hitchcock's *Vertigo*', p. 71.

56 Christopher Morris, 'Feminism, Desconstruction', and the Pursuit of the Tenable in *Vertigo*', *Hitchcock Annual* (1996–97), p. 3.

57 Morris, 'Feminism, Desconstruction', p. 3. He cites Judith Butler, *Gender Trouble: Feminism and the Subversion of Identity*, New York: Routledge, 1990.

58 Morris, 'Feminism, Desconstruction', p. 4.

59 Morris, 'Feminism, Desconstruction', p. 16.

60 Morris, 'Feminism, Desconstruction', p. 20, n. 5.

61 Morris, 'Feminism, Desconstruction', p. 19.
62 See Richard Allen and Murray Smith (eds.), 'Introduction', in *Film Theory and Philosophy*, Oxford: Clarendon Press, 1997, p. 16.
63 Laura Hinton, 'A Woman's View: the Vertigo Frame-Up', *Film Criticism* 19, no. 2, 1994, p. 3.
64 Hinton, 'A Woman's View,' p. 19.
65 Jennifer Hammett, 'The Ideological Impediment: Epistemology, Feminism, and Film Theory' in Richard Allen and Murray Smith (eds.), *Film Theory and Philosophy*, Oxford, Clarendon Press, 1997, p. 255.
66 Hammett, 'The Ideological Impediment', p. 256.
67 Hammett, 'The Ideological Impediment', p. 256.
68 Hammett, 'The Ideological Impediment', p. 257.
69 Judith Butler, *Bodies That Matter: On the Discursive Limits of 'Sex'*, New York: Routledge, 1993. See especially the chapter entitled 'Arguing with the Real' (pp. 187–222). Butler's discussion of Slavoj Žižek is particularly useful for those interested in his work on Hitchcock.
70 Butler, *Bodies That Matter*, p. x.
71 Butler, *Bodies That Matter*, p. 188.

Fear of the invisible subversive – Kim Novak as Judy Barton

Chapter 19
'You wanna check my thumbprints?': *Vertigo*, the Trope of Invisibility and Cold War Nationalism

Robert J. Corber

In the wake of the McCarthy witch-hunts of the early 1950s, Americans became obsessed with identifying the difference between the American and the unAmerican. One of the purposes of the witch-hunts was to show that even ordinary Americans might harbour subversive political beliefs, or worse, engage in counterespionage for the Soviet Union, and the invisibility of subversives emerged as one of the master tropes of the discourse of national security. In the 1920s and 1930s, communism was thought to appeal either to Greenwich Village bohemians who believed in free love or to immigrant Jewish intellectuals with ties to Yiddish culture. But with the adoption of the Popular Front in 1935, in which communists joined forces with liberals in the struggle against Fascism, the sort of Americans who were drawn to the Communist party became less easy to identify.[1] Abandoning the category of the worker in favour of that of the people, the party embraced mainstream American values and engaged in a cultural politics intended to demonstrate its patriotism. In his sensationalistic, tell-all memoir *I Led Three Lives*, one of many such memoirs published in the 1950s in which FBI informers provided dubious accounts of life 'underground' in the Communist party, Herbert Philbrick captured the paranoia and suspicion the invisibility of communists instilled in many Americans: 'Anyone can be a Communist. Anyone can suddenly appear in a meeting as a Communist party member – close friend, brother, employee, or even employer, leading citizen, trusted public servant.'[2]

The fear of the invisible subversive that gripped the nation was not confined to communists and fellow travellers, however. In 1950, after holding highly publicised hearings in which the chief officer of the District of Columbia vice squad testified that thousands of government employees had been arrested on morals charges, many of them across from the White House in Lafayette Square, a notorious cruising venue, the Senate Appropriations Committee issued a deeply homophobic report in which it asserted that male and female homosexuals posed a serious threat to national security and should be expelled from the government.[3] At the same time, the committee stressed how difficult exposing such employees would be if they did not already have a police record. Citing medical evidence that disputed the stereotypes of the effeminate gay man and the manly lesbian, the report stated that there were 'no outward characteristics or physical traits' that identified homosexuals.[4] Indeed, homosexuals were virtually indistinguishable from heterosexuals: 'Many male homosexuals are very masculine in their physical appearance and general demeanor, and many female homosexuals have every appearance of femininity in their outward behavior'.[5] In emphasising the invisibility of homosexuals, the report linked them to the communists and fellow travellers who where then also being investigated by Congress.[6] For if homosexuals could not be easily identified, then they too could infiltrate the government without being detected and subvert it from within by perverting 'normal' employees. Because they lacked distinguishing characteristics, the report asserted, 'one homosexual can pollute a Government office'.[7]

The trope of the invisible subversive, which was so central to cold-war political rhetoric, worked to contain opposition to cold-war ideologies in two ways. First, it insured that identifying the difference between the American and the unAmerican, the purported goal of the anti-communist and the anti-homosexual witch-hunts that transfixed the nation in the late 1940s and 1950s, could never be accomplished with any certainty. Assailed by sensationalistic accounts of the Communist party like Philbrick's, many Americans came to believe that they could trust no one, not even members of their own families. Second, the trope elevated issues of gender and sexuality to the level of national security. Any American who deviated from the dominant norms of masculinity and femininity risked construction as unAmerican, not just gays and lesbians. Thus heterosexual women who did not contain their sexuality to the domestic sphere or who worked outside of the home despite being married were denounced by a variety of experts because they supposedly threatened the nuclear family, which was considered the foundation of national life.[8]

In what follows, I explore the cold-war trope of invisibility in relation to *Vertigo* (1958). Despite the fact that it was neither a critical nor a box-office success when it was initially released, many critics consider *Vertigo* Hitchcock's masterpiece, as though it transcended the ideological conditions of its production.[9] Yet *Vertigo* elaborates the trope of invisibility in particularly complex ways, simultaneously underwriting and contesting cold-war ideologies. The film centres on a tawdry working-class white woman, Judy Barton (Kim Novak), who impersonates a glamorous heiress of Mexican descent, Madeleine Elster. Despite the enormous differences between her and the heiress, Judy's impersonation is so believable that Scottie (James Stewart), a former police detective hired to investigate her, falls deeply in love with her and fails to prevent Madeleine's avaricious husband from murdering her. But Judy's ability to impersonate Madeleine depends on the heiress embodying a mass-produced style of femininity that Anglicises her. Because of the way in which it elaborates the trope of invisibility, the film sheds considerable light on the relations of looking that governed the production of national subjectivity during the cold-war era. Scottie's love for Judy places her in a double bind. It is contingent upon her reassuming her glamorous look as Madeleine, but in so doing she renders her working-class identity invisible and thus re-engages in the very duplicity that made her vulnerable to exposure in the first place. What does this double bind indicate about one of the most troubling legacies of cold-war nationalism, the massive expansion of state power of which the anti-communist and anti-homosexual witch-hunts were symptomatic? How did the fear of the invisible subversive contribute to that expansion? In seeking to answer these questions, I hope not only to illuminate what is arguably one of Hitchcock's most haunting and complex films by situating it in relation to cold-war nationalism, but I also hope to elucidate the ideological conditions that led the mass of Americans to consent to a virtually unprecedented contraction of their freedoms in the name of national security.

A crime of passing

When Scottie finally locates Judy in a seedy residential hotel where after being ditched by Elster (Tom Helmore), she has reassumed her proper identity, he refuses to believe that she is who she claims to be. Although she provides him with detailed information about herself ('My name is Judy Barton, I come from Salinas, Kansas, I work at Magnin's, and I live here'), he persists in questioning her about her identity. Pressing her for more information, he tells her, 'I just want to know who you are,' as though none of the facts she has mentioned (her name, her place of birth, where she lives and works) are sufficient to establish her identity. Even when out of desperation she shows him her driver's license with the hotel's address on it, he does not seem satisfied. She finally asks, 'You wanna check my thumbprints?' as though they would provide irrefutable proof of her identity. But the point is she can provide no proof of her identity that would wholly satisfy Scottie. With this scene, the film renders Judy's identity suspicious *before* it reveals her involvement in Elster's murderous plot. Exactly who is this woman who looks enough like the 'dead' Madeleine to catch Scottie's eye while on her way home from work? Does she really live in a seedy residential hotel and work as a salesclerk in a department store? Or is her identity a cover designed to conceal a shady past?

Of course, her identity as Judy Barton is a cover. Her look is so different from the upper-class Madeleine's that no one, including Scottie, would connect her with the heiress brutally murdered by Elster. But by withholding knowledge of her complicity with the murder until the following scene where, in a flashback, we see her scream as Elster throws the real Madeleine from the bell tower of the mission at San Juan Bautista, the film complicates her guilt. Her implication in the murder does not seem nearly as incriminating as her deception of Scottie. Because her impersonation is so convincing, it makes her 'real' identity impossible to detect. If she was able to deceive Scottie, a former police detective, how can she really be Judy Barton? In raising this question, the film links her to the invisible subversive of the discourses of national security.

If it is impossible to determine conclusively Judy's 'real' identity, that is because the contrast between her and Madeleine could not be more sharply drawn. The film ascribes to Judy some of the most negative stereotypes of working-class femininity. Spectators would have associated her style of glamour with the pin-up. Such a style seems intended to translate her working-class identity into visual terms. She wears garish-colored clothes (vibrant greens and purples), cheaply made jewellery, heavy eye make-up, and even a beauty mark, a look that seems designed to advertise her sexual availability. When Scottie asks her out, she at first hesitates but then admits, 'I've been picked up before,' indicating a history of illicit sexual liaisons. By contrast, Madeleine's look resembles that of a glamorous Hollywood star. Her clothes are elegantly subdued in colour, and she wears her hair in a French twist, a signifier in the 1950s of sophistication and taste. Such a look, although it allows her to circulate as an object of desire, is not a sign that she is sexually available. On the contrary, her sexual capital, unlike Judy's, depends upon her limiting access to her body. But the differences between Judy and Madeleine are more than visual. Unlike Judy, Madeleine speaks with an upper-class accent and has a refined manner. Such a sharp contrast between the two women seems meant to heighten Scottie's sense of betrayal. Not only does Judy ensnare Scottie in Elster's plot by diverting his attention from the investigation. She also conceals from him her working-class identity. A self-described 'man of independent means', Scottie is a Stanford-educated lawyer who once hoped to become chief of police. He would never be attracted to a woman as cheap and tawdry as Judy, let alone fall in love with her.

Further complicating the question of her guilt, Judy seems unwilling to relinquish her working-class identity, even though Scottie's love is contingent upon her doing so. In the scene following the flashback Judy begins a letter to Scottie but then tears it up. We hear her say in a voice-over, 'If I had the nerve, I'd stay and be hoping that I could make you love me again as I am, for myself, and so forget the other, forget the past.' She hopes, in other words, to make Scottie fall in love with her, despite her working-class identity. But it is precisely that identity that he tries to erase by making her over as the 'dead' Madeleine. When he first proposes the make-over, she pleads, 'Couldn't you like me, just me, the way I am?' But it is obvious even to her that he would never have been attracted to her if she did not remind him of Madeleine. He even avoids touching her, except when coaxing her about the make-over. Desperate for his love, she finally agrees. 'If I let you change me, will that do it?' she asks, repressing her own desire. But despite her claim to the contrary ('I don't care anymore about me'), she struggles to retain at least some of her working-class style. She returns from the salon, for example, with her hair dyed the same color as Madeleine's, but hanging down around her shoulders as before. When Scottie reminds her that he told the beautician how her hair was supposed to be done, she explains, 'We tried it, it just didn't suit me.' Even when she finally yields to Scottie's entreaty and emerges from the bathroom with her hair in a French twist like Madeleine's, her transformation into the 'dead' woman remains incomplete. She resembles her in looks only. As Scottie bitterly remarks after discovering her duplicity, Elster did a better job of making her over, teaching her 'the manner and the words' as well as the glamorous style. Judy looks like Madeleine but she does not act like her, and thus her working-class identity can still be detected.

Judy's reluctance to be made over by Scottie emerges as a perverse desire to register visually the class differences between her and Madeleine. Even as it fetishises Madeleine as an object of visual pleasure, the film suggests that her glamorous style was widely available to women in the 1950s, regardless of their class. In the sequence of shots in which Scottie obsessively revisits sites associated with Madeleine (the Mission Dolores, the Palace of Fine Arts, and so on) after being released from the sanitarium, he mistakes one women after another for her: a woman emerging from Madeleine's apartment building who wears a coat similar to Madeleine's in the scene in the redwood forest; a woman at Ernie's, the restaurant where he first caught a glimpse of Madeleine, who is dressed in a grey suit that recalls the one Madeleine wore in the scene at the Palace of Fine Arts; and so on. Moreover, the film represents Judy's make-over as a form of mass production. In the sequence of shots in which we see the make-over, the beauty salon resembles an assembly line. Judy seems to be merely one of many women being made over in the same style, and she has her hair dyed and her nails manicured simultaneously. This emphasis on how easily mass-produced Madeleine's look is has the effect of stigmatising Judy further for being working-class. Why would she prefer a look that is so markedly working-class when Madeleine's can be obtained so easily, as Judy herself demonstrates through her impersonation of her? Thus the film's representation of Judy is profoundly contradictory. On the one hand, her concealment of her working-class identity is supposedly even more incriminating than her willingness to act as Elster's decoy. On the other hand, she is too visibly working-class and therefore cannot function as an object of visual pleasure for Scottie.

Nowhere are the contradictions more apparent than in Scottie's romanticisation of Madeleine's Mexican heritage. Through his investigation, Scottie learns that Madeleine is descended from Carlotta Valdez, a Mexican woman who went mad and killed herself after being abandoned by her Anglo lover in what Scottie's former fiancée, Midge (Barbara Bel Geddes), calls 'gay old Bohemian' San Francisco. After Carlotta's lover abandoned her, he took custody of their illegitimate daughter whom he raised as an Anglo, while Carlotta wandered the streets, pitifully stopping strangers and asking if they had seen her child. Scottie's discovery of Madeleine's Mexican heritage underlies his increasingly fetishistic relation to her. It emerges as a mystery that he must solve in order to prevent her from committing suicide. Why has Madeleine become so obsessed with Carlotta Valdez when, according to Elster, she does not even know that she is descended from her? Can Scottie persuade her that there is a reasonable explanation for her memories of the mission at San Juan Bautista and that she is not herself going mad? But the film's eroticisation of Madeleine's Mexican heritage is contingent upon its remaining invisible. As I have already indicated, one of the most important differences between her and Judy is that her look, although it marks her as upper-class, is mass-produced, and thus her Mexican heritage cannot be detected. The only visible trace of her relation to Carlotta Valdez is her hairstyle, which she copies from her portrait in the Palace of the Legion of Honor. But, as we will see, decoding this trace requires an arcane knowledge of San Francisco's past, and so it does not call into question her claims to whiteness. Thus there is an inconsistency in the film's elaboration of the trope of invisibility with respect to racial and class identity. For whereas Judy's working-class identity detracts from her erotic allure, Madeleine's Mexican heritage underpins hers.

Imperial melodrama

Despite the way in which it increases Madeleine's value as a fetish object, it would be difficult to exaggerate the significance of *Vertigo*'s representation of her Mexican heritage.[10] I know of no other Hollywood film from the cold-war era that goes so far in demonstrating how interwoven the histories of Anglos and Mexicans are in the American West.[11] But *Vertigo* does more than acknowledge this aspect of the nation's history and culture. It also exposes how its erasure has distorted the nation's self-imagining. When Scottie is unable to discover the identity of Carlotta Valdez, he asks Midge if she knows anyone who specialises in California's history. But when she mentions a professor at Berkeley, he replies, 'No, no, I don't mean that kind of history, I mean the small stuff. You know, people you never heard of.' The information he needs should not be confused with 'real' history, so Midge introduces him to Pop Liebl (Konstantine Shayne), the owner of the Argossy bookstore. She understands that by 'small stuff' Scottie means 'juicy stories like who shot who on the Embarcadero in August 1879'. With his vast knowledge of San Francisco lore, Liebl has no difficulty recalling Carlotta's story. He explains that in 'gay old Bohemian' San Francisco, 'there were many such stories' as hers. Liebl cannot even recall her lover's name, as if to underscore how typical it was for Anglos to abandon their Mexican mistresses.

In recovering Carlotta's story, the film constructs a counternarrative of the nation's history and culture. It shows that despite being 'small stuff', stories like Carlotta's provide crucial evidence of the miscegenated formation of the American people, thereby shattering the national myth of racial purity. Yet such stories have been relegated to the status of lore, an inferior form of historical narrative professors at Berkeley do not have to take into account. The exhibition of Carlotta's portrait in the Palace of the Legion of Honor, known simply as *Portrait of Carlotta*, serves as a case in point. The exhibition represses the nation's history of miscegenation even as it acknowledges it. The catalogue provides no information about Carlotta, thereby rendering her anonymous.

But the film does more than construct a counternarrative of the nation's history and culture in which the exploitation of Mexicans figures prominently. It also stresses the consequences of the nation's refusal to acknowledge its history of miscegenation. One of the reasons why Scottie is so easily deceived by Elster is because he romanticises Madeleine's Mexican heritage. He does not see her miscegenated identity as the product of racial and gender hierarchies that justified the sexual exploitation of Mexican women. For him, such exploitation is part of the colourful past described by Pop Liebl and has no bearing on the present. Consequently, he fails to prevent the real Madeleine's murder. Without a better understanding of the entanglement of race and gender, he is unable to see the connection between Carlotta and the real Madeleine. Instead, he thinks that Madeleine's obsession with her family's miscegenated past drove her mad and that she committed suicide. Ironically, he is himself driven mad by Madeleine's past. Following the 'suicide', he succumbs to what his doctor describes as 'acute melancholia together with a guilt complex'. He thinks that if he could have convinced Madeleine that Carlotta had not taken possession of her but that she was remembering childhood visits to San Juan Bautista where Carlotta was born, he could have prevented her 'suicide'. In this way, the film suggests that because it has been so distorted, the nation's history of empire building can only express itself in ways that resemble the Freudian uncanny. Repressed rather than assimilated, it constantly threatens to return and unsettle the parameters of American national identity.

But despite its exposure of the exclusions upon which the parameters of American national identity have been constructed, *Vertigo* misrepresents the nation's history of miscegenation, even as it returns it to consciousness. Imperialism emerges as a melodramatic subplot in the nation's history. The film's only allusion to the genocidal violence against racialised others that national expansion and empire building involved is in Pop Liebl's description of Carlotta's sexual exploitation. He explains that her Anglo lover simply 'threw her away' after she gave birth to their child, because 'a man could do that in those days. They had the power and the freedom.' The film undercuts this acknowledgement that Anglo power and freedom were asserted at the expense of Mexicans by turning it into the stuff of melodrama. As I have already noted, we learn that after going mad, Carlotta roamed San Francisco's streets in search of the daughter callously taken from her by her lover. Even more problematic, the nation's imperial past emerges as a source of nostalgia for the characters. The abandonment of Mexican women by their Anglo lovers was simply part of San Francisco's bohemian past, the disappearance of which the male characters in particular seem to regret. In the scene in which Elster asks Scottie to follow Madeleine, he says wistfully, 'The things that spell San Francisco to me are disappearing fast, the color, excitement, power, freedom.' Given that it was made during the cold war, it is hardly surprising that *Vertigo* avoided engaging the nation's history of imperialism more directly. After all, the cold war ushered in a new phase in that history, one in which the United States was able to expand its colonial power even as it lost its colonial possessions by positioning itself as the leader of the 'free world'.[12] The film's representation of the nation's imperial past performed important cultural work by diverting attention from the emergence of this new form of colonial expansion. It represented the nation's empire building and exploitation of racialised others as part of a past that had been occluded.

The declassification of race

To clarify the cultural work performed by the film's representation of the nation's history of miscegenation, it is necessary to return to its inconsistencies with respect to racial and class identity. As we have seen, the film elaborates the cold-war trope of invisibility only in relation to Judy. Scottie feels no sense of betrayal when he discovers that Madeleine is part Mexican. If anything, her miscegenated identity only increases his desire for her because it means that their relationship crosses racial boundaries. By contrast, he feels deeply betrayed when he discovers that the upper-class Madeleine was really the working-class Judy: his relationship with Madeleine did not cross racial boundaries, as he thought, but those of class. In this way, the film displaces the threat ordinarily posed by the mixing of races in Hollywood films onto the mixing of classes.[13] For Scottie, the discovery that the woman with whom he fell in love was not part Mexican but working class is more horrifying than his simultaneous discovery that she is an accomplice to a murder. He experiences the discovery as itself a kind of murder: the woman with whom he fell in love did not even exist. How do we account for *Vertigo*'s double standard with respect to racial and class identity? Why did its counternarrative of American national identity acknowledge the exploitation of racial and ethnic minorities but not that of the working class? Put differently, why would the film represent Scottie and Judy's coupling as a form of miscegenation?

As a number of historians have shown, the impact of the cold war on the nation's racial and ethnic minorities was deeply contradictory. On the one hand, the cold war gave new urgency to the struggle to end racial segregation in the South. White liberal intellectuals argued that segregation made the United States vulnerable to ideological attack by the Soviet Union. How could the US claim to be the leader of the 'free world' when African-Americans were denied basic civil rights? Even some African-American intellectuals worried that segregation would alienate Third World peoples, thus allowing the Soviet Union to extend its sphere of influence. For example, in an interview with *Paris Review* in 1955 Ralph Ellison claimed that 'our so-called race problem has now lined up with the world problem of colonialism and the struggle of the West to gain the allegiance of the remaining non-white people who have thus far remained outside the Communist sphere'.[14]

On the other hand, racial and ethnic minorities encountered new obstacles to achieving equality because of the cold war. White liberal support of civil rights was contingent upon the disarticulation of race and class. In the 1930s, the Communist party managed to link the struggle against capitalism with the struggle for racial equality by showing how entangled race and class are in American society.[15] But with the rise of anti-communism in the late 1940s, the alliance between communists and civil rights activists became a serious liability. White liberals feared that civil rights organisations were fronts for the Communist party, and to demonstrate their commitment to the 'American way', these organisations became militantly anti-communist. They not only expressed support for the witch-hunts but also conducted their own purges of suspected communists and fellow travellers.[16] Granted, the organisations needed to broaden their base of support among whites in order to achieve their goals. But in caving in to anti-communist hysteria, they surrendered one of their most useful categories.[17] For without a discourse of class, they could not adequately address the disenfranchisement of African-Americans and other minoritised groups, a shortcoming that continues to hinder them.

The inconsistencies in *Vertigo*'s elaboration of the trope of invisibility need to be understood in the context of the cold-war project to disarticulate race from class. The film elaborates the trope of invisibility in ways that converge with this project. This is perhaps most apparent in the parallels between Carlotta and Judy, parallels the film carefully lays out. Like Carlotta, Judy is sexually exploited by a lover who has the power and freedom to throw her away. As I have already discussed, Elster longs to recapture the 'color, excitement, power, freedom' of San Francisco's bohemian past. With his wife dead, he is able to satisfy this longing. He not only inherits the fortune from her father's shipbuilding business, thus enabling him to live however he chooses, but he treats Judy as callously as Carlotta's lover treated her. Judy's relationship with Scottie duplicates the exploitative structure of her relationship with Elster. Like Elster, Scottie makes her over so that she conforms to his sexual fantasy and then discards her after discovering the truth about her identity. Finally, in the film's final scene Judy throws herself away by jumping from the bell tower of the mission at San Juan Bautista, an act that links her not only to Carlotta but also to the real Madeleine who is thrown from the bell tower by Elster. These parallels would seem to suggest that Judy's working-class identity plays a role in her exploitation that is analogous to the one Carlotta's Mexican identity played in hers. In so doing, they acknowledge that working-class women are vulnerable to sexual exploitation by upper-class men. In the light of the ways in which cold-war ideologies obscured the formation of identity in relation to class, this acknowledgement is certainly remarkable. At the same time, however, the parallels occlude the entanglement of racial and class hierarchies in American society. Race and class emerge as discrete categories of identity rather than mutually constitutive ones. There is no recognition that because of her racial privilege Judy's exploitation differs significantly from Carlotta's.

The cold-war gaze

Thus far, I have shown how *Vertigo* elaborates the trope of invisibility in relation to racial and class identity, particularly pressing issues for cold-war nationalism. Now I want to show how the film elaborates another, closely related trope of cold-war political discourse, surveillance. Feminist film critics have argued that perhaps more than any of

Hitchcock's other films except *Rear Window* (1954), *Vertigo* thematises the organisation of the look in classic Hollywood cinema.[18] Scottie's voyeuristic relation to Madeleine, established in the scenes in which he follows her around San Francisco, allows him to achieve a fetishistic distance from her. His glimpses of her through the windshield of his car frame her as an icon, or object to be looked at, that interrupts the film's narrative flow. Thus he is able to evade the threat of castration her image poses as a signifier of sexual difference. But this argument does not adequately consider how the scopic regime of cold-war nationalism transformed relations of looking. For the film's thematisation of the voyeuristic economy of filmic pleasure is profoundly shaped by the cold-war fear of the invisible subversive. After all, Scottie's fetishistic distance from Madeleine prevents him from seeing through her duplicity and preventing the real Madeleine's murder. Captivated by her glamorous beauty, he fails to maintain a clear distinction between surveillance and voyeurism. Consequently, he overlooks clues that might have enabled him to detect Elster's murderous intentions. To understand fully the ideological project underlying the film's elaboration of the trope of invisibility, it is necessary to examine Scottie's confusion of surveillance and voyeurism in some detail. For in making that confusion central to the plot, the film legitimated the paranoid organisation of the look that grounded the cold-war political imaginary even as it exposed its enormous political and psychological costs.

The shift in Scottie's relation to Madeleine, from an investigative to a voyeuristic one, suggests that far from evading the threat of castration signified by her image, he has succumbed to it. His nearly fatal fall in the film's famous opening sequence of shots throws his subjectivity into crisis by unsettling the organisation of his look. While he and a uniformed police officer are jumping from one building to another in pursuit of a suspect, he stumbles and begins to slide off the roof until he catches himself on a gutter. The officer reaches down to pull him up, but he cannot maintain his grip, and he plunges to his death. The camera's vertiginous movement in this sequence emphasises the fall's impact on the organisation of Scottie's look. The film cuts from a shot of him looking down as he dangles perilously from the gutter to a shot of the street far below. Capturing his dizzying loss of perspective, the camera simultaneously tracks out and zooms in. Following the fall, Scottie occupies an increasingly feminine position in the film's hierarchy of masculinity. Because of his vertigo, he is no longer able to perform effectively as a detective, and in order to remain on the police force, he must accept a desk job. But he questions whether he can perform effectively even in that capacity, and he decides to retire early. When he tells Midge about his decision, she expresses her disapproval by reminding him, 'Weren't you the bright young lawyer who was going to be chief of police?' Moreover, Scottie must wear a corset as part of his recuperation, and he asks Midge, 'Do you suppose many men wear corsets?', as though he were ashamed to be wearing one. The corset signifies, if not his feminisation, then his immobilisation in the face of self-doubt.

The fall's impact on the organisation of his look does not become fully apparent until he begins to investigate Madeleine and he blurs the boundaries between surveillance and voyeurism. From the first moment he catches a glimpse of Madeleine at Ernie's, she transfixes his look. To underscore this point, the camera carefully traces the movement of his look. It cuts from a shot of him turning toward the table where she is seated with her back to him, tracks slowly across the room, and lingers there until she and Elster get up from the table. Scottie does not get a full view of her until she walks into the bar and emerges fully into the light. As she waits for Elster to finish paying the bill, the camera cuts to a close-up of her face, indicating the intensity of Scottie's desire for her. In light of the fall's destabilisation of his look, it is hardly surprising that Scottie is so easily transfixed by Madeleine. In undertaking an investigation before he has fully recovered from his vertigo, he risks having to perform some action that will retrigger it, which is, of course, precisely what Elster calculates on. But in achieving a fetishistic distance from Madeleine, he seems to forestall this possibility. The camera's movement in this sequence, which is governed by his look, indicates that his voyeuristic relation to her enables him, at least temporarily, to regain visual mastery and, by extension, his masculinity.

Scottie's vexed relation to masculinity explains more fully why the discovery of Judy's crossing of class boundaries is so traumatic. The restabilisation of his look and the recovery of his masculinity are purely illusory. He realises that he occupies a position in relation to Elster that is not so different from Judy's. Because of his vertigo, Elster has been able to exploit him in ways that further undermine his masculinity. His deception by Elster seems to confirm his loss of control over his look. As we have seen, Elster anticipates Pop Liebl's description of the exploitation of Mexicans by Anglos in the scene in which he expresses nostalgia for the 'the color, excitement, power, freedom' of San Francisco's past. Scottie is so distracted by Madeleine's beauty, however, that he fails to make a connection between Elster and Carlotta's lover. The film expresses Scottie's failure to recover his masculinity primarily at the level of form. During the first part of the film, Scottie's look controls the camera's movement. Following his first glimpse of Madeleine at Ernie's, most of the sequences are composed of shots of him looking, cross-cut by shots of the objects he is looking at. But beginning with Judy's flashback, in which we, but not Scottie, learn of her complicity with the real Madeleine's murder, the camera abruptly shifts to her point of view, registering Scottie's loss of control over the camera. As if to mark the significance of this loss, Judy turns and looks directly into the camera, thereby violating the classic Hollywood taboo against the direct solicitation of the spectator's look.

More than any other aspect of the film, including the parallels between Carlotta, Madeleine and Judy, the destabilisation of Scottie's look helps to clarify the film's complex relation to cold-war nationalism. For in thematising the consequences of confusing surveillance with voyeurism, the film simaltaneously underwrites and contests the cold-war organisation of the look. The fear of the invisible subversive promoted relations of looking which were governed by an economy of surveillance. The ability to distinguish the American and the unAmerican depended on a look capable of penetrating an individual's outward appearance to the 'real' core of her/his identity. As if to ratify this necessity, Scottie's discovery of Judy's duplicity restores the organisation of his look. In the film's final sequence of shots, Scottie is able to mount the bell tower's precipitous stairs without experiencing a vertiginous loss of perspective. When he reaches the top of the stairs and looks down, there is no dizzying movement of the camera, indicating that he has finally regained visual mastery. Yet as an object of visual pleasure Judy does not have the same capacity as Madeleine to transfix his gaze. Thus seeing through her duplicity is not as difficult for him as it is when she impersonates Madeleine, which would seem to suggest that the restabilisation of his look is tenuous.

The ambivalence of the film's ratification of the cold-war look surfaces most fully in the paranoid subject position it constructs for the spectator. The revelation of Judy's duplicity substantially reduces the spectator's visual pleasure. After all, Scottie's look has served as a relay for the spectator's. Madeleine has been an object of visual pleasure for her/him as well as for Scottie. Indeed, in the scenes in which he follows Madeleine around San Francisco, Scottie, who is simultaneously stationary and mobile, functions as a diegetic substitute for the spectator. Though seated in his car, he is able to indulge his voyeuristic desire as he drives. Moreover, his car's windshield performs a function similar to that of the camera, yielding him a surplus of visual pleasure by framing Madeleine as an icon.

But with the revelation, the spectator discovers that voyeuristic pleasure has a price. Judy's flashback interrupts her/his perceptual placement in the film's narrative space by providing her/him with a knowledge that Scottie lacks. Consequently, s/he experiences a disorienting loss of perspective from which they never wholly recover. The spectator has been deceived by Scottie as well as by Judy. Because Scottie's look has until this scene controlled the camera's movement, Scottie has provided the spectator with her/his main point of entry into the narrative. But with the flashback the spectator discovers that the voyeuristic pleasure he or she has experienced by identifying with Scottie has prevented her/him from questioning Scottie's point of view. By interrupting her/his absorption in the diegesis so abruptly, the flashback works to bring her/his look into alignment with the scopic regime of cold-war nationalism. The loss of the spectator's main point of identification is so disorienting that it calls into question the look as a source of knowledge and instills a desire to regain visual mastery. At the same time, the film's adoption of Judy's point of view partially counteracts this legitimation of the cold-war gaze. By encouraging the spectator to identify with Judy, the film prevents her/him from judging her as harshly as Scottie does. Her deception, though hardly justifiable, seems understandable. In this way, the film provides a subtle reminder that in the scopic regime of cold-war nationalism the spectator is as much an object as a subject of surveillance.

The state of paranoia

In National Security Council Memorandum No. 68, which provided the blueprint for the coordination of United States foreign and domestic policy during the cold war, Paul Nitze warned ominously that containing the threat of Soviet subversion depended upon the American people sacrificing 'some of the benefits which they have come to associate with their freedoms'.[19] But in supporting the anti-communist and anti-homosexual witch-hunts of the late 1940s and 1950s, the mass of Americans showed that they were willing to sacrifice more than just some of the 'benefits' associated with democracy. For in the name of national security, they consented to a massive and virtually unprecedented expansion of state power.[20] Legislation such as the National Security Act of 1947, which allowed the executive branch to coordinate military and economic policy without congressional approval or public accountability, consolidated the state's power to regulate the production of national subjectivity.

In focusing on *Vertigo*'s elaboration of the cold-war trope of invisibility, I have tried to illuminate the ideological conditions that led the mass of Americans to consent to this contraction of their freedoms, a contraction that continues to shape American political culture, despite the end of the cold war. Because of its complex relation to cold-war nationalism, the film sheds considerable light on those conditions. As we have seen, Judy's make-over by Scottie forces her to re-engage in the very duplicity that originally linked her to the invisible subversive of the discourses of national security. For this reason, it exposes the double bind in which the discourses of national security placed those Americans who functioned as the national other during the cold war (communists, homosexuals, lesbians and heterosexual women who, like Judy, did not contain their sexuality to the domestic sphere). The construction of these Americans as the 'enemy within' forced them to conceal their identities, but in concealing their identities, they positioned themselves as 'subversives' who needed to be exposed in order to preserve the nation's security. Thus the paranoid look promoted by the fear of the invisible subversive was crucial to the cold-war expansion of state power. It insured that the parameters of American national identity remained unsettled throughout the cold-war era. Because subversives were by definition invisible, the boundaries between the American and the unAmerican could never be satisfactorily determined, except by a state endowed with virtually unlimited powers of surveillance and detection.

Notes

1 On the 'invisibility' of communists, see Andrew Ross, *No Respect: Intellectuals and Popular Culture,* New York: Routledge, 1989, pp. 15–41. The best discussion of the political and rhetorical strategies of the Popular Front is Michael Denning's *The Cultural Front,* London: Verso, 1996.

2 Quoted in Ellen Schrecker, *Many Are the Crimes: McCarthyism in America*, New York: Little, Brown, 1998, p. 141.

3 For a more detailed discussion of the report, see John D'Emilio, *Sexual Politics, Sexual Communities: The Making of a Homosexual Minority in the United States, 1940–1970,* Chicago: University of Chicago Press, 1983, pp. 41–3; and Robert J. Corber, *In the Name of National Security: Hitchcock, Homophobia, and the Political Construction of Gender in Postwar America,* Durham, NC: Duke University Press, 1993, pp. 61–9.

4 US Senate, 81st Cong., 2nd sess., Committee on Expenditures in Executive Departments, *The Employment of Homosexuals and Other Sex Perverts in Government*, Washington, DC: Government Printing Office, 1950, p. 2.

5 Ibid., pp. 2–3.

6 Ibid., p. 5.

7 It is important to point out that the intensification of national homophobia during the cold war can also be traced to the publication of the Kinsey reports on male and female sexuality in the late 1940s and early 1950s, although Kinsey, who was himself homosexual, hoped that they would promote greater tolerance of homosexuality by challenging the stereotypes of the 'effeminate gay' and the 'manly lesbian'. I discuss the relation between the Kinsey reports and the 'homosexual menace' in detail in *Homosexuality in Cold War America: Resistance and the Crisis of Masculinity,* Durham, NC: Duke University Press, 1997, pp. 1–19.

8 For a detailed account of this aspect of cold-war ideology, see Elaine Tyler May,

Homeward Bound: American Families in the Cold War Era, New York: Basic Books, 1988.

9 Indeed, the reviews could not have been more scathing. The reviewer for the *New Yorker* dismissed the film as 'farfetched nonsense'. John McCarten, '*Vertigo*', the *New Yorker*, 7 June 1958, p. 65. The reviewer for *The Nation* complained that the film made him feel 'slow-witted' and that 'it was a little too difficult for me'. Robert Hatch, 'Films', *The Nation* 14 June 1958, p. 551. The reviewer for *Newsweek* was even more critical. 'This time,' he asserted, 'Hitchcock has overdone his deviousness, overreached the limits of credibility, and, in his plot-twists, passed beyond the point of no return.' 'The Hitchcock Twist', *Newsweek*, 2 June 1958, p. 91.

10 The following represents a significant revision of my earlier discussion of the film's representation of the tangled relations between Anglos and Mexicans in *In The Name of National Security*, pp. 154–60.

11 With its exploration of interracial relationships, *Touch of Evil* (Orson Welles, 1958) is a possible exception, but its focus is on the permeability of the border between the United States and Mexico, or rather the impossibility of maintaining a border between them. Unlike *Vertigo*, it does not reference US imperialism nor its by-product, a miscegenated people and culture that rendered the distinction between American and Mexican problematic from the beginning.

12 For a particularly useful discussion of cold-war empire building, see Mike Davis, 'The Political Economy of Late Imperial America', in *Prisoners of the American Dream*, London: Verso, 1986, pp. 181–230.

13 For example, in the postwar films *Pinky* (Elia Kazan, 1949) and *Imitation of Life* (Douglas Sirk, 1959) the refusal of the mulatto characters, Pinky (Jeanne Crain) and Sara Jane (Susan Kohner), to identify as black is cast in moral terms. They engage in passing, not because the lure of enjoying white privilege is too powerful for them to resist, but because they suffer from internalised racism. Yet they eventually learn to accept themselves as 'really' black and to embrace their black heritage. This shift in their self-understanding contains the threat their rejection of their black heritage poses to white patriarchal privilege. Passing enables them to become romantically involved with white men, which raises the specter of racial mixing. Embracing their black heritage lays this spectre to rest by ensuring that they will marry black men.

14 *Conversations with Ralph Ellison*, Maryemma Graham and Amritjit Singh (eds.), Jackson, MS: University of Mississippi Press, 1995, pp. 18–19.

15 On the Communist party's articulation of race and class, see Mark Naison, *Communists in Harlem during the Depression*, New York: Grove Press, 1983; and Robin D. G. Kelley, *Hammer and Hoe: Alabama Communists during the Great Depression*, Chapel Hill, NC: University of North Carolina Press, 1990.

16 On the impact of the cold war on civil rights organisations, see Manning Marable, *Race, Reform, and Rebellion: The Second Reconstruction in Black America, 1945–1990*, Jackson, MS: University Press of Mississippi, 1991, pp. 13–39.

17 On the continuing impact of the cold-war disarticulation of race and class, see Schrecker, *Many Are The Crimes*, pp. 359–415.

18 See, for example, Laura Mulvey, 'Visual Pleasure and Narrative Cinema' in *Feminism and Film Theory*, Constance Penley (ed.), New York: Routledge, 1988, pp. 57–66; Teresa

de Lauretis, *Alice Doesn't: Feminism, Semiotics, Cinema,* Bloomington, IN: Indiana University Press, 1984, pp. 153–5; and Tania Modleski, *The Woman Who Knew Too Much: Hitchcock and Feminist Theory,* New York: Methuen, 1988, pp. 85–101. See also Robin Wood, *Hitchcock's Films Revisited,* New York: Columbia University Press, 1989, pp. 108–30.

19 Quoted in Frederick M. Dolan, *Allegories of America: Narratives, Metaphysics, Politics,* Ithaca, NY: Cornell University Press, 1994, p. 73.

20 Despite its continuing impact, the cold-war expansion of the state has been all but ignored by American studies scholars. For an important exception, see Dolan, *Allegories of America*, pp. 60–113.

The 39 Steps – 'Is your name Hannay?' 'No.'

Chapter 20
39 Steps to 'The Borders of the Possible': Alfred Hitchcock, Amateur Observer and the New Cultural History

Toby Miller

> In 1909, the sensational novelist William Le Queux published *Spies for the Kaiser: Plotting the Downfall of England*, in which two lawyers expose 'the vast army of German spies spread over our smiling land of England'. When the novel was serialised in the *Weekly News*, the paper appointed a spy editor, and ran the headlines: 'FOREIGN SPIES IN BRITAIN./10 Pounds Given For Information./Have You Seen a Spy?' – (David Trotter)[1]

> 'While Europe was tensely watching the crisis over Czechoslovakia, Herr Hitler, accompanied by eight of his generals, paid a surprise visit to the French frontier to-day.' That is the way the newspapers talk about the world. These actual words were splashed across the *Star* on 29 August 1938. Of course, that is assuming that Britain, and the rest of Europe, really were at that time 'tensely watching'. But were they? How many were more tensely watching the racing news and daily horoscope? – (Mass-Observation)[2]

The first of these quotations details a shift in discourse between fiction and fact. This transformation happened because Le Queux claimed his novel was founded on fact, that thousands of Germans were 'planted' as barbers and waiters across the Edwardian Jerusalem. Fear of traitors and spies also gained expression in drama, film and comics, and when a newspaper reported in 1914 that enamelled advertisements for Maggi soup on telegraph poles contained messages to German spies, London suburbs became sites for 'screwdriver parties' at which loyal citizens would remove suspect signs.[3] Clearly, an early case of semiotic guerrilla warfare. The *Weekly News*' spy editor drew an extraordinary public response. And the British Government was persuaded to establish a Secret Services bureau, which rounded up a grand total of twenty to thirty suspects during the Great War from among the 75–90,000 citizens of the Central Powers allegedly resident in the UK – even though evidence from both then and now suggests there were no German plans to invade Britain and little inclination to spy on it.[4] Le Queux's novel and its reception can be read as signs of a realisation that an overreaching Empire was in decline,[5] as other powers sought to displace British 'civilisation'. Such an allegorical reading is one defence of the accusation that espionage fiction is a simple-minded genre because it chooses as 'protagonists men of action, not administrators, and least of all intelligence analysts'. (The latter are held to do the real work of spying.)[6]

The second quotation that begins this chapter, Mass-Observation's plea for the power of the quotidian as a counter to grand generalities about the public mind, mitigates a second charge against espionage fiction, that Le Queux, John Buchan, Alfred Hitchcock, and their ilk manipulate simple folk through the romantic evocation of a myth 'almost as ancient as man himself – the overcoming of the monster'.[7] Decidedly asymptomatic, Mass-Observation (M-O) proposes that the alleged apoplectic 1930s rush to militarism and spy mania was a fantasy of élites, not of everyday folk. The same might be said of the pre-World War I British public, who were busy with much more than espionage panic. They devoured P. G. Wodehouse's parody of Le Queux, *The Swoop! Or How Clarence Saved England* (also 1909), in which a boy scout defeats nine enemy armies.[8] More seriously, Norman Angell's tracts on economic pacificism had huge sales and great influence. He claimed that national prosperity derived from credit and commercial exchange rather than imperialism, and that it was therefore not in the interests of an economy to go to war.[9]

How might we historicise and evaluate espionage fiction? Allen Dulles, a vicious cold warrior who ran the Central Intelligence Agency (CIA) at the height of its 1950s infamy, claimed that 'the clandestine nature' of spying necessitated no 'exposure to outsiders'. This 'vacuum' created the conditions of existence for 'highly exaggerated ... short stories, novels, motion pictures and television series' that diminished 'the comprehensive craft of intelligence' to romantic individualism.[10] Dulles's knowledge of literary and espionage history was on a par with his judgement in advocating the pathetic Bay of Pigs invasion, which cost him his job.[11] For just as he had earlier orchestrated, through manipulation of the mass media, the very formation of the CIA against Presidential will, so popular culture and its figural norms had always been critical of the creation and conduct of social knowledges of spying. Somerset Maugham, Ian Fleming, Graham Greene and John le Carré were spies who later redisposed their experiences in fiction, adding a flavour of personal authenticity. Buchan himself went the other way, from novelist to agent.[12]

This complex intrication of the factual and the fictional forms the backdrop to my argument here: that Hitchcock's spy film *The 39 Steps* (1935) is a conservative text because of its faith in the 'talented amateur' and its abhorrence of the crowd, but is notable for showing interest in the detail of everyday life. *The 39 Steps* offers cues to a new cultural history that I find preferable to *Zeitgeist* interpretation. Accurate or otherwise in their descriptions, popular texts are more than symptoms – they are also signposts and metaphors, deployed in a variety of circumstances, and frequently with real-life references and effects. Walter Scott's *Lay of the Last Minstrel* asks readers whether any man has refrained from saying to himself: 'This is my own, my native land,' suggesting that if such a person were encountered, one must 'mark him well'. This canto was extracted by the US State Department in its 1980 legal case against Philip Agee, a whistleblowing ex-CIA agent.[13] (Agee also had the distinction of being described by George Bush as 'a traitor' at the televised fiftieth anniversary of the Agency, in 1997.) Similarly, the London *Times* used espionage fiction to make sense of Soviet spy George Blake's escape from Wormwood Scrubs in 1966 – devotees of 007 would assume he had used a two-way radio, while Smiley's readers would view the event as an elaborate ruse by the British Secret Service.[14] Nicholas Hiley goes so far as to allege that the period up to the 1930s saw 'most British intelligence officers [take] the greater part of their ideas of secret service directly from fictional sources'.[15] So this is not a case of spy fiction allegorising or adequating to the real, but of *contributing* to it.

As noted earlier, the quotation from M-O at the head of this chapter suggests 'state-of-the-nation' impressions are best understood as debating points among an élite, not as social symptoms. M-O started in the late 1930s as an antidote to such diagnostics. Its founders, a bizarre blend of surrealists and empiricists, enlisted 1,500 'amateur Observers', who went about Britain 'observing and analysing the ordinary' to compensate for the blind spots of their academic counterparts, who were thought to 'have contributed literally nothing to the anthropology of ourselves'.[16] During the War, MI5 distinguished itself by raiding the offices of M-O on instruction from Winston Churchill, who believed the observers were 'criminally liable' for asking ordinary Britons their opinions on the conflict.[17]

It seems to me that Hitchcock is like one of M-O's amateur observers. He is always present in his films as an extra (seen littering in *The 39 Steps* as he walks past a bus stop). His presence is utterly ordinary, yet strange at the same time – hardly a case of hidden enunciation as per orthodox film theory. Hitchcock focuses as a storyteller on small signs of life – the empiricist's eye for detail – and finds them bizarre – the surrealist's eye for distortion. For example, the electric intensity of protagonist Richard Hannay's (Robert Donat) flying from the police across rough country in *The 39 Steps* is visually speeded up, like latter-day screenings of silent cinema. This draws the viewer's attention to the nature of observation and plays with the filmic apparatus poetically.

In this chapter, I argue that Hitchcock's *The 39 Steps*, and its 1915 literary antecedent, Buchan's *The Thirty-Nine Steps*, had homologous relations to the social world (I shall distinguish between the two texts by using their different spellings and 'authors', even though the screenplay was attributed to Charles Bennett and Ian Hay, and some suggest Alma Reville should also be acknowledged beyond her continuity credit).[18] Just as Buchan's novel drew upon, and itself inflected, texts of the public mind, so did Hitchcock's film, adapted as much for the 1930s as the screen. Each embodied prevailing issues of their day to do with class, race, gender and national security. Each made especially powerful arguments for the value of the Dominions to Britain in a hostile world as a supply of talented amateurs to assist blundering professional worthies. And each pointed to the danger of the quotidian as a contradictory source of mass frenzy, pulverising *ennui* and mimetic deception – in short, as a site of norms that are inevitably polysemous and hence uncontrollable. To make these points, I consider the general relationship of espionage fiction to the real, and locate the texts of the *Steps* and its protagonist in fictional and historical space and time, before evaluating the film.

In so doing, I am following the method of Roger Chartier: (a) a reconstruction of 'the diversity of older readings from their sparse and multiple traces'; (b) a focus on 'the text itself, the object that conveys it, and the act that grasps it'; and (c) an identification of 'the strategies by which authors and publishers tried to impose an orthodoxy or a prescribed reading on the text'.[19] This grid from the new cultural history turns away from reflectionism, which argues that a text's key meaning lies in its overt or covert capacity to capture the *Zeitgeist*. It also rejects formalism's claim that a close reading of sound and image cues provides a film's meaning. Instead, I look at the passage of the text through space and time, noting how it accretes and attenuates meanings on its travels as it rubs up against, tropes, and is troped by other fictional and social texts. But first, a word on the British genre's location and morphology is due.

Genre

We can trace the origins of the spy novel to James Fenimore Cooper's *The Spy* of 1821. There was a jump then to the late nineteenth century and the first decade of the twentieth, when British fiction descended on the threat of invasion in a series of anti-Semitic, anti-German and xenophobic novels, such as Le Queux's, that borrowed from science fiction and detection.[20] Wesley K. Wark connects innovations in cheap popular fiction, journalistic and governmental campaigns of xenophobia, shifts in the formation of classes and the division of labour, and the emergence of British moral panics about foreigners and spying in the decade following the Dreyfus affair:

> The enemy could be the Jew, the foreigner, the not-quite gentleman, the corrupted, the bomb-throwers, the women. Why the day needed to be saved was very much a product of national insecurities that began to mount at the turn of the century. At their heart were fears about the pace of technological and societal change caused by the impact of the industrial revolution. In the wake of its manifold upheavals, traditional measures of the international balance of power were threatened and the domestic structures of government upset.[21]

For conservative critics, the success of espionage fiction demonstrates that its consumers approve of their governments acting covertly in the interest of state security. For other critics, the appeal lies in the romance of citizenship: readers and viewers test and enjoy limit cases presented by the comparative anarchy of international relations, where loyalty and patriotism, and even the mundanity of public employment, are suddenly reforged as plays with death and doom. The genre is equally associated with the question of subjectivity under technologisation and bureaucratisation, an existential dilemma that is not about an abstract absurdity, but part of material relations that form the everyday.[22]

Of course, there is no absolute one-to-one correspondence between economic and literary relations and representations. Although the era of multinational capitalism commenced a century ago, Ernest Mandel argues for a time-lag between its emergence as the substructure of society and its appearance in the superstructure of ideology. In fact, he dates the literary recognition of this change to the publication of *The Thirty-Nine Steps*. From that point on, the ratiocination characteristic of detection is insufficient. New heroes, operating as servants of a sovereign power, must act; they are *doing*, rather than *thinking*, creatures.[23] Just as that book was part of a slew of Edwardian and post-Edwardian novels, the second great conflict was also presaged textually. Mandel argues that the period between the two world wars was an epistemological watershed for the British reading public. Perceptions of the power of organised crime shifted to allow for a new force. It was directed against the sovereign-state, rather than property or individuals. These were crimes by one state against another, with the body of government personified in undercover figures seeking to undermine rival states.

As the genre developed, espionage thrillers focused on the identification and defeat of wrongdoers through participation and exploration, a practical reasoning that ultimately explained irregular, undesirable events. As figures of modernity, both villains and heroes lost their individual identities through cloaks of substitution – paradigm changes of costume, task, face, voice and history. Identity was assumed and discarded, in keeping with the self-actualising, transcendent subject who moved at will across time and space. This division of the self also divided the subject internally. Good and evil came to depend on each other through an overarching third term: the law and its embodiment in the state, which villains must elude, and heroes either convince that justice should be meted out or delegated, so they could mete it out themselves. But the latter's assumption of false personae weakened their truth claims and their identification with transparent valour. The genre's nexus of 'spectacular violence and social vacuousness' leads critics to blame it for modelling anti-social conduct, heroising the capitalist state, or delighting in base consumerism.[24] In response, supporters argue from a functionalist perspective that espionage fiction models the struggle between bad and good and displays democratic values. This seems difficult to sustain given the shadowy parallel universe occupied by spies, which is messily complicit with despised others and frequently involves indulgent evacuations to exotic locales.[25]

In film, the stock generic components are suspense, adventure, romance and humour, played out over repeated problems in the relationship of person to state: loyalty, paranoia, war and politics.[26] Films about the First World War made during the 1930s mostly turn on love affairs between spies who work for competing countries. These were regarded as scandalous tales of treason at the time. Today, they look like politically decontextualised melodramas. During this inter-war period, the future Axis powers made only a smattering of espionage movies, but they were a staple in France and Britain.[27] Hitchcock is a key figure in this boom, with *The Man Who Knew Too Much* (1934), *The 39 Steps*, *Sabotage* (1936), *Secret Agent* (1936) and *The Lady Vanishes* (1938). A third boost to the espionage genre comes via the crisis of empire and industry after the 1960s, when governments can only do so much next to movements of capital that are as significant as the movements of armies, and it is clear that traitors within are as common as enemies without.[28] Today, 'rogue' terrorism, rather than its state equivalent, is most common as a theme.

Espionage fiction often evokes 'instinctive dread'; heroes are forced to deal with elemental fears, most notably a personal, professional and frequently physical claustrophobia. Because open space is central to much cinema, when protagonists are restricted – Sean Connery in Crab Key's shaft from *Dr No* (Terence Young, 1962), Orson Welles in the Viennese sewers of *The Third Man* (Carol Reed, 1949) and *The Saint*'s Val Kilmer and Elisabeth Shue in Moscow tunnels (Phillip Noyce, 1997) – the spaces they occupy illustrate the impossibility of ever truly relaxing as a spy. Inevitably, they find themselves in a site that emblematises the gruesome interiority and tension of their calling.[29] Other typical ingredients include 'sexual conflict, spectacle, and suspense' via a particular formula. Attractive travellers, often in disguise but ultimately with stereotypical national characteristics, meet and pass information. Despite the openness of their good looks, their secret identities bespeak an untrustworthy world where threats are not just personal. Misrecognition is endemic, while the very act of travel shows that the apparently eternal verities and loyalties of blood and soil may be compromised. The great ability of the protagonist is to see through the fictions of others and uncover truth. This is no easy task, as violence is diffused throughout the text and its presiding source is rarely obvious – *The 39 Steps*' Mr Memory (Wylie Watson), a music-hall act who holds intelligence about a conspiracy of foreign spies and is himself their method of smuggling information about British *matériel* out of the country, embodies the struggle for knowledge characteristic of the genre,[30] while the fact that the gang's mastermind is a Professor Jordan (Godfrey Tearle) underscores the dubious nature of intellectuals versus men of action.

The Janus-face of professionalism is central here, as both good and bad are frequently represented via expertise: scientific, bureaucratic, corporate or legal.[31] The element of mystery in espionage derives from identifying the enemy and her or his alliances, supporters, methods and reasons. There is always a 'triple search for identity: who has done it; under what assumed identity is the villain hiding; what is the murderer – or spy, or mad billionaire, or conspirator – like as a "person"'.[32] In Hitchcock's text, the arch-villain is described as having 'a dozen names. And he can look like a hundred people.' Just as identity is uncertain, perfect knowledge seems unattainable. How can real understanding of an environment be reached when the latter is itself a labyrinth? Place is a crucial motif here. While conspiracies may take effect in the city, where government, business and population can be found, they are often hatched in the country. Arcady itself is brought into question. Presumptively a site of renewal, the countryside turns out to be especially risky when its redemptive sign value is misused by forces of evil.

Mandel argues that the search for identity and perfect knowledge is a necessary process for fiction produced in bourgeois societies, because individuals are divided among a variety of selves: the worker, the consumer and the capitalist are utilitarian figures who calculate the benefits to themselves of their actions. As property owners, they uphold and even materialise laws of ownership of both objects and people. As citizens, they are concerned with the general good, not their own, however. And as sexual subjects, they are driven by needs that take them beyond reason, the family and property. For Mandel, the spy story enacts the dilemmas posed by this contradictory, split subjectivity,[33] implicitly penetrating the mystique of law and order to go beyond sovereignty. Such issues are materialised in the daily actions of spies as delegates in foreign camps of a people, monarchy or army. The arbitrariness of this delegation, and its requirement of instant decision and action, is paradoxically cynical. Loading up one person with that power and responsibility, signing away the right to democracy, makes the myth of bourgeois society – popular endorsement of overt governmental processes under the publicly ratified rule of law – unsustainable.[34]

When allied to Mandel's claim for its representative status in marking transformations in global capitalism, this is quite an interpretative burden for the *Steps*, which some critics say does 'not really constitute adult reading'.[35] Buchan himself referred to it variously as a 'dime novel',[36] a 'shocker' and a 'romance where the incidents defy the probabilities, and march just inside the borders of the possible'.[37] But it continues to resonate. The book has never been out of print and as of 1990 had sold a million and a half copies, negotiating the space between critical derision as genre fiction and a significant uptake by literary studies as an 'improving' text.[38] Its uneven repute characterises the genre, as does its popularity with certain elite, white, male readers whom it so fulsomely represents.

Talented amateurs

One clear aspect to the talented male amateur who populates the ranks of British espionage-fiction heroes up to the 1960s is not bothering his head too much with abstraction. He embodies pragmatism, utilitarianism and an untheorised commitment to liberty. This is in keeping with the trope of accidental discovery that recurs in the genre's early novels and films – a mystery lands in the lap of a bright young man who proceeds to solve it and save his country from a conspiracy.[39] Through action, he generates ideas and reveals his principles.[40]

Of course, amateurism has economic preconditions. A clubbish atmosphere is clear in the nicknames that early members of the British secret service used to refer to one another: 'Woolly, Buster, Biffy, Bubbles, Blinker, Barmy, [and] Tin-Eye' head one list. Apart from attesting to the claim that the public schools *produce* children rather than develop them, this roll call signifies *joie de vivre*, not taking things too seriously, and never losing a sense of self that can transcend its environment. This accompanied a righteousness that came from a mix of race, class and gender. Buchan's novel was much beloved by Theodore Roosevelt, A. J. Balfour, Clement Attlee, George V and Robert Baden-Powell. Woolly and his 'chums' overtly modelled themselves on Hannay, and wrote racist 'yarns' based on his story (one of these men was allegedly in turn the basis for 'M' of the Bond books).[41] They also engaged in public self-mythification, via autobiographies that saluted their role in World War II very much as per Buchan's hero.[42]

But there is an added element to the *Steps*, a *distance* from privilege that derives from Hannay's colonial status. He stands to one side of the English ruling class, for he hails from the Old Dominions: Rhodesia in Buchan and Canada in Hitchcock. In the novel, he ascribes a capacity to escape danger to the fact that 'I'm a colonial and travel light'. In the film, his transience in the UK is signified by the list of residents in his apartment building. Unlike other names, Hannay's is written on a temporary board. This is very conspicuous, and he stares at it in desperation while escaping the building. The first newspaper photograph of him as a suspect shows Hannay in a bush hat and farming gear. The quality of the Old Dominions as special (and paradigmatic) attains additional colour in the novel with his introduction to a Scottish audience as a 'trusted leader of Australian thought' (whatever that might be).[43] In the film, he receives polite applause from the music-hall crowd when identified by Mr Memory as a Canadian. A need to leave London and return to the land is central to Hannay, who made his money in the Dominions and found his subjectivity there. Donat's fresh-faced beauty is crucial to capturing the look of 'dispassionate amusement'[44] that comes with being not quite English. In London, Hannay is a lost soul. The countryside allows him to track the secret he seeks and also avoid capture.

This places him squarely in the tradition of empire. Hannay carries the full burden of the civilising impulse in his body[45] – in the novel, one character calls him 'a white man' approvingly.[46] Britain's putative goal in World War I – the liberation of Europe from Prussian militarism – was structurally homologous to the putative goal of its

Empire – to displace barbarism with a 'higher' form of life.[47] Same discourse, new object, with Hannay the model subject who helped bring capitalism and government to Africa/North America and would now do the same for Europe. In each case, deliverance from demons within would come from angels without. This may seem bizarre today, given our disparagement of colonialism as nothing more than rapacious expropriation and enslavement. But the British élite was committed to uplift. Just after the First War, David Lloyd George told the Imperial Conference that the Empire was 'the most hopeful experiment in human organisation which the world has yet seen' because its *modus operandi* was not so much coercive as ethical: 'It is based not on force but on goodwill and a common understanding. Liberty is its binding principle.'[48] This mission was crucial to Hannay's life in the colonies and explains his unease when presented with the lack of a challenge 'at home'. It fitted Buchan's firm Calvinism, which found the dystopic in the utopic and vice versa. Sloth lay around the corner from pleasure.[49]

This restlessness presumably took Hannay across class lines and cultural capital to the music hall, where signifiers of clothing and accent point to his not belonging. (In the novel, the audience is full of 'capering women and monkey-faced men'.[50]) While this is partly a narrative device, it is also an index of his liminal status. Before he can adopt the mantle of an imperial hero transposed to Europe, Hannay must undergo a transformation. When he encounters the dying and then suddenly lifeless body of Franklin P. Scudder, in Buchan, and Annabella Smith (Lucie Mannheim), in Hitchcock, Hannay realises he has simultaneously become a suspect and a target. The police will believe him to be a killer, and the spies will take him for a confederate of the corpse. The change in gender of the dying spy from novel to film is crucial, part of Hitchcock's adaptation of Buchan's homosociality into a story world where female characters are powerful figures on whom men must rely for direction, ideas and succour. Hannay 'assumes her [Smith's] obligations and her furtiveness',[51] suddenly enlivened from his *ennui* and scepticism by Scudder's/Smith's sacrifice. This merges with the Edenic return, a kind of perverse *Bildungsroman*, that places him in the wilds of Scotland. In Buchan, this is a choice made out of familiarity and consanguinity, paralleling the flight from the city to redemption-through-peril in John Bunyan's *Pilgrim's Progress*. Romance meets Protestant morality in search of salvation through good deeds.[52] In Hitchcock, it is born of necessity, because the few clues to the mystery Hannay must solve lead him there. But again, he seems at home in a way that he was not in London – rurality brings freedom.

The film

That flight also took Hannay away from the crowds of the metropolis. The crowd was a figure of great anxiety in early twentieth-century public policy. This period sees the emergence of élite theory, through the work of Gaetano Mosca, Vilfredo Pareto and Robert Michels, along with pessimistic proto-social-psychologists such as Gustav le Bon. Their terror is of mob rule, which they both deplore and, quaintly, doubt – for behind every public tumult of mass energy lies one more group of agitators ready to displace existing rulers with their own power-mongering. For élite theorists, the demotic side to audiences is a sham – the herd mentality is ultimately an orchestrated one. Buchan's Hannay finds that 'the talk of the ordinary Englishman made me sick'.[53] Throughout the novel, he refers disparagingly to the first-person narration he is giving us, likening it to 'wild melodrama', 'a penny novelette', a 'crazy game of hide-and-seek', and 'pure Rider Haggard and Conan Doyle'.[54] In the film, Hannay reacts to Annabella's revelations about 'a certain foreign power' with an incredulous '[I]t sounds like a spy story', and later explains being saved from a bullet by a hymn book as something he's never witnessed 'except in the movies', while the initially hostile young woman, Pamela (Madeleine Carroll), calls his version of events a 'petty novelette spy story'. Hitchcock seems to share Buchan's pessimism about the masses – the panic of a music-hall crowd out of control in the film's opening sequence has rarely been matched in popular cinema (*pace* the equally stunning start to *Raging Bull* [Martin Scorsese, 1980]). Even prior to the riot, the questions asked of Mr Memory are trivial in the extreme. And when Hannay later addresses a political gathering, as per élite theory, he rouses the stolid Scots with demagoguery, not policies and programmes. Finally, the second and ultimate music-hall sequence sees further chaos and a riot.

The 39 Steps was described as the most popular British film of 1935.[55] It brought Hitchcock his initial acclaim by New York film critics,[56] spawned over thirty stage adaptations in Manhattan between 1935 and 1938,[57] encouraged Hergé to write a chase sequence for Tintin, and continues to appeal. *Time Out* voted *The 39 Steps* 76 in its 100 best films in 1987–8, *Movieline* positions it on an equivalent list, the *Arizona Republic* ranked it 87th in its 1998 'Top 100 Foreign Films', the staff of the *Star Tribune* voted it number 38 of *all* films in 1995, and the Ed McMahon Mass Communications Center rates it among '100 of the Best Films of the 20th Century'.[58] At the same time, the egregious *National Review* put it among the '100 Best Conservative Movies' in 1996, and a 1998 dramatisation of the film for the stage left the high-Tory Auberon Waugh, who thought Hannay was based on his maternal grandfather, 'proud to be English again'.[59] This achievement is as dubious as they come. The raft of latter-day homages includes: plans for a Robert Towne-directed version,[60] adding to 1959 (Ralph Thomas) and 1978 (Don Sharp) remakes; the storyline borrowed for *12 Monkeys* (Terry Gilliam, 1996); and spoofing citations in *High Anxiety* (Mel Brooks, 1977) and *Foul Play* (Colin Higgins, 1978). The original continues to attract viewers in both VHS and DVD formats, the latter complete with an introduction by Tony Curtis (you work out the link – perhaps because he and Donat share Polish ancestry!). Commemorated by a hotel in Edinburgh and a bar in Barbados, *The 39 Steps* stands out among Hitchcock's British films for its worldwide public esteem, perhaps in part because the text is available for uptake from a variety of perspectives.

In keeping with the tenets of empiricism and the perversity of surrealism, the film's cultural politics are all over the place. Buchan was a class snob, a racist, an anti-Semite and anti-gay. These tendencies are on display in the novel,[61] while women are almost entirely absent.[62] The film is different, not surprisingly given Hitchcock's views on women and spying: '[T]he international spy has multiplied a thousand fold. Scientists or street sweepers may act as spies, for money, for patriotism, for adventure. Women, with their eye for detail and their acting ability, make excellent spies.'[63]

The ambivalence of the film is nicely brought out in its gender relations. Annabella accosts Hannay during the riot with 'May I come home with you?'. When he inquires why, she replies, 'Well, I'd like to.' She comes to his rooms for what he flirtatiously, but presciently, calls 'your funeral'. Hannay assumes Annabella is an actor, to which she enigmatically responds, '[n]ot in the way that you mean'. This interplay of gender, sex and death repeats as he escapes Portland Place when his milkman is persuaded that he needs a disguise to conceal an infidelity. Hannay then enters a railway carriage where his fellow occupants carry on a discourse about ladies' underwear.[64] And consider the effect when his landlady screams on discovering the initial murder, which Hitchcock articulates with the whistle of Hannay's train escaping north in one of the most famous match-on-action cuts in cinema. Then we meet a crofter's game and sexy wife (Peggy Ashcroft), who hides and romances Hannay at great personal cost – retributive domestic violence, shot in slow-motion silhouette for horrifying effect. The focus on male–female relations happens again when Hannay and Pamela are handcuffed together ('There are 20 million women in this island and I get to be chained to you'). This unwelcome bracketing becomes a sign of their transformation into a couple, the 'concrete object' of the cuffs expressing a 'concrete relation' that is undergoing change[65] as an innkeeper's wife opens the way for the 'young couple' to be alone together. The film's final shot, from the rear, sees Hannay's becuffed hand reaching for Pamela, all in black satin. This moment of paradoxical and almost kinky romance[66] is nicely reprised in *Tomorrow Never Dies* (Roger Spottiswoode, 1997). It also gives Hitchcock claims to utilising 'The Method', given the story that he left the actors, who had never met before, locked together for hours on the pretence of having mislaid the key![67] Gender is subtly foregrounded whenever Hannay is absent from the action, in that we either know or are later shown that he is asleep or unconscious,[68] a classic warning about men letting down their guard, failing to be alert and showing vulnerability. Last, the famous camera movement in on the spymaster's missing fingers (quoted in Hitchcock's own television work)[69] references the need to compensate in political machinations for lacking a 'normal' masculine body – just the opposite of a guileless, open subject from the Dominions.

These qualities are all unique to the film. Hitchcock liked the book, but deemed the narrative segments inappropriate for cinema, not least because many scenes would have been difficult to film convincingly even though they read well. An instance is a sequence where Hannay sees a car coming towards him and is immediately able to disguise himself as a stone-breaking worker nearby. Descriptive prose makes up the time for the car to meet the person, but this was not available on film. In the novel, 'the thirty-nine steps' refer to the number of stairs leading down to the water level at a particular point on the English coast where evil deeds will be done. They are adapted here to streamline the plot and centre Hannay.[70] Similarly, Buchan's opening description of strolling through London and experiencing a number of diversions is cleverly concentrated by Hitchcock in the music-hall scene, which is also the site (though this time at the London Palladium) for the denouement. Like the occasion of Hannay's accidental political speech, the music-hall sequences are also opportunities to show his capacity to win over a crowd. Eric Rohmer and Claude Chabrol say that the ultimate moment of revelation begins Hitchcock's long line of confessional keys, characteristic of so many of his films. The relationships between people, the possibility of trust, are foregrounded throughout, as in the genre more broadly. The depthless character typical of spy-genre protagonists is to the fore in Hannay's memorable utterance, 'I'm nobody.' He proceeds to be a milkman, a mechanic, a parade marcher, a politician and a criminal, the perfectly depthless figure who can be anyone and be inconspicuous anywhere, paradoxically so secure in his very shallowness that he could pass as ordinary wherever he went.[71] At the same time, this sets up the conditions of possibility for comedy, as a series of misunderstandings produce chaos then a happy resolution. Supposedly joyous settings which go wrong, such as a music hall and a party, nevertheless show that the space for happiness exists somewhere, a lost pleasure that can be regained if Hannay keeps reasoning while all around him appears mad.[72]

Hannay's relationship to the country he defends and represents is ambivalent – he 'slums it' in attending vaudeville and is 'an outsider' matched against an aristocratic don, whose evil is hidden by his class position. It has even been suggested that Hitchcock's decades of oscillation between adoration and detestation for the ruling class 'are a kind of contour map of the middle-class mind'.[73] This social ambivalence is matched by a leitmotif in the films, whereby protagonists are accused of crimes they did not commit[74] and must come to terms with this new-found status – not only the unwarranted and unwanted condition of a criminal, but its corollary of hyper-competence, which suddenly lifts them up from ordinary life to an extraordinary stature as they adopt the subject position of the skilled spy and fugitive. Not only is this a recurring theme in the genre – of the innocent person tapping untold qualities when faced with peril – it is also the recto–verso of the very spying process itself. For just as the true professional must be able to slide easily into an unsuspecting world of trust in order to achieve the tasks of espionage, so the genuine amateur must find unknown personal resources with which to respond.

As noted earlier, the grand confusion and anonymity of the city, and the beautiful but ruggedly threatening toughness of the land, are both on vivid display here. Listlessness and *ennui* in the face of urban life are juxtaposed with the bracing revival of hostile heather, as Hannay gains in competence by leaving the decadence of the metropole and finding himself spiritually and physically renewed by the country and the chase.[75] The nomadism of which the British were so proud as a key to their empire comes back to him as a redemptive cue. At the same time, Hannay must return to the seat of power in order to thwart crimes against the state. The patriotism that animates him is exemplified in the sequence when he pretends to be a politician – lacking ideas, which makes him a figure of goodwill to those similarly inclined, his speech to a party meeting is essentially phatic rather than ideological, with modal shifters substituting for policy. At the same time as he plays this slightly odd character from the Dominions, Donat's status as a theatrical lead, and his silky, asthma-afflicted voice, imbue the part with key signs of the English gentleman fitted to the great tasks of history.[76] There is reassurance for the film audience that he can be trusted with the fate of the country because a 'live' audience is converted by his non-ideological decency (the flip-side to the negative notion of demagoguery winning them over, mentioned above). And there is a softness in Donat, his aspirated tones and matinée-idol looks, that connects to the aesthete and surrealist (M-O's flip-side to its doughty empiricist).

Hitchcock's gift in *The 39 Steps* is, in contradictory fashion: to create a generous *bricolage* of *opposition* to the masses, with *affection* for them; to touch on the wholesale ambiguity of the colonial subject returned and disappointed; and to allow gender play to substitute for xenophobia. He is like an 'amateur observer' from the ranks of Mass-Observation, even as his protagonist is a grand amateur. It is as though the director, like so many audience members, yearned to be like Hannay but knew that he belonged with the polloi. These lessons point us in the direction of cultural history in place of film studies' symptomatic norms.

Notes

Thanks to Richard Allen for his helpful comments.

1 David Trotter, 'The Politics of Adventure in the Early British Spy Novel', in Wesley K. Wark, ed., *Spy Fiction, Spy Films, and Real Intelligence,* London: Frank Cass, 1991, p. 31.

2 Mass-Observation, *Britain*, Harmondsworth: Penguin, 1939, p. 8.

3 Nicholas Hiley, 'Decoding German Spies: British Spy Fiction, 1908–18', in Wark, *Spy Fiction, Spy Films, and Real Intelligence*, pp. 55, 73.

4 Trotter, 'Politics', p. 31; Bernard Porter, *Plots and Paranoia: A History of Political Espionage in Britain 1790–1988,* London: Unwin Hyman, 1989, pp. 126, 128–9; James Rusbridger, *The Intelligence Game: The Illusions and Delusions of International Espionage*, London: The Bodley Head, 1989, p. 12; Phillip Knightley, *The Second Oldest Profession: Spies and Spying in the Twentieth Century,* New York: W. W. Norton, 1987, pp. 9–27, 35; Richard Wilmer Rowan with Robert G. Deindorfer, *Secret Service: Thirty-Three Centuries of Espionage,* New York: Hawthorn Books, 1967, pp. 467–73.

5 Hiley, 'Decoding', p. 56.

6 Walter Laqueur, *A World of Secrets: The Uses and Limits of Intelligence*, New York: Basic Books, 1985, p. 6.

7 Knightley, *The Second Oldest Profession*, p. 27.

8 Porter, *Plots and Paranoia*, p. 126.

9 J. D. B. Miller, *Norman Angell and the Futility of War: Peace and the Public Mind,* London: Macmillan, 1986; Norman Angell, *The Great Illusion: A Study of the Relations of Military Power to National Advantage*, London: William Heinemann, 1912, pp. vii–viii.

10 Allen Dulles, 'Foreword', in Rowan with Deindorfer, *Secret Service*, p. xi.

11 Knightley, *The Second Oldest Profession*, p. 318.

12 Ernest Mandel, *Delightful Murder: A Social History of the Crime Story*, London: Pluto Press, 1984, pp. 60–1; James Der Derian, *Antidiplomacy: Spies, Terror, Speed, and War*, Cambridge, MA: Blackwell, 1992, pp. 50–1.

13 Rosamund M. Thomas, *Espionage and Secrecy: The Official Secrets Acts 1911–1989 of the United Kingdom*, London: Routledge, 1991, p. ii, n. 1.

14 John Atkins, *The British Spy Novel: Styles in Treachery*, London: John Calder; New York: Riverrun Press, 1984, pp. 10–11.

15 Hiley, 'Decoding German Spies', p. 57.

16 Mass-Observation, *Britain*, pp. 10, 12.

17 John Crossland, 'MI5 Ordered to Spy on "Subversive" Opinion Poll', *Independent*, 21 July 1997, p. 6.

18 Jane E. Sloan, *Alfred Hitchcock: A Guide to References and Resources*, New York: GK Hall; Toronto: Maxwell Macmillan Canada; New York: Maxwell Macmillan International, 1993, p. 128 n.

19 Roger Chartier, 'Texts, Printings, Readings', in Lynn Hunt ed., *The New Cultural History*, Berkeley: University of California Press, 1989, pp. 157, 161–3, 166.
20 Hiley, 'Decoding German Spies', p. 56.
21 Wesley K. Wark, 'The Intelligence Revolution and the Future', *Queen's Quarterly*, vol. 100 no. 2, 1993, p. 275.
22 Der Derian, *Antidiplomacy*, pp. 53–4, 57–8.
23 Mandel, *Delightful Murder*, pp. 85–7.
24 Mike Westlake, 'The Classic TV Detective Genre', *Framework*, no. 13, 1980, p. 37; Paul Kerr, 'Watching the Detectives', *Primetime* 1, no. 1, 1981, p. 2; Grant Morrison, 'Un monde de miraculeuses métamorphoses', trans. David Fakrikian and Bruno Billion, in Alain Carrazé and Jean-Luc Putheaud (eds), *Chapeau melon et bottes de cuir*, Paris: Huitième Art, 1990, p. 21; Alain Dewerpe, *Espion: Une anthropologie historique du secret d'état contemporain*, Paris: Gallimard, 1994, p. 11.
25 Hiley, 'Decoding German Spies', p. 68.
26 Lenny Rubenstein, 'The Politics of Spy Films', *Cineaste* 9, no. 3, 1979, p. 16.
27 Pierre Sorlin, *European Cinemas, European Societies 1939–1990*, London: Routledge, 1991, pp. 31–40.
28 David Stafford, 'Spies and Gentlemen: The Birth of the British Spy Novel, 1893–1914', *Victorian Studies* 24, no. 4, 1981, p. 496; Wark, 'Intelligence', p. 280; Philip Schlesinger, Graham Murdock and Philip Elliott, *Televising 'Terrorism': Political Violence in Popular Culture*, London: Comedia, 1983, p. 81.
29 Gordon Gow, *Suspense in the Cinema*, New York: A. S. Barnes, 1968, pp. 53–4.
30 Marcia Landy, *British Genres: Cinema and Society, 1930–1960*, Princeton: Princeton University Press, 1991, pp. 124, 127, 138.
31 Landy, *British Genres*, p. 181.
32 Mandel, *Delightful Murder*, pp. 62, 65.
33 Mandel, *Delightful Murder*, p. 65.
34 Mandel, *Delightful Murder*, p. 122.
35 Atkins, *The British Spy Novel*, p. 31.
36 Quoted in Laqueur, *A World of Secrets*, p. 6.
37 Quoted in David Stafford, *The Silent Game: The Real World of Imaginary Spies*, rev. edn, Athens: University of Georgia Press, 1991, pp. 56–7.
38 Stafford, *The Silent Game*, pp. 57–8.
39 Dennis Butts, 'The Hunter and the Hunted: The Suspense Novels of John Buchan', in Clive Bloom ed., *Spy Thrillers: From Buchan to le Carré*, New York: St. Martin's Press, 1990, p. 46.
40 LeRoy L. Panek, *The Special Branch: The British Spy Novel, 1890–1980*, Bowling Green: Bowling Green University Popular Press, 1981, p. 47.
41 Porter, *Plots and Paranoia*, pp. 169, 171–2.
42 Knightley, *The Second Oldest Profession*, p. 122; Trotter, 'The Politics of Adventure', p. 52; Stafford, *The Silent Game*, p. 57.
43 John Buchan, *The Thirty-Nine Steps*, New York: Popular Library, 1977, pp. 51, 54. Also, http://www.cc.columbia.edu/acis/bartleby/buchan/.
44 William Rothman, *Hitchcock – The Murderous Gaze*, Cambridge, MA: Harvard University Press, 1982, pp. 114–5.

45 Panek, *The Special Branch*, p. 44.
46 Buchan, *The Thirty-Nine Steps*, p. 15.
47 V. G. Kiernan, *European Empires from Conquest to Collapse, 1815–1960*, n. p.: Fontana, 1982, p. 181.
48 Quoted in Nicholas Mansergh, *The Commonwealth Experience*, London: Weidenfeld & Nicolson, 1969, p. 158.
49 Butts, 'The Hunter and the Hunted', p. 55; Anthony Masters, *Literary Agents: The Novelist as Spy*, New York: Basil Blackwell, 1987, p. 33.
50 Buchan, *The Thirty-Nine Steps*, p. 7.
51 Mark Crispin Miller, *Boxed In: The Culture of TV*, Evanston: Northwestern University Press, 1988, p. 238.
52 Panek, *Special*, p. 52; Jeanne F. Bedell, 'Romance and Moral Certainty: The Espionage Fiction of John Buchan', *Midwest Quarterly* 22, no. 3, 1981, p. 231.
53 Buchan, *Thirty-Nine*, p. 5.
54 Ibid., pp. 103, 39.
55 Tom Ryall, *Alfred Hitchcock and the British Cinema*, rev. edn, London: Athlone Press, 1996, p. 105.
56 Robert Kapsis, *Hitchcock: The Making of a Reputation*, Chicago: University of Chicago Press, 1992, p. 23.
57 Ryall, *Alfred Hitchcock and the British Cinema*, p. 175.
58 Susannah Herbert, 'International: Tintin Artist "copied from films"', *Daily Telegraph*, 16 July 1998; *Time Out*, http://www–personal.monash;edu;au/~gstephen/London.html; *Movieline*, http://www.filmsite.org/movieline.html; *Arizona Republic*, 'Top 100 Foreign Films', 3 July 1998, p. D4; Neal Justin, 'It's a Wonderful Life', *Star Tribune*, 11 June 1995; Ed McMahon Mass Communications Center, http://www.quinnipiac.edu/libarts/films.html.
59 Warren Spencer, 'Your 100 Best Conservative Movies', *National Review*, 11 March 1996; Auberon Waugh, 'Way of the World: Moment of Joy', *Daily Telegraph*, 7 July 1998.
60 *Los Angeles Times*, 'Alfred Hitchcock Films are Being Mined for New Projects as Hollywood is Remaking the Master', 30 May 1998, p. 1.
61 J. P. Parry, 'From the Thirty-Nine Articles to the *Thirty-Nine Steps*: Reflections on the Thought of John Buchan', in Michael Bentley ed., *Public and Private Doctrine: Essays in British History Presented to Maurice Cowling*, Cambridge: Cambridge University Press, 1993, p. 218; Trotter, 'The Politics of Adventure', p. 30; Buchan, *The Thirty-Nine Steps*, pp. 10, 68.
62 Panek, *The Special Branch*, p. 45.
63 Quoted in Atkins, *The British Spy Novel*, p. 9.
64 Charles L. P. Silet, 'Through a Woman's Eyes: Sexuality and Memory in *The 39 Steps*', in Marshall Deutelbaum and Leland Poague eds., *A Hitchcock Reader*, Ames: Iowa State University Press, 1986, p. 110.
65 Gilles Deleuze, *Cinema 1: The Movement–Image*, trans. Hugh Tomlinson and Barbara Habberjam, Minneapolis: University of Minnesota Press, 1986, p. 204.
66 Louis Phillips, 'The Hitchcock Universe: *Thirty-Nine Steps* and Then Some', *Films in Review*, 1995, p. 23.

67 Donald Spoto, *The Dark Side of Genius: The Life of Alfred Hitchcock*, Boston: Little, Brown, 1983, p. 148.

68 Charles Barr, 'Hitchcock's British Films Revisited', in Andrew Higson ed., *Dissolving Views: Key Writings on British Cinema*, London: Cassell, 1996, p. 14.

69 Kapsis, *Hitchcock*, pp. 41–2.

70 Alfred Hitchcock, *Hitchcock on Hitchcock: Selected Writings and Interviews*, Sidney Gottlieb ed., Berkeley: University of California Press, 1995, p. 21.

71 Eric Rohmer and Claude Chabrol, *Hitchcock: The First Forty-Four Films*, trans. Stanley Hochman, New York: Ungar, 1979; Parry, 'From', p. 223.

72 Lesley Brill, *The Hitchcock Romance: Love and Irony in Hitchcock's Films*, Princeton: Princeton University Press, 1988, pp. 26–8.

73 O. B. Hardison, 'The Rhetoric of Hitchcock's Thrillers', in W. R. Robinson with assistance from George Garrett ed., *Man and the Movies*, Baltimore: Penguin, 1967, pp. 147, 150.

74 Brill, *The Hitchcock Romance*, p. 23.

75 Trotter, 'The Politics of Adventure', p. 51.

76 Landy, *British Film Genres*, p. 126.

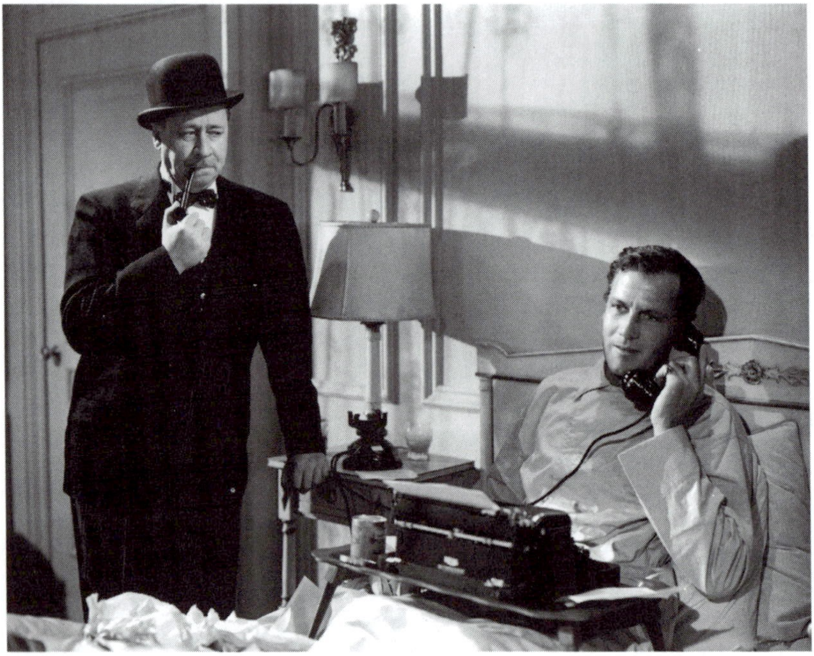

Foreign Correspondent – democracy under threat

Chapter 21
'We Might Even Get in the Newsreels': The Press and Democracy in Hitchcock's World War II Anti-Fascist Films

Ina Rae Hark

In my 1990 article 'Keeping Your Amateur Standing: Audience Participation and Good Citizenship in Hitchcock's Political Films',[1] I argued that Hitchcock throughout his career displays a profound distrust in democratic governments' abilities to ensure their own citizens the democratic freedoms that they espouse. The individual's salvation resides solely in his or her hands. Hitchcock formulated this paradigm primarily in his 1930s British espionage thrillers, where he emphasised the threats to specific 'innocent bystander' individuals by the machinations of foreign powers engaged in political intrigue.

When World War II broke out shortly after Hitchcock relocated to the United States, the director was faced with a situation that did not fit the paradigm so comfortably. Clearly, one man or woman's speaking up to expose covert Fascism would not suffice when it was not merely this or that citizen's welfare that was at stake but the preservation of democracy itself. The war brought a threat to the individual that was not simply unintended collateral damage from the political process. Depriving innumerable individual citizens of democratic rights, often including the right to literal survival, now became a primary aim of the Fascist project. The Nazi blitzkrieg targeted whole nations, Britain not the least.

As a result, Hitchcock's skepticism about political activism disappeared in the face of Fascism. As Rohmer and Chabrol have noted, 'Hitch, who is ordinarily not at all a "committed" auteur, made an exception where Nazism was concerned'.[2] Later scholars have seconded this insight. Sam Simone insists that 'the unifying theme of [Hitchcock's] World War II films is the perpetuation of freedom framed in the political ideology of democracy'.[3] Sidney Gottlieb observes that the repeated use of Fascist organisations to trigger the action in the British thrillers adds up to a 'fundamental' political theme, not merely a set of 'MacGuffins, texts [or] pretexts'.[4] The outbreak of hostilities moved this theme to the forefront of several of the director's films of the 1940s. Stung by unwarranted criticism[5] from fellow Britons for not returning home, Hitchcock made three anti-Fascist films during the wartime period that aimed to arouse support for the beleaguered European democracies and to forge a collective democratic consciousness in his American audiences. These films, *Foreign Correspondent* (1940), *Saboteur* (1942) and *Lifeboat* (1944), encounter, however, a number of roadblocks on the way to their goal. For they still portray democratic institutions as disorganised, incompetent, rent by internal dissension and easily infiltrated by the enemy. The task Hitchcock sets himself is to imagine an efficient democracy that does not achieve such efficiency at the cost of becoming that very Fascism it opposes. In what follows I will argue that, because of various elements inherent in his skeptical world view, the task eventually defeats him.

In demonstrating this hypothesis, I will focus on Hitchcock's portrayal of news organisations and news reporting in these films. Whereas the British films tended to explore the relationship between audiences and performers as an analogue for that between citizens and government, the American films made during the war add the relationship between readers/listeners/viewers and the press to that mix. In choosing the press as his metonymy for the functioning of democratic governments, Hitchcock makes use of the centrality of freedom of the press to the American democratic ideal, by virtue of its privileged status in the First Amendment to the US Constitution. United in the Bill of Rights with freedom of speech and freedom of worship, the free press stands unique as the only private, for-profit institution mentioned in that founding document. Hitchcock points the viewer toward a heightened scrutiny of press functions in the films through his cameo appearances in them. In *Foreign Correspondent,* we find the director walking down the street reading a newspaper; in *Saboteur* he is a customer at a news-stand; and in *Lifeboat* he famously appears in before and after pictures in a newspaper advertisement for the weight-loss aid Reduco.

The director's threefold identification with newspapers in these films might appear to signal his advocacy of the press as guardian of American freedoms. To come to this conclusion would be in line with Thomas Leitch's assertion that the Hitchcock cameos serve more 'as a contract equally binding on director and audience than as a means of inscribing either into the discourse on the basis of unconscious motives'.[6] If we think that is the narrative contract being offered here, however, the anti-Fascist films quickly disabuse us of that assumption, unless we are paying so little attention as to be classed with the 'moron millions' scorned by *Saboteur*'s American Fascist, Charles Tobin – in a phrase screenwriter Peter Viertel adapted from Hitchcock's frequent comment about his audiences;[7] for in reality, Hitchcock is announcing his intention to step in where the free press has failed.

A number of prominent Americans in the early 1940s had serious concerns about the ability of the US press to perform its function as guardian of democracy. Roosevelt's Secretary of the Interior, Harold Ickes, frustrated at the inverse relationship between newspapers' editorial endorsements of the President and the percentage of the electorate casting votes to re-elect him in the 1940 presidential contest, invited twenty-eight 'persons eminent in the field of journalism and of public opinion' to weigh in on 'the question of the freedom of the press in broad outline'. Ickes, of course, had a partisan axe to grind, and the preponderance of respondents who excoriate press-chain monopolies; the undue influence on editorial policy of advertisers; financial capitalists and 'the country-club set'; and the press's failure to represent accurately the concerns of organised labour indicates that he did not choose a totally balanced sample of contributors. Nevertheless, Ickes earns dissent from several quarters who point out that disagreeing with the government, including those officials the public elects, is precisely – and solely – the freedom that the Constitution guarantees to the press: '[Newspapers] are free as long as they can go on saying what they please without interference from the authorities. If they choose to represent only the local banker or the local bund, that is their business. So long as freedom is defined exclusively by the Bill of Rights, Mr. Ickes hasn't a liberal leg to stand on'.[8]

Yet few, not merely those with 'liberal legs', wished for a press that supported, or did not confront, the 'local bund'. Whatever their political orientation, many of these journalists believed that whatever impediments might constrain the present-day press, at the current moment, with democracy under siege everywhere, its continued functioning as a potent weapon for freedom could not be abandoned. 'These abuses are hard to curb without destroying what is good in the freedom of the press,' Herbert Agar writes. 'Yet they must be curbed, because they have become such a scandal that they are breeding a revolt against the whole concept of a free press. Today's world revolution against democracy must be resisted not only on the battlefield, but also by reform within democracy itself, so that it may become worthy to survive'.[9] Even without significant reforms, however, Richard J. Wilson asserts that the American press can serve its essential function: 'Freedom of the press today has one practical meaning. Whatever else the press may be subservient to, it is not subservient to the government ... Certainly, it is better to have a few newspapers out of step with the times than three thousand executing an editorial goosestep'.[10] Similarly, when George Gallup polled regular newspaper readers about their opinions regarding editorial partisanship following the 1940 election, 73 per cent found it quite acceptable for newspapers to take sides and opposed any move to curtail that right. A frequent comment, Gallup found, was 'Hitler, Stalin, and Mussolini put a stop to freedom of the press – and look what happened'.[11]

Just as the contributors to Ickes's 'clinical examination' often note that 'functioning as a means of information in a democracy, [the press] is an essential part of a successful democratic system',[12] Hitchcock's wartime films often use the free American press as a template that foregrounds the differences between democracy and Fascism. Despite the films' overt goal of propagandising against Fascism, however, he frequently dwells on the way the press reflects the larger failings of democratic institutions. The director depicts American democracy's greatest handicap as its inefficiency, its incompetence, its lack of direction. Likewise, Johnny Jones, the reporter in *Foreign Correspondent*, keeps losing track of his hat and is long deceived as to the true perfidy of the undercover Nazi, Fisher.[13] The authorities in *Saboteur* pursue the innocent Barry Kane rather than the true criminal, Fry, just as the news media broadcast Kane's supposed guilt from coast to coast. Poring over a useless, because weeks old, newspaper, the combined non-Nazi contingent on the lifeboat can't decide on a proper course to steer, and the journalist heroine is in the forefront of urging them to hand over navigation to the Captain of the U-Boat which torpedoed them. Fascism, by contrast, is extremely well disciplined and organised. Like Willy in *Lifeboat*, it knows where it's going and has the ability to head straight for its destination. The only problem is that no freedom-loving individual wants to go there.

As Hitchcock portrays the press, its 'democratic' shortcomings take several distinct forms. First of all, the press often fails to get its facts right. A newspaper's displaying a front-page photo of a wrongly accused man is a recurring Hitchcock trope, both before, during and after the war years. In this regard newspapers err by regarding the ever-bumbling legal authorities as competent. As Harold Lasswell warned his contemporaries, 'There was a day when we thought that a free press was a sufficient guaranty of democracy. But that day is gone. We know that a free press in not enough, since democracy needs intelligence as well as freedom'.[14] Besides simply conveying erroneous information passed on by others, the press is also vulnerable to the temptation to misrepresent the facts it has right in order to increase readership.

Second, journalists often think more about how getting a story will benefit them than the reader whom it is their democratic mandate to alert and inform. Third, efficient Fascists have very little trouble infiltrating and subverting the news media. And finally, when newspapers do provide competent and informative hard-news coverage, it often has less impact on the citizenry than news packaged in the more entertaining context of radio and newsreel. In comparing the three news sources, Hitchcock suggests the primacy of image over sound and sound over print in getting a message across. He also indicates that the relative capacity to misrepresent and deceive unfortunately follows precisely this same trajectory. Given Hitchcock's own preference for the visual expressiveness of 'pure cinema', this is an indictment likely to boomerang upon the films' director. It will not be the only one.

Foreign Correspondent and *Lifeboat* both have journalist protagonists, but deal with them in diametrically opposite ways. *Foreign Correspondent*'s Johnny Jones represents the democratic press doing its job to alert complacent Americans about the Nazi menace; the film's opening titles salute 'those intrepid ones who went across the sea to be the eyes and ears of America . . . Those forthright ones who early saw the clouds of war while many of us at home were seeing rainbows'.[15] By contrast, for *Lifeboat*'s Constance Porter, Nazism and its attendant tragedies merely provide opportunities for the reportage that has gotten her out of the working-class neighbourhoods of Chicago, introduced her to the rich and famous, and garnered her mink coats and diamond bracelets. *Saboteur*, on the other hand, deals less with the production of news than its reception, with people's relationships to the newspapers, radio broadcasts and newsreels that surround them as part of the litmus test for democratic citizenship.

Since *Foreign Correspondent* is the one of these films to deal with the democratic press at its most effective, it is telling to observe the considerable flaws of the fourth estate pointed out even here, in a movie whose first lines, exchanged between a foreign-desk staffer and a pressman, are 'What's new?' 'Same old daily bunkeroo.' The scene soon switches to Mr Powers, the editor of the *New York Morning Globe*, telling his associate editor Bradley that the foreign news appearing in his paper is virtually useless, 'a daily guessing game' instead of 'facts'. He diagnoses the problem as emanating from the tendency of foreign correspondents to view themselves as experts in world affairs who busy themselves in erudite analysis when they need to be reporting the news: 'I don't want any more economists, sages or oracles bombinating over our cables. I want a reporter, someone who doesn't know the difference between an -ism and a kangaroo.' In his search for a such a reporter with no intellectual pretensions to investigate the 'crime hatching' on the 'bedeviled continent' of Europe, he seizes upon crime-beat writer Johnny Jones, who is blissfully ignorant about world affairs but zealous in his pursuit of a story.

Despite Powers's apparent good sense and commitment to journalism as a means of uncovering the facts for his frustrated readers, however, the film soon reveals other tendencies in his ideology that compromise such a mission. Although Powers insists on sending a plain reporter instead of an élitist correspondent, he baulks at the proletarian name that his choice would make the byline for the *Globe*'s man in Europe. He therefore requires the reluctant Jones to assume the absurd but aristocratic *nom de plume* of Huntley Haverstock. Frustrated with intellectual snobbery, Powers is thus quite susceptible to social snobbery. Johnny may have the street-smart instincts to make him a good reporter, but, as shown by the departure scene on the *Queen Mary* in which the numerous short, plump, rumpled and bespectacled Jones relatives contrast with the tall, handsome Joel McCrea, he can also 'pass' as Haverstock. Moreover, just as for Constance Porter, being a foreign correspondent provides an entrée into élite society for the working-class Jones. We later see that this would not be the case with the current *Globe* reporter on the spot, Stebbins, a womanising alcoholic,[16] with a similarly unprepossessing surname and a distinct resemblance in physique to the lumpen Joneses. Thus, before Johnny has filed a single story, he has already consented to a deception upon his readers.

Powers perpetrates a far more serious deception on his readership through giving a forum to another 'passer', the urbane and upper-class Stephen Fisher, a German agent posing as an English peace activist. Not only does he advise Johnny to rely on Fisher as his means for obtaining an interview with the Dutch statesman Van Meer, but he publishes Fisher's op-ed pieces ('your Sunday articles') in the *Globe*. The paper's London man for twenty-five years, Stebbins, has provided a conduit for misinformation in another way. 'All you do,' he confides in Johnny, 'is cable back the government handouts and sign 'em "our London correspondent".' While finding much of the film highly unrealistic, Eugene Lyons in a 1940 *American Mercury* editorial confirms the accuracy of this portrayal of foreign correspondents' primary news sources: 'They get most of it, frequently all of it, from the local newspapers and radio broadcasts, official handouts, cut-and-dried press conferences, and occasional interviews with third secretaries of legation'.[17] Given the Hitler regime's penchant for churning out all manner of pamphlets and press releases, it is thus fairly certain that some of Stebbins's cables contain unadulterated Nazi propaganda.

Although the film offers us Johnny as a welcome antidote to Stebbins, his journalistic integrity is hardly beyond reproach. He takes the job with the promise 'Give me an expense account and I'll cover anything'. Scott ffolliott has to talk him out of filing his story at a time that might endanger Van Meer's life, and he is conversely willing to suppress the entire exposé of the Fisher organisation for the sake of the spy's daughter, and Johnny's fiancée, Carol, until she urges him to print it. Hitchcock's journalist heroes Haverstock and ffolliott do contribute to the cause of democracy by rescuing Van Meer before he can reveal the secret treaty clause and bringing Fisher's undercover Nazi organisation to light. However, they are most effective in taking up for the typically Hitchcockian failures of the Dutch and English police, of Scotland Yard, and of British Intelligence to do anything about the danger these men and women pose rather than through their efforts as newspapermen. A montage sequence shows us the various news stories the fictional Huntley Haverstock files after his return to London, but they significantly only chronicle Hitler's successes. Actual 1940s journalist Lyons, for one, was convinced that the nation's newspapers likewise could or would do little more:

> With a few notable exceptions, the American press has allowed itself to be bulldozed and hamstrung by foreign dictatorships . . . The scope of foreign reporting is being narrowed every day, as the blight of totalitarianism spreads. The foreign correspondent is being eliminated because his trade, in the final analysis, is an aspect of that freedom of the press now everywhere being extinguished.[18]

As the last line of the title card that introduced the film reads, the foreign correspondents can only 'stand as recording angels among the dead and dying', a motif echoed at the film's conclusion when Johnny tells a radio audience, 'All that noise you hear isn't static; it's death, coming to London.'

Significantly, Johnny's exhortation to his countrymen to keep democracy armed and protected as the lights go out in Europe doesn't come in an article or editorial, but on the radio, in the vein of Edward R. Murrow's famed broadcasts from London during the blitz.[19] This switch in media becomes necessary to serve the film's dramatic purposes, since a speech stirringly delivered by an actor has far greater impact than a close-up of a headline. But that is precisely the point about the efficacy of newspapers that the two other anti-Nazi films will expand upon.

The picture of Hitchcock in the advertisement for the 'Obesity Slayer' Reduco appears next to a headline about a fire at a state arsenal (shades of the defense plant in *Saboteur*), on a back page of the salvaged newspaper Gus Smith is reading. Gus informs his fellow lifeboat passengers that he has found a story about people who had to spend eighty days adrift. Rather than postulating that they, too, might find themselves featured in the paper after their rescue if they 'beat that record', he instead muses, 'We might even get in the newsreels.' This in turn leads him in the direction to which his mind inevitably turns, to thoughts of his girlfriend Rosie, and their appearance in a newsreel for winning a dance marathon by staying on their feet for eighty hours. The repetition of the number eighty stresses the transformation of a life-and-death struggle reported in print to a frivolous, leisure-time competition disseminated by newsreel, suggesting that, for the average American, the latter will necessarily have a stronger impact than the former. Constance Porter, a freelance journalist rather than a reporter on the beat, both writes books and gathers newsreel footage. However, her activities as film documentarist receive more discussion and scrutiny than do the written texts she authors.

As the film opens, we see the crewman Kovac swimming toward the lifeboat through Connie's viewfinder. In his study of Hitchcock as a political activist, Sam Simone claims, 'The newsreel was and is accepted as reality or selected reality. Hitchcock was aware that his audience's visual understanding of World War II was closely linked to the newsreels they viewed along with regular feature films. With this awareness, he inserted the newsreel technique at the beginning of *Lifeboat* to visually inform his audience that this film is closer to "a slice of life" than to "a slice of cake" '.[20] Although the director may well have used this technique to acknowledge that his audience took the newsreel view of the war for reality, the film is hardly as sanguine about that phenomenon as Simone implies. Once the initially admiring Kovac listens to Connie's breathlessly melodramatic description of the footage she has taken thus far, a parody of some of the more overwrought voice-overs that newsreels of the time employed, he is clearly sickened. He reaches the limit of his disgust when she rushes to obtain pictures of a drifting baby bottle: 'Why didn't you wait for the baby to float by and photograph that!'

If ordinary citizens mistook newsreels for news, they were sadly mistaken, according to critics of the time who lambasted them for their staged events and faked soundtracks and images. In his history of the American newsreel, Raymond Fielding quotes a newsreel editor who observed that the newsreel companies 'have formed the lazy habit of prearranging and rehearsing events, and, instead of going hunting in the jungles where history lurks or even waiting until she goes by, they have tamed the once camera-shy muse so that she will now turn up and show her profile at the studio by appointment'.[21] Indicating Hitchcock's knowledge of such chicanery, the film has Kovac respond to Connie's despair of ever getting footage to match what she has lost when the camera fell overboard by suggesting sarcastically that they'll just have to arrange another shipwreck for her.

Newsreels may have represented themselves as an offshoot of print journalism, but Fielding concludes that 'most evidence indicates that their values belonged to show business rather than to journalism and that they viewed their "readership" or "circulation" as being an entertainment-hungry audience rather than a well-informed public'.[22] Newsreels, after all, showed as appendages to regular feature films or served as sufficiently entertaining on their own to keep going all-newsreel theatres like New York's Embassy and Trans-Lux. W. French Githens, co-owner of the Embassy, reported that when the great historical figures of the 1930s and 1940s appeared on his screen, audiences responded to them like characters in fiction films. Anti-New Dealers came to hiss at Roosevelt, and each world leader such as Hitler, Stalin, Mussolini or Chiang Kai-shek 'had his adherents in the city, who flocked to the Embassy Theater when their favorite was on the screen', the newsreel equivalent of the star system.[23] Moreover, exhibitors reacted very strongly to newsreels taking any controversial stands on world events. The editorial staff of *The Motion Picture Herald* inveighed against 'controversial political material which is calculated to destroy the theatre as the public's escape from the bitter realities, the anguishes and the turmoil of life'.[24] Twentieth-Century Fox, whose Movietone News was the largest newsreel division in America, banned any controversial footage from the theatres it operated as early as 1931. Likewise all exhibitors in the state of Pennsylvania agreed in 1936 not to show any newsreels bearing upon political issues.[25]

Given these facts, Hitchcock's decision to shoot some of the opening footage of *Lifeboat* through a newsreel camera viewfinder would seem far more likely a caution to his audience that newsreels were not very different from the entertainment pictures they accompanied than any claim the comparison might make for his film's greater authenticity. *Lifeboat* clearly views the public's appetite for seeing its news through a camera lens with uneasiness. Nevertheless the film does not necessarily valorise print journalism either. Connie's typewriter soon follows her camera to the bottom of the ocean, and Kovac eventually attacks her journalistic integrity wholesale. If Mrs Porter stands in for the wider press corps in the microcosm of society the lifeboat contains, then the film finds the media guilty of using their trade for self-aggrandisement and egocentrism rather than truthfully reporting what democratic citizens need to know: 'You've been all over the world, and you've met all kinds of people – but you never write about them.

You only write about yourself. You think the whole war's a show put on for you to cover, like a Broadway play, and if enough people die before the last act, maybe you might give it four stars.'

Both *Foreign Correspondent* and *Lifeboat* therefore concentrate primarily on the personal characteristics of journalists, and both posit their function during the war as chroniclers of the dead and dying, although the former regards them as recording angels, while the latter sees them more as heartless vultures.[26] The really extensive Hitchcockian take on the press's effectiveness *vis-à-vis* the preservation of freedom in a democracy comes, however, in *Saboteur*, the one of these three films that does not include a journalist among its characters. The news is not encouraging. Newspapers in *Saboteur* spread erroneous information, printing the picture of an innocent man as a saboteur while another front-page photo celebrates the philanthropy of a society matron whose house is actually a refuge for native-born American Fascists. Besides being in all the papers, the incorrect reports of Barry Kane's guilt are 'on all the radios and everything'. The saboteurs use the 'American Newsreel Company' as a front for their activities and even place explosives in one of the newsreel cameras (just as the assassin in *Foreign Correspondent* concealed his gun within a photojournalist's camera).

The salvation of the hero and the foiling of the saboteurs happen in large part only because people pay very little serious attention to any of the news media. One of Ickes's contributors, David J. Stern, observed that 'in normal times we read newspapers or listen to the radio for relaxation'.[27] These normal-time practices have accustomed the media to essentially presenting 'vaudeville features' which are of no use in the current international crisis. Stern concludes, as does *Saboteur,* that it is therefore a good thing that the public does not take editorial opinion seriously. Thus, the truck driver who gives Barry a lift and later misdirects the police as Barry escapes on the bridge uses a newspaper to stop the clanking of his fire extinguisher, but he apparently has not read it. He confesses a total first-hand ignorance of important events: 'I never see anything happen. I don't even hear about anything except when my wife tells me what she sees in the movin' pictures.' The preternaturally wise blind man, Philip Martin, who sees 'intangible things, like innocence', can't read a paper and apparently does not own one of the radios that provide background noise throughout Barry's journey, from the neighbours' houses that surround that of Ken Mason's bereaved mother, to Tobin's poolside, to a Rockefeller Center office, to taxicabs, to the military police offices at the Brooklyn Navy Yard.

By contrast, close attention to (or manipulation of) the news characterises Kane's, and democracy's, enemies. The one person among the sideshow entertainers Mr Bones does not consider 'ignorant of the facts and therefore confused' is the Fascist midget, the Major, who significantly carries a newspaper under his arm. The biggest swipe at the press comes when Barry uses his picture on the front page of the Las Vegas paper – an incongruous shot of him grinning idiotically under the joky caption 'Uncle Sam Wants This Man!' – to convince the saboteur Freeman that he is one of the gang and deserves Freeman's protection from the police. While none of the good folks who help Kane has ever noticed that he is front-page news, the Fascists accept the accuracy of the free press without question.

Within its general skepticism about both the accuracy of the news media and their influence, *Saboteur* does differentiate among them. As my previous examples demonstrate, Hitchcock here stresses the misdirection inherent in the visual image. He begins by making the moral compass of the narrative a blind man, a man unimpressed by his niece's career as queen of the coast-to-coast billboard: 'Haven't you got your picture stuck up in enough places now?'[28] As in *Foreign Correspondent*, non-imagistic radio reveals somewhat more promise in sounding the clarion call for democracy. Because people can listen to radio while pursuing other activities that require their eyes and hands, it commands wider attention. Hitchcock uses the broadcast of the ship-christening ceremony at the Brooklyn Navy Yard to unify the sequence in which Barry races to prevent the sabotage while Pat tries to alert passers-by of her detention by the spies with a note dropped from the window of a skyscraper. Key to both endeavours are cab-drivers whose car radios are all tuned to the broadcast.

If radio is more compelling to the average citizen than newsprint, however, it is often no more reliable. Indeed the vast majority of radio news derived from local newspapers or nationwide wire services that fed the same dispatches to both media.[29] More people in *Saboteur* learn of Barry's supposed crime from the radio than anywhere else. Moreover, the covert Fascists can as easily appropriate the airwaves to their purposes as Fisher can place his articles in the Sunday *Globe*. The radio broadcast from the Yard plays also in Fry's truck to cue him when to set off the detonator, and part of the saboteur's equipment at Soda City consists of a radio transmitter.

Since newsreels didn't report breaking news,[30] we don't find them contributing to the misinformation about Barry's guilt. Nevertheless the spies use a newsreel company in Rockefeller Center as their cover, and *Saboteur* contains a famous sequence in which a movie audience in that same building's Radio City Music Hall mistakes shots fired in the theatre for those fired onscreen in an apparent sex farce. These events stress that this form of 'news' is even more susceptible to deception, fictionalisation and infiltration than the papers, while at the same time turning citizens' attention from the serious to the frivolous, as *Lifeboat* confirms. In a fortuitous conjunction of practices, the early history of the newsreel medium reveals that even genuine newsreel companies had an affinity for saboteurs of another sort: 'In that intensely competitive era, zealous newsreel cameramen were not above sabotaging their fellow photographers to secure exclusive footage'.[31]

So when all is said and done, the three anti-Fascist films abandon hope that the free press as currently constituted can save democracy, any more than law enforcement and government can. All of these institutions, as Hitchcock presents them, deserve Tobin's scathing indictment: 'When you think about it, Mr Kane, the competence of the totalitarian nations is much higher than ours. They get things done.' Many of the pundits in the *Freedom of the Press* volume similarly contrast the ineffectualness of the press in America with its chilling efficiency when co-opted by totalitarian leaders. Most eloquent of that volume's contributors on this score is not a journalist, but an artist, the poet Archibald MacLeish. His description of the perversion of the press by Fascist infiltration, and the only way to oppose it, resonates strongly with Hitchcock's themes in *Saboteur*. The true enemy of democratic freedoms, MacLeish says, 'destroys these things as the saboteur destroys them – secretly, by defamation of character, by falsification of fact, by excitement or rumor. There is no possible denial of the press, no form of statute and no method of enforcement, which will close the press to him and leave it open to his adversaries'.[32] MacLeish therefore calls for the 'partisans of democracy' to triumph by 'employing the press ourselves more skillfully and more persistently and more effectively than the saboteurs can employ it against us'.[33]

Perhaps convinced that average Americans paid more attention to alarms sounded in the cinema than printed in the daily papers, Hitchcock seems compelled to turn his own film-making to the purpose of exposing the apparently respectable and charming saboteurs in their midst. All of his espionage films since the 1930s had in fact used that revelation to structure their plots. With this minatory function fulfilled admirably, however, the anti-Fascist films still try to do more, to imagine a way to render democracy as a whole more skilful and effective and thus to imagine its ability to subdue the Nazi menace as well as merely to identify it. *Foreign Correspondent* and *Saboteur* suggest one possibility for accomplishing this goal, *Lifeboat* a very different one. Neither can survive serious scrutiny. Hitchcock's abiding scepticism about politics defeats him, no matter how eager he was on another level to propagandise for the good cause.

Saboteur presents us with a supposed model of participatory democracy leading to truth, as the plebiscite among the sideshow freaks exonerates Barry. Yet the way it is conducted hardly inspires confidence. Mr Bones announces the votes of everyone except Esmeralda the bearded lady, pre-empting their right to speak for themselves. Esmeralda, in turn, votes on the flimsiest of sentimental reasons, that if Pat Martin is so much in love with Barry, he must be innocent. Yet sentimentalism is ultimately all that *Foreign Correspondent* and *Saboteur* put forward to counter the Fascist menace. Barry assures Tobin that democracy will triumph because 'people who are helpful and eager to do the right thing, people that get a kick out of helping each other fight the bad guys' will combine their considerable strength to defeat people like the Nazis. If Barry sounds like someone giving a Capra or Ford populist elegy of the time, Van Meer, who assigns this function to 'little people everywhere who give crumbs to birds', belongs more to latter-day Disney.

To be sure, recourse to the power of the people is a frequent trope of pro-democracy rhetoric. Several of those criticising the press in Ickes's collection make this same move. Raymond Clapper cites 'the democratic formula, the formula upon which we depend to keep our political affairs on an even keel – alert and discriminating criticism by the public'.[34] Richard J. Finnigan proclaims, 'Newspapers are owned by individuals or corporations, but freedom of the press belongs to the people ... as much as the people's tongues for free speech and petition, or the people's churches for free worship'.[35]

Such stirring democratic sentiment doesn't last out the anti-Fascist films, however. In *Lifeboat*, Hitchcock undermines both majority rule and the good will of ordinary folks. The two most steadfast advocates of democratic process, Connie Porter and millionaire C. J. Rittenhouse, are the two for whom American democracy has produced the greatest capitalist success,[36] and the two most willing to play into Willy's hand. Although Willy does not in fact win the vote of confidence 'Rit' demands they take, the victor, Kovac, cannot steer the boat to safe harbor. It is tempting to see 'Joe' Spencer, the devoutly religious black steward and only passenger not to take part in killing Willy, as equivalent to the good-hearted but marginalised circus performers or the beatific birdfeeders, and to identify with this Christian pacifist who opts out of the political process entirely. Truffaut reports to Hitchcock that he had initially read the film this way but now believes that he was mistaken to derive from it the message that no man has the right to pass judgement on others. Casting his lot with Willy's executioners, even though acknowledging that 'they're like a pack of dogs', Hitchcock responds:

> We wanted to show that at that moment there were two world forces confronting each other, the democracies and the Nazis, and while the democracies were completely disorganized, all of the Germans were clearly headed in the same direction. So here was a statement telling the democracies to put their differences aside temporarily and to gather their forces to concentrate on the common enemy, whose strength was precisely derived from a spirit of unity and determination.[37]

Lifeboat tips the director's hand in a way that the other films disguise. I wrote in 1990 that 'because Hitchcock could so easily bend his audiences to his cinematic will, he had considerable concern about the ease with which dictators could trick free citizens out of their democratic rights'.[38] Having worked more extensively with the three wartime films now, I would modify that statement to include the possibility that Hitchcock was advocating a combination of Fascist methods with democratic goals as the only way to save democracy. So we hear his words echoing from Charles Tobin's mouth, and perhaps see Hitch's sardonic cherub countenance mirrored in the pudgy, baby-faced Nazi 'director' of the lifeboat as played by Walter Slezak. Indeed Nazi propaganda minister Joseph Goebbels praised *Foreign Correspondent* as 'a first-class production … which no doubt will make a certain impression upon the broad masses of the people in enemy countries'.[39] Likewise, Bosley Crowther, spearheading the storm of controversy that greeted the première of *Lifeboat*, claimed that 'we have a sneaking suspicion that the Nazis, with some cutting here and there, could turn *Lifeboat* into a whiplash against the "decadent democracies"'.[40] These reactions in turn remind us that the very populism *Foreign Correspondent* and *Saboteur* espouse is quite easily turned to Fascist purposes, as Frank Capra admits in *Meet John Doe* (1941), several years after learning that Hitler was a huge fan of *It Happened One Night* (1934). What does separate 'the little people', from '*das Volk*', after all?[41]

Hitchcock was, to be sure, not alone in envying Fascist organisation and single-mindedness. A number of press critics pointed to the insidious effectiveness of the Nazi-controlled newspapers and newsreels *vis-à-vis* their American counterparts. Fielding maintains that Hitler's propagandistic *Die Deutsche Wochenschau* 'despite the purpose to which it was put, provided a much more intellectually exciting and cinematically appropriate model for newsreel production'.[42] The Nazi newsreels used sophisticated filmic techniques, were structured and edited for continuity and took the subject matter seriously, while the fragmented and frivolous American newsreels presented an entertaining but ultimately shallow rendition of the events they chronicled.

What the anti-Fascist films never consider, however, is that disorganisation, inefficiency and frequent bumbling, no matter how frustrating, may constitute the essence of democracy, that which ultimately keeps Fascism at bay. It is after all not democracy that famously makes the trains run on time. To demand that democracies adopt a Nazi-like singleness of purpose may but simply transform them into that which they oppose. So, while Hitchcock makes a strong case that his audience should never quite believe what it reads in the papers, hears on the radio or sees in the newsreels, he fails to persuade it to abandon such caution in regards to those very films of his that carry the warning; for the wartime anti-Fascist films convey uncertainty, internal contradiction and no firm sense that the prescription offered for defeating the Nazi menace is the one Americans should take.

As was the case with his 1940s output overall, each of the films has an equivocal ending.[43] The rescue of Van Meer and the apprehension of Fisher's spy ring do nothing to stop the war from breaking out, prevent many of the airplane passengers from drowning, or persuade the stubbornly neutral American ship captain to allow Johnny to file his story without resorting to subterfuge. Although the murderer Fry falls to his death and the FBI rounds up Tobin's underlings, Tobin himself sails off to the Caribbean for a bittersweet exile in Havana. The lifeboat passengers dispose of Willy and are rescued by chance, but when the young Nazi sailor they pull into the boat asks, 'Aren't you going to kill me?' the passengers are still stymied as to how to offer a convincing counter-argument when confronted by the Fascist mentality ('What are you going to do with people like that?'). The best they can do is refer the question to Gus and Mrs Higley, dead at Nazi hands, whose heavenly perspective may perhaps provide insight unattainable by those still among the living.

I do not mean to suggest that Hitchcock's anti-Fascist activism in these three films was consciously insincere or disingenuous. As documented by Sidney Gottlieb, throughout the 1940s he remained committed to furthering the cinematic campaign against the Nazis in any way he could. Yet his divided sensibilities kept sabotaging the results, particularly in the two celebrations of French Resistance heroics, *Bon Voyage* and *Aventure Malgache,* which Gottlieb describes as 'chastening and monitory as well as uplifting' and 'not . . . the simple "stand up and cheer" films the government may have wanted and expected'.[44] Gottlieb could well be describing the overall impression left by the anti-Fascist fiction films as well.

In the end, the director's inability to reconcile a belief in the desirability of preserving democracy's freedoms with his conviction that democratically constituted populations can't take on their enemies effectively without adopting those enemies' methods, inevitably sabotages his attempts to allocate to himself the mission of the democratic press whose various inadequacies his wartime films delineate. When VE day finally arrived, and the European and American democracies *had* managed to defeat Fascism, one imagines that Hitchcock, the expatriate Briton who'd spent five years trying to convey pro-democracy propaganda, was relieved and overjoyed, while Hitchcock the skeptical artist, whose attitudes echo eerily from the mouths of Tobin and Willy, was merely surprised.

Notes

1 Ina Rae Hark, 'Keep Your Amateur Standing: Audience Participation and Good Citizenship in Hitchcock's Political Films', *Cinema Journal* 29, no. 2, 1990.

2 Eric Rohmer and Claude Chabrol, *Hitchcock: The First Forty-Four Films*, New York: Ungar, 1979, p. 60.

3 Sam Simone, 'Hitchcock as Activist: Politics and the War Films', Ann Arbor: UMI Research Press, 1985, p. 28.

4 Sidney Gottlieb, 'Hitchcock's Wartime Work: Bon Voyage and Adventure Malgache', *Hitchcock Annual* (1994), p. 158.

5 Hitchcock was ineligible for military service by virtue of being 'overweight and over age' (Francois Truffaut, *Hitchcock*, New York: Simon and Schuster, 1966, p. 113) but was very much upset by old friend Michael Balcon's criticism for not coming home to mobilise the British film industry for the fight against the Nazis. Leonard Leff believes 'Hitchcock may have pressed his friend [Sidney] Bernstein to search for a dramatic or documentary project that might serve the English cause and salve a troubled conscience' (Hitchcock and Selznick, New York: Weidenfeld and Nicholson, 1987, p. 99).

6 Thomas Leitch, *Find the Director and Other Hitchcock Games*, Athens: University of Georgia Press, 1991, pp. 6–7.

7 John Russell Taylor, *Hitch: The Life and Work of Alfred Hitchcock*, London: Faber, 1978, p. 181.

8 Freda Kirchwey, 'How to Get a Free Press', in Harold Ickes, ed., *Freedom of the Press Today*, New York: Vanguard Press, 1941, p. 156.

9 Herbert Agar, 'Rights Are Responsibilities', in Ickes, ed., *Freedom of the Press Today,* p. 21.

10 Richard Wilson, 'Freedom of the Press: Its Practical Meaning' in Ickes, ed., *Freedom of the Press Today*, p. 301.

11 George M. Gallup, 'The People of the Press', in Ickes, ed., *Freedom of the Press Today*, p. 301.

12 Ickes, ed., *Freedom of the Press Today,* p. 167.

13 In a patriotic gesture, the director gives Jones's English journalistic counterpart Scott ffolliott the heroic task of confronting the spies in their hideout in order to keep Van Meer from revealing the secret to the Nazi agents and effecting the Dutchman's rescue. *American Mercury* columnist Eugene Lyons in fact complained of Johnny that 'a British colleague also does most of the work for him' (Lyons, 'The State of the Union: the Truth about Foreign Correspondents', *American Mercury* 51, Nov 1940, p. 359).

14 Harold D. Lasswell, 'The Achievement Standards of a Democratic Press', in Ickes, ed., *Freedom of the Press Today*, p. 171.

15 The film was inspired by *Personal History*, the memoirs of veteran foreign correspondent Vincent Sheean. Producer Walter Wanger was eager to transform these into an extremely timely piece of anti-Nazi propaganda, but he encountered frustration after frustration in trying to have various writers come up with a workable script. Finally Hitchcock called in his veteran collaborators from the days of the British thrillers, Charles Bennett and Joan Harrison (see Spoto, *The Dark Side of the Genius: The Life of Alfred Hitchcock*, New York: Little, Brown, 1983, pp. 227–30). Thus, like the other two anti-Fascist films, for which Hitchcock respectively wrote the scenario and rewrote much of the dialogue, *Foreign Correspondent*, despite originating as Wanger's personal project, was a thoroughly Hitchcockian product in the end.

16 Stebbins displays what Lesley Brill identifies as conventional attributes of movie reporters: 'idle, cynical, dissolute, and/or incompetent' (Brill, ' "A Hero For Our Times" Foreign Correspondent Hero and The Bonfire of Vanities', *Hitchcock Annual,* 1995–6, p. 5). Several of the contributors to the *Freedom of the Press* volume note the increasing number of college graduates among reporters and point out that 'the pint flask has disappeared from the overcoat pocket of American journalism' (Wilson, *Freedom of the Press*, p. 296). Nevertheless, Eugene Lyons, editor of *The American Mercury*, noted that 'a composite of actual foreign reporters remains closer to Bob Benchley than McCrea, alas' (p. 358). Lyons also insists that Powers is wrong to prefer facts over analysis, because the current crisis requires not fearless police reporters but expert interpretation (Lyons, 'The State of the Union', p. 360).

17 Lyons, 'The State of the Union', p. 360

18 Lyons, 'The State of the Union', p. 363

19 For the relationship between foreign newspaper correspondents and the new breed of broadcast journalists who cut their teeth on European politics in the 1930s, see David Hosley, *As Good as Any: Foreign Correspondents on American Radio, 1930–40*, Westport, CT: Greenwood, 1984.

20 Simone, 'Hitchcock as Activist', p. 90

21 Raymond Fielding, *The American Newsreel 1911–1967*, Norman: University of Oklahoma Press, 1972, p. 235.

22 Fielding, *The American Newsreel*, p. 225.

23 Quoted in Fielding, *The American Newsreel*, p. 201.

24 Martin Quigley, 'The Exhibitor's Screen – How Shall it be used?', *Motion Picture Herald* 5, Feb 1938, p. 7.

25 Fielding, *The American Newsreel*, pp. 223, 233.

26 In Hitchcock's own final propaganda effort during the war the director would once again, as at the conclusions to *Foreign Correspondent* and *Lifeboat*, function primarily as a recording angel among the dead and dying. He served as a consultant on a project to shape 'atrocity' footage taken at the liberated Nazi concentration camps that was to be used to make the conquered German people face up to the enormity of their government's wartime actions. The film was never completed and never shown to its intended audience. In a moment of true Hitchcockian irony, a Foreign Office political intelligence bureaucrat warned that although there was great need to convert the raw concentration camp footage into 'a first-class documentary record' to supersede a 'rather crude and unthought-out newsreel' that had been produced in America, to show it to the defeated and demoralised German people would conflict with the standing policy of 'encouraging, stimulating, and interesting' them (Elizabeth Sussex, 'The Fate of F3080', *Sight and Sound* 53 no. 2, 1989, p. 97).

27 David J. Stern, 'The Newspaper Publisher Moves Across the Railroad', in Ickes, ed. *Freedom of the Press Today*, p. 249.

28 For more on the critique of visual perception in *Saboteur*, see Marshall Deutelbaum. 'Seeing in *Saboteur*', *Literature/Film Quarterly* 12, no. 1, 1984.

29 Hosley, *As Good as Any*, p. 18.

30 Indeed they failed to cover a large proportion of news of any sort. Charles Grinley observed in *Life and Letters Today*: 'The great proportion of important events are not

recorded, or at most given cursory notice. So for all its apparent "service," the newsreel isn't giving us the real news' (Grinley, 'Notes on the News-Reels', *Life and Letters Today*, Winter, 1937, p. 127).

31 Fielding, *The American Newsreel*, p. 144.

32 Archibald MacLeish, 'The Duty of Freeedom', in Ickes, ed., *Freedon of the Press Today*, p. 190.

33 MacLeish, 'The Duty of Freedom', p. 190.

34 Raymond Clapper, 'A Free Press Needs Discriminating Public Criticism', in Ickes, ed., *Freedom of the Press Today*, p. 93.

35 Richard J. Finnigan, 'An Experiment Goes On', in Ickes, ed., *Freedom of the Press Today*, p. 103.

36 Legendary publisher William Allen White, attempting to defuse fears about the increasing ownership of newspapers by financial capitalists, asserts in 1941 that 'World capitalism . . . has established world credit based on the faith of man in man around the globe. Capitalism, for all its ruthlessness, and for all its apparent greeds, still has acquired a lot of benevolence. In the world democracies, capitalism represents somewhat the self-respect inherent in democracy' (White, 'From Horace Greeley to Henry Luce' in Ickes, ed., '*Freedom of the Press Today*, p. 274). This is a fairly accurate assessment of what Rittenhouse, especially, represents in the film, a complex intertwining of genuine belief in democracy, a benevolence tinged with *noblesse oblige*, and a capitalistic self-interest. Hitchcock's verdict to Truffaut that Rit is 'more or less a Fascist' (Truffaut, *Hitchcock*, p. 113) isn't really borne out in the film itself.

37 Truffaut, *Hitchcock*, p. 113.

38 Hark, 'Keeping Your Amateur Standing', p. 13.

39 Quoted in Simone, *Hitchcock as Activist*, p. 55.

40 Quoted in Spotto, *The Dark Side of the Genius*, p. 269

41 See Bennet Schaber, ' "Hitler Can't Keep 'Em That Long": the Road, the People', in Stevan Cohan and Ina Rae Hark, ed., *The Road Movie Book*, London: Routledge, 1997, for a discussion of the ties between cinematic populism and Fascism in the 1930s and 1940s.

42 Fielding, *The American Newsreel*, p. 229.

43 Leitch discusses the problematic endings of all the 1940s films in *Find the Director*, pp. 127–30.

44 Gottlieb, 'Hitchcock's Wartime Work', p. 160.

Bibliography

1990–1999

What follows is a list of English-language publications of books and critical essays of the last decade which are focused primarily if not exclusively on the works of Alfred Hitchcock. It is meant, in part, to serve as a supplement to Jane Sloan's invaluable annotated bibliography (see below) of the director's œuvre. It is also meant to indicate to our reader the continuing prosperity and productivity of Hitchcock Studies. Reprints in anthologies of essays whose original publication has already been noted (either here or in Sloan's book) are *not* included in this bibliography. For an ongoing discussion of the most recent Hitchcock scholarship visit The MacGuffin website at <www.labyrinth.net.au/~muffin>.

Books

Aulier, Dan, *Hitchcock's Notebooks* (New York: Avon Books, 1999).

——, *Vertigo: The Making of a Hitchcock Classic* (New York: St. Martin's Press, 1998).

Barr, Charles, *English Hitchcock* (Moffat, Scotland: Cameron and Hollis, 1999).

Boyd, David (ed.), *Perspectives on Alfred Hitchcock* (New York: G.K. Hall, 1995).

Brougher, Kerry, Michael Tarantino and Astrid Bowron (eds), *Notorious: Alfred Hitchcock and Contemporary Art* (Oxford: Museum of Modern Art, 1999).

Cohen, Paula Marantz, *Alfred Hitchcock: The Legacy of Victorianism* (Lexington: U of Kentucky P, 1995).

Condon, Paul and Jim Sangster, *The Complete Alfred Hitchcock* (London: Virgin Books, 1999).

Corber, Robert J., *In the Name of National Security: Hitchcock, Homophobia, and the Political Construction of Gender in Postwar America* (Durham: Duke UP, 1993).

Finler, Joel W., *Hitchcock in Hollywood* (New York: Continuum, 1992).

Freedman, Jonathan and Richard Millington (eds), *Hitchcock's America* (New York and Oxford: Oxford UP, 1999).

Hitchcock, Alfred, *Hitchcock on Hitchcock: Selected Writings and Interviews*, ed., Sidney Gottlieb (Berkeley: U of California P, 1995).

Hunter, Evan, *Me and Hitch* (London and Boston: Faber and Faber, 1997).

Hurley, Neil P., *Soul in Suspense: Hitchcock's Fright and Delight* (Metuchen, NJ: Scarecrow Press, 1993).

Kapsis, Robert E., *Hitchcock: The Making of a Reputation* (Chicago: U of Chicago P, 1992).

Leitch, Thomas M., *Find the Director and Other Hitchcock Games* (Athens: U of Georgia P, 1991).

Mogg, Ken, *The Alfred Hitchcock Story* (New York: Taylor Publishing, 1999).

Naremore, James (ed.), *North by Northwest: Alfred Hitchcock, Director* (New Brunswick, NJ: Rutgers UP, 1993).

Paglia, Camille, *The Birds* (London: BFI, 1998).

Price, Theodore, *Hitchcock and Homosexuality: His 50-Year Obsession with Jack the Ripper and the Superbitch Prostitute: A Psychoanalytic View* (Metuchen, NJ: Scarecrow Press, 1992).

Raubicheck, Walter and Walter Srebnick (eds), *Hitchcock's Rereleased Films: From Rope to Vertigo* (Detroit: Wayne State UP, 1991).

Rebello, Stephen, *Alfred Hitchcock and the Making of Psycho* (New York: Dembner, 1990).

Ryall, Tom, *Alfred Hitchcock and the British Cinema*, revised edition (London and Atlantic Highlands, NJ: Athlone, 1996).
——, *Blackmail* (London: BFI, 1993).
Samuels, Robert, *Hitchcock's Bi-Textuality: Lacan, Feminisms, and Queer Theory* (Albany: State University of New York P, 1998).
Sharff, Stefan, *Alfred Hitchcock's High Vernacular: Theory and Practice* (New York: Columbia UP, 1991).
——, *The Art of Looking in Hitchcock's Rear Window* (New York: Limelight, 1997).
Sloan, Jane E., *Alfred Hitchcock: The Definitive Filmography* (Berkeley: U of California P, 1995).
Sterritt, David, *The Films of Alfred Hitchcock* (Cambridge, UK and New York: Cambridge UP, 1993).
Žižek, Slavoj (ed.), *Everything You Always Wanted to Know About Lacan (But Were Afraid to Ask Hitchcock)* (London: Verso, 1992).

Essays

Allen, Richard, 'Avian Metaphor in *The Birds*', *Hitchcock Annual*, 1997–98, pp. 40–67.
Almansi, Renato J., 'Alfred Hitchcock's Disappearing Woman: A Study in Scopophilia and Object Loss', *International Review of Psychoanalysis*, vol. 19 no. 1, 1992, pp. 81–90.
Ames, Deborah Lee, '*Vertigo*: The Nomenclature of Despair', *Hitchcock Annual*, 1997–98, pp. 153–67.
Ardolini, Frank and Deloy Simper, 'The Iconic Influence of the Dead: Iconoclasm and Idolatry in Hitchcock's *Rebecca, Vertigo*, and *Psycho*', *Journal of Evolutionary Psychology*, vol. 12 nos. 1–2, March 1991, pp. 130–41.
Atkinson, David, 'Hitchcock's Techniques Tell *Rear Window* Story', *American Cinematographer*, vol. 71 no. 1, January 1990, pp. 34–40.
Barr, Charles, 'Hitchcock's British Films Revisited', in Andrew Higson (ed.) *Dissolving Views: Key Writings on British Cinema* (London and New York: Cassell, 1996), pp. 9–19.
Barton, Sabrina, '"Crisscross": Paranoia and Projection in *Strangers on a Train*', *Camera Obscura*, vol. 25–6, January–May 1991, pp. 74–100.
Bauso, Tom, 'Mother Knows Best: The Voices of Mrs. Bates in *Psycho*', *Hitchcock Annual*, 1994, pp. 3–17.
——, '*Rope*: Hitchcock's Unkindest Cut', in Raubicheck and Srebnick (eds), *Hitchcock's Rereleased Films: From Rope to Vertigo*, pp. 226–39.
Beckman, Karen, 'Violent Vanishings: Hitchcock, Harlan, and the Disappearing Woman', *Camera Obscura*, 39, September 1996, pp. 78–103.
Beebe, John, 'The *Notorious* Postwar Psyche', *Journal of Popular Film and Television*, vol. 18 no. 1, Spring 1990, pp. 28–35.
Belton, John, 'The Space of *Rear Window*', in Raubicheck and Srebnick (eds), *Hitchcock's Rereleased Films: From Rope to Vertigo*, pp. 176–94.
——, 'Charles Bennett and the Typical Hitchcock Scenario', *Film History*, vol 9, 1997, pp. 320–32.
Berenstein, Rhona J., 'Adaptation, Censorship, and Audiences of Questionable Type: Lesbian Sightings in *Rebecca* (1940) and *The Uninvited* (1944)', *Cinema Journal*, vol. 37 no. 3, Spring 1998), pp. 16–37.
——, '"I'm Not the Sort of Person Men Marry": Monsters, Queers, and Hitchcock's *Rebecca*', *CineAction*, 29, Fall 1992, pp. 82–96.
Bertolini, John A., '*Rear Window*, or the Reciprocated Glance', *Hitchcock Annual*, 1994, pp. 55–75.
Bigwood, James, 'Solving a *Spellbound* Puzzle', *American Cinematographer*, vol. 72 no. 6, June 1991, pp. 34–40.
Bogdanovich, Peter, 'Alfred Hitchcock', in Bogdanovich, *Who the Devil Made It* (New York: Alfred A. Knopf, 1997), pp. 471–557.
Bonitzer, Pascal, 'Hitchcockian Suspense', in Žižek (ed.), *Everything You Always Wanted to Know About Lacan (But Were Afraid to Ask Hitchcock)*, pp. 15–30.

——, '*Notorious*', in Žižek (ed.), *Everything You Always Wanted to Know About Lacan (But Were Afraid to Ask Hitchcock)*, pp. 151–4.

——, 'The Skin and the Straw', in Žižek (ed.), *Everything You Always Wanted to Know About Lacan (But Were Afraid to Ask Hitchcock)*, pp. 178–84.

Bozovic, Miran, 'The Man Behind the Retina', in Žižek (ed.), *Everything You Always Wanted to Know About Lacan (But Were Afraid to Ask Hitchcock)*, pp. 161–77.

Brand, Dana, 'Rear-View Mirror: Hitchcock, Poe, and the Flaneur in America', in Freedman and Millington (eds), *Hitchcock's America*, pp. 123–34.

Brill, Lesley, 'A Hero for our Times: *Foreign Correspondent*, *Hero*, and *The Bonfire of the Vanities*', *Hitchcock Annual*, 1995, pp. 3–22.

——, '"Love's Not Time's Fool": *The Trouble with Harry*', in Raubicheck and Srebnick (eds), *Hitchcock's Rereleased Films: From Rope to Vertigo*, pp. 269–81.

Brisseau, Jean-Claude, '*Psycho*', in John Boorman and Walter Donahue (eds), *Projections 4 1/2*, trans. Yves Baignères (London and Boston: Faber and Faber, 1995), pp. 33–5.

Brougher, Kerry, 'Hitch-Hiking in Dreamscapes', in Brougher, Tarantino and Bowron (eds.), *Notorious: Alfred Hitchcock and Contemporary Art*, pp. 6–20.

Brown, Royal S., 'Herrmann, Hitchcock and the Music of the Irrational', pp. 148–74, in Brown, *Overtones and Undertones: Reading Film Music* (Berkeley: U of California P, 1994).

Butte, George, 'Theatricality and the Comedy of the Mutual Gaze in Hitchcock's Cary Grant Films', *Hitchcock Annual*, 1997–98, pp. 114–36.

Chankin, Donald O., 'Delusions and Dreams in Hitchcock's *Vertigo*', *Hitchcock Annual*, 1993, pp. 28–40.

Chion, Michel. 'The Cipher of Destiny', in Žižek (ed.), *Everything You Always Wanted to Know About Lacan (But Were Afraid to Ask Hitchcock)*, pp. 137–42.

——, 'The Fourth Side', in Žižek (ed.), *Everything You Always Wanted to Know About Lacan (But Were Afraid to Ask Hitchcock)*, pp. 155–60.

——, 'The Impossible Embodiment', in Žižek (ed.), *Everything You Always Wanted to Know About Lacan (But Were Afraid to Ask Hitchcock)*, pp. 195–207.

——, 'Norman; or, the Impossible Anacousmêtre', in Michel Chion, *The Voice in Cinema*, trans. Claudia Gorbman (New York: Columbia UP, 1999), pp. 125–61

Chumo, Peter N., '*The Crying Game*, Hitchcockian Romance, and the Quest for Identity', *Literature/Film Quarterly*, vol. 23 no. 4, October 1995, pp. 247–53.

Cohen, Paula Marantz, 'The Ideological Transformation of Conrad's *The Secret Agent* into Hitchcock's *Sabotage*', *Literature/Film Quarterly*, vol. 22 no. 3, 1994, pp. 199–209.

Cohan, Steven, 'The Spy in the Gray Flannel Suit', in Steven Cohan, *Masked Men: Masculinity and the Movies in the Fifties* (Bloomington and Indianapolis: Indiana UP, 1997), pp. 1–33.

Cohen, Tom, 'Beyond 'the Gaze': Hitchcock, Žižek, and the Ideological Sublime', in Tom Cohen, *Ideology and Inscription: 'Cultural Studies' after Benjamin, De Man, and Bakhtin* (New York: Cambridge UP, 1998), pp. 143–68.

——, 'Graphics, Letters, and Hitchcock's "Steps"', *Hitchcock Annual*, 1992, pp. 68–105.

——, 'Hitchcock and the death of (Mr.) Memory', *Qui Parle*, vol. 6 no. 2, Spring 1993, pp. 41–75.

——, 'Sabotaging the Ocularist State', in Cohen, *Ideology and Inscription*, pp. 169–200.

Cvetkovich, Ann, 'Postmodern *Vertigo*: The Sexual Politics of Allusion in De Palma's *Body Double*', in Raubicheck and Srebnick (eds), *Hitchcock's Rereleased Films*, pp. 147–62.

Dolar, Mladen, 'A Father Who Is Not Quite Dead', in Žižek (ed.), *Everything You*

Always Wanted to Know About Lacan (But Were Afraid to Ask Hitchcock), pp. 143–50.
——, 'Hitchcock's Objects', in Žižek (ed.), *Everything You Always Wanted to Know About Lacan (But Were Afraid to Ask Hitchcock)*, pp. 31–46.
——, 'The Spectator Who Knew Too Much', in Žižek (ed.), *Everything You Always Wanted to Know About Lacan (But Were Afraid to Ask Hitchcock)*, pp. 129–36.
Edelman, Lee, 'Piss Elegant: Freud, Hitchcock, and the Micturating Penis', *GLQ*, vol. 2 nos. 1–2, 1995, pp. 149–77.
——, '*Rear Window*'s Glasshole', in Ellis Hanson (ed.), *Out Takes: Essays on Queer Theory and Film* (Durham and London: Duke UP, 1999), pp. 72–96.
Eyüboglu, Selim, 'The Authorial Text and Postmodernism: Hitchcock's *Blackmail*', *Screen*, vol. 32 no. 1, Spring 1991, pp. 58–78.
Fletcher, John, 'Primal Scenes and Female Gothic: *Rebecca* and *Gaslight*', *Screen*, vol. 36 no. 4, Winter 1995, pp. 341–70.
Freedman, Jonathan, 'From *Spellbound* to *Vertigo*: Alfred Hitchcock and Therapeutic Culture in America', in Freedman and Millington (eds), *Hitchcock's America*, pp. 77–98.
Fried, Debra, 'Love, American Style: Hitchcock's Hollywood', in Freedman and Millington (eds), *Hitchcock's America*, pp. 15–28.
Garrett, Greg, 'The Men Who Knew Too Much: The Unmade Films of Hitchcock and Lehman', *North Dakota Quarterly*, vol. 61 no. 2, Spring 1993, pp. 47–58.
Gordon, Paul, 'Sometimes a Cigar is Not Just a Cigar: A Freudian Analysis of Uncle Charles in Hitchcock's *Shadow of a Doubt*', *Literature/Film Quarterly*, vol. 19 no. 4, October 1991, pp. 267–76.
Gottlieb, Sidney, 'Alfred Hitchcock's *Easy Virtue* (1927): A Descriptive Shot List', *Hitchcock Annual*, 1993, pp. 41–95.
——, 'Hitchcock and the Art of the Kiss: A Preliminary Survey', *Hitchcock Annual*, 1997–98, pp. 68–86.
——, 'Hitchcock's Wartime Work: *Bon Voyage* and *Aventure Malgache*', *Hitchcock Annual*, 1994, pp. 158–67.
——, 'Kissing and Telling in Hitchcock's *Easy Virtue*', *Hitchcock Annual*, 1992, pp. 1–38.
——, 'The Unknown Hitchcock: *Watchtower Over Tomorrow*', *Hitchcock Annual*, 1996—97, pp. 117–30.
Goulet, Robert G., 'Life With(out) Father: The Ideological Masculine in *Rope* and Other Hitchcock Films', in Raubicheck and Srebnick (eds), *Hitchcock's Rereleased Films*, pp. 240–52.
Grimes, Larry E., 'Shall These Bones Live? The Problem of Bodies in Alfred Hitchcock's Psycho and Joel Cohen's Blood Simple', in Joel W. Martin and Conrad E. Ostwalt, Jr. (eds.), *Screening the Sacred: Religion, Myth and Ideology in Popular American Film* (Boulder, Co: Westview Press, 1995), pp. 19–29.
Groh, Fred, '*Vertigo*'s Three Towers', *Hitchcock Annual*, 1992, pp. 106–14.
Gustainis, J. Justin and Jay DeSilva, 'Archetypes as Propaganda in Alfred Hitchcock's "Lost" World War II Films', *Film and History*, vol. 27 nos. 1–4, 1997, pp. 80–7.
Guthey, Eric, 'Guilty Pleasures in Hitchcock's *The Lodger*', *New Observations*, 90, July 1992, pp. 30–5.
Hall, John W., 'Touch of *Psycho*? Hitchcock's Debt to Welles', *Bright Lights*, 14, 1995, pp. 18–22.
Hansen, Phil, 'The Misogynist at Rest: Women in Hitchcock's *Lifeboat*', *Hitchcock Annual*, 1996–97, pp. 110–16.
Hark, Ina Rae, 'Keeping Your Amateur Standing: Audience Participation and Good Citizenship in Hitchcock's Political Films', *Cinema Journal*, vol. 29 no. 2, Winter 1990, pp. 8–22.
——, 'Revalidating Patriarchy: Why Hitchcock Remade *The Man Who Knew Too Much*', in Raubicheck and Srebnick (eds), *Hitchcock's Rereleased Films*, pp. 209–20.
Heimpel, Rod S., 'Hitchcock's *Psycho* in Stephen Frear's *The Grifters*', *Canadian Journal of Film Studies*, vol. 3 no. 1, Spring 1994, pp. 45–65.

Hemmeter, Thomas, 'Hitchcock the Feminist: Rereading *Shadow of a Doubt*', *Hitchcock Annual*, 1993, pp. 12–27.

——, 'Hitchcock's Melodramatic Silence', *Journal of Film and Video*, vol. 48 nos 1–2, Spring 1996, pp. 32–40.

——, 'Twisted Writing: *Rope* as Experimental Film', in Raubicheck and Srebnick (eds), *Hitchcock's Rereleased Films*, pp. 253–65.

Hepworth, John, 'Hitchcock's Homophobia', in Corey K. Creekmur and Alexander Doty (eds), *Out in Culture: Gay, Lesbian, and Queer Essays on Popular Culture* (Durham and London: Duke UP, 1995), pp. 186–94.

Hinton, Laura, 'A "Woman's" View: the *Vertigo* Frame-Up', *Film Criticism*, vol. 19 no. 2, Winter 1994–95, pp. 2–22.

Hollinger, Karen, 'The Female Oedipal Drama of *Rebecca* from Novel to Film', *Quarterly Review of Film and Video*, vol. 14 no. 4, August 1993, pp. 17–30.

Infante, G. Cabera, 'Peeper, Parish!', 'Macabracadabra', '1 Hitch + 1 Arm = 2 x X', 'Hitch Hitches Hitch', 'In Search of Long Lost Love', '*The Thirty-Nine Steps*', in G. Cabera Infante, *A Twentieth Century Job*, trans. Kenneth Hall and G. Cabera Infante (London: Faber and Faber, 1991), pp. 35–6, 80–2, 87–8, 276–8, 278–85, 349. Originally published as *Un Oficio del Siglo XX* (Havana: Ediciones R, 1963).

Jameson, Frederic, 'Spatial Systems in *North by Northwest*', in Žižek (ed.), *Everything You Always Wanted to Know About Lacan (But Were Afraid to Ask Hitchcock)*, pp. 47–72.

Klopcic, Matjaz, '*Vertigo*', in Boorman and Donahue (eds), *Projections 4 1/2*, pp. 105–6.

Knapp, Lucretia, 'The Queer Voice in *Marnie*', *Cinema Journal*, vol. 32 no. 4, Summer 1993, pp. 6–23.

Kolker, Robert P., 'Algebraic Figures: Recalculating the Hitchcock Formula', in Andrew Horton and Stuart Y. McDougal (eds.), *Play It Again, Sam: Retakes on Remakes* (Berkeley: U of California P, 1998), pp. 34–51.

Kuhns, J.L., 'Comments on 'Alfred Hitchcock's *Easy Virtue* (1927): A Descriptive Shot List', *Hitchcock Annual*, 1995, pp. 126–33.

Lawrence, Amy, 'Jimmy Stewart is Being Beaten: *Rope* and the Postwar Crisis in American Masculinity', *Quarterly Review of Film & Video*, vol. 16 no. 1, 1995, pp. 41–58.

Leff, Leonard, 'Into the Archives: Some Thoughts on Hitchcock, the Truffaut Interview, and Radio', *Hitchcock Annual*, 1997–98, pp. 87–95.

Leff, Leonard, 'Ingrid in the Lion's Den: Recutting *Notorious*', *Film Comment*, March/April 1999, pp. 26–9.

Leitch, Thomas M., 'The Hitchcock Moment', *Hitchcock Annual*, 1997–98, pp. 19–39.

——, 'Self and World at Paramount', in Raubicheck and Srebnick (eds), *Hitchcock's Rereleased Films*, pp. 36–51.

——, 'It's the Cold War, Stupid: An Obvious History of the Political Hitchcock', *Literature/Film Quarterly*, vol.27 no. 1, 1999, pp. 3–15.

Leonard, Garry M., 'A Fall from Grace: The Fragmentation of Masculine Subjectivity and the Impossibility of Femininity in Hitchcock's *Vertigo*', *American Imago*, vol. 47 nos 3–4, Fall–Winter 1990, pp. 271–91.

Lesser, Wendy, 'Hitchcock's Couples', in Wendy Lesser, *His Other Half: Men Looking at Women Through Art* (Cambridge, MA: Harvard UP), pp. 121–44.

Linderman, Deborah, 'The *Mise-en-Abîme* in Hitchcock's *Vertigo*', *Cinema Journal*, vol. 30 no. 4, Summer 1991, 51–74.

McDougal, Stuart, 'The Director Who Knew Too Much: Hitchcock Remakes Himself', in Horton and McDougal (eds.), *Play It Again, Sam*, pp. 52–69.

Marker, Chris, 'A Free Replay (Notes on *Vertigo*)', in Boorman and Donahue (eds), *Projections 4 1/2*, pp. 123–30.

Maxfield, James F., 'A Dreamer and His Dream: Another Way of Looking at Hitchcock's *Vertigo*', *Film Criticism*, vol. 14 no. 3, Spring 1990, pp. 3–13.

Mazzella, Anthony J., 'Author, Auteur: Reading *Rear Window* from Woolrich to Hitchcock', in Raubicheck and Srebnick (eds), *Hitchcock's Rereleased Films*, pp. 62–75.

Michie, Elsie B., 'Unveiling Maternal Desires: Hitchcock and American Domesticity', in Freedman and Millington (eds), *Hitchcock's America*, pp. 29–53.

Miller, D.A., 'Anal *Rope*', *Representations*, 32, Fall 1990, pp. 114–33.

Millington, Richard H., 'Hitchcock and American Culture: The Comedy of Self-Construction in *North by Northwest*', in Freedman and Millington (eds), *Hitchcock's America*, pp. 135–54.

Mogg, Ken, 'Hitchcock's *The Lodger*: A Theory', *Hitchcock Annual*, 1992, pp. 115–27.

——, 'South by Southeast: Hitchcock's *Rich and Strange* (1932)', *MacGuffin*, no. 22, May–August 1997, p. 17–24.

——, 'The Universal Hitchcock: *The Trouble With Harry* (1956)', *MacGuffin*, no. 21, February 1997, pp. 9–25.

Morris, Christopher, '*Psycho's* Allegory of Seeing', *Literature/Film Quarterly*, vol. 24 no. 1, 1996, pp. 47–51.

——, 'The Direction of *North by Northwest*', *Cinema Journal*, vol. 36 no. 4, Summer 1997, 43–56.

——, 'Feminism, Deconstruction, and the Pursuit of the Tenable in *Vertigo*', *Hitchcock Annual*, 1996–97, pp. 3–25.

——, 'The Allegory of Seeing in Hitchcock's Silent Films', *Film Criticism*, vol. 22 no. 2, Winter 1997–98, pp. 27–50.

——, 'Torn Curtain's Futile Talk', *Cinema Journal*, vol 39 no. 1, Fall 1999, pp. 54–73.

Morrison, Ken, 'The Technology of Homicide: Construction of Evidence and Truth in American Murder Films', *CineAction*, 38, September 1995, pp. 16–24.

Naremore, James, 'Spies and Lovers', in Naremore (ed.), *North by Northwest: Alfred Hitchcock, Director*, pp. 3–19.

Negra, Diane, 'Coveting the Feminine: Victor Frankenstein, Norman Bates, and Buffalo Bill', *Literature/Film Quarterly*, vol. 24 no. 2, April 1996, pp. 193–200.

Ness, Richard, 'Alfred Hitchcock's *The Manxman* (1929): A Descriptive Shot List', *Hitchcock Annual*, 1995, pp. 61–116.

Nochimson, Martha P., 'Amnesia 'R' Us: The Retold Melodrama, Soap Opera, and the Representation of Reality', *Film Quarterly*, vol. 50 no. 3, Spring 1997, pp. 27–38.

Odabashian, Barbara, 'The Unspeakable Crime in Hitchcock's *Rear Window*: Hero as Lay Detective, Spectator as Lay Analyst', *Hitchcock Annual*, 1993, pp. 3–11.

Paulin, Scott D., 'Unheard Sexualities?: Queer Theory and the Soundtrack', *Spectator*, vol. 17 no. 2, Spring/Summer 1997, pp. 37–49.

Pelko, Stojan, '*Punctum Caecum*, or, Of Insight and Blindness', in Žižek (ed.), *Everything You Always Wanted to Know About Lacan (But Were Afraid to Ask Hitchcock)*, pp. 106–21.

Perry, Dennis R., 'Imps of the Perverse: Discovering the Poe/Hitchcock Connection', *Literature/Film Quarterly*, vol. 24 no. 4, October 1996, pp. 393–9.

Phillips, Louis, 'The Hitchcock Universe: *Thirty-Nine Steps* and Then Some', *Films in Review*, vol. 56 nos. 3–4, March 1995, pp. 22–7.

Poague, Leland, 'Engendering *Vertigo*', *Hitchcock Annual*, 1994, pp. 18–54.

Polan, Dana, 'The Light Side of Genius: Hitchcock's *Mr. and Mrs. Smith* in the Screwball Tradition', in Andrew Horton (ed.), *Comedy/Cinema/Theory* (Berkeley: U of California P, 1991), pp. 131–52.

Recchia, Edward, 'Through a Shower Curtain Darkly: Reflexivity as a Dramatic Component of *Psycho*', *Literature/Film Quarterly*, vol. 19 no. 4, October 1991, pp. 258–66.

Roberts, John W., 'Survival versus Salvation: The Conflicting Visions of Welles and Hitchcock', *Midwest Quarterly*, vol. 32 no. 2, December 1991, pp. 197–210.

Roche, M.W., 'Hitchcock and the Transcendence of Tragedy: *I Confess* as Speculative Art', *Post Script*, vol. 10 no. 3, Summer 1991, pp. 30–7.

Roth, Marty, 'Hitchcock's Secret Agency', *Camera Obscura*, 30, May 1992, pp. 34–48.

Rubin, Stan Sanvel, '"Artifice that Deepens and Humanizes": An Interview with Donald Spoto', *Hitchcock Annual*, 1996–97, pp. 26–48.

Saito, Ayako, 'Hitchcock's Trilogy: A Logic of Mise en Scène', in Janet Bergstrom (ed.), *Endless Night: Cinema and Psychoanalysis, Parallel Histories* (Berkeley: U of California P, 1999), pp. 200–48.

Salecl, Renata, 'The Right Man and the Wrong Woman', in Žižek (ed.), *Everything You Always Wanted to Know About Lacan (But Were Afraid to Ask Hitchcock)*, pp. 185–94.

Sandler, Kevin S., 'The Concept of Shame in the Films of Alfred Hitchcock', *Hitchcock Annual*, 1997–98, pp. 137–52.

Schneider, Kirk J., 'Hitchcock's *Vertigo*: The Existential View of Spirituality', *Journal of Humanistic Psychology*, vol. 33 no. 2, Spring 1993, pp. 91–100.

Sevastakis, Michael, 'Alfred Hitchcock's *Number 17* (1932): A Descriptive Shot List', *Hitchcock Annual*, 1994, pp. 76–148.

Sharrett, Christopher, 'The Myth of Apocalypse and the Horror Film: The Primacy of *Psycho* and *The Birds*', *Hitchcock Annual*, 1995, pp. 38–60.

Silet, Charles L.P., 'Alfred Hitchcock's *The Lodger, A Story of the London Fog* (1926): A Descriptive Shot List', *Hitchcock Annual*, 1996–97, pp. 49–109.

——, 'Writing with Hitch: An Interview with Evan Hunter', *Hitchcock Annual*, 1995, pp. 117–25.

Simon, William G., 'Hitchcock: The Languages of Madness', in Raubicheck and Srebnick (eds), *Hitchcock's Rereleased Films*, pp. 109–15.

Smith, Murray, 'Altered States: Character and Emotional Response in the Cinema', *Cinema Journal*, vol. 33 no. 4, Summer 1994, pp. 34–56.

——, 'Technological Determination, Aesthetic Resistance, or A Cottage on Dartmoor: Goat-Gland Talkie or Masterpiece?', *Wide Angle*, vol. 12 no. 3, July 1990, pp. 80–97.

Stam, Robert, 'Hitchcock and Buñuel: Authority, Desire, and the Absurd', in Raubicheck and Srebnick (eds), *Hitchcock's Rereleased Films*, pp. 116–46.

Sterritt, David, 'Alfred Hitchcock: Registrar of Births and Deaths', *Hitchcock Annual*, 1997–1998, pp. 3–18.

——, 'The Diabolic Imagination: Hitchcock, Bakhtin, and the Carnivalization of Cinema', *Hitchcock Annual*, 1992, pp. 39–67.

Street, Sarah, 'Hitchcockian Haberdashery', *Hitchcock Annual*, 1995, pp. 23–37.

Swaab, Peter, 'Hitchcock's Homophobia? The Case of *Murder!*', *Perversions*, 4, Spring 1995, pp. 6–40.

Tarantino, Michael, 'How He Does It (1976), or The Case of the Missing Gloves (1999)' in Brougher, Tarantino and Bowron (eds.), *Notorious: Alfred Hitchcock and Contemporary Art*, pp. 21–33.

Teachout, Terry, 'The Genius of Pure Effect', *Civilization*, vol. 5 no. 1, February 1998, pp. 43–4.

Tharp, Julie, 'The Transvestite as Monster: Gender Horror in *The Silence of the Lambs* and *Psycho*', *Journal of Popular Film and Television*, vol. 19 no. 3, Fall 1991, pp. 106–13.

Thomas, Deborah, 'Confession as Betrayal: Hitchcock's *I Confess* as Enigmatic Text', *CineAction*, 49, May 1996, pp. 32–7.

——, 'On Being Norman: Performance and Inner Life in Hitchcock's Psycho', *CineAction*, vol. 44, July 1997, pp. 66–72.

Tomlinson, Doug, '"They Should Be Treated Like Cattle": Hitchcock and the Question of Performance', in Raubicheck and Srebnick (eds), *Hitchcock's Rereleased Films*, pp. 95–108.

Trumpener, Katie, 'Fragments of the Mirror: Self-Reference, Mise-en-Abyme, *Vertigo*', in Raubicheck and Srebnick (eds), *Hitchcock's Rereleased Films*, pp. 175–88.

Turner, George, '*Foreign Correspondent* – The Best Spy Thriller of All', *American Cinematographer*, vol. 76 no. 8, August 1995, pp. 75–81.

——, 'Hitchcock's Acrophobic Vision', *American Cinematographer*, vol. 77 no. 11, November 1996, pp. 86–91.

——, 'Hitchcock's Mastery is Beyond Doubt', *American Cinematographer*, vol. 74 no. 5, May 1993, pp. 62–7.

——, '*Saboteur*: Hitchcock Set Free', *American Cinematographer*, vol. 74 no. 11, November 1993, pp. 67–74.

Vest, James M., 'Echoes of Alfred Hitchcock's *Vertigo*, *The Birds*, and *Frenzy* in François Truffaut's *Story of Adèle H*', *Hitchcock Annual*, 1997–98, pp. 96–113.

Weinstock, Jane, '5 Minutes to Alexanderplatz', *Camera Obscura*, 27, September 1991, pp. 76–87.

West, Ann, 'The Concept of the Fantastic in *Vertigo*', in Raubicheck and Srebnick (eds), *Hitchcock's Rereleased Films*, pp. 163–74.

White, Susan, 'Allegory and Referentiality: *Vertigo* and Feminist Criticism', *MLN*, vol. 106 no. 5, December 1991, pp. 910–32.

Williams, Linda, 'Learning to Scream', *Sight and Sound*, vol. 4 no. 12, December 1994, pp. 14–17.

Wollen, Peter, 'Theme Park and Variations', *Sight and Sound*, vol. 3 no. 7, July 1993, pp. 6–9.

——, 'Compulsion', *Sight and Sound*, vol. 7 no. 4, April 1997, pp. 14–19.

Wood, Bret, 'Foreign Correspondence: The Rediscovered War Films of Alfred Hitchcock', *Film Comment*, vol. 29 no. 4, July 1993, pp. 54–8.

Wood, Michael, 'Fearful Cemetery', in Freedman and Millington (eds), *Hitchcock's America*, pp. 173–80.

Wood, Robin, 'The Men Who Knew Too Much (and the Women Who Knew Much Better)', in Raubicheck and Srebnick (eds), *Hitchcock's Rereleased Films*, pp. 194–208.

——, 'Why We Should (Still) Take Hitchcock Seriously', *CineAction*, 31, Spring 1993, pp. 44–9.

Žižek, Slavoj, 'Alfred Hitchcock, or The Form and its Historical Mediation', Žižek (ed.), *Everything You Always Wanted to Know About Lacan (But Were Afraid to Ask Hitchcock)*, pp. 1–12.

——, 'Hitchcockian *Sinthoms*', in Žižek (ed.), *Everything You Always Wanted to Know About Lacan (But Were Afraid to Ask Hitchcock)*, pp. 125–28

——, '"In His Bold Gaze My Ruin Is Writ Large"', in Žižek (ed.), *Everything You Always Wanted to Know About Lacan (But Were Afraid to Ask Hitchcock)*, pp. 211–72.

——, 'One Can Never Know Too Much about Hitchcock', in Slavoj Žižek, *Looking Awry: An Introduction to Jacques Lacan through Popular Culture* (Cambridge, MA: MIT Press, 1991), pp. 67–122.

Zupancic, Alenka, 'A Perfect Place to Die: Theater in Hitchcock's Films', in Žižek (ed.), *Everything You Always Wanted to Know About Lacan (But Were Afraid to Ask Hitchcock)*, pp. 73–105.

Index